Inside Out and
Outside In

Inside Out and Outside In

Psychodynamic Clinical Theory and Psychopathology in Contemporary Multicultural Contexts

SECOND EDITION

Edited by Joan Berzoff,
Laura Melano Flanagan,
and Patricia Hertz

JASON ARONSON
Lanham • Boulder • New York • Toronto • Plymouth, UK

Published in the United States of America
by Jason Aronson
An imprint of Rowman & Littlefield Publishers, Inc.

A wholly owned subsidiary of
The Rowman & Littlefield Publishing Group, Inc.
4501 Forbes Boulevard, Suite 200, Lanham, Maryland 20706
www.rowmanlittlefield.com

Estover Road
Plymouth PL6 7PY
United Kingdom

Copyright © 2008 by Jason Aronson

British Library Cataloguing in Publication Information Available

Library of Congress Cataloging-in-Publication Data

Inside out and outside in : psychodynamic clinical theory and psychopathology
in contemporary multicultural contexts / edited by Joan Berzoff, Laura Melano
Flanagan, and Patricia Hertz.—2nd ed.
        p.   ; cm.
    Includes bibliographical references and index.
    ISBN-13: 978-0-7657-0431-3 (cloth : alk. paper)
    ISBN-10: 0-7657-0431-5 (cloth : alk. paper)
    ISBN-13: 978-0-7657-0432-0 (pbk. : alk. paper)
    ISBN-10: 0-7657-0432-3 (pbk. : alk. paper)
    1. Psychodynamic psychotherapy.   2. Personality development.
3. Psychoanalytic interpretation.   4. Psychology, Pathological.   I. Berzoff,
Joan.   II. Flanagan, Laura Melano.   III. Hertz, Patricia.   IV. Berzoff, Joan. Inside
out and outside in.
    [DNLM: 1. Psychoanalytic Therapy.   2. Cultural Diversity.   3. Personality
Development.   4. Psychoanalytic Theory. WM 460.6 I59 2007]
    RC489.P72B47 2007
    616.89'14—dc22   2006100210

Printed in the United States of America

∞ ™The paper used in this publication meets the minimum requirements of
American National Standard for Information Sciences—Permanence of Paper for
Printed Library Materials, ANSI/NISO Z39.48-1992.

Contents

Acknowledgments

This second edition of *Inside Out and Outside In* has been a pleasure to write, largely because of the very enthusiastic responses of so many students and colleagues around the country and at Smith College, and because the three coauthors who have coedited it have shared such similar clinical and theoretical sensibilities with each other, and with you, the reader. We have enjoyed the ongoing process of trying to make this work even more biopsychosocial and hope that this edition surpasses the first in doing so.

The person who deserves my greatest thanks is Lew Cohen, my husband, friend, and co-parent. Somehow, from the beginning of this book in 1989 to the present, we have raised two wonderful children, all the while wondering: "What did we do right?" Those children, Zeke and Jake, have been sources of inspiration, pleasure, and humor, and their childhood experiences are models of development, interwoven into the pages of this book. They have watched their parents develop as academics, and have themselves become scholars and joyful, creative, and kind people.

I have been blessed with friendships as well. Jaine Darwin has given her love, her heart, and her undying loyalty to every chapter of my life. Merry Nasser has offered wise counsel and been wonderful ballast. Kathryn Basham has been an intellectual and teaching model whose humor and insight have been invaluable. Bob and Cynthia Shilkret have been like family. Cathy Hanauer has been a funny, smart, and wonderful support with whom I can truly complain about writing, while we walk our tootsies off and indulge in chocolate. Wendy Salkind, my old friend, has, as always, provided me continuity and an abiding sense that from our roots, somehow, we could create good works. Elly Winniger has also restored my own history to me, being the longest-term friend, dating from in utero.

I thank my mother, Myra Berzoff, who has shown me how complex and ultimately possible ongoing adult development can be. She has been a model of strength and enormous support, encouraging me throughout this and other creative endeavors. My two nieces, Sarah and Kate Shapiro, and my nephew, Zach Shapiro, have taught me so much about loss and about living. I feel like they are also my children. I am indebted to my sisters-in-law, Toby Tider and Felice Grunberger, and my brother-in-law, David Noah Cohen, who have always allowed my wackiness to be a part of their families. I also want to acknowledge three people who are no longer with me but very much within me: Sydney Berzoff, my father; Barbara Shapiro, my sister; and Vera Cohen, my mother-in-law.

There are many people and institutions to thank as well. Three deans were a part of this book. Ann Hartman, Anita Lightburn, and Carolyn Jacobs created a climate at the Smith College School for Social Work that valued scholarship and productivity and gave me the time to do this work. I thank my colleagues at the school, both resident faculty and adjunct, for their support of this book and help when I was away working on it. And I cannot thank my students enough, both master's and doctoral, who have offered so many insights, case experiences, questions, probes, and ideas.

Anna Marie Russo, my administrative assistant, has been enormously helpful: editing, typing, organizing, and creating this manuscript. She has formidable organizational and technical skills without which this truly would have been impossible. Gerry Schamess and I first developed the course that later became this book and I thank him for his ideas, scholarly approach, and mentorship in those years.

Joan Berzoff
Northampton, Massachusetts

Although ten years have passed (unimaginably quickly) since this book was first published, my acknowledgments have not changed that much because I am fortunate to have a core group of people who support me in my learning and my work.

Starting closest to home, I owe Judy Levin the same debt of gratitude that I still cannot fully articulate in words. She read, she typed, she listened, she sent and received innumerable e-mails, she edited brilliantly, and she was a major part of this process from beginning to end. Without her special insight into the material and her consistent, loving encouragement I would not have been able to persevere. Her unswerving belief in all of us made the book better.

I thank my wonderful sons, Michael and Brian. They are now fully embarked on their own meaningful, productive, loving lives. Last time I thanked them for their patience and forbearance during the lengthy process of writing the first version of this book. This time, I thank them for graciously ignoring altogether the fact that this book (or "The Book," as they call it) was being rewritten. What remains true is that I continue to learn invaluable lessons from the steadfast and courageous ways they pursued their own hopes and dreams.

My mother, Maria Melano, has died in the interim, but I still owe her my profound thanks for having been a great enabler of my teaching and writing, both through her financial generosity, which bought me precious time, and by the example of her vibrant, active life. I am still inspired by the memory of how at eighty-five, two weeks before her death, she still traveled alone by bus to audit classes at her alma mater, Barnard College.

To my dear friends, thank you for having the grace and the kindness to stop asking, "Why in heaven's name are you doing that book again?" while at the same time lovingly encouraging me to continue.

At the Smith College School for Social Work, I am forever indebted to Ann Hartman and Joan Laird for pushing, prodding, and coaxing me to expand my thinking about sociocultural concepts. That "stretch" has enriched both my teaching and my contributions to this book. My thanks also go to Michael Hayes, who was with us for a while as an author, is still with us as a teacher, and whose inspiration has endured. His ability to combine a sophisticated grasp of the fine points of psychodynamic theory with a loving, gentle application of that theory to practice helped me retain the belief that this theory is indeed worth teaching.

New thanks go to Denis Miehls who became the coordinator of the courses on which this book is based and managed that arduous task in a skillful, nurturing, energizing way. His deep knowledge of theory and his clear vision of how to make use of it to help people heal infuses much of my new work.

To the able, talented AnnaMarie Russo, who loves and beautifully uses both words and computers, all I can say is that, given my dread of technology, I would have been frozen into silence without her editing, formatting, and organizing skills. Many, many thanks.

Finally, and most important, my deepest gratitude still and always goes to Joan Berzoff and Pat Hertz—colleagues, collaborators, dear friends. There were moments when I thought we would not survive the writing of this new edition, but somehow one of us always came up with the enthusiasm, vision, sanity, or commitment to help the others out. What I said ten years ago remains true today: the path we walked to create this book has been joyful, arduous, exciting, frustrating, fun, and sometimes infuriating, but ultimately we walked it together.

Laura Melano Flanagan
Brooklyn, New York

In addition to making me feel older, writing a second edition of this book underscores how grateful I am that, after all of these years in the mental health field, I have been able to sustain my passion for this work. What has made this possible? I am indebted to the many patients who have had the generosity and courage to let themselves be known—to themselves and to me—in a clinical space where our lives have intersected in a deeply personal and hopefully transformative way for all of us. I am appreciative of the many students whose inquisitive minds forced me to articulate why I think and do what I do, and continually reminded me of what I have yet to learn. My colleagues at Smith College School of Social Work trusted me to teach long before I knew I had something to offer, and the staff at the "old" Revere Community Counseling and in the Social Work Department at Beth Israel Deaconess Medical Center have modeled a commitment, enthusiasm, and dedication to patients that bring forth what is most meaningful in clinical practice.

I want to thank those who have been so close to me personally, who may not have read every draft of these chapters, but without whom I could never have sustained the energy to complete this project. The love and support of my friends and family have made me what I am today and have helped give me the voice that is captured in some of these pages. This includes my mother, Marilyn, whose steady patience, love, and common-sense vision continue to shape my life and my parenting; my incredible sisters, Meg and Marcia, and their families (Glenn, Seth, Aaron, Bob, and Josh); and Heather and Michael (like family) who know me at times better than I know myself, and whose closeness has provided me with an understanding of all that can be wonderful about relationships; my husband, Bob, whose loving spirit, optimism, selfless support, editing, and endless late-night cups of tea (delivered with the question "when will you be done with this book?") enabled me to complete this work with my self-esteem intact; my special group of friends who helped me in countless ways through both of these editions, offering babysitting, distraction, guidance, and perspective; my coauthors, Joan and Laura, who had the vision and perseverance to encourage me to do "one more round"; and the generous multifaceted help of Judy Levin, Ann Stauble, Kathy Jungreis, Jonathan Slavin, and of course the amazing AnnaMarie Russo, whose organizational and editing skills turned this disparate group of chapters into a coherent whole.

My greatest appreciation is to my daughter, Sofia, who, for better (hopefully) and worse, has accommodated the rhythms of life with a working mom. Her quiet empathy, deep sensitivity and kindness, lively spirit, remarkable intuitiveness, and playful sense of humor have nurtured, centered, and inspired me. This one is for you.

Patricia Hertz
Newton, Massachusetts

1

Inside Out, Outside In:
An Introduction

Joan Berzoff, Laura Melano Flanagan, and Patricia Hertz

In this second edition of *Inside Out and Outside In*, we attempt to explain the complexities of human psychological functioning and human suffering from psychological, social, and biological perspectives. Many schools of psychology, counseling, and social work have turned away from the idea that the psychological lives of individuals, families, or groups can be understood from the "inside out." These schools no longer attend to what motivates human behaviors from an unconscious point of view. Many schools have joined with current managed care practices to argue that only what can be observed, measured, manualized, and empirically tested can be said to be of clinical value. Solution-focused short-term treatments, cognitive behavioral therapies, behavioral therapies, and biological treatments that are quantifiable and empirically grounded are at times preempting the use of psychodynamic approaches, even when these approaches may be equally effective either on their own or in conjunction with other forms of treatment.

An intense debate has been going on about the relative importance of biological etiologies and biological solutions in the treatment of mental illnesses, due in part to our improved diagnostic tools and in part to the problems of financing mental health services. With mandates to cut costs by reducing the access to and frequency of mental health services, the treatment of mental illness and psychological suffering has been increasingly dominated by shorter-term managed care; a heavier reliance on the use of medications; and brief, even single-session, therapy. This, in time, exerts

1

pressure on many clinicians to turn away from theories that try to describe and understand the forces in the mysterious internal world that govern human behavior. Many schools of social work, counseling programs, and psychiatric residencies have cut back or dropped their psychodynamic curricula. We believe that, ultimately, this results in a disservice to clients because a knowledge of psychodynamic forces can illuminate what is going on in any human interaction or communication, no matter how brief it is. If Prozac is prescribed for five people, it will have a different meaning for each, and the meaning (relief, insult, hope, failure, care) will have been shaped, at least partly, by psychodynamic forces. When two men on Social Security disability were given carfare for clinic appointments, one accepted the money gratefully as a sign of concern and care, and the other felt belittled and ashamed. Again, the meaning of the benefit was radically different because of each man's internal and external life experience.

Many schools have turned away from ideas that individuals may be driven by desires or fears that they do not understand, that people may act out of conflicts about which they are unaware, or that they may be compelled to enact old relational templates. They have turned away from looking at the psychic costs of trauma or from the messy and often complex understanding of what constitutes a person's psyche and even soul. They have turned away from developmental models and even from relational models that focus on the importance of the therapeutic relationship for change. Ideological battles over whether to emphasize the importance of social factors or psychological factors are also legion in many schools. Even in the school in which these authors teach, there is no longer consensus about whether a master's-level practice teacher needs to be able to teach about the value of the unconscious in determining behavior.

But as much as the current field of clinical practice is dominated by splits—long term versus short term, behavioral versus intrapsychic, biological, or social—we believe that these are false dichotomies. How can we hold the complexity of our clients' lives if we are compelled to see our clients through only one lens, that is, as problems embedded in the external environment or as biological vulnerabilities, as needs that must be addressed on the concrete or manifest level, or by only attending to their inner lives. To work therapeutically with another human being, we must use multiple lenses, simultaneously, and address external realities: the social contexts of race, class, gender, age, ability, and sexual orientation; the biological determinants of genes and brain chemistry; and the complexity of a person's inner world. In this edition, we attempt, albeit not always successfully, to hold ourselves to this standard of care as we invite the reader to share these lenses with us.

Why, then, do we dichotomize so much? Melanie Klein tells us it is very hard to maintain psychological complexity, especially when we feel helpless or afraid. As clinicians, we often feel helpless. Klein tells us that little children are drawn to seeing the world in black and white terms, where there is only right and wrong, or good and bad. We now actually live in a country that has a similar way of viewing others: good, evil; worthy, unworthy. Melanie Klein tells us that it is a developmental achievement, in fact, to realize that different and even opposing points of views can be held. Klein calls this the depressive position, because it is depressing to realize that there is no one hold on truth. It's hard to hold complexity. It is easier to split.

In this book, then, we try to maintain that every human life is shaped by the interplay of forces that arise from both within and without. We introduce the reader to psychodynamic theories of psychological development, which help us understand the inner world, and we enrich the usefulness of those theories by adding the biological and social aspects that they often lack. Psychodynamic theories do not purport to be all-inclusive. They look through a rather narrow lens deep into an individual's inner psychological world. And yet, to know a person more fully, or to do any kind of clinical work, the lens has to include the biological and the social factors that interweave throughout a client's life. This is why we so strongly believe in what is called the biopsychosocial approach to clinical work.

Each newborn arrives in this world with certain individual physical characteristics—green eyes or chocolate-colored skin or big feet or sweetly shaped ears. Even these seemingly "outside," objective, concrete characteristics are deeply formative, because they would be viewed and valued in vastly different ways in different cultures, thereby shaping the inner world right from the first moment of life outside the womb. And what of gender? Mary is a girl. John is a boy. These simple statements seem to describe objective facts, and yet they belie enormous complexity. Cultures, religions, social classes, even locales have different definitions of what it is to be a boy or to be a girl—as does each different individual. When Freud (1925) noted that biology is destiny, he meant that anatomical and biological differences shape goals, wishes, and personality traits. He was somewhat right, but also very wrong. Gender is one of dozens of variables that will shape a life, but only one. The more correct statement would be "everything is destiny": every factor—biological, psychological, and social—makes its impact.

Every baby is born with innate, highly individual, idiosyncratic inner characteristics, some of them biologically based. These traits—a quickness to anger, an easy smile, a way of being calm or fidgety, a lively curiosity, a tendency to melancholy—are not so easily visible, much harder to get to know, and ultimately always somewhat mysterious. Yet, they too play a crucial, complex role in shaping the course of a person's life. And the web grows. All babies with their own inner and outer characteristics are then born into an outer world with great specificities of its own: time, place, class, race, family, community, country, ethnic group, religion, political climate.

To be born a Caucasian middle-class girl of European descent in New York City in 2007 is to be born into a different world and a different life than a Caucasian middle-class girl of European descent born in New York City in 1940 or 1911. At a breakfast honoring young women in their twenties who had achieved rising-star status, the New York Women's Agenda organization also honored women in their eighties and nineties who had not been able to become stars in their field simply because of when they were born. Many of the older women were in tears, speaking about the pride, the envy, and the loss they felt listening to the opportunities being made by and for the younger women today.

And these are only small examples of the variable of time. Every other variable is just as powerful. An African American baby and a Korean American baby and a Swedish American baby born on the same day in the same hospital in Kansas City will each be strengthened or assaulted by very different outside forces.

We believe strongly in holding a balanced, comprehensive biopsychosocial view of assessment and treatment, valuing each of the components equally. We hope in this book to challenge some of the false dichotomies, and try instead to teach the subtle and ever-changing interweaving of all the factors, the relative weight of which can change from moment to moment.

WHAT IS PSYCHODYNAMIC THEORY?

Since this book focuses predominantly on the psychodynamic part of the biopsychosocial matrix, we need to explain what we mean by the word *psychodynamic*. *Webster's Third International Dictionary* (1963, p. 711) defines *dynamic* as "pertaining to energy or power in motion . . . the motive and controlling forces, physical and moral, of any kind; also, the study of such forces," and "characterized by continuous change, tending to produce change." *Psychodynamic* is defined by *Webster's* (p. 1833) as relating to "the science of dealing with the laws of mental action" and "motivational forces, especially unconscious motives, and relating to or concerned with mental or emotional forces or processes developing especially in early childhood and their effects on behavior and mental states."

The many theories that fall under the term *psychodynamic*, then, have to do with inner energies that motivate, dominate, and control people's behavior. These energies are based in past experiences and present reality. We use the term psychodynamic because it is broad enough to encompass any theory that deals with psychological forces that underlie most human behavior.

We also wish to distinguish *psychodynamic* theory from *psychoanalytic* theory, although this is by no means easy to do. The two terms are often mistaken for one another. Some clinicians use them interchangeably. Others · insist they are vastly different. There is disagreement even among psychoanalysts as to what the term *psychoanalysis* encompasses—some reserving the term for the Freudian theory of unconscious conflicts about drives and desires, others including all theories that deal with anything in the unconscious.

There continues to be, in psychoanalysis, a sharp debate about its nature, purposes, and goals. Some, as Freud did, describe it as a branch of natural science and others, such as Lacan, as a form of hermeneutics in which personal narrative, not objective data, is the only subject of interest.

Richard Chessick (1993) in *A Dictionary for Psychotherapists* says the following about psychoanalysis:

> Psychoanalysis is in some ways very simple to define and in other ways very difficult. All psychoanalytic models have the same conceptual base, the dynamic unconscious, although they may differ in certain fundamental ways. All deal with transference and countertransference and use the method of free association. All view infantile and childhood experiences as crucial and stress preoedipal and oedipal factors to one degree or another. All in various ways and to varying degrees emphasize repetition, the role of the analyst, and the importance of interpretation. (p. 306)

Many of the theories presented in this book include these psychoanalytic concepts, and clinicians who use these theories in their practice often call themselves psychoanalysts. Yet we are not calling this a book on psychoanalysis, because we are including dynamics that are not unconscious, and also because we want to pay more attention to outside social and cultural forces. We view *psychodynamic* as a much broader, more inclusive term and *psychoanalytic* as having a more limited focus. To go back to the dictionary definition, *psychodynamic* applies to all forces at play in shaping the personality. In this book, we use it to mean *any forces*, internal or external, that have an impact on mental and emotional development.

Our hope is that this book will be useful and relevant for a wide range of mental health practitioners, including those who work in settings where transference issues or unconscious conflicts are not the main focus of treatment, either because of time constraints or the needs and goals of the clients. Psychodynamically informed treatment might focus absolutely appropriately on cultural struggles or issues of oppression, or on concrete and reality-based needs.

We believe that a knowledge of psychodynamic theory is not only useful but also invaluable, whether a clinician is treating someone in long-term psychotherapy or conducting diagnostic evaluations, whether one is making a hospital discharge plan or completing a housing application. Clinical knowledge grounded in psychodynamic theory is one of the most powerful ways we have to look inside someone's heart and mind. Without it, we are almost blind, limited to the surface, the concrete, the manifest.

Let us give two examples of why this is so. One of our authors taught in a post-master's program for advanced clinical social workers for over ten years. The students in the program had all received master's degrees in social work from fine schools, but schools that no longer taught psychodynamic theory. All of the students had been in practice for at least several years and many were still receiving supervision in their places of employment, which included hospitals, family service agencies, mental health clinics, addiction programs, prisons, and schools. The students were very knowledgeable and highly skilled in understanding and changing systems (including family systems), in helping clients get necessary services, and in empowering groups whose voices were not being heard. They were, in fact, expert at working from the "outside in." Yet they all applied for additional training, citing a painful and frustrating dearth of knowledge about what was going on inside clients. They felt that they had never been taught to work from the "inside out" and that this lack greatly limited and hampered their clinical work.

In one particular case discussion, a student described trying to work with Michael, a twenty-four-year-old Latino man who was living in a halfway house after psychiatric hospitalization. His history revealed severe and persistent abuse at the hands of his stepfather and abandonment by his mother, who fled from the home and left him with cousins when she herself was abused by the same man. Michael's main emotional problem was that he had divided himself into three parts, which he had named Good Michael, Bad Michael, and Middle Michael. Because of the fragmentation within him, members of the psychiatric team argued about his diagnosis. Some thought he was schizophrenic, others believed he suffered from multiple personality disorder, and still others saw him as having a borderline personality.

The post-master's student assigned to be Michael's clinician did excellent work helping Michael to adjust to life outside the hospital and get started in a sheltered workshop. But he was mystified about the meaning of the three different Michaels and uncomfortable when the patient referred to them. The student felt he had no vocabulary and no tools to understand the reason for the nature of the fragmentation, especially because Michael seemed at times to be very pleased to have these selves and other times to be in great pain because he was "so messed up."

A psychodynamically informed view of Michael's inner world ultimately allowed his therapist to enter into and understand Michael's separate selves. Michael spoke nervously about how his family held very strict Catholic views that he felt were almost impossible to reconcile with some of their own behavior and with the appeal of drugs and sexual activity so easily available in his neighborhood. At home, he heard that giving in to the Devil would lead to an eternity in Hell, while on the streets his peers tried to lure him into drugs and sex. Early in his life, Michael became overwhelmed by these confusing and conflicting forces that were both outside and inside himself, for he wanted to be good and close to God and his family, but he also wanted to experience the pleasure and power of the streets. Hence, the creation of the three Michaels to reflect and embody these disparate, seemingly irreconcilable parts of himself. When the therapist truly understood Michael's need to divide his inner experiences into parts, as well as the risks of integrating them, she was able to help Michael begin to weave the parts of himself together.

Another example is that of Martin, a twenty-eight-year-old black Haitian man, who came seeking mental health treatment because he could not stop worrying about what was to befall him next. His anguish had caused him to drop out of graduate school, he had lost his part-time job, and his marriage was in deep emotional trouble.

Martin, the son of a policeman, had grown up in a Caribbean Catholic culture with a father who expected his son to bring honor to the family. At age twenty, Martin had emigrated to the United States to pursue an advanced degree, and was by all standards doing well. One evening he attended a party in a racially mixed part of the city that was rife with racism. The party became loud, and the police were called. Martin, although quiet and soft-spoken, was physically large, and the officers who arrested him placed him overnight in jail. Fellow white prisoners assaulted him with racial epithets and doused him with buckets of urine. When released (with no charges), he was unable to function or concentrate. He lost considerable weight and could not stop dwelling on the humiliating experience. He berated himself and felt that somehow he deserved the punishment.

While the postgraduate student did an excellent job of connecting Martin to legal services and advocating on Martin's behalf educationally, she was bewildered about why Martin remained emotionally immobilized despite the resolution of his legal and educational concerns and his taking psychiatric medication. The student lacked the theoretical tools to understand that Martin had experienced the external racial assaults *internally*, and how the oppressive environment, which was once outside, was now introjected inside, continuing to cause tremendous anxiety and self-reproach.

For Michael, and for Martin, as perhaps for all clients, there is often no more profound experience than being heard, understood, and accepted. This requires that the clinician have empathy—the ability to project oneself into the experience of another. Empathy requires knowledge and skill. In this book we hope to tackle the first element of this formula, showing how knowledge about a client's inner life helps us enter into the client's whole experience. We hope to demonstrate how an understanding of internal psychological factors, as they are interwoven with external factors such as culture, gender, race, class, and biology, helps us understand the tapestry that becomes an individual self. It is from this perspective that we begin to learn how the outside comes to be inside a person, and, in turn, how the inner world shapes a person's outer reality.

WHO IS THIS BOOK FOR?

This book has been written for beginning clinicians who are about to make the long and challenging journey into clinical work. It is also written for those more experienced practitioners who may never have had a comprehensive understanding of psychodynamic theories and their uses in a multicultural world. It is for all students who want to understand how internal life is conceptualized within biological and social contexts, and for those practitioners and continuing students who want to learn to thoughtfully critique these theories. It is written for those practitioners who are challenged by the limits of managed care and who want to understand how what is inside and outside an individual comes to be metabolized as psychological strengths and disturbances. For many, we hope that it will serve as a useful review.

There are many psychological texts that discuss drive theory, ego psychology, life cycle theory, trauma theory, object relations, self psychology, attachment theory, and relational theory, and there are many texts about culture, race, and ethnicity. In this book, however, we combine a psychodynamic understanding of individuals with an understanding of how they function within their social contexts. To our knowledge, this is one of the few attempts to look at the inside *and* outside concurrently, or at least with equal weight, which is difficult to accomplish because most psychodynamic theories are more heavily weighted toward the inner world. For years, as teachers, we would become defensive when those more interested in teaching about external realities and oppression would tell us that what we said about race, class, gender, and culture was always "just tacked on at the end." What we finally realized is that it sounds tacked on because it is. In fact, that is precisely the contribution we are trying to make. We are adding, completing, enriching, and, we hope, integrating knowledge from biology, sociology, anthropology, and folklore to psychodynamic theory. Starting with Freud, through Erikson, to Greenberg and Mitchell in the present, theoreticians have been aware of and interested in the role of culture. However, to date, psychodynamic theories of development are still in their infancy, and clinicians continue to grapple with how to integrate fully the issues of race, class, gender, and culture (Altman 2000, Chodorow 1991, Moss 2006, Perez-Foster et al. 1996, Roland 1996, Wachtel 2002).

Similarly, there are many books that review the characteristics of different psychopathologies. *DSM-IV-TR*, while demonstrating a greater awareness of cultural influence on diagnoses than previous editions, remains an atheoretical, descriptive text of objective criteria for mental illnesses. A more recent text, the *PDM* (2006), is the first to try to offer a developmental understanding of each of the psychological disorders. Some other texts offer an understanding of emotional disturbances by looking at them through a biological, cognitive, or psychodynamic lens alone, or by critiquing the current explanations of the etiologies of the disorders. We attempt, once again, to hold biological, psychological, and social lenses *concurrently* as we look at several, somewhat arbitrarily chosen, diagnostic entities. We try to resist the tendency toward polarization by exploring the contributions of psychodynamic, biological, and social factors in the development of emotional difficulties. Once again, while acknowledging that equal weight is not always given to each of these factors, our commitment is to demonstrate the relevance of both external and internal forces in shaping the lives of individuals and the mental disturbances that plague them.

A CRITICAL THINKING STANCE

In this book we study psychodynamic concepts and theories of psychopathology from the perspective of human behavior. Psychodynamic theories represent approximations of human experience, metaphors that have developed within particular cultures, during particular social times, and with particular social values. As such, we state and restate our conviction that every theory is a social construction. By this we mean that all theories are, of necessity, products of their time and place and culture. No thinker or writer or practitioner lives in a vacuum. Every theoretician is inevitably influenced by all the experiences of his or her life and, therefore, constructs theories out of the raw material of those experiences. Many theoreticians find it difficult to acknowledge that their ideas are socially constructed and culture bound. They often fall prey to the rather grandiose notion that their theories are universal and apply to all people at all times. We believe that no one theory or even any combination of theories can fully describe something as unique and complex as a human being. Even while using a comprehensive biopsychosocial approach, it is necessary for clinicians to recognize that all the theories in the world are not sufficient to explain everything about a person's feelings, strengths, or weaknesses. As Hamlet says to Horatio, "There are more things in heaven and earth, Horatio, than are dreamt of in your philosophy."

As we study each theory and pathology, we ask: Who created this theory? What dominant ideologies does the theory represent? Who is not represented? What gender or racial biases are embedded in the theory of psychopathology? Does this theory apply to all people at all times?

Because many psychodynamic theories have been silent about issues of race and gender, while other theorists have openly devalued oppressed groups such as women or people of color, we provide a gender and a racial critique of psychodynamic theories. Many students and their professors are tempted, when a theory is biased, to throw out the baby with the bath water. We are critical of some of the psychodynamic theories for their biases or omissions in terms of race or gender, for their devaluation of oppressed groups, and for who they include and exclude in the theory. But we also see how some psychodynamic theories are invaluable in helping us understand how people experience oppression psychologically.

THEORY AND CULTURE

As we present psychodynamic theories and psychopathologies throughout this book, we want to remind the reader that definitions of health and pathology are always culture bound. In predominantly white Western cultures, for example, considerable value is placed on autonomy and individuation as the psychological developmental goal. Many Eastern, African, and Hispanic cultures, however, define health as the achievement of interdependence. This was brought home to us in the description of a normal psychological development class held in Iran in 1984. Iranian psychology students were asked to observe two mother-child dyads: one American and the other Iranian. The American mother brought her toddler to class dressed in a pair of ragged jeans and dirty sneakers. Within minutes, the toddler was wandering among the students, eating candy they offered, straying far from the mother, who smiled as her daughter wandered from student to student. By contrast, the Iranian baby was extremely well groomed, her dress was formal, and she and her mother never left the elegant rug that her mother had so carefully set down. While the Iranian baby sat silently on her mother's lap, the students were asked to assess the psychological health of the dyads. Uniformly, the first mother-child pair was diagnosed by the Iranian students as highly pathological given the mother's "neglect" and the child's obvious "lack of attachment." The second pair was seen as normal and healthy because the child and mother were so tightly bound. American observers would have arrived at opposite conclusions. They would have seen the Iranian baby as too passive, dependent, and enmeshed; the American baby as healthily active and independent. Whereas in predominantly white Western cultures, the baby is viewed as a dependent creature needing to begin the healthy journey toward independence and autonomy, in Iranian culture, the baby is seen as already too separate and distinct, needing to be bound to the community. In this book, we take the stance that normality is always in the eyes of the observer.

Consider another cautionary tale about the errors that can ensue when a well-intentioned clinician is unfamiliar with cultural traditions and so defines health in her terms.

Two years after receiving her MSW, the clinician was working in a large city hospital, assigned to the inpatient unit of the department of psychiatry. She had been working with the parents and young wife of a medical student who had become psychotic. The patient was suicidal and had been hospitalized on the very ward where he had been a promising and successful intern. The social worker had been seeing the parents together and the young wife alone for over six months.

Despite being medicated and having someone with him, the medical student committed suicide by throwing himself off the roof of the hospital. The task of notifying the family fell to the social worker. After spending some time with each shocked and grieved family member, the social worker was asked if she would pay a call to the parents' house the next evening, which she agreed to do.

Feeling quite shaken, she arrived promptly at 6:00 PM and observed the following: the door was propped open, the mirrors were covered with what looked like burlap, and several women were sitting on wooden crates. The women wore no makeup and their hair was uncombed; the men wore suits, but their feet were in sneakers; the men also wore ties that looked ripped or cut up.

Despite coming from a bicultural, bilingual family and living in a multicultural city, the worker saw only strangeness and unfamiliarity, and instantly diagnosed the entire family as suffering from a simultaneous psychotic break. She remained frozen in the doorway while actually beginning to count the number of people in the room in order to tell 911 how many ambulances to send!

The mother of the dead medical student, however, was able to assess the clinician's predicament and very gently said, "No, it's not what you think. We have not all gone mad. We are sitting Shiva and this is our way of mourning. Come in and let us explain it to you."

The importance of this vignette is that it illustrates how, in the clinician's own anxiety, she saw pathology in what was, in fact, cultural strength—the strength of a family to use their beliefs and rituals to engage in the process of grieving.

This book attends to both the cultural relativity of our theories and our diagnoses, and to the ways different racial, ethnic, and cultural groups have of coping with, and finding solutions to, what others may define as pathology.

An essential part of making a diagnosis and of ensuing clinical work is the capacity to identify strengths—of the individual, the family, the community, and the culture. No matter what degree of disturbance we encounter in our clients, there will also be in them sources of joy, ideals, flexibility, humor, ambition, and hope that give them strength, solace, and the potential for growth. These must be elicited, heard, respected, and understood with the same vigor we use in pursuing the deficits, developmental arrests, and maladaptation that characterize their psychopathology.

HOW THIS BOOK IS ORGANIZED

First, a word about language. We originally tried to write the book using the female pronoun *she* exclusively, in order to correct the centuries of books written only about *he*. Eventually, this came to sound as stilted as any book written using only the male pronoun. We then tried *he or she*, and *she or he*, and even *s/he*, but these combinations sounded forced and unnatural. What we finally settled on is our own idiosyncratic combinations of *she* and *he*, which, after all, more accurately reflect the composition of the human race and the way people actually speak in real life.

In the first half of the book, the authors examine and illuminate core concepts drawn from psychodynamic theories: drive theory, ego psychology, life-cycle theory, object relations, self psychology, attachment theory, control mastery theory, and relational theories. Each of these theories offers different lenses, many complementary and some contradictory, for understanding how the self develops in many contexts. We study these concepts historically and in terms of their applicability to clinical practice. We learn how each theory developed within its unique social context and is therefore a product of that milieu. We also learn how each theory was revised by internal critiques within the theory itself and by external critiques outside of the theory, and how those critiques led to new theory development. We especially attend, in separate chapters, to the approach (or lack thereof) to race and gender in psychodynamic theories. In summary, the first half of the book examines different ways in which psychodynamic theories have conceptualized human problems from the inside out.

Because we think that psychodynamic concepts help us understand people in different social contexts, we have chosen to use cases drawn from our own practices in multicultural settings. Many books on psychodynamic theory illustrate their concepts using white and privileged middle-class clients who may be shielded from discrimination, poverty, homelessness, disabilities, discrimination based on sexual orientation, and severe and persistent mental illness. Our intent is to show how psychodynamic concepts are useful and apply to populations that are not so privileged. Hence we have chosen cases for their variations in race, class, gender, culture, and sexual orientation.

In the second half of the book, we use the theories and concepts discussed in the first half to understand five major psychopathologies. We do not study all of the diagnoses in the *DSM-IV-TR*. Rather, we have chosen to study those diagnoses for which a knowledge of psychodynamic theories seems to be the best way to help the clinician into the internal world of the client. These five broad categories are the psychoses, personality disorders, depression, anxiety, and trauma. With an increasing appreciation for the importance of neurobiology in understanding psychopathology, we introduce those concepts as they relate to each of these diagnostic categories.

Psychodynamic explanations alone do not account for all of human suffering. Social and biological influences are also factored into the study of each of these disorders. As is true in the first half of the book, when we study the psychopathologies, we continue to ask: How does the diagnosis reflect the dominant values and ideologies of the social times in which it developed? Who does it privilege? Who does it marginalize? What biases are inherent in the diagnosis? In addition, as we study each of these five major psychological conditions, we attend not only to the experience of the client, but also to the experience of the helper. We try to remember that not only are definitions of psychopathology socially constructed, but beliefs about health are also culture bound.

In this book we hope to convey some appreciation for the mysteries of another person's humanness. Respect for the mysteries inherent in clinical work can be particularly difficult when one is trying to learn a theory and its application. The developmental theories we study here are by nature causal and linear. They postulate that if certain experiences occur during certain stages of development, certain results are likely to follow. Sometimes they do, but often they do not, which must always be remembered to keep us honest, open, and alive to the sense of wonder with which human phenomena must be clinically approached.

There is a passage in Mary Gordon's *Men and Angels* (1985) that expresses how little can really be known about the relationship between a traumatic event in childhood and its effects on personality development. A mother, stunned after she has discovered the dead body of their babysitter who has committed suicide, holds her sleepy children in her arms. She thinks about the kinds of trauma that mothering sometimes inflicts and about how little we can know about its results. She muses:

And what could you say of it [mothering] that was true? She used to think it was of all loves the most innocent, but now she knew she had been wrong. There were mothers who loved their children in a way that cut the children's breath and stopped their hearts; there were mothers who, in a passion of love, took the children and pressed them to their bosoms and in the next moment threw the children screaming from them, covering them with blows. There were mothers for whom the sight of their children meant nothing; no love stirred, no part of their heart lifted. There were mothers who hated their children from the moment of their births; who hated the first touch of flesh on flesh and went on hating. There were mothers who loved their children but could not love them, for they bent to kiss the children's flesh and felt the flesh stop in their mouths and make them fear for their next breaths. *And children throve or starved, and no one knew why, or what killed or saved.* (p. 238, italics added)

What a frightening, yet freeing, statement for a clinician, and what an excellent reminder that theory cannot possibly explain everything. There is, then, always mystery in clinical work.

It is crucial that when we learn developmental psychodynamic theories, we are careful not to define the person's pathology by a specific deficit or trauma that occurred in one particular stage of development (e.g., there was a trauma when the client was two years old; therefore, he must have difficulties in separation and individuation and must be borderline). Instead, in every case, we need to know how the individual emotionally, constitutionally, and socially comes to be who she is and to explore the subtle, complex interplay between who the person is and what her environment provides. This is why a biopsychosocial approach to diagnosis offers the best chance for understanding a person in all her fullness.

This second edition has added new content on trauma, attachment, relational theories, and control mastery theory, and has revised all of the previous content to include newer knowledge about both neurobiological and social factors. This book, then, has many purposes. In it, we hope to convey an appreciation for the value of psychodynamic theories as students try to learn how to enter into something as unique and complex as the inner life of another human being. We hope to show how a person takes in her environment and acts upon her environment based upon both her strengths and weaknesses, which she has developed from a complex web of experiences, relationships, innate abilities, biological endowments, and social conditions. We hope to articulate what motivates human behavior and some of the life experience and healing environments that promote psychological growth. We want to stress the importance of social factors—culture, class, race, gender, and the physical surround—on experiences of self and identity, and to emphasize how social work can powerfully contribute to or undermine optimal development. In addition, we hope that students will think critically about the theories they use and about the social and political contexts in which they always develop.

REFERENCES

Altman, N. (2000). Black and white thinking: A psychoanalyst reconsiders race. *Psychoanalytic Dialogues* 10(4):589–605.

Chessick, R. (1993). *A Dictionary for Psychotherapists: Dynamic Concepts in Psychotherapy*. Northvale, NJ: Jason Aronson.

Chodorow, N. (1991). Feminism, femininity, and Freud. In *Feminism and Psychoanalytic Theory*. New Haven, CT: Yale University Press.

Freud, S. (1925). Some psychical consequences of the anatomical distinction between the sexes. *Standard Edition* 19.

Gordon, M. (1985). *Men and Angels*. New York: Random House.

Moss, D. (2006). Mapping racism. *Psychoanalytic Quarterly* 75:271–95.

PDM Task Force. (2006). *Psychodynamic Diagnostic Manual*. Silver Spring, MD: Alliance of Psychoanalytic Organizations.

Perez-Foster, R., Moskowitz, M., and Javier, R. A. (1996). *Reaching across Boundaries of Culture and Class: Widening the Scope of Psychotherapy*. Northvale, NJ: Jason Aronson, Inc.

Roland, A. (1996). How universal is the psychoanalytic self? In *Cultural Pluralism and Psychoanalysis: The Asian and North American Experience*, pp. 3–21. New York: Routledge.

Wachtel, P. L. (2002). Psychoanalysis and the disenfranchised: From therapy to justice. *Psychoanalytic Psychology* 19(1): 199–215.

Webster's Third New International Dictionary. (1963). Springfield, MA: G. & C. Merriam Company.

2

Freud's Psychoanalytic Concepts

Joan Berzoff

We said in our introduction that we live in a world in which mental health practices are being evaluated almost exclusively through the lens of quantifiable goals (i.e., the reduction of measurable symptoms, but not necessarily the improvement of the quality of a person's life). We live in an era in which empirical validation trumps a more philosophical, imaginative, or interpretive way of understanding human behavior. We live in a period in which social work education devalues psychoanalytic theories, either caricaturing them as endless navel gazing, or favoring theories and practices that are manualized and measurable. Why have so many schools abandoned psychoanalytic theories and practices?

Perhaps one reason is that we do not like to view people as conflicted within themselves, nor are we comfortable admitting that our clients' inner worlds, let alone our own, may be full of hate, sexuality, desire, rage, envy, aggression, or other passions of which we are largely unaware. We may not welcome the idea that early trauma shapes our subsequent behavior in ways that we may live out, often destructively, in unconscious relationships within ourselves and with others. We may not like the idea that our everyday dream life, slips of the tongue, or behaviors—of which we are totally unaware—have meanings that, when decoded, may reveal our frailties or vulnerabilities. We may not welcome the thought that difficulties at one stage of development may have lasting effects on our character, relationships, and sense of the world and of others. We may not want to acknowledge that we have an unconscious life that may propel us to act in ways that are irrational, not in our best interests, or even contrary to our own ideals. We may not like to think about the sensual or sexual lives of children. We may not want to confront the ways in which our minds disavow unpleasant truths. We may not want to embrace a psychological view that is inexact, messy, and ambiguous. While the zeitgeist of Freud's time forced him to try to make his work a science, a more postmodern view of Freud holds that, like Karl Marx, he was trying to alleviate human suffering, alienation, and conflict, based on a humanistic view that people, unaware of the origins of their suffering, were unlikely to be able to change them.

Take for example, Paul White, a fifty-year-old white, male computer technician who came to treatment actively suicidal and unable to work after having hacked into his wife's computer and learned of her affair, which had been going on for the last two years. She would not come to treatment with him and told him that she was not interested in ending the affair either. Paul envisioned hanging himself, using a computer cable.

Paul soon revealed having grown up in a home in which he felt powerless in the face of an economically and emotionally impoverished single mother, who was sixteen when he was born. She told him often that he had destroyed her childhood, and conveyed her rage and disappointment for her difficult life and his by withdrawing from him. His solution was to enslave himself to her, and in the face of her distance and terrible economic circumstances, he learned to do whatever was asked of him. As soon as he was able, he took on all the household chores from folding laundry to cooking meals. He was not allowed to leave the perimeter of his yard, though he longed to be with other children on his street. When he was ten, his mother remarried, subsequently bearing two more children, whom both parents, he felt, treated preferentially. Paul felt that his parents expected him to be a "man," as they increased his responsibilities to include taking care of his siblings. When his mother later divorced her husband and abandoned the family, she left Paul in charge of his two younger brothers.

At eighteen, Paul left his brothers behind and joined the army, where he thrived on the order and discipline. He had long planned to marry his high school girlfriend, until his mother interfered and encouraged his girlfriend to end the engagement. Soon thereafter, Paul took up with a single mother who, at age sixteen, had had her own child. Unmindful of the likeness to his own mother, he set about rescuing her from a life of poverty, paying for her divorce, and buying her a home. During their twenties, she engaged in many extramarital affairs while he supported her. Now he was ready to kill himself, largely unaware of how the present repeated the past.

It was Freud who first unlocked a way of looking at Paul's life and behavior and who offered some understanding of what drove Paul, what motivated his behavior, how his rage was turned inward rather than outward, how his early traumatic events had shaped his character, and how his modes of relating were not working for him now. It was Freud who first wrote a set of assumptions about psychic life that explained the power of the unconscious mind, the ways in which early experiences are repeated in the present, the ways in which psychological conflicts shape development while repudiated aspects of past relationships emerge in present life. It was Freud who first saw the relationship between past and present, who first articulated developmental models that shaped symptoms and behaviors, and who first assumed that there was even something called an unconscious life.

Freud's work is often maligned because he is perceived to have been pseudo-scientific, distant, neutral or omniscient, and sexist. Yet Freud was intimately involved with his patients, seeing them many times a week, often in unorthodox treatments, experimenting with and trying to understand what motivated their behaviors. Bruno Bettelheim (1983) argues that Freud wrote of psychoanalysis as not only a science but also a cure through love, a way of taking the work personally and not at a safe distance of anonymity and neutrality. He thought that Freud chose the symbol of *psyche*, for psychoanalysis, from the myth of Psyche, the goddess of love, who had to enter the dark underworld in order to better understand herself. He argued that Freud's work was truly about pathways to self-discovery, and that the German word that had been translated into English as "psychoanalysis" should have been translated as the "analysis of the soul."

Bettleheim reminds us that Freud admonished his readers to know themselves. If we could really face our hateful feelings, and our loving feelings, we might not be compelled to act in ways that are destructive, narcissistic, or self-defeating. It is through self-awareness that we may change the ways in which we act unconsciously, freeing us up to love and work successfully.

Freud, then, was among the first psychological theorists to posit that human beings are driven by powerful instinctual biological forces of which they are largely unaware. These forces—of love or hate, of sexuality and aggression—express themselves differently in each individual, and ultimately shape how each individual functions and develops. In his fifty-three-year career, Freud developed a psychology of the mind in which he identified how the drives (both sexual and aggressive) seek expression and result in characteristic ways of being and living. He showed how the drives influence the development of symptoms and relationships with others.

In his evolving view of human behavior, Freud viewed humans as bestial in their natures (Mitchell 1988), fueled by forces, fantasies, longings, and passions beyond their control. He hypothesized that most psychological problems occur when the drives are opposed by other forces in the mind. His psychodynamic theory became the first one to posit that powerful forces, urges, and wishes exist within the mind and are perpetually in conflict with the self and society. His theory became the first psychological theory to organize those passions into a system of human behavior.

This chapter introduces some of Freud's core concepts that are still relevant to clinicians practicing today. We begin our study with Freud's first insights into the nature of psychological symptoms, using the case of Anna O. This is really the first trauma case, and we will look at the disagreements the case generated, the methods Freud developed for "curing" people, and the absolute importance he placed on the therapeutic relationship for producing psychological change. As his career developed, Freud came to appreciate the importance of the therapist's self-knowledge for understanding the passions and yearnings that might exist in the client. In our study of his ideas, we will examine how Freud used his self-knowledge and his clinical mistakes to revise his theories when the clinical data did not fit. Freud developed many therapeutic methods, such as the analysis of transference/resistance, free association, and the analysis of dreams, as ways of gaining access into the psyches of his clients. We will study how Freud evolved a theory of how drives differ at each stage of childhood development, and how this psychosexual theory explains distinct kinds of character traits, relationships, and potential problems that may emerge. We will examine some of Freud's economic ideas and his conviction that when psychic energies are bound up in one part of the mind, they are depleted for other functions. We will consider Freud's topographic ideas—that there are layers in the mind, which need to be excavated to be understood. Finally, we will show how Freud came to think of psychopathology and of most of human suffering as arising from dynamic conflicts within and between structures of the mind, which he would call his structural theory. Freud was always influenced by the belief that insight, self-awareness, and self-knowledge promote psychological development.

Although Freud used highly scientific and empirical language, his clinical theories were deeply grounded in the actual life experiences of his patients. In his clinical practice, he listened with what he came to call *evenly suspended attention*, trying to be open to hearing what his clients said in ways that allowed the theory to evolve from the data.

INTELLECTUAL TRADITIONS

Freud was a physician and a scientist interested in the investigation of the psyche. Many disciplines influenced his thinking. Because Freud was a neurologist, he conceptualized the mind in terms of neural excitations that were stored and needed to be discharged or tamed. Neurology also influenced his thinking that psychological functions occur in discrete or separate parts of the brain. From his neurological background, he envisioned each function of the mind as interdependent and acting upon the others. Physics had a profound influence on Freud, leading him to view human behavior as a function of predetermined and predictable forces. Physics also contributed a hydraulic metaphor to Freud's thinking—that there were finite amounts of energy in the mind that, if used in one place, were not available for other functions. Archaeology and geology also influenced him. He saw the mind as having a *prehistory* that needed to be *excavated* to be understood. Freud's scientific leanings were also leavened with a love of art, literature, religion, and philosophy, all of which contributed to his appreciation of the symbolic aspects of human behavior. Shakespeare influenced the romantic elements of Freud's thinking, especially about human tragedy and suffering. From Judaism emerged other strains: deep pessimism about the human condition, cultural prescriptions about the value of an individual life, and deep meaning assigned to the value of the nuclear family. Judaism also influenced the mystical side of Freud that probed deeply into the inner workings of the soul.

SOCIOCULTURAL INFLUENCES

Throughout this book, we will emphasize that every theory can be understood as a social construction emerging from the unique economic, cultural, religious, and political forces of the times in which it is developed. Thus, to understand Freud's earliest psychoanalytic concepts, we have to look at how his culture informed his thinking, and how the social times in which he lived contributed to his worldview. Freud was born in 1856 in Freiberg, Moravia (now a part of the Czech Republic), to the family of a wool merchant. When he was four years old, Freud moved with his family to Vienna. At the height of the Victorian era, this city was considered to be the seat of licentiousness and sexuality in Europe. There was a facade of control and repression of sexuality within a largely Catholic culture. Yet men routinely went to prostitutes, and likewise, women had lovers. Women in Victorian Vienna were viewed either as sexual property, among the working classes, or as sexless objects with carefully prescribed social roles (Lerman 1986). In either case, women rarely were expected to fulfill their potential for whole human experience. Furthermore, the absence of means for birth control made the expression of sexuality in all social classes a dangerous enterprise. Thus, Freud grew up in a cultural context of sexual contradictions. It was within this social context that the concept of repressed sexuality, so central to Freud's thinking, emerged.

It is also important to note that as a Jew in Vienna, Freud was the victim of rampant anti-Semitism, which marginalized him professionally and impeded his professional recognition. Many of his ideas remained outside mainstream medicine. Some of his views reflected his own experiences of oppression, so that by the end of his career, when he was forced to flee from Vienna in the face of Nazism, he came even more to believe that aggression was a central force, not only in human development but in national development as well.

FREUD'S EVOLUTION OF A THEORY AND METHOD FOR UNDERSTANDING HYSTERIA AND TRAUMA

Freud completed medical school in Vienna within three years and went on to study with Charcot, a Parisian neurologist who treated women suffering from hysteria. Charcot's female patients suffered many symptoms, including paralysis and blindness, for which there was no known organic cause. At that time, it was thought that the symptoms these "madwomen" suffered had a particularly female etiology. Indeed the very word *hysteria* in Latin meant "wandering uterus," and so it was common in those days to attribute a sexual etiology to certain kinds of madness. Charcot experimented with treating hysterical symptoms by such methods as hypnosis and the application of pressure to sensitive spots, such as the ovaries. Freud studied hypnosis with him and began to suspect that hysteria was not solely a woman's disease and that hysterical symptoms were not simply fabrications of women's minds (Brill 1921). Freud made enormous intellectual leaps, however, when he went from hypnotizing women in Charcot's clinic in Salpêtrière to discovering key concepts in psychoanalysis that are still alive in our practices today. Let us then turn to one of the cases in which he discovered so many of these concepts.

Anna O.: The Case in Which Freud Conceptualized Free Association, Symptoms as Disguised Wishes, Transference, Countertransference, Resistance, and Repression

In 1882, early in Freud's career, his colleague Josef Breuer consulted with him about a woman who came to be called "Anna O." This was a troubling case that had ended badly. Anna O. was a beautiful, intelligent, and willful twenty-one-year-old woman whose symptoms included a nervous cough, difficulty swallowing, anorexia, suicidal ideation, sleepwalking, rages at her governess, tics, squints, paralyses of her arms and neck, temporary blindness, an inability to speak in her native German, and episodes of changed consciousness. The patient was an intellectually gifted woman from an upper-middle-class Jewish family. Yet the choices available to young women in her day were to marry, become a governess, or tend to the sick. For such a creative and gifted young woman, these options were particularly oppressive.

When her father fell ill of pneumonia, she was charged with his care.

After nursing him until his death, her symptoms became so overwhelming as to affect every aspect of her waking life. These symptoms continued for over two years. Anna O. also had a family history of psychological instability among her more distant relatives and had two siblings who had died.

Her internist, Josef Breuer, was a handsome, middle-aged physician who began treating Anna's physical symptoms by hypnotizing her in the late afternoons at her bedside. He visited her three to four times a week and held her hand as he invited her to enter into a hypnotic state. When he asked her about what may have caused a particular symptom, she would say whatever came to mind, without censorship. Often she would not recognize him, and would drift into trances, or following his visits, fall into deep sleep, or her "clouds." During these late afternoon meetings, she spoke easily (Freeman 1979).

It was Anna O. who called this a "talking cure" and likened telling everything on her mind to "chimney sweeping." In fact, Breuer and Anna O. were actually developing a method that would become central to psychoanalysis, that of *free association*, in which access to hidden or forgotten feelings, memories, and wishes could be gained from saying, without censorship, whatever came to mind.

In the course of Breuer's work with Anna O., many ideas that gave rise to the field of psychoanalysis emerged. Breuer thought that by letting his patient speak freely and in a hypnotic state, she could revisit the traumatic events of the past two years, and abreact, or rid herself of those memories. Without any formal training in psychoanalysis, or even the existence of such a field, Breuer intuited that her fantasies might be texts that might unlock secrets about how and why her illness had developed.

Until his collaboration with Freud, however, Breuer still had no way of making sense of the many fantasies Anna O. produced. For example, in his paper with Freud, he wrote:

[In] July, 1880, while he [Breuer] was in the country, her father fell seriously ill of a sub-pleural abscess. Anna shared the duties of nursing him with her mother. She once woke up during the night in great anxiety about the patient, who was in a high fever. . . . Her mother had gone away for a short time and Anna was sitting at the bedside with her right arm over the back of the chair. She fell into a waking dream and saw a black snake coming towards the sick man from the wall to bite him. . . . (In reality, she had been recently frightened by *actual* snakes behind her house.) She tried to keep the snake off, but it was as though she was paralysed. Her right arm, over the back of the chair, had gone to sleep and had become anesthetic and paretic; when she looked at it the fingers turned into little snakes with death's heads. . . . When the snake vanished, in her terror she tried to pray. But language failed her: she could find no tongue in which to speak. . . . The whistle of the train that was bringing the doctor whom she expected broke the spell. (Freud and Breuer 1893, p. 39)

Imagine a woman reporting such a hallucination! Without a pre-existing theoretical model, how would one give meaning to the symbol of the snake or to her experiences of paralysis and muteness?

Freud and Breuer began to hypothesize that this "waking dream" contained conflicts. Today we might speculate that Anna O. wished her father's suffering to end and, hence, wished for his death. Perhaps Anna O. was angry at being left to care for her father and wished that snakes would kill him. However, such aggressive wishes, especially at her own hands, would have conflicted with her role as caretaker and so would need to be kept out of consciousness. Perhaps, having nursed her father in the most intimate of circumstances, alone and at night, separated from her mother and deprived of any opportunities to be with men her own age, Anna O. felt sexual feelings toward her father. The snakes, which came out of her own hands, might have not only a biting and aggressive component, they might also represent forbidden sexual wishes that she had for her father, or perhaps masturbatory impulses. Since these sexual feelings might have been unacceptable to her, they might have been out of her conscious awareness. It is even possible, given the nature of her episodes—her difficulty swallowing and her anorexia—that she might have been the victim of sexual abuse and that the snakes might have represented memories of previous sexual trauma. But all of these ideas were to follow later with the development of drive theory.

At this time in history what Anna O. consciously experienced was paralysis and muteness. Freud would later hypothesize that, in a condensed way, her physical symptoms expressed both her sexual and aggressive wishes as well as their prohibitions. Freud now began to think that physical symptoms were internal psychological conflicts that were converted into physical pathways. He later called these kinds of symptoms *conversion hysteria*, and they are currently classified under the general rubric of somatoform disorders.

As Anna O. and Breuer continued their work, many of her conversion symptoms began to have some association to previous trauma. Her difficulty hearing seemed related to her father having asked her in vain for some wine. Her squint appeared related to a time when she couldn't see her father because of the tears in her eyes. Her cough seemed related to wishes to be elsewhere than with her dying father. Each symptom seemed to have some association with wishes or feelings that were consciously unacceptable and had been transformed into physical states. As the associations were discovered, examined, and understood, many of her symptoms abated.

Over time, a deep relationship developed between Anna O. and her doctor. When he went on vacation, leaving another physician to look in on her, she went into a deep depression, becoming paralyzed and mute again. As she had been paralyzed under the weight of feelings toward her father, some of her intense feelings now appeared to be occurring within her current relationship with her physician. This experience of bringing to the therapeutic relationship feelings, wishes, and assumptions from past relationships was the phenomenon that we now refer to as *transference*. Although neither Freud nor Breuer named it as such, transference refers to reexperiencing and reenacting in current relationships the wishes, feelings, and experiences from past relationships. This takes place in all relationships, but is a particularly useful tool for understanding the internal and *unconscious* aspects of clients' inner lives as they are lived out in the treatment process.

As episodes from the previous year in which she tended her sick father were repeated, remembered, and talked through, Anna O. seemed to improve, and Breuer attempted to terminate the treatment. To his great dismay, however, he was summoned to Anna O.'s bedside in the middle of the night to find her in the midst of a hysterical pregnancy. As she screamed and groaned in labor, she accused Breuer of being the father of the baby. Breuer was unaware of and certainly unprepared for the intensity of Anna's feelings toward him. Given that he had no theoretical model in which to conceptualize her sexual feelings for him, he hypnotized her a final time and is reported to have left for a second honeymoon, never to see her again (Jones 1953).

What Breuer could not know, and what Freud was to discover, was just how powerful, real, and urgent Anna O.'s sexual feelings were. These powerful transference feelings had flourished during their regressive late afternoon sessions. Anna O.'s sexual and aggressive fantasies had been transferred to her current therapist and were experienced as if they were actually happening in their relationship. Because those feelings were not acknowledged, they became represented in her hysterical pregnancy. And because Breuer did not recognize his own feelings in himself, he wrote of his beautiful patient, "The element of sexuality was astonishingly undeveloped in her" (Freud and Breuer 1893, p. 21). A therapist's own sexual and aggressive fantasies and feelings toward the client are called *countertransference reactions*. Breuer's unawareness of his own countertransference reactions probably resulted in his disavowed attraction to her and in the premature termination.

Today, we know that denying, avoiding, or repressing countertransference feelings interferes with the therapeutic process. In fact, the patient's growing conscious awareness of feelings for the therapist, and the therapist's awareness of feelings for the patient, provide some of the most useful data in clinical work. This process—in which the client examines her own feelings, fantasies, and reactions to the therapist, and the therapist does the same toward the client, either inwardly or in supervision—requires honesty, vigilance, and self-knowledge. When these intense feelings are recognized, Freud thought, they can be controlled. But when they are denied, resisted, or avoided, as Breuer did, they can negatively affect the course of treatment. Freud initially thought that transference should and could be avoided, but he would shortly discover, in the case of Dora, that transference was an unavoidable part of the talking cure. Later, he came to see transference not as an impediment, but as *the* major vehicle for psychoanalysis.

Anna O. did not do well immediately after her treatment with Breuer. She was hospitalized and even addicted to morphine for a time. But she later became a great feminist social worker, advocating on behalf of women who had been exploited—prostitutes, unmarried mothers, and young girls in the white slave trade. Perhaps her commitment to working with women oppressed by men had its roots in her unequal relationships with her brother and her father, as well as with Breuer. We do know that she did not value psychoanalysis for her own clients and that she appeared never to have forgiven Breuer for "not knowing" (Freeman 1979).

Yet, the irony is that, because Breuer did not know, and because he dared explore an inner world that neither she nor he could understand, he unknowingly discovered the phenomena of transference and countertransference. Because he did not know, and because he dared to share his clinical errors with Freud, Freud was later able to use this case to begin to develop core concepts still used in psychodynamic practice today.

THE BEGINNINGS OF CONFLICT THEORY

Let us now examine several of the concepts from this case that led Freud to develop his theory of the mind. First, the case of Anna O. led Freud to think that by free-associating, by reliving the past, and by verbalizing repressed feelings, past trauma could be worked through, and some symptoms could be relieved. Second, this case illustrated that traumatic experiences, when repressed, sought expression through physical symptoms. Freud would later show that by freely associating in the context of a trusting relationship, clients could gain access to powerful sexual and aggressive wishes. Freud also began to discover in his work with other hysterical women that their wishes and urges that sought release were always opposed by counterforces in the mind that resisted coming into consciousness. This was the essence of his idea of a conflict theory, that unconscious sexual and aggressive wishes seek expression but are kept out of consciousness by other forces in the mind. Freud envisioned a censor in the mind that *resisted* unacceptable thoughts, feelings, and wishes. Later, he identified the central mechanism for keeping unacceptable thoughts, urges, and feelings out of conscious awareness as *repression*. Repression is the defense that keeps out of consciousness that which is too painful, shameful, or dangerous to know or feel. The idea that there might be forces in the mind that keep unbearable feelings out of consciousness began to account for why hypnosis alone did not bring enduring relief of symptoms. Bringing unconscious material to light was not enough. Clients needed help in overcoming their resistances and their repression in order to work through what was unconscious, dreaded, and feared. Psychological conflicts, Freud began to realize, were an inevitable part of psychic life.

In Freud's earliest cases, then, were the precursors to many critical concepts: *free association*, freely reporting whatever comes to mind; *resistance*, the forces that oppose the striving toward recovery (Freud 1912); *repression*, the unconscious mechanism that keeps unacceptable wishes and feelings out of consciousness; *symptom formation*, the nature of symptoms as symbolic, unconscious expressions of conflicts; *conversion*, the transformation of aggressive or sexual wishes into somatic pathways; *transference*, thoughts and feelings for a therapist that have their roots in earlier relationships and in subsequent emotional experiences with others; *countertransference*, thoughts and feelings and reactions to the client rooted in one's own history and current world; *symbolic content*, fantasies, hallucinations, and dreams containing symbols, which may condense many wishes and feelings; and *unconscious conflict*, unconscious wishes and fears that seek expression but meet with repression. Every one of these concepts is still a vital part of psychodynamic clinical work today.

THE EVOLUTION OF FREUD'S UNDERSTANDING OF PSYCHOPATHOLOGY

While Freud initially continued to hypnotize hysterical patients, he found that much of the same material was also accessible via free association in the analytic setting. In *Studies in Hysteria* (1895), he began to evolve a number of theories drawn from patterns in the hysterical women he treated. He noted that their symptoms, such as dissociation, amnesia, and conversion disorders, seemed related to *real* sexual traumatic events that they had experienced as children. Memories that could not be expressed emerged as symptoms. The cure for hysteria involved gaining access to unconscious memories through free association. The talking cure became a way to allow *strangulated affects*, or feelings, to be discharged through speech. Cure involved "remembering the sexual trauma, making it conscious despite resistance, repeating it in the transference, and working it through" in the context of a therapeutic relationship. It should be noted that Breuer held a complementary but different view from Freud about Anna O.'s symptoms. He suggested that, after a trauma, the affects or feelings are dissociated and show up in hypnoid states. What ensues is a splitting of the mind, and the role of hypnosis is not so much to lift repression but to integrate these dissociative states. This view underlies much current trauma theory today (see chapter 17).

However, between the publication of *Studies in Hysteria* in 1895 and its reception in 1905, Freud retracted his view that all hysterical women had suffered from real sexual trauma. Instead, he began to view sexual seductions in childhood as wishes that were the products of his female patients' own desires. That a real event should so simply be disclaimed as a fantasized realization of a wish was problematic then, and remains a difficult part of the theory now. Indeed, discriminating memory from fantasy continues to be a raging debate in the trauma literature today (Loftus and Ketcham 1994). Freud's abandonment of the seduction theory, however, led to many decades in which the importance of real trauma was minimized or denied (Masson 1984).

To review, then, Freud came to see hysteria as a function of a patient being traumatized, followed by intense feelings that were stirred up. These feelings were forms of excitation that could be painful. The traumatic memories also represented something that was incompatible with the person's mind, and that incompatible idea was repressed (or dissociated). The excitation then took a somatic (physical) pathway, and what was left in consciousness was a symbol. If the traumatic memory could be brought to consciousness, then the painful affects (feelings) could be released and the patient would be less symptomatic. We can see this somatization in the following example.

Gloria, a single, forty-year-old Polish, Catholic woman, came to treatment having heard one of the authors give a talk about dissociative identity disorders at a national conference. She said that she had been stirred up by the talk, but stated in the first session that she was very skeptical of ever having experienced sexual abuse. She complained of low energy, constant headaches, and a lack of memory or focus. She lived at home with her eighty-year-old father; her mother and four brothers had moved out of the home ten years before because of her father's chronic alcoholism and physical abuse. Her sister had married at eighteen, and had left home for good.

Now she took care of him, providing his meals and shopping and cleaning for him, with a very limited life outside of her work and home. Her father mostly sat in the dark, in his easy chair, watching television, bitter and depressed. She described herself as still sleeping with the sheets wrapped around her like a mummy and that said she fitfully slept as far against the wall as she could.

In about the sixth session, Gloria brought in a hard plastic doll whose ears and feet she had literally chewed off in childhood. Talking about the doll, and wondering why a child might chew something so hard, led her to wonder about what she might have been feeling. She then recalled a memory of a man in the doorway, smoking a cigarette, where all she could see was the red dot of the flame of the cigarette. This memory unleashed a flood of other memories, which were extremely painful and which she would alternately embrace and then dismiss.

But as the memories began to surface, she remembered hearing rustling in the bed closest to the door, which her sister occupied. She recalled knowing and not knowing that her father was in her sister's bed, and only later was able to remember that her father's advances had been made toward her as well. But Gloria resisted bringing memories to consciousness because they were too painful to bear. Her need to know and not know at the same time were further compounded because she had experienced some excitement, and remembering those feelings provoked some guilt and self-reproach. When Gloria was able to feel and empathize with what a child must have felt: the terror, the confusion, and even the excitement of a parent in her bed, she regained some of her energy and began making plans to bring in a housekeeper, and move out of her family home.

Hence, Freud began to conceive of traumatic events (or fantasies) producing a conflict in the mind. One part of the mind seeks to keep such memories from conscious awareness (repression); another part of the mind resists the fantasies or memories becoming conscious because they are too painful, and so what is left in the conscious mind is some excitation that is incompatible with the conscious mind. Usually, the symptom represents the conflict. Freud's view was that hysterics suffer from *reminisces*, or from memories that produced dammed-up or strangulated affects (feelings). The goal of treatment was to remove symptoms by accessing and recovering repressed memories and verbalizing them with the associated feelings. This, too, is fundamental to trauma theory today.

Furthermore, with these insights, Freud was beginning to see symptoms as compromises between repressed memories and the conscious mind. While the conscious mind struggles to keep what is painful out of consciousness, symptoms emerge because of strangulated affects that cannot be extinguished.

THE ANALYSIS OF DREAMS

Freud continued to investigate the internal lives of individuals by exploring their dreams (1900). As he continued to study dreams he thought that dreams were actually like symptoms. He noted that under the relaxation and regression of sleep, dreams expressed unconscious fantasies or wishes, which were often encoded in symbols that expressed desires in disguise. Every dream, he thought, expressed a wish or an impulse that may be infantile. What we often see in dreams is that wishes are condensed or projected or displaced or symbolized, so that the wish is disguised. What is consciously remembered from our dreams is called the *manifest content*. Dreams occur in the unconscious, but undergo a *secondary elaboration* as they make their way through the censor of the mind and into consciousness. Like symptoms, but in a more normative way, dreams allow for the discharge of sexual and aggressive drives, wishes, and impulses. The work of dream analysis, then, lies in making connections between the manifest content of a dream and *latent* or *symbolic content*, which includes urges, impulses, and feelings that are unacceptable to the conscious mind. Dreams provide access into some of the fragmentary, primitive, shameful, secret aspects of unconscious life. Freud believed that by following patients' associations to dreams, we can decode their meanings.

Freud also continued to remain aware of a *censor* that keeps the forbidden meaning of dreams out of consciousness. During sleep, the censor relaxes, permitting the instinctual impulses of childhood to be expressed without regard to the concerns that operate in conscious life (Freud 1900).

THE ROLE OF SELF-KNOWLEDGE

Freud continued to refine his methods of free association through his own dream analysis and the analyses of his patients' dreams. However, he was not satisfied to look at the passions of others only from the safe distance afforded the clinician toward the client, and so, he undertook his own self-analysis. He began to identify within himself some of the passions and conflicts he was finding in his patients. He remembered, for example, his own shame as a boy at seeing his once powerful father humiliated by an anti-Semitic attack. He remembered his arousal at seeing his mother's naked body, and his guilt for having these feelings. What Freud uncovered in himself were his own repressed sexual feelings for his mother, wishes to be rid of his father, and fears of retribution or punishment for his incestuous wishes. Referring to *Oedipus Rex* by Sophocles, Freud conceptualized these themes as being *oedipal* in nature. From his own self-analysis, he began to develop a theory that there were universal themes of sexuality and aggression, as well as their prohibitions, at different levels of child development.

A GENETIC MODEL OF PSYCHOSEXUAL DEVELOPMENT

Freud used the word *genetic* to refer to the ways in which early history is laid down and unfolds over time. He evolved a model for understanding how normal child development is shaped by the two powerful drives of sexuality (or libido) and aggression. He understood these drives to be biologically based phenomena that seek discharge or expression. There are many drives: hunger, sleep, and other biological regulatory functions. Freud postulated that the drives arise in the body, that they are unconscious, and that they become conscious as they seek expression. Toward the beginning of his career, he emphasized sexuality as the major drive and an important factor in psychopathology. Later, he introduced the importance of the aggressive drive.

Freud proposed that sexuality and aggression seek expression in the everyday lives of children. That children were sexual was a radical idea. That their sexual and aggressive drives evolve and become increasingly complex with their physical and psychological maturation was a substantive and creative leap. Freud's theory about the developmental course of the drives united embryological and developmental theories with neurological concepts of drives that seek discharge.

Freud's theory of *infantile sexuality*, or *psychosexual development*, as he called it, was epigenetic. It held that everything that grew had a predetermined ground plan. Developmental periods require that the individual meet and surmount critical tasks at the proper time and in the proper sequence. Development is hierarchical, invariant, and sequential. Each new stage of psychosexual development depends on the preceding stage. Within this paradigm, there are *regressions* (or returns) to earlier stages of functioning, and there can be *fixations* (getting stuck) at each stage of development, which may form the basis for pathological relationships or character traits in later life.

According to psychosexual drive theory, each phase of child development is shaped by an *erogenous zone* (a physical zone of sexual pleasure), a *drive*, an *object* (usually a person) toward whom the drive is aimed, the *psychosexual issue* that the individual faces at that stage of development, the cluster of *character traits* that emerge at each juncture of childhood development, and the kinds of symptoms that might occur at each stage of development.

Freud now began to articulate a model of child development that viewed childhood as governed by internal sexual and aggressive urges, by physical maturation, by the passage of time, and by events in the real external world. Thus, his psychosexual drive theory synthesized the concept of children's erogenous zones as being associated with the kinds of relationships and attachments, symptoms, character traits, and psychological preoccupations they face at each stage of development.

Freud divided childhood psychosexual development into five stages: infancy, toddlerhood, the phallic or oedipal stage, latency, and adolescence (the genital stage). Let us consider each of them individually. Before doing so, however, we want to issue a caveat. This theory about psychological stages often sounds vastly oversimplified—and it is. For example, descriptions of the oral stage make it sound as if the infant is simply one big mouth with no other interests and experiences. To focus on the fulfillment or frustration of oral needs, nothing else is described, which gives a very limited and distorted picture of that particular time in life. In reading about any particular stage, it is important to remember that many other things are going on and that what happens developmentally also depends on the individuality of the person and all the other factors influencing his or her life. Fred Pine (1990) offers the term *developmental moments* to replace the more rigid, monolithic idea of *developmental stages*. We find this concept useful because it is so much more fluid. The oral stage can then be understood as having many oral developmental moments and perhaps more oral moments than at any other time in life, but room is left to imagine the baby at that time as a multifaceted, complex little person.

The Oral Stage

Freud proposed that at the oral stage (birth to one and a half years of age), babies experience pleasure and aggression primarily through their mouths, the first erogenous zone. Babies will stimulate themselves by sucking on a breast, fingers, or toys. Their needs, perceptions, and pleasurable and painful feelings are expressed principally through their mouths and tongues. Babies will scream to be fed. They will derive great pleasure from sucking, and they will be satiated through their mouths. There are aggressive aspects to orality. Babies use their mouths to spit, to bite, or to chew. Some aggressive feelings can be pleasurable as well. Babies depend on relationships with their parents, their caregivers, or others, to regulate their tensions, and to soothe, feed, and comfort them. Freud thought that, to the degree that babies can love, their love is invested in themselves. Other people are valued as the parts that serve the baby as need-fulfillers or neglecters, as breasts or bottle carriers rather than as persons in their own right. The central psychosexual issue at this stage is to get basic needs met and to satisfy oral drives, both loving and aggressive. The healthy character traits that may emerge include the capacity for trust (Erikson 1950), self-reliance, and self-esteem. When oral issues are unresolvable, they show themselves in adult problems. Let us look for some of the oral themes that emerged with a therapy patient.

> William, a thirty-one-year-old graduate student, came to treatment complaining of "glaring at people." He described a fantasy life populated by alligators. He imagined these vicious animals in a moat protecting him from the intrusions of others—anyone who tried to get close would be devoured.

William had been an only child, born to two middle-aged parents. He described his own mother as excessively dependent on his grandmother, who lived with them until her death when he was eight years old. His father was described as a rigid, removed, and distant military man. Neither parent was seen as reliably comforting. When William's grandmother died, he gained about forty pounds. He remembers that no one noticed. He grew up feeling chronically empty, hungry, and lonely.

When it came time to apply to college, William had his mother write his applications, including his autobiographical statement. She chose his college, and her choice reflected her own conservative values rather than William's values. Throughout college, his mother baked sugar cookies and sent them to him. He would reciprocate by sending her his laundry halfway across the country, believing that he could not do it for himself.

He described a worldview of relationships summed up by: I'll feed you if you feed me. True reciprocity was impossible, and his relationships were often marked by rage when he felt any deprivation. For example, when his landlord raised the rent, William threatened to pour boiling oil through the pipes. When a girlfriend became pregnant with his baby, he ended the relationship because her plan for an abortion was simply, as he saw it, an attempt to kill a part of him. At work, he expected immediate rewards. When, during a blizzard, a computer program he had written could not be read immediately, he became irate and careened through the icy streets endangering himself and others. Often William would give presents, but then would become disappointed by the lack of immediate payback, and so would demand them back. Like the oral child who bites and rages when his needs are unmet, William was not able to see relationships in any terms but his own.

Over the course of treatment, there emerged a gulf of loneliness and unfulfilled needs. Often, he would bring a knapsack filled with bananas and milk and eat them in sessions as he recounted incidents of his emotional hunger. In fact, one of the more notable gains in treatment came when he was able to delay and anticipate his hunger, and discuss with me the ice cream cone he would like to have after the session. The ability to delay and, ultimately, to feed himself took many years. After four years of treatment, William was able to get the recipe for sugar cookies and actually bake them for himself. He stopped sending his laundry home, and he even entered into a work situation where he could be admired, while not having to work closely with people. His interpersonal relationships remained distant, but he was less driven by the intensity of his hunger, dependency, and rage.

William had serious difficulties tolerating his own oral needs: to be loved, to be satisfied, or to be appropriately gratified at the most basic level. Because his basic needs had been both overly gratified and not gratified enough, he could not see himself or others as whole. He had difficulty with empathy, with mutuality, and with love. In drive theory terms, William struggled with excessive and unneutralized oral drives—biting, hunger, oral greed—coupled with a need for immediate gratification. This resulted in his prominent character traits of narcissism, dependency, envy, and rage.

The Anal Stage

By the second year of life (ages one and a half to three), the capacity to walk and climb gives a toddler some degree of autonomy. Toddlers, however, are notable for their self-centeredness and limited capacity for reason. They do not see value in waiting to cross the street. They have not internalized a set of controls that prevent them from hanging from a light cord, putting a knife into an electric socket, kicking, biting, screaming, or lying down in a crowded airport or supermarket. Almost all of their behaviors seem aggressively intensified and directed toward testing the boundaries of what is acceptable and what is not. Toddlers must learn not only what is prohibited, but also how to internalize the prohibitions of others, thus making them their own. Their psychosexual tasks, then, are around the development of internal control. This usually occurs first around toilet training. Ultimately toddlers must begin to manage their anal struggles over independence and autonomy by internalizing parental wishes and prohibitions. What motivates children at this stage to accommodate to social demands, Freud thought, is shame and the fear of loss of the parents' love.

The erogenous zone identified with the anal stage, is, as the name implies, the anus. Freud hypothesized that there was both erotic pleasure in, and heightened aggression over, the production of excrement. Two-year-old children, for example, show *anal eroticism* by delighting in, and expecting caregivers to equally applaud, the products of their bowels or bladders. They may show equal curiosity and delight in caregivers' toileting behaviors, following them to the bathroom, and discussing or insisting on inspecting their caregivers' excrement. Toddlers may show *anal aggression* in retaining, expelling, or even smearing their feces or urine. They may express these feelings through play with dump trucks, puddles, play dough, or finger paint.

Freud thought that both the loving and aggressive drives in the anal stage are aimed at trying to gain control, first, over their sphincter muscles, and then, over the important objects (people) in their lives. Relationships at this stage involve two people; that is, they are *dyadic* in nature. The quality of their relationships is marked by struggles over self-control. Take, for example, Martin, whose account of himself when he was a child indicates that at age five, he was still fixated at the anal stage.

His father was a naval officer, and Martin's favorite form of play was floating his toy boats in the bathtub and torpedoing them. Both parents had become frustrated with Martin because he consistently expelled his feces in his pants and not in the toilet. In desperation, they offered him twenty-five cents for every bowel movement he made in the toilet. Martin soon calculated that it was not in his best interest to become toilet trained, because to do so would mean that he would ultimately lose money. Instead he would use the toilet for three days to earn the money. But the only way to keep the money flowing was to lose control periodically, and this he would do at home or at the homes of his friends. One day, Martin's best friend's mother insisted that, at her house, he use the toilet. There, she overheard him muttering to himself about Napoleon's battles. When he came out of the bathroom he informed her, "I'm Napoleon, and Napoleon shits wherever he pleases!"

For Martin, toileting had become the battleground to control and dominate others. Not surprisingly, some of Martin's adult character traits were shaped by his early anal fixation. He had difficulty completing his master's thesis because he could only write "in spurts." He tended to have difficulty interpersonally, especially in control struggles with his advisors and in close relationships. Other anal character traits that Freud identified may include excessive cleanliness, hoarding, or frugality.

The Phallic Phase

By ages three to five, children have entered an exciting world of fantasy, imagination, and budding romance. Suddenly, their preoccupations are no longer around "poop" or "pee." Rather, they begin to have romantic feelings and sexual fantasies, often directed toward their parent or parent surrogate of the opposite sex. Children at this stage are just beginning to discover their own genitals. As pretend princes and princesses, kings and queens, husbands and wives, oedipal children become cognizant of sex roles and play out games of love and marriage on the playground and in the nursery school. One nursery school teacher reported that when she would instruct boys and girls to put their hands on their heads, on their toes, or the air, some little boy inevitably would call out, "Put your hands on your penis!" This preoccupation with genitals as the erogenous zone at the oedipal stage is natural and normative.

It is hard to imagine a three- to five-year-old as sexual, or as having sexual feelings, but they often have erotic longings for an adult of the opposite sex. Often, they play out their fantasies in which there is some sort of retribution from the parent or parent-surrogate of the same sex. For example, a colleague described this conversation with her four-year-old son, which took place in the bathtub:

Son: I love you so much even my two arms can't show you enough.
Mother: I love you so much my arms can't show it either.
Son (said with a little discomfort): And Daddy too.
Mother: And Daddy too.
Son: You're so beautiful. I'd like to marry you. You know, Daddy could live down the street in a smaller house. In fact, you know, I've noticed lately that sometimes Daddy smells. Have you?

Mother: You know, sweetie, as much as you love me, and I love you, you really can't marry me. I'm married to Daddy. But I bet that when you grow up, you'll marry someone even more beautiful than me.

Son (now fondling his genitals): Do you really think I'll ever be bigger than him anyway?

Another mother described her son admiring her as she dressed to go out. He said, "You look lovely, my princess bride. May I suggest that you wear this (pointing to a necklace) to go out with me."

Indeed, in a wonderful poem by A. A. Milne (1924, 1952), a little boy is described at the height of oedipal longing:

James James
Morrison Morrison
Weatherby George Dupree.
Took great
Care of his Mother
Though he was only three.
James James
Said to his Mother,
"Mother," he said, said he,
"You must never go down to the end of the town if you don't go down with me."

(p. 521)

A third mother remembered this event between her daughter and her husband. Four-year-old Lilly, who had been dressed for bed, suddenly began to take off her nightgown in a kind of strip tease before her father, saying, "Bosom dance. Bosom dance."

Her father responded, "Lilly, put your nightgown back on! What are you doing?"

Lilly replied, "Daddy, you know I've been thinking that a three-year-old couldn't marry you, but I bet a four-year-old can!"

For the oedipal child, the penis or the vagina becomes the erogenous zone. According to drive theory, children experience their sexual desires directed toward the parent or parent-substitute of the opposite sex; aggression is directed toward the same-sex parent. The oedipal child's world is not made up simply of dyadic relationships of the self and another, but includes *triadic* relationships. The oedipal child's world now requires reconciling sexual feelings and aggressive feelings that involve three people: the child, the mother, and the father (or parent-substitute).

According to most societies, the child must not realize her own incestuous wishes for the opposite-sex parent, and therefore, these feelings need to be renounced and repressed. In addition, because the child also loves the parent or parent-surrogate toward whom she feels competition and aggression, she begins to direct the aggression once felt for the same-sex parent against the self. Freud thought that children were motivated to give up their erotic feelings for their opposite-sex parent because they feared retribution coming from the same-sex parent. Often, this is represented as some physical harm that may come to the child. He called this *castration anxiety* and saw it as a precursor to guilt. It is important to mention that castration threats to children were not uncommon in Freud's era. Castration anxiety later becomes an extremely important concept in Freud's understanding of guilt and the superego (see chapter 3). While he viewed boys as fearing castration, he saw girls as feeling already castrated. (See chapter 10 for a fuller explication of Freud's views on women.)

Freud hypothesized that children ultimately resolve their oedipal conflicts through developing a conscience. Through the process of *identifying* with the same-sex parent and by taking on the attributes, values, and ideals of that parent, a child's gender-role identity is solidified. At the same time, by identifying with parental injunctions of right and wrong, a child at the oedipal stage develops an internalized set of moral principles. No longer motivated only by fears of loss of love, children at this stage are now motivated by *guilt*. This is a feeling that emerges when internal moral prohibitions are violated.

With the development of a conscience, or what Freud called a *superego*, morality for the oedipal child now becomes an internal concern. No longer governed by external prohibitions only, the oedipal child now experiences the unpleasant feeling of guilt when she or he encounters sexual and aggressive longings that violate internal moral injunctions and social prohibitions.

Hence, the goal of the oedipal period is to establish, through identification, one's own gender-role identity and to develop a conscience. Many kinds of neurotic disturbances derive from fixations at the oedipal stage. These include excessive competitiveness, emotionality, over-sexualization, inhibition, and a sense of inadequacy or inferiority. While pathology may emerge as a result of a fixation at this stage, children's incestuous and aggressive wishes toward parents and parent surrogates are not, in and of themselves, pathological.

Brenner (1955) has written of oedipal feelings that "the single most important fact to bear [about the intensity of oedipal feelings] is the strength and force of the feelings of the people involved. This is the love of a real love affair. For many, it is the most intense of their entire lives. The intensity of deepest passion of love and hate, yearning and jealousy, fury and fear, rage within the child" (p. 106). Selma Fraiberg (1959) adds, "Yet this is a dream which must end in renunciation and reconciliation" (p. 204).

Oedipal children are often drawn to fairy tales because these stories provide in fantasy both oedipal wishes and their resolutions. In the fairy tale "Jack and the Beanstalk," Jack is a young boy left alone to care for his widowed mother. Already, this fact contains an oedipal boy's wish to have his mother exclusively. Jack trades in his mother's cow (Milky White—an oral image) for three beans. Jack brings the beans to his mother but she rejects these signs of his manhood, and throws the beans out the window. To Jack's phallic delight, up sprouts a large beanstalk, which he climbs three times (three being a symbol of triadic relationships) to do battle with a giant ogre (his rival and competitor, who is bigger than he) so that he can support his mother. While Jack is sometimes saved by the ogre's wife, and regresses by hiding in her oven (womb), he is finally betrayed by her and must climb down the ogre's beanstalk. At the bottom, he looks up to see an image many oedipal boys experience when they view their own naked fathers—that of a giant man with a beanstalk (phallus) through his legs. Jack is terrified of being hurt, even devoured, by the giant who will punish him for trying to steal what is not his (the golden harp). And so Jack chops the beanstalk down with an axe, steals enough gold to provide for his mother, and marries a princess of his own.

"Jack and the Beanstalk" has a moral tale to tell to the oedipal child. Jack must come to terms with his wishes to have his mother exclusively, with his aggressive feelings toward a symbolic father (the giant), as well as with his fears that the giant will harm him. To deal with his forbidden sexual wishes toward his mother, he takes on the manly attributes of the giant (or father) and tries to kill him. Jack has expressed a universal oedipal fantasy of coveting what is not his. But by identifying with the giant's manly strengths, he ultimately gets rewarded by having a princess of his own.

Bettelheim (1983) has proposed that Freud's choice of the Oedipus myth as a guiding metaphor for psychoanalysis was not accidental. The myth of Oedipus is, in fact, the story of a boy who acts to kill his father due to a metaphorical blindness. He kills his father because he does not know himself.

The tragedy of Oedipus tells of a boy born to a king and queen, who are warned that their son will murder his father. To avert that tragedy, they drive a spike through their son's foot and send him away to be killed. He is then adopted by the king and queen of Corinth, whom he believes are his real parents. When he consults an oracle, he is told that he will slay his father. To avoid that fate, he leaves Corinth, only to meet and murder a stranger on the road. Of course, that stranger is his true father. Oedipus, a seeming hero, then answers the riddle of the sphinx and is made king of Thebes, where he unknowingly marries his own mother. When a plague befalls his city, he tries to discover its source and in the process uncovers the truth, that by not knowing himself, he has, in fact, murdered his father and married his mother. In his grief and despair, he blinds himself, and his mother kills herself. Bettelheim (1983) writes:

> This is a crucial part of the myth: as soon as the unknown is made known—as soon as the secret of the father's murder and the incest with the mother are brought to light and the hero purges himself—the pernicious consequences of the oedipal deeds disappear. The myth also warns that the longer one defends oneself against knowing these secrets, the greater is the damage to oneself and to others. The psychoanalytic construct of the Oedipus complex contains this implicit warning too. Freud discovered both in his self-analysis and in his work with patients that when one has the courage to face one's own unconscious patricidal and incestuous desires—which is tantamount to purging oneself of them—the evil consequences of these feelings subside. *Becoming aware of our unconscious feelings—which makes them no longer unconscious but part of our conscious mind—is the best protection against an oedipal catastrophe.* (p. 15)

In trying to develop a corollary theory about the oedipal situation for girls, Freud's own self-analysis was not helpful. Indeed, both Freud and his female patients were embedded in a culture and a social milieu that devalued women. Within this culture (and his patients gave him plenty of evidence for his theory), he postulated that girls viewed their genitals as "inferior" and as evidence of having already been castrated. He believed that girls were angry with their mothers for having given them an inferior organ, and that they envied boys; that they turned to their fathers as heterosexual object choices because they wanted a baby as a compensation for their disappointment and anger with their mothers; and that because girls saw themselves as already castrated, and hence inferior, they developed penis envy and the character traits of passivity, receptivity, narcissism, and masochism. Freud's mistake was not in seeing penis envy, but in minimizing its cultural sources. We will discuss the phallocentrism of this theory extensively in our gender critique in chapter 10, but that Freud's theory was phallocentric is incontrovertible. It also did not allow for a healthy homosexual object-choice as the outcome of this period, which we know, today, to be the case. Freud's articulation of different psychological development for girls and boys has provoked reactions from women that have lasted over three-quarters of a century. Again, a discussion of these issues can be found in chapter 10.

Latency

Freud thought of latency (six to eleven years of age) as a time in which the sexual and aggressive drives are relatively quiescent. In latency, sexual and aggressive energy is no longer directed toward parents. The recently intense oedipal passions of romance, longing, and rivalry are transformed into behaviors that are calmer, more pliable, and directed toward peers (Noshpitz and King 1991).

As school-age children move out beyond the bounds of their nuclear families and into the world of school, their sexual and aggressive energies are expressed as a drive to gain mastery of physical skills and cognitive learning. This is a time when children, through identification with peers, are socialized into the culture's sex roles—when boys learn what the society values as masculine and girls learn what a feminine role means. In latency, one sees games, classrooms, and neighborhood configurations organized around same-sex segregation. These games often involve fantasies of super-heroes, good guys, and bad guys. For boys, there can be endless delight in being Toxic Crusaders, Superman, or Power Rangers; for girls, April O'Neill, Wonder Woman, or Barbie may express identification with the culture's same-sex ideals. What captivates the literary imaginations of latency-aged boys and girls are myths, legends, or mysteries, such as *The Knights of the Round Table*, the Hardy Boys, or Nancy Drew. In all of these stories, themes of adventure and rescue can be found.

Peter Pan might be considered the quintessential latency-aged boy. Peter Pan lives with a tribe of lost boys in Never-Never Land, a world character-ized by endless battles and chases made up of same-sex peers. In this story, Peter enlists Wendy and her two brothers to leave the real world and join him in his adventures involving pirates and Indians. But when Wendy expresses mildly romantic feelings for Peter, he is willing to lose her forever and even to forsake his tribe of lost boys, so that he can continue to live in a same-sex world of exploits and rescue. Sadly for Peter, Wendy returns to the real world of sexuality where she grows beyond the pleasures of latency and can never rejoin Peter. When Peter returns to find her, he discovers a world that has advanced developmentally beyond him.

In latency, aggression is freed from within the bounds of the nuclear fam-ily, and is expressed through competition with peers. Children at this age define their identities by virtue of their place among their peers—in spelling bees, team games, crafts, and sports. Loving and sexual feelings, once directed toward the opposite-sex parent, are often turned into idealizations of the same-sex parent or surrogate (teachers, coaches, etc.). Often latency-age boys and girls will insist that their fathers or mothers and coaches or counselors are the strongest, bravest, best in the world.

Because sexual and aggressive drives tend to be transformed into activity, the latency-age child is notable for exploring, skill building, learning, and socializing beyond the bounds of the nuclear family. This is a stage where children will collect rocks, stamps, baseball cards, bottle caps, dolls, mod-els, and so forth. Freud considered these behaviors to be in the service of controlling unconscious sexual and aggressive impulses. These sorting activities, he hypothesized, were purposeful behaviors to defend against unacceptable sexual and aggressive impulses.

Unlike the exhibitionistic phallic child, the latency-age child tends to be modest about his or her body. Now the child's body becomes a means for achieving in sports, for acquiring skills, and for developing muscles for games. When there are difficulties in body mastery, in learning, or in social interactions, there can be the potential for long-lasting character traits of inferiority, failure, and defeat. Freud also thought that some of the obsessive behaviors of this stage could lead to lifelong character traits marked by rigid thoughts and behaviors.

The Genital Stage (Adolescence)

Freud proposed that, in contrast to latency, during which the sexual drives are quiescent, adolescence is a tumultuous stage of biological changes in which there is an upsurge of aggressive and sexual impulses. With rises of sex hormones and resultant physical maturation, boys and girls become keenly aware of their bodies and those of the opposite sex. Boys develop facial and pubic hair, their voices change, and they experience nocturnal emissions. Girls develop breasts and pubic hair, and begin to menstruate. These physical changes affect cognition, emotion, and fantasy. In the cognitive realm, adolescents may be flooded with sexual and aggressive feelings that may interfere with learning. At the same time, this affective flooding may enrich their curiosity and creativity. Adolescents tend to be highly emotional and often regress to earlier oedipal themes of grief, unrequited love, rage, longing, desire, and revenge. Given sudden hormonal changes, their mood swings are often intense, confusing, and overwhelming. Given the sexual transformations in their bodies, adolescents gravitate toward peers who can help them develop norms around sexuality. They voraciously seek out literature, movies, music, and other forms of popular culture that are sexually and aggressively explicit. For the adolescent, the world now becomes filled with sexually charged feelings about siblings, teachers, coaches, and peers. Whereas oedipal feelings and fantasies were repressed in latency, they are revived in adolescence. Since one of the goals of adolescence is to separate from the family of origin, sexual attraction to peers promotes disengagement from the adolescent's family. Adolescents also experience grandiosity and invulnerability in their thinking and judgment, believing that they have all the answers in contrast to their "over the hill" parents and teachers.

As the objects of their sexual drives shift, so too, their aggression is redirected. Adolescents are known for their acting-out and rebellious behaviors, their political and ethical stances that are in opposition to those of their parents, and their devaluation of authority in general. All of these expressions of their aggression, Freud suggested, are in the service of the goal of adolescence—that of separation from the family of origin.

Adolescence is also a time for the consolidation of a conscience and of aspirations and goals. Adolescents may go through an ascetic phase characterized by rigid morals and ideals. Their idealizations of idols, movie stars, music figures, and even saints present them with opportunities to experiment with new values and new kinds of ideals.

Janna's parents called the community counseling center alarmed by the changes in their daughter's behavior. They reported that the school principal had suspended Janna that day for cutting class with her boyfriend and for smoking pot. Her parents lamented that their once responsible, sweet, cooperative girl had turned into a sullen, uncommunicative, and angry fifteen-year-old. Whereas she had once returned from school filled with stories to tell her family, she now spent most of her time at home barricaded behind a closed bedroom door, talking on the phone with friends. She plastered her bedroom walls with posters of the rock group Metallica. She wore a nose ring, ripped jeans, and tattered shirts. She spent most of her spare time with her leather-clad boyfriend.

In the initial session, her father described how his daughter had been his "special girl," but how he refused to talk with her now while she was dating "that bum." Janna responded to the clinician's questions with shrugs, monosyllabic replies, and a gaze transfixed on a tree outside the office window. She noted that she just wanted "space . . . to live my own life and make my own decisions."

Janna's psychological goal was to separate from her family and to define her separate identity. Her sexual and aggressive acting-out was her unconscious effort to deal with revived oedipal feelings. Freud would maintain that the way she expressed, modulated, and sublimated her aggressive and sexual drives would ultimately affect the course of her adult personality integration. Were she to remain fixated at this stage of adolescent development, some of the pathological character traits that might emerge include violations of social norms through acting-out behaviors, a lack of neutralized aggressive and libidinal drives, and a lack of age-appropriate identifications.

It must also be remembered that we now know that the task of each of these stages is not only biologically and psychologically determined, but also culturally and socially determined. Environmental influences may advance or assault personality development. While this will be more fully addressed in our discussion of Erikson's life-cycle theory (chapter 5) and in our chapters on gender and racial development (chapters 10 and 11), Freud's psychosexual theory did provide a way of viewing development as both biologically and psychologically determined.

ECONOMIC THEORY

Freud evolved another way of thinking about the forces in the mind. Using physics as a model, he thought that there were finite amounts of psychic energy, which, if used in one place, would not be available in others. This was a more quantitative way of understanding human behavior (Brandell 2004) than some of his other theories.

In his trying to understand the two phenomena of narcissism and depression, we see his economic theory at play. Freud understood narcissism as a form of excessive self-love, which did not leave room for the love of others. Using the myth of Narcissus, who fell so in love with his own image that he drowned, the problem was of having too much libido (or love) invested inward (1914). When we are ill, when we are in mourning, even when we are asleep, we often withdraw our energy from the outside world and invest that energy in ourselves. That is considered healthy narcissism. But when too much energy is invested in the self, there is not sufficient energy for connecting to others, and this may leave the self impoverished. When Freud considered depression, he again used the lens of economic theory. He believed that in mourning (as with a profound loss), a person turns inward, investing her energy in the work of grief while also hypercathecting (holding on to) the memories of the object or person she has lost. But slowly and with time, one decathects (divests) one's energy in the loved person and begins to experience energy for new love and for work. For the person who is depressed or melancholic, however, energies that are bound up in another are harder to free. Because we always experience ambivalence in every relationship, when there has been a loss, there is also always anger at the person who is gone. But when this anger or aggression is disavowed or entirely denied, then the unconscious aggression is turned inward, and the disavowed hatred is turned against the self. This can result in lowered self-esteem, or even in self-hatred. (For a fuller explanation, see chapter 6 on object relations, and chapter 15 on depression.)

TOPOGRAPHIC THEORY

Freud's archeological roots were never more obvious than in his first understanding of the mind as layered. Freud envisioned the mind as a map. In this map, conflict theory was implicit but underdeveloped. Given his interest in archeological and geological principles, he began to think of the mind as if it were in layers, consisting of an unconscious, a preconscious, and a conscious mind. According to this model, the *unconscious mind* is governed by the *pleasure principle*. The unconscious is the unruly part of the mind not governed by the constraints of reality; it is the part of the mind in which wishing will make it so. It operates according to *primary process thinking*. This refers to the chaotic, disjointed world James Joyce so eloquently described in *Finnegan's Wake*. It is a world of free association and fantasy, governed minimally by logic or reality. It is the world in which dreams take place that express fantastical desires, wishes, and urges.

The *preconscious mind* is that part of the mind that can be brought to attention, but that is largely out of consciousness. Jokes and slips of the tongue are evidence of preconscious processes. The *conscious mind* is governed not by pleasure, but by the *reality principle*. The conscious mind refers to the logical, orderly, rational, cognitive operations of everyday waking life. Within the conscious mind is the capacity for self-evaluation, reason, judgment, and delay. The conscious mind uses a logical and sequential kind of thinking that Freud called *secondary process thinking*. Freud envisioned the conscious mind as striving to reduce excitation. He proposed that these parts of the mind try to achieve homeostasis whereby excitement is made neutral. These ideas became central to his understanding of hysteria. They also contribute to the idea of a mind that is always in conflict with itself. It reinforces the basic Freudian idea that unconscious processes always underlie and motivate conscious thinking and behavior.

STRUCTURAL THEORY: AN INTRODUCTION

By 1923, Freud began to observe that symptoms could not be explained solely as regressions or fixations of the drives at different stages of psychological development. Neither could symptoms be explained only as expressing interactions between the three layers of the mind, as his topographic theory had proposed. Rather, symptoms and related psychopathology seemed to occur both developmentally and as a result of conflicts between sexual or aggressive wishes, reality, and internal moral prohibitions. These internal, unconscious psychological conflicts seemed to result in problems of depression, anxiety, lowered self-esteem, and diminished psychological capacity to function freely. At the most extreme, conflicts between structures of the mind seemed to lead to breaks with reality. Freud began, then, to envision a theory of the mind in which psychopathology was related to conflicts among wishes, reality, and ideas, each represented by a different agency of the mind. Using this paradigm, he organized the mind into three agencies: the *id*, the *ego*, and the *superego*. These are not physical entities; they exist only metaphorically.

We have lost some of the passion and immediacy of Freud's writing in the process of translation from German to English, which has rendered it mechanistic and abstract. The very term *psychoanalysis* in German refers not to a medical science but to the investigation of the psyche or soul. While

Freud spent a lifetime investigating the inner souls of individuals, we are left with abstract translations that make our most passionate urges and conflicts read as if they were foreign structures. Freud used the mythological character of Psyche as the symbol of having to enter a mysterious underworld to find oneself, because he believed that in exploring unconscious conflicts, we come to know and ultimately control ourselves.

As we begin to study Freud's structural theory, let us also keep in mind that when American physicians appropriated psychoanalysis and excluded non-physicians from its practice, Freud's actual language and meaning became lost in the translation into a medical model (Bettelheim 1983). We are about to be introduced to a language of ids, egos, and superegos— words that do not capture the intensity of pleasure, love, anger, and ambition, or the conflicts between darkest wishes and their prohibitions. So, while Freud's writings in German captured the ambiguity of the human heart, American medicine has developed a highly technical language that often fails to capture the complex longings of the human soul.

FREUD'S THEORY OF THE MIND: REVISITED

Before pursuing a formal discussion of the structural theory as it explains unconscious conflict and symptom formation, let us review Freud's original theory of the mind. As Freud studied the interplay between unconscious desire and conscious prohibition as it was played out in the mental life of his patients, he developed the following explanatory paradigms:

1. A theory that all human thought and behavior is motivated by genetically determined, somatically rooted instinctual drives that achieve mental representation in the form of sexual and aggressive impulses.
2. A theory of unconscious influence that describes three strata of mental activity interconnected along a vertical continuum: a deep stratum composed of thoughts, feelings, and memories that are entirely unconscious; an intermediate (preconscious) stratum composed of mental contents that are neither fully unconscious nor fully conscious; and a relatively small stratum in which all mental activity is logical, reality oriented, and consciously perceived (topographic theory).
3. A theory of psychosexual development emphasizing that, from the moment of birth, children pursue sexual and aggressive aims that evolve predictably through well-defined psychosexual stages.
4. An economic theory, which holds that the mind has finite energy that when used in one place may deplete sources of energy for other functions.

5. A theory that explains psychopathology in terms of unconscious mental conflict between socially unacceptable impulses that reflect the *pleasure principle* (the search for gratification without concern for realistic constraints), and the efforts of a *censor* (repression), whose job it is to ensure that every conscious thought, feeling, and behavior is experienced and expressed in morally and socially acceptable terms.

These concepts focused attention on the essential role that unconscious mental processes play in both pathological and normal mental functioning. The first four formulations, in versions that are only slightly modified, inform psychodynamic thinking to this day. The fourth, having been substantially revised, provides a flexible and complex explanation of how mental conflict originates and how it is resolved within the mind. Together, these five theories emphasize the causal relationship between early developmental experiences and the thoughts, feelings, and behaviors that characterize the mental life of adults. By his insistence on integrating past and present into a unified theory of mental functioning, Freud established a compelling agenda to which contemporary students of the mind must refer, whether they agree or disagree with his specific formulations.

While contemporary therapists tend to talk about developmentally early desires such as *wishes* or *passions*, Freud and his colleagues always used more forceful terms, especially in their early writings. They termed sexual and aggressive wishes as *drives, impulses,* or *instincts,* biologically based words that emphasize that the wishes actually motivate thought, feeling, and behavior. This view argues that we are often driven by psychological impulses that we do not understand and, therefore, cannot control through conscious thought. When viewed from this perspective, Freud's drive theory advanced the ideas that both sexual and aggressive impulses seek expression but are in conflict with reality and with society. Drive theory led to his development of a theory of the mind as being in conflict with itself. Freud termed his theory a structural theory, which will be the object of our study in chapter 3.

REFERENCES

Bettelheim, B. (1983). *Freud and Man's Soul.* New York: Knopf.

Brandell, J. (2004). Psychodynamic Social Work. N.Y.: Columbia University Press.

Brenner, C. (1955). *An Elementary Textbook in Psychoanalysis.* New York: International Universities Press.

Breuer, J., and Freud, S. (1895). *Studies in Hysteria,* ed. A. A. Brill. Boston: Beacon, 1950.

Brill, A. A. (1921). *Fundamental Conceptions of Psychoanalysis.* New York: Harcourt-Brace.

Erikson, E. (1950). *Childhood and Society.* New York: Norton.

Fraiberg, S. (1959). *The Magic Years.* New York: Scribner.

Freeman, L. (1979). Immortal Anna O. *The New York Times Magazine,* November 11, pp. 30–38.

Freud, S. (1900). The interpretation of dreams. *Standard Edition* 4/5:1–626.

———. (1912). A note on the unconscious in psychoanalysis. *Standard Edition* 12:255–67.

———. (1914). On narcissism, an introduction. *Standard Edition* 14:67–102.

Freud, S., and Breuer, J. (1893). Psychical mechanisms of hysterical phenomena: preliminary communication, in "Studies in hysteria." *Standard Edition* 2:1–48.

Jones, E. (1953). *The Life and Work of Sigmund Freud,* vol. 1. New York: Basic Books.

Lerman, H. (1986). *A Mote on Freud's Eye: From Psychoanalysis to the Psychology of Women.* New York: Springer.

Loftus, E., and Ketcham, K. (1994). *The Myth of Repressed Memory.* New York: St. Martins.

Masson, J. M. (1984). *The Assault on Truth.* New York: Farrar, Straus & Giroux.

Milne, A. A. (1924, 1952). *When We Were Very Young.* New York: Dutton.

Mitchell, S. (1988). Drive theory and the metaphor of the beast. In *Relational Concepts in Psychoanalysis.* Cambridge, MA: Harvard University Press.

Noshpitz, J., and King, R. (1991). Latency. In *Pathways of Growth: Essentials of Child Psychiatry, Normal Development,* vol. 1, ed. J. Noshpitz and R. King. New York: Wiley.

Pine, F. (1990). *Drive, Ego, Object Self.* New York: Basic Books.

3

Structural Theory

Gerald Schamess

This chapter presents an overview of structural theory as first articulated in Freud's "The Ego and the Id" (1923). In its original formulation, structural theory supplements and expands classical drive theory. It addresses a number of difficult theoretical and clinical issues that had been recognized during the first twenty-five years of psychoanalysis. The theory is called structural theory because it refers literally to structures—the three structures that Freud believed make up the human psyche: the id, ego, and superego. Structural theory presents us both with great contributions to the field and with problems. On the one hand, it is clear and lucid in its explanatory power. On the other hand, it is too concrete and rigid to explain anything as complex and fluid as the inner workings of a human being. The solid, architectural metaphor of the self as composed, indeed constructed, like a building out of three interrelated parts works well, but not fully.

This new theory affirms Freud's view that unconscious sexual and aggressive wishes motivate most, if not all, human behaviors. At the same time, however, it directs attention toward the central role the ego plays in organizing and synthesizing mental functioning. At its core, structural theory calls attention to the processes through which the ego regulates unconscious wishes that are morally and/or socially unacceptable. In their original form, such wishes are repugnant to the adult self and, in addition, violate the norms of ordinary social interaction. By emphasizing the ego's central role in organizing and balancing conflictual forces that arise within the mind, the structural hypothesis markedly expands the range of human behavior that can be explained by psychodynamic theory.

Over the course of the first twenty-five years of psychoanalytic practice,

Freud began to recognize that his original ideas did not adequately explain his patients' psychological problems. The clinical data were particularly confounding in regard to two emotional states: depression and anxiety. Freud was keenly aware that, at best, these states are quite distressing, and, at worst, they disorganize mental functioning in extreme ways. Depression presented a serious theoretical problem because Freud's first theory of unconscious mental conflict did not provide a reasonable explanation of why aggression might be directed against the self. Since guilt and self-hatred are hallmarks of depressive illness, the lack of a viable explanation was quite disconcerting to patients and therapists alike. Anxiety was problematic because the early theoretical formulations suggested that it arose as a consequence of unsatisfied sexual desires. This formulation suggested that anxiety would disappear when clients uncovered the unconscious wishes they had previously repressed. While these ideas seemed reasonable from a theoretical perspective, it gradually became apparent that a significant number of clients became more, rather than less, anxious when they began to recognize their unconscious desires.

The theoretical and practical importance of these problems can best be illustrated by a case example (Hayes 1991, personal communication):

> A therapist reported the treatment of a nine-year-old African American girl, Shovanna, who suffered from episodic rages accompanied by the temporary loss of well-established psychological functions such as the capacity to speak. These difficulties had severely disrupted her life both at home and at school. Shovanna had seen her mother shoot and kill her father when she was four years old. Prior to the killing she had regularly witnessed violent fights between her parents. During a play therapy session, she had her doll shoot an adult doll and then begin to drown a baby doll in a sink of water. As the play progressed, she panicked, screaming as if she were being killed. Quickly she became even more disorganized, perspiring profusely, wetting herself, and speaking incoherently. When the therapist realized what was happening he intervened to "save" the baby doll from "drowning."

An early drive theorist would explain Shovanna's disorganization in terms of unconscious wishes or memories breaking through the repression barrier into consciousness. This explanation would assume unconscious content related to either repressed aggressive wishes directed toward one or both of her parents or repressed memories of a traumatic event she had actually lived through. However, neither of these formulations explains why she turned her aggression against the baby doll after shooting the adult doll (it seems likely that, in fantasy play, the baby doll represented herself), or why she so quickly regressed to an almost infantile level of functioning, wetting herself and losing the capacity to speak coherently. Certainly, her anxiety did not decrease or disappear as she became aware of her aggressive wishes, nor were her depressive feelings ameliorated by her expression of anger (in the play situation) against the adult caregiver (doll).

Later in this chapter we will see that Freud's structural theory provides a more useful explanation of such dilemmas by postulating an unconscious conflict among the different *agencies* (id, ego, and superego) of the mind, with the ego mediating between the opposing forces. In chapter 4 we will see that ego psychology suggests still another explanation by emphasizing the study of defense mechanisms and the importance of overall ego functioning. Although drive theory, structural theory, and ego psychology complement one another, each framework advances a somewhat different explanation for the same clinical problem. As we will see over the course of this book, the most useful explanations, from both the therapist's and the client's perspectives, are the ones that best take into account the client's level of emotional development, internal (psychological) organization, and capacity for object relations, as well as the social/economic and political contexts in which the client lives.

If we now return to the case vignette, we can probably agree that regardless of the theoretical perspective utilized to understand Shovanna's terror, "remembering" the wishes and/or events she had previously repressed initially made her worse. As her defenses crumbled, she was immediately overwhelmed by a combination of anxiety and terror. When she could no longer repress what had been unconscious, she became younger and younger in her emotional functioning in a desperate effort to reestablish her psychological equilibrium. By regressing to a more and more infantile level of functioning, Shovanna clearly communicated her need for a caring adult who would protect her against the memories, feelings, and wishes she had worked so hard and so long to "forget." Since her emotional response made it clear that she was incapable of managing the terrifying inner world she had thus far concealed both from herself and the world around her, the therapist acted quickly to support her ego by rescuing the baby doll, at which point Shovanna was able to pull herself together. We will discuss the concept of ego support in more detail in chapter 4.

Freud addressed the theoretical problems related to depression, anxiety, and symptom formation in three major publications: "Mourning and Melancholia" (1917), "The Ego and the Id" (1923), and "Inhibitions, Symptoms and Anxiety" (1926). He was sixty-one when he published the first of these papers and seventy when he completed the third, quite an accomplishment for a man of his age. In these works he proposed a new and more complex model of the mind that has come to be known as structural theory. He also markedly revised his views about the nature of depression and anxiety, and about the roles these powerful emotions play in mental functioning.

TERMINOLOGY

Before discussing structural theory as it is currently conceptualized, it seems appropriate to revisit what we said in chapter 2. In discussing how Freud's ideas were translated from German into English, Bettelheim (1983) contends that many of the original concepts were seriously distorted to make them seem more scientific, and therefore more acceptable to the American medical profession. He notes that in "naming" the structures of the mind that we now call the id and the ego, the origin of the words *id*, *ego*, and *superego* were actually rooted in the everyday language of German children. *Das es*, German for the *id*, referred to that which is irrational, uncontrolled. *Das ich*, German for *I*, actually referred to the self, to the idea of *me*. Both the *id* and the *I* were imbued with feeling and meaning, which, when translated to the Latin, became cold, mechanistic, and technical.

> No word has greater and more intimate connotations than the pronoun "I." It is one of the most frequently used words in spoken language—and more important, it is the most personal word. To mistranslate *Ich* as "ego" is to transform it into jargon that no longer conveys the personal commitment we make when we say "I" or "me"—not to mention our subconscious memories of deep emotional experience we have when, in infancy, we learned to say "I." (Bettelheim 1983, p. 53)

Bettelheim goes on to explain that in choosing the term *superego* the translators rendered that concept more sterile also. The term Freud chose was *uber Ich*, and again he used it as a noun. In English it would be the "over I." In German *uber Ich* conveys the notion of mature conscience but also carries the feel of the tyrannical persecutory, immature inner forces that can be inappropriately self-blaming. *Superego*, not even being an English word, has no such resonance for us.

This commentary should be kept clearly in mind when studying structural theory. While the theory in its (mis)translated form has considerable explanatory power, Bettelheim is right in saying that the "scientific" language we currently use objectifies the intimate, emotionally powerful mental processes that define who we are as individuals, and what each of us shares with humanity at large. In the process, it distances therapists both from their own and their clients' inner lives. For these reasons, it is important to balance a thorough cognitive understanding of mental structure and organization with a keen appreciation for the personal meanings and the intensity of feeling that vitalize our inner lives. One way to stay as close as possible to Freud's original meaning is to remember the colloquial, child-like evocative words that he so purposely chose.

FREUD'S STRUCTURAL THEORY

Structural theory postulates that "recurring and enduring psychological phenomena are systematically represented and organized within the mind, and, that the nature of this organization can be usefully described" (Moore and Fine 1990, p. 120). Following from this principle, the theory proposes that all mental activity is organized around the interaction of three relatively stable and enduring structures or agencies of the mind: the id, the ego, and the superego. Each of these structures has a set of unique functions. Although the structures are interdependent, their aims and functions frequently conflict. As a result, their interaction within the mind generates considerable dynamic tension, or what is known as intrapsychic conflict. By studying their interaction, therapists have come to understand unconscious mental conflict, particularly as it leads to neurotic symptom formation (hysteria, phobias, compulsions, etc.). In addition, therapists have learned that the processes that synthesize inherently incompatible wishes and fears also lead to healthy adaptation, even among individuals who have been severely traumatized. Finally, structural theory has taught us to empathize with the unconscious struggles that our clients experience, even when the clients themselves know nothing more than that their symptoms make them feel utterly miserable.

Let us now turn to a fuller description of each of the three psychic agencies.

The Id

The id is described as the source and repository of sexual and aggressive impulses, the seat of all desire. It is the part of the mind that wants what it wants when it wants it. It is also the part of the mind that makes sure there is hell to pay if the gratifications it seeks are either delayed or denied. It is governed by the pleasure/unpleasure principle, the concept that the sole aim of all mental activity is to seek pleasure and avoid pain. It is not directly influenced by reality, morality, logic, or social convention. Classical drive theory assumes that its contents do not change after adolescent development has been completed. In spite of this formidable description, it is assumed theoretically that id impulses can be contained, rechanneled, or transformed as a result of ongoing interaction with the ego. Substantial evidence drawn from clinical practice supports that view.

The id is thought to be rooted in physiological processes that cannot be represented in the conscious mind. Accordingly, only derivative expressions of id aims and objectives reach conscious awareness. When derivatives become conscious, they do so in the form of sexual and aggressive fantasies (and/or impulses to act), and this allows dynamically oriented practitioners to make inferences about the influences the id is exerting on mental processes at given moments in time.

A forty-four-year-old divorced woman who had been in treatment for six months told of a dream in which she had watched her highly respected and admired minister argue vehemently with his wife. At the height of the argument he turned to the client saying, "Let's go off together. I'm fed up with my wife and I'll be a lot happier with you than I ever was with her." The dream ended with the client and the minister going off happily together while his wife receded noisily into the background. Not surprisingly, the client felt considerable shame and guilt as she described the dream.

Even though this dream comes close to conveying the underlying id wishes, it is derivative in that the "real" objects of the client's passion, competition, and disdain are still disguised. As treatment progressed, she revealed that her mother had been seriously ill when she was an adolescent, and that she had spent a great deal of time trying to care for her alcoholic father. She imagined that she would be able to convince him to stop drinking, and she remembers thinking when she was thirteen or fourteen that she could have been a much better wife to him than her mother ever was. Over time the underlying oedipal dynamics became quite clear, as did the fact that the minister and his wife were stand-ins for her father and mother.

Freud's (1940) formal definition states that the id "contains everything that is inherited, that is present at birth, that is laid down in the constitution—above all therefore, the instincts which originate from the somatic organization and which find a first Psychical expression here (in the id)" (p. 145). Earlier, Freud (1933) had described the id as "the dark inaccessible part of our personality. . . . We approach the id with analogies: we call it a chaos, a cauldron full of seething excitation" (p. 73). Since Freud never modified his view of the id, it is worth emphasizing that the concept of the id, over and above its usefulness as a theoretical paradigm, reflects a philosophical view of basic human nature—no exceptions and no apologies, at least not from Freud.

The Superego

The superego is conceived of as a relatively enduring organization of moral beliefs and prohibitions within the mind. Although psychodynamic practitioners tend to think of it as conscience (in the adult sense of the term), it also represents developmentally early, punitive, and persecutory tendencies. In essence it tells us how we ought to think and act, and how we may not think or act. It "sets up and maintains an intricate system of ideas, values, prohibitions and commands. . . . [It] observes and evaluates the self. . . . [It] compares [the self] with the ideal. . . . [It] either criticizes, reproaches and punishes, or [conversely] praises and rewards" (Moore and Fine 1990, p. 189).

While the superego can represent morality and civilized behavior, it can be as demanding and unreasonable as the id is in the pursuit of pleasure and vengeance. Depending on how and when moral expectations and prohibitions are internalized, the superego may or may not demonstrate an appreciation of moral complexity. In early childhood, it tends to be harsh, rigid, and punitive, often reflecting the principle that an eye for an eye and a tooth for a tooth is the only possible form of justice. If development progresses reasonably well, persecutory fantasies diminish and the superego gradually becomes more flexible, more reasonable in its expectations, and better able to appreciate realistic constraints on moral behavior. As this occurs, the punishments it demands become less harsh, and within broad limits it becomes more tolerant of moral ambiguity. A ten-year-old may believe that it is "never, ever, ever okay to tell even the teeniest lie," while an adult may realize that it is sometimes appropriate or even necessary to tell a fib to protect or spare someone.

In performing its functions the superego may diminish or enhance self-esteem, often in extreme ways. In the psychodynamic literature it is frequently described as an internal authority or judge that functions below the level of conscious awareness. Typically, individuals do not recognize the ongoing mental processes of self-evaluation that so acutely affect how they feel about themselves. However, derivatives of these processes regularly become conscious in the form of fluctuations in self esteem. When, as frequently happens, these fluctuations occur without apparent cause, individuals experience good or bad feelings about themselves that seem unrelated to anything happening in their day-to-day experience. Similarly, individuals may punish or endanger themselves in serious ways, without any conscious awareness that they are doing so.

A thirty-seven-year-old divorced man entered treatment because of depression and the feeling that he could never develop a positive relationship with a woman. He had grown up in a very religious family with an abusive, alcoholic father and a resigned, long-suffering mother. His mother never acknowledged her husband's drinking or his abusive behavior. Although the client expressed a great deal of anger toward both his mother and his former wife, he maintained the view that he had been mostly, if not entirely, responsible for the breakup of his marriage and for the problems in his subsequent relationships with women. Well into the second year of treatment, he acknowledged, with enormous shame and guilt, that he had been sexually involved with prostitutes during his senior year in college. Although he had renounced his family's religious beliefs many years previously, he still felt strongly that his "unclean" sexual activities in college made him unfit to be with a "decent" woman.

In the course of discussing these feelings and memories, he acknowledged for the first time that some of his recent sexual encounters with women had bordered on sexual harassment. It occurred to him that such encounters not only confirmed his view that no decent woman would want him, but also endangered his career. It was only then that he realized that if he had been sued and/or fired from his job, he would have finally succeeded in punishing himself as he thought he deserved to be punished ("ruined forever"), for his "sinful" sexuality. It had never occurred to him that the behavior that for so many years had kept him at the edge of ruin might be related to guilt, shame, or a need to punish himself. Since sexual harassment is a problem rooted in social inequality as well as individual psychology, the psychodynamic examination of this client's behavior, while accurate for him, does not constitute a general explanation for harassing behavior, nor does understanding these dynamics in any way excuse it.

Freud first proposed the concept of the superego in his 1923 monograph, "The Ego and the Id." In that work he attempted to solve a number of theoretical problems related to guilt, self-hatred, and the workings of an internal conscience. As stated in chapter 2, he thought that the superego came into existence through identification with the parent of the same sex during the resolution of the oedipus complex. He also thought that, once the superego had been established, its contents remained relatively constant throughout life. In the psychoanalytic literature, identification is viewed both as an ego defense and as a process that contributes to intrapsychic *structuralization*—the creation and maintenance of psychic structure. In this second meaning, identification involves taking in selected aspects of a beloved person and incorporating those aspects as functional parts of the self, without conscious awareness of their origin.

Contemporary theorists think that the contents of the superego change throughout the life cycle. In addition, they view the *ego ideal* as a functional part of the superego. In structural theory the ego ideal plays a significant role because it is thought to contain representations of the attributes we value most in the people we love. It thus functions as the repository of our most cherished ideals, strongly influencing how we wish to lead our lives and whom we want most to emulate.

The Ego

Structural theory starts by postulating that, within the mind, the aims of the id and the superego are diametrically opposed. If structural theory is to work as a general explanation of personality organization, it must then postulate the existence of a third structure. This third structure is needed to mediate the conflicts generated by the two structures that oppose each other. Without a third structure, the mind would be constantly divided against itself, and it would be impossible to conceive of a coherent functioning personality or of cohesive individual identity.

Structural theory, then, postulates the existence of the ego. If we think about the theory as a model of the mind in conflict, we recognize that the ego functions as a kind of internal gyroscope. Its most important task is to maintain psychological cohesion and stability in the face of the powerful, conflictual forces that arise when id, superego, and/or external reality clash, that is, when people experience a combination of wishes, moral demands, social expectations, and fears that are inherently incompatible.

Technically speaking, the ego is described in terms of a relatively stable group of functions that organize, synthesize, and integrate mental processes. In the early formulations (Freud 1923), its central role involved mediating between the conflicting demands of the id, the superego, and external (social) reality. Contemporary theorists have markedly expanded its functions to include: (1) perceiving the physical and psychological needs of the self as well as the qualities and attitudes of the environment; (2) evaluating, coordinating, and integrating perceptions of the self and external reality, so internal demands can be adjusted to better correspond with external requirements; (3) finding ways of achieving optimal gratification of the sexual and aggressive wishes that are compatible with moral constraints and social norms; (4) repressing or rechanneling those wishes that offend or defy social norms; and (5) preserving a reasonable level of self-esteem by maintaining good relations with the superego. To accomplish these tasks, the ego must be as sensitively attuned to the demands of the physical world and social reality as it is to the demands of the id and the superego. Note that the first four ego functions listed above place as much emphasis on the ego's relationship with external reality as they do on its relationship with the other structures of the mind.

Over the course of psychosexual development, the ego develops a characteristic defensive organization that protects the self from what it perceives as internal and external danger. Different defense mechanisms operate below the level of conscious awareness and are brought into play automatically whenever the ego begins to experience feelings of anxiety. Anxiety, as Freud reconceptualized it in 1926, is engendered when the different psychic structures come into conflict either with each other or with external reality. Generally speaking, defense mechanisms assist the ego in its efforts to resolve mental conflict. When a specific conflict cannot be resolved, the defense mechanisms work to encapsulate the conflict and reduce its effect on overall mental functioning. We will describe the defense mechanisms and their effect on functioning in some detail in chapter 4.

COMMON MISINTERPRETATIONS

The concept of enduring mental structures can be quite misleading since it is easily misinterpreted. The first common misinterpretation is based on the idea that the id, ego, and superego are physiological entities located in specific areas of the brain. This idea leads practitioners to talk about the composition, contents, and functions of the various mental structures as if they were organ systems that can be isolated, mapped, and manipulated. The second misconception proceeds on the assumption that the structures of the mind are homunculi (imaginary, diminutive people) who live inside the brain where they perform specific tasks and fight with one another when their aims or functions conflict. When this way of thinking predominates, as it often does, even among knowledgeable clinicians, discussions of intrapsychic conflict take on the quality of battlefield dramas in which opposing armies attempt to defeat or dominate each other (e.g., a powerful id that overwhelms a poorly defended ego and a weak superego in the pursuit of sexual gratification).

In considering this problem, it is important to recognize that Freud and his colleagues deliberately used metaphors to convey complicated ideas about mental functioning that did not lend themselves to ordinary methods of exposition. For example, structural theory draws on architectural and/or anatomical metaphors. Conflict theory evokes images of warfare, while topographical theory (see chapter 2) is rooted in the concepts and methods originally developed for the study of archeology and embryology.

In spite of their usefulness, metaphorical explanations are also problematic. They lack precision and they mean different things to different people. As a result, they are interpreted in a variety of idiosyncratic ways. For that reason if for no other, it is essential to remember that when we talk about structures of the mind, we are describing very complex mental processes in an evocative rather than a precise way. At its most useful, the structural metaphor encourages us to think in terms of mental functions that cluster together more or less consistently, and that therefore lend themselves to conceptualization as coherent agencies of the mind. In using the concept metaphorically, we are encouraged to imagine how our own and our clients' mental lives might be organized. Such acts of imagination make it possible to temporarily enter the minds of our clients, and they are thus beneficial both to therapists and clients. That is, they are beneficial as long as the therapist remembers that structures of the mind are metaphors not metropolises or organ systems.

The following case example demonstrates how structural theory may be used to explain unconscious mental conflict and neurotic symptom formation. It describes how the ego reduces conflict within the mind by creating symptoms that are both pathological and, within the context of an individual's life history, adaptive. This paradox is intrinsic to the theory and is intentional. Freud believed that neurosis is the price humans beings pay for civilization.

A caveat is in order. Freudian theory, especially structural theory, can sometimes sound like a parody of itself. With its metaphors of pipes and dams and eruptions it easily lends itself to ridicule and has been the butt, as it were, of many jokes. It is attributed to Freud that even he said a cigar is sometimes just a cigar. Yet a cigar is sometimes a symbol for the penis and an explosion for an orgasm. In the following case it just so happens that structural theory was the most useful tool to illuminate and alleviate the client's suffering.

Mr. Johannson, a fifty-seven-year-old married Caucasian man of Scandinavian descent, requested treatment for compulsive symptoms and obsessive thoughts that interfered with his normal functioning and caused him considerable mental distress. He worked alone on the night shift as a technician in a hydroelectric generating plant, a responsible, well-paying job that he had held for almost twenty years. His final task was to turn off fifteen valves that controlled the passage of water through the turbines that generated electricity. He was supposed to complete this task at 1:00 AM, the time of day when electricity demand was at its lowest point and his work shift ended.

In describing himself, Mr. Johannson recognized that he had always been a very "careful" person and a conscientious employee. In the past years it had taken him approximately half an hour to shut off and check the valves. That was twice the time it took the technician who relieved him on his days off. However, it was important to him that he do his work "correctly," so he was wanting to take the extra time.

For six months prior to his request for treatment, he had been spending more and more time turning off the valves. The night before his first therapeutic appointment, it had taken him almost three hours to shut down the generating station. As a result he got home well after 4:00 AM. In addition to his concerns about the extra time spent on the job and about getting home to his wife so late, Mr. J. said that he was consumed with anxiety about making a mistake. He felt that if he made an error in shutting down the plant, he would cause a massive flood that would injure people and destroy property. "Rationally" he knew this could not happen. Nonetheless, the prospect made him so anxious that he would return to the beginning of the sequence twenty or thirty times a night to make certain that he had not left a valve open. For example, he said, no sooner had he closed valve six, than he began to worry about whether he had fully closed valve two. This made no sense to him because even if he did leave a valve open, the only consequence would be that water would continue flowing through the turbines, drawing down the reservoir and perhaps, reducing the amount of water available to produce electricity the next day. In fact, one of the weekend technicians had done just that and had received a mild reprimand from the supervisor.

This compulsive symptom was making Mr. J. miserable. He complained that it interfered with his relationships with his wife and grown children, as well as with the daytime activities he enjoyed. However, he felt he had absolutely no control over the symptom, and that in fact the symptom was controlling him.

He had begun to dread going to work, a feeling that was extremely distressing to him since he had always enjoyed his work.

Over the first three months of treatment Mr. J. explored how his symptom had affected relations with other family members. He remembered that the compulsion had begun at about the time he found he could not maintain an erection when attempting sexual intercourse with his wife. This had happened on two or three occasions, for the first time in his life. He had no idea of why he might have experienced this difficulty and was extremely upset by it. He had consulted his family physician, who assured him that occasional impotence was not unusual for a man of his age and that there was no reason for him to be concerned. He had not been reassured by the physician's advice.

As he continued to talk about his feelings, he realized that in fact, he had been avoiding sexual relations with his wife because he feared being impotent again. He also recognized that his compulsion at work reduced the opportunities for sexual relations with his wife, who in the past had waited up for him until he returned from work but could not wait for him until 4:00 or 4:30 AM. She worked during the day and needed a reasonable amount of uninterrupted sleep, a need Mr. J. accepted without question or complaint.

As treatment progressed, he gradually recalled that his impotence had first occurred at a time when he and his wife were having a serious disagreement about how much financial support to offer a son who had lost his job. It was unusual for Mr. and Mrs. J. to have serious disagreements, but in this instance he felt his wife was being too indulgent. At one point he found himself secretly wondering whether his wife preferred his son to him, a thought he was quite ashamed of. In spite of his angry and jealous feeling, he had decided to "give in" to his wife's wishes because he remembered how stern and ungiving he felt his own father had been when he was growing up.

In discussing these feelings and memories, he recognized how hurt, angry, and upset he had been, both about his wife's attitude and his son's "inability to take care of himself." When the therapist suggested that these feelings might have contributed to his impotence, he expressed considerable interest in the idea. He decided to discuss his feelings with his wife and promptly did so. She had been unaware of how strongly he felt and was quite concerned about his hurt feelings. Over the next six months, his compulsion gradually disappeared and his relationship with his wife improved markedly. His fears about being impotent diminished, and he was able to resume a mutually satisfying sexual relationship with his wife.

As this case suggests, it would be possible to explain Mr. J.'s compulsion by applying Freud's first theory, that is, that his frustrated sexual impulses had been transformed into anxiety and symptomatic behavior. Yet the clinical material in its fullness required a more complex explanation. Using structural theory, Mr. J. and his therapist came to understand that the initial incidents of impotence stemmed directly from a conscious attempt on Mr. J.'s part to control his angry feelings (aggressive impulses) toward his wife and son. While this attempt was overtly successful, it had serious consequences at the level of unconscious mental functioning. The first consequence appears to have been his impotence, which was accompanied by guilt and a profound loss of self-esteem, as his superego "reproached" him for being so angry with his wife and son. Concurrently, his sexual desires were frustrated as a result of his impotence, and to make matters worse, his self-esteem (ego ideal) was injured when he was unable to live up to his own standard of masculinity. His ego, faced with a serious disruption of intrapsychic equilibrium, an upsurge of libidinal and aggressive impulses, and a significant loss of self-esteem, automatically instituted defensive measures. We will discuss the specific defenses he employed in chapter 4. Suffice it to say at this point that the ego's work so far (note the anthropomorphism) kept Mr. Johannson's aggressive feelings toward his wife and son outside the realm of conscious awareness and prevented him from acting on them. However, the ego had not addressed the sexual frustration and loss of self-esteem that accompanied his impotence. His inability to maintain an erection threatened Mr. J.'s ideal image of himself (*ego ideal*), and interfered with the id's demand for genital orgasm. In attempting to provide the id with some measure of substitute gratification, the ego offered a compromise that involved regression to an earlier stage of psychosexual development. In doing so it temporarily diverted the id from its original aim (genital orgasm). With sadness and relief, Mr. J. realized that his wish for sexual intercourse was replaced by fantasies of phallic exhibitionism (see chapter 2). These fantasies were expressed symbolically through his fear of opening a giant pipe and causing a destructive flood. At this point in the process of symptom formation, the ego was attempting to work cooperatively with the id to provide the best form of gratification that could be achieved within the context of superego and reality constraints.

As the foregoing analysis indicates, the process of symptom formation involves both effort and creativity on the ego's part. Often a symptom is a *compromise formation*, combining, in symbolic form (so that different elements will not enter conscious awareness), a forbidden impulse, a threatened punishment, and a solution that attempts to reconcile the conflicting forces. Even when, as in Mr. Johannson's case, the solution is pathological and creates a great deal of psychological misery, it constitutes the best compromise the ego can devise at a particular moment in time given the client's idiosyncratic psychosexual history and the environmental context in which he functions. When symptoms successfully perform the function the ego intends, they encapsulate a troublesome intrapsychic conflict without unduly disrupting overall psychic functioning. For example, a mild hand-washing compulsion will, for some people, stabilize unconscious conflict over forbidden sexual or aggressive impulses, without seriously interfering with the individual's day-to-day activities or relationships.

In Mr. J.'s case, however, the symptom did not perform this function effectively, as evidenced by his increasing level of anxiety and the fact that, night by night, it was taking him longer to complete the ritual the ego had devised to deal with the conflict. Treatment was thus necessary to help Mr. J. deal more adaptively with this conflict. The case discussion illustrates the usefulness of structural theory in studying and understanding complex mental processes, especially those that lead to symptom formation.

OVERVIEW AND EVALUATION

In creating structural theory, Freud viewed the mind as an arena in which inherently incompatible forces contend with each other for primacy. He viewed the ego as a crucible in which wishes, fears, moral demands, and social expectations are synthesized. The structural hypothesis is thus a theory that explains how the mind is organized and how its different parts interact with one another. It is also a philosophical treatise that proposes a thought-provoking, but not entirely satisfactory, view of the relationship between individuals and the societies in which they live.

Structural theory, like drive theory before it, made a significant contribution to understanding human suffering as a result of intrapsychic conflict. It utilized and expanded drive theory, but gave more primacy to the role of the ego over the id, and eventually laid the groundwork for psychology of the ego. Let us now turn to the development of ego psychology to understand more fully the role the ego plays in maintaining healthy and adaptive functioning.

REFERENCES

Bettelheim, B. (1983). *Freud and Man's Soul*. New York: Knopf.
Freud, S. (1917). Mourning and melancholia. *Standard Edition* 14:243–58.
———. (1923). The ego and the id. *Standard Edition* 19:3–66.
———. (1926). Inhibitions, symptoms and anxiety. *Standard Edition* 20:75–175.
———. (1933). New introductory lectures on psychoanalysis. *Standard Edition* 22:5–182.
———. (1940). An outline of psychoanalysis. *Standard Edition* 23:144–207.
Moore, B. E., and Fine, B. D., eds. (1990). *Psychoanalytic Terms and Concepts*. New Haven, CT: Yale University Press.

4

Ego Psychology

Gerald Schamess and Robert Shilkret

Structural theory was forged in the aftermath of the First World War, a cataclysmic event in human history. Between 1918 and 1936, Freud and his colleagues witnessed one unthinkable disaster after another: the war itself, the widespread destruction left in the aftermath of the war, the deadly flu epidemic of 1918, the dismemberment of the Austro-Hungarian Empire, the Great Depression, the rise of Nazism, the beginnings of the Holocaust, and the preparations for World War II. Deeply pessimistic about human nature at its core, structural theory teaches practitioners about the primitive desires that drive human experience, about archaic codes of justice and retribution, and about the uniquely human struggle to transform amoral childhood wishes and fears into civilized adult behavior.

In contrast, ego psychology began to take shape in Vienna and England toward the end of the period between the two world wars, and it was elaborated after World War II, mostly by European expatriates who emigrated to the United States to escape Nazi persecution. Buoyed by their newfound political freedom and encouraged by the optimism that characterizes American society, they were considerably more hopeful in their fundamental view of human nature and more pragmatic in their approach to understanding mental processes. They shared certain beliefs with the Freudians about the powerful forces in the id, but were far more interested in the ego, which they saw as the preeminent psychic agency. For the most part, they studied and theorized about how the mind accomplishes particular tasks. As a result, ego psychology encourages practitioners to think about developmental processes across the life cycle, about the unfolding of human capacities in response to the interaction between environmental influences and inborn developmental potentials, about the internal forces that propel individuals toward ever more complex and goal-directed patterns of organization, and about the ways individuals either adapt to their social and physical environments or modify those environments to make them more compatible with personal needs and wishes. Because ego psychology focuses attention on the mind's development in interaction with the social and physical world, it provides therapists with a theoretical framework for (1) repairing the effects of arrested, incomplete, or distorted psychosocial development, and (2) facilitating a better fit between the psychological needs of the individual and the normative expectations of society.

CONCEPTUALIZATIONS OF THE EGO

The ego has been conceptualized in different ways over time. Freud's (1923) original formulation was, simultaneously, the most elegant and the most constricting.

> In its relation to the id [the ego] is like a person on horseback, who has to hold in check the superior strength of the horse; with this difference, that the rider tries to do so with his own strength while the ego uses borrowed forces. The analogy may be carried a little further. Often a rider, if he is not to be parted from his horse, is obliged to guide it where IT wants to go; so in the same way the ego is in the habit of transforming the id's will into action as if it were his own. (p. 25)

In this quotation, Freud emphasizes the ego's relative lack of strength in relation to the id. He notes that the horse (id) has most of the energy and power, and that the rider (ego) must depend on the horse's power if he hopes to arrive at his chosen destination. The metaphor suggests that most of the time, but not always, the ego is capable of harnessing the id's energy toward its own purposes.

Eloquent though the imagery is, Freud's view of the ego's relationship to the id and to the external world does not adequately convey how the ego is organized or how it functions. Because the metaphor assumes that the ego's fundamental job is to regulate id impulses, it does not recognize that other ego activities such as perception, cognition, judgment, reality testing, and affect regulation also play vital roles in helping individuals achieve their chosen objectives, that is, if we wish to preserve Freud's imagery of directing the horse where the rider wants it to go. In other words, the metaphor does not recognize that the rider has strength, knowledge, goals, and a range of inborn capacities that contribute to his effectiveness in regulating the horse's behavior.

Contemporary conceptualizations focus on the ego's executive and synthesizing functions. These conceptualizations assume that the ego performs a variety of different tasks that, when combined, allow it to organize and manage mental experience and functioning. The ego attempts to stabilize mental equilibrium, in much the same way as a gyroscope orients and stabilizes the path of a rocket in flight. Since each individual gradually constructs an idiosyncratic style of ego organization over the course of his/her psychosocial development, each individual's ego has idiosyncratic strengths and weaknesses. These particular strengths and weakness reflect the techniques and processes the ego utilizes to manage internal and external stimuli. Over time, the ego organizes the techniques into a stable, repetitive pattern called character structure. This pattern makes it possible for individuals to think, feel, and act in predictable ways throughout the life cycle.

Conceptualizing the ego in terms of its organizing and synthesizing functions focuses attention on the large number of specific tasks that must be accomplished, which people take for granted as they go about their day-to-day lives. The most important of these are: (1) perceiving, filtering, and selectively remembering the enormous amounts of information that originate both inside and outside the mind; (2) organizing (editing) the filtered information in ways that allow individuals to think, feel, and act coherently; (3) finding socially acceptable ways of satisfying the conflicting demands of the id and the superego; (4) facilitating all of the routine mental activities (loving, learning, playing, acquiring new skills and capabilities, etc.) that characterize human experience; (5) mastering the developmental and social challenges that arise normatively over the course of the life cycle; (6) developing capacities that make it possible to deal adaptively with the ordinary stresses of everyday life; and (7) finding ways of minimizing the disruptive effects that trauma has on overall functioning.

While a number of specific ego functions are listed in the section that follows, it is important to keep in mind that the concept of *ego* cannot be understood simply as the sum of its component parts, or even as the sum of its many functions. Contemporary ego psychologists assume that the ego has successfully accomplished its organizing and synthesizing functions when individuals experience themselves as coherent, functional human beings with an enduring sense of personal identity. When viewed from this perspective, the concept of ego closely resembles Erikson's concept of *ego identity* (see chapter 5), and Kohut 's concept of the *self* (see chapter 7).

The following vignette illustrates adaptive, synthetic functioning under stress:

A forty-seven-year-old divorced woman moved to a new job in a new community where she had no friends or family. Her twenty-two-year-old son, an only child, had decided to pursue his career in their hometown, several thousand miles away. The woman was the oldest child in a large family that had always celebrated Christmas with ceremony and enthusiasm. The Christmas following her move she decided not to go home, fearing she would realize how lonely she was in her new community. To cope with her loneliness, she invited a number of acquaintances to her home for Christmas dinner. She chose people she knew who did not have other plans for the holiday. The dinner was potluck, and she advised her guests to bring one present to be given to another guest after dinner. When the time for gift giving arrived, she stipulated that none of the guests could open a gift until they had answered a personal question asked by another guest. Her guests, many of whom barely knew each other, were delighted by the game and enthusiastically engaged in asking and answering questions. By the end of the evening the party had generated considerable good feeling, much to the hostess's delight. The lively interaction and good cheer temporarily overcame her loneliness and reminded her of the family gatherings she had enjoyed so much. She also realized that she had gotten to know quite a lot about her various guests. Although she still missed her son and siblings, she felt she had begun to make a place for herself in her new community.

EGO FUNCTIONS

The ego's ability to organize and synthesize mental activity is based on the interaction of a number of interrelated capacities called *ego functions*. The most important of these are described below. A working understanding of ego functions is enormously helpful both in evaluating clients' strengths and weaknesses, and in predicting how they are likely to respond to different therapeutic interventions. In addition, periodic review of a client's ego functioning provides the therapist with a systematic way of evaluating treatment progress.

Reality Testing

This function involves the individual's capacity to understand and accept both physical and social reality as it is consensually defined within a given culture or cultural subgroup. In large measure, the function hinges on the individual's capacity to distinguish between her own wishes or fears (*internal reality*) and events that occur in the real world (*external reality*). The ability to make distinctions that are consensually validated determines the ego's capacity to distinguish and mediate between personal expectations, on the one hand, and social expectations or laws of nature on the other. Individuals vary considerably in how they manage this function. When the function is seriously compromised, individuals may withdraw from contact with reality for extended periods of time. This degree of withdrawal is most frequently seen in psychotic conditions. Most times, however, the function is mildly or moderately compromised for a limited period of time, with far less drastic consequences. The following vignette describes someone whose reality testing was severely compromised:

> A young volunteer entered a locked, padded, seclusion room in a state mental hospital. The room was occupied by a ten-year-old boy who crouched, trembling, in a corner. An aide explained that the boy had become violent that morning, attacking everyone who approached him. Having placed him in seclusion, the staff thought it might comfort him if someone kept him company. Since the boy conveyed nonverbally that he did not want to be approached, the volunteer sat quietly in the corner furthest away from him. After an hour, the boy asked why the volunteer was there. The volunteer answered frankly and asked if the boy was frightened. The boy asked why the volunteer wasn't afraid of the snakes. Startled, the volunteer looked around the room. The boy volunteered that the room was crawling with poisonous snakes which were trying to kill him. The only safe place was where he was sitting, since he was saying "magic words." However, he didn't see any snakes where the volunteer was sitting and asked how the volunteer kept the snakes away.

A second example describes a less severe loss of reality testing:

> A young professional woman, Mary, had been living with her aged mother, who died suddenly. The estate was not large, and the will divided the assets equally among Mary and her siblings. Mary mourned her mother intensely. In addition, she needed money desperately since she had not worked during the years she lived, rent free, with her mother. She had cared for her mother, and with her mother's approval, had pursued an interest in painting. Among her mother's possessions was an heirloom chest that the siblings decided to sell to raise cash. Citing her knowledge of antiques, Mary estimated the chest's worth. Much to everyone's surprise, two professional appraisers evaluated it at half of Mary's estimate. For the next six months, Mary refused to accept the professional evaluations, thereby making it impossible to sell the chest. It was only after her grief had moderated and she had found a full-time job that she accepted the "realistic" appraisal and allowed the chest to be sold. Her temporary loss of reality testing was a result of her ego's depletion in the process of mourning her mother.

Judgment

This function involves the capacity to reach "reasonable" conclusions about what is and what is not "appropriate " behavior. Typically, arriving at a "reasonable" conclusion involves the following steps: (1) correlating wishes, feeling states, and memories about prior life experiences with current circumstances; (2) evaluating current circumstances in the context of social expectations and laws of nature (e.g., it is not possible to transport oneself instantly out of an embarrassing situation, no matter how much one wishes to do so); and (3) drawing realistic conclusions about the likely consequences of different possible courses of action. As the definition suggests, judgment is closely related to reality testing, and the two functions are usually evaluated in tandem.

We have placed the quotation marks around "reasonable" and "appropriate" because sound judgment is a social construct. Clinicians who understand the contextual nature of judgment think carefully about their own cultural values, as well as about the particular social and cultural contexts within which their clients live. For example, the "appropriate" response to a schoolyard threat from peers is quite different for middle-class, suburban high school students than for inner-city students. The middle-class students would, at worst, have to consider the possible implications of being drawn into a fistfight. The inner-city student with good judgment would have to consider the possibility of being shot. The "appropriate" action for the two teenagers would be quite different, and would depend not only on their internal (psychological) organization but on the realistic dangers they face and the social norms that characterize their particular communities.

On a day-to-day basis, judgment plays a central role in deciding whether one has drunk too much to drive safely; whether one is adequately prepared to pass a test at school; whether the man or woman one has fallen in love with is likely to be a loving, reliable partner; or, at the most basic level, whether one is dressed warmly enough to go out in the cold (you and your mother might disagree about whether you are properly dressed).

Modulating and Controlling Impulses

This function is based on the capacity to hold sexual and aggressive feelings in check without acting on them until the ego has evaluated whether they meet the individual's own moral standards and are acceptable in terms of social norms. Adequate functioning in this area depends on the individual's capacity to tolerate frustration, to delay gratification, and to tolerate anxiety without immediately acting to ameliorate it. Impulse control also depends on the ability to exercise appropriate judgment in situations where the individual is strongly motivated to seek relief from psychological tension and/or to pursue some pleasurable activity (sex, power, fame, money, etc.). Problems in modulation may involve either too little or too much control over impulses.

> A group of adolescent male gang members were on a therapeutic camping trip and were cooking shish kebab for dinner over an open fire. Having delayed

preparing the fire until they were famished and desperate to eat, they were only able to cook the meat until it was lightly browned on the outside, before they tried to eat it. With each bite, they yelled and cursed, blaming the counselors because the meat was raw. This sequence was repeated again and again because the boys could not control their appetites long enough to cook the meat adequately. The only gang member who enjoyed his meal was a boy accurately nicknamed "Joe Fats" because of his love of food. Of all the boys, he alone listened carefully to the counselor's instructions and waited patiently until the meat was cooked. He feasted royally while his friends cursed.

An intellectually precocious eight-year-old boy was referred for treatment because he regularly defecated in his pants. During a treatment session that opened with a discussion of his inability to control himself, he began to talk about his interest in Napoleon's military campaigns. Recognizing his admiration for and identification with Napoleon, the therapist asked whether he thought Napoleon "pooped" in his pants. He fixed the therapist with a withering stare and said "Napoleon pooped any time and anywhere he pleased." The interchange highlights the boy's unwillingness to exercise age-appropriate control over his bowel functions.

Therapists who work with eating disorders regularly see problems that arise from excessive impulse control. A common but extreme example involves the anorexic teenager who, on eating half a carrot, feels compelled to exercise for several hours to burn off the calories she has consumed. Clients who are severely anorexic may have great difficulty in tolerating any kind of oral pleasure, feeling that food will make them fat and ugly, and that they have to punish themselves severely whenever they eat.

Modulation of Affect

The ego performs this function by preventing painful or unacceptable emotional reactions from entering conscious awareness, or by managing the expression of such feelings in ways that do not disrupt either emotional equilibrium or social relationships. To adequately perform this function, the ego constantly monitors the source, intensity, and direction of feeling states, as well as the people toward whom feelings will be directed. Monitoring determines whether such states will be acknowledged or expressed and, if so, in what form. The basic principle to remember in evaluating how well the ego manages this function is that affect modulation may be problematic because of too much or too little expression.

As an integral part of the monitoring process, the ego evaluates the type of expression that is most congruent with established social norms. For example, in white American culture it is assumed that individuals will contain themselves and maintain a high level of personal/vocational functioning, except in extremely traumatic situations such as the death of a family member, very serious illness, or terrible accident. This standard is not necessarily the norm in other cultures. For example, when Arabic women mourn the death of a loved one, their culture expects them to scream and wail publicly, tear their garments, and pull out their hair. Women who do not publicly express intense grief are viewed with suspicion. Their restraint is thought to be inappropriate, suggesting they may not have really loved the family member who died. Compare the Arabic norm for mourning among women with the vignette cited below, which describes an American man who is mourning his mother's death. In doing so, keep in mind the gender differences within American culture; men who mourn are expected to behave differently from women who mourn. Using a cultural standard, the behavior described in this vignette would have been even more problematic had the client been a woman. This first vignette illustrates constriction in the expression of affect:

> A man calmly told his therapist that he was relieved about his beloved mother's death. He noted that she had suffered greatly from a degenerative neurological illness during the last years of her life. He added that his religious beliefs assured him that she has passed on to her "just reward" in Heaven. During the memorial service and funeral he did not shed a tear, and after the service he disposed of her household possessions without the slightest conscious awareness of grief. Some weeks later he entered treatment. He was perplexed about the reasons for his reduced work effectiveness and for his difficulty concentrating, even on such simple tasks as reading the newspaper.

The second example involves excessive and inappropriate expression:

> A photographer felt his supervisor had unjustly reprimanded him. Consumed with anger, he told the supervisor, "You're not fit to be a pimple on a real photographer's ass." He told friends about this incident, who worried about his future, yet he was the only one surprised when he was fired. On being asked to reflect on this behavior, he commented that he had every right to be angry and to express it openly. His only regret was that the remark overestimated his supervisor's competence.

In evaluating this man's overall ego functioning, it would be necessary to consider not only his capacity to modulate affect but also his reality testing, judgment, and capacity for impulse control. As the example illustrates, all of these functions were seriously compromised.

Object Relations

This function is discussed as a separate theory in chapter 6. For now, it is sufficient to say that this function involves the ability to form and maintain coherent representations of others and of the self. The concept refers not only to the people one interacts with in the external world but also to significant others who are remembered and represented within the mind. Adequate functioning implies the ability to maintain a basically positive view of the other, even when one feels disappointed, frustrated, or angered by the other's behavior. Disturbances in object relations may manifest themselves through an inability to fall in love, emotional coldness, lack of interest in or withdrawal from interaction with others, intense dependency, and/or an excessive need to control relationships.

Self-Esteem Regulation

This function involves the capacity to maintain a steady and reasonable level of positive self-regard in the face of distressing or frustrating external events. Painful affective states, including anxiety, depression, shame, and guilt, as well as exhilarating emotions such as triumph, glee, and ecstasy may also undermine self-esteem. Generally speaking, in dominant American culture a measured expression of both pain and pleasure is expressed; excess in either direction is a cause for concern. White Western culture tends to assume that individuals will maintain a consistent and steady level of self-esteem, regardless of external events or internally generated feeling states.

A thirty-five-year-old professional man who had grown up with rejecting parents had always assumed that his wife sometimes ignored him because she didn't love him. His perception caused him enormous emotional pain and confirmed his private view that he was less than fully human. His idea that he was basically a "loathsome" creature reflected his serious problems in self-esteem. After discussing his feelings in treatment, he asked his wife whether she was avoiding him, and if so, why. To his surprise, he discovered that during childhood she had suffered from a serious learning disability, and still had difficulty focusing her attention when she felt "overstimulated." Since she knew that she loved him and he loved her, she had always assumed he would understand if she was sometimes inattentive. He responded to these revelations by further examining his reasons for viewing himself as a person "with whom no one would voluntarily associate." Thereafter, he found it easier to maintain a positive sense of self-esteem, even when his wife was distracted and temporarily unavailable to him.

Mastery

When conceptualized as an ego function, mastery reflects the epigenetic view that individuals achieve more advanced levels of ego organization by mastering successive developmental challenges. Each stage of psychosexual development (oral, anal, phallic, genital) presents a particular challenge that must be adequately addressed before the individual can move on to the next higher stage. By mastering stage-specific challenges, the ego gains strength in relation to the other structures of the mind and thereby becomes more effective in organizing and synthesizing mental processes. Freud expressed this principle in his statement, "Where id was, shall ego be."

An underdeveloped capacity for mastery can be seen, for example, in infants who have not been adequately nourished, stimulated, and protected during the first year of life, in the oral stage of development. When they enter the anal stage, such infants are not well prepared to learn socially acceptable behavior or to control the pleasure they derive from defecating at will. As a result, some of them will experience delays in achieving bowel control and will have difficulty in controlling temper tantrums, while others will sink into a passive, joyless compliance with parental demands that compromises their ability to explore, learn, and become physically competent. Conversely, infants who have been well gratified and adequately stimulated during the oral stage enter the anal stage feeling relatively secure and confident. For the most part, they cooperate in curbing their anal desires, and are eager to win parental approval for doing so. In addition, they are physically active, free to learn, and eager to explore. As they gain confidence in their increasingly autonomous physical and mental abilities, they also learn to follow the rules their parents establish and, in doing so, win parental approval. As they master the specific tasks related to the anal stage, they are well prepared to move on to the next stage of development and the next set of challenges. When adults have problems with mastery, they usually enact them in derivative or symbolic ways.

> Over a two-year period, prior to each of her therapist's three vacations, an intelligent, well-educated client from an upper-class family canceled the last appointment prior to the therapist's departure. She had been abandoned repeatedly by her parents and other caregivers during childhood and had unconsciously established a pattern of leaving relationships before the person she cared about could leave her. Well in advance of his next planned vacation, the therapist pointed out the pattern of missed appointments. She was surprised by the therapist's comment since she was totally unaware both of what she had done and of the feelings connected with her behavior. As a result of the interpretation, she kept all her appointments, including the last one before the therapist left. After the therapist's return she commented that it had taken her more than two years to believe he would actually come back. Moreover, in his absence she realized she had never believed he would want to see her again, even if he did return. The interview material suggests that, over the course of treatment, she had begun to master the separation anxiety that had, until then, interfered with her attempts to establish intimate relationships. From that point onward she could talk more openly about her fears of loss

and abandonment. Over time, her attention gradually turned to issues of sexuality and intimacy.

THE USE OF DEFENSE MECHANISMS

Up to now we have discussed the ego in terms of the specific functions it performs. In doing so, we have paid particular attention to the superordinate functions that involve organizing and synthesizing mental processes. We now consider the ego's role in protecting the self from both real and perceived danger, and the methods (*defenses*) by which it fulfills that task. Defense mechanisms are among the most important of the ego functions.

The ego requires protection from four kinds of danger: (1) conflict among the different agencies of the mind (id, ego, superego); (2) conflict in interpersonal relationships; (3) conflict in relation to social norms and institutions; and (4) the disruption of psychological equilibrium that occurs in response to trauma. As noted in chapter 3, conflicts among the agencies of the mind arises when there is a clash between developmentally early, unconscious, sexual, and aggressive wishes (emanating from the id), and the ethical and moral standards represented by internalized conscience (emanating from the superego). Interpersonal conflict arises when an individual's unconscious wishes and fears are incompatible with the behavioral expectations and needs of caregivers, family members, friends, and/or lovers. Social conflict arises when unconscious wishes or fears and the behaviors associated with them challenge consensually accepted social norms. Trauma occurs when psychological equilibrium is disrupted (at least temporarily) by an inescapable need to cope with terrifying external events.

When faced with one or more such dangers, the ego uses defense mechanisms to protect the self. Defense mechanisms automatically and unconsciously modify the individual's perception of and/or reaction to danger. The specific mechanisms that are employed reflect the ego's evaluation of the perceived danger and the level of psychosocial development the individual has achieved. Ego psychologists believe that the conscious self feels threatened whenever it becomes aware of unconscious wishes and fears, regardless of whether they originate in the id or superego. Every defense mechanism is designed to keep unconscious content from entering conscious awareness. However, each defense mechanism accomplishes the task in a different way.

While defense mechanisms protect the self from perceived danger, they do so at a certain cost. The cost varies, depending on the mechanisms employed. As one would expect in a hierarchical theory that emphasizes the mastery of stage-specific developmental tasks, it is assumed that individuals employ defense mechanisms that are congruent with their achieved levels of ego organization. At the lower levels of ego organization, the ego uses defenses that significantly interfere with reality testing. Defenses such as denial and projection interfere with overall ego functioning even though they protect the self to a limited degree. At intermediate levels of organization, the ego employs defenses that interfere with impulse control and judgment, turn wishes and fears into their opposites, redirect feelings away from their original objects, impede cognitive functioning, and/or undermine memory. Defenses such as acting out, reaction formation, displacement, and repression interfere less with overall functioning and usually provide the self with better protection. However, the cost of utilizing them may still be considerable. At higher levels of organization, the ego uses defenses (e.g., sublimation and humor) that protect the self quite well and enhance rather than interfere with overall functioning.

Although the distinctions between the defenses used at higher and lower levels of ego organization are important, clinicians should remember that individuals *always* use the *most adaptive* defenses available to them. The unconscious use of a defense or set of defenses depends on the individual's developmental history, the nature of his/her significant relationships, and the stresses and supports inherent in his/her social environment. Within that context, the defenses reflect the best choices that the individual is capable of making. Descriptions of defenses in the literature and in the classroom often sound pejorative, almost as if the person employing them were doing something bad or weak. Nothing could be further from the truth, since defenses are always attempts (often gallant attempts) to preserve psychic integrity and survival under the pressure of stress and fears. It is important for clinicians to remember this principle when deciding how they will deal with specific defenses that interfere with overall functioning.

Anxiety and Defense Mechanisms

Before listing and describing the defense mechanisms used by the ego, it is important to explain how they relate to anxiety. Defense mechanisms are automatically triggered when the ego becomes conscious of anxiety, an inherently distressing emotion that individuals experience along a continuum ranging from mild discomfort to intolerable panic. Unpleasant though it is, anxiety serves a necessary and useful function in regulating mental processes. In much the way that pain alerts us to problems that are likely to affect our bodily functions, anxiety alerts us to problems that are likely to affect our emotional well-being. It is effective as a warning precisely because most people find it so painful and unsettling. When the ego perceives anxiety, it responds by mobilizing the defense mechanisms available to it with the aim of preserving emotional well-being and limiting the degree of functional impairment.

In his monograph "Inhibitions, Symptoms, and Anxiety," Freud (1926) identified five types of anxiety. Each type is associated with a particular stage of psychosexual development and with a normal developmental task that must be mastered if the individual is to progress to the next, more advanced, developmental stage.

Freud thought that the first and most overwhelming kind of anxiety was experienced in early infancy, particularly during the initial twelve months of life. He named it *automatic anxiety* to distinguish it from *signal anxiety*, which he viewed as developmentally more advanced. Automatic anxiety arises in response to excessive levels of frustration, such as hunger, or threatening kinds of stimulation, such as fever, loud noises, or noxious odors, which the infant can neither escape nor modulate. When faced with such painful stimulation, infants have no recourse except to cry, kick, and flail about. Fortunately, they can usually be consoled by an attuned caregiver, even when they are extremely distressed. If outside help is not forthcoming, they can only cry until they exhaust themselves and fall asleep. By doing so they shut off both outside stimuli and internal mental processes.

Contemporary ego psychologists assume that infants experience these terrifying moments at the level of excruciating organic distress, accompanied by inchoate fears that overwhelm them. If this type of anxiety is re-evoked in adulthood, it frequently leads to psychotic decompensation. However, some traumatized individuals are able to limit the degree of decompensation, even when so stressed, by utilizing dissociation as a defense. Dissociation, which also shuts off internal and external stimulation, has serious but far less drastic consequences (see chapter 16 on the anxiety disorders). Because this type of anxiety threatens the total loss of ego functioning, contemporary theorists refer to it as *annihilation anxiety*, a term chosen in an attempt to capture the depth of the overwhelming, disorganizing terror involved.

A second, developmentally more advanced level of anxiety often referred to as "fear of loss of the object " is originally experienced during the second and third years of life. It involves the fear of being abandoned by a primary caregiver. Since young children depend on adults both for survival and for emotional well-being, abandonment anxiety is quite terrifying. In spite of the degree of terror that the threat of abandonment evokes, therapists should remember that abandonment anxiety is an important marker of developmental progress. Abandonment anxiety can occur only when normal development has progressed far enough for the child to recognize that the primary caregiver exists separately in the world, and therefore is not under the child's omnipotent control. Generally speaking, if this kind of anxiety is re-evoked in adults, it is enacted through intensely dependent and/or clinging behavior, or through acting out, which may be antisocial in nature. Acting out unconsciously asserts that the individual does not need a caregiver, is not anxious, and is capable of taking perfectly good care of himself without any assistance from anyone else.

The third level of anxiety, called "fear of loss of the object's love" is associated with the threat of losing the caregiver's love and esteem. Children ordinarily become aware of this danger during their third and fourth years of life. It is evoked by their attempts to (1) curb childhood sexual and aggressive desires and (2) accept the behavioral rules and constraints their parents endorse. This type of anxiety is allayed when children can maintain a stable internal representation of the caregiver (*object constancy*) and are willing to change their behavior in order to win the caregiver's approval.

At a still more advanced level of development, we see an anxiety that is specific to the phallic and oedipal stages of development. This type of anxiety, unfortunately still often referred to as *castration anxiety*, involves a fear of retribution, bodily harm, or the loss of an essential, highly valued physical or mental capacity. It is based on the child's projected fear of retribution for hostile wishes against a parent. The theory postulates that such wishes are directed against the parent who prevents the child from conceiving a baby with the other parent. Adults who re-experience this kind of anxiety tend to use neurotic defenses and to function at a neurotic level of intrapsychic organization (see chapter 16). In spite of the psychic pain associated with *castration anxiety*, its appearance indicates that the individual has successfully mastered the previous stages of psychosocial development and has achieved a high level of ego integration.

And finally, during latency, children may selectively experience anxiety associated with any or all of the earlier stages of psychosexual development (annihilation, abandonment, loss of the caregiver's love, retribution, bodily injury, and/or loss of valued capacities). Different levels of anxiety are evoked because the internalized parental representation, the superego, has assumed responsibility for making moral judgments and meting out punishment. In this role, the superego threatens the ego with phase-specific punishments, based on how it views particular wishes, feelings, and memories. Ego psychologists believe that after latency, if development has progressed reasonably well, the superego will be less punitive in responding both to forbidden wishes and to situations that threaten its moral standards. The mature superego's increased flexibility reduces pressure on the ego, thereby making it possible for the ego to consider a greater range of options in attempting to resolve intrapsychic and interpersonal conflict. Since contemporary theory states that the ego continues to mature during latency and thereafter, people who have mastered the developmental tasks intrinsic to the oral, anal, phallic, and genital stages of development tend to experience anxiety in more transient ways, to employ healthier (higher-level) defenses, and to become less dysfunctional in the face of perceived psychological danger.

Defenses are activated by anxiety in the following way. When the ego perceives anxiety, it responds automatically, first by evaluating the nature of the danger, and second, by reviewing its repertoire of defenses. It employs a defense or set of defenses that had been effective in managing a similar threat earlier in life. Since all defenses are unconscious, individuals do not ordinarily recognize either the danger they are defending against or the protective mechanisms that have been activated. While the activation of defenses is painful, it must be understood that it happens unconsciously, totally outside the individual's conscious awareness. If defenses work as intended, anxiety disappears from conscious awareness. However if the defenses fail and do not eliminate or at least diminish the threat of danger, anxiety increases and additional defenses are called into play. Generally speaking, the most threatening perceived dangers are those that re-evoke real and/or imagined childhood fears. To illustrate how this process works it is useful to reconsider Mr. Johannson, the power plant engineer who was discussed in chapter 3.

> Mr. J. obsessed endlessly over whether he had actually turned off the water outtake valves he was responsible for turning off. During treatment he remembered that he had been very angry at his wife because she had sided with his son in a family disagreement. With considerable shame, he also remembered his feeling that his wife preferred his son to him. This incident re-evoked childhood experiences of his own with an indulgent mother and a stern, punitive father. When, some months later, he became impotent for the first time, his childhood anxieties returned. Unconsciously, he viewed his impotence as the punishment he had feared when he was five—castration. In thinking about his impotence, he was consciously aware of concerns about his sexual functioning, but not of his childhood memories or anxieties.

In attempting to deal with both the current and historical threats to his manhood, Johannson's ego employed several defense mechanisms that had previously protected him from similar dangers (the defenses italicized here are explained in more detail below). When his anger at his wife threatened his childhood defense of *repression* (he remembered nothing about his childhood oedipal wishes and fears), he *regressed* to a developmentally earlier level of psychosexual organization, replacing the wish for genital intercourse with a compensatory wish to exhibit his phallic prowess by creating an enormous flood. (There is a wonderful description of a similar fantasy in Rabelais's [1532] classic book *Gargantua and Pantagruel*, 1946 edition, pp. 41–43.) Realizing that the compensatory wish was also unacceptable, he defended against it through *reaction formation* and *undoing*; that is, in his conscious mind he was determined not to cause a flood (*reaction formation*), even if he had to turn the valves on and off for hours at a time (*doing and undoing*). Given the strength of the wish and the intensity of his castration anxiety, the combination of defenses available to him did not work adequately. His levels of anxiety and functional impairment increased, and he finally entered treatment.

Defense mechanisms are easy to understand once their unconscious content is revealed. Before the client has recognized and acknowledged unconscious content, however, the underlying meaning of any given defense mechanism is, by definition, unclear. In fact, there is no way a therapist can be certain that a defense mechanism is being utilized until the client acknowledges the defense in some fashion. For example, if the client does not remember an event or a feeling (repression), how can the therapist know that the patient is not remembering something? Similarly, if a client says she loves her mother, how can the therapist determine whether she does in fact, love her mother, or whether she unconsciously hates her mother (reaction formation)? While it is useful for therapists to develop hypotheses based on other information the client has presented, it is important to remember that hypotheses are no more than informed speculations, until they are confirmed or disconfirmed by the client. This way of approaching the unconscious material encoded in defense mechanisms encourages therapists to be respectful of the protective role that defenses play and to remember that clients voluntarily (albeit unconsciously) give up defenses when they feel it is safe to do so. From an ego psychological viewpoint, patience, respect, and careful observation are the crucial elements that permit clients to feel safe enough to recognize the underlying meaning of the defenses they employ.

A HIERARCHY OF DEFENSES

We can now consider specific defense mechanisms and how they operate. Of the twenty or more defense mechanisms identified by Anna Freud (1936) and George Vaillant (1992), we will present eleven. In doing so, we will follow the well-established tradition of categorizing defenses hierarchically. Vaillant (1992) classifies defenses as developmentally early/psychotic, immature, neurotic, and mature/healthy. These categories parallel the stages of psychosexual development that have been discussed previously. Note that the classification reflects a continuum. It begins by describing defenses that drastically impair functioning, continues with defenses that are less disruptive, and ends with defenses that enhance functioning.

Although we will use Vaillant's classification system, we do so with a proviso. Vaillant contends that people who function at the higher levels of ego organization always employ higher-level defenses, the ones he classifies as neurotic or mature/healthy. In contrast, clinical reports suggest that highly functioning clients actually employ a wide range of defenses, including some that are categorized as developmentally early or immature. It seems likely that the ability to call on, as needed, a wide range of different defenses is an indication of emotional health. Vaillant's hierarchical system seems slightly more reliable in describing clients who function at lower levels of ego organization. Such clients seem to have fewer defenses available to them, and therefore rely almost exclusively on developmentally early and/or immature mechanisms; however, clinicians have seen many examples of clients with poor ego organization who also have a rich array of defenses at their disposal depending on the level of anxiety they are experiencing.

Developmentally Early/Psychotic Defenses

Denial

The ego ignores or disavows a painful event or the meaning connected with it. When denial is operating, the ego simply does not acknowledge the existence or implications of threatening aspects of external reality. In its most extreme forms, denial contributes to the development of psychotic delusions and hallucinations. However, in most instances it simply blocks out specific events or stimuli that are overwhelmingly threatening to the ego. Denial is ubiquitous among alcoholics and drug abusers who, even in the face of overwhelming evidence, refuse either to admit their addictions or to acknowledge that the addictions interfere with their functioning. For example, in an inpatient alcohol rehabilitation program, it was customary to videotape the original intake interview with every client. Two weeks later, when the clients had "dried out" and regained their health to some degree, they were shown their own videotapes. Approximately a third of them insisted they were not the person who appeared in the videotape. They could not or would not believe they had ever looked so desperate, so down-and-out (Rohan, personal communication about the alcohol treatment program at the Northampton, Massachusetts, Veterans' Administration Hospital, 1984).

Like every other defense mechanism, denial can be adaptive under certain circumstances, especially in realistically dangerous situations where there is no means of escape. Soldiers in combat use denial adaptively to minimize their terror and to keep fighting. Patients suffering from slow, debilitating, and fatal illnesses often use adaptive denial to sustain their will to live. People with impaired hearing who communicate through sign language will, sometimes, when they don't want to understand what is said to them, simply close their eyes.

Projection

The ego deals with unacceptable impulses and/or terrifying anxieties by attributing them to someone in the external world. In this defense, individuals do not experience or acknowledge the projected impulses or anxieties as their own. They feel victimized by some other person who, inexplicably, wishes to injure them, or who blames them for some terrible deed. In its most extreme form, projection dominates the mental life of psychotic or paranoid clients whose relationships with external reality may be seriously compromised. Even when it is utilized by healthier people, projection can be a startling and disconcerting defense. For example, a Caucasian recreation worker tells of having to restrain a six-year-old African American boy who had been throwing pool balls around the game room. When the boy had finally been carefully restrained, he turned around, spat in the worker's face, and said, "You black boogie bastard." The worker, who was quite fond of the child, later told his supervisor, "I was near tears. I don't know much psychology, but I do know that if one of us sees himself as a 'black boogie bastard,' it's not me."

Because projection can have such a profound negative effect on the people toward whom it is directed, it is important to emphasize the important constructive role it plays in everyday human interactions. Projection makes it possible to fall in love, to care for children, and to empathize with people whose inner lives and cultural experiences are different from our own. All of these quintessential human activities are based on the ability to put one's own thoughts and feelings into someone else's mind and to retrieve them as needed. The process can be more or less healthy, depending on the degree to which the projected thoughts and feelings are congruent with the other person's actual thoughts and feelings.

Immature Defenses

Acting Out

This defense involves the direct expression of wishes, impulses, and fantasies through overt behavior. Immediate action makes it possible for individuals to avoid conscious recognition of distressing feelings they unconsciously experience as intolerable. "Acting out involves chronically giving in to impulses in order to avoid the tension that would result were there any postponement of expression" (Vaillant 1992, p. 245). Addicts who drink because they cannot tolerate depressive feelings, patients who engage in self-mutilation because they feel unsure of whether they are actually alive, and the adolescent who steals a leather jacket because he can't tolerate wanting but not having a jacket of his own are all using acting out as a defense.

Dissociation

In dissociation, a painful idea or memory is separated from the feelings attached to it, thereby altering the idea's emotional meaning and impact. It is a core defense among incest survivors and among adults who were abused as children.

> A thirty-eight-year-old woman who had been sexually abused repeatedly as a latency-age child could remember the details of the abuse but did not experience any feelings in relation to the abuse. She knew intellectually that she must have bad feelings, but could feel nothing. After a period of treatment she became aware that when she started to experience feelings connected with the abuse she simply disappeared emotionally, even in the middle of a conversation. "I just go away in my head. Sometimes when I'm driving, I look around and realize I've lost half an hour. I don't know where I am, how I got there, or what's been going on in my head. I've just been gone, even though I've been driving the car. I get scared about that. I wonder whether someday I'll have a serious accident."

Regression

This defense involves a retreat to an earlier level of psychosexual functioning and/or ego organization. Typically, it appears when a specific developmental challenge cannot be mastered or when an environmental stressor creates high levels of anxiety. While it usually makes its first appearance as a defense during the anal stage of development, it is utilized throughout life regardless of the individual's level of ego organization. In childhood, regression is frequently seen after the birth of a sibling. For example, an older child temporarily loses bowel or bladder control, even though control had previously been well established. In such instances, the regression is caused by jealousy of the new baby and by the older child's fantasy that he would be equally loved and fussed over if he were a baby.

Regression may also take place "in the service of the ego." When adults become physically ill and need care, they frequently take to their beds, asking to be fed, bathed, and pampered. While such behavior reflects a transitory wish to be a baby again, it may also facilitate healing. When regression is temporary, as in this example, it enhances ego functioning by providing individuals with a moratorium during which they do not feel they have to act in mature and responsible ways. As a result they are able to reassess their emotional problems, recover their strength, and return more rapidly to prior levels of functioning. When this occurs, stress on the ego is reduced, and the degree of functional impairment is limited. Under such circumstances regression not only protects the self from danger but also enhances the ego's adaptive capacity. In therapy, regression can be beneficial if it helps clients get in touch with their developmentally early wishes and fears, and with pre-verbal bodily needs. Generally speaking, however, when regression continues over long periods of time, it significantly impairs ego functioning. The duration and degree of regression markedly affects the "cost-benefit" ratio and may make use of the defense counterproductive.

Neurotic Defenses

Repression

This defense simply involves complete forgetting. Thoughts, memories, and feelings that are repressed simply do not exist in the person's conscious mind. Repression protects the self from unwelcome knowledge such as the awareness of desires that defy moral standards, or fears that are too terrifying to contemplate, or disappointments that are too difficult to bear.

One young woman in treatment began talking about how much she had suffered in school from her serious, yet undiagnosed, learning disabilities. She described not only feeling stupid and ashamed but also alone and unprotected because no family member or teacher paid enough attention to help her figure out what was wrong. As the patient described those painful feelings and events, the therapist was thinking rather smugly about how vigilant and active she had been regarding her own children's learning disabilities and what excellent help she had gotten them. After the session, the therapist expected to feel compassionate toward the patient and pleased with herself, and was therefore surprised when she felt very frightened and ill at ease. She was even more surprised during the next session when she sat there nervously, hoping the subject of learning disabilities would not come up. Her anxiety grew until several days after the second session she suddenly remembered that she too had struggled with learning disabilities as a child and that no one had been aware of her difficulties or helped her with them. Like her patient she had learned to get decent grades by paying very careful attention in class and compensating in every way possible for her visual-motor impairment. She had repressed these painful memories because she had not wanted to recognize how angry and hurt she was at her parents for their neglect. During the first session, during which her client talked about learning disabilities the therapist recalled how good she was with her own children, a reaction formation that, among its other functions, allowed her to forget the ways in which her parents had failed her. Her attempt at repression failed, however, when the patient's story made her aware of the painful memories she had unconsciously banished.

Reaction Formation

This defense transforms an unacceptable wish into an acceptable one, a "bad" wish into a "good" one. When individuals employ reaction formation as a defense, the wishes of which they are consciously aware are the exact opposites of the wishes they actually want to fulfill. To understand this defense one must recognize that expressed love can conceal hatred, expressed mercy can conceal cruelty, and expressed obedience can conceal defiance. For example, parents who are very angry at their children will often be overly solicitous about the child's health and well-being, some-times to the point of emotionally suffocating the child. Similarly, people who feel sexual desire for an unavailable partner will often describe pub-licly, at great length, in very derogatory terms, how sexually unattractive the object of their desire is. Although such talk may be part of a conscious strat-egy to challenge and attract a partner, when the underlying attraction is unconscious the negative comments serve a defensive purpose.

Displacement

In this defense unacceptable sexual and aggressive wishes are directed away from one person and redirected toward another. Usually, wishes and impulses are directed away from a person who is perceived as inappropriate and/or dangerous, and redirected toward a person who is perceived as appropriate and/or safe.

> A young therapist working in a mental health clinic was unconsciously angry at his supervisor. He was unaware of his anger, in part because he was afraid the supervisor would evaluate him poorly. During his supervisory meetings, he complained bitterly about the clinic administration. Even though he was expressing intense anger he was unconcerned about his supervisor's response, since he knew she shared many of his negative opinions. He was quite sur-prised one day when his supervisor quietly asked him whether he might also be angry at her. At that point, he could no longer maintain the displacement, and he became consciously aware of his angry feelings for the first time.

Displacement occurs predictably and normatively during adolescent development. One frequently sees adolescents of both genders dating peo-ple who bear a distinct resemblance to the parent they had most loved when they were young children. Since one of the fundamental develop-mental tasks of adolescence is to find a partner, outside the family, toward whom one can feel passion, and with whom who can share one's most pri-vate thoughts and feelings, the adolescent's use of displacement is an essen-tial and constructive component in his/her attempt to master this essential stage-specific task. Displacement is also the mechanism that takes place in transference and countertransference. Greenson (1965) described it best when he said that transference is "a new edition of an old relationship . . . an anachronism, an error in time. A displacement has taken place; impulses, feelings and defenses to a person in the past have been shifted onto a person in the present" (p. 201).

Undoing

This defense involves acting in ways that symbolically or actually make amends for prior thoughts, feelings, or behaviors that one feels guilty about and/or that threaten punishment. Mr. Johannson's inability to decide whether he had closed the water outtake valves at the power plant is a prime example of undoing. Having actually closed the valves, his unconscious wish to create a flood undermined his certainty about whether they really were closed. To make sure he had closed them, he had to reopen them. Having reopened them, he needed to close them again. On proceeding to the next valve, his unconscious wishes again made him feel uncertain about whether the last valve was open or closed, so it was necessary for him to start over again. As with Mr. Johannson, this process can go on for very long periods of time. Undoing is a defense most often seen in clients with obsessive-compulsive symptomatology (see chapter 16). When it operates to a limited degree, it can be quite adaptive. For example, accountants and computer programmers who are expected to make as few errors as possible are often praised for their use of doing and undoing, which is viewed by their supervisors as evidence of carefulness. When the defense gets out of hand, however, it disrupts ego functioning and relationships with others in profound ways.

Mature Defenses

Sublimation

This defense involves a process in which the ego transforms asocial, sexual, and aggressive wishes into derivative behaviors that are socially acceptable, or valuable.

> A gangly adolescent, who at fifteen is six-and-a-half feet tall and weighs a hundred and forty pounds, feels awkward, unattractive, and unlovable. He hates his peers, all of whom are better looking and more popular than he is. Three years later, he has learned how to dress, and by emphasizing his height, has made himself into a very handsome young man. He has worked on his coordination by studying dance and has developed some undiscovered talents as an actor. Instead of avoiding people and hiding in shame, he now participates in public theater performances and has become popular with his peers. He has quite literally transformed himself, and the self-hatred he thought he would carry to his grave has metamorphosed into a healthy, if somewhat exhibitionistic, appreciation of how wonderful he has become.

Another example shows how socially sanctioned behavior can demonstrate sublimation.

Professional football players routinely display levels of aggression that, if enacted anywhere but in a football stadium, would quickly bring them to trial for assault and battery. As professional athletes, however, they are extremely well paid for their talents. As long as they follow the rules, they are encouraged to knock people down and run over them in a kind of controlled mayhem. If they are good at the sport, they become role models as well as sex symbols for a sizable percentage of the population. The kind of aggressive behavior that, under other circumstances, would cause them and society enormous trouble, has been transformed into a socially desirable activity.

Humor

This defense permits the overt expression of painful or socially unacceptable wishes and feelings without discomforting the individual who is being humorous or (in most instances) offending the listeners. Like sublimation, humor frequently enhances overall functioning.

An extremely intelligent seven-year-old boy whose parents were engaged in a bitter custody battle was referred for treatment because of problems with peers and poor schoolwork. On settling in for his first treatment interview, he asked whether the therapist had heard the story of the "Titchenstein monster." The therapist had not, and the boy told the following story. "Long ago and far away, nine children were playing on top of a high dam that was holding back a huge reservoir of water. Suddenly the dam began to crack, and the children realized they could not save themselves, since they had been playing in the middle of the dam. Their parents, half of whom were on one side and half on the other, could not reach them either. Just when they feared they were doomed, out of the water rose the Titchenstein monster, an enormous beast with red eyes, and flames coming out of his mouth. With one great, hairy claw he scooped up all the children, depositing half on one side of the dam, and half on the other. The children and parents were delighted to be reunited." At this point the child stopped, and asked the therapist if he had guessed the moral to the story. The therapist had not, and the child said, "You should have! . . . The moral is, a Titchenstein saves nine."

THE AUTONOMOUS EGO FUNCTIONS

Any serious discussion of ego psychology requires careful consideration of the work done by Heinz Hartmann. Among his other contributions, Hartmann (1939) articulated the view that a number of important ego functions are genetically programmed (inborn), and that these functions normally operate outside the sphere of intrapsychic conflict. This formulation made ego psychology into an independent, freestanding theory with important theoretical and clinical practice implications. When Hartmann first proposed it, the formulation was startling and innovative. It revised the prior view that at the beginning of life all psychic energy is concentrated in the id. The earlier formulation stated that it was necessary for the ego to acquire energy from the id, as id impulses were tamed during the course of psychosexual development. In that formulation, the ego's capacity to influence mental life depended entirely on its ability first to neutralize id energy, and then to use that energy for its own purposes. In constructing the horse and rider metaphor cited earlier, Freud tried to show that the rider (ego) could pursue life goals only if he could control, direct, and manage the horse's (id's) superior strength and energy.

By postulating an autonomous, conflict-free sphere of ego functioning, Hartmann revised Freud's view, persuasively arguing that from birth onward the ego is endowed with energy and power of its own, allowing it to perform a number of essential mental functions, independent of id wishes or superego constraints. The functions that have primary autonomy include intellectual ability, perception, and motor activity (motility), as well as inborn capacities that facilitate the acquisition of language and make it possible to plan and initiate goal-directed behavior. Under ordinary circumstances, the autonomous functions are not affected by conflict of any kind. The ego is capable of maintaining and further developing these functions during the various phases of psychosexual development, except in instances where children are born with genetic limitations or have been subjected to severe and persistent mistreatment (neglect, abuse, rejection, or other trauma) early in life.

In this context, Hartmann proposed the view that autonomous ego functions develop within normal limits if the infant's genetic endowment is adequate, and if the infant's caregivers provide an "average expectable environment." Because the infant is totally dependent on its caregivers, normal development unfolds in the context of a human environment that recognizes and meets the infant's basic needs for nurturance, protection, care, and stimulation. Hartmann suggested that the "fit" between an infant's inborn temperament and the caregivers' ability to understand and address the infant's idiosyncratic ways of conveying need states is crucial in determining the infant's subsequent developmental course. The concept of an average expectable environment assumes that when there is a reasonably good fit between infant and caregiver, and the caregiver provides the infant with a reasonably protective and gratifying environment, the infant's physical and psychological capacities will develop within what are consensually considered to be normal limits. As noted above, however, in instances where the child's genetic endowment is compromised, or when the social environment is less than average and expectable, even autonomous ego functions can be disrupted. When this occurs, children experience significant emotional distress and suffer from serious functional impairments.

Shovanna, the nine-year-old African American girl who had seen her mother kill her father when she was four years old (see chapter 3), had well-developed language ability for a child her age. However, when her spontaneous play unexpectedly reminded her of her father's murder and of her overwhelming fear for her own and her mother's safety, she instantaneously lost the capacity to speak coherently. She could say nothing about what she was experiencing and began to make the sounds an infant would. Because the killing occurred when Shovanna was four, her capacity to use language had developed adequately before the trauma occurred. When the trauma was re-experienced, however, she temporarily lost the function, even though it had previously been well established. Had the original trauma occurred at an earlier age, she might well have become mute, an outcome that could have permanently compromised her language development. Without language, her overall ego functioning would have been seriously, and perhaps permanently, impaired.

In considering the concept of the average expectable environment, consider how children are affected when they grow up poor, ill fed, ill housed, ill educated, with inadequate medical care, and with little or no protection from the violence that permeates their communities. Shameful though it is in a society as rich as ours, this litany of deprivation describes the average expectable environment for the substantial number of American children (25 percent) who grow up in poverty. Consider how parents are affected when they face the reality that they cannot provide adequate food and shelter for their children. Consider what it means when parents have to acknowledge to themselves that the environment in which they live not only deprives their children of adequate food, shelter, and health care but may also be life threatening on a day-to-day basis.

Given what we know about the effects of severe deprivation and trauma, it is remarkable that so many children who grow up poor and who are surrounded by violence throughout childhood and adolescence reach adulthood with their ego functioning intact. The capacity for adaptive functioning that we see in these children is a tribute both to their innate resilience and to the efforts of caregivers who, against all odds, somehow provide them with a human environment that is good enough to promote healthy growth. Certainly, the conditions under which they live do not provide them with an average expectable environment as defined by middle-class standards. And just as certainly, the environment these children live in is not the one their parents would choose for them, if their parents had a choice.

Hartmann's other major contribution to ego psychology was the concept of *adaptation*, a term clinicians use regularly to describe behavior that allows individuals to cope advantageously with the environments in which they live. In Hartmann's view, adaptation can involve "alloplastic behavior," behavior through which individuals change the external environment to better fit their own wishes and needs. Adaptation can also be "autoplastic" in nature. In autoplastic adaptations, individuals change how they feel and act to better fit the demands and expectations of the external world. In either case, adaptation is desirable when it creates a more harmonious relationship between the individual and the external world. Clinicians assess adaptive capacity by evaluating the client's ability to be productive in love and work, to enjoy life, to maintain mental equilibrium under stress, and to change when change is called for in ways that preserve an inner sense of ego integrity. Adaptive capacity is a fundamental attribute of healthy ego functioning. Successful adaptation is well illustrated by the parents and children described earlier who achieve high levels of ego integration in spite of dangerous physical and social environments that are unsupportive at best, dangerous most of the time, and deadly with disconcerting frequency.

MASTERY RECONCEPTUALIZED

In a significant elaboration of the concept of autonomous ego function, White (1959, 1960/1971) proposes that mastery be viewed as a primary motivational force, equal in importance to sexuality and aggression. He argues that there is an inborn human need to master developmental, interpersonal, and environmental challenges. From his perspective, human beings work toward achieving higher and higher levels of competence for the sheer pleasure of doing so. People who study, learn, theorize, challenge themselves, overcome difficulties, and change their environments to conform better to personal wishes and needs are simply being true to their species-specific basic nature.

White (1959) emphasizes that humans are born with a strong desire for "effectance" and "competence." Those concepts can be understood in terms of "what the neuromuscular system wants to do when it is otherwise unoccupied or is gently (rather than intensely) stimulated by the environment" (p. 321). Through this definition, White emphasizes that as a species we are intrinsically motivated to do a great many things that are not directly or indirectly related to need states. When we are not actively seeking gratification or avoiding pain and punishment, we work, play, interact, explore, and learn things. In White's view we engage in these different activities because we belong to an intelligent and curious species, which experiences pleasure in exercising and developing the capacities we are born with. White is eloquent in arguing for "effectance" as a basic motivating force. He states:

> The infant's play is indeed serious business. If he did not while away his time pulling strings, shaking rattles, examining wooden parrots, dropping pieces of bread . . . when would he learn to discriminate visual patterns, to catch and throw, and to build up his concept of the object? . . . [Infancy is] a time of active and continuous learning, during which the basis is laid for all those

processes, cognitive and motor, whereby the child becomes able to establish effective transactions with his environment and move toward a greater degree of autonomy. Helpless as he may seem until he begins to toddle, he has by that time already made substantial gains in the achievement of competence. (p. 326)

CONTROL-MASTERY THEORY

This chapter will conclude with an introduction to a late-twentieth-century development in ego psychology, an approach known as control-mastery theory. The approach was developed in the 1960s and 1970s by psychoanalysts Joseph Weiss and Harold Sampson, who began first to talk with each other about their clinical case observations and how those observations often did not fit with their traditional training. They began to include others in these discussions and to undertake research studies that would test out their ideas. Their approach can be seen as a further development of the changes Freud made in the 1920s, which emphasized the greater role of ego functions and defenses and initiated the development of ego psychology. But control-mastery theory can also be seen as a radical critique of drive theory. As a contemporary ego psychological theory, control-mastery assumes that we all have considerable unconscious "control" over our mental lives, in contrast with drive theory's assumption that unregulated and unconscious sexual and aggressive drives are predominant. Second, rather than offering various resistances to change, it assumes that clients in treatment seek to *master* their conflicts, rather than offering various resistances to change. Drive theorists thought that resistances reflected the client's desire to continue the compromise gratifications that were assumed to be the basis of psychopathological behavior.

Closely related to Robert White's assumptions about mastery, control-mastery theory assumes that the primary motivations are adaptation and survival. To survive, the human infant needs a great deal of help from caregivers, and attachment to early caregivers is thus assumed to be a primary motivation both early in life, and later as well, because residues persist later in life. Adaptation involves not simply the development of confidence that basic biological needs will be met in reasonable ways (Silberschatz 2005a). It also involves the development of beliefs about how the world works, about one's family and oneself in relation to the people important in one's life. While many beliefs are conscious, some of the most important ones are not. For example, a child who has a parent who becomes upset whenever she expresses a desire to do things with friends may develop the belief that her parent needs her to be nearby (the unconscious component in this example), not simply that her parent is strict about friends (the conscious component).

Control-mastery theory also assumes that behavior is regulated by judgments (often unconscious) about safety and danger. Traumatic experiences are examples of dangerous situations. The theory addresses obvious extreme dangers such as traumas (e.g., abuse or neglect), but it also includes more moderate, but ultimately pathogenic patterns of behavior in its concept of what can be traumatic. For example, if a parent has a pattern of becoming upset and depressed whenever the child expresses interests in developing friendships, the child might eventually renounce the developmental goal of wanting friends. On a conscious level, she would most likely simply experience a loss of interest in making new friends and perhaps a corresponding new interest in doing something that keeps her close to home. In this scenario, she would be unlikely to have the insight that her parent's depression is related to her new interest (recall that often the most problematic aspects of a belief are unconscious). Unconsciously, the child judges the safety/danger of various possible actions on her part in terms of the parent's reactions. The child will choose to do those things that reduce the danger and increase her sense of safety. Here, as in many formulations in this model, the danger is one that presents a threat to a loved one, the parent, who has the potential to become anxious or depressed in response to the child's behavior. The child acts in a way that preserves the attachment to the parent or, in this instance, protects the parent from becoming depressed.

Inferences such as these, often developed over considerable periods of time from the dense texture of everyday life, are called "unconscious pathogenic beliefs" when they result in behaviors that are not in the person's best interest (e.g., renouncing a normal developmental goal). Because the theory emphasizes the attachment between child and parent, as well as motives such as empathy and concern for loved ones, particular emphasis is given to pathogenic beliefs that threaten these most important early relationships. Three kinds of such beliefs are distinguished. *Separation guilt* refers to the anxiety surrounding having different ideas, different values, indeed, a different life than one's loved ones. This can occur when the person has come to believe that developing differently than the attachment figure(s) wants, threatens those loved ones. Thus, separation guilt is far more than guilt toward a parent, for example, about moving away from the parent; it involves guilt about leaving in a psychological sense rather than simply physically. A college student may, for example, become very depressed about developing a new value (e.g., about his career plan) if he believes a parent would become upset by the new direction. The student may well not make the connection between his new value and his depression. Rather, he may become tired, study less, and begin to do poorly in courses that might prepare him for this new career, as a way, interestingly, of sabotaging his own new interest.

Survivor guilt comes from the child's belief that he deserves the same fate as a loved one who is suffering or, that if one has a better life than one deserves, the loved one suffers as a consequence (see Bush 2005 for a fuller discussion). For example, women incarcerated for nonviolent crimes (e.g., prostitution, drug offenses) often have families that directly and overtly elicit survivor guilt (e.g., the accusation, "You think you're better than us" when the woman tries to kick her drug habit), making improvement more difficult (Simone and Shilkret 2001). College students are vulnerable to survivor guilt when they have parents whom they perceive as weak or having difficulty with a life crisis (e.g., divorce), especially if they believe their successes in college will deprive the suffering or weak parent of their help (Shilkret and Nigrosh 1997). In such circumstances, a student might fail academically without being aware of the guilt-based dynamic of her loss of interest in her work or in doing well.

Thirdly, children often develop beliefs about themselves to comply with their parents' beliefs about them. Such "compliances" can also be the basis of current and later difficulties. Parents who consistently are harshly critical of a child often have children who believe critical things about themselves. For example, it is not unusual for a parent with an alcohol problem to blame the child directly for this problem ("If you were easier to raise, I wouldn't drink so much"). Often such beliefs are more subtle. Even negative views of a child held by the parent in a well-intentioned attempt to protect the child from failure can still be inaccurate and pernicious (e.g., the parent who concludes that a four-year-old will be bad at math because she, herself, was). It does not require direct statements for such beliefs to develop; children often make inferences on their own in an attempt to understand important relationships and to protect relationships with loved ones.

Therapeutic Implications

As a result of its view that people strive for adaptation and mastery, control-mastery theory assumes that clients enter therapy with a "plan" for the therapy, significant aspects of which may be unconscious. The plan consists of such elements as the client's "goals" for the therapy and the "pathogenic beliefs" that have impeded her in everyday life. The therapist's task is to understand what the client's plan is. This discovery process is ongoing as therapy proceeds. It is useful in the therapist's own thinking, however, to formulate the client's plan very early in therapy, keeping in mind that the therapist's understanding will be continuously refined as she learns more about the client.

In therapy informed by control-mastery theory, therapist and client work together to disconfirm the client's pathogenic beliefs (see Silberschatz

2005a for a fuller version of this description). A good deal of research has demonstrated that the process of disconfirming pathogenic beliefs is therapeutic. The therapeutic work is accomplished in three ways: First, the relationship with the therapist itself may be therapeutic. A client who has been routinely ignored by parents, for example, may find it quite therapeutic to have a therapist who pays careful attention. Second, the therapist's interpretations, if they are congruent with the client's plan, are therapeutic. Third, the client usually presents the therapist with certain tests; these tests usually arise as a result of earlier traumas, which may be repeated patterns of responses by parents or others of importance in the client's past.

Tests are particularly important in this treatment model and are of two kinds. *Transference* tests occur when the client acts with the therapist as she did earlier with a parent, in the hope that the therapist will *not* respond in the traumatizing way a parent did. For example, a client whose parent was highly critical even of very minor things and needed to have his children do everything his way, and like everything he did, might engage in a transference test by committing relatively minor offenses, such as coming a bit late to appointments. If the lateness is a test, the client is particularly affected by the therapist's response. If the therapist is unbothered or makes only a passing reference to the tardiness, the therapist's response might be sufficient to disconfirm the pathogenic belief that doing things wrong will upset an important person. If so, the therapeutic work will deepen, the client will progress in making this particular issue clearer, or might reveal more about the origins of this trauma. In such ways, the therapist continuously refines her inferences about what the client's plan is. On the other hand, if the therapist focuses on the tardiness in a heavy-handed way, by, for example, offering a rapid, deep interpretation, the client may think the therapist was, indeed, upset by her lateness. The client's narrative might become confusing; she might object to the therapist's interpretation; she might shift the topic to something safer for her, or to some other issue the therapist has handled more successfully.

The second way clients test in therapy is called "passive-into-active" testing. The client above might test in this way by, for example, by being highly critical of a minor mistake on the therapist's part. Here, the client is acting toward her therapist in the way a parent acted toward her. Her hope, often unconscious, is that the therapist will not be as traumatized as she was earlier at the hands of her domineering parent. Again, by observing how she handles the therapist's response to her criticism, the therapist can confirm (or disconfirm) the idea that this, indeed, was the dynamic between the client and her parent. Since many clients in therapy have had highly critical parents, there is a good deal of unreasonable criticism of therapists, and it is useful to think of much of this behavior as passive-into-active testing. That is not to say, of course, that therapists do not engage in behavior that is truly worthy of criticism! If a client's criticism is truly a test, it usually is considerably greater than the therapist's supposed or real transgression warrants. Further, even some positive behavior toward the therapist may involve passive-into-active testing. An example of this is the client who was seduced or sexually abused as a child, and who becomes seductive with a therapist, in the hope that the therapist will not allow herself to be seduced. Often, the therapist can use her own reactions to make the judgment about whether a client's behavior is a test or not. But one cannot judge simply from whether the client's behavior toward the therapist is negative rather than positive, whether the behavior is or is not a test.

Clients often have been traumatized in numerous relatively small ways over many months and years. Sometimes the process of testing in therapy, as well as the other ways therapy can be transformative (e.g., the therapist's attitude; the therapist's interpretations), may take a long time before the client finally comes to the conclusion that she is not as responsible for the misfortunes of others, for example, as she had originally thought. However, the control-mastery approach has also been very effective in short-term therapy. If the client enters therapy knowing that time is limited, she then decides, often unconsciously, to work on goals and pathogenic beliefs that are more paramount at that moment for her. Control-mastery theory can be seen, then, as having important similarities with earlier post-Freudian developments in ego psychology as well as with more contemporary cognitive and relational approaches to psychotherapy. Unlike most psychodynamic theories, control-mastery theory is supported by a large research base as well as detailed clinical observations (see Shilkret and Shilkret 1993; Silberschatz 2005b for summaries of the research).

OVERVIEW AND SUMMARY

Ego psychology markedly expands the range of psychodynamic formulations that attempt to explain motivation. While childhood sexual and aggressive wishes are still viewed as primary, ego psychology adds the autonomous ego functions and the desire for "effectance" to the list of variables thought to motivate behavior. This significant change encourages a fuller, more balanced view of human activity and provides support for assessments of human behavior that emphasize the importance of positive, growth-inducing capacities. In evaluating the problems that a client brings to treatment, cognitive capacities, goal-directed behaviors, and the desire to overcome difficulties are all viewed as indications of health. An appreciation of the client's strengths and latent capacities makes it possible to approach treatment in an optimistic and respectful way without losing sight of underlying problems in ego functioning and adaptation. Control-mastery theory expands these theoretical developments and proposes a radically different explanation of basic human motivation, while still utilizing principles drawn from ego psychology.

By focusing on specific ego functions, carefully examining defense mechanisms, and placing anxiety in a developmental context, ego psychologists emphasize the ego's supraordinate role as the organizing and synthesizing agency within the mind. The ego manages what we think, what we do, and how we feel. This theoretical framework emphasizes that treatment is best directed toward strengthening the ego both in terms of its relationship to reality and its relationship to the other agencies of the mind. Ego psychologists thus reaffirm the complementarity between individuals and society. The concept of adaptation makes it unmistakably clear that individuals do not exist separately from their social and biological contexts. As a species we are not only capable of changing our own behavior to suit a range of different environments but can also change the environments we live in, to better suit the wishes and needs we bring to them.

The theoretical changes outlined above have profoundly changed therapeutic practice. Instead of focusing on uncovering unconscious impulses, ego-oriented treatment emphasizes the importance of intervening in ways that strengthen ego functioning and thereby enhance adaptive capacity. Therapy based on control-mastery theory works from a notably different premise. It emphasizes the ways in which clients test their therapists as they attempt to fulfill their unconscious plans for the treatment. When therapists disconfirm the pathogenic beliefs that clients develop to deal with unconscious guilt and to preserve their attachments to primary caregivers, ego functioning is repaired and their capacity for healthy development is restored. The case example presented below reflects a traditional ego psychological approach to treatment. It focused on trying to repair object relations, strengthen reality testing, and enhance self-esteem.

Some years into treatment Ms. R., a forty-seven-year-old woman suffering from a serious depression, feelings of being "unreal," and the conviction that she was "crazy" in spite of the "normal" facade she maintained at work and in her social relations, began to talk about how worried she was about the safety and well-being of her thirty-four-year-old, drug-addicted brother, Colin. Colin no longer was in contact with her or with any other member of her family, having disappeared at least a decade before after a violent argument with their father (who had abused him repeatedly). Although their father had long since died, Colin had not made any attempt to reunite with the family. Ms. R. had information which suggested that Colin was living in an impoverished neighborhood of a large city, and she often thought about visiting that city and walking through the "skid row" areas in the hope of finding and helping him.

When Ms. R.'s male therapist commented on her love for and concern about Colin, Ms. R. continued for a time to talk about her plan to rescue him, and then stopped in mid-sentence to stare intently at the therapist. After several minutes of silence, she continued by saying, "I don't think I've ever talked to you about this. When I was thirteen, Colin was born. My mother stayed in the hospital for at least a week, and my father invited me into his bed to sleep with him. I don't think he did anything overtly sexual, but I was very uncomfortable being there, and a night or two after my mother returned home, I told her about what had happened. She must have talked with my father that same day because the night after I told my mother, he told me that I needn't come to bed with him that night. After that, my relationship with him changed drastically. Until then, he and I had always been close. From that time onward, throughout my adolescence, he criticized me constantly, calling me a slut and a whore. He would ask me, in front of the entire family, who I was sleeping with. Of course, as a good Catholic girl, I was hardly dating. I wasn't kissing boys, let alone sleeping with them. My mother never said a word on my behalf, and as you know, by the time I was seventeen, I felt my survival depended on getting away from the family. When I left for college, I felt certain that both my father and mother were glad to see me go.

"Whenever I've tried to think about this time in my life, it was like stepping into a black, swampy pit where I would be sucked down and drowned. I don't know why, but when I heard you say that I love my brother, I suddenly imagined you would take my hand and walk with me into the pit, so I wouldn't be alone anymore. I thought if you held my hand the pit would still be horrible and dangerous, but that somehow that I would be able to get out alive; I wouldn't drown. Looking back on all this, it seems strange. My mother was so exhausted after taking care of all my other sisters and brothers, that, being the oldest child, I raised Colin almost as if he were my own. I think that taking care of him made it possible for me to survive those awful years until I left home. During all of that time, I never knew whether my father's accusations about my being a slut were true. Mostly, I think I believed him."

This vignette is noteworthy because the client spontaneously remembered the traumatic events of her adolescence after she was convinced that the therapist understood and accepted the love she felt for her brother. That knowledge gave her hope that the therapist would stand by her during her worst moments of terror. The growing strength of her relationship with the therapist, and the image she created in her mind—of his taking her hand much as a parent takes the hand of a frightened child—gave her the courage to remember that her father had not only invited her into his bed but had also abused her psychologically throughout adolescence. In subsequent sessions, she could talk in a feeling way about how the changed relationship with her father and mother (who, she felt, had not protected her from her father) had affected her view of herself. She recognized that she felt crazy in the face of her father's accusations and that she has felt crazy ever since, no matter how she tries to conceal it.

Assessing Ms. R.'s functioning from an ego psychological perspective highlights her ego organization and adaptive functioning. Ms. R.'s social and vocational functioning was relatively intact in spite of her underlying view of herself as crazy. She experienced serious problems in maintaining self-esteem, as well as some encapsulated difficulties with reality testing, evidenced by her continuing uncertainty about whether she actually had been/still was a whore and a slut. Judgment, affect regulation, and impulse regulation were all intact, with some tendencies toward constricted expression. Her capacity for mastery was well developed in the intellectual, social, and vocational spheres. Under ordinary circumstances her primary anxiety focused on the dangers inherent in losing the love and esteem of a significant other, but when memories of her adolescent abuse were triggered, she briefly regressed to fears of annihilation. By the end of adolescence when she left home to go to college, her ego had regained its capacity for synthetic functioning and had successfully defended against the memories of abuse by repressing them.

Ms. R.'s capacity for relationships was superficially well developed. On a deeper level, relationships were dangerous for her because she could only relate to people by molding herself to their expectations. This adaptation made it possible for her to avoid the danger of subsequent abuse, but foreclosed the possibility of genuine intimacy. Her experience in treatment made it possible for her to imagine a relationship in which another person would be interested in and attuned to her needs and feelings, without exploiting her.

As the treatment summary indicates, the ego psychological approach did not focus on uncovering her unconscious sexual and aggressive desires, but instead encouraged the development of a new relationship that strengthened her overall ego functioning. This is among the most important contributions ego psychology has made to contemporary treatment technique. It is no overstatement to say that the effects of that contribution are profound.

COMMENTARY

Ego psychology adds complexity and nuance to Freud's original formulations about drives and intrapsychic structures. In spite of its impressive utility, however, like all theories of mind, it has significant limitations.

First, except for its emphasis on adaptation, it does not attempt to address fundamental issues about why people think, feel, and act in the ways they do. By utilizing drive theory explanations about basic human motivation, it ignores the limitations that have become increasingly apparent in those formulations. In recent years, control-mastery theory presents a theory of causality organized around the concept of *pathogenic beliefs* engendered in formative relationships with parents and/or other primary caregivers. Over time, it will be interesting to see to what degree that formulation proves compelling and useful to contemporary practitioners and theorists.

Second, because ego psychology focuses on how rather than why the mind works as it does, it tends to encourage mechanistic ways of thinking about human behavior, a tendency that can be problematically reductionist.

Third, although ego psychology recognizes that object relations and self-esteem are important aspects of intrapsychic functioning, it does not emphasize their centrality and developmental significance, an omission that was later addressed through the development of object relations theory and self psychology (see chapters 6 and 7).

And finally, therapists now know that people who utilize "mature" defenses, demonstrate high levels of ego functioning, and appear well adapted to their environments can nonetheless experience significant emotional distress and live lives they experience as unhappy and unfilled. That observation has spurred the development of theoretical models that attempt to understand and address ego psychology's inherent limitations.

The next chapter considers the work of ego psychologist Erik Erikson, who expanded the concept of the ego to include self and identity and who described how the ego develops over the course of life.

REFERENCES

Bush, M. (2005). The role of unconscious guilt in psychopathology and in psychotherapy. In *Transformative Relationships: The Control-Mastery Theory of Psychotherapy*, ed. G. Silberschatz, pp. 43–66. New York: Routledge.

Freud, A. (1936). *The Ego and the Mechanisms of Defense*. New York: International Universities Press.

Freud, S. (1923). The ego and the id. *Standard Edition* 19:3–66.

———. (1926). Inhibitions, symptoms and anxiety. *Standard Edition* 20:75–175.

Greenson, R. (1965). The working alliance and the transferences neurosis. In *Explorations in Psychoanalysis*, ed. R. Greenson, pp. 199–225. New York: International Universities Press, 1978.

Hartmann, H. (1939). *Ego Psychology and the Problem of Adaptation*. New York: International Universities Press.

Rabelais, F. (1532). *Gargantua and Pantagruel*. New York: Dutton, 1946.

Rohan, B. (1984). Personal communication.

Shilkret, R., and Nigrosh, E. E. (1997). Assessing students' plans for college. *Journal of Consulting Psychology* 44:222–31.

Shilkret, R., and Shilkret, C. J. (1993). How does psychotherapy work? Findings of the San Francisco Psychotherapy Research Group. *Smith College Studies in Social Work* 64:35–53.

Silberschatz, G. (2005a). The control-mastery theory. In *Transformative Relationships: The Control-Mastery Theory of Psychotherapy*, ed. G. Silberschatz, pp. 3–30. New York: Routledge.

———. (2005b). An overview of research on control-mastery theory. In *Transformative Relationships: The Control-Mastery Theory of Psychotherapy*, ed. G. Silberschatz, pp. 189–218. New York: Routledge.

Simone, R., and Shilkret, R. (2001, April) Attachment, guilt, and symptomatology among incarcerated women. Poster presented at the biennial meeting of Society for Research in Child Development (SRCD), Minneapolis, MN.

Vaillant, G. E. (1992). *Ego Mechanisms of Defense*. Washington, DC: American Psychiatric Press.

White, R. W. (1959). Motivation reconsidered: the concept of competence. *Psychological Review* 66:297–333.

———. (1960/1971). The core of personality: Fulfillment model. In *Perspectives on Personality*, ed. S. R. Maddi, pp. 85–146. Boston: Little, Brown.

5

Psychosocial Ego Development

The Theory of Erik Erikson

Joan Berzoff

In chapter 4, we considered the functions of the ego: to organize; to synthesize; to defend against unwanted impulses, feelings, and anxiety; and to adapt to internal demands and societal realities. We looked at how the ego tries to master the forces within the internal world and adapt to, or even change the forces from without that are in the external environment. We considered some of the ways in which the ego functions independently of psychological conflict, and we saw how the ego provides many functions, not the least of which are mastery, coherence, and continuity to the self.

ERIKSON: THE EGO PSYCHOLOGIST

Erik Erikson was a particularly unique ego psychologist who examined how the ego maintains coherence over the course of an average expectable human life cycle. He theorized that the ego itself is shaped and transformed, not only by biological and psychological forces but also by social forces. Erikson was the first to develop a truly psychosocial theory, modeled on Freud's model of psychosexual theory, but one that joined principles of ego psychology with Freud's epigenetic principles from drive theory.

Erikson made a lasting impact on our understanding of human functioning and dysfunction by expanding the principles of psychological development beyond childhood. He linked biological, erogenous zones with particular modes of ego functioning, and demonstrated how self and identity are biologically, psychologically, and socially determined.

In this chapter, then, we examine how Erikson's psychosocial perspective expanded Freud's premise that all of psychological development occurs within the first fifteen years of life. Erikson, unlike Freud, saw development occurring from birth to death, within the contexts of social relationships and social institutions that either foster or hinder ego development.

How did Erikson define ego identity? He viewed identity as a sense of personal continuity and sameness, personal integrity and social status, which occurs as a result of the interactions between the self and the environment. He was the first psychoanalyst to articulate the interaction between the person and her environment and to consider the influence of culture and society on identity formation. Erikson was also the first lifespan developmentalist who maintained that personality development was not fixed in childhood, but involved an unfolding of ego psychological developmental tasks over the life cycle. He wrote, "If everything goes back to childhood then everything is someone's fault and trust in the power of taking responsibility for oneself is undermined" (Evans 1981, p. 27).

Like Freud, Erikson's theory of ego development was epigenetic. Each developmental stage unfolds from infancy through old age; each stage builds on previous stages and affects later stages. Development is invariant, sequential, and hierarchical. Every individual negotiates basic developmental tasks and basic biopsychosocial crises from birth to death in a predictable developmental sequence. Erikson clustered these tasks into "eight ages of man" [sic], which he defined as infancy, early childhood, play stage, school age, adolescence, young adulthood, adulthood, and old age.

A Strengths Perspective

As an ego psychologist, Erikson's interest was not so much in pathology as it was in health, and so he identified the ego strengths as well as vulnerabilities that a person faces at each junction of life-cycle development. Erikson defined health in terms of the ways in which a person (1) masters her environment, (2) has a unified personality, and (3) perceives herself and her world accurately.

As stated previously, identity was as central to Erikson's thinking as sexuality was to Freud's. Erikson's theories were, of course, very much a product of his own biography and identity struggles. Born in Frankfurt, Germany, in 1901, Erikson had been abandoned by his biological father, who was Danish. He was raised by his mother, a German Jew, and his stepfather, a German-Jewish pediatrician, neither of whom told him about his biological origins until he was eighteen. In fact, his mother acted as if his biological father never existed, although Erikson clearly had some awareness of him based on his own sense of difference. As a child, then, Erikson suffered a series of identity crises. He was a blond, blue-eyed son of a Jew, thought to be Jewish by non-Jews and non-Jewish by Jews. His sense of not belonging, within his community or within his own family, became a central theme in his work. Interestingly, in adulthood he reinvented himself with a Danish name, that of the son of Erik, or "Erikson." When he fled to America in the 1930s to escape the Nazis, he first attempted to immigrate to Denmark. Refused entry there, he subsequently came to America, once again having had the experience of being an outsider who had been excluded from what he considered his real homeland.

Erikson did poorly in school and, in fact, dropped out for a time. He would later conceptualize such periods as "psychosocial moratoria" during which adolescents temporarily suspend their identities, to discover and redefine themselves before making adult commitments. During his own psychosocial moratorium at age seventeen, he traveled around Europe as an artist. In 1927, he met Peter Blos, a later leader in ego psychology and adolescent development, who was then tutoring the children with whom analyst Dorothy Burlingham and Anna Freud were working. Erikson became a teacher in their Montessori school. Soon after, he was analyzed by Anna Freud. With neither a medical degree nor any formal training beyond high school, he was invited into the Viennese analytic circle. Without professional credentials, however, he continued to remain an outsider. Although his marginal identity was costly to him, it also afforded him a certain degree of flexibility within psychoanalysis and propelled him toward interdisciplinary pursuits (Monte 1980).

In 1933, taking with him the theoretical viewpoints from both ego psychology and drive theory, Erikson moved to Boston, Massachusetts, where he collaborated with anthropologists Margaret Mead and Ruth Benedict. This led to his cross-fertilization of anthropological, psychoanalytic, and ego psychological ideas. After teaching at Harvard and at Yale, he traveled to South Dakota, where he worked with anthropologists in understanding Sioux and Yurok Indians from both psychological and social perspectives. It was in this collaboration that he began to articulate how identity development occurs as a *psychosocial* phenomenon.

With these biographical footnotes as a backdrop, let us examine Erikson's most lasting and important contribution: that of his theory of the eight ages of man [sic]. According to Erikson, there is a progression of development over the life cycle which is also epigenetic. Each developmental stage is defined by an individual's facing an age-specific crisis, at an age-specific time, with an age-specific concern. The past and the present crystallize into new developmental tasks. In the negotiation and resolution of each developmental crisis along the life cycle, every person has the opportunity for new development. Psychological and social crises increase a person's vulnerability, but heighten his or her potential. At each stage of psychosocial development, then, there is the potential for the emergence of a unique kind of ego strength, or what Erikson called a "virtue," although he did not use this word as it is most commonly used. Erikson (1964) wrote, "I'm not speaking of values; I am only speaking of a developing capacity to preview and abide by values established by a particular living system" (p. 113).

According to Erikson, each stage of development affords the possibility for a negative outcome, or a positive one. But Erikson cautioned against viewing the stages of psychosocial development as either negative or positive. "Actually," he wrote, "a certain ratio of [positive and negative outcomes] is the critical factor. . . . [For example] when we enter a situation, we must be able to differentiate how much we can trust and how much we can mistrust in the sense of a readiness for danger and anticipation of discomfort" (Erikson 1968, p. 105).

Although Erikson did not challenge Freud's formulations, he changed the focus of attention, making each stage of psychological development about social values and emphasizing the adaptive, positive character traits that can emerge when particular developmental tasks are mastered. He also expanded the original psychosexual model of development by adding ego psychological concepts (such as ego strengths, adaptation, mastery, and identity), and by emphasizing the importance of the person in her environment. He brought time as a construct into his theory and with it the idea that everyone relates to themselves and others at different stages of the life cycle in unique ways, depending upon their different intersecting life stages and identities. Most important, he brought social context into every aspect of psychological development, so that social contexts of oppression, disenfranchisement, poverty, violence, war, discrimination, and natural disasters all interact with a child's developing psyche.

Let us turn now to his theory of psychosocial development to illustrate how ego identity emerges over the life cycle.

THE EIGHT AGES OF MAN

Erikson's psychosocial developmental timetable roughly corresponds to Freud's theory of psychosexual development until adolescence. However, whereas Freud thought that psychosexual development ended with adolescence, Erikson added three more important life stages that shape identity over the life cycle. He thus created a developmental theory that suggests that people grow, change, and develop throughout their entire lives (table 5-1).

At each stage of physical, psychological, and social development, there

Table 5-1. Erikson's Epigenetic Stages

Basic Stages	Psychosexual Stages and Modes	Psychosocial Crisis	Significant Relations
I. Infancy	Oral-Respiratory, Sensory Kinesthetic (Incorporative Modes)	Basic Trust vs. Basic Mistrust	Maternal Person
II. Early Childhood	Anal-Urethral, Muscular (Retentive-Eliminative)	Autonomy vs. Shame and Doubt	Parental Persons
III. Play Stage	Infantile-Genital, Locomotive (Intrusive, Inclusive)	Initiative vs. Guilt	Basic Family
IV. School Age	Latency	Industry vs. Inferiority	Neighborhood
V. Adolescence	Puberty	Identity vs. Confusion	Peer Groups and Outgroups/Models of Leadership
VI. Young Adulthood	Genitality	Intimacy vs. Isolation	Partners in Love, Friendship, Competition, Cooperation, Sex
VII. Adulthood	(Procreativity)	Generativity vs. Stagnation	Divided Labor, and Shared Household
VIII. Old Age	(Generalization of Sensual Modes)	Integrity vs. Despair	"Mankind"/"My Kind"

are psychological and social tasks to be mastered and conflicts to be negotiated. Like Freud's psychosexual stages, Erikson's early stages associate the tasks of ego development with dominant biological organs or zones of pleasure. But his genius lay in expanding biological timetables with the ways in which individual development took place in the context of interactions with larger social institutions, societal values, and social and cultural expectations. Once he went beyond adolescence and into adult development, however, he identified biological processes that shape psychosocial tasks and outcomes, but no longer defined them as erogenous because Freud conceptualized erogenous zones as ending with adolescence.

Let us consider each of Erikson's eight epigenetic stages.

Infancy: Trust vs. Mistrust (Birth to Eighteen Months)

In the first stage of infancy, a baby's mouth is her source of nourishment as well as her medium for relating to caregivers. Erikson describes infants as social, interactive, and incorporative from the beginning. A baby drinks in her mother with her eyes and her skin. The baby comes to expect to be nurtured and taken in, as caregivers come to expect to give love and to be loved. Erikson views the infant as developing her identity in the context of a relationship in which she learns about being cared for and loved. The reciprocity that occurs between the child and her caregiver ultimately forms the basis for basic trust. We saw in Freud's description of a baby that the mouth is the central organ and the zone of pleasure, which is also true in Erikson's epigenetic plan. By nature, infants take in the outside world through their mouths. They also bite, which reflects aggressive aspects of their interactions with caregivers. Ultimately, infants need to form relationships with caregivers in which they can manage both their incorporative and sadistic modes. Sufficient trust in a caregiver's recognition and affirmation leads to what Erikson calls "the virtue of hope." Without sufficient basic trust, a child develops an enduring mistrust and pessimism. The challenge of this stage is to achieve some balance between trust and mistrust. If this development task cannot be mastered, the negative outcome will be dependent, unthinking, rigid adulation of others, or its opposite, the pervasive mistrust of others. Basic trust develops from the interaction between the self and the social world, and forms the foundation for all other stages of development.

To illustrate the relevance of Erikson's theory of infancy, let's turn to Frances, whose identity was shaped during her earliest years in ways that left her both dependent upon and mistrustful of others.

Frances was a fifty-year-old white occupational therapist from a working-class background who could not develop even the most basic trust with others. While having gone on to complete many life-cycle tasks, including commitment to an adult relationship and a career, she felt a deep sense of hopelessness and mistrust. She described her relationship with her own mother as fraught with confusion. As early as she could remember, her mother, who was alcoholic, would swear at her, break lamps, and "be crazy." When her mother was finished with one of her outbursts, she would tell Frances that she (the mother) had a twin sister, and that it was the twin who had been raging and not herself. Frances grew up with a very deep mistrust of others, which she tried to overcome by seeing those in authority as always being correct and as having her best interests at heart. When, however, her boss transferred her to another part of the hospital for what she thought were capricious reasons, she felt hopelessly betrayed. Incapable of mastering her own disappointment, and unable to reconcile the belief that her boss was watching out for her with the feeling that he had betrayed her, she became so mistrustful that she left her job and never worked again.

While Frances's earliest childhood experiences of mistrust culminated in a profound psychological disorganization, Maxine, by comparison, also suffered great fear in early childhood, which resulted in a different outcome.

Maxine was a sixty-one-year-old white Jewish music critic and mother of two children. She survived World War II by being hidden in a cellar in Austria. For the first eight months of her life, she had little food or light and lived with a family that feared being sent to a concentration camp and killed.

To this day, Maxine feels physical fear when faced with dangers on the subways or on the streets. In a visceral way, she is hypervigilant, noticing even a menacing look and always aware of acts of violence around her. While she does not have memories of what it meant to be cold, hungry, or in severe peril, she carries a bodily feeling of mistrust within herself. But given a life context peopled with family members, teachers, and mentors, given her strong and abiding spiritual faith, and given her community, in which physical, psychological, and social needs were met, her mistrust has evolved into a healthy skepticism that mostly serves her well in her life career as a critic.

Early Childhood: Autonomy vs. Shame and Doubt (Eighteen Months to Three Years)

This second stage of child development corresponds with Freud's anal stage. While Freud's "anal" baby took sexual and aggressive pleasure in the retention and the expulsion of feces, Erikson's toddler learns to control his or her sphincter muscles in relationship to others and to the social world. The toddler tries to master his or her environment by controlling caregivers and others in that world. Biologically, a toddler needs to negotiate two muscular actions: holding on and letting go. Children at this stage need to achieve a sense of independence over their own bodies, including some control and autonomy over what is inside and what is outside of them. This includes not only the ways a toddler retains or eliminates feces, but also the ways in which toddlers hold on to and let go of toys, food, or other objects (in ways that often exhaust even the most patient caregivers). If a child experiences some autonomy in walking, exploration, and sphincter control, she may gain some confidence and pride, which becomes a part of her ego identity. If she experiences herself as overly controlled, or without any controls, she may feel excessive shame and doubt.

Evan, a white twenty-six-year-old lawyer, was recently reminded by his parents of his initial delight in an especially large production of feces. At age two and a half, he had called his mother and father into the bathroom to examine and admire his opus. Both parents exclaimed with pride about its size and quantity. But when he called in his brother to look, the brother responded by saying, "That's not very big at all. In fact, that's one of the tiniest poops I've ever seen!"

Evan's mother also recalled preparing a family dinner when, as she watched in horror, two-and-a-half-year-old Evan peed all over the newly cleaned floor. His mother remembers her look of disgust and his of shame as he slinked away from her and hid in the bathroom. But given many other factors that supported his self-esteem—a sustaining day-care situation, a cultural milieu that encouraged the more playful and creative aspects of his willfulness—Evan developed an identity of willful independence rather than one of self-constriction, shame, and doubt. In fact, Evan continues to be admired for his achievements, having chosen a profession that encourages him to engage in struggles and battles for which he is paid. These battles are now fought in courtrooms and not in toilets or on the kitchen floor.

Ideally, a child at this stage develops a sense of identity based on social experiences of cooperation and self-expression. But a child who is filled with doubts will not feel autonomous; she will feel compelled by the will of others.

Michael was the seventh child in a lower-working-class, Irish-Catholic family. Both of his parents were financially and emotionally overwhelmed. They were living far from extended kin, which increased their isolation. Michael's father worked a day job as a security guard, and his mother cleaned office buildings at night. Michael had little sense of protection and little supervision.

Michael remembers not being able to defecate until his mother returned home from work. As he grew older, he became concerned about encopresis (involuntary defecation). He would soil himself at school or worry that he would soil himself with friends. He felt exposed and without inner or outer control.

These feelings became manifest later in a number of adult feelings and behaviors. As an adult, Michael chronically doubted himself. He felt potentially invaded by others and felt he needed to protect himself from others. Friends and family were barred from his apartment or his workplace. Any time he was in public places he felt exposed. He was unable to use the bathroom at his girlfriend's house or at his workplace, as any toilets other than his own made him feel at the mercy of others, exposed and ashamed. These symptoms constricted his bodily, psychological, and social functioning.

The virtue at this stage is will: "The unbroken determinant to exercise free choice as well as self restraint" (Erikson 1964, p. 119). Where Evan's willfulness became transformed into a strong and determined will, Michael experienced himself as without good will or free will.

Play Stage: Initiative vs. Guilt (Three to Six Years)

Like Freud, who depicted an oedipal stage, Erikson noted how children between the ages of three and six enter into a period rich with imagination and creativity, ushered in by locomotion and language. This is a time of family romance and of conflicts between what a child may want in fantasy and what he may have in reality. It is during the oedipal stage that Erikson saw children's modes of action as "on the make, the attack and the conquest," and it is within this stage that children face the ego-psychological tasks of identifying with their parents' and their society's values. In their social worlds, children who successfully negotiate both internal psychological demands and social expectations learn to plan and to discover. But they must also learn what they may and what they may not do or have. The virtue in this stage is the development of a sense of purpose, that is, "the courage to envisage and pursue valued goals uninhibited by defeat of infantile fantasy, by guilt or by the foiling fear of punishment" (Erikson 1964, p. 122). In this stage, Erikson thought, children begin to develop the ability to make enduring commitments.

> Raoul, age four, was a purposeful and delightful working-class Hispanic boy. At his day-care center, he'd initiate the building of enormous block structures, which he'd lead his friends in knocking down. On the playground, he'd boldly slide down the steepest slide, delighting in and conquering this scary structure. Each night he'd play a card game with his dad, who would often allow Raoul to outwit him and win. "I'm really good! I'm great," he'd say.

Where Erikson's theory has the most value is in considering Raoul's sense of initiative in the context of his social environment. But if he had been living in, let us say, Iraq, growing up in a culture where most children have seen dead bodies of people they knew, seen corpses hanging from lampposts or on the doors of former houses, or lying in the streets, the social surround might have an impact on Raoul's initiative. Likewise, what if Raoul had grown up in the Henry Horner Housing Project, only one of many notorious projects in South Chicago (Kotlowitz 1991)? By age five, virtually all children there have seen a shooting or have known someone involved in one. In fact, 30 percent of children in American inner cities have witnessed a killing by the time they are fifteen years old, and more than 70 percent have seen someone beaten. Erikson might expect that there would be children who would find ways to master the environment, achieve relative safety, and maintain ego coherence. That is to say pathogenic environments alone do not create pathological children. Rather, Erikson would assess Raoul's ego strengths and their effects on mediating his environment for him. Therefore, it is important to remember that Erikson's life stages and the potential for psychopathology do not have a direct correspondence. However, serious difficulties during one of the first three stages of life may form the basis for enduring and serious dysfunction. Without basic controls at the anal stage, for example, a child may bring that experience of excessive doubt into all subsequent life stages, doubting himself as a learner, as a sexual partner, as a worker, parent, or friend. The child who feels excessively guilty will lack initiative not only in this stage, but all the stages to follow.

School Age: Industry vs. Inferiority (Six to Eleven Years)

This stage corresponds to Freud's psychosexual stage of latency. As children enter school, their social worlds widen. Developmentally, they begin to reason deductively, to use adult tools to complete tasks with steady attention and with diligence. They are invested in making things and making them well. Children now move beyond the bounds of the nuclear family and develop play skills, cognitive skills, and skills about group life, including learning to express and integrate their own feelings. If a child's efforts are thwarted, for example, by inhospitable schools or by social conditions such as racism or homophobia, then relationships with parents, teachers, or peers may be threatened, and an enduring sense of inferiority can become a feature of the child's identity. If a child can learn to work and play successfully in a supportive culture and social milieu, the groundwork can be laid for an identity based on a sense of industry and achievement. The virtue that may emerge at this developmental stage is competence, which Erikson (1964) defines as "the free exercise of dexterity and intelligence in the completion of tasks unimpaired by intellectual inferiority" (p. 124).

Learning disabilities or some other kind of developmental interference at this stage may present children with particular challenges in latency, where educational support from schools or lack thereof can make a profound difference.

> Eric was a wonderfully busy and industrious eight-year-old boy. But when he was faced with the task of understanding the printed word at school, he was unable to comprehend or decode the symbols. He began to feel stupid in the classroom and to kick and hit other children. Whereas this behavior could have been defined as pathological in and of itself, his school recognized that his was not a behavioral problem, but a reaction to frustration in mastering reading tasks. With a tutor and resource room to provide some academic support, as well as with emotional support from his single mother, he was able to reenter group life easily, without his sense of competence with peers being undermined. Here the social milieu was necessary to counter his identity as an incompetent learner and to help him achieve a more positive identity as a growing master of his learning.

Other kinds of societal pressures can lead to a sense of inferiority unless counteracted by other supports and forces within the family and the community.

Lucy was an industrious and competent seven-year-old daughter of a divorced lesbian mother who had been in a relationship with a female co-parent for six years. Her family lived in a politically conservative, working-class rural community. Lucy's mother could not reveal her sexual orientation at work, in Lucy's school, or to the larger community, as she was embattled in a custody case and feared losing her daughter if her sexual orientation were known. When Lucy broke her arm at school, her co-parent was invisible as a significant other. There was no place to identify Lucy's second mother on the hospital forms. Only her biological mother was invited to attend parental conferences. Lucy was careful about whom she invited home. Despite the fact that there was no socially approved language to define the role of co-parent, and in spite of the homophobia Lucy faced when dealing with social institutions, her own identity as a competent student and friend was stable. This stemmed largely from her co-parents' clarity about their own identities as well as the support her family drew from an extended friendship network of other lesbian families.

Here again, we see Erikson's emphasis on how the social milieu mediates and supports an individual's identity.

Jake, age eleven, experienced much security in both his school and in his home environments. He had few impingements psychologically, physically, or socially. Robust, endowed with a strong intellect, and very pleased with himself for graduating from the same school that he had attended since he was three, he wrote an alphabet journal about the school's significance for him. Note his language of conquering new material, of the importance he places on peers for his development, of the role of teachers, and of the importance of mastering new knowledge as he reflects on his development.

"Q" stands for quest. I feel that the Campus School has been like a quest to me. It has obstacles and it has easy, wide open roads. It has had its up and its downs, but altogether it turns out as a success. I have loved this school so, so much.

"R" stands for reading. When I was younger and this may be due to the fact that I skipped Kindergarten, I couldn't read well. Actually I could barely read at all. But luckily I had a good friend, Annie. She would go over the alphabet many times with me and then we would read words. My parents and teacher also taught me but Annie was the one who really stuck with me. Now I consider myself to be an excellent reader and I would like to thank Annie so much for helping me.

"S" stands for spelling and studying. I love spelling. Spelling came easily to me after I learned how to read. At the campus school, they really stress studying for tests. I guess they do that at any other school but here if I get a bad score on a test, I feel awful. Not bad, but awful. I also feel bad if I don't study.

"T" stands for talent show. It is only for 6th graders and I remember going to the performance every year and wishing that I were the one on stage. This year I finally was.

"U" stands for united. At the campus school, teachers are united when it comes to bad language and such. They are always fighting a battle to rid the school of it. This is a losing battle. If a teacher catches you swearing you may be sent out of the room, given the hairy eyeball or if it happens a number of times, you may lose your recess. Recess is really fun so you try not to lose it.

"V" stands for visiting. I visited many schools this year. I felt this thrill because my life was totally in my hands.

"W" stands for Ms. Wickles. She was our substitute teacher and she was really nice, for example, when she was done teaching she gave us gift certificates. She was also really strict, like one day she told us that all she wanted to hear was the scratch of the pencil on paper. After that, we all laughed.

"Y" stands for year. This year we studied the Industrial Revolution and simple machines. It was a lot of fun and we had to make a project that, with the power of a hair-blower, would lift an egg. During all of this, we had been writing, reading, and learning. In math we learned distributive property, algebra, equations, fractions, decimals, and percents. Currently we are doing acid rain. Altogether, this has been an amazing year.

"Z" stands for Zeke. He is my brother. He isn't always a nice boy. We fight a lot but what do you expect brothers to do? I mean he plays with me. We joke around and he usually does not physically hurt me.

Conclusion. Oh no, this essay is ending! Anytime you feel lonely, feel free to read this Alphabet book again. This essay has been very gratifying. I have had bundles of joy in writing it. It has taken time, energy and a sharp mind to write all of this. I hope that you have licked up every last scrap of my school life and still have its delicious flavor on your tongue. Savor this. I won't make another one. And finally, I thank my school for giving me six great years of a near-perfect life!

In Erikson's view, Jake's narrative about his life would look different had he had biological problems with learning, an environment that was ill equipped to nurture his learning, or a set of family circumstances (loss, family violence, trauma) that undermined his sense of mastery.

Adolescence: Identity vs. Role Confusion (Eleven to Eighteen Years)

Almost universally, adolescence is a difficult time. Adolescents face rapid hormonal changes. Their reference groups shift from parents to peers. They are deeply concerned with themselves. Erikson saw their efforts to fall in love, with other people or with ideas, as efforts to also define themselves.

Adolescents engage in painful struggles over self-acceptance and acceptance from others. They are deeply concerned about who is "in" and who is "out." Adolescence provides a time of achieving individual identity through a group identity.

In Erikson's schema, adolescence presents a pivotal crisis around the development of a sense of a personal identity. Adolescents are often in a state of suspended morality, as they begin to formulate personal ideologies based upon values that differ from those of their parents. Adolescent drug experimentation and sexual experimentation are attempts to construct individual values, based on group identity. The psychosocial task of this stage is that of identity vs. role confusion. The task of adolescence is to achieve a stable sense of self, which must fit with an image of the individual's past, present, and future of larger possibilities. What must be achieved in adolescence is the accrued confidence that one's identity will remain stable over time.

Erikson did not set a standard for the development of a "healthy" identity. Again, he always argued that the meaning of an adolescent's behavior had to be understood within the sociocultural and historical contexts in which the adolescent develops. In his studies of the Sioux Indians, for example, he demonstrated how an adolescent's identity might be shaped in the context of a disenfranchised culture. However, Erikson was careful to state that simply because an adolescent was socially or economically disenfranchised, she should not be seen as deviant. If adolescents, as was true for many Sioux Indians, engage in seemingly pathological behaviors such as truancy, alcohol abuse, or passive aggression, these are adaptive responses to the disruption of their continuous identities and communities.

Consider this poem by Rosario Morales, an adolescent immigrant, whose identity is being forged in a new culture, a new social class, and in both Puerto Rican and Jewish ethnicities. She writes:

> I am what I am and I am U. S. American. I haven't wanted to say it because if I did you'd take away the Puerto Rican but now I say go to hell. I am what I am and you can't take it away with all the words and sneers at your command. I am what I am. I am Puerto Rican. I am U. S. American. I am New York Manhattan and the Bronx.
>
> I love the sound and look of Yiddish in the air in the air in the body in the streets in the English language.
>
> I am what I am and I'm naturalized Jewish-American. and its me dears its me bagels blintzes and all
>
> I am what I am
> Take it or leave me alone
> (Morales 2002, pp. 14–15)

While Morales celebrates her identity for all of its discontinuities in ethnicity, class, and culture, sometimes an adolescent may develop what Erikson calls a negative identity. A negative identity may be forged around those "identifications and roles which at critical stages of development had been presented to them as most undesirable or dangerous and yet also as most real" (Erikson 1959, p. 131). Some adolescents form socially deviant identities with groups who may be dangerous, such as antisocial gangs or cults. A negative identity may also develop in opposition to the excessive idealism of a parent. While an adolescent may turn to antisocial groups, cults, or gangs, not all gang membership results in a negative identity. In fact, gangs can provide community, fraternity, fidelity, and loyalty.

> Mark was a thirteen-year-old Chicano boy in an urban housing project who began to hang out with the Warlords. Their leader was a drug dealer who, under less socially impoverished conditions, would have been a positive role model in the community. Mark was drawn to the drug dealer's savvy, strength, and leadership skills. His identification with the dealer had aspects that were both positive and negative, as he learned to assess his situation and to protect himself on the streets.

Erikson proposed that as adolescents struggle with who they are, they may need, as he did, a psychosocial moratorium, or period of time in which it may be adaptive to drop out and explore one's identity without making premature commitments. But if adolescents are not supported in forming coherent identities through their personal strengths and societal supports, they run the risk of prematurely foreclosing on their identities or of losing themselves in fanatical or exclusive commitments or through negative identifications. But if an individual's strengths and social world support the emergence of a coherent identity, fidelity can be the virtue. Fidelity is defined as the ability to sustain loyalties freely pledged in spite of differences in values.

Young Adulthood: Intimacy vs. Isolation

To achieve intimacy in relationships in young adulthood, a solid sense of identity is needed. Intimacy involves mutuality, which requires the ability to lose oneself and find oneself in another without losing one's own identity. When identity is shaky, attempts at intimacy "become desperate attempts at delineating the fuzzy outlines of identity by mutual narcissistic mirroring: to fall in love often means to fall into one's mirror image" (Erikson 1964, p. 18). Without the capacity to share with loved ones, including friends, there can be a tendency toward isolation. In a sociocultural time such as the 1980s and 1990s, when individualism was so highly valued and the narcissistic pursuit of self-gratification so socially sanctioned, isolation may have represented a socially acceptable feature of what, in fact, were poorly consolidated identities of many young adults.

As part of intimacy, Erikson identified the role of genitality, which he defined as the capacity for orgasm with a partner who is loved, trusted, and competent, and with whom one is willing to regulate one's work and play for the purposes of procreation. Real intimacy requires having ego boundaries that are strong enough so that one is able to temporarily suspend them in the service of connection to others. For people whose identities are fragmented, rigid, or brittle, the capacity for real intimacy may be limited or impossible. The virtue of this stage is love, which Erikson (1964) defined as "the strength of the ego to share identity for mutual verification of one's chosen identity while taking from this supportive relationship the opportunity to be a separate self" (p. 129). It should be noted that Erikson saw intimacy as achieved in a partnership that was heterosexual, and that he privileged one form of sexual expression and commitment over others.

Adulthood: Generativity vs. Stagnation

Loving and working adults need to feel concern for, and interest in, the next generation if they are to maintain their continuous identities. The abilities to extend interests both within and outside the home, and to establish and guide future generations, are particular challenges to men and women in midlife. To be generative, however, does not mean that one must produce biological children. Consider the coaches, troop leaders, clergy, and teachers who serve and work in their communities. Then reflect upon the ways in which they have shared their interests, guided, organized community or church activities, mentored, cured, and showed concern for others. Generativity ultimately involves finding one's place in the life cycle of generations. The opposite of generativity is stagnation and self-absorption, pseudo-intimacy, or self-indulgence.

In this developmental stage, the virtue is care. Care is "the widening concern for what has been generated by love, necessity, or accident" (Erikson 1964, p. 131). The guiding parent, friend, teacher, mentor, or even storekeeper needs to have the conviction that "I know what I am doing and I am doing it right" (p. 131). The opposite may be authoritarianism, self-indulgence, or insensitivity to the needs of others.

Dorothy was a forty-two-year-old African American schoolteacher and single parent. The mother of two boys, she had worked since her sons were infants. In the school in which she taught, Dorothy spent long afternoons, evenings, and weekends with her students, working on community issues, giving freely of her skills by tutoring, and by providing encouragement, guidance, feedback, and love. Her colleagues benefited from her effusive and generous nature. She wrote an important and widely used handbook on working with minority adolescents; she provided major leadership in curricular development, and she was consulted widely and often. Her generativity extended far beyond her nuclear family, although her two children also thrived within the richness of her life.

By contrast, T. S. Eliot's poem, "The Love Song of J. Alfred Prufrock" (1917) captures some of the self-absorption, somatic preoccupations, self-consciousness, and stagnation of a midlife man who is not generative. It is interesting to note that Eliot wrote this poem when he was an undergraduate, containing within it his own concerns about a stagnant identity that had already begun in adolescence. J. Alfred Prufrock lamented:

> "Do I dare?" and, "Do I dare?"
> Time to turn back and descend the stair,
> With a bald spot in the middle of my hair. . . .
> Do I dare
> Disturb the universe? . . .
> Should I, after tea and cake and ices
> Have the strength to force a moment to its crisis? . . .
> Do I dare to eat a peach? . . .
> I have heard the mermaids singing, each to each.
> I do not think that they will sing to me.
> (Eliot 1917, p. 18)

Here, we see how the difficulties in negotiating earlier stages (initiative, intimacy) contribute to Prufrock's midlife experience of stagnation, fear, and a lack of capacity to care beyond himself.

Old Age: Integrity vs. Despair

Old age requires acceptance that death is an inevitable part of life. Whether having lived as a Sioux, an African American, Irish Catholic, or Protestant, the finality of death in old age is inescapable. Each culture mediates the meaning and significance of old age differently. Asian cultures venerate the old and accord a great deal of respect and wisdom to people at this life stage. Many Western cultures respond to old age with fear and denial, warehousing old people in substandard nursing homes and isolating them from their communities and social supports. How a person negotiates this stage of life in the face of death is mediated by the individual's ego strengths, the culture, and the historical time.

In this stage, adults who have been cared for and who have cared for others may now care for themselves. In this last stage of life, integrity is the opposite of self-centered love. Integrity is a sense of acceptance that this is one's only life. This is the time (and last time) for emotional integration. An infant first learns to trust herself as she trusts the world, and so in the beginning relies on another's integrity. With the achievement of integrity in old age, the life cycle is complete. Erikson wrote that healthy children should not fear life if their elders are integrated enough not to fear death.

> If, at the end, the life cycle turns back on its own beginnings so that the very old become again like children, the question is whether the return is to a child-likeness seasoned with wisdom or to a finite childishness. The old may become (and want to become) too old too fast or remain too young too long. Here only some sense of integrity can bind things together . . . and by integrity we do not mean only an occasional outstanding quality of personal character, but above all, a simple proclivity for understanding or hearing those who understand the integrative ways of human life. . . . [With integrity] there emerges a different, a timeless love for those few others who have become the main counter-players in life's most significant contexts. (Erikson 1950, p. 46)

The virtue of old age is wisdom, defined as a "detached concern with life itself in the face of death itself." The opposite is disgust and despair, which implies a sense of futility about one's life, a meaninglessness, and ultimately an inability to care for oneself or for others. Consider the ways in which Mrs. Frank approached the end of her life.

> Mrs. Frank was an eighty-six year-old woman who had lived in the same neighborhood most of her life. She had been married at twenty, widowed at sixty, and had raised two daughters who had families and careers of their own. Every week she attended a book group comprising women of different ages. She often had young neighbors in for tea and was deeply interested in their relationships and their lives. Local kin would be invited for Sunday dinner. She was still involved in social action and she attended musical events regularly. Although her children and grandchildren were geographically distant, she maintained regular contact with them. She even came to speak to a psychology class on Erikson's final life stage and enjoyed her own presentation immensely!
>
> While Mrs. Frank was in relatively good health, save rheumatoid arthritis, she also recognized that her own life was nearly over. She had prepared for her home to be sold when she became unable to function independently and had arranged for residential care when necessary. She had decided which books she hoped would go to which grandchildren, and which furniture would go to which daughter, had been able to talk with her children about her life and impending death, and appeared to accept her death as an ultimate finality.

While Mrs. Frank was able to approach the end of her life with wisdom and responsibility, integrating the many successful earliest resolutions of identity crises, Ira Marks, by contrast, met the psychosocial tasks at the end of his life with pessimism and despair.

> Ira Marks, a Jewish former shoe salesman, was seventy when he developed Parkinson's disease. Formerly dapper, his personal attractiveness had been essential to his work and life, but he now had a disease that made him unable to eat without spilling his food on his clothes. He was also incontinent.
>
> Ira had been deeply involved in his Orthodox Jewish congregation and knew most of the members of his community. His wife had recently died of cancer and his children were living far away. Now isolated despite his religious community, he was cared for by strangers in his home. His speech was impaired, and when his children came to visit or when members of the congregation did stop by, he would turn away, put his head in his hands, and wail. Deep guttural sounds of despair, like those of a wounded animal, would emerge from him.
>
> Prior to his wife's death, he had relied heavily on his own mother, and later on his wife. He had always felt unprepared to make any life decision without consultation with his rabbi. In the absence of any current relationship in which he could feel taken care of, either within his family or within his community, he was deeply depressed. Ira could not evoke memories of past achievements or take pleasure in the achievements of his children or many grandchildren. Ultimately his lack of interest in his life culminated in anorexia. When he got a cold, it quickly became the pneumonia from which he died. He appeared to have died without feeling that his life had been worth living.

CRITIQUES OF ERIKSON

Erikson made an enduring contribution to understanding human development in ways that incorporated culture, class, ethnicity, race, and historical oppression. He vastly expanded the idea that health and psychopathology derived from the nuclear family alone, and he came to identify the importance of strengths and impingements from the social environment. But over the last few decades, Erikson has been faulted for the gender biases in his theory of life cycle development. For example, Erikson proposed that male and female life cycle development differed in childhood, adolescence, young adulthood, and midlife, but the differences often looked like girls and women were less developed than boys and men.

In describing childhood, for example, Erikson identified gender difference in the spatial organization and play of boys and girls. He noted that boys' play tends toward creating high towers and protrusions, and that their play was independent and aggressive. Girls at play tended to be preoccupied with interior, closed space, and their play was more receptive. Erikson understood these differences to be a result of the interface between anatomy, social roles, and psychosexual tasks. His underlying assumption of female passivity and receptivity, however, unwittingly reflected the sex role stereotypes and expectations for women in the 1950s and early 1960s, the decades in which he wrote.

Erikson also proposed that, in adolescence, women lag behind men in the development of a gendered identity. In fact, he wrote that for a woman identity is not actually achieved in adolescence but rather occurs in early adulthood and is defined by the man she will marry, who will fill her inner space. This idea captures another gender stereotype—that women are defined by their relationships with men. His theory normalized this stereotype and made it a developmental goal. It also implied that female identity is less articulated and less differentiated than is male identity, with the disconcerting suggestion that this might result from a deficiency in women rather than from the unequal social world in which women are raised.

In describing the state of generativity, Erikson suggested that female identity was defined by motherhood. Once again, the gender stereotype of a woman caring for children at home was viewed as a developmental goal. If female identity in midlife is defined by motherhood, then why is male identity at the same stage not defined by fatherhood? As has been true in so many of the psychodynamic theories we have studied, then, male development was the prototype for all development, and female development was considered a deviation from the norm. Recall that Erikson postulated that normally (read "for men") identity precedes intimacy. By the end of adolescence, a man has a sufficiently separate and bounded identity that he can form a relationship with a woman with whom he shares life's pleasures and with whom he can lose and find himself. On the other hand, Erikson posited, a woman's identity occurs later. It is defined in early adulthood by the man she will marry and by the children who will fill her inner space. Hence, women were seen as less developed than men.

Jean Baker Miller (1984) argued that Erikson's theory neglected the role of relationships and attachments throughout the life cycle. In an effort to balance what she saw as an overemphasis on separation (with developmental goals such as autonomy, initiative, and industry), Miller proposed adding a relational component to each of Erikson's eight stages of man. For example, in infancy, a girl develops not only trust but also a sense of herself in a relationship, giving her the capacity for emotional empathy. In the second stage of autonomy vs. shame, Miller noted that a girl never becomes autonomous, but instead develops a sense of her own agency within a community of relationships with others. At the oedipal stage, girls in Western cultures begin to learn about their mothers' devalued place in society and to identify with them.

> Lizzie, a six-year-old girl, noticed that in her basketball games, boys tended to shoot the baskets while girls were trained to pass the ball. She went to her

school principal to tell her what she had discovered. Her principal responded that this was the "normal" way that girls learn to be girls. In effect, her principal codified that gender inequality was a normal part of Lizzie's development and that Lizzie should accept her devalued place in the game and in society.

In latency, Miller maintained, a girl's relationships with female friends play an important part in self-definition. And yet, it has been noted that when girls on the playground who are engaged with female friends are asked what they are doing, they invariably reply, "Nothing." Clearly, girls in latency also learn to devalue, as their society does, their relational ties. By adolescence, Miller noted, girls begin to see their own needs as conflicting with the needs of others. Gilligan (1982) has also noted that in adolescence girls begin to silence themselves academically, conforming to societal expectations to tend to the needs of men.

In a similar vein, Franz and White (1985) criticized Erikson for his overarching emphasis on separation and individuation in his life-cycle theory. In fact, his emphasis on separateness unconsciously privileged male development. Franz and White suggested, as did Miller, that Erikson's stages of development be viewed as two pathways: one of individuation and the other of attachment. For example, using Mahler's ideas about separation and individuation, they noted that a two-year-old child becomes autonomous only when she masters the relational achievement of object constancy. As a child develops within Erikson's stage of initiative, she develops greater relational complexity, taking the initiative to engage with others in play. By school age, a child develops the capacity for industry and also for collaboration with other children. Adolescence is a time when a child develops a separate identity, but it is also a time for interdependence. Thus, many of his stages, such as autonomy, initiative, industry, and identity, reflected the values of a Western, male-dominated, competitive, industrialized culture (Berzoff 1989). Miller, then, and Franz and White offered relational correctives to what they saw as an overemphasis on separation and individuation.

Another critique of Erikson elucidated a problem that every theorist has faced: all theorists are embedded in their unique culture and moment in sociohistorical time. Hence, when Erikson referred to intimacy, he referred only to heterosexual intimacy, which he defined as occurring through mutual, genital, heterosexual orgasm. But is this the only form of adult intimacy or love? We would argue emphatically that genital orgasm with a heterosexual partner is not the hallmark of intimacy, but that the ability to lose oneself and find oneself in another, in mutually regulated ways, constitutes the highest form of adult intimacy and love. We imagine that Erikson, who paid such close attention to cultural variance, would have been more inclusive of variance in sexual orientation were he writing today.

An additional critique comes from the current discourse in postmodernism (see chapter 10 on gender). Many theorists are beginning to question the value of stage theories such as Erikson's, which are both linear and hierarchical. They question the validity of a continuous construct such as "the self" and "identity." They ask whether a core self truly exists or whether we are constituted as multiple "selves" that continue to develop in the contexts in which we grow, live, and work. In this latter view, we carry multiple identities, in multiple situations (Mitchell 1993). Postmodern theorists question whether a coherent and continuous identity is possible or even desirable in a technological world that requires multiplicity (Gergen 1991). We are students, and teachers, and fax numbers, e-mail addresses, workers, siblings, bosses, children. We contain multiple selves in the instant when the telephone rings, the fax machine intrudes, or we step onto an airplane that within hours will transport us into an entirely different context that calls for different parts of ourselves and identities. In a postmodern view, the self is continuously oscillating, based on the many social and relational contexts in which it is expressed (for further discussion, see chapter 9 on relational theories, and chapter 10 on gender).

Despite these critiques, it is important to recognize that Erikson was one of the first developmental theorists to add gender to the definition of identity. Erikson was also the first to emphasize the importance of a person's location in the social structure and to recognize the degree to which a person's identity was shaped by culture, religion, place in the social structure, and by social history, including oppression. His theory is more open to critique precisely because it is more inclusive.

CONCLUSION

In spite of these critiques, Erikson's life-cycle model of ego development remains very valuable for psychodynamic practitioners. First, it brings child development out of the narrowly defined bounds of the nuclear family and into a social world in which developing children interact not only with parents, but also with peers and teachers, with day-care providers and community members in the context of larger social and cultural expectations. Second, it provides a developmental framework that projects personality development beyond infantile sexuality and concentrates on development throughout the adult life cycle until death. Third, it focuses on identity, as opposed to sexuality, as a central determinant of psychological well-being. Fourth, it begins to unite ego psychology with object relations, so that an individual is seen as increasingly mastering inner and outer reality as she moves through the life-cycle tasks, individual stages, and relationships crucial to the developmental tasks of those stages. Finally, Erikson's theory is more psychosocial than Freud's or that of any other ego psychologists. His theory is the first, and still the strongest, to expand the discourse on development by adding the variables of culture, race, class, gender, and time to how a person develops a coherent sense of identity.

While Erikson was constrained by his own cultural constructs and values, his era, and by a linear view of development, his work has provided us with a theory that takes race, class, and gender into consideration far more than any previous psychodynamic theory. His inclusion of the sociocultural surround in which individual identity develops makes a profound contribution to clinical practice. While Erikson sought to explain the confluence of gender and identity, it is an ongoing task of our current and future theories to continue to articulate the ebbs and flows of separation and connection as they occur in the identities of girls, boys, men, and women in differing sociocultural contexts.

REFERENCES

Berzoff, J. (1989). Fusion and heterosexual women's friendships: Implications for expanding adult developmental theories. *Women and Therapy* 8(4):93–107.

Eliot, T. S. (1917). The love song of J. Alfred Prufrock. In *T. S. Eliot: Poems, 1909–1925*. New York: Harcourt, Brace, 1926.

Erikson, E. (1950). *Childhood and Society*. New York: Norton.

———. (1959). Identity and the life cycle: Selected papers. *Psychological Issues Monograph* 1(1). New York: International Universities Press.

———. (1964). *Insight and Responsibility*. New York: Norton.

———. (1968). *Identity, Youth and Crisis*. New York: Norton.

Evans, R. (1981). *Dialogue with Erik Erikson*. New York: Praeger.

Franz, C. E., and White, D. (1985). Individuation and attachment in personality development: Extending Erikson's theory. *Journal of Personality* 53(2):82–106.

Gergen, K. J. (1991). *The Saturated Self: Dilemmas of Identity in Contemporary Life*. New York: Basic Books.

Gilligan, C. (1982). *In a Different Voice*. Cambridge, MA: Harvard University Press.

Kotlowitz, A. (1991). *There Are No Children Here*. New York: Doubleday.

Miller, J. B. (1984). The development of women's sense of self. In *Essential Papers in the Psychology of Women*, ed. C. Zanardi. New York: New York University Press.

Mitchell, S. J. (1993). *Hope and Dread in Psychoanalysts*. New York: Basic Books.

Monte, C. F. (1980). *Beneath the Mask*. New York: Holt, Rinehart.

Morales, R. (2002). I am what I am. In *This Bridge Called My Back*, eds. C. Moraga and G. Anzaldua. Berkeley CA: Third Woman Press.

6

Object Relations Theory

Laura Melano Flanagan

Object relations theory continues the study of psychological development and contributes its own special lens with which to look into a person's inner world. The focus of object relations theory is not on the forces of libido and aggression or on the adaptive functions of the ego. Rather, it is on the complex relationship of self to other. Object relations theory explores the process whereby people come to experience themselves as separate and independent from others, while at the same time needing profound attachment to others. Melanie Klein (1952) summarized the core tenet of this theory: "there is no instinctual urge, no anxiety situation, no mental process which does not involve objects, external or internal; in other words, object relations are at the center of emotional life" (p. 53).

WHAT IS OBJECT RELATIONS THEORY?

Object relations theory is the term that has come to describe the work of a group of psychodynamic thinkers, both in England and in the United States. Although almost always written in the singular, object relations theory is not actually *a* theory, because it refers to the work of many writers, who did not necessarily identify themselves as part of any given school and who often argued and disagreed quite passionately with one another. Object relations theory is now so called in order to distinguish some of its central tenets from drive theory, ego psychology, and self psychology.

Object relations theory is based on the belief that all people have within them an internal, often unconscious world of relationships that is different

121

and in many ways more powerful and compelling than what is going on in their external world of interactions with "real" and present people. Object relations theories focus on the interactions that individuals have with other people, on the processes through which individuals internalize those inter-actions, and on the enormous role these internalized object relations play in psychological life. The term "object relations" thus refers not only to "real" relationships with others, but also to the internal mental representa-tions of others and to internal images of self as well. While other theories have attended to how libido and aggression may seek discharge, expression, and satisfaction or to how the ego copes with life stressors and adapts to conflicts between intrapsychic structures, object relations theory adds an inner mysterious world, with its own story, plot, drama, and, above all, cast of characters.

When thinking about object relations in psychodynamic theory it is important to remember that the term is not synonymous with the com-monly used term "relationships." Object relations does refer, in part, to the complexity of external relationships with others, but it also includes a whole internal world of relations between self and other, and the ways in which others have become part of the self. This can be seen in peoples' fan-tasies, desires, and fears, which invariably include images or representa-tions of other people. One's internal world, then, includes the mental representations of self and other. When object relations are assessed in the process of diagnosis, it is to examine both the quality of real, external, inter-personal relationships and the internal self and object representations as well.

When confusing object relations and relationships, people may say, "Mr. Smith must have good object relations because he has been married twenty years," or "Ms. Jones must have poor object relations because she is not involved with anyone." The mere fact that someone has been married for twenty years or that someone is not involved does not necessarily tell the clinician much about object relations. For instance, Mr. Smith could have remained married for twenty years because his object relations are troubled, because he believes that others are dangerous or bad. His self-representa-tion, his view of himself, could be that of a weak man desperately needing the protection of one good object, his wife. Ms. Jones, on the other hand, might have healthily and adaptively come to know herself as a person who benefits from solitude and separateness. Her self-representation could include a balanced view of both her strengths and needs, and her internal world might be filled with benign object representations that keep her from being too lonely while not involved with an intimate other.

The use of the word *object* to mean "person" is traditional in psychoana-lytic literature. This choice may seem odd and is perhaps unfortunate because *object* usually refers to a thing. Each of the authors has had the experience of giving a lecture on object relations with students and colleagues from other fields who eventually, incredulously ask: "When she uses the word *object*, does she mean a person?" When the answer is yes, the response is always some variant of "What a weird choice of words for professionals who are supposed to be interested in people!"

Object, when used in reference to a person, can sound depersonalizing and static. In fact, the word has been chosen to capture an important facet of human relations—that people outside the self can be many things, including objects of desire and fear, rather than simply the people they are. The word *object* is also chosen because it clearly differentiates object from subject. In this way it becomes clear that the subject is the self and the object is the thing outside of the self that the self perceives, experiences, desires, fears, rejects, or takes in. Webster (1963) offers several definitions for the word *object*: "Something that is sought for." "Something of which the mind by any of its activities takes cognizance, whether a thing external in space or time or a conception formed by the mind itself." And, simplest of all, "what is aimed at" (p. 1555). In psychodynamic theory the word *object* usually refers to people, but other things such as music, art, the weather, or even medications can become objects when they are deeply and symbolically connected to powerful object experiences in the inner world. An antidepressant being given to a patient may function not only as a pill but also as the symbol of care, nurture, and even feeding, since it is taken by mouth.

In Freudian drive theory and in ego psychology, the term "object" is usually but not always used in reference to people. Yet the word *object* in drive theory can be somewhat depersonalized. Sometimes the word actually does refer to a thing: the object of an oral impulse can literally be the breast; the object used by a shoe fetishist is literally the shoe. Even when drive theory refers to objects as people, it is referring to people as representing the targets of the drives, and as such they become the means or object by which a drive can be satisfied or frustrated.

In object relations theory the personal aspect of the object becomes more fully fleshed out. *Object* no longer refers to the person or thing outside of the self as the gratifier of an instinctual wish. *Object* refers much more to the person, real or internalized, with his qualities, with his contribution to the interaction.

Another distinction between object relations theory, drive theory, and ego psychology is that object relations theory looks more closely at how needs are met or not met in relationships, rather than at the satisfaction or frustration of particular impulses. In fact, this theory is the first to make a very clear and important distinction between need and impulse, with need being understood as a far broader concept.

D. W. Winnicott (1956), a major object relations theorist, believed that drives and impulses can be gratified without the relationship being all that important, whereas needs have to be met by a person, thereby placing the relationship at the center of the experience. For optimum development to take place, important needs have to be met including the need to be seen and valued as a unique individual, to be accepted as a whole with both good and bad aspects, to be held tight and to be let go, and to be cared for, protected, and loved.

Object relations theory postulates that human beings are incorporative by nature, both physically and psychologically. Just as the body takes in food and drink and then metabolizes it, so too does the psyche take in what it experiences with others and process it to become part of the psychological self. In the physical realm what happens when a body takes in food depends in part on the individual body. So, too, in the psychological realm, there are individual variations in what happens to what is taken in emotionally. Ten people eating the same amount of salad or steak or chocolate cake will not gain or lose the same amount of weight or extract the same kinds and amounts of nutrients. What happens will be determined by each person's complex physical condition at the time. Ten people being criticized or being given a hug will similarly react in ten different ways depending on what psychological strengths, vulnerabilities, past experiences, and social and cultural influences have made them unique.

When a clinician is getting to know a client and beginning to make an assessment, in any setting, no matter what service is going to be provided, it is very useful, indeed necessary, for her to consider both the nature and nurture of the person. We believe that it is important always to look both at what the person has experienced from the outside and who the person is who is taking those things in. As clinicians we also believe that what is taken in from the outside are not just the personal experiences in a client's life but also the social forces at play in her culture and society. Oppression, prejudice, hatred, discrimination, being looked down on—all these messages get inside the internal world just as powerfully as interactions with immediate family members. Racism, sexism, ageism, heterosexism, ableism, classism, all the isms in our society, need to be fought against not only as external evils but also because they get inside the people who suffer from them, and then shape and color their internal world.

Rose, a successful professional thirty-five-year-old African American businesswoman, feeling ill, dreads the thought of asking her boss for some time off. She not only imagines the boss rejecting her request but is also convinced she will be shamed and humiliated. For several nights she dreams that she is "bleeding to death from the heart" on her boss's desk while the boss chats and laughs with his white friends on the phone. When Rose actually asks for the time off she is surprised and confused by the gentle, concerned manner in which she is encouraged to take a few sick days.

This example shows us how a person's internal representations of object experiences from the past, coupled with discrimination and racism, can dominate the present inner world to such a degree as to render life painful and confusing by distorting present relationships. Rose is a person who often cannot tell what is inside and what is out, or even what is present and what is past. She was raised by a family that consisted of rigid, controlling, often sadistic grandparents, a schizophrenic mother, and a severely depressed father. The family lived in crushing poverty and therefore offered limited economic and cultural opportunities, which caused further frustration and despair. There was a great deal of illness as well, and Rose suffered as each family member was hospitalized for serious physical and emotional breakdowns. All of her caregivers were dead by the time she was twenty. Nothing ever seemed stable, clear, clean, or safe. Therefore, Rose now carries within her the expectation (what object relation theorists call "object expectations") that bad things will come *at* her (fearing the boss's rejection) and that this will result in life coming *out* of her (bleeding to death). Although Rose is very bright and has a quick, perceptive mind, which she uses successfully in her work, her judgment fails her when it comes to herself and her needs. Having taken in the badness around her, she still experiences herself as a neglected, invisible, and bad girl in that chaotic, racist, hostile, frightening world in which she grew up.

Led by social work, which has always valued the biopsychosocial approach, the mental health disciplines are becoming more aware of the importance of looking not only at the person, but also at the "person-in-situation." The striking, invaluable contribution made by object relations theory is that it helps the clinician to look at the "situation-in-person" and to understand the power of that phenomenon. In other words, what is "outside" often gets "inside" and shapes the way a person grows, thinks, and feels.

BEGINNINGS

In chapter 2, we saw that Freud's genius lay in his appreciation of the passions that "drive" humankind, passions both sexual and aggressive. However, he was also aware of the role that real objects play in development. In 1917 he published "Mourning and Melancholia," a paper that for the first time addressed the role of the object as much more than simply the target of the drives and stressed the importance of the object in psychological development. Freud distinguished the process of normal mourning from that of melancholia. In mourning, the sorrow is about loss and, once the loss is worked through, the self remains basically unchanged or perhaps even strengthened through internalization of the lost "good" object. In

melancholia, which looks like a mourning that doesn't end, harsh or negative feelings toward a lost loved one become internalized, are turned
against the self, and actually change the self into a self-hating human being.
This is the first time in psychoanalytic theory that change in psychic structure is seen as coming from an object relation rather than from the success
or failure of the gratification of a drive.

In the time immediately after someone's death, the person in mourning
is dejected, full of sorrow, and uninterested in present-day life. But that
same person will often be passionately interested in memories of the dead
person, who may seem more vividly alive and important than anyone else.
The memory of the loved one's voice or of her smile, of the way she loved
spaghetti or woke up in the morning—all these details are present, sometimes unbearably so. Places become filled with meaning, beauty, and pain
because of past experiences with the dead person. It is as if the mourner
makes one last desperate attempt to keep the person alive, to defy and deny
the reality of loss. In time, however, as each memory is seized and cherished, reality ultimately requires letting the object go, allowing the mourner
to return to the present, to the self, and to new objects.

Melancholia looks the same at first. There is the same dejection, the loss
of energy and interest, but in melancholia these things do not pass. There
is no sense of anything being worked through. The mourner remains in
mourning, unable to move forward and, strikingly, in addition to being sad
about the loss, seems full of complaints about the self. The mourner seems
to be suffering from a disturbance in self-regard that often reaches the level
of self-hatred.

What accounts for this melancholia, this drop in self-esteem? Freud postulated that the complaints about the self were actually plaints about the
lost person turned against the self. In this condition, the loss of a significant
other, occurring through death, abandonment, or emotional unavailability,
is accompanied by strong feelings of ambivalence. To preserve a positive
image of the other, the mourner takes in and identifies with the ego of the
abandoned object and then directs feelings of anger and disappointment
toward that internalized image. Self-reproach and self-punishment become
ways of dealing with anger toward the ambivalently held other, as that
anger is now turned against the self. Rather than letting the loved one go
and creating inner space for new objects and experiences, the melancholic
turns her energies away from the world and toward the self.

To explain this process, Freud (1917) wrote one of the most dramatic and
beautiful sentences in psychodynamic literature: "Thus the shadow of the
object fell upon the ego" (p. 119). Here we encounter for the first time the
potent idea that the nature of the relationship with an object influences the
nature of psychic structure. We can see how the mental representation of
another is created in the self and how it serves to shape a person's sense of

self and ability to relate to others. The concept of the shadow of the object falling upon the ego, of something in a relationship beyond instinctual gratification or frustration profoundly affecting the structure of the self, represented an enormous expansion of psychodynamic theory and eventually became the heart of object relations theory.

The process of how and why a person identifies with others, takes in others, and turns feelings about others into ways of feeling about the self is being examined, discussed, and debated about by object relations theorists to this day.

BASIC CONCEPTS

In the rich and varied field of object relations there are several schools of thought or theoretical groups. From the beginning there has existed a lively tradition of dialogue, interaction, and even sometimes quite fierce arguments within and between the schools. The simplest division of the schools is into the British and the American traditions. Main proponents of the British school are Melanie Klein, Ronald Fairbairn, Harry Guntrip, Donald Winnicott, and John Bowlby. Chief among the Americans are Margaret Mahler, Otto Kernberg, Thomas Ogden, and James Masterson.

Primary, Basic Attachment

Object relations theory fundamentally addresses the absolute, primary need for attachment and the harm that can come if that need is not met. Several theorists have explored this concept through direct observation of infants and children.

Bowlby (1969) concluded that attachment is a primary, biological, and absolute need in human beings, necessary for the survival of the species. Unlike the theoreticians who believe that the mother or primary caregiver becomes important because she takes care of the child's needs, Bowlby believed that she is important from the very beginning in an absolute, built-in, biological way that is part of the "archaic heritage" of the race. He argued that children can suffer true mourning due to loss of the caregiver, rather than merely frustration because wishes are not gratified, because the primary caregiver is crucial to their very existence. Before Bowlby, Winnicott had already recognized the importance of not using the word *gratify* for the needs of the infant. It is instinctual wishes that are either gratified or frustrated. Real needs for object relations must be either met or not met. What Bowlby proposed from his extensive and voluminous study of behavior across many cultures is that attachment is an absolute *need* (see chapter 8 on attachment theory).

Earlier still, Spitz (1946) published a study describing the psychological harm that can come to children who are deprived of adequate emotional care. He observed approximately 100 infants of mothers in a penal institution. For the first six to eight months the babies were cared for by their mothers. Then there ensued a three-month separation from their mothers, during which the infants received adequate physical care from the nursery staff but were not cuddled or held in the same way as they had been when they were with their mothers. Slowly but surely the babies began to withdraw into themselves. They lost interest in and responsiveness to the world around them. A sizable proportion developed what is called "anaclitic depression"—a severe, total withdrawal from the environment, characterized by turning away from objects, and a going inward somewhere so far away that there can be no return. Suffering this kind of severe depression, some of the infants became anorexic and simply lay in their cribs, inert and drained of energy. A few actually died. Of those that survived, many showed severe developmental abnormalities in the use of motor skills and language, even at eighteen months. Attachment theory has received renewed attention in the last ten years and new theoreticians have emerged whose research has greatly expanded our understanding of attachment and illustrated its usefulness for clinical practice, so much so that you will see this book now includes a separate chapter devoted to attachment theory (chapter 8).

A vignette from the treatment of a forty-five-year-old professional woman illustrates the theory of the universal need for attachment and the enduring emptiness and sorrow that can result from a paucity of early attachment:

> Sandy, a forty-five-year-old African American woman, entered treatment complaining of an inability to take care of herself properly despite a seemingly successful and well-organized life. The truth of the matter was that she almost never cooked for herself, rarely even went to the market, and was quite unable to clean her house or keep her clothes in order. She lived alone, and her dinner often consisted of buying a can of franks and beans and eating it out of the container barely warm. She slept in her underwear and took quick showers in the morning, but only out of necessity. She had been left alone and neglected a great deal as a child, and the therapist correctly determined that she lacked self-parenting skills because of that deprivation. Together therapist and patient worked on helping her learn to market, cook, clean, and take long, luxurious baths. Despite good progress Sandy still seemed very sad. When asked what was wrong she said, "I am really glad I have learned to take care of myself better. Every evening now I buy good food and cook it well and set the table with pretty things. I read a good book and bathe in my bath salts and powder myself and put on a soft nightgown and nice face cream. *And then I sit on the edge of my bed and cry pitifully and wonder when the grown-ups are going to come home.*"

Sandy had learned all about the comforts and joys of physical care, but still felt terribly and tragically lonely inside because of never having had enough inner attachments. Sandy was born to a sixteen-year-old, single black mother who was in many ways still a needy child herself. Her mother became clinically depressed and unable to care for Sandy when she was six months old. The child welfare system intervened, but, having neither the policies nor the resources to help keep mothers and babies together, the system placed Sandy in the first of a long series of foster homes. Sandy's great-grandmother fought fiercely to be allowed to raise her, but was deemed "too old" at fifty-nine. Profound connections were therefore severed that were not to be replaced in the foster homes where Sandy lived for varying periods of time, always feeling like the outsider despite what often was adequate care.

In object relations terms we would say that Sandy's inner loneliness was due to her lack of soothing introjects. Introjects are the result of what one has taken in from others. They are the inner people we all carry within us. Their quality and quantity can vary tremendously. They can be helpful or harmful or absent or any complex combination thereof. Sandy teaches us that attachment is necessary for more than simple physical survival. The fullness and quality of a person's inner world is greatly influenced by the quality of early relationships, and Sandy had been left feeling too alone and unattended to.

THE NATURE AND QUALITY OF ATTACHMENT: "HOLDING" AND GROWTH—DONALD WINNICOTT (1896–1971)

We now turn to Winnicott's contribution, which highlights the importance of the quality of relationships, and to how the nature of object experiences influence development. We will also evaluate the way in which his theory stresses the need to balance attachment with the capacity to be separate.

Winnicott (1958b) was especially interested in the capacity to be together as a prerequisite for the ability to be alone and to enjoy solitude. His work explored the complex interplay between the need for attachment and the need for separateness in development. He realized that both needs are profound and that, because they are almost opposites, there is a tremendous amount of tension between the two. Louise J. Kaplan, in a book entitled *Oneness and Separateness* (1978), captures some of the intensity of this basic dilemma:

Where does the dialogue begin? In his first partnership outside of the womb, the infant is filled up with the bliss of unconditional love—the bliss of oneness with his mother. This is the basic dialogue of human love. The next series of mother-infant dialogues concern the way the infant separates from the state of oneness with the mother. All later human love and dialogue is a striving to reconcile with our longings to restore the lost bliss of oneness with our equally intense need for separateness and individual selfhood. (p. 27)

Regarding the "bliss of oneness," Winnicott did place a rather heavy burden on the shoulders, or rather the bosoms, of mothers. He postulated that at the very beginning of life the infant thrives with a mother (we would say caregiver, not just mother) who can allow herself to merge into the kind of blissful union and total merger that, if it were not so healthy and fundamental to development, would be seen as abnormal. Winnicott (1956) calls it "primary maternal preoccupation" and, in fact, describes it as a "normal illness" (p. 302). By this he means that a healthy mother must allow herself to lose herself completely in her baby. The state described is akin to being totally, consumedly in love, and, as such, eases the shock of the transition from the perfect state of oneness in the womb to separate, extrauterine life. In fact, Winnicott says that this merger with the baby ideally needs to start during pregnancy so that this almost totally safe surround is ready for the infant when she is born.

The critique of this theory is that it is highly culture bound, placing at its center the idealized stay-at-home mother of the 1950s—a totally different world from that of 2006, when it is estimated that in the United States, 76 percent of mothers either choose to, or must, work outside the home. Taken too literally, it can sound as if the child's healthy psychological development is doomed unless the child's mother can achieve that state of primary maternal preoccupation. Taken in perspective, however, the value of this concept is that it can help the clinician appreciate the kind of closeness and attachment that needs to occur at least some of the time in early life, and, sometimes, later in treatment, for development to proceed well. In other words, it is probably true that all babies and all people need to feel some moments of complete safety, union, and love, provided by someone. It must also be remembered that it was Winnicott himself who qualified all his statements about mothers by saying that the mother does not have to be perfect for healthy development to occur. She just has to be "good enough," and the most important quality the good-enough mother possesses is a capacity for attunement to the baby's changing developmental needs, a daunting task in and of itself.

This period of mother-child union shifts as the infant begins to recognize her separateness, and her individuality grows. Her sense of being in a good-enough "holding environment" continues to be necessary, but it must be subtle enough to be protective without being overly impinging or limiting. By holding environment, Winnicott did not mean only the literal holding, but the capacity of the mother to create the world in such a way for the baby that she feels held, safe, and protected from the dangers without and protected as well from the danger of emotions within. The concept of the holding environment is also an extremely useful one for the clinical encounter. Clients, too, need the therapist to construct a holding environment that creates a safe physical and psychological space wherein they feel protected so that spontaneous interactions, feelings, and experiences can occur. As it is for children, that space must be created in such a way that clients benefit from it without necessarily being aware that it is being created for them.

A therapist tells the touching story of being pleased when a very shy four-year-old boy, whose trust he had worked hard to gain, came and sat on the floor near him and started to color. The atmosphere was calm and peaceful, and then the clinician made what he himself calls a treatment error. Out of his own kindness and his wish to acknowledge closeness, he simply leaned forward and said, "What a pretty picture you have made, Steven." And that was the end of that. Steven folded up his paper, put away the crayons, and went to sit at the far side of the room, from which he did not return for several weeks. What Steven had needed was to be allowed to keep the illusion that nothing was being given to him or being done for him. He needed to feel that he had the power and the efficacy to create the moment of closeness and peace. He did not need the therapist to point it out. The clinician admits that in this instance he forgot Winnicott's nuanced and creative thinking, which posits that sometimes what seems like a good thing, such as the offering of love and praise, can actually take something precious away.

Now that we have looked at the state of blissful attachment to the object, we need also to understand how the child moves toward a state of separateness. In looking at children's strivings to reconcile these two needs, Winnicott observed that children turn to the use of what he called "transitional objects." The worn, scruffy teddy bear, the beloved chewed-up piece of blanket, the humming of Mom's favorite tune—these are the things that children literally carry with them in order to begin to cross that great gap away from complete union toward the sense of self as a separate entity. These transitional objects offer ways for the child to hold on to the internal representations of others when she is not yet able to do so on her own. In other words, when the child does not yet have the capacity for internal representations, a separation can be experienced as a disappearance, as a ceasing to exist, as a permanent void. The transitional object then is literally the only bridge to the possibility that a person continues to exist even if absent.

Clinically the concept of transitional objects is extremely useful in helping those clients who have trouble holding on to the mental representations of others in their absence and cannot, like the healthy child, create a transitional object from within. When there are no internal representations of the therapist, vacations or even the time between sessions can leave the client with a sense of complete emptiness. The strengthening of the client's capacity for internal representation during a separation from the clinician can often be achieved if the clinician offers the client a picture, an address, a postcard—anything that will represent the object of the clinician while she is away. The purpose of the offer is to create a bridge, a transition to the time when the object can be retained in its absence without the need for pictures or cards.

One client tearfully reported that when her husband went away on a business trip she "could not hold on to the idea of his existence." The therapist suggested that she create a little booklet with pictures of him and a narrative of some of the things they like to do together and carry it with her at all times. This transitional object turned out to be so immensely helpful to her that she developed better object permanence and eventually said, "I don't need the booklet any more. I can carry his picture inside me."

From a cultural point of view it is interesting to note that the need for a transitional object to facilitate separation is by no means a universal phenomenon or a sign of emotional health. Not surprisingly, the phenomenon is found chiefly in groups that value independence and privacy and therefore encourage their children to tolerate being alone at a very early age. Jeffrey Applegate (1989) reports on several fascinating studies about the use of transitional objects that factor in such variables as sleeping arrangements, feeding patterns, and the extent of rhythmic physical contact. In one study he observed Italian rural families, Italian city families, and Anglo-Saxon families living in Rome. In the rural group, 77 percent of the children slept either in the same bed or same room as their parents and only 5 percent of them developed transitional objects. In the city group, almost as many children slept in the same room as their parents but they were rocked and patted much less frequently, and 31 percent turned to toys or blankets for comfort. In the Anglo-Saxon families, only 17 percent of the children slept in their parents' room and 61 percent developed attachments to transitional objects. Having reminded the reader of the inevitable ethnocentricity of theory formation, Applegate urges clinicians to pay close attention to culture in developmental achievements. He recalls his training in which he was taught that the failure to develop transitional objects was an indicator of probable developmental arrest and subsequent psychopathology.

Winnicott (1958a) gave a great deal of thought to the capacity to be alone. He came to believe that the ability to tolerate, enjoy, and make use of healthy solitude could be developed, paradoxically, only in the presence of another. If aloneness is experienced as too empty, separate, or bleak, it becomes unbearable. This can happen if a child has been left alone too much either physically or through gross misattunement to psychological needs. Aloneness and loneliness become synonymous. The inner world is not peopled with enough comforting figures. Conversely, it can also happen that aloneness becomes painful or intolerable if the inner world is too crowded with threatening, controlling figures who offer neither safety, comfort, nor peace. The ideal, then, is for the growing child to experience being near someone while also being separate and apart, to be allowed to simply *be* in the presence of someone who is neither too stimulating nor too frustrating.

Regarding the quality of attachment, Winnicott (1960) made one additional important point. He believed that attachment needed to be flexible and genuine enough to nurture what he called the "True Self," which is at the core of the personality. The True Self is the repository of individuality, uniqueness, difference. In relationships characterized by genuine attachment, the separate individuality of both persons is seen, respected, and encouraged to flourish. But if the child's striving for separateness is thwarted, the holding environment can become a prison, a limiting rather than an expansive force. A True Self cannot emerge if the child feels she must be attuned to the needs of others in the family system and if she needs to be a certain way in order to be recognized and acknowledged. The highly individuated True Self will not emerge when the environment fails to be genuinely attuned to the child's uniqueness. What happens instead is that the child may develop a "False Self," one that seeks to suppress individuality and molds itself to the needs of others. This False Self, trying so hard to be responsive and to take care of others, ultimately becomes overly compliant. Uniqueness, vibrancy, idiosyncrasy, difference are all submerged. In this debilitating, constricting process the energy, the power, the "wildness" of the True Self is lost.

Adam entered treatment for mild but chronic depression. In his early forties he had what he called a "seemingly perfect American life—a lovely wife, two great kids, and a successful career as a lawyer." It turned out, however, after months of exploration, that Adam hated being a lawyer. He had never liked it. The aggression, organization, and linear thinking that are so useful in a law practice had always "felt foreign" to him. With encouragement and acceptance he was able to come to know himself as a much gentler, more creative person. He discovered/remembered that what he really wanted to be was a florist, but that such a wish could not even be "known" to him, much less mentioned in his upwardly mobile family. At the current time, Adam is trying to figure out ways to leave the law and eventually work as a horticulturist. He has realized that he developed a False Self to comply with family expectations and to protect the family from disappointment if he did not realize their dreams.

THE BRITISH SCHOOL OF OBJECT RELATIONS—MELANIE KLEIN, RONALD FAIRBAIRN, HARRY GUNTRIP

The British object relations theorists Melanie Klein, Ronald Fairbairn, and Harry Guntrip present us with very specific and useful ideas about what the internal object world can be like. The internal world comprises representations of self and other, representations formed by ideas, memories, and experiences with the external world. A representation has an enduring existence, and although it begins as a cognitive construction, it ultimately takes on a deep emotional resonance. For example, memory images of a mother feeding, hugging, cooing, and so forth, coalesce into an object representation of the mother. Similarly, the various images of the self as they are experienced within, for example, warm and loving, or selfish and repulsive, make up the self-representation. These representations are not observable and may not reflect the actual situation, but they are the content of the internal world and the building blocks from which relationships with the self and with others are ultimately formed.

Melanie Klein (1882–1960)

Although a drive theorist, Melanie Klein was most interested in the internal "relatedness" of infants from birth. She saw the drives as "inherently and inseparably directed towards objects" (Greenberg and Mitchell 1983, p. 136) from the earliest moments of neonatal life, and not merely for the reduction of bodily tensions but for fuller passionate relatedness to another person. In Freud's view, no phantasy (this is the way Klein always spelled it) will take place if real gratification is available. Klein offered a radically different view. She did not see phantasy as a substitute for real gratification, but as a basic characteristic of human beings. And for her, phantasies were always "peopled," were always full of yearning for objects and object relations.

Klein's theory about the internal world was also developmental. However, unlike Freud, who postulated the oral, anal, phallic, and genital phases, Klein talked about internal "positions." The term "positions" made it clear that she was not simply describing a phase or a stage to be passed through, negotiated, and resolved, but rather internal states, ways of perceiving the world, ways of feeling that can and will be experienced throughout the life cycle. The two positions presented by Klein are the paranoid-schizoid position and the depressive position. Each describes a state of object relations that occurs early in life but can also be present in adult life.

Problems arise from the fact that developmental theorists from Freud onward use terms such as "phases," "stages," or "positions" because they sound so fixed and static. One writer, Pine (1985), proposes the more fluid, more useful concept of "developmental moments." If a child in the second year of life is said to be in the anal phase, does that mean that every moment of her existence is focused on anal issues of being clean versus dirty, of giving and withholding? Surely not. And what about the fact that age two is considered to be the separation-individuation phase by Mahler? How many phases or stages can a child be in at once? Surely more than one. Pine suggests the idea of "moments" to solve this dilemma by trying to capture the fact that during certain times in life there are periods of "peak intensity and peak developmental significance of certain phenomena" (p. 40). Therefore, although the so-called anal child has many other important things going on in her life, there are probably more moments at age two when issues of surrender and control are of compelling interest to her than at other times in her life.

Pine's concept of developmental moments is also useful as we look at Klein's description of positions. The first position she defined, the earliest way of being, is the paranoid-schizoid position. The name itself is frightening and describes terrifying moments in the neonatal period that can be filled with feelings of fragmentation, surprise, and fear. Even the most cherished, protected, and nurtured baby cannot feel safe and connected all of the time, simply because it is so little, delicate, and dependent in a stimulating and startling world. The child in the paranoid-schizoid position lives in a land of shadows and pieces, of noise and light, of moments that feel blissful and moments of great fear.

The main anxiety of this paranoid-schizoid position is that persecutory parts of objects will get inside the self, overwhelm it, and even annihilate it. Again, the possibility of a baby's experiencing persecution is hard to understand; but if a baby gets very hungry, waits too long, gets panicky, then gulps down the milk so fast as to choke, then one can begin to understand how even something good from the outside can feel like an attack inside.

Klein postulated that there was no such thing as a totally objectless autistic phase. The early world of the infant is full of impressions of "things out there" and "things inside" without clarity or accuracy of what's where or what's what. The things out there are not even remotely experienced as what adults can come to know as whole objects or real people, but they are nonetheless present and important. Klein named objects as they are experienced in the paranoid-schizoid position "part objects" in order to capture the fragmented way the world looks when a person is, or feels, too little to perceive the whole.

An eight-year-old boy away from home at sleep-away camp for the first time writes to his mother:

Dear Mom I miss you. a lot of times I think about you I almost always cry. I
wish you were here. Miss Flule always tries to kiss us good night so does miss
lever. I wish you could kiss me good night. I'll love you even blu even wen
you're spaced out. Oh if I could just see a part of your face then I would be
OK. Your son Brian Dantona Kelly.

Under the painful pressure of separation, eight-year-old Brian is trying
desperately to get enough comfort from the counselor's good night kisses,
but it isn't quite enough to soothe away the pain and fear. He then remembers some of the mother's bad qualities ("blu" and "spaced out") and
declares himself capable of loving her even with faults—interestingly, faults
of distance. Then, with the strongest cry from the heart, he states that he
would be OK if he could just see a part of her face. By age eight Brian has
achieved some sense of wholeness of others (which he demonstrates with
the "I'll love you even blu"). However, in his vulnerable state, he has
regressed to the world and the longings of a much younger child. A whole,
complex, real object is not needed—just a piece, a fragment, a part will do.
During a subsequent camp visit, his mother asked him what part he would
liked to have seen. He pondered awhile and the answer did not come easily
because at first he couldn't decide between her mouth or her eyes, but then
he said, "Oh, it doesn't matter, any old tiny part would have helped."

Brian also makes sure that he signs his full name (as if his mother
wouldn't know who just "Brian" was), probably to reassure himself about
his wholeness, his solidity, and substance on this earth. He will not fall
apart in fragments. As we will see later in the chapter, this is a good description of a person trying to hold on to what Mahler called "self and object
constancy."

In describing the second position, the depressive position, Klein tried to
capture some of the sadness that can occur, paradoxically, just at the time
that there is growth in the internal world. She saw the depressive position
starting when the toddler begins to have enough experience to realize that
the good person who feeds him and nuzzles him and keeps him warm and
the bad person who sometimes puts him down harshly or keeps him waiting for his food or his diaper change are one and the same. Perhaps even
more upsetting is that the person, the self, who loves is also the person who
hates. The loss that comes from this developmental step of seeing both others and the self as complex and multifaceted is basically a loss of innocence,
a loss of the belief in the possibility of perfection.

For many, this theory is disconcerting because the thought of a depressed
eighteen-month-old is not a particularly welcome one, especially when the
depression comes from normal development itself, rather than from any
misfortune. However, the developmental phases of infancy do include
these intense feelings. Even for mature adults there can be pain in trying to

reconcile being both full of love and at the same time full of hate for the same person. It is a struggle and at times depressing not to experience oneself or an other as simply and totally good or bad.

The clinical utility of Klein's work lies in understanding that the eighteen-month-old is beginning to experience the first faint traces of one of life's most difficult and enduring dilemmas—that of both wanting and fearing to be whole.

> Melissa, a twenty-year-old daughter of an alcoholic father, describes vowing three things to herself as a little girl: (1) that she would always "totally and completely" hate her father, (2) that she would "always be utterly different from him," and (3) that she would never need anyone and would never cry. With a stony face and great tension she reports that she has succeeded, but her presenting problem is that she is so tense and rigid that she feels "made of stone." After a few meetings, when she is asked what would happen if she finds out that she does have some softness in her and does love her father a little, her answer is a terrible cry of despair: "First I would want to hit you and then I would get so depressed. I wouldn't be able to live."

Melissa is trying hard to keep her internal world very simple, with only the seeming clarity of black and white. She is struggling to ward off the depression that would ensue if she had to face both goodness and badness in her father and therefore in herself. The only way she had found to survive and distance herself from the traumas of her home was to think of herself as totally different from her "bad" father. Until entering therapy she believed it would be too confusing, too sad, and ultimately too unbearable to face the complexity that she and her father were each both good and bad. Her conflict, as it is for all of us, is the dilemma inherent in wholeness. To be whole one must give up the purity of ideal goodness and total badness. As a patient of Klein's said to her, "With wholeness you gain a lot. But some of the luster is gone."

Despite the loss of luster, Melissa eventually learned the benefits of wholeness and concluded, "I can love myself as a real person with some faults as well as lots of goodness." Her internal world, then, became peopled with images of self and others that were complex, full of goodness and badness, love and hate. This captures the essence of how the depressive position is mastered through the development of tolerance for an integrated sense of self and others. This concept is central to object relations theory.

An important critique of Klein's theory is that it collapses and condenses too many later feelings and experiences into preverbal infancy and ascribes to babies clear-cut internal experiences that they probably do not actually have in the form that Klein postulates. While there is validity to this critique, Klein's insights into the fears and desires, connections and disruptions at the beginning of life are both evocative and clinically useful. If a client is struggling with some of these feelings it does not matter in exactly what month they first felt them or whether they have words to describe them. It is also important to remember that Klein is not giving diagnostic labels to these positions (although the terms chosen can sound pathological), but rather describing normal, universal states.

Ronald Fairbairn (1899–1964)

More than any of the other object relations theorists, Fairbairn believed that what is inside the self, what actually becomes part of the internal world and the structure of the self, is taken in from experience with "outside others." He saw the ego itself as composed of parts: the central ego of everyday living, the libidinal ego, and the antilibidinal ego. While the terms are awkward, they describe a complex self composed of many parts, both conscious and unconscious. He describes these parts as splits in the ego and, along with Guntrip, considers them to be schizoid phenomena. This can be a confusing and unfortunate phrase because schizoid personality disorder now appears in the *Diagnostic and Statistical Manual* as a mental illness. Fairbairn and Guntrip do not mean it that way; rather, they consider schizoid phenomena as part of the human experience. They are using the word *schizoid*, as derived from ancient Greek, meaning fragments or splits or divisions, and they believe that we all have these in our internal world.

Fairbairn's internal world comprises the following parts. The central ego is primarily conscious and assumes the responsibility of the ego functions. The primarily unconscious libidinal ego refers to the part of the self that is loving and expansive, and grows in relation to good, positive experiences with others. The even more unconscious antilibidinal ego is the repository of bad object experiences that have now been introjected to become part of the self.

Dreams often reveal how internalized object relations express the different aspects of a person's internal world.

A twenty-nine-year-old secretary dreams she is walking on "a dark and evil plain." In the distance she sees a group of hoboes sitting around a fire and at first she is drawn to the warmth and the light. As she goes closer, however, she realizes that the hoboes are engaged in a brutal task. They are roasting puppies ("adorable, innocent, little puppies") on the fire. Some seem already dead and some are still struggling. Controlling her fear and horror, the woman figures out how much money she has and begins to bargain with the hoboes for the lives of the puppies that can still be saved. She does this with considerable mathematical skill, arriving at a precise amount per puppy. Even while still dreaming she is quite impressed by her skill, because she has always considered herself to be a "weak moron at math." As the dream ends she is carrying a bunch of living puppies to safety.

Working with this dream transformed the woman's therapy and has been an enduring metaphor for who she is and what she means to work toward. She understands all the characters in the dream to be parts of herself. The puppies were her "baby self," full of innocence and potential (libidinal ego). The cruel hoboes, *now within her*, were introjected from her parents who were, in her memory, extremely harsh toward anything infantile, weak, or tender (antilibidinal ego). What was most useful, however, was not another reminder that she had experienced her parents' rejection, but seeing that part of her was now similarly cruel toward her own weakness and babyishness. Helped by this dream, she became much more aware of the times when she was harshly lacking in compassion toward her own vulnerability and neediness. She began to alter her relationship to herself at those times by saying "my hoboes are at it again." This allowed room for true growth, and also enhanced the functioning of her more adult self, which the dream had also revealed to be more competent than she had known (central ego of everyday living). Her view of herself as a "poor little math idiot" diminished as she joyfully began to acknowledge her skills and strengths.

This example shows us how potent the positive and negative internalizations of others can be, how they can rule the internal world, and how they can change through new object experiences and the growth of consciousness.

Harry Guntrip (1901–1974)

Harry Guntrip added yet another dimension to the drama between internalized and actual relationships. He shed light on a different part of the internal world—the part he understood as the final splitting off of the self, the most deeply hidden schizoid self, which he called "the lost heart of the self." Guntrip believed that many people are terrified that their neediness, their hunger, indeed their greed for love, will paradoxically destroy them when they get it. They need love so much; they fear that they will allow themselves to be swallowed up and lose their identity if it is offered. Guntrip's particular sensitivity was to the most vulnerable and weakened parts of the self. He described what he termed the struggle with "ego weakness" and the "regressed self" that takes place in everyone as they attempt to develop and thrive. Guntrip believed that "the core of psychological distress is simply elementary fear, . . . fear carrying with it the feeling of weakness and inability to cope with life" (Guntrip 1968). Much of the work done today on recognizing and healing the "inner child" comes from Guntrip's attunement to this "baby self" in all of us.

Although not completely disavowing the drives as powerful motivating factors in human motivation, Guntrip believed that they retained a central place in psychological theory only because people would rather think of themselves as filled with mighty instincts than face the greater universal truth of being tiny and vulnerable in a powerful and mysterious universe. He also believed that people can very easily become overwhelmed when they are loved.

Just as it is difficult to accept the Kleinian notion about the depressive position (that there is sadness in seeing the self and others as whole), so too it is painful to understand that people can be so frightened and needy that they cannot bear love when it is there. It is much easier to think of a needy person suffering because care and love are not available to him or her. Suffering because of the terror that love is there confronts us with a much more complex human dilemma.

Tom, a forty-four-year-old CEO of a multimillion dollar corporation, came for therapy because he "couldn't ever rest or be still." A recent medical examination had revealed high blood pressure and a rapid heartbeat, and the physician had insisted on therapy. Tom was the kind of person who exulted in "never doing just one thing at a time." He was praised at work for his boundless energy, although his relationships at home were strained by his intensity and perpetual motion. He always arrived late for sessions and could barely sit in his chair. After many months, which were spent trying to help Tom calm down a bit, he was finally able to respond to the therapist's request that he be still for a minute to see what that experience would be like. Since Tom had been pacing, he was standing at the time. When he remained still and closed his eyes, he began to rock ever so slightly and two silent little tears began to flow down his cheeks. In a tiny voice he said, "I feel like a nerd, I feel just like a nerd." The therapist was immensely moved by the sight of this powerfully built, well-dressed, self-described "captain of industry" revealing his suffering in such a poignant way. She was about to say something accepting and responsive when Tom added in a desperately tight tone "and please, please, don't be nice to me because then I will be nothing at all."

It took Tom a long time to accept and love the part of himself that, in the language of childhood, he called a "nerd." When he was able to make peace with his littleness and his intense neediness, his behavior became much less driven. Eventually he also became less terrified at the loss of strength and autonomy, the loss of self, which he had believed would occur if he allowed someone to care.

One of the greatest contributions of object relations theory has been a rethinking of independence and autonomy as developmental goals that define mental health and maturity. In the belief system offered by object relations theorists, connection is highly valued, whereas absolute independence is seen as unhealthy and not psychologically sound. Mature dependence is considered to be the ideal. Having achieved mature dependence, a person could survive for a while without dependence on others, but would not actually want to. Development is understood to proceed from infantile (total) dependence to mature dependence, but never to the independence and autonomy so beloved by the ego psychologists and some of the American object relations theorists, or so valued in Western ideals of mental health.

EARLY PROCESSES AND DEFENSES

In the chapters on drive theory (chapter 2) and ego psychology (chapter 4), we introduced the concept of defenses, defined some of the defenses, and described the role they play in development. We will now turn to the contribution of object relations theorists to our understanding of the defenses. Since all the theorists discuss the defenses, we will not present each author's point of view but will look instead at the defenses that play the most important roles in object relations theory.

Object relations theorists wrote extensively about the defenses, paying particular attention to how they pertain to relational issues. Because of their interest in the creation of the internal world and the processes whereby object relations are organized, they worked most on the defenses that begin to be organized in the earliest months and years of life. These defenses, known as the primitive defenses, are introjection, projection, projective identification, denial, splitting, idealization, and devaluation. As the names themselves imply, all these mechanisms exist to ward off and cope with anxieties inherent in object relations. These processes serve to manage fragments and parts of the self and others—to keep them in, to get them out, to control them.

There are, however, problems in using the term "defense," and even more so, the term "primitive defense," to define these processes. The term "defense" is most often used to describe the mechanisms that people develop within themselves to ward off anxiety. Yet what is referred to especially when the words *introjection* and *splitting* are used is simply the way the infant *is* at the beginning of life. Babies and young children just do not have the capacity at first to know what is inside and what is outside, or even remotely to experience themselves or others as whole. They are too little and too new to do anything but live in a world of fragments and beginning impressions, so they are actually not warding anything off or "defending" against anything.

With regard to the characterization of certain defenses as "primitive," the word itself is problematic because in everyday language it has a pejorative ring to it. Indeed, in modern anthropology and folklore, care is taken not to describe cultures as "primitive" because of the connotations of being crude, unsophisticated, or inferior. In developmental theory, the term is meant purely descriptively as "pertaining to the beginning or the earliest time" (*Webster's* 1963). It is also meant to elicit compassion for the very young child trying to cope with a very complicated world with very simple inner mechanisms.

These issues become important when we attempt to do a full biopsychosocial assessment. When, for example, an adult is observed to be "doing a lot of splitting," we must assess whether we are looking at a constellation of primitive defenses (regression under stress), or a developmental arrest (failure to progress, either fully or in part, to a more advanced developmental level). It is an exceedingly difficult distinction to make since the words, feelings, and behavior of the client look and feel very similar. One way of trying to find out the difference is testing out whether the client welcomes or fears the possibility of integrating fragmented parts of self and others.

For example, if it is pointed out to a client that the boss she is experiencing today as a "total devil" is the very same person whose kindness she was describing last week, and that observation is welcomed as useful, then one can speculate that the person was not previously helped to see others as complex and whole human beings and that the splitting was a developmental arrest.

If, on the other hand, suggestions that human beings contain good and bad aspects are not only unwelcome but actually rejected, one can begin to think along the lines of defense—that there is some reason why the person needs to keep various aspects apart and separate. There is a *desire* to avoid or control something. This is quite different from experiencing the world as being in bits and pieces. There is a real wish, often experienced as a need, to keep the pieces apart to avoid the suffering that comes from seeing objects as whole and therefore flawed or disappointing. The term "conflict model" is used when psychological dysfunction seems to be caused by unresolved conflicts between desires and the defenses that are the prohibitions against them. The term "deficit model" applies to those instances when the dysfunction is understood as being caused by developmental arrest due to early failures in object relations.

We will now look in some detail at the contribution that object relations theories have made to our understanding of the defenses, seeing them as both part of a normative developmental process and as mechanisms to ward off anxiety.

Splitting

"Splitting" is the term used to describe the process by which the good and bad or positive and negative aspects of the self and others are experienced as separate or are kept apart. The word *splitting* can be very misleading because it implies that something was once whole and was then split apart, but in object relations theory *splitting* is meant to describe a way of seeing the self and objects *prior* to seeing them whole. It is central to the way in which infants first organize their world—into good and bad or frustrating and gratifying experiences. Infants make use of splitting to help order chaotic early life experiences. Splitting allows infants to let in as much of the environment as they can manage when they still lack maturational ability to synthesize incompatible or complex experiences into a whole.

When splitting becomes a defense it is an indication of an unconscious desire to keep things apart and separate. Splitting roughly runs along the lines of good and bad, but is often a very complex phenomenon and is not usually as simple as, for example, perceiving one's mother as all good or all bad at different times. Splitting can apply to one's self-representation or to one's object representations. For some people, splitting is an enduring way of organizing the world, whereas, for others, it can be a temporary regression to a more simplistic, "black and white" way of looking at things during times of stress.

Jim was sent to therapy by his supervisor at the Metropolitan Transit Authority where he worked as a subway conductor. His supervisor had noticed that he seemed chronically depressed and was having increasing difficulty getting along with coworkers. All went well for the first few sessions, despite Jim's reluctance to "see a shrink," and he told the therapist that she seemed like "a very good person." However, this changed abruptly when the therapist told him that it might be useful for him to have a medication consultation. She had done so sensitively and compassionately, acknowledging that another referral might be difficult for him. The care she took in making this intervention did not matter. Jim instantly became furious, said that she was "no good after all," and that he was sorry he had ever thought that she might be a decent human being. The therapist accepted his anger calmly and in a spirit of inquiry, asking him what had happened inside when she made the referral. Jim was then able to describe that this kind of thing happened to him all the time. "It's like a switch going on and off and I can't control it." Now that she had been kind to him, he thought she was great again.

Jim's history revealed that he had grown up in a very rough, working-class Italian-American Brooklyn neighborhood in which there was a Mafia presence. He recalled that even as a little boy he was terrified that he could not "tell the good guys from the bad guys." He gained the insight that his current difficulties, turning on people at work or feeling that they were turning on him, became much worse after the attacks of September 11 when he was stuck underground in a subway knowing that people "really were trying to kill us." After that day his capacity to evaluate people's intentions toward him, already fragile, diminished. Jim presents us with an example of someone who needs to use splitting because he is unable to manage complex feelings that are not easily integrated.

Like all defenses, splitting has adaptive, useful functions. Splitting attempts to put some order into chaos, even if it is simple ordering into good and bad. Splitting can be the basis for the adult faculty of discrimination and the capacity to differentiate good and bad. It is also needed as the precursor to the more developmentally sophisticated defense of repression because it is a young way of keeping things apart, keeping away something that is feared as bad and unacceptable.

Incorporation, Introjection, and Identification

Central to object relations theory is the belief that human beings are incorporative by nature. This means that we are constantly taking in from the world outside ourselves messages, ideas, attitudes, feelings, whole people, parts of people, and good and bad experiences. Psychodynamic theories propose various kinds of internalizations, the three main ones being incorporation, introjection, and identification. These are the dreaded *I*-words of theory exams because these processes sound and, in fact, are quite similar. Do we take things in to hold on to them, to control them, to deny them, to remember them, to make them part of ourselves? Do we take things in out of love or hate or fear or need? These questions are still part of a lively debate to this day, and once again underscore how psychodynamic theories reflect the philosophic view each author holds about human nature and the human condition.

The terms "incorporation," "introjection," and "identification" are often confused with one other and they are used in many different ways by different authors. We understand these processes to exist on a fluid continuum with introjection somewhere in the middle.

Incorporation occurs when the distinction between self and other has only barely been achieved and when there is a sense of the object being swallowed in part or whole. It has the quality of an almost cannibalistic oral ingestion and is the earliest, most primitive form of taking in. A schizophrenic man who cannot tolerate being separated from his mother may say to his therapist that he has eaten her.

Introjection describes the process of internalizing aspects of the object or whole relationships with objects. We can think of introjects, for example, as the taking into the self of the warmth of a mother's joyful smile or the coldness of her angry frown. Introjection is a type of internalization that is more advanced than incorporation. Freud originally understood introjection as a process in which the lost object is taken in, in order to retain it as part of one's psychic structure. In contrast, Fairbairn did not believe that good objects or object experiences need to be introjected because they can simply exist in memory. He believed that only bad objects need to be introjected in order to split them off from consciousness and to control them. Most theoreticians however believe that the mechanism of introjection is needed for both good and bad object experiences and that our internal world is filled with both.

Introjection is less advanced than identification, a much more selective process in which what is taken in are valued parts of another. An example of identification would be a man whose father was a Quaker activist in Latin America choosing to work among street gangs in Spanish Harlem. In introjection what is taken in from outside objects and object experiences becomes part of the person's self-representation. In identification, selective and valued parts of another are internalized, but remain unconscious. In Freud's view, the taking in of parental rules through the process of identification results in the formation of the superego. Mature identification is not merely a copying of someone else's traits, but actually making those traits uniquely a part of the self. We will hear distinct echoes and elaboration of this idea in Heinz Kohut's use of the term "transmuting internalization" (yet another *I*) in the chapter on self psychology (chapter 7).

Object relations theorists have focused primarily on how introjection helps us master our experiences with painful and disappointing objects in our lives in order to be able to bear the anguish that the people we love and depend on can also at times be experienced as hateful to us. The "badness" of the other is "taken in" in an attempt to control and master the situation, in an attempt not to feel so powerless and to preserve the positive image of the needed other. This part of object relations theory is of great use clinically and helps explain why the victims of neglect, abuse, crime, or brutality often end up hating themselves rather than their abusers. It would seem much more logical that the person being hurt would be angry at the person doing the hurting, but that is often not the case. Children who are taken away from abusing parents almost always ask to be allowed to return home, claiming that they are the ones who are bad. Surviving victims of the Holocaust have often described being filled with self-loathing rather than hating their torturers.

In *A Taste for Death*, P. D. James (1986) describes a character who shielded the object representation from possessing any "badness" at great expense to herself:

> Miss Wharton had been taught to fear in her childhood, and it isn't a lesson children can ever unlearn. Her father, a schoolmaster in an elementary school,

had managed to maintain a precarious tolerance in the classroom by a compensating tyranny in his own home. His wife and three children were all afraid of him. But shared fear hadn't brought the children closer. When, with his usual irrationality, he would single out one child for his displeasure, the siblings would see in each other's shamed eyes their relief at this reprieve. They learned to lie to protect themselves, and were beaten for lying. They learned to be afraid, and were punished for cowardice. And yet, Miss Wharton kept on her side table a silver-framed photograph of both her parents. She never blamed her father for past or present unhappiness. She had learned her lesson well. She blamed herself. (p. 162)

To illustrate the power of introjection, Fairbairn (1952) wrote poignantly of how profoundly people needed to believe that "God's in His Heaven— All's right with the world," of how crucial it is to feel that the world *outside* is good, even if the "badness" must be felt in the self in order to preserve that belief. At least then there is hope of redemption and love. A child can only survive believing that there are good objects because "it is better to be a sinner in a world ruled by God than to live in a world ruled by the Devil" (p. 66). In a world ruled by the Devil "the individual may escape the badness of being a sinner" but the psychological price to be paid is very high because the world becomes a place without the possibility of hope, rescue, or salvation. With introjection the power and influence of the real external object diminishes because it is now controlled in fantasy within the self. Often this compromise lies at the heart of depression—"I dare not hate you, my parent; I will keep you as a good object but I will hate myself and therefore there will be no joy in life." Tragically, this phenomenon also sometimes explains why certain people do not get better in therapy—their need to protect their parents' "goodness" prevents them from facing the truth and finding the goodness in themselves.

As always, there are adaptive and useful aspects to introjection, beyond that of warding off of anxiety. Introjection helps in the later, more sophisticated process of identification, as it is necessary to be able to take something in, in order to identify with it.

Projection

Projection refers to the process of expelling, sending outward, and getting rid of unwanted or bad feelings (parts of the self), and placing them in others. The purpose of projection is to disavow those aspects of the self. Projection is a defense that can cause a lot of trouble in a person's life since it distorts reality. It is at the heart of illnesses such as paranoia with the classic example being the murderously angry patient who goes through the world thinking everyone is going to kill her. The aim of projection is to make the self feel all right, devoid of badness. This can make the outside world seem very dangerous. It can also leave the self feeling empty, depleted, and sterile (for further explanation, see chapter 4 on defenses).

Projective Identification

Projective identification is one of the hardest defenses to define and understand. A complex phenomenon, it has several parts and serves a variety of functions. It is, in fact, not just a defense, but also the manifestation of a fantasied object relationship (Moore and Fine 1968).

The projective part of projective identification is the same as in simple projection, in which the aim is to get rid of something within the self that is uncomfortable and unacceptable. But in projective identification the projector does not want to lose the projected part completely—hence the identification.

Ogden (1979) offers some definitive work on the subject. He proposes that projective identification serves four functions and, as such, plays a large part in much of psychic life:

1. A defense to distance oneself from an unwanted part of the self, while in fantasy keeping the part alive in the recipient.
2. A mode of communication in which the projector hopes to be understood by making the recipient feel the same way.
3. A type of object relation in which the projector has achieved a certain degree of separateness but is still in some ways merged with or undifferentiated from the object.
4. An important pathway for psychological change and growth since the process is by no means static and the projector can learn much from the identification with the other.

The following are two examples of projective identification:

A wife talks constantly with her friends about her husband's intense anger and depression. She focuses in particular on the way he curses and then despairs when little things go wrong, such as the kids spilling their milk or a light bulb burning out, often screaming "God damn it—I can't stand it." In their arguments he always vehemently denies that he is depressed. In contrast, she describes herself as efficient, hopeful, and happy most of the time. A month after the couple separates the wife finds herself shouting "God damn it—I can't take it" over and over again as she frantically pounds the light switch to a bulb that has blown out. To her dismay she realizes in that moment that she too is depressed, that she is behaving exactly the way her husband did, and that she had wanted to "place" all her frustrations and despair into her husband in order not to face them in herself. However, she had remained intensely interested in depression by constantly thinking and worrying about his. In subsequent marital counseling both partners learned to acknowledge and accept their own anger and depression, and the projective identification was no longer needed as a defense.

A client accuses her therapist of being a "greedy pig" when the therapist proposes a fee increase based on the fact that the woman's salary has doubled after a job change. Rather than feeling greedy, the therapist is feeling quite virtuous because she has proposed only a moderate raise, despite having charged a very low fee for years. She thinks that patient is greedy for not wanting to pay more now that she has more. The argument about who is greedy and who is not consumes a great deal of the therapy time and goes on for weeks. Only when the therapist's supervisor points out that perhaps she is feeling greedy and secretly desires a much higher fee does the impasse begin to be resolved. The therapist can then talk with acceptance of her own greediness to the patient enabling the patient to stop defending against that feeling in herself and to start exploring it instead. For the first time, the patient is able to recount how she felt growing up "on the edge of poverty" in a South American country where many of her friends and classmates flaunted considerable wealth. She had always hated "being a have-not among the haves" and now recognizes that she had "grown greedier and angrier every day"; hence, her projective identification with the therapist's request for more money.

Both these examples illustrate an important aspect of projective identification—that "it takes two to tango." If no one in the dyad can take responsibility for the unwanted feeling, it will be batted back and forth between the two like a hot potato. When one person can comfortably "own" the feeling and no longer needs to disavow it, the pathway for psychological change can begin and the troublesome feeling can be integrated into both self and object representations. Another adaptive and useful function of projective identification is that of "staying in touch with" and "feeling with" the other person, capacities that later lead to the formation of mature empathy.

Idealization

Idealization is sometimes difficult to understand as a defense since the word itself has so many different meanings. For instance, we will see in the next chapter that self psychology views the capacity for idealization and the availability of objects to idealize as essential to the development of a vibrant, cohesive self.

Idealization is a defense when, like all the defenses, it is used to keep painful and unacceptable feelings out of consciousness. The feelings that are troublesome are usually the same ones that people often want to disavow: anger, disappointment, envy, sadness, desire, greed.

Dawn, at age twenty-one, came to New York to study ballet with a renowned teacher. She had auditioned with him in the Midwest and had been impressed by his knowledge and his rigor. Even before leaving her hometown, she began to idealize her teacher as "the most wonderful ballet master in the entire universe." At this point she was idealizing him because she was afraid of such a big move and had to convince herself and everyone else that it was a good decision to go because her teacher would be "perfect." When she got to class in New York, she saw that the teacher had far too many students and was both unclear and sadistic in his way of conducting practice sessions. Because she could not yet face the painful truth of her disappointment, fear, and anger, she idealized him further, telling everyone that she admired his courage to be true to his art as he yelled at students and humiliated them. She spoke about the "purity of his standards." Only when several students quit the class because of his cruelty was she able to begin to face the fact that his behavior was abusive and unacceptable. Eventually she was also able to leave and find a more helpful and creative class.

Idealization is particularly maladaptive when it is used as a defense against envy. When someone idealizes a person in an attempt not to feel envy toward him or her, the idealization can actually make the envy grow, because the more wonderful the person is perceived to be, the more there is to envy.

Devaluation

Devaluation is the converse of idealization and is used as a defense for the same purpose—to disavow troublesome feelings such as neediness, weakness, insecurity, envy, or desire. Most people have at one time or another said, "I wouldn't go out with him if he asked me" or "She thinks she's so beautiful but I don't want her," when in fact they are very attracted to the other person but fear their advances would be rejected. If a person denies desire through devaluation they end up feeling smug and superior but quite alone.

In the previous example, Dawn might have begun to devalue her teacher in an attempt to feel "I didn't want to study with him anyway," thereby denying the pain of dashed hopes. Both idealization and devaluation, when used as defenses, rob people of connection to their authentic feelings.

While we have not presented individual theorists' definitions of these defenses, we will mention here that some of the most vibrant, incisive, deeply understood work on these primitive defenses and early ways of being can be found in the writings of Otto Kernberg (1975). Kernberg is described in various ways, either as a contemporary Freudian revisionist (Mitchell and Black 1995) or as an American object relations theorist. He actually was both, because in his system the drives do not exist at birth. Libido develops over time from experiences with good, gratifying objects, and aggression consolidates over time from experiences with bad, unsatisfying objects. His work with the defenses as correlated to developmental levels and subsequently to diagnosis is invaluable. Hence more of his work will be presented in chapter 14 on borderline personality disorders.

THE AMERICAN SCHOOL OF OBJECT RELATIONS: SEPARATION-INDIVIDUATION AND THE DEVELOPMENT OF SELF AND OBJECT CONSTANCY—MARGARET MAHLER (1897–1985)

Thus far in this chapter we have discussed some of the most central concepts of object relations theory: the need for attachment, the importance of the quality of relationships with others, the nature of the internal object world, and the role of the early defenses. Another important facet of object relations theory centers around how the self develops through relationships toward greater differentiation and individuation. Margaret Mahler, an American object relations theorist, added to the study of psychological development a schema that explains how a child makes attachments to significant others, internalizes those attachments and yet ultimately blossoms into a separate, autonomous individual. Mahler preferred to think of herself as an ego psychologist, but we have included her in this chapter because her work emphasizes the development of self and object constancy so well, because her ideas fit well with object relations theory, and because her work is often cited as a further elaboration of it.

Mahler called her developmental schema the process of separation-individuation. These are two different, but similar, interrelated and interwoven processes. She believed these led to the "psychological birth" of the human infant. Her work presents us with a Western, white middle-class, male belief system of mental health. Autonomy and independence are highly valued and made synonymous with health and maturity. It is not a view of healthy development that would be shared by all cultures. We can harken back here to the example cited in chapter 1 of the Iranian students observing an Iranian and an American mother-child dyad. Mahler's conclusions would be exactly the opposite of the Iranian students'. The American child would be seen as growing appropriately in autonomy, becoming comfortable with separateness and independence. The Iranian child would be viewed as overly "clingy" and dependent and headed for developmental trouble. Hence, Mahler's image of the baby captures uniquely American themes. The baby, in Mahler's theory, is seen as "an explorer of the New World," even as "a conquering hero". Surely pathology and normality are in the eyes of the beholder.

Because of this very Western overvaluing of independence and autonomy and the shift to more relational theories, Mahler's work is not as much in vogue as it was twenty years ago. Nevertheless, because patients routinely bring into treatment unresolved issues and problems stemming from the developmental challenges of Mahler's various "phases," her work has great clinical utility. Separation is defined as the process by which a growing child comes to experience herself as a separate, distinct entity who "stands alone," so to speak. It is the process of moving away from union/oneness with mother. Individuation is defined as the process of coming to experience oneself as the unique individual self one is. It includes very specific self-knowledge about the traits, qualities, characteristics, and idiosyncrasies that make one oneself and no one else.

Mahler delineated phases in the separation-individuation process that she tied to specific moments of a child's life and related to the physiological maturation of the child. Applied in too concrete a fashion, her theory can be linear and static. A similar problem can arise when particular pathologies are traced in a linear way to certain phases of development. Strict adherence to Mahler's phases is not useful and can lead to "cookie cutter" diagnoses. It would be better, once again, to think of them as Pine (1990) suggests, in terms of "developmental moments." What Mahler describes does not happen in set phases or only in specific months, but it does happen. Here then is a description of Mahler's phases of development.

The Autistic Phase (Birth to Twelve Weeks)

It is important to note that Mahler's stages are not fixed and linear. Rather the ages for various phases often overlap. An autistic phase is postulated by Mahler (Mahler et al. 1975) as an objectless and, in fact, even selfless phase. If this phase exists, it would be a time of almost complete nonrelatedness and nonmeaning. Mahler correlates problems during, or regression to, this phase with the development of psychosis later in life, which is highly problematic, especially in view of the current state of knowledge about biological factors in the most severe mental disorders.

Many theoreticians reject the idea of an autistic phase since they believe instead in the infant's capacity to relate from the moment of birth. Mahler's conclusions about this phase in particular are also the most challenged by current infant research (Beebe and Lachmann 1988, Lyons 1991, Stern 1985). Their work reveals a subtlety and intensity of recognition, interaction, imposition of self, alertness, and relatedness in infants heretofore unknown. These observations refute that a baby is ever completely in an autistic or unrelated phase. Despite this, it must be remembered that some children do suffer from autism and seem to be living away from relatedness in a land of mysterious shadow. There are also certainly autistic moments of nonrelatedness experienced by all babies and adults.

The Symbiotic Phase (Six Weeks to Ten Months)

Mahler (Mahler et al. 1975) calls the symbiotic phase "the primal soil from which all subsequent human relationships form" (p. 48). "Symbiosis" is the term used to describe a time in life when caregiver and baby seemingly exist in one orbit. It is the time of the most complete union, of healthy merger. The holding environment is the most encompassing at this time and from it stems the feeling of being safe in the world. *Symbiosis* refers not only to the actual relationship with the caregiver in the first months of life, but also to the perhaps universal fantasy of a time of total omnipotent union and bliss. In Mahler's view the hallmark of symbiosis is "omnipotent fusion with the representation of the mother and, in particular, the delusion of a common boundary between two physically separate individuals" (p. 450).

Having looked earlier in this chapter at Winnicott's ideas about the quality of attachment, we can see how this phase coincides with his views about the need of the baby to experience "primary maternal preoccupation." However, we also know that this is the same time in life that Klein saw as the beginning of the paranoid-schizoid position. Again, there are undoubtedly moments of each—when the baby experiences blissful oneness, but also when she feels frightened by experiencing the seeming bigness, fragmentation, and chaos of the world around her.

Separation-Individuation Proper

According to Mahler, the baby begins to "hatch" out of symbiosis, entering what she calls separation-individuation proper. This includes the subphases of (1) differentiation, (2) practicing, (3) rapprochement, and (4) on the way to object constancy.

Differentiation (Five to Twelve Months)

This period is marked by the infant's beginning separation out of the symbiotic unity. Growing interest in the world outside of the primary caregiver is stimulated by the new ability to crawl or creep or roll, and eventually to stand. The chief caregivers are still tremendously important, but they are no longer the center of the universe in the same way.

Practicing (Ten to Twenty-four Months)

Practicing coincides with increased locomotion and ever-increasing bodily skills. Learning to walk is of enormous consequence, not just in terms of physical mastery but because it ushers in the psychological correlates of being able to stand alone and walk both toward and away. This era of new cognitive and motor skills is often filled with elation on the part of the toddler. It is a time of triumph, exhilaration, grandiosity, omnipotence, narcissism. "No" and "bye-bye" are often favorite words. The child feels like "the world is her oyster." She is "the gleam in her mother's eye." Sometimes, though, that new world out there becomes frightening or tiring; it is then that the caregivers need to be there for emotional refueling. It is best for the child if the adults in her environment can accept with good grace her omnipotence and grandiosity so that the child's eventual disillusionment can be gradual and so that some of the power and exhilaration of this phase remains available throughout the life cycle.

> A group of adults is walking toward the ocean with an eighteen-month-old boy. As they reach the top of the dune they are all struck by the roaring of the rough ocean waves that day. The little boy looks momentarily startled but then squares his shoulders, holds up his head, and in a very imperious manner proclaims, "Stop, waves." He does it with such power that the adults almost expect the waves to stop. Naturally they do not. To really underscore the grandiosity of the toddler, he is not even fazed by it. Anyone else exerting such force to make something happen would be crushed, but not the child in this phase. He is perfectly happy with the power of the gesture and the fantasy, and so, ignoring the crashing waves, goes off contentedly to play in the sand.

Rapprochement (Twenty-four to Thirty-six Months)

Rapprochement is probably the most complex and complicated of the phases for both parent/caregiver and child. This is because it is the time that the child has very opposing needs—the need to cling and be close as well as the need to separate, to be off on her own exploring the world. Gone is the blithe exploring of the practicing days when separation seemed so triumphant. Yet the wish is not for total symbiosis either, because that would mean giving up too much selfhood. Because of this complexity of needs, this phase can often be the most trying for caregivers. A needy parent might cling too hard when the child needs to be let go, while an overburdened parent might push the child away too soon when she needs to be held close a little while longer. From this phase is derived the idea that the parent needs to be both optimally frustrating and optimally gratifying, another of those daunting-sounding tasks for parents.

One of the developmental struggles of the rapprochement subphase is called "ambitendency." This term in psychodynamic theory captures the tendency to swing between two intense wishes—the wish to be close and the wish to be separate—and the two enduring, intense fears—the fear of engulfment and the fear of abandonment. These twin fears arise most potently as challenges during rapprochement, but vestiges of this dilemma often remain present throughout life, and for some, ambitendency becomes central to psychological problems and dysfunction.

Ambitendency needs to be carefully distinguished from ambivalence, with which it is sometimes confused. Whereas ambivalence refers to a person's mixed or contradictory feelings toward another person, ambitendency describes a person's fluctuating states of desire for and fear of both merger and distance. In a state of ambivalence a person has simultaneous and opposite feelings, usually love and hate, about another. This can be difficult to bear and to come to terms with. Ambivalence causes discomfort because it represents the struggle to integrate good and bad feelings about another object. Ambitendency also causes discomfort, but it is the discomfort of an earlier time developmentally. In ambitendency, the developmental challenge is not to reconcile the positive and negative aspects of the other, but rather to overcome fears about the dissolution of the self. The developmental opportunity in ambitendency is to discover that one need not be engulfed and destroyed by closeness and that distance does not necessarily mean abandonment and unbearable aloneness.

People often experience a resurgence of ambitendent feelings at the beginning of falling in love. This proved to be the case with Richard, who came for brief, focused therapy due to the wild, intense mood swings he could not control at the beginning of his relationships with Peter.

Richard had felt ready for a serious, committed relationship for some time. He believed himself prepared to proceed wisely when he met Peter and realized that he liked him a great deal. He was dismayed when he soon "started acting like a nut case." On one date Richard would feel very loving and close toward Peter and talk with him about the possibility of a long-term, committed relationship. On the next date he would be aloof and distant and talk about himself as a loner with little interest in engagement or closeness. Despite these shifts, which he could not control, Richard was having a wonderful time with Peter and recognized that he was learning to love him deeply. In therapy, Richard kept talking about his "ambivalence" about Peter, but he soon realized that he did not have mixed feelings about Peter at all. What he did have was deep fears about what degree of closeness and separateness he desired and could tolerate. He could not find a comfortable way of being that included a good balance of union and separateness. When he felt close to Peter he wanted to "merge with him forever," but then that would scare him because he feared he would lose "all energy, individuality, and ambition." Impelled by these fears he would distance, but distance too much, and then become frightened about having gone too far away and being too alone.

Once Richard understood these fears he was able to confront them, realize how young they were, and work on achieving a comfortable way of being with Peter in a long-term partnership. Over the years Richard has returned to therapy occasionally for short-term work on other issues, career changes, aging parents, and so forth. After twelve years he is still in a happy, fulfilling relationship with Peter. He states he still struggles occasionally with fears of engulfment and abandonment, but he recognizes what they are and works through them successfully.

In this example Richard has worked out and grown beyond rapprochement issues. These developmental tasks will be revisited in chapter 14, where we talk about the borderline condition, since many of the developmental tasks and problems of rapprochement appear in people suffering from that disorder.

On the Way to Object Constancy (Thirty-six Months to the End of Life)

"On the way to object constancy" is the name chosen by Mahler to denote the last subphase of separation-individuation. The fluid nature of the concept has been welcomed by many practitioners because it denotes that developmental achievements are not fixed and rigid but come and go depending on the various stresses and strains in different periods of a person's life.

Object constancy refers to the establishment in the psyche of a relatively stable, benign, and positive representation first of the mother, and eventually of others, that "holds" even in the face of absence, disappointment, or anger. It is a crucial capacity to develop in order to have an even reasonably healthy, mature psychological life. It is one of the most important cornerstones of mental health, but even those who have achieved it lose it from time to time, some more severely and enduringly than others.

Simply put, object constancy provides security and strength from the feeling that the self can endure and be well whether or not the object is meeting its needs at the moment. Object constancy is related to object permanence but is not the same thing. Piaget (1937) coined the term "object permanence" to denote a purely cognitive achievement, that is, the capacity to retain a mental representation of an object even when the object is not present. Object permanence has no affective coloration. Object constancy adds that affective dimension because its achievement introduces the capacity to retain belief in the goodness of the object even when it is not being gratifying in the moment.

Many people struggle with weak object permanence and wavering object constancy. Clinicians hear this from clients when they say, "I can't even remember that you exist when I am not in the office with you" (lack of permanence), or "I can't believe you are there for me and care about me if we disagree about something" (lack of constancy). In treatment the achievement of object permanence and object constancy are often worthwhile and attainable goals.

Mary Lou suffered from the lack of a well-developed object constancy as well as from occasional lapses in object permanence. The world, therefore, was often an overwhelming and frightening place for her. If a friend or coworker became annoyed with her, she could not remember that they basically liked her. Although she tried, she could not summon an image of the therapist to help her out internally when she was getting lost in the belief that no one liked her. Mary Lou came up with the idea that it might help her if she could call the therapist's answering machine every day, not to talk and leave a message, but to hear the outgoing message. Mary Lou meant this quite literally and said, "Perhaps if I really hear your voice on the outgoing message every day and that therefore that you exist and are basically a decent, courteous person, I will finally get the message that there is someone out there in a constant relationship with me no matter what is going on." Mary Lou called the machine daily for approximately three weeks and discussed the changes occurring within her in her weekly sessions. One day she stated simply, "It's done; I've got it now, I don't need to call any more," and from that day forward felt transformed by her developmental achievement. For the first time in her life, she was able to form friendships and get along with supervisors, because she could retain the idea and feeling that (a) they still existed even when not present, and (b) that they liked her even when they were at odds with her.

This vignette also illustrates the use of what Winnicott called the "transitional object" to achieve object permanence and constancy.

A CRITIQUE OF OBJECT RELATIONS THEORY IN ITS SOCIAL CONTEXT

It is important, as with all theories we study, to place object relations theory in its historical and cultural contexts. The heart of object relations theory was developed in England and in the United States during a decade when belief in the existence and the value of the nuclear family was at its height. It is no accident, then, that the theory focuses with great intensity and specificity on the mother-baby relationship, assuming not only that mothers would be the primary caregivers but also that mothers would be able to be at home during almost *all* of the early child rearing.

Like any other theory, then, this theory must be understood to be limited by when and where and by whom it was constructed. One of the most important critiques to bear in mind is that object relations theory can sound like, or actually become, a potentially mother-blaming theory. Since the vicissitudes of development are tied so closely to the quality of the mother-child interaction, there is a danger of interpreting this to mean that whatever goes wrong is primarily the mother's fault. This does not seem to have been the intent of the theoreticians, but in paying such intense, microscopic attention to mother and child, they did at times lose the forest for the trees. The forest encompasses other relationships within and outside of the family—the social, cultural, religious, and economic forces at play, and the innate temperament, personality strengths, weaknesses (and therefore *input*) of the baby itself. When Winnicott said, "There is no such thing as a baby," he meant that there is no such thing as a baby without a mother. We would say there is no such thing as a baby without a mother and/or father, siblings, grandparents, extended family, and, ultimately, a neighborhood, school, and religious and cultural affiliations. There is also no such thing as a baby who grows up without being profoundly influenced by the prevailing realities of and attitudes toward gender, race, ethnicity, sexual orientation, and class. A baby always grows up in a specific country within its political and economic system, and the values of that system have a profound impact on its development.

Object relations theory can sound as if every child grows up in a traditional nuclear family consisting of a biological mother and father and a couple of kids. This resonates with the universal romanticized fantasy within our culture of the perfect *Father Knows Best, Ozzie and Harriet* type of family. It is probably the fantasy of the family we all wish we had grown up in—and that fantasy dies hard. However, many children do not grow up that way, and we must take that into account in our reading of past theories, in our future development of theory, and in our clinical work.

Here are some facts, not fantasies, about current living arrangements of families in the United States. The U.S. Census Bureau (2001) reports:

In 2001, 72.5 million children under 18 lived in households. The majority of these children (51.1 million) lived with two parents. Three percent (2.1 million) of all children lived with two parents who were not married to each other.

Among the 18.5 million children living with only one unmarried parent, 2.2 million lived with their father.

Of the 1.4 million children living in households with at least one adoptive parent, 44 percent lived with two adoptive parents.

Fifteen percent of children (10.6 million) lived in blended families. About half of these children, 5.1 million, lived with at least one stepparent.

6.2 million children lived with at least one grandparent, and 1.4 million of these children had no parent present. (p. 2)

These figures begin to give us an idea of what complicated relational lives children lead. They remind us that object relations theory often describes an almost impossibly idealized family structure.

Another limitation of object relations theory (and, in fact, of all psychological theories) is that it was developed largely by white, Jewish or Christian, middle- to upper-class clinicians treating patients primarily from the same racial, socioeconomic, and religious backgrounds as their own. These theories, then, are not derived by, or from, a study of the poor, the disadvantaged, or racial or religious minorities or non-Western cultures, and do not in any way capture the richness, heterogeneity, and diversity of the current population of the United States. For this reason great care must be taken to evaluate what aspects of these theories are irrelevant or actually harmful to the care and treatment of specific individuals or groups within our society.

In a *New York Times Magazine* article (Smith 1990) entitled "Mothers: Tired of Taking the Rap," a clinical social worker and mother writes poignantly of how a rigid, narrow adherence to the belief that mothers are responsible for everything can be misleading and damaging.

> As part of my work I have made many home visits to very poor women in housing projects. I witness the obstacles these mothers must overcome to arrange a day's worth of juice and Pampers for their toddlers. They have no money, bad housing, no day care, no way to earn a living, no physical safety, few reliable relationships and no social support. But when their children are evaluated at mental-health clinics the all-too-common requiem for the mother's effort is simply "neglectful and unmotivated." The fact that mothers have had primary responsibility for raising children does not mean they have had the power and the resources to protect children from the world's tricks and perils—nor from their own circumstances and limitations. Primary responsibility for raising children cannot be simply equated with primary responsibility for harming children.
>
> Such fantasy notions of the good mother harm all mothers and cause them to assume too much blame for damaging their children. Mothers imagine irreparable psychological consequences whenever they yell, stay late at a meeting, use the TV as a baby-sitter, forget to serve a vegetable, let a child share a bed, or leave a bad marriage. I cannot remember ever working with a mother—wealthy, middle class or poor—who did not have secret theories about how behaviors, or choices, or feelings of hers had deeply harmed her children. While some part of such worry and guilt is appropriate to the task of child rearing, it is increased unfairly and exponentially by the pervasive and unremitting image of what a really good mother would have done in her place.

CONCLUSION

What then has object relations theory contributed to our knowledge of the client's inner world? Most simply, it has provided a number of basic concepts for understanding psychological development.

The first and most basic concept of object relations theory is that of the primary, absolute need of human beings for attachment. The second central concept is that the child's inner world is shaped by internal representations of others. The third important concept is that human beings need to be both alone and with others, and that the struggle to balance and meet these seemingly contradictory needs lasts throughout the life cycle. Fourth, object relations theory looks at why we need others, how we take them in, and how we relate to them internally. It looks at the consequences of loss on the development of selfhood. It looks at the influences of relationships on the internal world. Being very much a theory about psychological processes, object relations theory pays particular attention to the earliest experiences and defenses—those that have to do with trying to distinguish between self and other, between what is inside and what is outside, and eventually with accepting and integrating both the good and the bad parts of the self and others.

Object relations theorists have also given us a new way to look at the therapeutic encounter. One of the most useful tools for learning about a client's early object relational experiences is the relationship that develops between client and therapist. Here the clinician learns in her bones about the client's feelings about separateness; here the clinician comes to know (often through projective identification), how the client's difficulties and strengths in relationships are re-experienced in the present. Here the client and therapist discover how in the transference, the client may hide true wishes while trying to conform to her perceptions of what the therapist wants the client to be. Here the therapist may experience the client's fear that if the client is too distant or too close, the therapist will no longer care. Here the clinician and client can begin to understand the costs and gains of separation and individuation and what these may have meant and now mean for the client.

Often the clinician cannot know and the client cannot express the complexity of her inner object world until both have experienced it together, in a relationship, over time. And although managed health care may push us toward solving problems using time-limited, intermittent treatment, it is ultimately object relations theories that remind us of the utter centrality of a relationship to psychological development and growth.

In chapter 7 we turn to a quite different view about how relationships with others shape development—that of self psychology.

REFERENCES

Applegate, J. (1989). The transitional object reconsidered: Some sociocultural variations and their implications. *Child and Adolescent Social Work* 6(1):38–51.

Beebe, B., and Lachmann, F. (1988). The contribution of mother-infant mutual influence to the origins of self-object representations. *Psychoanalytic Psychology* 5:305–37.

Bowlby, J. (1969). *Attachment and Loss*, Vol. 1: Attachment. New York: Basic Books.

Fairbairn, R. (1952). *Psychoanalytic Studies of the Personality*. London: Routledge & Kegan Paul.

Freud, S. (1917). Mourning and melancholia. *Standard Edition* 14:237–58.

Greenberg, J. R., and Mitchell, S. A. (1983). *Object Relations in Psychoanalytic Theory*. Cambridge, MA: Harvard University Press.

Guntrip, B. (1968). *Schizoid Phenomena, Object Relations and the Self*. London: Hogarth.

James, P. D. (1986). *A Taste for Death*. New York: Warner.

Kaplan, L. (1978). *Oneness and Separateness*. New York: Simon & Schuster.

Kernberg, O. (1975). *Borderline Conditions and Pathological Narcissism*. New York: Jason Aronson.

Klein, M. (1952). The origins of transference. In *Envy and Gratitude and Other Works, 1946–1963*. New York: Delacorte.

Lyons, R. (1991). Rapprochement on approachement: Mahler's theory reconsidered from the vantage point of recent research on early attachment relationships. *Psychoanalytic Psychology* 8(1):1–23.

Mahler, M., Pine, F., and Bergman, A. (1975). *The Psychological Birth of the Human Infant*. New York: Basic Books.

Mitchell, S. A., and Black, M. J. (1995). *Freud and Beyond*. New York: Basic Books.

Moore, B. W., and Fine, B. D. (1968). *A Glossary of Psychoanalytic Terms and Concepts*. New York: American Psychiatric Association.

Ogden, T. H. (1979). On projective identification. *International Journal of Psycho-Analysis* 60:357–73.

Piaget, J. (1937). *The Construction of Reality in the Child*. New York: Basic Books.

Pine, F. (1985). *Developmental Theory and Clinical Practice*. New Haven, CT: Yale University Press.

———. (1990). *Drive, Ego, Object, and Self*. New York: Basic Books.

Smith, J. M. (1990). Mothers: Tired of taking the rap. *New York Times Magazine*, June 10, pp. 32–38.

Spitz, R. (1946). Anaclitic depression: An inquiry into the genesis of psychiatric conditions in early childhood. *Psychoanalytic Study of the Child* 2:313–42.

Stern, D. (1985). *The Interpersonal World of the Infant*. New York: Basic Books.

United States Department of Commerce, Bureau of the Census. (2001). *Living Arrangements of Children*. Washington, DC: Department of Commerce.

Webster's Third New International Dictionary. (1963). Springfield, MA: G. & C. Merriam Company.

Winnicott, D. (1956). *Primary Maternal Preoccupation*. London: Hogarth.

———. (1958a). *Through Paediatrics to Psycho-Analysis*. London. Hogarth.

———. (1958b). *The Capacity to Be Alone*. London: Hogarth.

———. (1960). *Ego Distortion in Terms of True and False Self*. London: Hogarth.

7

The Theory of Self Psychology

Laura Melano Flanagan

Until now, we have examined very different views of the self. In drive theory, the self is a cauldron of seething impulses of sexuality and aggression. In ego psychology, the self is that agency that mediates between the drives, reality, and morality. In object relations theories, the self is made up of internal representations of relationships with others. This chapter presents the theory of self psychology, which attends with its own specificity to the kinds of life experiences that contribute to the formation of a vibrant, cohesive self, and describes the tenets of self psychology, which focus with a different lens on how the self develops in the context of relationships with others.

Throughout the history of philosophy, literature, psychology, and the social sciences, there have been many ways of defining and constructing ideas of self, no two exactly alike. Indeed, all psychodynamic theories talk about the self in one way or another. What distinguishes self psychology (and the reason it is called self psychology) is its focus on understanding the self as a cohesive whole. The emphasis is on the person's *subjective* sense of cohesion and well-being rather than on the supposedly *objective* functioning of various aspects or parts of the self, such as the id, ego, and superego. Self psychologists try to understand the experience of self from the inside out, rather than from the outside in.

In *Webster's Third New International Dictionary* (1963) there are many definitions of self. The three most congruent with self psychology are "the entire person of an individual," "the union of elements (body, emotions, thoughts, sensations) that constitute the individuality and identity of a person," and "the source of social adaptation and growth of the individual personality" (p. 2059).

The theory of self psychology was first developed by Heinz Kohut (1923–1981), whose main body of work was published in the 1970s and early 1980s. His work gave birth to what has become a separate and distinct school of thought and a specific way of conducting treatment. Self psychology has become one of what are known as the "four psychologies" (Pine 1990), the other three being drive theory, ego psychology, and object relations theory. In some ways self psychology flows out of and incorporates some of the ideas of those theories, but it also critiques, rejects, changes, and modifies many tenets of the other theories and makes its own unique and creative contributions.

Kohut was born in 1923 in Vienna to a middle-class Jewish family. He showed intellectual promise early but was only reluctantly allowed to finish his medical studies as a neurologist because he was Jewish. In 1939 he fled Nazi persecution to Chicago but had to bear the tragedy of several relatives dying in the death camps. He became a prominent, controversial member of the Chicago Institute for Psychoanalysis, where he did his groundbreaking work.

Kohut began his career as a classical Freudian analyst and kept close ties throughout his life with Anna Freud and Heinz Hartmann. Kohut, who wrote in German, did not publish his first book until he was in his fifties, but then he radically changed psychoanalysis with his new theory of self psychology, which was the first significant psychoanalytic movement to originate in the United States. His theories were constantly evolving and he was often at the storm center of controversy. Many in the classical establishment stopped thinking of him as a psychoanalyst altogether because he deemphasized the importance of the drives and of internal conflict. For instance, Slap and Levine (1978) stated rather harshly, "Although Kohut refers to it as a psychoanalysis, his therapeutic method depends on suggestion and learning, but not insight, conflict resolution, or making the unconscious conscious." It is indeed true that Kohut (1971) formulated a radically different view of the unconscious, stating that people repress not impulses and wishes in the id but rather "unfulfilled archaic narcissistic demands, related to the mother's rejection of the child's independent narcissism" (p. 185).

Kohut also proposed new definitions of transference, naming his the narcissistic transferences, which he understood as based on needs rather than on conflict. In terms of technique, he taught that interpretations are often not only unhelpful but even destructive.

Kohut's work significantly changed psychoanalytic thinking for many clinicians and the currently popular schools of intersubjectivity and relational theory flow out of his innovative work.

Rather remarkably, and to the annoyance of many, Kohut did little to acknowledge the theorists who came before him. In a recent book on self psychology, Lessem (2005) titled his chapter on the thinkers who influenced Kohut, "Theorists Who Anticipated Self Psychology," explaining that he had to choose that name for the chapter because we can only deduce whose work Kohut built his upon. Kohut himself did not tell us. Lessem names Ferenczi, Balint, Fairbairn, and Winnicott as "theorists whose work in important respects can safely be said to have anticipated Kohut's, even though it is not known if they directly influenced him" (p. 221). He also mentions that Fairbairn, Winnicott, and Balint were "particularly offended" because several of Kohut's key concepts bear a strong similarity to theirs.

At first Kohut postulated that the development of the self coexisted with the development of the ego as a separate but equally important line of development. However, by the end of his life, he rejected classical structural theory altogether and placed what he called a tripartite self with its own structure at the center of the personality. In Kohut's final metapsychology, the self is a supraordinate configuration that exists from birth. It is the source "for our sense of being an independent center of initiative and perception, integrated with our most central ambitions and ideals and with our experience that our body and mind form a unit in space and a continuum in time" (Kohut 1977, p. 177). We will see later in the chapter that this supraordinate self as described by Kohut has its own structure, needs, and driving forces. Id, ego, and superego are replaced by the concept of the tripartite self driven by ambition, pulled by ideals, and needing to recognize itself in similar others. Also central to Kohut's theory is the belief that the self can best come to be understood through empathy rather than through insight. Indeed, according to self psychologists, the self can only develop within a manageable empathic matrix of relationships that offer a combination of optimal empathic responsiveness and manageable empathic failures.

INTELLECTUAL AND CULTURAL CONTEXTS FOR SELF PSYCHOLOGY

As was discussed in chapter 1 and as has been true of all the other theories we have looked at, the themes presented in the theories are always congruent with the cultural themes of the time in which they develop. In a review of Strozier's (2001) biography of Kohut, Mark Edmundson, a professor at the University of Virginia, writes:

> Kohut came to believe that he was reshaping psychoanalysis to respond to the cultural climate in which he found himself. Freud's emphasis on the Oedipal complex might have been apt in a society that almost totally repressed sexuality and where many patients grew up in hothouse families, with three genera-

tions living under a single Viennese roof, along with a clutch of maids, nurses, manservants and other potential objects or initiators of seduction. But times had changed. In mid-century America the self was the central preoccupation, narcissism was the central pitfall, and analysts had to reset their instruments.

It is important to remember that the very concept of "self" is itself a social construct rooted in time, place, and culture. The value placed on the development of an individuated, autonomous, flourishing self varies widely from culture to culture. The notion of an enduring individual self has always been central in Western Judeo-Christian tradition and is still very much a part of the ethos of the modern, Western, largely male-dominated, industrialized world, which values autonomy over community. In Christian theology the individual self and, therefore, the individual soul remain individual for all eternity and will be reunited with the individual body at the end of time. Many other major systems of belief, such as Buddhism, to name just one, view the individuated self as an impediment to spiritual growth and enlightenment. In those religions the soul is always but a part of the whole universe, and if the belief system includes reincarnation, the soul returns not to become more individuated but to become a more evolved part of the whole.

The historical context in which self psychology developed is the 1970s and 1980s, decades known for an almost fierce focus on individual self-definition, fulfillment, and well-being. This was a time of self-aggrandizement, overindulgence, excessive power, in which "perfecting" the self became its own goal. Magazines such as *Self* flourished; popular novels such as *The Bonfire of the Vanities* and movies such as *Wall Street* chronicle society's preoccupations with power, individuality, and greed. Christopher Lasch's *The Culture of Narcissism* (1978) describes Americans in that era as living in "a state of restless, perpetually unsatisfied desire" (p. xvi). The ascendance of self psychology coincides with the era when many people in the United States valued commitment to self-actualization above all else. Not surprisingly, the pathologies of the times became "self" pathologies: the empty self, the fragile self, the fragmented self.

Today, self psychology is considered to be a useful clinical theory precisely because it is very open and positive in its view of human nature and focus on the individual. There are almost no dark forces in self psychology since the self is viewed as having a tremendous desire and capacity to grow if its needs are met. There are no drives or unruly impulses originating from within, but rather there is an innate, vigorous, motivating "push" toward health.

Early in his career Kohut observed that he was treating a group of patients who were not helped by his interpretations of drive and conflict. They did not feel better about themselves, nor were their symptoms alleviated even though they gained a certain amount of insight. Kohut suggested that many of these patients struggled with dilemmas of narcissism. On one hand, they were arrogant, aloof, and felt superior to others; on the other, they seemed not to have achieved a sound, cohesive sense of self or healthy, balanced self-regard. In the transference relationship, these patients needed either to be admired profusely or to find perfection in the clinician or sometimes both. In examining his own countertransference, Kohut realized that these patients often left him feeling listless, bored, and disconnected. They were so wrapped up in themselves that the therapist could not feel useful or sometimes even real. They seemed not to need anyone at all and yet paradoxically seemed very fragile and prone to shame. Later Modell (1975) was to write about narcissistic pathology as "the illusion of self sufficiency," a phrase that poignantly captures the narcissistic struggle to appear strong and invulnerable while hiding tremendous neediness and lack of cohesion.

Because of these observations, Kohut began to rethink the question of what constitutes a healthy self. Eventually he abandoned the drives as the motivating force in growth and personality formation, and placed the impetus to become a cohesive self at the center of psychological development. He also rejected the Freudian notion that psychological structure is composed of the id, the ego, and the superego, and the idea that the resolution of intrapsychic conflict produces health. Instead, a healthy self is derived from experiences in which caregiving others, known as "selfobjects," meet the specific needs of the emerging self. Rage and aggression are no longer seen as intrinsic forces flowing from distinct, innate drives, but rather as reactions to unmet needs. Needless to say, this radically different view of human nature met with great opposition, and the discussion about whether aggression and therefore rage are innate forces or only occur as a reaction to life's vicissitudes continues to this day.

At first, Kohut believed that his new insights applied only to certain patients who suffered from narcissistic character problems. He still saw the validity of drive, ego, and object relations theories for problems of a neurotic nature. However, by the end of his life he believed that all psychopathology was based on flaws in the self and that "all these flaws in the self are due to disturbances of self-selfobject relationships in childhood" (Kohut 1984, p. 53). Here again we see the phenomenon that we discussed in the chapter 1 and have pointed out already several times in the book: the apparently natural but unfortunate tendency of major theoreticians and their followers to come to postulate that their theories are true for everyone at all times. Again we reiterate our belief that this is not possible. Human nature is too complex and human experience too diverse for one theory to even begin to explain everything about development or psychological health and illness.

THEORIES ABOUT NARCISSISM

Before turning to the actual building blocks of self psychology, it is necessary to understand the profoundly new and different view of narcissism that is offered by Kohut and that lies at the heart of self psychology. Freud's view of narcissism was drive centered, based on energetic concepts, and, as such, was both quantitative and linear. It was quantitative in that he believed that each person has a finite amount of libidinal energy. What was directed toward another must be taken away from the self. If a person has only a certain amount of libido to divide between self and others, then she will need to replace self-love and self-involvement with object love in order to move forward in development. It was a linear theory for related reasons. In Freudian psychology healthy narcissism has only one line of forward development—from self-love to object love. Pathological narcissism occurs when too much libido remains invested in the self, and the shift to object love does not occur.

Freud also differentiated primary narcissism from secondary narcissism. Primary narcissism exists in the earliest phases of life when all libido is attached to the ego. For the infant, this state is considered natural; it is the starting point of development. Secondary narcissism occurs later in life when the libido that has been directed toward others is withdrawn from objects back into the self due to thwarted growth opportunities, disappointments, illness, trauma, or old age. Thus, in secondary narcissism an infantile state of self-involvement is re-created, and Freud considered this to be unhealthy and in need of resolution. Throughout Freudian theory, narcissism has a mostly pejorative connotation; it is something to be outgrown, avoided, or treated.

Since Freud, debate and controversy have swirled around this subject. Many of the ego psychologists and object relation theorists have also described primary narcissism as a state of utter self-absorption and absolute infantile omnipotence to be modified or outgrown. But they are by no means in agreement with Freud or with each other about how, when, or why narcissism develops or what an ultimate, healthy resolution might be. To give just a few examples, Klein denied the existence of any period of primary narcissism whatsoever. The Blancks, major ego psychologists, wrote about the possibility of "sound" secondary narcissism and defined this as the acquisition of healthy self-regard wherein self-representations are cathected with value (Blanck and Blanck 1979). In all these definitions, however, there still exists the implied belief that narcissism is something to be outgrown in favor of a more adult interest in others.

Kohut, on the other hand, eventually described narcissism in much less pejorative and much more expansive ways, differentiating between the crucial development of healthy narcissism and the pathology of narcissism. He postulated a separate and central line of development for normal, healthy narcissism. His view was less linear, polarized, and quantitative than that of the other developmental theorists. He did not believe that libidinal energy was finite. In fact, self psychology is based on the belief that the more attunement and love people have for themselves, the more they will have for others. Pathological narcissism only occurs when insufficient love and attunement are received from others, thereby forcing the person to become overly interested and invested in his or herself. Kohut did not view self love and object love as mutually exclusive. He did not posit object love or separation-individuation as primary goals of development or as important signs of health and maturity. On the contrary, he valued a much wider range of possible choices, seeing them as equally healthy and worthwhile ways of living.

> Although the attainment of genitality and the capacity for unambivalent object love have been features of many, perhaps most, satisfying and significant lives, there are many other good lives, including some of the greatest and most fulfilling lives recorded in history that were not lived by individuals whose psychosexual organization was heterosexual-genital or whose major commitment was to unambivalent object love. (Kohut 1984, p. 7)

Kohut did not view independence from others as a hallmark of maturity, since he believed that we are all mutually dependent on others throughout life.

THE THEORY OF SELF PSYCHOLOGY

Despite devoting a considerable amount of attention to the concept of narcissism, Freud began the first section of his paper "On Narcissism" (1914) with the following statement: "The disturbances to which a child's original narcissism is exposed, the reactions with which he seeks to protect himself from them and the paths into which he is forced in doing so—these are themes which I propose to leave on one side, as an important field of work which still awaits exploration" (p. 92). To the exploration of these themes Kohut devoted his life, in his study of what he called "the science of the self" (1978, p. 752). From his explorations he concluded that the plight of "Tragic Man" was at the heart of the human condition. For Kohut, the term "Tragic Man" described the suffering that all individuals struggle with when empathic failures thwart their efforts to achieve self-cohesion and self-realization. He contrasted his view to what he called Freud's notion of the pleasure-seeking "Guilty Man" who struggles with conflicts that arise between desires and prohibitions.

Whereas Freud was interested in the phenomenon of guilt, Kohut turned his attention to the exploration of shame. Guilt occurs when a person feels he or she has transgressed against the prohibitions of society, usually contained in the superego or against one's ego ideal, which is contained in the ego. Guilt has to do with rules and codes of conduct and morality made by persons outside the self and brings with it fear of punishment. Once the rules have been internalized, guilt can be based on not living up to one's own ideals. Shame is a much younger, nonverbal, less conceptual experience. It is the feeling within the self of being inadequate, embarrassed, humiliated, "less than." It is felt more in the body rather than in the mind and often has somatic manifestations such as blushing, trembling, and crying. Shame often comes about from narcissistic wounding, which is one of the reasons why Kohut was so interested in it. Patients can often be helped to face and grow out of their shame if they can use the language of childhood comfortably while talking about it. They often describe the feeling as "icky," "puny," "empty," or "nerdy." One client began to call his experience of shame "my slimy, little wormy feelings" and, once named, began to deal with them.

Several new, key concepts are central to Kohut's understanding of psychological development: (1) the importance of empathy not only as the main tool in clinical work but as the matrix within which all growth takes place, (2) the notion of the structure of the tripolar self, and (3) the existence and crucial role that selfobjects play in psychological development.

The Role of Empathy

The role of empathy in development and in clinical work is not a new concept, but Kohut elevated it to a position of supreme importance and considered it to be the primary clinical tool. Kohut did not use the term *empathy* according to the current, lay usage of the word, which often includes notions of warmth, sympathy, or approval. He meant something much closer to the dictionary definition of the word: "The projection of one's own personality into the personality of another in order to understand him better: intellectual identification of oneself with another." According to the dictionary definition, one could have empathy for an ax murderer, and that is precisely the way Kohut used it—to "understand" from within the experience of another, no matter what the experience. Much more than a feeling, empathy is a way of "knowing."

Kohut wrote a great deal about the use of empathy, or what he called "vicarious introspection," as a tool in clinical work. He also described his belief that all human beings need an empathic matrix within which to grow and that only an empathic environment can provide the psychological nutriment and sustenance essential for mental health. Kohut did not envision the environment, however, as being always empathic. He knew full well that perfect empathy is impossible. Sooner or later human beings always disappoint or fail each other to some degree. What he did say was that there had to be an optimal balance of empathic gratification and empathic failure for the developing self to flourish and eventually experience itself as energetic and cohesive. Both in life and in clinical treatment, reactions to failures in empathy can be worked through if the disappointment and anger over unmet needs can be expressed and understood. This leads to a stronger and firmer sense of self. According to self psychology, empathic attunement is the necessary facilitator of development; repeated empathic failures are the roots of disturbance and thwarted growth.

A children's book that always gets a joyous response from youngsters is *I Hate It When . . .* (Preston 1969). The "when" refers to necessary parental endeavors such as "when you scrub my face" or "when you make me eat my spinach." This is an example of empathy for children because it acknowledges the truth of what children feel even when someone is doing something for their own good. The book does not say, "Because you hate it, I won't scrub your face" or "You shouldn't hate it when I do necessary things for you." It merely, through empathy, acknowledges what *is* and therefore validates something in the sense of self in the child. Caregivers scrub faces and sometimes children hate it; that simple reality offers true empathy to both. In some ways this is akin to Melanie Klein's beautiful point that if you can name troublesome feelings you can begin to master and transform them, because you have a fuller, more accepting knowledge of yourself. Empathy does not necessarily make a person feel good, but it does help people feel genuine and authentic.

The following example illustrates the inner impoverishment that can ensue when there is a lack of empathy.

Lisa, a thirty-seven-year-old woman from El Barrio, a Latino section of New York City, joined a support group at a women's center. The group decided to focus on identifying and healing the "inner child." Participants encouraged each other to remember and tell their stories of neglect, mistreatment, and abuse. Lisa, who was the sixth child of an exhausted, struggling, poor single mother, became alarmed when she could summon no specific memories of her early childhood. Every time the group turned to her, she felt "gray and empty." She secretly feared that she had undiagnosed memory problems or that she was stupid. After many weeks she and the group began to realize that the gray empty feeling *was* the memory. Her childhood had been characterized by an absence of empathy for anything about her—good, bad, or indifferent. She realized that her sense of herself was vague and diffuse, and lacked specificity. The group members realized that they did not have to help Lisa heal the wounds of overt trauma; rather, they had to help her see and explore with specificity what did not blossom in her due to years of inattention.

Kohut looked to the lack of empathy to explain narcissistic rage, which he believed to be the most destructive form of anger and sadism. He did not believe that anger was an innate drive but rather that it resulted from the intense, sometimes violent reaction to the kind of hurt that makes people feel powerless and ashamed. He considered narcissistic rage to be pathological because it emerges when the very fabric of the self has been injured. Kohut (1977) called narcissistic rage a "disintegration product" because it occurs when a person feels he or she is literally falling apart and has returned to a state of primitive disorganization.

Self Objects and the Tripolar Self

When it came to defining the structure of the self, Kohut made a radical departure from the Freudian view that a person's structure is made up of the id, ego, and superego. He introduced a major new piece of metapsychology by postulating that the self is made up of three distinct poles. Just as the Latin words *id, ego*, and *superego* were probably not the best choices to identify parts of the self in English (see chapters 3 and 4), so too the choice of the word *pole* for parts of the self is awkward. However, Kohut chose *pole* to refer to an aspect or a pathway of development within the self that has its own energy and needs. He initially identified two poles in the self: the pole of the grandiose self and the pole of the idealized parent imago, and thus labeled the self "bipolar." Toward the end of his life Kohut added a third pole, the pole of twinship, and considered the developmental needs of this pole to be equal in power and necessity to the other two. Confusingly, some of the literature of self psychology still refers to the bipolar self. But the full structure that Kohut eventually envisioned was tripolar.

Perhaps the best way to understand the tripolar self is to turn to Kohut's concept of selfobjects, for it is selfobjects that are needed to meet the needs of each aspect or pole of the self. In *A Dictionary for Psychotherapists*, Chessick (1993) defines selfobjects as follows:

> An object may be defined as a selfobject when it is experienced intrapsychically as providing functions in an interpersonal relationship that add to or maintain the cohesive self. This includes affect attunement, consensual validation, tension regulation and soothing, recognition of one's autonomous potential, and restoration of a temporarily threatened fragmentation of the self through a variety of activities and comments. (p. 357)

Kohut believed that the formation, cohesion, and health of the self actually occur from the taking in of good psychological nutrients from selfobjects. That is their function—to create and build a strong, vibrant self. The need is not simply to be seen or to have an ideal person to merge with or to have alter ego experiences, the need is to actually be created, *be made.* Phyllis Greenacre perhaps put it best when she sent Kohut a thank-you letter after he had introduced her as a speaker. She wrote:

> Something happened to me with your introduction of me that Sunday. I have tried to think of what it was: I thought "I was greatly touched"—"No, I was moved"—and then it occurred to me that perhaps it was not so much one of these, as that I was gently and reassuringly solidified. (quoted in Cocks 1994, 90–91)

"Gently and reassuringly solidified"—what a beautiful and evocative way to capture what happens when selfobjects function well.

Self psychological theory postulates that selfobjects, understood as people or things outside of the self, are vitally necessary to every individual as sources of mirroring, sources of perfection and grandeur to merge with, and as similar selves to feel at one with. Selfobjects are needed to fulfill these functions throughout the life cycle and are called selfobjects because they stand not as objects to be related to in and of themselves but as objects that function to give the self what it needs in order to become and remain energetic and cohesive.

Although selfobjects are most often other people, it is important to realize that other things such as art, literature, music, and a variety of symbols can serve selfobject functions. For example, a client who is particularly attuned to the weather may use it as a selfobject.

> Susan, whose sense of a well-functioning, cohesive self is very fragile, begins feeling "lost and panicky" if there are several rainy or cloudy days in a row. When the sun returns, she experiences a restoration of hope and well-being. For her, the sun is a symbol of the warmth and beneficence we need to take in from the loving gaze of a selfobject. It is also a symbol of power and her sense of merger with it is one of the few sources of well-being in her life.

There is a psychiatric diagnosis called seasonal affective disorder (known as SAD), which identifies patients whose brain function is affected by the shorter amount of daylight in the dark winter months. However, even that biologically based diagnosis would not preclude the *meaning* of light and warmth in Susan's internal world. This particular patient, who became quite attuned to the interweaving of psyche and soma, was helped immeasurably by the combination of light therapy and talking about what strengths blossom in her when she feels that the "light and warmth" in her relationship with the therapist are sufficient to nourish her energy and hope, and thereby make more substantive her sense of self.

Conversely, another patient, Matthew, often becomes depressed and agitated on a bright, sunny day. To him the light seems piercing and harsh and reawakens the pain of his mother's gaze, which he experienced as fierce, critical, and oppressive. Sunshine, for Matthew, does not serve a helpful selfobject function because the person it evokes was harmful to the development of a strong, cohesive self, and made him feel more fragmented.

The Tripolar Self

To understand the main contribution of self psychology, we will now turn to the selfobject needs of each of the three poles of the tripolar self—the pole of the grandiose self, the pole of the idealized parent imago, and the twinship pole. Each needs empathic responses from selfobjects in order to flourish and grow. Each is necessary for the development of a cohesive self. Each has its own selfobject transference based on the selfobject experiences needed in childhood by this part of the personality. Again, although the language of self psychology is cumbersome, the theory describes poignant human needs and yearnings. The word *pole* sounds rigid, but what it is attempting to capture is not a fixed tripartite structure but rather the idea of a flexible, ever-changing, relational web of aspects or polarities of the self.

The first part or pole of the self described by Kohut, the pole of the grandiose self, needs mirroring selfobjects, people who will reflect and identify its unique capacities, talents, and characteristics. Some clinicians prefer to call this the pole of ambitions. The grandiose self is the self that wants to feel special and full of well-being. It is the repository of natural, healthy exhibitionism. It also includes a great deal of specificity about characteristics of the self and therefore forms the core of identity and individuality. People with sound grandiose selves are vibrant, full of confidence, hopeful, ambitious, and productive. They don't quite believe they can do anything, but they often have the courage and the vision to try. There are echoes here of Mahler's practicing child crowing that the world is her oyster, being the gleam in everyone's eye. There is also a similarity to Winnicott's concept of the "True Self," full of raw vitality, fantastic feelings, and fervent wishes.

If we think back to the story of the little boy in chapter 6 who needed to feel he could stop the waves when he was frightened, we can see how harmful a lack of empathy for grandiosity could be. If the adults had said, "Don't be silly—you can't stop the waves," he might have experienced his littleness or helplessness as overwhelming or shameful and humiliating. Empathic attunement to his need to feel powerful, on the other hand, allowed him to go off and play with a sense of wholeness and well-being.

The concept of the grandiose self can best be illustrated in clinical examples where there has been an absence of delighted mirroring or an active thwarting of the child's wish to shine on the part of the selfobject.

Mary, a forty-two-year-old woman beginning treatment, was surprised, moved, and a little scared when her therapist reacted with delight at the way she described an event of the previous day. With a keen sense of observation and a twinge of humor, she recounted how her meditation teacher, who had been sitting on the floor dressed in a sweat suit humming a mantra, suddenly jumped up, changed into a ball gown, and went rushing off to meet her diplomat husband at a white-tie event for dignitaries of the United Nations. The therapist laughed at the humorous description and smiled warmly at Mary as she recounted this tale. She pointed out Mary's excellent sense of humor and skill in describing the moment. She observed that Mary seemed very stirred by this attention. Mary responded to this mirroring by stating sadly that no one in her family ever seemed to identify or care about any of her qualities, except if she was bad. No one had ever noticed or enjoyed her humor, her way with words, or her vitality. She then began to recount the story of her childhood in a very rigid army family. The standards of behavior for the children centered around silence and self-effacement. "Children should be seen and not heard" was actually embroidered on a sampler hanging in the living room. Grandiosity was not only seen as unhealthy, but was feared as unruly, disruptive, and possibly leading to evil. Boasting and pride in oneself were "works of the devil"—traits to be tamed, controlled, and, if possible, rooted out. Naturally, through the course of her life, Mary had become a good listener, but she felt that she "had lost myself in paying attention to others." She had entered treatment after reading a book on shamanism and realizing that she could "no longer find my soul." She felt that, "The flame of my spirit was flickering out because no one recognized or cared what it was like."

Subsequent treatment has revealed to Mary many specifics about herself that she now thoroughly enjoys: she is very funny, she can be sarcastic when she wants to be, she has a true gift of imagery, she sometimes would rather talk than listen, and she likes being the center of attention.

Because self psychology is not a drive theory, one still needs to ask about what energies or forces fuel the wish or need for a healthy, grandiose self. Kohut never fully offered a substitute for the drives, but did speak of the pole of the grandiose self as "driven by ambition." This fits in with his general concept that there is something in each person akin to a biological growth force that pushes the individual toward the completion of maturational tasks. Kohut believed this inner motivation, or tension, to be the innate, embryonic push every individual has toward the development of a cohesive self.

Anxiety is also understood differently in self psychology than in drive, ego, or object relations theories. As in relational theory (see chapter 9), anxiety is not seen as arising from intrapsychic conflict, but rather from loss of contact with the self or selfobjects. It is experienced not so much as tension or nervousness, but rather as fear and dread. In the pole of the grandiose self there can be fear of loss of contact with one's authentic self if grandiosity becomes too exaggerated and unreal. The authentic self needs to feel special or strong in a real way based on genuine qualities. A person who has become overly grandiose may feel so filled with energy and power that these become painful and frightening. The anxiety is akin to that experienced by people in manic states who feel they might burst or disintegrate.

> When Yvonne, a hard working, talented, inner-city teenager earned a full scholarship to a prestigious college, she received so much attention in her school and from the media that she began to feel "high and wild." She no longer paced herself well in her studies, becoming obsessed with getting higher grades even though they were no longer necessary. She began to daydream of getting straight A's in college and "becoming famous on campus." With just a little help she realized she had become overstimulated by all the admiration. She learned to meditate as a source of needed self-soothing and within a period of weeks was considerably less anxious. In this example, Yvonne recaptured the mature qualities that derive from the pole of the grandiose self, which are enthusiasm over appropriate goals and the ability to pursue these ambitions with joy and self confidence.

Kohut called the transference that occurs when the needs of the grandiose self have not been well met the "mirroring transference." The client needs mirroring and the clinician must respond to this need not by interpreting it but by meeting it. Mitchell and Black (1995) describe it in the following way:

> Some patients . . . establish a powerful attachment to the analyst based on the need for the analyst to grasp and reflect back their experience of themselves, their excitements, their perceptions, as well as their disappointments. Although the analyst may seem to be insignificant to the patient in the traditional way, she is actually essential as a kind of nurturing context (much like Winnicott's "holding environment") within which the patient can begin to feel more seen, more real, and more internally substantial. (pp. 160–61)

Of course Kohut knew that no therapist could gratify patients' needs perfectly and, in fact, what he recommended for growth (not only for the patient but for the developing child) was a balance of optimal gratification and optimual frustration.

The second pole that Kohut described is that of the idealized parent imago or, less awkwardly, the pole of ideals. By imago he meant an internal, sometimes unconscious, object representation of an idealized other, usually from the early history of an individual (Chessick 1993). Again, the choice of words is unfortunate and misleading. First, the word *imago* is awkward, unfamiliar, and not used in common parlance. Second, calling it a "parent imago" is misleading because it implies that the experience is limited to childhood and that the representations are limited to early caregivers. This contradicts one of the strengths of self psychological theory, which postulates that selfobject needs can and should be met by a variety of people and experiences throughout the life cycle.

The idealized parent imago aspect of the self contains what Kohut proposed as the second, universal, selfobject need—the need to have someone strong, calm, and wonderful to idealize and merge with in order to feel safe and complete within the self. Just as the pole of the grandiose self needs to feel that the beauty and the splendor within is mirrored by others, the pole of the idealized parent imago needs to see strength and wonder outside of the self, in others, in order to merge with their growth-enhancing qualities. The pole of the grandiose self needs to be shown qualities within the self that are wonderful, while the pole of the idealized parent imago needs to find qualities in others that are wonderful.

> Annie, a fifty-four-year-old Caucasian woman, came to treatment because of anxiety and depression so crippling she could barely function. The therapist had been highly recommended to her by a trusted friend and had been described as a caring, skilled practitioner. Annie was very pleased with the first meeting and said she experienced the therapist as "warm, important, and smart." By the second session Annie was paying close attention to the therapist, gazing at her intensely in the hope of seeing something good, which because of her need (and because the therapist is a genuinely nice person) she found. By the third session she would start speaking about the therapist while coming down the corridor before even entering the office. She would say things like, "Oh, you look so pretty today. You look so calm. I feel better already" or "You're so smart. I just know you are going to be able to help me today." She always said these things with a piercing childlike sweetness and her whole being seemed filled with the hope of having found someone wonderful to merge with. In speaking about her early experiences, she described a family she was ashamed of. Her father was an alcoholic tyrant and her mother a "wifty socialite with no substance." As her treatment progressed, Annie often remarked on what a difference it made to her that she now had "someone special who makes me feel that I too can be calm, hopeful, and strong."

Kohut described the energy that motivated this part of the self as a "pull." The pole of the parent imago is "pulled by ideals." By merging with the calmness and competence of the selfobject, those qualities can be established within the self.

There can be anxiety in this pole also, and one form is the potential loss of self. This may happen if the merger with the idealized selfobject becomes total. Anxiety arises from trying to maintain the delicate balance between merger experiences that enhance the self because one feels protected and strengthened by the power and calm of another, and merger experiences

that lead to loss of self cohesion because too much of the self has disappeared into the bigness and greatness of another. Probably everyone can
think of a time when he or she needed to "sink into" the calm and strength
of a parent, a spouse, a lover, a friend, or even a TV program at the end of
a hard day. Finding such a selfobject to merge with is a wonderful experience that can, however, become frightening if the immersion in the other
results in a loss of self so complete that disorientation or panic ensues.

> A teenage African American boy, Jim, began to feel much better about himself
> once he started idealizing Michael Jordan's skill and prowess. He discovered a
> sense of power and possibility and applied himself much more diligently to
> his studies and to training for the basketball team. However, he scared himself
> at times when he realized that there were moments when he was thinking
> about Jordan's prowess so intensely that he "kind of lost it" and forgot who he
> himself was. He realized that he had to learn to balance seeing Jordan's skills
> as a source of strength while maintaining a realistic awareness of himself and
> without losing his own sense of identity.

Aside from problems of merger, self psychologists see other risks inherent
in idealization. If others are idealized too much, the self can be left devalued, feeling little, worthless, and ashamed. This is a new way of looking at
the psychological dangers of idealization. Drive theorists understood idealization primarily as a defense, as a way of denying hostile impulses against
a loved one. "See, I don't hate you. I think you're great." Ego psychologists
understood that idealization could potentially interfere with the regulation
of self-esteem. Self psychologists saw the potential problems with idealization but chose to focus more attention on the contribution healthy idealization can make to a person's very sense of self.

When there are sufficient selfobjects in a person's life to idealize, the
mature qualities of the pole of the idealized parent imago can develop.
These are the ability to delight in and grow from qualities in others and
eventually to experience pleasure and pride in one's own qualities, standards, and values. The qualities of the idealized selfobject are taken into the
self as a result of successful merger experiences.

Kohut called the selfobject transference that develops from the need to
merge with an ideal object the "idealizing transference." Chessick (1993)
says of this transference: "The goal of the idealizing selfobject transference
is to share, via a merger, in the power and omnipotence of the therapist"
(p. 164). The need here, as illustrated in the cases of Annie and Jim, is for
the patient to be able to feel strong and important and safe by virtue of a
connection to a good, powerful, important therapist.

The third pole, the pole of twinship, refers to the need to feel that there
are others in the world who are similar to oneself. This mutual recognition,

this finding of a sameness in a pal or a soulmate, provides another kind of universal sustenance from selfobjects. The need for a twin is related to, but also subtly different from, the need for the grandiose self to be mirrored or the need of the pole of the idealized parent imago to have strong and wondrous selfobjects. Kohut came to consider the selfobject needs of the twinship pole to be as vital as the need of the other two poles for developing a vigorous and cohesive self, and therefore he eventually designated it as a distinct pole in its own right.

> Peter, a thirty-five-year-old Caucasian man from a working-class background, was immensely moved, and formed an instant, powerful, and permanent bond with his therapist, when he asked her what her major had been in college and it turned out to be the same as his—French literature. His family and his peers had ridiculed him throughout his childhood about his love of words and reading. He had been strongly advised against majoring in French, not only by his parents, but also by his guidance counselor in high school who had called his interest "an esoteric, useless pursuit." The fact that the therapist had also been a French major was seldom talked about in therapy. It just remained there as a precious and reassuring similarity and, by its power, enabled him to see how little his need to be understood had been met in the course of his growing up. Oddly enough, this same therapist had had an unusual number of patients over the years who turned out to have been French majors and to whom that bond had great meaning.

Because Kohut developed his ideas about the importance of the twinship pole toward the end of his life, he never did posit the energy that motivates that part of the self or the anxiety it experiences. We would say that the energy is born of the need not to be different or isolated or weird, and that anxiety arises when there is no one "the same as me."

> One young woman described suffering greatly from the fact that all her siblings were retarded. She talked about the embarrassment she felt when she was out in public with them. She expressed how wonderful she would feel in the hospital where she is a physician if one of her siblings were a doctor also. Poignantly, she stated, "If only one of them could walk beside me and be like me, I wouldn't feel so different anymore. I wouldn't feel so alone." Not being able to establish a feeling of twinship with her own siblings made her feel so "different and strange" that she did not realize she could establish a sense of twinship with colleagues. When this was pointed out to her in a support group, she was able to mourn her lack of twinship opportunities within her immediate family and start trying to find twinship selfobjects elsewhere.

Another example that many people can identify with is how welcome it is to encounter a fellow citizen when traveling abroad, especially for an extended period of time. A graduate student engaged in folklore fieldwork in Afghanistan described the pure joy he felt at meeting an American after living many months in a small native village. He laughed at the fact that the two would never have been friends back home in the United States because they disagreed wildly on many philosophical, cultural, and political issues. However, it was "worth its weight in gold" to be able to talk to someone who missed hot dogs, wondered what team had won the Orange Bowl, and remembered spending Sunday mornings in pajamas reading the *New York Times*. Too much time spent without a feeling of twinship can make people feel like they are unraveling and losing touch with themselves.

The mature qualities that develop when the selfobject needs of the twinship pole are met are security and a sense of belonging and legitimacy. These enhance the nuclear self and all its endeavors.

Yoshi, a twenty-eight-year-old Asian-American man who played catcher on his Little League, high school, and college baseball teams, developed a great bond with other catchers, whether they were competing for his spot or playing for the opposing team. At tryout camps and baseball clinics he would always seek out the other catchers to talk about their mutual love of playing that particular position, so central to the action, so physical, dirty, and painful. They would compare notes about knee operations and the soreness after games and swap funny stories about what prima donnas certain pitchers were. Yoshi observed that it was almost as if the catchers had a secret language that only they understood. Although as an adult Yoshi no longer plays baseball, he believes that these twinship experiences have made him very confident in the world. A successful salesman, he can walk into any company and feel "I am not alone or different on this earth." He is part of a brotherhood that provides him with sustenance and strength.

The selfobject transference that develops from the needs of this pole is called the "twinship" or "alter ego" transference. If it is allowed to flourish, the client will feel a likeness, a sameness, with the therapist and therefore more known to herself and less alone.

Self psychology does not postulate specific childhood developmental phases for the three parts of the self that are closely tied to certain months or years of life. However, Kohut did believe that there was a general sequence in development, with the needs of the grandiose self being predominant until around the age of four, and the need for ideal selfobjects to be at its most intense from four to six. He did not suggest an age-specific time for twinship needs, although we believe that they are particularly strong in latency and adolescence. It is important to remember that his main belief about selfobject needs from the three poles is that they continue to exist in some form, naturally and appropriately, throughout the entire life cycle.

Transmuting Internalization

What is the process by which a person takes in the qualities and functions of selfobjects that are necessary for the development of a healthy, cohesive, vibrant self? Kohut called it "transmuting internalization," which is defined as "the process through which a function formerly performed by another (selfobject) is taken into the self through optimal mirroring, interaction, and frustration" (Elson 1986, p. 252). As the self takes in the functions of selfobjects, they are gradually changed and made one's own so that the healthy self is not a replica of selfobjects but a unique self in its own right. The word *transmuting* was carefully chosen by Kohut to try to capture the transformative nature of internalization. The meeting of selfobject needs does not simply fill a person with well-being, strength, and a sense of cohesion. Rather, the meeting of selfobject needs acts as a catalyst for development so that the qualities that are internalized become a genuine, integral part of the self that has taken them in, in specific, personal, and unique ways. Some critics of self psychology hear the theory as advocating that they simply "give" to patients to help them heal, but a careful reading of Kohut and his followers contradicts this view. Empathic attunement to needs is not meant merely to fill or soothe; it is meant to stimulate the needed energy for clients to work and grow in their own ways to become more fully themselves.

It is important to note that although Kohut often spoke about the desirability of optimal gratification for selfobject needs, he also often spoke of the need for—indeed the inevitability of—optimal frustration. He understood full well that perfect empathic attunement is not possible in human relationships and believed that empathic failures were actually necessary to stimulate growth. When there is optimal frustration, the developing child is challenged to find strength and comfort within the self. Handling difficult moments well on ones own can contribute to the experience of a vital, cohesive self.

In the section of *Childhood and Society* on "Initiative versus Guilt," Erikson (1950) tells the wonderful story of the day Freud was asked what he thought a normal person should be able to do well. "The questioner probably expected a complicated answer. But Freud simply said, 'To love and to work.' . . . Thus we may ponder but cannot improve on the professor's formula." To love and to work—surely one of the greatest answers of all time. But, Kohut did want to improve on "the professor's formula." What he wanted to add was that people needed to be able to love and, especially, to work creatively and with vitality and joy—whether laying a brick wall, making a meatloaf, driving a truck, or writing the great American novel. For Kohut, the ability to work creatively was the supraordinate motivation in human nature and the hallmark of mental health.

Thus, to follow up on some of the cases mentioned earlier in this chapter, Mary eventually grew to experience her skill in storytelling with delight, but with her own "take" on it. She was ultimately amused by different things than the therapist was, and became aware of her capacity for observation at different times and in her own unique way, which was always somewhat wry and subdued. Annie's pain was never fully soothed by her merger with the intelligence and calm of her therapist, but she found hope in the fact that a better selfobject was available to her. Peter derived a sense of legitimacy and "sameness" that allowed him to explore the specifics of what he was really like as a person in his own right, with his own special love of language and literature. All of these transmuting internalizations seemed to potentiate self-knowledge, growth, and cohesion in the nuclear self, and, very important, a sense of joy.

Kohut often used the term *microinternalizations* to capture the flavor of the myriad number of times the self needs to take in psychological nutriment from selfobjects. The empathetic attunement of selfobjects, including the willingness to admit and repair empathic failures, is the necessary groundwork for transmuting internalizations to occur.

A SELF PSYCHOLOGICAL VIEW OF PSYCHOPATHOLOGY: DISORDERS OF THE SELF

When it comes to psychological suffering and illness, Kohut and the self psychologists speak of "disorders of the self" and offer various ways of classifying these disorders. Underlying all the disorders is the belief that psychological illness occurs when the legitimate developmental needs of the three poles are not met with optimal empathy and optimal frustration. This puts self psychology squarely in the "deficit model" of psychopathology rather than the "conflict model." In the conflict model, psychological problems and illnesses arise when internal impulses and desires clash with reality or with prohibitions and guilt. In the deficit model, human beings are viewed as much more vulnerable to hurt, neglect, and deprivation than to being disturbed by tumultuous forces from the drives within. Self psychologists (Kohut and Wolf 1978) distinguish between (1) primary and secondary disorders, (2) a variety of typical self states, and (3) a variety of character or personality types. Notwithstanding the fact that they are offering a system of classification, they take care to point out that these are merely outlines and that no individual can ever be completely categorized by any of these classifications.

The primary disorders of the self include the familiar categories from the American Psychiatric Association's *DSM-IV-TR* (2000): the psychoses, borderline states, narcissistic behavior disorders, and narcissistic personality disorders. The self psychological view of the etiology of these disorders is that severe deficits occur in the cohesion of the self when the mirroring, idealizing, and twinship needs of the developing individual have not been met due to chronic deprivation or severe trauma. Biological and social causes are not ruled out and are seen as contributing to the fragmentation of the inner world. More will be said about the self psychological view of these major diagnostic categories in the later chapters on psychopathology.

The secondary disorders that Kohut and Wolf refer to are "reactions of a structurally undamaged self to the vicissitudes of life" (p. 414), or the transient drop in self-esteem, depression, nervousness, elation, detachment, and so forth that individuals feel due to the inevitable stresses in life. These are called secondary because they do not shake the core of the person's sense of herself as an integrated, whole human being.

The self states identified by Kohut and Wolf do not follow psychiatric diagnostic criteria or categories. Instead they are descriptive categories of disorders of the self that are useful in clinical work especially in enhancing empathy and identifying the unmet selfobject needs of the client. The categories described are the understimulated self, the overstimulated self, the fragmenting self, and the overburdened self. These categories are not absolute. They refer to ways of experiencing oneself in the world that have become pervasive and enduring. Particular deficits are thought to have a tendency to lead to particular disorders but there is a great deal of fluidity among all the categories.

The understimulated self describes those individuals who often feel empty, bored, listless, or apathetic. Their selfobjects have not been able to mirror and nourish their grandiosity sufficiently. They feel flat, robbed of their buoyancy, their sense of aliveness and richness. Mary, whose case was presented earlier in this chapter, is, in fact, a painter who struggles mightily to "find something inside to put on canvas." She came into treatment describing herself as "arid, barren, and gray." She felt hopeless and inept about the prospect of ever finding selfobjects that would awaken her to life.

The overstimulated self describes those who have suffered from the opposite problem—intense, excessive, inappropriate, or erratic mirroring. Intense but not consistent behavior on the part of selfobjects can leave the developing self feeling overwhelmed and too full of feeling. There is not space or peace enough for transmuting internalization to take place because the person is always being crowded with demands and stimulation from the outside. In this case the person often also feels robbed, but robbed of the sense that her own unique strength and vigor reside within herself and are her own.

An overstimulated self can also develop as a result of idealized selfobjects being too powerful, vibrant, or famous. In such instances there is no ideal calmness to merge with, and learning self-soothing becomes a problem. Sometimes the result is a kind of flatness, underachievement in the service of keeping the self-system regulated. Sometimes the result can be an oversensitivity to anything new or stimulating.

Syrie, the daughter of a well-known, highly grandiose musician, feels constantly "full of ideas and projects and worries and pain." A performer in her own right, she can't shake either the wildly erratic praise or the self-aggrandizing attitudes of her father. She grew up in a household where the doors were always open and no one had any privacy. Her father seemed larger than life and "took up all the space in the family." He was also wildly inappropriate, watching pornography with the children, totally unattuned to how much this confused and upset them. At other times both parents seemed not to notice that the children were there at all and left them alone, bored, and eventually listless for hours on end.

Syrie is often so overstimulated that she jumps if the phone machine clicks in the office or a car horn sounds in the distance. She becomes flooded with ideas, plans, and ambitions, but these often quickly drain away, leaving her feeling small, empty, and worthless. A beautiful, talented, highly educated woman, she constantly becomes overexcited but then underachieves, trying to seek invisibility and peace. She cannot connect to other musicians, partners, friends, or herself.

In treatment she hopes to develop a clearer, more realistic, sense of her own talents and resources. She already feels helped by the notion that it is possible to distinguish between real qualities or achievements and grandiose fantasies and beliefs. She is comforted by the example of the therapist's quiet, solid pride in her own achievements and would like to develop the ability to merge with the therapist's joyful yet appropriate sense of self-esteem.

While in healthy self states there is a basic cohesion, the fragmenting self has little sense of cohesion. Individuals with this disorder have not been related to as a whole by their selfobjects. They have received attention but it has been erratic, inconsistent, and unpredictable. The caregivers are often worried and distractable themselves, their attention flitting from one thing to another.

Vicki, the daughter of a very anxious mother, has trouble paying attention to one subject at a time in treatment. She will sometimes fly out of the office at the end of a session leaving the door to the building wide open. She experiences herself as a "bunch of pieces—like a puzzle thrown on the floor." She remembers with pain that her parents and all her older siblings would always interject "odd things" into conversations. One of them would say, "Your sweater is the wrong color" or "Wasn't the weather nice today" when she would be trying to tell them about her day in school. She understands that it is hard for her to experience herself as a unified whole when people were always behaving and paying attention in a random, scattered way as she was growing up.

The overburdened self, on the other hand, has felt too alone and unsupported. Perhaps a person's problems or neediness were not accepted or even allowed. Perhaps her idealized selfobjects were not calm and reliable. Perhaps there were no twinship selfobjects who seemed to be going through similar difficulties. Whatever the case, the overburdened self feels he must "go it alone" in what is experienced as an unnerving, demanding, even hostile world. Neediness is experienced with guilt rather than with compassion.

> Nancy feels she has to be responsible for all the problems of her family. "I have to take care of them—they need me to be strong." She is also hyperalert to "the pain and suffering in the universe" while very reluctant to reveal her own, believing that no one could possibly ever want to help her. Both her parents suffered from major depression throughout her life, and family interactions revolved around the parents' neediness and despair.

The character types identified by self psychologists are mirror-hungry personalities, ideal-hungry personalities, alter-ego-hungry personalities, merger-hungry personalities, and contact-shunning personalities. This way of looking at various personality types is self-explanatory and the very use of the word *hungry* captures the poignancy of what can occur when the needs of each pole of the individual are not met or are met inadequately or traumatically. The resultant yearning can shape personality and leave the person in a perpetual state of craving and/or fear.

SELF PSYCHOLOGY TODAY

Kohut's new and stimulating ideas about the importance of the development of the self revolutionized psychodynamic thinking and treatment for many clinicians. Peter Fonagy (2001) described this revolution succinctly when he wrote, "He broke the iron grip of ego psychology by forcing psychoanalysts to think in less mechanistic terms, in terms of selfhood rather than psychological function, in terms of selfobjects rather than drive gratification that the object fulfilled" (p. 108). This shift in focus gave rise to an invigorated interest in infant observation and research as theoreticians sought to identify the building blocks of the self from the moment of birth. Daniel Stern (1985), for example, has done extensive, pioneering work in the field of infant research. Upon direct observation he has found that the human baby can indeed experience moments of intense connectedness and intense differentiation from birth on. This seems to contradict some of the object relations theorists' beliefs about the neonatal, symbiotic period of complete merger with the mother. Stern observed the baby to be deeply connected to the mother but also "outward looking" from the beginning.

Two other self psychologists, Beatrice Beebe and Frank Lachmann (1994), have formulated their theories about the structuralization of the self. They have been profoundly influenced by the research that shows that what infants remember are interactions. They have developed "three principles of salience" that describe how internalization, representation, and structuralization begin in infancy. They name these principles "ongoing regulations," "disruption and repair of ongoing regulations," and "heightened affective moments." They believe these experiences both in childhood development and in therapy are the stimuli for the developing of psychic structure.

Although they began as self psychologists Beebe and Lachmann have been joined by other theoreticians such as Robert Stolorow and George Atwood and have moved on to the study of intersubjectivity, which they describe as a metatheory—a metatheory because the idea that human beings always co-construct their relationships can be applied to any clinical theory or treatment model. As Lessem (2005) says, "It is as not as much a theory as a sensibility" (p. 173). Orange, Atwood, and Stolorow (1997), three of the major creators of this theory, describe it thus: "[I]t is an attitude of continuing sensitivity to the inescapable interplay of observer and observed. It assumes that instead of entering and immersing ourselves in the experience of another (the position of self psychology), we join the other in the intersubjective space" (p. 9). It is based on the concept of "the intersubjective field," which will be discussed more fully in the chapter on relational theory (chapter 9).

A CRITIQUE OF SELF-PSYCHOLOGY IN ITS SOCIAL CONTEXT

Like most other psychodynamic theories, self-psychology does not pay much attention to specific issues of race, class, culture, gender development, sexual orientation, or even biology. That having been said, it must be noted that self psychology has been well received by those with feminist, gay and lesbian, and sociocultural concerns. One reason for this is that mental health is defined by the subjective experience of well-being, cohesion, and vigor within the individual self. In the self psychological model, for instance, heterosexuality is not held out to be any more healthy than homosexuality. The goal of sexual development is for everyone to become more fully and vibrantly who they believe and experience themselves to be at any given point in time. This is a construct that allows greater fluidity in this area than many of the other theories, which postulate much more fixed psychosexual stages and outcomes.

For many feminists, self psychological theory is welcome because it broadens the parenting role to include fathers and all significant others. Kohut did not believe in the existence of a symbiotic phase between mother and infant and, unlike Winnicott, did not think mothers have to regress to form attachments with their babies. Thus, aspects of the mother-child bond become demystified, less sacred and magical, and more available to any person in the baby's life with parenting skills.

The oedipal drama is also reformulated in significant ways. It is seen as less of a drama and it is not necessarily a time filled with desire, competition, acquiescence, loss, guilt, or fears of revenge. For self psychologists the story can be one of joyful self-discovery. Having people of different genders to love and be loved by and to identify with is seen as offering wonderful opportunities rather than painful choices.

The impact of sociocultural factors can also be easily folded into self psychological theory. It can be used to understand the suffering to the self caused by social ills. Groups that are oppressed can be seen as suffering from selfobject failures on the part of society. People of color, the poor, many women, homosexuals, the disabled—to name a few groups—are rarely mirrored for their special qualities and their talents and often do not have good, strong, calm role models to idealize and merge with. Hence, society, when it is oppressive, can be seen as a selfobject that has tremendous power to destroy and that often contributes to a lack of self cohesion. There are a growing number of opportunities for twinship experiences in grassroots organizations and support groups, but, for some young people, the only twinship opportunities ever offered may tragically be on the street in gangs. A thorough understanding of the selfobject needs of the tripartite self would be a sound beginning in the formulation of better mental health and social policies as well as better clinical skills.

Some critiques of self psychology center precisely on the fact that the theory places such a high value on individual development. Although such a value fits snugly with certain aspects of current American culture, it is certainly not espoused by all cultures. There are many other constructs that place the good of the group or the community far above the good of the individual. In such cultures, the mirroring of individual qualities would be seen as far less important than teaching individuals what they have to sacrifice in themselves for the benefit of the community.

Another critique of self psychology focuses on its belief about the nature of the human condition, which it sees as basically tragic. There is great compassion in the theory for the vulnerability and neediness of the human infant but for some this is too passive and empty a vision of what it means to be and to become a person. Self psychology does not seem comprehensive and complex enough to those who believe that there are innate negative and destructive forces within people that need to be acknowledged and worked with, and who still want to look at the important role that guilt plays in the range of experiences to be understood. While self psychology suggests that pathologies arise from deficits in the environment, it has been critiqued for neglecting the intrapsychic conflicts *within* human beings. Some clinicians feel that self psychology does little to address the pain of those struggling with more innate affective instability, rage, and darkness. Attunement does not always soothe the soul.

Current postmodern clinicians who are interested in developing a vigorous two-person psychology, fully co-constructed by client and therapist, find self psychology to be too much of a one-person psychology. Although much of the work of a self psychologically informed treatment takes place in the narcissistic transferences, thereby paying a great deal of attention to the therapeutic relationship, critics of the theory find that there still exists too much of a distinction between the empathic, attuned, giving therapist and the injured, needy, passive, receptive client.

Nevertheless, despite what some see as its flaws or shortcomings, self psychology has made an enormous contribution to psychodynamic theory. Even those who do not see it as a comprehensive theory often make use of its concepts in their clinical work and find themselves enriched in their capacity for attunement and empathy.

CONCLUSION

What then does self psychology contribute to our knowledge of human psychological development? Self psychology offers a particular view of human nature and therefore of development. It offers new beliefs about the structure of the self. It offers a way of conducting treatment based on empathic attunement to selfobject needs. Self psychology posits that the achievement of a cohesive, well-regulated, empathic, and vigorous self is the goal of all psychological development. The health and well-being of the self derives from empathic attunement on the part of selfobjects, as well as the working through of empathic failures. According to self psychologists, the self is tripartite, with each part of the self having specific selfobject needs. The grandiose part of the self needs mirroring. The idealized part of the self needs wonderful people and things with which to merge. The twinship part needs to experience others as similar in order to recognize oneself in another and to be comforted. Qualities and functions of selfobjects are taken in by the process of transmuting internalizations; these then help the self grow strong and whole, enjoying a sense of genuineness, authenticity, and individuality.

In the absence of, or through excessive disappointments with, selfobjects we all experience difficulties with healthy self-regard, with ambitions, values, or goals. In the absence of mirroring selfobjects, there may be difficulty recognizing and valuing the self and valuing others. In the absence of a strong other with whom to merge, there may be a sense of frailness and emotional vulnerability. In the absence of twinship experiences, there can be difficulties in achieving a sense of connectedness.

As is true in object relations theory, empathic failures are necessary and are inevitable. Self psychology provides us with a way to learn about how selfobjects were or were not available to perform self functions. Self psychology provides a new lens to help us understand empathy's potential to promote emotional growth in the present. Self psychology offers a way of understanding not only what was missing, but what can be provided via new relationships (therapeutic and other) to make healing and growth possible. It is very much a theory of how the "outside" affects the "inside" and how the inside grows into selfhood. As with all of the psychodynamic theories there are clinicians who rely primarily or solely on self psychology to inform their treatment. We prefer to think of self psychology as one more useful lens to help us look into the experiences and struggles of another. It is a particularly useful lens for the many moments in therapy when clients come to us not so much with conflicts, or deficits in ego functions, or impaired self- and object-representations, but rather with unmet needs in mirroring, idealization, and twinship.

REFERENCES

American Psychiatric Association. (2000). *Diagnostic and Statistical Manual of Mental Disorders*, 4th edition, Text Revision. Washington, DC: American Psychiatric Association.

Beebe, B., and Lachmann, F. (1994). Representation and internalization in infancy: Three principles of salience. *Psychoanalytic Psychology* 11:127-65.

Blanck, G., and Blanck, R. (1979). *Ego Psychology II: Psychoanalytic Developmental Psychology*. New York: Columbia University Press.

Chessick, R. (1993). *A Dictionary for Psychotherapists*. Northvale, NJ: Jason Aronson.

Cocks, G. (1994). *The Curve of Life: The Correspondence of Heinz Kohut, 1923–1981*. Chicago: Chicago University Press.

Edmundson, M. (2001). I'm O.K., and then some. Review of C. B. Strozier, *Heinz Kohut: The Making of a Psychoanalyst*. *New York Times* on the Web, June 3, 2001.

Elson, M. (1986). *Self Psychology in Clinical Social Work*. New York: Norton.

Erikson, E. (1950). *Childhood and Society*. New York: Norton.

Fonagy, P. (2001). *Attachment Theory and Psychoanalysis*. New York: Other Press.

Freud, S. (1914). On narcissism: An introduction. *Standard Edition* 14:67–104.

Kohut, H. (1971). *The Analysis of the Self*. New York: International Universities Press.

———. (1977). *Restoration of the Self*. New York: International Universities Press.

———. (1978). *The Search for the Self*. New York: International Universities Press.

———. (1984). *How Does Analysis Cure?* Chicago: University of Chicago Press.

Kohut, H., and Wolf, E. (1978). The disorders of the self and their treatment: An outline. *International Journal of Psycho-Analysis* 59:413–25.

Lasch, C. (1978). *The Culture of Narcissism*. New York: Norton.

Lessem, P. (2005). *Self Psychology: An Introduction*. New York: Jason Aronson.

Mitchell, S., and Black, M. (1995). *Freud and Beyond: a History of Modern Psychoanalytic Thought*. New York: Basic Books.

Modell, A. A. (1975). A narcissistic defense against affect and the illusion of self-sufficiency. *International Journal of Psycho-Analysis* 56:275–82.

Orange, D., Atwood, G., and Stolorow, R. (1997). *Working Intersubjectively: Contextualism in Psychoanalytic Practice*. Hillsdale, NJ: Analytic Press.

Pine, F. (1990). *Drive, Ego, Object and Self*. New York: Basic Books.

Preston, E. M. (1969). *I Hate It When . . .* New York: Viking.

Slap, J., and Levine, F. (1978). On hybrid concepts in psychoanalysis. *Psychoanalytic Quarterly* 47:499–523.

Stern, D. (1985). *The Interpersonal World of the Infant*. New York: Basic Books.

Webster's Third New International Dictionary. (1963). Springfield, MA: G. & C. Merriam Company.

8

Attachment Theory

Robert Shilkret and Cynthia Shilkret

Unlike many of the chapters in this volume, which deal with theories that were formulated for psychotherapy practice, attachment theory began and still is primarily a theory of development, perhaps the most widely studied and influential developmental theory of the second half of the twentieth century. It has been very influential in several aspects of clinical work and attachment ideas and findings that are clinically relevant are emphasized in this chapter. The theory sometimes seems difficult to teach clinicians because it was not developed as a theory of psychopathology or of clinical intervention. However, it has become relevant in several ways for clinicians, as it has been applied to difficulties in interpersonal relationships throughout the lifespan. We will emphasize the clinical importance of the theory in this chapter, while reviewing the basic propositions and findings of the theory.

BACKGROUND AND HISTORY OF ATTACHMENT THEORY

Attachment theory began in the middle of the twentieth century with the work of John Bowlby (1907–1990), a British psychoanalyst, and this approach was developed by Mary Ainsworth (1913–1999), an American psychologist. After graduating from Cambridge University in 1928, Bowlby volunteered at a school for maladjusted children. This experience, as well as his questions about the cool, distant parenting he had experienced himself, common in his culture and socioeconomic group, convinced him of the importance of early parenting experiences in the subsequent development of the child, and it set his professional course. He became a child psychiatrist and received psychoanalytic training at the British Psychoanalytic Institute. There he was supervised by Melanie Klein, who emphasized the role of fantasy, rather than reality, in children's difficulties. Bowlby had serious questions about Klein's lack of concern for the child's real world. In one case (Bretherton 1992), Klein forbade Bowlby to talk with the mother of a three-year-old child he had in treatment. Bowlby, upset by Klein's lack of attention to the child's real world, argued and showed with clinical case material that disturbed young children can be helped by working with their parents. While today this seems self-evident, ideas about the importance of the child's real experiences and the critical importance of their parents' interactions with them were scandalous in the British psychoanalytic community of the 1940s. The fact that they are so common today is largely a testament to the influence of Bowlby's and Ainsworth's work.

In his early work, Bowlby drew on evolutionary theory and work with animals. He noted, for example, the important work of ethologists such as Konrad Lorenz, who had studied the "imprinting" in newly hatched ducklings and goslings: shortly after hatching, they follow their mothers. Lorenz had shown that this very early behavior was a response to the particular speed (relatively slow) that the mother walked, and not due to the mother's shape, her odor, or other characteristics. The picture of Lorenz walking slowly around his laboratory followed by a line of ducklings, having been removed from their mother immediately after hatching and having imprinted on Lorenz instead, made him famous. Bowlby proposed that all complex organisms have an attachment system, one that is highly adaptive in that it keeps the young in close proximity to a critical older animal, and to whom the young seeks to return at times of danger.

But Bowlby's own work was not with animals; it was with much more complex human children. He wrote "Forty-Four Juvenile Thieves," documenting the affectionless character and antisocial behavior of a group of children at his clinic, which he related to earlier maternal deprivation and separation. World War II interrupted his career as a child psychiatrist; instead, he was assigned to a research group studying officer selection criteria, and it was there that he learned research procedures. But the British Secret Service, long before attachment theory was developed, knew about at least one result of impaired attachments. When they needed to find men who could work behind enemy lines and engage in very violent behaviors such as cold-blooded murder of an enemy, they tried to find soldiers who had been raised in orphanages. These men were, it was known, likely to have few feelings for others, and little guilt or concern about the tasks they would be asked to do. Later, Bowlby and his colleagues would demonstrate the deleterious effects of orphanages, in that most of them met the social needs of children quite minimally if at all, and this work would be highly influential in the decline of the orphanage as a social institution, in favor of foster care.

Bowlby joined the Tavistock Clinic after World War II and continued his work with maladjusted children and teenagers and their families. In one of the most fortuitous partnerships in all of developmental and clinical psychology, Mary Salter Ainsworth was in London in 1950 and looking for a job, having completed her PhD at the University of Toronto with Blatz's "security theory," emphasizing the importance of early dependence on parents. Bowlby had advertised in the London newspapers for a research assistant, and Ainsworth, having followed her new husband to London, answered the ad. Ainsworth became the research partner Bowlby needed.

Following her husband again, Ainsworth, now in collaboration with Bowlby, found herself in Uganda, in east Africa, in the early 1950s. There she engaged in a major cross-cultural research project, which would become the first true attachment theory research. She studied twenty-six families with nursing infants by long home visits (with an interpreter) every two weeks for nine months. When this work was eventually published, it outlined the sequence of behaviors characterizing the development of attachment to a primary caretaker. Some of these infant/mother relationships were better than others. Security of the infants' attachment was correlated with mothers' sensitivity (that is, the mothers' degree of attunement to the infants' needs and their appropriate responses to those expressed needs). Less sensitive mothers had insecure babies. To this day, attachment theorists do not speak in terms of "strength" of attachments; rather, attachments are described in terms of their quality: secure or insecure. The insecure ones would soon be conceptualized as several subtypes. The function of attachment around the first birthday, particularly a secure attachment, seemed to give the infant a "secure base," from which she could move away from the mother and explore the environment.

Back in London, Bowlby's work continued with a talented group of colleagues. Particularly noteworthy was the work of James and Joyce Robertson, who studied the effects of mother-child separation. They addressed, for example, the question of what happens when a separation occurs after a secure attachment has formed. They studied maternal separations prompted by the hospitalization of a mother for the birth of a second child. Earlier work had shown the deleterious effects of long hospitalizations on children themselves. For example, Rene Spitz had published controversial work on depression in hospitalized children in the mid-1950s. The Robertsons extended this theme with graphic films of how infants cope or fail to cope when separated from mothers in infancy and early childhood. They argued, actually against Bowlby, that another sensitive adult could largely compensate for the negative effects of early mother-infant separation. They demonstrated this by taking infants into their own home for the nine- or ten-day hospitalizations that were then routine for childbirth. The famous film *John: Nine Days in a Residential Nursery* was part of this project. John's family rejected the Robertsons' offer to have John stay with them, but agreed to allow them to study John in the small orphanage in which they placed him, following their own pediatrician's advice. John graphically illustrated the sequence of protest/despair/detachment that Bowlby had outlined earlier. The deterioration of this securely attached, nondeprived seventeen-month-old was now not simply the word *trauma* on the printed page in a research or clinical report. The visible trauma of John's separation with no single stable figure to take his mother's place still upsets those who see it: John's protest in banging his cup and refusing to eat; his dismay when his father leaves; his increasingly disorganized behaviors with other children; his futile attempt to cuddle into the lap of a nurse; his weak, final cries of despair at his failure to find a stable substitute mother figure. This dramatic illustration of the effects of the trauma of early separation once attachment had formed and other work of the Robertsons became influential in shortening hospital stays for young children, and in allowing frequent parental visits and in having a parent stay with a child in the hospital.

After leaving Uganda in 1955, Mary Ainsworth settled in Baltimore, and soon divorced. Based at Johns Hopkins University (eventually, she would move to the University of Virginia, where she completed her career), she conducted a second large-scale longitudinal (same participants observed over time) attachment study. The Baltimore Project, like the Uganda work, involved twenty-six families, who were now recruited prenatally. She and a team of research colleagues conducted eighteen four-hour home visits during the infants' first year, recording many aspects of mother/infant interaction for subsequent analysis. Thus, the original attachment research involved detailed, home-based observations of mother-infant behavior during the first year, one group from Uganda, another from the United States.

The basic attachment findings were that attachment, now defined as "proximity seeking" by the infant toward the mother or other primary caregiver, develops rapidly during ages six to twelve months. It is preceded by differential behaviors toward the primary caregiver (e.g., smiling and vocalizing more toward the mother than toward others). By the first birthday, attachment could be demonstrated; all infants were shown to develop some kind of attachment to a caregiver, even those with rejecting or neglectful mothers. Research soon followed from other investigators showing that attachments could form toward fathers even when mothers were the primary caregivers if the father had had some role in the infant's early experience. A small number of such attachments could form by the first year, but one secure one would be sufficient for optimal development. Later work showed that adoptive parents of all kinds could produce securely attached infants if their caregiving was sufficiently attuned to the infant's changing needs.

ATTACHMENTS: SECURE AND INSECURE

During the Baltimore study, Mary Ainsworth and her team, almost as an afterthought, wanted a quick way in the laboratory to confirm the quality of mother-infant interactions they were observing in the homes. They designed a half-hour procedure, the Strange Situation, which did confirm what they found in their home observations and became one of the most widely used procedures in developmental research. In the Strange Situation procedure, mother and infant come to a comfortably furnished room with several toys scattered about. They are joined by a friendly female. The novel room, toys, and new person are "strange" to the year-old infant, and the experience typically is mildly anxiety arousing for such a young child. The mother leaves the stranger and infant alone for a few minutes, then returns for awhile. There are a few more comings and goings, each for a few minutes. It is all observed. A securely attached infant at this age typically becomes upset, often crying when the mother leaves. One of the most important things Mary Ainsworth taught us was that, as important as the infant's reaction to the mother's leaving is, even more important is how the infant responds to the mother's return. A secure attachment is marked by the upset infant's welcome of the mother's return and his use of the mother to calm down and to begin to explore the novel environment at her encouragement. Thus, it is a developmental milestone at this age for the infant to be upset by the mother's leaving in a strange environment. This would not happen at home, where the environment is familiar and the caregiver's coming and going is routine. But the quality of the overall interaction is quite similar between home and laboratory. An older child, even a two-year-old, would not respond like this; an older securely attached child would not be as bothered by the mother's brief absence. Thus, the Strange Situation procedure is appropriate only for infants from twelve to eighteen months.

In Ainsworth's families, replicated in many subsequent samples, about two-thirds of the infants were securely attached. Of the one-third insecure attachments, Ainsworth differentiated two types. "Avoidant" infants did not protest their mother's leaving and did not respond to her immediately upon her return. At an earlier time, some critics thought these infants were prematurely independent, and not insecure at all. But they typically had later difficulties in preschool, often acting out against peers. Further physiological studies demonstrated that avoidant infants in the Strange Situation had biological markers of anxiety higher even than the overtly upset secure infants when their mothers left. Ainsworth's second type of insecurity, "ambivalent" infants (also called resistant) also were upset when their mothers left and seemed to welcome their return, but did not calm down readily and they often resisted their mother's attempts to calm them. For ambivalent infants, clinginess alternated with anger. Of these two types of insecurity in infancy, in American samples avoidance is more frequent than ambivalence. This asymmetry of the frequency of different types of insecure attachments is different in other cultures, to be discussed later.

Bowlby and Ainsworth did not think that the differences in attachment styles observed for life's first relationships were simply a catalog of interesting and important behavioral differences in infancy. They proposed that the earliest attachment styles (and an infant can form a small number of attachments, as noted earlier) become the basis of "internal working models" of attachment (IWMs), which are internal templates or schemas of interactions, defining the expectations of infant and young child of what close relationships are like. In later childhood, adolescence, and adulthood, these IWMs, significant parts of which function unconsciously, determine interpersonal expectations and behavior, especially with important people in one's life—one's friends, lovers, children, teachers, bosses, therapists.

Mary Main (1995), a student of Mary Ainsworth, extended the IWM idea through adult life. She developed the Adult Attachment Interview (AAI) for assessment of attachment styles in adolescence and adulthood, corresponding to the Strange Situation for assessment of attachment in infancy. The AAI is a clinically sensitive semistructured interview, inquiring about important attachment figures, instances of separation, and how earlier attachments influenced later development. Main identified adult attachment styles corresponding to Ainsworth's categories: "Secure" adults are clear, consistent, and relatively succinct in their descriptions of their histories of close relationships; they are not defensive and when they are angry, they are not overwhelmed by anger. This is not to say that secure attachment cannot be preceded by considerable trauma; but a secure resolution involves the ability to discuss such trauma calmly with some attempt to understand it.

In contrast, "dismissing" adults (corresponding to Ainsworth's avoidant infant attachments) remember little about early attachments, minimize their importance, often are superficial and contradictory within the interview, and may idealize their parents.

Ed, a working-class Irish-American in his late twenties, entered therapy because his wife had an affair. He wanted to decide whether or not to end the marriage. In therapy he focused on her behavior as he struggled to make a decision. The therapist's attempts to connect this decision to other psychologically relevant material were politely ignored. He denied that his numerous dreams had any meaning, and he also denied that his family history was relevant even though he mentioned that his father had had numerous affairs. When he did discuss his early life he usually emphasized how independent he was as a child. He presented memories in an upbeat way no matter what the content. For example, he reported approvingly that his mother was a no-nonsense, "get on with business" type of person. He remembered one time when he was about seven years old. He came home from school upset because the teacher had criticized him. He was looking for comfort by following his mother around as she cleaned the house. She finally got annoyed and said, "Just get over it and stop following me."

Ed's memory of this interaction with his mother suggests that he developed an avoidant attachment style as an infant to enhance his attachment to a mother who had little tolerance for displays of neediness. As an adult in therapy he enacted his dismissing style with the therapist, minimizing the affective impact of her comments. Knowing Ed's attachment style helped the therapist to understand that he was not uninterested in the therapy; rather, he was attached to her in the way that had worked best with his mother earlier. The therapist had to tolerate Ed's minimization of their relationship as he slowly increased his ability to tolerate feelings of dependence.

The dismissing form of insecurity is distinguished from "preoccupied" adults (an adult version of Ainsworth's ambivalent infants), who dwell on early childhood conflicts without resolving them; they are often angry and preoccupied with earlier and/or current attachment figures.

Anna, the forty-year-old daughter of Italian immigrants, began therapy by presenting herself as desperate for the therapist's help. Her husband was threatening to leave her because he could no longer tolerate her treatment of him. Sometimes she would go out with her friends after work without even calling him, while at other times she would get very upset if he did not want to stay at home with her. In therapy she found it difficult to discuss anything other than the way everyone mistreated her. The therapy was marked by frequent demands that she needed immediate answers to her problems but she was rarely satisfied with any suggestions that the therapist made. Anna described a volatile and chaotic family life. When not focused on her own problems, her mother was usually overcontrolling. Her parents fought constantly and sometimes violently and this was frightening for the children. When the parents were fighting, her mother typically ignored Anna's increasing upset until Anna began to sob hysterically. Her mother would then try to calm her, but by that point Anna felt quite out of control and was hard to soothe.

Anna's early experience of inconsistent mothering resulted in the development of a preoccupied attachment style as an adult. As a young child she could not be sure that her mother would be consistently available and so she had to intensify her upset to be sure she truly had her mother's attention. As an adult in therapy she enacted her preoccupied attachment style to be sure of holding her therapist's attention. The therapist often felt barraged and burdened by Anna's demands. Understanding Anna's preoccupied attachment style helped the therapist to recognize that Anna did not believe that the therapist would remain a consistent attachment figure unless she exaggerated her suffering. That understanding helped the therapist to worry less about Anna's demands.

Mary Main also reanalyzed Ainsworth's Baltimore results and articulated a fourth infant category, called "disorganized" attachment, for the small percentage of those who were unclassifiable in Ainsworth's original system. These infants showed the absence of a consistent strategy to deal with anxiety about separations. Only about 5 percent of the sample was so classified, but these were infants who were quite worrisome. Sometimes, obviously upset, they would approach their mothers but freeze midway toward them, appearing frightened. Other times, they might demonstrate equally puzzling behavior, such as moving in a very slow manner, as if underwater. Because these infants behaved in these unusual ways only under stress, they were given a secondary classification (e.g., disorganized/avoidant) to describe their attachment behaviors more fully. Main also found a similarly small group of "unresolved/disorganized" adults from her AAI assessments. Such adults showed episodes of extreme disorganization in their discussion of early trauma or a recent upset, in the context of an interview that might also be characterized as generally conforming to one of the other styles.

> Grace, a middle-class white lesbian, came to therapy because she was very depressed about her inability to develop a stable relationship with a partner. She was able to discuss her family history in a general way. However, when asked for details about specific family interactions, she often became vague and confusing and was frequently unable to remember events even if they had happened the previous week. Sometimes, as she tried to recall events, she felt increasingly frightened in the session and she did not know why. She often appeared to fall asleep in the sessions. Occasionally she reported strange bodily sensations during a session, such as the feeling that her body was changing size and floating away. After a very long period of not being able to remember many details of her early life, Grace began to recall that her mother had been seriously depressed for much of her childhood. Her mother left Grace in the care of the maid, and on the maid's day off her mother did not seem to know what to do with her. If Grace got upset or had a tantrum, her mother stood by helplessly and did nothing. Grace remembered long periods of being alone.

Grace's difficulties in forming stable relationships and her extreme fearfulness in therapy suggested an early history of inadequate attachment figures.

Her mother had been unavailable due to her severe depression, and the maid, although caring for her physical needs, was not an adequate substitute. Because she had not been able to develop a consistent attachment style, relationships were frightening and mystifying. As Grace alternated between different affect states, her therapist often felt confused and very worried, unsure of what would be most helpful for her. Understanding Grace's disorganized attachment history enabled her therapist to master her own uncertainties and to stay calm in the sessions; her consistency countered Grace's experiences with her frighteningly unavailable mother.

What about Ed's, Anna's, and Grace's developmental continuities? What is the correspondence more generally between the earliest attachments and subsequent adult attachment? There are several large-scale longitudinal samples now, and the concordance, or degree of correspondence, is in the 70–80 percent range, which is quite impressive. This is understood in terms of continuity of care; the parent who is attuned (or misattuned) to the infant is likely to be similarly attuned (or not) to the older child and adolescent. Studies of the 20–30 percent lack of correspondence of attachment style over development have shown that insecure attachments might be improved (and the move from earlier insecurity to later security is called "earned security") by (1) an advantageous change in parenting (e.g., divorce in a high-conflict family, marriage of a beleaguered single parent to a caring new partner); (2) introduction of a helpful other, such as a concerned family member, teacher, or clergy person; (3) psychotherapy. Likewise, the converse change (secure to insecure) can occur by trauma (e.g., the Robertsons' "John") or other deleterious change in parenting. But the majority of cases demonstrate attachment continuity across the lifespan.

Continuity is also influenced by the peers and adults a child or adult encounters. Particular behavior toward others evokes responses that often recapitulate earlier attachment patterns. For example, relationships with child care workers and later with teachers are consistent with earlier relationships with parents (Howes 2000).

Another kind of developmental continuity is the intergenerational transmission of attachment patterns from parents to children and beyond. Mary Main's original AAI study of adult attachment was done with first-time mothers. Their infants were assessed independently by the Strange Situation, and the degree of correspondence between mothers' and infants' attachment styles was quite high. Several other studies have confirmed this intergenerational correspondence (in the 70–80 percent range), even when mother's attachment status is assessed prenatally.

Attachment researchers are loath to regard insecurity, especially in infancy, as a "diagnosis" in itself. Rather, insecurity is seen as an exquisite adaptation to a particular history of parenting experiences, and it is formed by the end of the first year. Avoidant infants typically have primary caregivers who have a great deal of difficulty with dependency themselves, due to their own attachment histories. These parents do not like "lap babies"; they discourage, even punish, crying and other expressions of dependence. By one year, their infants have developed a striking capacity to inhibit their expression of distress.

Yet, why should avoidance be considered an attachment at all? Recall Ainsworth's original definition of attachment in terms of proximity seeking in infancy. The avoidant adaptation keeps a parent who does not like dependency as close as possible. These are not necessarily neglectful parents; they are often quite responsive to independence bids by the child. For example, Ed's mother (discussed previously) was an adequate mother in many ways. She cared about her children and proudly recounted their successes. However, she was consistently disapproving of "weak" emotions such as sadness, neediness, or dependency.

In contrast with the avoidant infant, the ambivalent infant typically has a parent who is inconsistent in her or his responses, generally, and sometimes quite chaotic. But this parent is more consistent in response to overtly expressed dependency needs (e.g., crying), although the intervention might be quite ineffective in calming the infant due to a lack of attunement. This infant's ambivalence in the Strange Situation directly follows from this history. The ambivalent infant may cry bitterly but is unsure she can be comforted by the parent's ministrations. She appears to want comfort, but may arch away when her parent makes an attempt to calm her. For example, Anna, the preoccupied client discussed earlier, reported that her mother was not always neglectful, but was caught up in her own dramas with Anna's father. She did respond to Anna's crying, but by the time she did, both mother and daughter were so tense and upset that Anna did not feel soothed.

Another reason why early insecure attachment is not seen as a diagnosis (but may be regarded as a risk factor) is that so much can change with a young infant over time. We know now the kinds of things likely to reduce insecurity, and, it is assumed, later difficulties. Disorganized attachment, on the other hand, is regarded as a matter of serious concern (similar to a diagnosis) in itself, because it is so clearly maladaptive. Recent studies have shown that disorganized attachment styles often develop under two surprisingly different circumstances: (1) when there is serious abuse or neglect; or, (2) when a parent appears to be afraid of the child or of imagined environmental dangers and conveys this fear and sense of danger in her caregiving (see Cassidy and Mohr 2001). Grace (the client with the disorganized attachment style, discussed previously) was not abused or physically neglected. However, her mother's inability to respond to Grace, as a result of her own severe depression, conveyed to Grace that her mother was afraid of being attached to her. That left Grace unable to find a safe attachment style to connect with her mother, and it left her fearful of attachments in general.

Another early criticism of attachment theory (before the infant adaptations to differential parenting experiences were fully articulated) was that attachment was a developmental consequence of biological differences at birth (called temperament). There are several kinds of evidence that have addressed this alternative hypothesis. For one thing, a child often has different attachments to different adults, even secure ones along with insecure ones, depending on differences between multiple caregivers. Most parenting couples are similar in their parenting styles, but a significant minority are not, and it is from those that we know about this kind of complexity. These different attachments suggest that attachment is not determined by temperament and that parenting can override differences in temperament.

A strikingly convincing study addressed this issue in the favor of the attachment explanation—that is, in terms of experiences after birth rather than inborn temperament. Dymphna van den Boom (1994) performed a critical experiment with 100 "difficult" infants, that is, infants who cry easily and are difficult to calm. (This was a heroic study in that it took her several hundred infant assessments to find this sample.) These were the very infants that the temperament hypothesis would expect to develop insecure attachments at one year and beyond. Half the infant/mother pairs (the control group) were left alone, with infant Strange Situation assessments done at one year. The other fifty infant/mother pairs received three interventions by van den Boom herself after the sixth month, helping mothers respond more effectively with their difficult infants. The choice to begin intervening midway through the first year was quite deliberate. It is around then that all those infant social behaviors begin to get organized as a discriminating response system to one or a small number of caregivers. Further, after six months with a difficult infant, the mothers were quite eager to receive help! The interventions were clinically sensitive, nonjudgmental, problem-solving sessions with each mother/infant pair. In the control group (no intervention), about two-thirds of the infants were insecure at one year. Note that if you stopped here, you might be tempted to conclude that the temperament hypothesis was valid: In everyday life, difficult infants *do* often end up insecurely attached, but, as it turns out, not primarily because of their temperament. In the intervention group, fully two-thirds were "secure," not insecure, at one year, a percentage no different from the population of infants at large. Thus, van den Boom demonstrated how to prevent what would likely have been many insecure attachments. The study has obvious implications for very early intervention policies as well as for the theoretical controversy it largely laid to rest.

There have been some findings showing specific psychopathological outcomes related to specific kinds of attachment styles among adolescents and adults. Borderline disorders have been related to disorganized attachment (see Cassidy and Mohr 2001, for further discussion). In a small group of hospitalized adolescents, Rosenstein and Horowitz (1996) found that those with dismissing attachments were more likely to have conduct or substance abuse disorders, narcissistic, or antisocial disorders, while those with preoccupied attachments were more likely to have affective disorders and obsessive-compulsive characteristics. This makes sense, in that dismissing attachment involves externalizing one's difficulties, whereas preoccupied attachment is characterized by a great deal of manifest anxiety and conflict. Virtually all of these hospitalized adolescents were insecurely attached, as were their mothers. But the relation between insecure attachment and diagnosis is far from one to one: There are many other insecurely attached adults who exhibit no consistent symptoms.

Although attachment theory is not a theory of psychotherapy, it has several implications for therapeutic practice. The AAI sensitizes clinicians to listen in a particular way to the descriptions clients give of their early attachments and current close relationships (see Main 1995, for a full description). Clients can be usefully seen in terms of their particular attachment styles in the therapeutic relationship. Clients with dismissing attachments minimize the importance of close relationships and see little relevance in discussing early history. In therapy, they may minimize the importance of the therapy itself and denigrate the therapist's comments. The therapist dealing with such a client may feel unimportant, even impotent. There are temptations to allow premature termination; short-term therapy may be all that is possible for some of these clients. In contrast, clients with preoccupied attachments may become preoccupied with the therapy, brooding over the meaning of the therapist's comments, vacillating between being overly needy and angrily defiant. Frequent countertransference reactions are the therapist's experiencing worry and frustration. (See Shilkret 2005, for a full discussion of transference and countertransference reactions characteristic of different attachment organizations, with several clinical examples.)

GENDER AND CULTURE

It may be surprising to some that in the many hundreds of studies of infant attachment there have been very few sex differences found. Boys and girls seem to develop insecure attachments at about the same rate (about one-third are insecure of one type or another at one year). Infants seem to develop their types of insecurities independent of their gender; that is, in American samples, there are often more avoidant insecure infants than ambivalent insecure infants, but this seems to be true both for boys and girls. This is understandable when one considers that the needs of the young infant are the same for both sexes—that is, all infants need a "good enough caregiver" for optimal development (and for secure attachment). It is also understandable when one considers that, while the parents' construction of gender begins at birth, developmentally the cultural imprint of gender really gets going somewhat after infancy.

It is more surprising, perhaps, then, that there are still few reports of gender differences in attachments of young children, older children, adolescents, and adults. The avoidant (dismissing) attachment might be expected to occur more among males and the ambivalent (preoccupied) attachment more among females. Perhaps the failure to find robust, well-replicated findings regarding gender differences in attachment speaks more to our stereotypes about gender than about real differences. There are a few reported gender differences in children, but these are subtle. For example, Turner (1991) found no differences between secure four-year-old boys and girls; but insecure attachment had different behavioral correlates for girls versus boys (e.g., insecure girls were more dependent; insecure boys showed off and boasted more). But even here, there were few gender differences in attachment styles themselves. The clinician, therefore, should be equally attuned to the possibility of any kind of attachment style in male and female clients.

Are attachment styles universal? Do the same kinds of attachment styles and distributions of attachment styles arise in cultures with different kinds of childrearing and differing expectations and values for children? Might what is considered insecure in Western culture be considered secure in some other? As usual with this kind of question, it is far easier to speculate about or imagine cultural differences than to demonstrate them. There have been a moderate number of attachment investigations in other cultures, and generalizations are difficult. Still, in many different cultures, the basic finding of about two-thirds of secure attachments in infancy and beyond has held. Mothers from cultures with different values, when asked which of the three types of infant they would prefer (Ainsworth's original secure, avoidant, and ambivalent), typically choose the "secure" description.

Nonetheless, there have been intriguing findings regarding more subtle differences in types of insecurity in different cultures. Consider the avoidant/ambivalent distinction as a continuum. Many Western cultures value independence (avoidance) more than dependence (ambivalence); some cultures have the opposite value. For example, in Western cultures that value independence and autonomy, it is not surprising that we find more avoidance than ambivalence among insecure attachments. In northern Germany, independence is valued even more than in American culture, and there seem to be even more avoidant attachments there (Grossman, Grossman et al. 1985). The Israeli kibbutz, in contrast, values interdependence, especially among the peer group, over independence and autonomy. The attachments of kibbutz-raised infants and children have typically found few, if any, avoidant attachments; nearly all the insecurity seems to be of the ambivalent type (e.g., Sagi et al. 1994). And it has been found that the peer group itself serves as an object of attachment in the kibbutz (Weiss and Shilkret 2005). Another culture that values interdependence more than Western culture is the traditional Japanese one; in childrearing, great value is placed on the mother's anticipation of the infant's needs and early response. When insecurity occurs, it is much more likely to be of the fussy, irritable sort characteristic of the ambivalent infant than the aloof avoidant one. Whether this supports attachment theory or questions it is currently a matter of healthy debate (Rothbaum, Weisz, et al. 2000; Rothbaum et al. 2001).

Attachment theorists tend to emphasize the universals of development; their critics emphasize cultural specificity. The fact is that there are still comparatively few large-scale attachment studies of a wide range of cultures, and this is still a "growing point" of attachment research. For the clinician, it is quite useful to know about differences in childrearing and different values that parents have for their children. What an adolescent might consider parental intrusiveness in American society might well be considered appropriate concern in some other part of the world, as well as in some subcultures in the United States.

In concluding, it is useful to recall where we have come in the past 100 years. Sigmund Freud, in his earliest psychoanalytic writings over a century ago, assumed the importance of early experience for personality development, both adaptive and maladaptive. But Freud did not observe young children systematically, and his speculations about them remained unpersuasive to many. It is an extraordinary irony that John Bowlby, reacting against his psychoanalytic training, began the program of work that by the end of the century had moved the idea of the importance of early parenting experience out of the realm of speculation onto the firm ground of demonstrated fact, thereby confirming one of Freud's earliest assumptions.

REFERENCES

Bretherton, I. (1992). The origins of attachment theory: John Bowlby and Mary Ainsworth. *Developmental Psychology* 28:759–75.

Cassidy, J., and Mohr, J. J. (2001). Unsolvable fear, trauma, and psychopathology: Theory, research, and clinical considerations related to disorganized attachments across the life span. *Clinical Psychology: Science and Practice* 8:275–98.

Grossman, K., Grossman, K. E., Spangler, G., Suess, G., and Unzer, J. (1985). Maternal sensitivity and newborns' orientation responses as related to quality of attachment in northern Germany. In *Growing Points in Attachment Theory and Research. Monographs of the Society for Research in Child Development* 50 (Serial No. 209), ed. I. Bretherton and E. Waters, pp. 233–56.

Howes, C. (2000). Attachment relationships in the context of multiple caregivers. In *Handbook of Attachment: Theory, Research, and Clinical Applications*, ed. J. Cassidy and P. R. Shaver, pp. 671–87. New York: Guilford.

Main, M. (1995). Discourse, prediction, and recent studies in attachment: Implications for psychoanalysis. In *Research in Psychoanalysis: Process, Development, Outcome*, ed. Shapiro and Emde, pp. 209–44. New York: International Universities Press.

Rosenstein, D. S., and Horowitz, H. A. (1996). Adolescent attachment and psychopathology. *Journal of Consulting and Clinical Psychology* 64:244–53.

Rothbaum, F., et al. (2001). Comments and a rejoinder. *American Psychologist* 56:821–29.

Rothbaum, F., Weisz, J., Pott, M., Miyake, K., and Morelli, G. (2000). Attachment and culture: Security in the United States and Japan. *American Psychologist* 55:1093–1104.

Sagi, A., Donnell, F., van IJzendoorn, M. H., Mayseless, O., and Aviezer, O. (1994). Sleeping out of home in a kibbutz communal arrangement: It makes a difference for infant-mother attachment. *Child Development* 65:992–1004.

Shilkret, C. J. (2005). Some clinical applications of attachment theory in adult psychotherapy. *Clinical Social Work Journal* 33:55–68.

Turner, P. T. (1991). Relations between attachment, gender, and behavior with peers in preschool. *Child Development* 62:1475–88.

van den Boom, D. (1994). The influence of temperament and mothering on attachment and exploration: An experimental manipulation of sensitive responsiveness among lower-class mothers with irritable infants. *Child Development* 65:1457–77.

Weiss, Y., and Shilkret, R. (2005). "The importance of the peer group in the Israeli kibbutz for the development of adult attachment style." Poster presented at Biennial Meeting of the Society for Research in Child Development, Atlanta, GA, April, 2005.

SUGGESTIONS FOR FURTHER READING

The best single book-length source for the clinician on attachment theory, research, and clinical implications is: Karen, R. (1998). *Becoming Attached: First Relationships and How They Shape Our Capacity to Love*. New York: Oxford.

The fullest treatment of attachment research, including relations to psychopathology and other clinical issues is: Cassidy, J., and Shaver, P. R., eds. (2000). *Handbook of Attachment: Theory, Research, and Clinical Applications*. New York: Guilford.

9

Relational Theory

Inside Out, Outside In, In-Between, and All Around

Martha Hadley

Relational theory, as it has emerged over the last twenty years, began with the recognition that a number of theories—object relations and interpersonal theories, self psychology, feminist and attachment theories, as well as other humanistic approaches—share an underlying relational perspective. The perspective they share is that we are born oriented to and seeking interaction with others. We come to experience and know ourselves in relationships with caretakers and families within particular social worlds and cultures. The "relational tradition" has emerged as a blend of and a discourse between theories and individuals and theories sharing a relational perspective on furthering the development of clinical work and, more generally, on the human condition.

What makes relational theory distinct from theories from which it developed? Clinical work between a therapist and client or in a group is inherently relational, but not all clinical approaches theorize about human relatedness or make it the focus of their practice and thinking about helping people to change in a therapeutic interaction. Further, clinical work always occurs in a social and cultural context, but not all psychodynamic theories consider self and other, clinician and client, and the experience they construct together in social context. Relational theory focuses on studying relatedness in context and makes this integral to a theory of practice. It views the self as more fluid than fixed, and as shaped in interaction relative to social or interpersonal settings and backgrounds.

> Embeddedness is endemic to human experience. I become the person I am in interaction with specific others. The way I feel it necessary to be with them is the person I take myself to be. That self organization becomes my nature. (Mitchell 1988, p. 276)

What initiated the development of relational theory? A shared perspective about the nature of human experience is only part of the story. As we will see, the milieu of psychodynamic ideas during the late twentieth century and the wider social/historical era in which relational theory developed were essential to the development of relational theory as a psychodynamic "sub-culture." The "relational tradition" has emerged as a blend of and discourse between these theories that, despite differences, share this perspective.

In order to set the stage and briefly review what you already know, consider the field of psychodynamic theory and practice during the late 1970s and 1980s in the United States. Many clinicians continued to practice using a classical or ego psychological model (chapters 2 and 4), others practiced using an object relations theory orientation (chapter 6), including the work of Klein, Winnicott, Fairbairn, Balint, Guntrip, Bion from Great Britain, and Kernberg from the United States. Kohut's self psychology (chapter 7) had provided a new lens and approach for many clinicians in the late 1970s and 1980s in the United States. Along the way, the growing body of work on attachment theory (chapter 8) and infancy research influenced the thinking of many clinicians, as did the work of humanistic and existential psychologists, family systems, and a number of feminist theorists. By the end of the twentieth century, the world of clinical theory, both psychodynamic and otherwise, was a rich collection of many different perspectives and approaches.

It was at this historical moment, in the mid- to late 1980s, that psychodynamically trained clinicians began to reflect on the range of theories and approaches to practice that were part of our clinical tradition. They began to ask critical questions about what these approaches had in common and how they differed, about the ways that they could be understood as building on each other, as compatible with and even as complementary to one another. These reflections were not about what is good or bad, what works or doesn't, but rather about deconstructing underlying principles or assumptions of theory and practice. It was a time when many people in different disciplines were asking questions about how we know what we know, and how assumptions about gender, race, or class influence the ways people think and behave, just as the language and categories we use shape our thinking. Psychodynamic clinicians from different backgrounds joined in this postmodern questioning and reflection.

At the center of this critique and discussion were several key topics:

- The importance of considering the experience and subjectivity of both the client/patient and the therapist as they influence each other. (We will elaborate later on this "two-person model" and other issues.)
- The nature of the space or interpersonal field between therapist and client, and the ways that therapist and client co-construct experiences together that can be reflected upon in order to further understanding and growth.
- A more fluid and complex conception of the self; a self influenced by changes in relationships and other contingencies throughout a person's life.
- The profound and inescapable impact of context, culture, race, gender, and class on human experiences, aspects that need to be acknowledged and deconstructed in our work with clients as well as in our theories.
- Following from the above, a recognition of the inherently social nature of the mind. This has implications for thinking about mind in social, interpersonal, as well as intrapsychic terms.

The dialogue about these and related topics varied depending on who was involved in the conversation. For several leaders in this dialogue, it was about integrating the more active engagement of interpersonal theory— with its emphasis on dynamics in the room between people—with ideas about the development of complex internal worlds from object relations theories. Others were invested in finding an alternative to drive and ego psychology, and their conversations tended to push away from the classical views and find an alternative in the relational approach. Still others were eager to explore and theorize about the implications of bringing social, racial, and gender issues into our understanding of the clinical dyad. Others found an opportunity in relational theorizing to explore topics like trauma, dissociation, agency, and aggression from new perspectives. Although they often had different agendas, most of the clinicians who have engaged in this dialogue, regardless of their original training, came to describe themselves as "relational." They have revisited ideas that we have explored in earlier chapters (projective identification, the role of the self object, transference and countertransference, oedipal dynamics, and many more), have challenged familiar assumptions, and have suggested new ways of theorizing about these ideas. They have had a lot to say about the nature of clinical relationships, and have theorized extensively about practice from a relational perspective.

In order to engage in this relational dialogue, consider the issues listed above as they might relate to any one of the theoretical approaches you have read about. For example, how might classical drive theorists think about a clinician's influence on an enactment in which both the client's and the therapist's own histories, cultural identities, and current behavior contribute? How might a clinician, trained as a Kleinian or a self psychologist, think about cultural or racial differences as they are woven into the interactions of therapist and client? Clinicians from these backgrounds and many others have tried to theorize about these complex dynamics. For many, it has meant change and growth in their views and work. The discussions over the last few decades have often been lively. Posing such questions has opened up a space for and an interest in meaningful dialogues that reflects the concerns of the era in which we live.

THE ORIGINS AND DEVELOPMENT OF RELATIONAL THEORY: NEW WAYS OF LOOKING AT FAMILIAR IDEAS, OR OPENING A SPACE FOR A DIFFERENT APPROACH TO THEORY AND PRACTICE?

The "relational turn" in psychodynamic theory began, then, with a review and critique of existing clinical theory. From this project a framework was developed that focused on self and other, therapist and client, and the interaction constructed between them. Using this framework, it was possible to acknowledge, integrate, and expand on ideas from previous theories, bringing in new considerations, including revised ways of thinking about clinical process in a "two-person" model. In this model, development is rethought as more flexible, diverse, and always shaped by the systems of social relations and context in which a child or person lives (Corbett 2001a, 2001b, Harris 2005).

During what has been described as the "second phase" of the development of relational theory (Aron and Harris 2005), what began as a critique of theory and practice evolved into a body of work—a relational theory—that has been described as " more than the sum of its parts" (Altman 2000). As is true of every theory discussed in this book, relational theory was generated in a social and historical context that shaped its efforts to both sustain diversity and find ways of theorizing that worked in our contemporary, more globalized world. As mentioned briefly above, this was and is an era in which many people from adjacent disciplines are studying and questioning the assumptions on which common concepts are based. For example: Is gender necessarily a binary category? What assumptions are we making in the concepts we use to describe psychopathology or abnormality? There is widespread recognition of the relativity of truth in relation to context, the need to consider different levels or kinds of analysis, as well as the limits of rationality. Many question the authority that is implicit in social practices and categories, and also challenge the dynamics of power and influence as they are negotiated between people. This is an era in which the impact of culture, race, class, and gender on a person's sense of themselves as well as on their interactions with others continues to be recognized and critiqued. This continues to be a period in which individuals from many fields engage in deconstructing theoretical ideas of all kinds along with familiar, everyday language or practice. This contemporary thinking and questioning, often referred to as postmodernism, involves different ways of looking at the world and building theory accordingly. Psychodynamic theory is no exception.

In the midst of this zeitgeist, relational theory was and continues to be influenced by feminism, gender studies, contemporary cognitive science and neuroscience, as well as infancy and attachment research, while being enriched by cultural theory and contemporary philosophy. New ideas about clinical theory and practice have also been shaped by the practical necessity of doing clinical work with a wide range of people struggling with many different kinds of trouble, in many different settings, including inner-city clinics and hospitals or private practices where the finances of managed care impact on clinical work.

Let us, then, consider some specifics of the emergence of the relational tradition in this contemporary context. During the early 1980s, a number of clinicians who had come of age in the 1960s and 1970s set themselves the task of reflecting on and writing about theories. A now classic overview and critical analysis of psychodynamic theories was published by Greenberg and Mitchell (1982). These authors initiated the distinction between two models or kinds of psychodynamic theories based on distinct assumptions. These two models are: (1) the "drive-conflict model" that underlies classical theory as well as ego psychology; and (2) the "relational model" that formed the basis of the object relations school, interpersonal and humanistic theories, as well as self psychology. The theories that share a relational model perceive the therapeutic situation as "inherently dyadic" with an emphasis on the therapeutic action being fostered by the relationship between the therapist and patient. The theories of Winnicott, Klein, Fairbairn, Sullivan, Jacobson, and Kohut are premised on a relational model. As we have read, there are many differences between these theoretical approaches, but they share an underlying relational model or view.

In relational clinical work, the pushes and pulls that the therapist experiences in her countertransference reactions are understood as communications from or about the patient's relational patterns and experiences (Hoffman 1998; Maroda 1991; Mitchell 1988, 1993, 2000; and others). Conversely, the patient's perception of the therapist can be actively used in the treatment to provide insight into the dynamics that develop between them and to lead to an awareness of the mutual influence they have on each other (Aron 1991, Hoffman 1983). Both client and clinician are contributing to and influencing the dynamics they construct together. It is interesting to note that it was in the 1980s that the clinical diaries of Sandor Ferenczi (a Hungarian analyst and an early colleague of Freud's, who fell from grace because of his views about the need for the therapist to be an active participant, and because of his reformulating of trauma theory) were finally translated and published (Aron and Harris 1993). The discovery of this foreshadowing in Ferenczi's work and method of what are now described as relational ideas have fascinated many, as if the tradition from which psychodynamic theory had developed was more varied and rich than we had known.

As the relational approach evolved, the framework of self, other, and the space between them was used in different ways—to conceptualize "earlier" developmental needs of the client, as well as the system in which the client's experiences and behaviors were developed and sustained (Harris 2005). These ways of thinking led to ways of theorizing about and doing clinical work in which both participants were considered in broader contexts and understood to be co-creating the therapeutic relationship in which they were embedded within these contexts (Aron 1991, Mitchell 1988). Further, the larger social and cultural milieus that both therapist and patient brought to their interaction was always "in the room," an inevitable part of their work together. Some, like Altman (1995, 2000) and Leary (1997) wrote and theorized about race and class as they were embedded in clinical practice. The social construction of gender, the nature of gender itself, and its significance in clinical encounters were discussed by Harris (1991), Dimen (2003), Dimen and Goldner (2002), Benjamin (1988, 1998), Layton (1998), and Corbett (1996, 2001a, 2001b). Following a long tradition in the field, psychodynamic conceptions of the human condition were also being used to gain deeper understanding of struggles outside the consulting room, from Columbine to racial conflict, women's roles, and political situations such as 9/11 and terrorism.

In sum, what began in the 1980s, as a now classic critical analysis of psychodynamic theories, has expanded in the context of the broader postmodern discourse that has furthered the development of theory. With this development came the challenge of a more engaged, aware, "two-person " approach to clinical work, in which the therapist's and client's subjectivities are understood to influence each other. Their personalities, as well as their constructions of gender, race, culture, and class, are an inevitable part of the co-constructed experience in the clinical dyad.

> In this vision the basic unit of study is not the individual as a separate entity whose desires clash with an external reality, but an interactional field within

which the individual arises and struggles to make contact and to articulate himself. Desire is experienced always in the context of relatedness and it is that context which defines its meaning. Mind is composed of relational configurations. The person is comprehensible only within the tapestry of relationships, past and present. Analytic inquiry entails a participation in, and an observation, uncovering, and transformation of, these relationships and their internal representations. (Mitchell 1988, p. 3)

The "relational turn" began with a dialogue about—and has evolved out of—existing psychodynamic theory. It is a dialogue to which many clinicians from different theoretical backgrounds have contributed. For some, this way of thinking about self and mind in the context of clinical work and the social world is viewed as a paradigm shift. Others see this dialogue and its subculture as an evolution of previous theory rather than a qualitative change. Either way, different kinds of questions have been and are being asked, and psychodynamic ideas have been brought into a contemporary discourse. Consider a brief example in order to illustrate some of these points. Then we will articulate some of the specific influences on the development of the relational theory.

HOW DOES RELATIONAL THEORY SHAPE PRACTICE?

In a practice setting, a relational perspective, or "two-person" model, focuses on the subjectivities of both the therapist and the patient, becoming embedded in a complex, rich dynamic. They construct this dynamic together, influenced by what each one brings to the dyad, including the influences of their experiences in the contexts in which each has lived. Whereas other psychodynamic approaches to practice tend to focus on the client's feelings, behaviors, and mind—delineating countertransference as the aspect of a therapist's experience of the client that is relevant to the work—a relational approach includes the mutually influential subjectivities of both participants, conscious and unconscious, in social context. This is not an alternative to, but an extension of, countertransference. Relational clinicians attend to the experience and mutual influence of each person in the dyad, acknowledging that there are difference in their roles as therapist and patient.

Consider an example, a brief clinical vignette that we can reflect upon.

As I entered the waiting room, I saw Tony seated with head leaned back against the wall. The tension and anger in Tony's face was palpable, as if containing the feelings was no longer possible. Her affect was expressed in details of stance, facial aspects, and a series of deep sighs. Her anger and despair were visceral. I could feel myself breathing in and stiffening, then trying to exhale and release the anxious expectations that were building inside me. Once seated in my office, Tony glowered at me and said, "There is no way you can help. This is bigger than talk."

"Tell me about it," I heard my voice saying in a practiced, even, interested way, trying to sustain equanimity. Inside, I was wondering if Tony wasn't right. I was feeling ill equipped and limited in my ability to address the parental abuse and trauma (from unpredictable rages triggered by alcoholism) that Tony had lived with for years. The incident in question had occurred the night before. Tony's intoxicated father had come home angry about several bills, blaming everyone in the family, in turn, and hurling a phone receiver at Tony. Tony understood the frustration with unemployment and threats of eviction that fueled his rant, but as I listened, I felt the anguish, the sense of being trapped and unable to do anything except absorb the rage and verbal abuse that was so often unloaded onto Tony. It occurred to me that the dread I had felt coming down the corridor was a small portion of what this family felt, and that my sense of inadequacy was mirrored in their own helplessness. It was hard to listen and not try to handle, placate, or minimize the force of feeling that Tony expressed and had been holding since last night when fear of retaliation had resulted in her shutting down, an adaptive response to this onslaught.

Working within a relational approach, this moment is understood as being lived and co-constructed between Tony and myself, as well as in the space between us. Relational theorists, like many clinicians, would say that Tony desperately needed to communicate complex, intense feelings, and to have them known by another. A clinician working from a relational perspective would suggest that her feelings needed to be expressed, felt, recognized, contained, metabolized, and eventually reflected on, between us, in ways that were authentic. The communication is not just verbal. It is also nonverbal and visceral. Who I am, my subjectivity and history, will shape our interactions in subtle ways, just as Tony's subjectivity and experiences, including her perceptions of me, will contribute to our dynamics at both conscious and unconscious levels. Eventually, we will wonder together about how we have influenced each other and will become slowly aware of what has emerged between us as a means of gaining insight into the issues and troubles that are at the heart of why Tony came for help.

The process is collaborative, often candid, and mutual in a way that acknowledges the "asymmetry" of a client-to-therapist relationship (Aron 1991). But it is not "wild," as some critics have suggested." The therapist is viewed as a person in the dyad, but her job is to facilitate the process so that both she and the client become able to recognize, understand, and reflect on their experiences together, as a "two-person" therapeutic dyad. Both therapist and client have their own subjectivity; neither is privileged as "the knower," but the roles are also different. It is the clinician's job to be responsible and to work at being in and conscious of patterns and shifts in the relationship, to be open to the client's reactions, and to recognize the feelings and dynamics that are behind the words, emotional tones, and gestures. It is our job as clinicians to survive and contain the dynamics that emerge, while trying our best to be aware of our own feelings as they evolve and shift. In other words, the therapist uses her subjectivity and counter-transference as a tool that can shed light on the dynamics between her and the client, leading to insight about the client's internal experience and relations with others.

In my work with Tony, I experienced awareness of my own subjectivity and countertransference. I reflected silently and sometimes out loud on what I felt and how my own history was integral to the process. Wondering about and asking her about how she felt and experienced her world, our interaction, and me, gradually enabled us to become aware of what happened within and between us. This awareness served as a means to gradually help us both understand her internal experience as well as her often antagonistic relation with others. This growing awareness along with different experiences in our work together enabled her to find alternative ways of being with others and knowing herself.

There were times when our shared gender and ethnic backgrounds, as well as our different class backgrounds, would come into play and be discussed. I would, at some point, acknowledge or disclose my own sense of helplessness in the face of repeated angry scenes in her home, and talk about my wish to rescue Tony. There were ironic, shared moments and even humor that helped us to find air in what, at times, became a space permeated with despair. As we experienced and reflected on the world in which Tony lived and felt trapped, I recognized that she struggled with the sense that many things are not possible, and that she could not imagine a future that I, from my background, believe can and will happen if a person has a sense of purpose and ability to work. Talking about and accepting these differences was a part of finding ways to relate to each other—part of coming to learn to appreciate what we each brought to relations with others. Throughout such processes of engagement and reflection there are changes, ruptures, and repairs.

How is this approach different or new compared to previous ways of thinking about and doing psychotherapy? Certainly the importance of relationship with another as integral to the process of healing or change has long been understood by shaman, priests, rabbis, doctors, teachers, social workers, and other clinicians, including Freud. Many professionals working with oppressed populations or studying social theory have focused on the enormity of the influence of social and cultural context on individuals, their troubles, and ways of life. What distinguishes relational theory as it has emerged out of the psychoanalytic tradition? First, it's theorizing about the nature and profundity of relational dynamics in a particular clinical dyad, acknowledging that both participants contribute to the construction of such dynamics in the clinical setting. Second, the influence of many aspects of the broader culture in this context are acknowledged and deconstructed in ways that increase recognition and understanding of the complexity of an individual's experience, feelings, and behaviors. Further, reflection on relational moments and patterns is considered to be a means to therapeutic change. Again, it is not simply the importance of a supportive relationship that distinguishes relational theory; it is the theoretical articulation of a "two-person" model in which the unconscious is understood in terms of patterns of relatedness and processes of constructing experience between self and other, or of experiencing oneself in relation to personal history and social/ cultural contexts.

Influences on Relational Theory: Feminism, Gender Theory, Attachment Theory, Infancy Research, and Work with Oppressed Populations

Feminist writers were very important in this developing discourse. They began to question the nature of gender as a fixed dichotomy, to critique assumptions about social roles and power linked to gender, as well as to challenge prejudices about sexual preferences (Benjamin 1998, Chodorow 1978, 1992, 1995, Corbett 2001a, 2001b, Dimen 2003, Goldner 1991, Harris 1991, 2005, and others).

At a time when gender roles were being challenged in the broader culture, inherent gender biases were being identified and deconstructed in more traditional psychodynamic theories. The idea that gender, like other aspects of self experience, was constructed in interpersonal and social contexts led to questioning of the nature of gender itself, challenging the culturally assumed gender dichotomy, and considering the negotiation of gender dynamics in the clinical situation (see chapter 10).

Clinicians working with people from a range of oppressed and marginalized populations in inner-city clinics and other settings have made important contributions to relational theory, not only pushing us to recognize the inevitability of race, class, and culture entering the therapeutic situation, but also extending our grasp of the biases that we bring into work with diverse groups (Altman 1995, 2000, Leary 1997). Race, from a relational perspective, is a social construction that becomes part of our unconscious as we grow and live in both our social world as well as in particular relationship. Altman (2000) suggests that "unconscious racism" is an inevitable part of our work at this point in history, and he writes about the dynamics of race in the transference/countertransference matrix of treatment. Altman (1995, 2000), Leary (1997), Suchet (2004), and others have taken the lead in discussing "racial enactments" and the ways that clinicians and patients construct them and can collaborate in learning from them (chapter 11).

Another important influence on the development of relational theory is the study of attachment (chapter 8) and infancy research, particularly research on caretaker/infant interactions that has been developed over the last thirty years (Fonagy 2001, Stern 1997, and others). It is not possible here to summarize the extensive findings of infancy research as it illuminates our understanding of early relational capacities and dynamics with caretakers. However, it should be acknowledged that evidence that specifies the remarkably early development of repeated, distinct patterns of relatedness between caretakers and infants has been found to correspond to later interactive patterns or intersubjective dynamics that are evidently internalized as schemas between self and caretaker, or what Stern (1997) has described as "RIGs" (repetitions of interactions generalized). There are strong connections between the early mutual regulatory patterns of infants with their caretakers and later capacities for self-regulation. These patterns can be experienced and understood in a therapeutic relationship.

The concept of "mentalization," or development of a capacity for "mind to mediate our experience of the world," has been one extension of research on attachment (Fonagy et al. 2004). It has been utilized to understand how interactions early in life can shape our capacity to interact and reflect on our experience with others. Many clinicians working from a relational perspective have extended their practice by understanding the developmental significance of encouraging "mentalization" in order to help patients learn to regulate intense feeling states. For example, Tony (from the earlier case vignette) was gradually able to both put her frustration and anger into words and then to reflect on ways that her father's often unpredictable rages destabilized the family, leaving them helpless and terrorized. As she became able to reflect on her own helplessness and have it recognized, her sense of agency began to develop, just as her anger acquired a voice that could be affirmed.

Infancy research has explored infants' inborn capacity and striving to relate and to sustain familiar patterns of relationship with others, along with caretakers' capacities to reflect and respond to the infant. Studies of these early relational dynamics between very small babies and their caretakers suggest that these experiences are integral to the emergence of an initially visceral sense of self as related to others. The implications for clinical work have been important to the development of relational theory.

THE SELF, THE OTHER, AND THE SPACE
BETWEEN: OPENING A DIALOGUE

Relational theory focuses on three aspects: The self, the other, and the space between the two. There is no "object" in a psychologically meaningful sense without some particular sense of oneself in relation to it. There is no "self," in a psychologically meaningful sense, in isolation, outside a matrix of relations with others. Neither the self nor the object (other) are meaningful dynamic concepts without presupposing some sense of psychic space in which they interact, in which they do things with or to each other (Mitchell 1988, p. 33)

Consider some key concepts developed in recent writings from a relational perspective with its focus on these three aspects.

The Relational Matrix

The relational matrix is the "unit of analysis" for clinical theory; it includes

the relational bonds and the relational matrix they form. At stake are different forms of relatedness, one mediated through burden and pain, one mediated through activity and spontaneity. Bodily processes, sexuality, aggression, are all important subjects of inquiry. (Mitchell 1988, p. 39)

Enactments in Clinical Work

As clinician and patient work together, they frequently find themselves unconsciously engaged in relational dynamics that repeat certain familiar patterns from the patient's past—often the origin of troubles that have brought the person to treatment. The therapist and patient are together involved in constructing such enactments, with the patient bringing old needs and ways of interaction to the work, and the therapist predictably responding in ways that are both similar to what the patient has experienced before and yet different. Being able to recognize enactments and reflect on them with interest rather than judgment is important to the application of relational ideas to clinical work. For example, if Tony, in our original example, had a repeated experience of others being unable to help her, then she would assume that I could not help and, initially, I would be likely to feel daunted by and helpless in the face of her situation and needs. The key is to be able to recognize such patterns as enactments and to reflect on them in order to become aware with the patient of their meaning, gradually enabling alternative relational possibilities to emerge.

Disclosure by the Therapist

If the therapist's subjectivity is integral to the work of psychotherapy and contributes to the co-construction of the dynamics between therapist and patient, then it is legitimate to ask: When is it appropriate for the therapist to be "up front" and disclose either the feelings or facts about her life when they are relevant to the current dynamics or impasse in the work? This is a topic that has often been discussed in relation to erotic transference and countertransference (Davies 1994, Davies and Frawley 1994), but it is also very relevant to situations in which the therapist's behavior is perceived by a patient as withholding, or authoritative, or hurtful, or somehow inappropriate, in part because the therapist's background or feelings (countertransference) have contributed to what she has said or done (Aron 1996, Hoffman 1998). Disclosure, *after careful consideration* by the therapist, and often after consultation with a supervisor, can be helpful in working through a therapeutic impasse or helping the patient to understand how the experience of the therapist may be very different than the patient's own, for reasons that can be understood in the context of such a disclosure (see chapter 17 on trauma for further elaboration).

A Relational Unconscious

Relational theory understands unconscious process in a different way than classical, Freudian theory. From a relational perspective, the unconscious is not a place of repressed wishes, desires, and conflicts. Instead, a relational view of unconscious process considers the "unthought known" (Bollas 1987) in terms of relational configurations or schemas, of which a person is largely unaware, but which are experientially familiar to the person and continue to evolve in the course of his or her life. Unconscious relational patterns shape how we know ourselves in relation to others, and shift as we develop and engage in new relationships. Early patterns may continue to be familiar, as when we find ourselves feeling and behaving in a certain way when we meet someone who reminds us of a parent, but the emphasis is on process and patterns rather than specific conflict or content. Relational theorists tend to understand these dynamics as "procedural," fluid, and non-verbal in nature, often first identified in patterns of interaction or enactments that a person can gradually become aware of and verbalize (Lyons-Ruth 1999).

Stolorow and Atwood (1992) characterize the Freudian unconscious as an "isolated mind," an "objective entity" that is "estranged" within the individual. From their perspective, the unconscious in classical theory is a "storehouse of what consciousness can't tolerate." They propose an alternative view of the unconscious based on a "two-person model" in which the process of exploring unconscious process is "dialogic" rather than "archaeo-logical." In this approach, the therapist works with the patient to wonder about and explore the "tacit preconceptions, expectations, and principles that shape the patient's experience." The unconscious material that emerges at one moment is related to the context of that moment; the possibility for becoming aware of unconscious processes is relative to the relational and circumstantial context of a person's life and to the dynamics emerging in the relationship with the therapist (Stolorow and Atwood 1992). This clini-cal process has been referred to by Stern (1997) as " courting surprise" or finding creative ways to encourage enactment and discovery. In this proc-ess, the therapist needs to be open to curiosity, awe, and new possibilities.

Trauma and Dissociation

How can we better understand the impact of trauma and dissociation from a relational perspective?

> Sitting with Dan in session was unsettling. He seemed wiser than his years, but at fifteen there was no sense of playfulness or bravado about him. As the son of a Cambodian immigrant family who had escaped the Khmer Rouge, he assumed the need to project strength and toughness in a world where violence was assumed. But there was a subtle sense of deadness in the room. While he spoke politely and easily there was a toughness that felt impenetrable—a wall between us, and feelings of dislocation and trauma that went back for genera-tions. He remained stoic, and I felt the deadening while sensing the unspeak-able feelings beneath or beyond our grasp.

If the defining mark of trauma is an experience so extreme in its intensity that a person cannot assimilate, symbolize, or metabolize it, then the after-math of trauma is anxiety, more or less specific to particular circumstances. The natural defense against such overwhelming experiences is dissociation. When sitting with a patient with a trauma history, the clinician often expe-riences anxiety or deadness, feelings that are, as yet, "unformulated" (Stern 1997). Gradually, experiencing and naming these feelings can give form and voice to the client's experience.

A number of relational theorists (Bromberg 1998, Davies and Frawley 1994, Stern 1997, Boulanger 2007) have discussed the kinds of dynamics that are clues to earlier trauma in a patient's life—dissociated states and blank moments or sudden shifts in affects that often emerge in the work of the therapeutic dyad. Learning to identify and work with dissociated states that are the aftermath of traumatic experiences often involves developing sensitivity to non-verbal shifts in state and changes in one's countertrans-ference that seem to co-occur simultaneously with such shifts in the client.

Returning to Tony, there were times when she would arrive in reasonably good spirits and then begin to talk about an incident related to anger at home. Her mood would shift to one of dejection, and I would find myself feeling empathic but "spacey," becoming aware of noises in the hallway, or the rain on the window. We would be at the brink of dealing with traumatic material that simultaneously and inexplicably shifted Tony's feeling state and challenged my ability to stay engaged between her experiential states as we worked toward integrating what had been dissociated.

Working with traumatized individuals often challenges us to "stand in the spaces" (Bromberg 1998) between a person's different experiential states while using our own subjective experience as clues in the process of integrating dissociated feelings and experiences (see chapter 17 on trauma).

Intersubjectivity

Intersubjectivity is a developmental achievement, and one that most of us take for granted in day-to-day communication. It is a defining focus and feature in thinking and practicing from a relational perspective. Intersubjectivity is the capacity to recognize that others have their own subjectivity, and the ability to grasp certain aspects of what the other is feeling or thinking. This leads to the possibility of engaging in shared subjectivity that is the basis of communication. Intersubjectivity enables us to consider the experience of each person (or subject) as he influences the experience of the other in ways that are reflexive, not unidirectional. The study of intersubjectivity has challenged us to broaden our understanding of development to include the emergence of the ability to recognize the other as a separate subject (Benjamin 1998) and to acknowledge the importance of a "mutuality of regulation, which refers to the reciprocal control that two people in a relationship continuously exert on each other" (Aron 1996). The relational approach to clinical work has been extended by theorizing about different "modes of intersubjectivity" (Mitchell 2000), and the renegotiation of the mutual impacts of client and therapist on each other in order to restore "the patient's sense of personal agency."

What does the relational model imply for our understanding of development, particularly the development of degrees and kinds of intersubjectivity? Mitchell (2000), in his book titled *Relationality*, describes qualitatively different "modes" of interaction that can evolve or shift back and forth in the course of relating to others. He includes some useful distinctions for clinicians to keep in mind when they are trying to hear the quality of relatedness in their interactions with clients. Consider the following case example as a means to explicate the evolution of different "modes" of inter-

subjectivity (quoted in italics) or relatedness (quoted in italics) in work
with an individual patient.

Marissa is a young woman, sixteen years of age, with whom I worked as a therapist in an inner-city clinic for about a year. She came seeking help for " feeling
depressed" and troubled with "overeating when I feel down." She had come
from the Caribbean to a city in the Northeast United States with her mother
and two older brothers three years earlier. Her father, grandmother, and
extended family, with whom she had been raised, were left behind, along with
everything that she had known as familiar. Her mother, who could work
legally, planned to make money and educate her children in the United States.
Although Marissa had adjusted in many ways to a new neighborhood and
school, she felt lonely much of the time. Her mother worked late, and she felt
she couldn't complain when they were together because she knew that her
mother was also struggling, and she was afraid to burden her. As I listened I
began to understand that she had spent years learning to stay cheerful and not
speaking about what hurt her.

Her quiet, considerate manner was compelling, and I realized by the end of
the first session that while I could feel the anger and frustration beneath her
surface, feelings that needed to be expressed, there was a charm and appeal
that I was reticent to challenge. I felt pulled into both wanting to engage with
her amiable self and feeling conscious of the need to pursue her more troubled
feelings. I was also aware of how important it was for me, in my own life, to
feel that I could keep the surfaces intact, to appear resilient and functional
while holding back troubling feelings because of their potential to disorganize
situations and upset others. Eventually, I shared my personal familiarity with
striving to maintain a calm surface in order to be responsible and avoid upset,
a way of being that I had learned in my culture and family, made up of Quak-
ers with a strong social and personal ethic. Marissa described the importance
in her family, particularly for women, of "presenting a good face" as a proud
daughter and granddaughter in a Catholic, Caribbean culture. As we spoke
about the intersection of similarity and difference, of how it felt to hold back
and carry on, she began to access the undertow of her own subjectivity.

It took time for Marissa to begin to speak freely. Interest in and inquiry
about details of her daily life (routines, relationships, social and cultural sur-
rounds), both now and before the move, helped her to open up. I have found
that beginning a therapeutic relationship with as few assumptions as possible,
with a self-imposed discipline of "not knowing," increases the chance that the
client might be candid. Marissa began to describe the many changes that had
taken place in her life over the past few years. At first, she spoke of events and
relationships as if reporting, and I felt her effort to hold back emotion, and
asked what it was like being her in the midst of these events. It was then that
she began to express despair and loss.

*Inquiry, interest and recognition can often help a person to move from a basic
mode of intersubjectivity in which they describe what they and others around*

them "actually do with each other in a nonreflective, presymbolic way " to a
mode marked by "shared experience of intense affect." (Mitchell 2000, p. 58)

As Marissa's experiences began to be described with increasing connection to her own feelings, the relationship between us began to grow. She spoke to me as a person whom she felt could respond, recognize, and engage her. She began to know and speak of her own loss, feelings of dislocation, and confusion. We spoke openly about what it meant for each of us to be from different backgrounds while being able to understand and share what it meant to be uprooted, to lose what is familiar, and to struggle through the confusion of a transition. Her shyness began to fade as she talked about the details of all the changes she had been through, and she expressed a growing awareness of the impact of these changes on both herself and her family. Her expression of agency grew as she voiced her experience of all that had happened, and I recognized its enormity.

What began as stories about specific troubles and circumstances gradually shifted to reflection and the capacity to express the feelings that went with these experiences. I grew sincerely fond of her and began to worry with her and, at times, for her. We spoke of this shared capacity for worry and began to understand it as a way of caring.

The emergence of "experience organized into self-other configurations" in ways
that can be relied upon and function to regulate emotion and connection suggests
a third mode of relational organization. (Mitchell 2000, p. 62)

Marissa often seemed younger than her age, asking me to help her in small ways. She would ask for directions to the bus stop, wanted reassurance about how she looked in a particular outfit, and requested to call me if she was lonely. I felt the pull to respond to her needs, and I did draw maps or reassure her. Arrangements were made so that she could leave messages and know that I would respond in a timely way. I became aware of feeling like I was filling a role that I didn't fully understand. It occurred to me that my countertransference was framed by my own cultural background with its value in closeness with a large dose of independence and clear differentiation, love that was expressed when mastery was achieved.

There came a point, however, when I wondered aloud with her about these ways that she expressed trust, or need, and kept her self tied to me. I shared with her (my disclosure) a brief memory of my own adolescent life in which the desire to be cared for and the need to be independent coexisted in a confusing moment. She smiled with recognition and began to talk about missing her grandmother who had cared for her much of the time when she was young, as well as her sense of longing for being in a place where she knew how to get places easily, to dress so that she fit in, and to feel less self-conscious or awkward. She had lost the person whom she felt comfortable leaning on, and was in a new environment with her mother whom she felt responsible to help and protect. I sensed that I was shifting back and forth between these two transferential positions, and eventually shared this with her.

The more she was able to articulate her feelings of both longing to be cared for and supported, and striving to be responsible as well as supportive, the more her confidence and agency grew. She could be both, with me and in her own mind. We were able to smile with recognition when she expressed a desire to "lean on me" or be "concerned about " me, or when I stepped in to "take care," anticipating her need for support and later appreciated her concern. She could be granddaughter and daughter, each with their particular relational configurations, and I could be grandmother and mother.

The subjective experience of both patient and therapist, or each self and other, are recognized in a "two person" dynamic along with their mutual, though "asymmetric," influence on each other in interaction. As mutual self-reflection and agency become possible the intersubjective process becomes more mutual and generative. (Mitchell 2000, pp. 64–65)

At one point when she had repeatedly requested to speak to me on the phone during the week, I asked her if she had been able to speak to her mother about some of the troubles she was talking about with me. She said that no, her mother was too tired, and in addition to not wanting to burden her, she didn't feel her mother would understand why she was struggling with certain situations at school. It occurred to me to ask whether her mother would have understood before, back at home where she had grown up. She began to share details of her life back home, including interactions that spoke to my question in ways that suggested that she knew what I had in mind. I asked if she had always felt that she needed to care for her mother, being careful not to upset her while relying on her grandmother for her own support. At first, she explained that it was a daughter' s duty to help and care for her mother. I said I understood, but wondered with her about what this meant for her, particularly now that her grandmother was far away, and she was here where daughters might have different ideas about their responsibilities. Bit by bit, we built an understanding about the complexity of being a responsible daughter who has needs herself, and the importance of her extended family in providing support while she was " being a good daughter." There were important cultural as well as personal dynamics grasped in this process. I learned a great deal about what it meant for Marissa to be a daughter in her culture, as well as how people within her extended family supported each other. We both grew to understand how such relations are culturally embedded and different for each person. Sharing selected moments in my life with her led her to become an active interpreter of my experience and to feel the reciprocity of our relationship. It was important for us to develop these insights together, for me to inquire but not to tell and thereby impose my own perspective. I invited her to wonder with me, to disagree and respond to my inquiries in ways that made sense to her so that she could take the lead.

There are many ways that a therapist could have worked with Marissa. Clinicians working from a relational approach strive to be open to alternatives and innovation, and engaged in a dialogue in which diversities of opinion, background, and perspective enrich the process. This approach is "a blending of . . . diverse currents into a broad, multidimensional vision of human intersubjectivity" (Mitchell 2000, p. 65).

THE IMPACT OF RELATIONAL THEORY

What does this new dialogue and relational approach mean for change in thinking about and working with patients? It means that the subjectivity of the client, along with that of the therapist, is integral to the work in what is referred to as a "two-person" psychology. Transference is not considered as a function of only one person—the patient—but as influenced in various ways by the therapist. *Countertransference is taken to be meaningful*, not something a clinician needs to rid herself of, but a critical part of the work and the learning. As "relational patterns" or "enactments" emerge in the relationship, like the patient feeling dominated, abandoned, or unheard by the other, these dynamics and feelings are ideally shared, recognized as valid, and reflected on by both client and therapist. An understanding is constructed between the two people, involving what is significant for both, linked to the patient's history, the kinds of issues he struggled with in daily life, as well as to the therapist and his experience of them. Part of the therapist's job is to inquire, to wonder with the patient about feelings and about changes in their relationship. The gradual renegotiation of their experience of each other always involves consideration of influence and subjectivity, remaining open to the possibility that while the therapist's experience may differ from the patient's, it doesn't necessarily make it "right." The truth of a given insight or the meaning of behaviors is always considered as relative to the context that each participant brings to the interaction.

The process of clinical work is obviously different depending on an individual's needs, developmental history, and circumstances. There are times when the therapist may disclose some aspect of his or her experience, and other times that the experience, as well as understanding of the other's vulnerability, will result in a decision to "hold" one's own reaction(s) and, reflect on them privately, considering their potential influence, and gradually working with the patient to move towards moments when they can step back, inquire, and reflect on *the way they have co-constructed the relational dynamics, making links to previous experience.* The phrase "asymmetric mutuality" (Aron 1996) has been aptly used to characterize the therapeutic relationship and the need for the therapist to be in the role of the therapist while also being a real person.

The *relationship*, the growth of mutual recognition, reflection, renegotiation, and regulation within the clinical dyad is understood as the primary means to change by those working from a relational perspective. Staying in the process while being able, at times, to step back and reflect on it, enables a "third" position to be experienced. The "third" has been thought about as emerging in the reverie of the therapist (Ogden 1994), as being a place of reflection on the process that is vulnerable to collapse when participants experience conflict in which dominance and submission to each other is enacted (Benjamin 1998). The "third" is that which can be grasped in reflective moments and can illuminate the process between and around the dyad, but often remains out of consciousness. Thirdness provides rich potential for reflection and insight when awareness can be achieved, and reflection becomes possible.

The relational approach, including intersubjectivity, is premised on process, on dialogue, and reflection. Both client and therapist work, when possible, to consider other viewpoints and to recognize that there is more than one possible perspective or truth. The experience of the patient and that of the therapist may be different and both may be "right" at the same time. An angry adolescent from a troubled home in an inner-city neighborhood, like Tony in the first brief clinical example, may initially experience the therapist as a privileged authority figure who cannot begin to understand her world. On the other hand, the therapist who has struggled to earn her way through school and experiences her own stress around finances, relationships with authority figures, and racial, class, or gender oppression may feel misunderstood in her efforts to help. The complexity of a "relational matrix" with all the issues of gender, race, class, age, ethnicity, culture, and the health care system are present in the room. Part of what moves the clinical process is recognition of each other's subjective states, particularly when the client and therapist may think or feel differently. *Grasping the subjectivity of self and other along with the reality they construct together is an essential part of the work.* Being able to negotiate feelings and relationship differently is crucial to feeling differently about oneself in a particular dyad and in the world outside the consulting room. Tony's doubt and frustration about my being able to help her was gradually mediated by her feeling my own doubt and despair, along with my hope and belief that change is possible. We moved between these poles and gradually were able to step back and recognize patterns in our own experience together in the context of the very real, overlapping, but distinct social, cultural worlds in which we were each embedded.

From this beginning, then, the "relational turn" in psychodynamic theory has never been about one theory or one voice. It has been a dialogue between clinicians working to understand the process that takes place between "the self, the other, and the space between the two" (Mitchell 1988). The basic unit of analysis in the relational model is the dynamics of relationship and relational patterns that a person has experienced, leading to ways of constructing with another.

> The relational model rests on the premise that the repetitive patterns within human experience are not derived, as in the drive model, from pursuing gratification of inherent pressure and pleasures (nor, as in Freud's post-1920 understanding, from the automatic workings of the death instinct), but from a pervasive tendency to preserve the continuity, connections, familiarity of one's personal, interactional world. There is a powerful need to preserve an abiding sense of oneself as associated with, positioned in terms of, related to, a matrix of other people, in terms of actual transaction as well as internal presences. (Aron 1991, p. 33)

A relational approach to clinical work includes efforts to theorize about the connections between interpersonal and intrapsychic dynamics within situational, social, and historical contexts. It is an approach that focuses on process and the ways people construct experience between each other. Within the clinical world, relational theory has opened up a space for many generative discussions on a range of theoretical, clinical, and social issues. Familiar concepts like "oedipal dynamics," "projective identification," and "gender identification" from the psychodynamic tradition have been reconsidered in relational terms. New ideas about development have been explored (Corbett 2001b, Harris 2005). Relational theory continues to evolve through reflection and dialogue about the "inside out and outside in" as well as the "in between" of relations as they are constructed between people both within and outside of the treatment situation.

Critiques of Relational Theory

Along with providing a space for dialogue, relational theory has also generated controversy. There are those who question the distinction between drive and relational assumptions about human nature. Some would argue that this is a false dichotomy, while others assert that there are clear differences in the implications of each. Relational theory maintains that theorizing about relationship, recognizing mutual influence in a two-person model, as well as valuing reflection on and re-negotiation of relational dynamics is distinct. While there are always some people who hold to a theoretical perspective as a source of identity and differentiation, most relational clinicians value differences in points-of-view and welcome dialogue about important concepts or aspects of human experience. They acknowledge that there are many possible views of most situations and often encourage the kinds of dialogue between views that leads to new understandings, just as they do in work with their clients.

REFERENCES

Altman, N. (1995). *The Analyst in the Inner City: Race, Class and Culture through a Psychoanalytic Lens*. Hillsdale, NJ: The Analytic Press.

———. (2000). Black and White thinking: A psychoanalyst reconsiders race. *Psychoanalytic Dialogues* 10:589–604.

Aron, L. (1991). The patient's experience of the analyst's subjectivity. *Psychoanalytic Dialogues* 1:29–51.

———. (1996). *A Meeting of Minds: Mutuality in Psychoanalysis*. Hillsdale, NJ: The Analytic Press.

Aron, L., and Harris, A. (1993). *The Legacy of Sandor Ferenczi*. New York: Analytic Press.

———. (2005). *Relational Psychoanalysis (Vol. 2): Innovation and Expansion*. Hillsdale, NJ: The Analytic Press.

Benjamin, J. (1988). *The Bonds of Love: Psychoanalysis, Feminism, and the Problem of Domination*. New York: Pantheon.

———. (1998). *The Shadow of the Other: Intersubjectivity and Gender in Psychoanalysis*. New York: Routledge.

Bollas, C. (1987). *The Shadow of the Object: Psychoanalysis of the Unknown Thought*. London: Free Association Books.

Boulanger, G. (2007) *Wounded by Reality:Understanding and Treating Adult Onset Trauma*. Hillsdale, NJ: Analytic Press.

Bromberg, P. M. (1998). *Standing in the Spaces: Essays on Clinical Process, Trauma, and Dissociation*. Hillsdale, NJ: The Analytic Press.

Chodorow, N. (1978). *The Reproduction of Mothering: Psychoanalysis and the Sociology of Gender*. Berkeley: University of California Press.

———. (1992). Heterosexuality as a compromise formation. *Psychoanalysis and Contemporary Thought* 15:267–304.

———. (1995). Gender as personal and cultural construction. *Signs* 20(31):516–44.

Corbett, K. (1996). Homosexual boyhood: Notes on girlyboys. *Gender and Psychoanalysis* 1:429–63.

———. (2001a). Faggot = Loser. *Studies in Gender and Sexuality* 2(1):3–28.

———. (2001b). More life: Centrality and marginality in human development. *Psychoanalytic Dialogues* 11:313–35.

Davies, J. M. (1994). Love in the afternoon: A relational reconsideration of desire and dread in the countertransference. *Psychoanalytic Dialogues* 4:153–70.

Davies, J. M., and Frawley, M. G. (1994). *Treating the Adult Survivor of Childhood Sexual Abuse: A Psychoanalytic Perspective*. New York: Basic Books.

Dimen, M. (2003). *Sexuality, Intimacy and Power*. Hillsdale, NJ: Analytic Press.

Dimen, M., and Goldner, V. (2002). *Gender in Psychoanalytic Space* . New York: Other Press.

Fonagy, P. (2001). *Attachment Theory and Psychoanalysis*. New York: Other Press.

Fonagy, P., Gergely, G., Jurist, E., and Target, M. (2004). *Affect Regulation, Mentalization, and the Development of the Self*. New York: Other Press.

Ghent, E. (1989). Credo: The dialectics of one-person and two-person psychologies. *Contemporary Psychoanalysis* 25:169–211.

Goldner, V. (1991). Towards a critical relational theory of gender. *Psychoanalytic Dialogues* 1:249–72.

Greenberg, J., and Mitchell, S. A. (1982). *Object Relations in Psychoanalytic Theory.* Cambridge, MA: Harvard University Press.

Harris, A. (1991). Gender as Contradiction. *Psychoanalytic Dialogues* 1:197–220.

———. (2005) *Gender as Soft Assembly.* Hillsdale NJ: Analytic Press.

Hoffman, I. Z. (1983). The patient as interpreter of the analyst's experience. *Contemporary Psychoanalysis* 19:389–422.

———. (1998). *Ritual and Spontaneity in the Psychoanalytic Process.* Hillsdale, NJ: The Analytic Press.

Layton, L. (1998). *Who's That Girl: Who's That Boy.* Hillsdale, NJ: Analytic Press.

———. (2002) "Cultural Hierarchies, Splitting, and the Heterosexist Unconscious" in Fairfield, S., Layton, L., and Stack, C. (2002). *Bringing the Plague: Toward a Postmodern Psychoanalysis.* New York: Other Press, pp 195–24.

Leary, K. (1997). Race, self-disclosure and "forbidden talk": Race and ethnicity in contemporary psychoanalytic practice. *Psychoanalytic Quarterly* 66:163–89.

Lyons-Ruth, K. (1999). The two-person unconscious: Intersubjective dialogue, enactive relational representation, and the emergence of new forms of relational organization. *Psychoanalytic Inquiry* 19:576–617.

Maroda, K. (1991). *The Power of Countertransference.* Northvale, NJ: Aronson.

Mitchell, S. (1988). *Relational Concepts in Psychoanalysis: An Integration.* Cambridge, MA: Harvard University Press.

———. (1993). *Hope and Dread in Psychoanalysis.* New York: Basic Books.

———. (2000). *Relationality: From Attachment to Intersubjectivity.* Hillsdale, NJ: Analytic Press.

Ogden, T. (1994). *Subjects of Analysis.* Northvale, NJ: Aronson.

Stern, D. B. (1997). *Unformulated Experience: From Dissociation to Imagination in Psychoanalysis.* Hillsdale, NJ: The Analytic Press.

Stolorow, R., and Atwood, G. (1992). Three realms of the unconscious. In *Contexts of Being: The Intersubjective Foundations of Psychological Life.* Hillsdale, NJ: Analytic Press.

Suchet, M. (2004). A relational encounter with race. *Psychoanalytic Dialogues* 14(4):423–38.

10

Psychodynamic Theory and Gender

Joan Berzoff

As we begin this chapter, we need to begin by asking ask what we mean by gender. While sex refers to being male or female based on the "objective" facts of a person's genitalia, gender has to do with the meaning ascribed to genital differences. One can be very masculine and have female genitals; one can be feminine and have male genitalia. One can have ambiguous sexual organs, as do hermaphrodites. The gender assigned to the genitals, however, comprises a series of meanings, of expected roles and behaviors that are often socially constructed. For example, being female, Asian, and poor at the turn of the twentieth century will differ from being female, Latina, and upper class at the turn of the twenty-first century. Gender is always situated in contexts of historical time, social class, ethnicity, and culture.

In 1903, Freud asked, "What does a woman want?" (Jones 1955, p. 421). Given that it has taken almost a century just to begin to answer the question, it is clear that the answer is anything but simple. In fact, the discourse on psychoanalysis and gender has produced a body of knowledge greater than Freud could have ever imagined.

Over the last hundred years, Freud has been both assailed and assimilated by feminists for his theories about women. He has been called misogynist and phallocentric for capturing the gender stereotypes of his Victorian times and labeling them normative. On the other hand, many of his ideas have been used by feminists who have critiqued, revised, and improved upon his formulations and who have articulated newer pathways for female psychological development. Current gender theorists still use Freud's ideas today to assert a postmodern construction of gender.

This chapter will look at the three waves in psychodynamic theorizing about gender, particularly about women. The first wave arose as a critique of Freud in the 1920s and 1930s in reaction to Freud's views of women as masochistic, narcissistic, and less morally developed. The second wave came between the 1960s and late 1980s, when white, middle-class feminism was at its height, and when women's differences (their moral development, their relationships, and their empathy) were celebrated as feminine strengths. During this second wave, as well, social structural theories, particularly Marxist theories, were used to understand the relationship between women's psychological differences and their place in the family and social structure. The third wave, from the 1990s to the present, has been a discourse by postmodernists and poststructuralists who assert that gender can never be understood outside of power relationships, that gender is always a socially constructed category, and that gender ambiguity and paradox are at the core of the self. Now gender is no longer viewed as a singular category, but one that is multiple, ever changing, multicultural, complex, and entirely dependent upon context.

THE FIRST WAVE: EARLY CRITIQUES OF FREUD

Let us begin, then, with Freud. As we said in chapter 2, Freud made some rather stunning statements about how psychosexual development occurs differently for little girls than for little boys at the oedipal stage of development. Freud began with the premise that little girls are really little men. He postulated that in early childhood, girls are unaware of their own vaginas and actually see their clitorises as small penises. When they discover the anatomical differences between themselves and boys, they feel envy. Girls become heterosexual, he postulated, almost by default. In trying to explain why girls break their pre-oedipal ties to their mothers and turn to men, Freud theorized that girls turn away from their original love objects, their mothers, when they discover that men have penises, and that neither they nor their mothers do. Disappointed in their mothers for not having provided them a penis, girls then turn toward their fathers in the hopes of restitution and with the fantasy that their fathers will provide them with a baby. Heterosexuality, in Freud's view, is a girl's consolation for not having a penis. Unlike boys, who renounce their oedipal desires for their mothers because of fears of being castrated by their rivals, girls do not ever fear castration because, in Freud's view, they are already castrated. As a result, girls can never fully resolve their oedipal issues and, therefore, develop weaker superegos than do boys. When girls do turn back to their mothers to identify with them, they identify with that which Freud thought was the essence of femininity: passivity, masochism, and narcissism. These features, he suggested, are essential hallmarks of female identity.

It is difficult to consider such a theory in the decade of the 2000s because Freud's claims are so embedded in his Victorian society's devalued view of women. Nonetheless, and despite how misogynistic he sounds, he actually identified some very important concepts that still contribute to our understanding of women's psychological development today.

It is interesting to note that while many of Freud's theories about women reflected the patriarchal culture in which he was embedded, he was also surrounded by women whom he trained and encouraged, including his own daughter, Anna. Many of these women went on to challenge his ideas about female development, particularly penis envy, and the development of female identification as weaker and lesser than men's (Hadley, personal communication, 2005).

Karen Horney (1924, 1926, 1967), for example, was among the first wave of Freud's contemporaries to challenge Freud's phallocentrism and to say that penis envy was not an intrapsychic event but rather a societal one. When a girl becomes aware of her anatomical difference, it is not the lack of a penis that makes her feel inferior. Instead it is the *symbolic* meaning of her difference from boys that makes her experience herself as inferior. In fact, Horney maintained that it was not the male anatomical apparatus that women want, but rather the access to what men have: power, opportunity, and resources. The idea that women's psychological development is inextricably linked to their unequal place in the social structure has dominated almost all subsequent thinking about the psychology of gender. Horney's critique was the first of many to argue that there is no such thing as a woman "born." Instead, a woman is "made." She is psychologically constructed by the society in which she develops (Rich 1976), as is her "inferiority." Further, Horney challenged Freud's view of penis envy altogether. In fact, she thought that boys envied girls, and later women, for their capacities to bear children, and she referred to this as "womb envy." She thought that this envy of men for women's reproductive abilities was one factor contributing to the domination of women by men.

In Freud's case of Little Hans (see chapter 16), we see Freud's blindness to womb envy. This five-year-old boy who has become phobic of horses, and who now clings to his mother after a new sibling is born, insists that he can have a baby. Although his father tries to dissuade him, Hans persists in the belief that he, like his mother, will give birth. Many, if not most, boys think that they can have babies, just as girls at four or five may express wishes for a penis. But in the case of Little Hans, Freud entirely ignored Hans's womb envy. Perhaps his blindness to this important part of the case history reflected his own defensive position. Perhaps by denying his own envy of women, Freud accorded the penis a more central place in all of psychological development than it deserved. Yet, envy is something to listen for in the clinical setting, be it envy of the penis or of the womb.

Bertha, a white, middle-class, three-year-old girl had been raised by two social workers. Her father shared half of the parenting responsibilities, and anatomical differences in the family were discussed and celebrated. That mommy had a vagina and daddy had a penis were taught to Bertha in the context of both sexual organs being beautiful and powerful. In fact, Bertha was very identified with the power and glory of her mother, who was now pregnant with her baby brother. However, one day while her mother was changing her newborn brother, Bertha burst into tears, saying, "I want one too! Why didn't you give me one?" pointing to his penis. She was held and comforted and reminded of all that her parents had explained. When, her parents, out of sheer curiosity, asked her what had upset her so much. She answered, "It just looks like more!" For both girls and boys, then, envy is ubiquitous.

While Horney was writing about men's dread of women (1926), Melanie Klein (Grosskurth 1986) was also suggesting that the Freud's views of women emerged out from a male fear of women' s power, not out of women's powerlessness. Noting that women are always the first love object of boys and girls, Klein maintained that women have tremendous power over their children to provide or withhold love. For little boys, this can be dangerous and threatening, and the threats of women's power may later lead to their denigration of women, and even to the abuse of women. Hence, psychological theories that diminish the power of women may be defensive in origin.

THE SECOND WAVE: WOMEN AS DIFFERENT BUT NOT DEFICIENT

From the 1960s to 1980s, much of the writing about the psychology of women was from a "difference" perspective, establishing women's separate sphere from men. At that time, a different and more contemporary critique of penis envy came out of cognitive developmental psychology, and although it was not a psychodynamic theory, per se, it was a way to try to understand gender identity. Irene Fast (1984) noted that "difference" has dominated most of the discourse on women. She suggested that envy was ubiquitous to both boys and to girls. Each gender wants what it cannot have, and envy is a result of a child's cognitive awareness of difference. In her view, the recognition of difference is a cognitive achievement, not an intrapsychic one.

Cognitively, little girls and boys are aware of sex differences by the end of the first year of life. Between the ages of one and two, little girls and boys begin to distinguish sex differences based on hair and dress. A little boy or girl might say, "He's a boy because he has short hair," or "She's a girl because she wears a dress." If a boy has long hair, or if a girl wears long pants or has short hair, the young child may have some difficulty identify-ing the gender. For the young child, the concept of gender is not fixed. Rather, the young child still sees gender as reversible and fluid. By ages three to five, however, boys and girls become aware that sex differences are not based on external characteristics but on genital differences, and then become curious about each other's genitals, and often explore the physical differences between them. However, the *meaning* of those anatomical dif-ferences does not actually develop until the child discovers that the genitals he or she has will remain constant forever. The awareness of gender con-stancy imposes limits. Having a penis means never giving birth to a baby; having a vagina means never having a penis. When children cognitively confront the limits of their own anatomy, they envy what they do not have. The awareness of the limits, and of gender constancy, leads to the develop-ment of a fixed gender identity. This view of envy as a cognitive develop-mental achievement depathologizes the concept of penis or womb envy.

During the 1960s to the 1980s, some very similar ideas about female relational capacities were emerging from psychoanalytic Marxist analyses. Recall that Melanie Klein described the infant as absolutely dependent on the mother, so that when a mother's milk is available, the infant feels loved. When the infant tries to drink too quickly and chokes on the mother's milk or when the mother is not available to the infant, the child can feel utter and complete dependency and hatred. The mother, in Western cultures, then, is the source of all of the infant's experiences of being worthy or unworthy. She can also be the source of the child's hatred, which may be experienced as an attack from without or within. Klein, and later Dorothy Dinnerstein (1976), noted that the mother, who is experienced as all-pow-erful, can be the source of gender oppression. Dinnerstein contended that the rigid sex roles and sex role ideologies that are so prevalent in Western culture stem from primitive fears about the power of women. Because nei-ther boys nor girls develop a realistic sense of their own mothers as an inde-pendent or autonomous agents, their fantasies about the power of their mothers become, paradoxically, greater. Because children need their moth-ers and are entirely dependent on them, they also wish to control them, so that the most pathological aspects of our current culture—violence against women, the devaluation of and humiliation of women—have their roots in earliest child-rearing arrangements.

Hence in the 1970s and 1980s, patriarchal societies were seen as creating and maintaining rigid gender roles as a societal defense against the power of women. Mothers were viewed as the source of human creation and blamed as the source of all human malaise (Dinnerstein 1976). As long as gender roles were perpetuated through child-care arrangements in which only mothers cared for children, women would continue to be feared, and men and women would be robbed of their fullest opportunities for human development (Chodorow 1974, Dinnerstein 1976).

Nancy Chodorow (1974), a Marxist sociologist who later became a psychoanalyst, was also interested in the gender inequities in American society. Rather than reject outright psychoanalytic theories, she used the very same theories to explain social inequality. She argued that in a society in which only women take care of children, boys and girls are socialized to develop a gendered senses of self in the context of an unequal nuclear family. Boys develop their gender identities by first separating and individuating from their primary love objects, their mothers. To develop his sense of self, a boy has to develop strong ego boundaries between himself and his mother. Thus, boys develop a self that is more boundaried, more differentiated, and more autonomous than that of girls. In the process of their gender identity development, a boy learns to repress or deny the parts of himself that were forged in close contact with his mother.

On the other hand, in the process of developing a female sense of self, a girl never needs to break her pre-oedipal ties to her mother. Her female sense of self develops in the context of a continuous relationship with her mother. As a result of this continuity, girls develop different kinds of relational skills and capacities than do boys. Girls develop more permeable ego boundaries with greater capacities for empathy than do boys. The beginning of the theory that girls are more relational, and boys more autonomous and independent, then, was argued in the context of an analysis of the social structure of mothering and of the heterosexual nuclear family.

Chodorow (1974) asserted that in a society in which women are predominantly mothers, girls and boys develop different relational skills that are then reproduced as asymmetrical gender roles. Boys, because they must separate and individuate from their mothers, reproduce a socialization process that fosters male autonomy, separateness, and individuation, while girls will reproduce a social structure in which they maintain a relational orientation and a more fluid sense of self. In a society that values autonomy over connectedness, this gender asymmetry does not serve women well. In the nuclear heterosexual family especially, gender asymmetry perpetuates unequal gender roles. Only a revolution in parenting, then, could solve gender inequities. In later theorizing, Chodorow began to wonder why nuclear families are ever heterosexual, given that girls never break their preoedipal ties. Instead, she begins to wonder, and why all girls and later women are not lesbian (Chodorow 1994).

Jessica Benjamin (1988), another Marxist psychoanalyst, began as a social historian who turned to psychoanalysis to understand how gender inequities in the social structure led to differences in gendered identities. She suggested that, for little boys, the father represents the pure and idealized love that comes with independence and freedom. Boys recognize, when their father leaves the family for work each day, the freedom that their father has, and they identify with their father and with their father's separateness. For girls, the task of separation is far more difficult, because in Western cultures, fathers represent separation and freedom to girls as well. But where boys identify with their fathers, girls must come to terms with being different from their fathers. What does a girl do with her own desire for freedom and separateness? Benjamin asserts that girls defensively begin to idealize men and to subjugate their own desires for agency and separateness to the desires of men. Rather than experience themselves as subjects in their own right, girls begin to learn to become objects of men's desire. We can see the evolution of subjugation and loss of agency in the following example.

> Gina, a twenty-one-year-old college student, described her mother as "bland, ugly, fat, and frumpy." Her father (who, it turns out, was all of these things), she described as "cool, brilliant, inventive, and creative." As treatment progressed, it became clear that Gina's mother was the more attuned and caring parent, whereas her father was quite self-involved and remote. Yet Gina found herself in sexual relationships in which she tried to think the deep and profound thoughts she assumed men expected of her. Invariably, she became silent with boys because she felt unworthy, and that they would and should control the relationship. She tried to dress seductively for men, but had no idea what style of dress *she* liked. She expended much energy becoming an object of men's desires, but said that she had little sense of who she was or what she wanted.

In this second wave of feminism, then, women began to be seen as oppressed by having to become objects of men's desire, and having difficulty being subjects of their own desire. A child who has some sense of socially sanctioned value will be less likely to be controlled by others. But girls, whose gender is devalued, learn to subsume their own desires. Perhaps this is why Margaret Mahler (1980) described how little girls in the rapprochement sub-phase lose some of their enthusiasm, and become more depressed than little boys. Like Chodorow, Dinnerstein, and others writing in this vein, Benjamin argued that, if female self and object representations are ever to become more robust and alive for girls and women, there would need to be changes in both the family structure and the social structure.

Jessica Benjamin (1995) also identified how psychoanalytic language further exacerbates the problem. When, for example, people are described as objects (as in object relations theories), they are rarely, if ever, seen as subjects in their own right. Our language of object relations theory often implies that a woman (read mother) is someone who is submissive, accommodating, and a passive object who exists to meet the needs of others, but not a person who is recognized as having her own agency and desire. In fact, Benjamin claims that the recognition of a mother's subjectivity is a critical developmental step for boys and girls, and that without such recognition, women continue to be treated as objects, not subjects, by men.

In summary, this second wave of psychodynamic feminist theorizing highlighted several critiques of earlier theories of female development. Feminist psychoanalytic theorists suggested that in nuclear family structures in which only one gender does the parenting, women may be feared. In a society that fears women, it is likely that they will be subjugated. In nuclear families, gender asymmetries may become codified as gender roles and become reproduced as social inequities. In family structures in which men represent freedom and separation, women may have to subjugate their own desires. In nuclear family arrangements, women are made powerfully responsible for the care of others, but are subordinated and experience powerlessness in the larger social world. As long as mothers remain the primary caretakers, they become the target of fear and loathing. Without recognition of women as subjects, and not only objects, they remain unrecognized as agents of their own desires.

SELF-IN-RELATION THEORIES: MORE
FROM THE SECOND WAVE

At the same time as the women's gendered senses of self were being understood as occurring within the social structure, self-in-relation theorists (Miller 1976, Gilligan 1982, Jordan, Surrey, and Kaplan 1983) began to claim women's relational capacities as strengths and as forms of survival. In this view, pejorative concepts such as female dependency were now turned upside down and were celebrated as the strengths of cooperation and creativity. From this self-in-relation perspective (Jordan et al. 1983, Jordan and Surrey 1986, Surrey and Kaplan 1990), the female infant was seen as never fully separating from her mother, but always developing a self in relation to others. Rather than pathologizing women's dependency in relationships from birth on, these theorists suggested that girls develop greater empathy and attunement to others by virtue of their continuous relationships with their mothers. A girl's sameness with her mother fosters her ability to see herself in her mother; her likeness catalyzes rather than impedes her development. In this analysis, there are echoes of self psychology—the belief that maternal empathy fosters psychological development.

Thus, during the same period of psychological theorizing in which Chodorow, Benjamin, and Dinnerstein were viewing women's differences based on inequality in parenting arrangements, other theorists were focusing on female development as a self-in-relation paradigm. Theorists from the Stone Center at Wellesley College (Jordan et al. 1983; Jordan and Surrey 1986; Miller 1976, 1990; Surrey and Kaplan 1990) were explaining that within a Western society, where women had been subordinate to men, they had found ways to act and react from their subordinate positions. Like any subjugated group, women tended to form intense affiliations and relationships with other women in the workplace, the community, and the family. These kinds of relational bonds, while in reaction to their subjugation, could also be seen as fostering their identities and leading to stronger senses of self. Yet while women were socialized to make and sustain relationships, this activity occurs in a society that devalued relationships and overvalued personal productivity (Berzoff 1989, Miller 1976).

In a related domain of moral development and at around the same time, Carol Gilligan (see chapter 5 on Erikson for further elaboration) began to question views of women's inferior moral development, arguing that women's moral reasoning was different from men's, but not deficient. Having been a protégé of Lawrence Kohlberg, who showed that children made moral decisions based on a rights and responsibilities orientation, Gilligan became interested in why the girls that Kohlberg studied often scored lower on his measures of moral development than boys. Gilligan posited that boys and girls simply approach moral issues differently, and that for girls, moral reasoning tended to be more relational and less legalistic. Gilligan had already noticed that in games, boys would argue about the rules, while girls would end the game, to preserve their relationships with one another. Hence when she systematically studied how women made moral decisions (1982), she found that their moral decisions were based on maintaining and keeping relationships, and that their perspectives on morality were based on an ethic of care rather than a rights and responsibilities orientation. Gilligan maintained that female moral decision making was different than from men's, but by no means inferior.

But as self-in-relation theorists tried to correct the devaluation of women, they also inadvertently tended to idealize women's relational skills. Stone Center theorists tended to valorize women as affiliative, nurturant, and maternal, so much so that by the 1990s, many feminists began to wonder if the "differences" theories were not "essentialist," meaning that they exaggerated the essences of maleness and femaleness in overly prescribed, stereotypic, and traditional ways. Women, in this view, were relegated to a separate sphere of maternal empathy and connectedness. How oppressive might this be for women who saw themselves as agentic, individuated, and not oriented only to care? In fact, many of the critics of self-in-relation theories also began to ask: Which women are we talking about? Were these descriptions of women as nurturant, relational, and empathic true for working-class women, for African American and Latina women, for all lesbian women? Were these essentialist qualities, in fact, not yet another form of gender conformity that did not allow for views of men and women as more complex, with identities that were more fluid and ambiguous? Were such views of men and women overly dichotomizing women's and men's roles in society?

> These tensions can be seen in the treatment of Emily, a twenty-four-year-old graduate of a feminist women's college, who had spent four years in college with a self-in-relation therapist. She described how very deficient she was made to feel because her nature and her personality strengths had to do with independence, critical thinking, control, and power. She felt that in her earlier therapy she had to hide her true self and her aspirations—to go into business, to be a "son of a bitch," to become a CEO—because those qualities were reviled as "male" in her therapy, and therefore as less good. By nature, she was a cool and distant person who did not like sharing and processing her feelings. Only in the second therapy could she begin to articulate how hemmed in she felt by the essentializing nature of feminism at that time.

Just as Freud had been critiqued for devaluing women's essential natures, the feminists of the 1960s and 1970s may have overzealously been guilty of glorifying women's essential natures, in response to the strong currents of early feminism.

POSTMODERN FEMINIST CRITIQUES: THE THIRD WAVE

Much of the third wave of psychoanalytic theorizing about gender, then, began as a critique of the second wave, noting that "differences" theorists seemed blind to social class, race, ethnicity, and sexual orientation as influencing gendered "identities." Postmodern theorists began to ask whether there was anything essential about being a woman (Abel 1990, Flax 1990, Greene 2000, Perez Foster, Moskowitz, and Javier 1996, Spelman 1988, Unger 1979). Do "female" qualities of nurturance and relationship apply to all women? Do they pertain to Asian women living in urban poverty, to Latina women, to single, married, lesbian, aging women, to women with disabilities, privileged women, physically ill women, rural women, urban women, disadvantaged women? In fact, the question emerged again whether there should be a category at all such as "woman"?

Peggy McIntosh (1988) pointed out that "white privilege" encouraged white feminist scholars to assume that their own middle-class experiences were universal, normative, and representative. In that way, white, heterosexual feminists assumed that all women were like them. As long as we assume that all women are empathic, or flexible, or affiliative, we lose sight of the ways that race, class, age, health, sexual orientation, and ethnicity mediate the many meanings of being female. As long as ways of being are dichotomized only as female or male, we privilege some sexual arrangements and marginalize others. As long as the only configuration that is valued is that of the nuclear and heterosexual family, then many women's experiences are marginalized. Many postmodern theorists call instead for "psychologies" of women, which are pluralistic, multicultural, contextual, and egalitarian.

Over the last decade, then, from the postmodern frontier has come the critique that the so-called essential attributes of women (and of men) need to be challenged. Do all women (mothers) produce boys who are separate and autonomous? Are all girls relational? Is all of society reducible to the nuclear family? Are there boys and men who are more relational and girls and women who are less socially constrained by gender norms? Is gender a stable construct across social classes, ethnicities, sexual orientations? Are women more nurturant, or is this a political means of maintaining the status quo? Were "difference" perspectives, in fact, inferiorizing women as "other"? Hence, the very concept of gender came into question as reifying and supporting the nuclear, heterosexual family. As long as psychological theories prescribe fixed gender categories that are dualistic and binary (i.e., males representing one set of behaviors, abilities, values, and capacities, and women another), realities would be structured accordingly, and we unwittingly perpetuate gender stereotypes (Abel 1990, Butler 1990, Dimen 2003, Dimen and Goldner 2002, Hare-Mustin and Marecek 1990, Spelman 1988).

Postmodern psychoanalytic theorists, therefore, began to encourage deconstructing the concept of gender, and challenging the hierarchical oppositions that legitimize power differentials. Hare-Mustin and Marecek (1990), for example, point to the alpha and beta biases in gender theorizing. Alpha biases exaggerate differences (e.g., all women are relational and nurturing; all men are autonomous and separate). Taken to the extreme, alpha biases valorize women for their relational skills, while relegating them to the domestic sphere of caregivers for children. This leads us away from changing their unequal social conditions. Beta biases obscure differences (e.g., men and women are androgynous and the same, and there are no differences between them). Beta biases in gender theorizing can ultimately result in creating social policies that treat men and women as exactly the same, despite their differences (such as eliminating pregnancy leaves for women in the workplace). Both kinds of biases tend to dichotomize gender possibilities, reducing human complexity, ambiguity, and paradox.

As long as gender is conceptualized only as binary, gender conformity will be the goal. When gender is dichotomized, there is a tendency toward relational "splitting" (Goldner 1991). In the course of any individual's development, parts of the self are encouraged for one gender, while other parts of the self are prohibited. But this kind of gender splitting is regressive, prohibitive, and ultimately limits human possibility and human potential (Goldner 1991).

Muriel Dimen (2003) has tried to capture gender complexity this way. She sees gender difference as a paradox of selfhood.

> Autonomy and dependence, activity and passivity, heterosexuality and homo-sexuality, body and mind, selfness and otherness, subjectivity and objectifica-tion, body superiority and inferiority, want and need and I could go on: these apparent polarities are but diverse aspects of the self, the passage between which might be regarded as pleasurable even though when we leave the pre-ferred polarity, when for example we transit from want to need, we are, as things now stand, extraordinarily uncomfortable. (pp. 197–98)

Postmodern theorists (Foucault 1980, 1990) have also noted that words create worlds; language constructs reality. Gender, then, is not a given, it is a series of cultural constructions created through language. But binary categories of male/female tend to encode these categories with social expec-tations of what women should be. We cannot know the "meaning" or "truth" of anyone's gender based on biology or development alone (Butler 1990), because cultures, environments, and relational contexts either encourage multiple kinds of expressions of gender, or constrict them.

The same argument, by the way, has been made about sexual orientation. Just as psychoanalytic theories posited a developmental theory of causality for why women were narcissistic and masochistic, so, too, did those same psychological theories posit causality for homosexuality, finding gays and lesbians to be immature, deviant, and perverse. But, like gender, sexual ori-entation is also not deviant, fixed, or immutable; instead, it changes over time within different kinds of relational contexts. Take, for example, Nina, who did not want to be constrained or limited by binary gender categories.

> Nina came to therapy to deal with the loss of her mother from cancer. She was in her mid-twenties, and thought that many of her problems with asserting her authority at work stemmed from difficulties she had asserting her autonomy at home, at a time when her mother was weakened and wasting away. While struggles with her female boss had brought her into treatment, there was one area of her life that was playful and pleasurable. Nina described, with some delight, dating both men and women. She liked this part of herself that could be spontaneous, less prescribed, and more flexible. In contrast to seeing herself "stuck" at work, especially in relation to any authority figures, her sexual life felt like the one area of freedom, experimentation, and choice she wished existed in other realms of her life.

Most lesbian women maintain that sexual orientation is not a choice, and that expressions of sexual orientation change over time. When straight relationships were structured according to gender roles, many lesbian women tended toward also being "butch or femme." That began to change (as it has in straight relationships) when the kinds of roles that men and women play became more fluid. When being bisexual was rejected by the gay community, the community itself pressured people to commit themselves to being gay only. Currently, there is much greater encouragement about a range of forms of sexuality, including lesbian, bisexual, and transgendered. While a full discussion of transgendered relationships is beyond the scope of this chapter, transgendered individuals experience gender dysphoria, and feel that the gender assigned to them does not match their own gender identity. For them, coming out involves acknowledging and disclosing their sexual orientation and gender identity to themselves and others. Often, it involves a process of gender reassignment that means making biological changes from male to female or female to male, along with a range of social, legal, and psychological changes. For gay, lesbian, and bisexual women, as for their straight counterparts, sexuality is about feeling empowered, finding support and community, achieving a healthy and positive identity, and developing as a cohesive, authentic, and whole human being. And while gender theorists extol the creativity of new forms of gendered expression, we must always remember that gay, lesbian, bisexual, and transgendered youth are regularly victims of verbal and physical assaults, and twice as likely to report having seriously considered suicide. For transsexuals, 53 percent had made suicide attempts (Education Report of the Massachusetts Governor's Commission on Gay and Lesbian Youth, National Gay and Lesbian Task Forces, Safe Schools Report).

Many postmodern theorists (Comas-Diaz and Greene 1994, Dimen and Goldner 2002, Harris 1995a, 1995b, Layton 2002) now focus on gender as discontinuous, on gender as a particular set of discourses that often have to do with coercion and power, and on gender as a personal construct that is always idiosyncratic. Even the very categories of masculinity and femininity are always constructed in relation to each other (Layton 2002). Postmodern perspectives on gender tend toward becoming liberating discourses, so that women are not constrained by dualities or limited by binary categories. We are always embedded in our culture and our times.

While much has been written on the need to deconstruct gender and to be open to gendered possibilities, there is still much work to be done on how this actually occurs in the clinical situation, especially with clients who may be more disturbed. While a postmodern perspective—positing identities as always shifting based on culture, gender, race, religion, ethnicity, class, and sexual orientations—is very valuable to the practitioner, there are still issues that postmodernists do not address, especially for those clients whose experiences of multiple identities contribute to unbearable fragmentation. Multiplicity can be playful, creative, and enlivening, but in those whose senses of self are not coherent, multiplicity may lead to further fragmentation. There is then a tension for the practitioner between fostering the paradox, and the ambiguities of gender identity, while also appreciating that, for some, discontinuities of self may be unbearable. Under the best of circumstances, living with a multiplicity of gendered possibilities may be freeing for both women and men in achieving their full relational potentials, but there will also always be those who come to us for help because such discontinuities are overwhelming and fragmenting.

And so, we are left with the question: What do women want? And the answer is: Anything or everything. Some women want to stay at home with their children; some women want to be president of the United States. Some women see themselves as affiliative, and others see themselves as instrumental. Some see themselves as both, depending on the context. Some women want a man, some women desire other women, and some women desire both men and women. Our answers about what women want must recognize that women are always embedded in particular power arrangements, unique social contexts, stages of development, particular forms of family life, sexual orientations, religions, ethnicities, social classes, races, and that these determine, as much as anything, their gendered self-states. Women move in and out of gendered categories and through different roles, often based on culture, religion, social conditions. Their capacities to tolerate fluidity may, in fact, be hallmarks of their mental health.

REFERENCES

Abel, E. (1990). Race, class and psychoanalysis? Opening questions. In *Conflicts in Feminism*, ed. M. Hirsch and E. F. Keller. New York: Routledge Press.

Benjamin, J. (1988). *The Bonds of Love: Psychoanalysts, Feminism and the Problem of Domination*. New York: Pantheon Books.

———. (1995). *Like Subjects; Love Objects: Essays on Recognition and Difference*. New Haven, CT: Yale University Press.

Berzoff, J. (1989). From separation to connection: Shifts in understanding women's development. *Affilia: Journal of Women and Social Work* 4:45–58.

Butler, J. (1990). *Gender Trouble: Feminism and the Subversion of Identity*. New York: Routledge.

Chodorow, N. (1974). Family structure and feminine personality. In *Woman, Culture, and Society*, ed. M. Z. Rosaldo, and K. Lamphere. Stanford, CA: Stanford University Press.

———. (1994). *Femininities, Masculinities, Sexualities: Freud and Beyond*. Lexington, KY: University of Kentucky Press.

Comas-Diaz, L., and Greene, B. (1994). *Women of Color: Integrating Ethnic and Gender Identities in Psychotherapy*. New York: Guilford.

Dimen, M. (2003). *Sexuality, Intimacy, Power*. Hillsdale, NJ: The Analytic Press.

Dimen, M., and Goldner, V., eds. (2002). *Gender in Psychoanalytic Space: Between Clinic and Culture*. New York: Other Press.

Dinnerstein, D. (1976). *The Mermaid and the Minotaur: Sexual Arrangements and Human Malaise*. New York: Harper and Row.

Fast, I. (1984). *Gender Identity: A Differentiation Model*. Hillsdale, NJ: Analytic Press.

Flax, J. (1990). *Thinking Fragments: Psychoanalysis, Feminism and Postmodernism in the Contemporary West*. Berkeley, CA: University of California Press.

Foucault, M. (1980). Truth and Power. In *Power/Knowledge: Selected Interviews and Other Writings of Michel Foucault, 1972–1977*, ed. C. Gordon. New York: Pantheon.

———. (1990). *The History of Sexuality*, Vol. I (trans. R. Hurley). New York: Vintage [English translation Copyright 1978 by Random House, Inc.].

Gilligan, C. (1982). *In A Different Voice: Psychological Theory and Women's Development*. Cambridge, MA: Harvard University Press.

Goldner, V. (1991). Toward a critical relational theory of gender. *Psychoanalytic Dialogues* 1(3):249–72.

Greene, B. (2000). African American lesbians and bisexual women in feminist-psychodynamic psychotherapies: Surviving and thriving between a rock and a hard place. In *Psychotherapy with African American Women: Innovations in Psychodynamic Perspectives and Practice*, eds. L. C. Jackson and B. Greene. New York: Guildford Press.

Grosskurth, P. (1986). *Melanie Klein: Her World and Her Work*. New York: Knopf.

Hare-Mustin, R., and Marecek, J. (1990). *On Making a Difference: Psychology and the Construction of Gender*. New Haven, CT: Yale University Press.

Harris, A. (1995a). Gender as contradiction. *Psychoanalytic Dialogues* 1:23–24.

———. (1995b) *Disorienting Sexuality: Psychoanalytic Reappraisals of Sexual Identities*, eds. T. Dominici and R. C. Lesser. New York: Routledge Press.

Horney, K. (1924). On the genesis of the castration complex in women. *International Journal of Psychoanalysis* 5:50–65.

———. (1926). The flight from womanhood: the masculinity complex in women as viewed by men and women. In *Woman and Analysis: Dialogues on Psychoanalytic Views of Femininity*, ed. J. Strouse. New York: Grossman, 1974.

———. (1967). *Feminine Psychology*. New York: Norton.

Jones, E. (1955). *The Life and Work of Sigmund Freud*, vol. III. New York: Basic Books.

Jordan, J., and Surrey, J. (1986). The self-in-relation: Empathy and the mother-daughter relationship. In *The Psychology of Today's Woman: New Psychoanalytic Visions*, ed. T. Bernay and D. W. Cantor. Hillsdale, NJ: Analytic Press.

Jordan, J., Surrey, J., and Kaplan, A. (1983). *Women and Empathy: Implications for Psychological Development and Empathy*. Stone Center for Developmental Services. Wellesley, MA: Wellesley College.

Layton, L. (2002). Gendered subjects, gendered agents: Toward an integration of postmodern theory and relational analytic practice. In *Gender in Psychoanalytic Space*, eds. M. Dimen and V. Goldner. New York: Other Press.

Mahler, M. (1980). *The Psychological Birth of the Human Infant.* New York: Basic Books.

McIntosh, P. (1988). White privilege and mate privilege: A personal account of coming to see correspondences through work in women's studies. Wellesley College Center for Research on Women, Working Paper 189, 1–19.

Miller, J. B. (1976). *Toward a New Psychology of Women.* Boston: Beacon.

———. (1990). The development of women's sense of self. In *Essential Papers on the Psychology of Women,* ed. C. Zanardi. New York: New York University Press.

Perez Foster, R. M., Moskowitz, M., and Javier, R. A., eds. (1996). *Reaching Across Boundaries of Culture and Class: Widening the Scope of Psychotherapy.* Northvale, NJ: Aronson.

Rich, A. (1976). *Of Woman Born: Motherhood as Experience and Institution.* New York: Norton.

Spelman, V. (1988). *Inessential Woman: Problems of Exclusion in Feminist Thought.* Boston: Beacon Press.

Surrey, J., and Kaplan, A. (1990). *Empathy Revisited,* no. 40, pp. 1–14. Wellesley, MA: Stone Center, Wellesley College.

Unger, R. (1979). Toward a redefinition of sex and gender. *American Psychologist* 34(11):1085–94.

11

Coloring Development

Race and Culture in Psychodynamic Theories

Lourdes Mattei

> *You are made of chocolate, and I'm vanilla.*
> Three-year-old boy's comment while playing with adult

Psychodynamic theories have a long, contradictory, and marginalized relationship with issues of race and culture. As has been true throughout this book, the insights and value preferences, the biases and prejudices of every sociohistorical time and place are embedded in our psychological theories, concepts, and ideas. Psychodynamic theories are no exception.

From Freud onward, a number of psychodynamic theorists who are discussed throughout this chapter and book have presented us with ways of understanding the relationship between society and the individual. There has been an inherent tension in the psychoanalytic discourse regarding the role of culture in psychological development. On the one hand, psychoanalysis, like any other "modern" discipline has aspired to be universal (that is, to be culture-free and color-blind) in its basic principles. On the other hand, a "culturalist" tradition exists. This "culturalist" position has taken two different paths: (1) the use of psychodynamic ideas to explain social dynamics, or (2) the use of psychodynamic concepts to help explain the influence of society on personality development. In this chapter, then, we will focus on the ways that psychoanalytic insights have been applied to the understanding of malignant psychosocial dynamics such as racism, bigotry, and ethnocentrism.

We will also explore the relationship between psychoanalysis, race, and culture. In order to illustrate this relationship, we will highlight critical ways of understanding race/racism. We will feature race in the context of two major metaphors used in psychoanalysis in the United States: the metaphor of the "beast" and the metaphor of the "baby" (Mitchell 1988). According to psychoanalyst, Stephen Mitchell, psychoanalysis has used two fundamental discourses to theorize about human development. The first sees the individual psyche as fundamentally "beastly" (drive and ego psychology); the other sees the individual as more like a baby with unmet developmental needs (object relations and self psychology). These discourses are based on fundamental differences in ideas about human nature, development, pathology, and motivation.

To make our psychoanalytic discourse even deeper and more complex, epistemological leaps and critiques have been—and are being—articulated with the advent of postmodernist ideas, which challenge the notion that development can ever be fully explained within either—or any one—metaphor. These postmodern perspectives imply drastic differences in epistemological positions. For example: How do we know what is in my/your/our mind(s)? Is it possible to know one mind from intrapsychic or one-person psychologies, or can we only know with any certainty or authority what is generated in our minds by the encounter of two minds, as described by intersubjective, interpersonal or two-person psychologies? Is psychic functioning universal or is it historically bound?

In the "case" of race and racism, the understanding of the relationship between the person and her society is inescapably linked. In addition, race, like gender, has been historically understood as a category that uses the body as its defining characteristic. Thus, the relationship between the body and the psyche comes into play in our theories and practices. Although we currently understand "race" as a "social construction," we have inherited a variety of ways in which the word/concept/fantasy condenses a multiplicity of meanings, both by groups and individuals (Lacan 1981).

We think that psychodynamic insights may be used to illuminate dialogues on race and racism. We do not think of psychodynamic or any other psychological theories as *the* explanation for such a complex and multiply determined human experience as race or racism. At the same time, we do believe psychodynamic ideas can help illuminate, deepen, and open up the debate about the persistence of racial dynamics in development, the clinical situation, and society-at-large. This chapter, then, represents a synthesis of the possibilities and limitations contributed by psychoanalytic knowledge to our understanding of race and racism.

Let us begin, then, with an overview of race and culture in the psychoanalytic tradition. Next, we will present specific interpretations from the dominant psychoanalytic psychologies in the United States. Case examples will be used throughout the chapter to illustrate how we might "listen" to race and understand racial dynamics in the therapeutic encounter.

RACE AND CULTURE IN THE PSYCHOANALYTIC TRADITION: CONTROVERSIES, USES, AND MISUSES

Psychoanalysis's interest in culture has taken many directions. Since its inception, psychoanalytic theorists have been interested in society or "civilization." Freud's later writing was characterized by a concern with the application of psychoanalysis to larger groups, communities, and social issues (Paul 1991). In fact, Freud's later books have been referred to as the "cultural books" (i.e., *Totem and Taboo* [1912/1913], *Civilizations and Its Discontent* [1930], *Group Psychology and the Analysis of the Ego* [1921], *Moses and Monotheism* [1939]). In addition, anthropologists have been interested in the debate over the universality of psychoanalytic concepts across cultures since its beginnings (e.g., Geertz 1973, Kurtz 1992, Malinowski 1927/1953). There is even a long-standing tradition of interdisciplinary work stemming from psychoanalysis, anthropology, and sociology, such as the "culture and personality" studies. (See Young-Bruehl 1996 for a comprehensive overview of this historical line of theoretical development.)

Two main controversies, however, exist in understanding the construction of race and racism. These controversies point to different fundamental epistemological and theoretical assumptions about human "nature" and society. The first controversy includes what we call the tension of universality. Are we humans all the same? How are we different? What do these differences mean? The second critical controversy revolves around power, or what I name "the conflict around determinacy." Where, we need to ask, is power located: in society; in the individual; in the body; in the mind; or in the society, culture, and institutions?. Which dimension is more important in determining development, pathology, or motivation? How is the psyche reflected in society? How is society reflected or "entered into" the psyche? Psychoanalytic interpretations of racial dynamics depend on answers to these questions.

Before continuing any further, we will borrow Clarke's (2003) definitions of the "old" and the "new" racism as points of departure. In his illuminating book, *Social Theory, Psychoanalysis, and Racism*, Clarke presents us with the following historical development in the definition of racism:

Cultural forms of racism, or what has been termed the "New Racism," are not dependent on racial stereotypes or typologies but are rooted in notions of cultural and ethnic difference. These, it could be argued are nothing new, rather there is a shift in emphasis. Biological racism uses . . . inferiority as a means of not only demonizing the subject but also the culture of that subject. Publicly and certainly politically it is unacceptable to talk of people as biologically inferior; the emphasis has therefore switched to a discourse of cultural difference in which the Other becomes demonized. (p. 28)

In the "old" version of racism, racism was defined by the body; "biological" differences came to mean inferiority or superiority among groups. In the "new" version, differences in culture define our prejudices. Racism at its core is about dehumanizing the "other," about negating another person's subjectivity. And, subjectivity, the many ways in which it is formed and deformed, is a main interest in psychoanalysis.

UNIVERSAL CONTROVERSY

Like many thinkers of his time, Freud claimed—and wanted to make a case for—modern principles for his emerging theory: finding universal laws for human nature and motivation as a new kind of science. His claim notwithstanding, the impact of Freud's own ethnicity in the development of his ideas has been a source of interest and controversy (see Brunner 1991, Gilman 1992). Furthermore, like many thinkers of his time, he held the ethnocentric belief that Western civilization represented the most advanced stage of human history. The comedian Dick Gregory aptly captures this prejudicial view in his joke:

You gotta say this for Whites, their self-confidence knows no bounds. Who else would go to a small island in the South Pacific, where there's no crime, poverty, unemployment, war, or worry—and call it a "primitive society?" (cited in Watkins 1994, p. 502)

Brickman (2003), in an exhaustive, interdisciplinary, and piercing book, draws our attention to the persistent use of the idea of the "primitive" in psychoanalysis. Linking a tightly woven line of historical and intellectual associations, Brickman highlights Freud's 1915 essay on the unconscious, where he refers explicitly to the content of the unconscious as an "aboriginal population in the mind." This author persuasively argues that the fantasy of the primitive is suffused in colonialist and racist discourses. While radically undermining European elitist thought of the day with the claim of universality (everyone has an unconscious, including the Europeans!), Freud reproduced the ethnocentric, evolutionary ideology of his time by marking the unconscious as a dark, regressive, infantile, and pathological place. This concept remains very much alive in our current psychoanalytic (clinical) discourse, while its use has faded when characterizing cultures. Frosch (1989) comments on the "misuse" of the psychoanalytic/evolutionary principle of primitivity when "assessing" cultures along a phylogenetic line, that is, when we contrast the development of cultures over time in contrast to the development of the individual:

> Using an evolutionary framework of doubtful validity, this involves an assumption that the current patterns of culture to be found in the non-industrialized peoples can be regarded as fossilized versions of the actual pre-history of Western culture . . . Indeed the strongest ideological determinant of this work is an assumed equivalence between so-called "primitive" people, children, and the insane . . . a related tendency common to many psychoanalytic studies is to view Western culture as the pinnacle of development, with non-industrialized societies representing either or both a fixation at childhood points of development, or pathological regressions. (pp. 212–13)

Although this colonialist use of psychoanalytic ideas to understand social groups or cultures has resulted in well-deserved criticisms of psychoanalytic thinking, the link with "dark" forces continues to plague or infest our clinical work (i.e., our writings, teachings, practices, interpretations) with racist and colonialist colorings. Hence, when we talk about "primitive urges" we are reproducing colonialist discourse.

With the slow and uneven integration of postmodern critiques in psychoanalysis, the question of universality has taken center stage once again (see chapter 9 on intersubjectivity, and chapter 10 on gender). Postmodern critiques have called into question concepts of essential identity that presume a fixed, pre-social, prehistorical idea. This critique of the concept of identity has been more fiercely articulated by feminists in relation to gender than race (see chapter 10 on gender).

WHERE IS THE POWER?

Another critical controversy in psychoanalytic theories is the debate about the relationship between the individual and the group/culture/society. This debate gets especially thorny when it gets polarized. For example, which realm has more power in determining what shapes our identities? In the case of racism, should we be looking more at society or at the individual's personal agency and psychological determinism? Other related questions that underlie intellectual discourses and have significant implications for understanding race and racism include: How is the psyche reflected in societal practices? How are social values reflected and/or reproduced in the psyche?

Psychoanalytic theories that rely heavily on the idea (fantasy/representation) of the body such as the classical (drive and ego psychology) and Kleinian theories have been used to "privilege," to emphasize as the most important, simplistic notions of biology. These ideas have been applied in ways that suggest that the "biological" realm (drives/instincts, erotogenic zones, "good"/"bad" breast, etc.) is fixed, inevitable, and immutable. In other words, this biological dimension of psychological life is typically considered "pre-social," that is, as belonging to a realm in opposition to, before, or even outside culture. The line between the body and the mind is starkly drawn, as well as it is between the individual and her environment (inside and outside) are starkly drawn.

One clinical implication of this polarization has led to a de-emphasis of culture in psychoanalytic inquiries. Culture, or the "external," or what is not intrapsychic (the special domain of one-person psychologies) tends to be considered a more superficial (surface, manifest) content than the core (deeper, latent) aspects of the mind. Some psychoanalytic accounts appear to reduce social factors to a "screen" or stage for the playing out of biologically determined and universal conflicts. Little substantive attention is paid to the very real ways the social context creates, shapes, and influences complex psychological processes. We consider this approach to be an extreme version of psychological determinism. Consequently, psychoanalytic ideas have been criticized for their psychological reductionism (the "reducing" of complex dynamics to the psychological level as *the* main source of understanding) and for their extreme individualism.

Moreover, and more recently, postmodern views in psychology, such as social constructivism, question the validity of the concept of the "individual" (e.g., see Gergen 1994, Hoffman 1991 for this view in psychoanalysis).

Paradoxically, important insights have emerged from one-person psychologies. Psychoanalytic theory has a very sophisticated idea of causality. For example, the concept of "over-determinism" or "multi-determinism" captures the complexity of psychic life in this definition: "a construct stating that a psychic event or an aspect of behavior may be caused by more than one factor and may serve more than one purpose in the psychic framework. . . ." (Moore and Fine 1990, p. 123). Examples of traditional psychoanalytic accounts applying these "intrapsychic" insights to our understanding of racial dynamics will be elaborated below.

As psychodynamic theories evolve and diversify, new ways of struggling with the tension between the person and her culture are being articulated. As Leary (2000) points out, "contemporary psychoanalysis now downplays any sharp distinctions between the social and the psychological" (p. 648). She observes that psychotherapists of "all stripes now regard the analytic situation as profoundly relational" (p. 648). Reflecting on the past, Leary suggests that psychoanalytic "slowness" in considering race had to do with the field's understanding of race as a sociological issue. Therefore, "it lay outside the analytic purview" (p. 648). This "positioning" of race as outside of the psychoanalytic domain persists today in many mental health disciplines. Accordingly, Leary concludes that race tends to be conceptualized as being "skin deep" and left marginalized if not invisible. In addition, race, until very recently, has been primarily thought of as "pertaining to people of color, rather than as a dynamic constellation with relevance to all persons" (p. 648).

In conceptualizing race primarily as a sociological concern, clinicians have missed the vast and profound opportunities that psychodynamic theories offer. In their approach to the development and understanding of subjectivity, psychoanalytic accounts are unprecedented in their complexity and depth. Rather than conceiving race as a static or preconceived idea, we can imagine race, like any other psychoanalytic idea, as being subject to condensation, affect/impulse (sex, hatred), defense, transitional space, fantasy, signifier, object relationship, self/identity. Examples of the uses of these psychoanalytic concepts when "listening" to race, when we attempt to understand the malignancy of racism, are presented in the following sections.

Drive Theory

Freud believed that humans are inevitably shaped by a fundamental, inherent antagonism between their wishes and societal prohibitions. Cultural norms and values become "individual" or internalized by the individual as the person develops a conscience. In Freud's tripartite model of the mind, the superego is the psychic system that enforces and passes on the group's rules. As an agent-within, the superego is typically in conflict with our beastly desires (id), which then mobilizes a mediator (ego) to achieve a compromise. The id is seen as a "cauldron" full of seething motivational forces fueled and filled by our beastly past. Psychoanalysis singles out two irreducible impulses in human development: the sexual and aggressive drives. These forces, particularly sexuality or libidinal strivings, enter into a life-long conflict with the demands of a socialized existence. Development—and pathology—are seen as the compromised results of a series of conflicts fought in a sequential progression of bodily battlegrounds. This view has come to be called the psychosexual theory of development. The passage through these psychosexual stages leads to fixations and regressions, whose outcomes come to be represented in symptoms and character traits and in compromise formations (see chapter 2).

Within a drive theory perspective, racist dynamics can be understood as expressions of psychosexual conflicts—in other words, racist dynamics (individual and/or group racist behaviors, attitudes, traits or character, transference and countertransference) are seen as manifestations of unconscious conflicts. Given this theoretical context, blackness colors powerful fantasies—the black body is psychically equated with the repressed. Kovel's 1970 book, titled *White Racism*, is a progressive example of the use of classical theory applied in this area (see his reflections on his thinking in the psychoanalytic journal, *Psychoanalytic Dialogues*, Special Issue on Race, 2000). Kovel places in historical context these fantasies and associations, an unconscious heritage that we all share. When Africans were brought as slaves to the American shore, contact with Europeans fueled racial fantasies and myths: "These people were black; they were naked; they were unchristian; ergo, they were damned" (p. 63). Using blackness and whiteness as "cardinal symbols," Kovel makes the following psychoanalytic interpretation:

> Spurred by the superego, the ego designates the id, which is unseen, as having the qualities that come from darkness; as being black. The id, then, is the referent for blackness within the personality; and the various partial trends within the id, all repressed, make themselves symbolically realized in the world as the forms of blackness embodied in the fantasy of race. (p. 66)

The unconscious, itself, becomes associated or symbolized by the psyche as Darkness. Our deepest fears and wishes—which in drive theory are, at their root, sexual and aggressive conflicts—get experienced through racial dynamics (see Dalal 2002 for a more recent and inverse argument and interpretation about the motivational thrust of what he calls the "racialization" process). Thus, Kovel argues, racism can, quite literally, embody anal as well as oedipal conflicts and anxieties; the black body comes to be perceived as dirty and/or castrated, both hated and desired.

Frantz Fanon, a pioneer psychiatrist from the Antilles, wrote passionately about this "embodiment," applying a psychoanalytic perspective to understand racial dynamics in colonized societies. The threat for the white person *is* the black body, he argues. "The Negro is the *beast*, a phobic object, the personification of The Other" (1967, p. 170, emphasis mine). Thus, the black body activates anxieties of the most dreaded, the most desired. The black person "symbolizes the biological danger. To suffer from a phobia of Negroes is to be afraid of the biological. The Negroes are animals" (p. 165). Focusing on the centrality of sexual or libidinal impulses, Fanon highlights how humans confront conflicts with "difference." In this case, skin color difference, a physical difference, arouses genital anxieties in the white man: the black body represents both sexual potency and danger. Fanon based his psychoanalytic interpretations on the French psychoanalytic tradition. This tradition has been seminally shaped by Lacan (1981), although Lacanian theory has been used more widely in the United States in the deconstruction of literary texts than in clinical practice. For a more recent example of Lacanian and postcolonial psychoanalytic theory on race, see Lane (1998).

A clinical example shows the emergence of the "black person" in a dream during the course of psychotherapy.

> Rey, a thirty-year-old Puerto Rican man who was severely traumatized as a child, often reported a "dark" man in his nightmares during his early months of recovery from a fifteen-year addiction to heroin. Associations to his dream, evoked memories of his father. When inebriated, using racial insults, Rey's father, a light-skinned man, brutally humiliated him, the darkest of ten siblings. Although at the time of the nightmares, Rey could not report having any "negative" feelings toward his father, working with his dreams evoked the following memory. Throughout his adolescence, Rey frequently had obsessive thoughts of revenge. A drive-derived psychodynamic interpretation would link the "darkness" in the dream with the repressed (unconscious or defended-against) aggressive conflicts "returning" to haunt him. Note how these kinds of interpretations would omit any understanding of the meaning of race or racism in relation to the "dark man" of Rey's nightmares.

In sum, drive theory has been used to understand racial dynamics by suggesting the following interpretations: racism is a symptom indicative of underlying psychosexual conflicts based on the unconscious association of darkness—the black body—with our beastly impulses (sexual and aggressive drives). These racial fantasies, then, are reactivated through psychosexual pressures. In a racist society, racism can be understood as a compromise formation, resulting from psychosexual conflicts and anxieties, a socially acceptable "solution" to the inherent and inevitable conflictual relationship between the mind and the body, the individual and society.

As we noted earlier, drive theory has been widely criticized for its ethnocentric and colonialist reductionism. Drive theory critics maintain that social as well as psychological dynamics are reduced to libidinal conflicts (conflicts and anxieties historically bounded to the European, nineteenth-century concerns of "civilized" society). Furthermore, explanations grounded in oedipal narratives have been deservedly critiqued as having a pervasive male bias (see chapter 2). Akin to the "anatomical differences between the sexes," the color difference between the races has been critiqued as an a-historical, simplistic, a-social view of the body and biology that can lead to malignant views of difference. At the same time, important insights can be derived from this perspective, including the central role played by unconscious conflicts in racist dynamics; more specifically, the association of blackness with the repressed, whiteness with the rational. In addition, drive theory's emphasis on the body and sexuality opens possibilities in the understanding of racial subjectivities given the centrality of physical characteristics as the marker for the experience of difference. Later theoretical development will come to place more emphasis on other psychoanalytic ideas, such as defense and object relations.

Ego Psychology

Psychoanalytic theory in the United States developed its own accent on Freud's structural theory of the mind. We have come to know this particular theoretical framework as ego psychology.

In contrast to Freud's tragic or pessimistic views of human nature, the evolving theory of ego psychology in the United States flourished with triumphant optimism, with its emphasis on the ego's capacity for "mastery" and "adaptation" (Hartmann 1958). In an ego psychological discourse, the concepts of "ego functions" and "defects" took a central role. The assessment of the ego's functions and, in particular, the ego's "defensive" maneuvers in the formation of "character structure" become a prominent feature of our clinical lens. In addition, the developmental thrust of this perspective shifts our focus to the importance of achieving an integrated "identity."

How does ego psychology understand prejudice and bigotry? We will begin by highlighting the insights derived from a now classic study of ethnocentrism by Adorno and his colleagues, *The Authoritarian Personality* (1950). Following the Holocaust, a group of social psychologists sought to explain the emergence and dynamics of anti-Semitic attitudes by applying psychoanalytic principles. (See Bettelheim and Janowitz's work [1964], for another critical example of these psychoanalytic applications.)

Combining ego psychology with social psychology, Adorno and his team of researchers established a relationship among a sociopolitical climate (fascism), family dynamics (authoritarian parenting style), and personality development (prejudiced individual). The authors explain:

> A basically hierarchical, authoritarian, exploitative parent-child relationship is apt to carry over into a power-oriented, exploitatively dependent attitude towards one's sex partner and one's God, and may well culminate in a political philosophy and social outlook which has no room for anything but a clinging to what appears to be the strong and disdainful rejection of whatever is relegated to the bottom. (p. 971)

A parenting style that relies primarily on domination and subordination through the exercise of rigid and punitive discipline significantly shapes a certain type of personality, the authoritarian personality. In turn, this type of personality is especially susceptible to ethnocentric, non-democratic ideas. The authoritarian family environment shapes a person's character with a tremendous amount of hostility and ambivalence toward authority. This personality structure struggles with fears and conflicts typical of the anal stage of psychosexual development, such as an extreme need for order, cleanliness, and control, as well as a limited tolerance for ambiguity and ambivalence. The intensity of hostility fueling these dynamics results in an excessive reliance on mechanisms of defense such as "projection" and "displacement." These unconscious defensive strategies protect the individual from internal conflict and, ultimately, from psychotic disintegration. Minority groups (for example, Jews and Blacks) become the perfect targets or substitutes for the externalization of aggression and hatred. Consequently, and paradoxically, Frosch (1989) reminds us "the prejudiced person *needs* her or his hated object in order to survive" (p. 234) [emphasis mine]. For other important attempts at combining psychoanalytic theory to illuminate "social character," see Fromm (1955) and, more recently, the exhaustive work of Young-Bruehl (1996).

In the application of ego psychology to understand ethnic prejudice, we see the critical importance of childhood experiences in the generation of hostility and hatred underlying racist dynamics. Defense mechanisms come to the rescue of an unconsciously fragile and embattled bigoted personality. These dynamics are exacerbated by the complexities and alienation of modern life. In this account, we also see a dominant psychoanalytic interpretation of racial and ethnic dynamics: the excessive use of defenses to ward off unacceptable hostile and aggressive impulses. Thus racial dynamics are understood as defensive and as derivatives of hatred.

Another major development in this theoretical line comes from the work of one of the most popular psychoanalytic writers, Erik Erikson (1963, 1968). Erikson placed "identity" at the center of psychosocial inquiry. Expanding Freud's theory of development to include the sociocultural realm, Erikson sees development as a life-long progression of stages in the context of the individual's culture. From this perspective, all of us pass through the same stagelike sequence, but our particular culture offers us its unique possibilities for resolving universal "crises" in development (see chapter 5). Erikson's writings include observations of minority groups in the United States, such as the Sioux, the Yurok, and the "Negroes." His observations are an example of another common psychoanalytic understanding of the psychodynamics of race. In his view, cultural beliefs such as racial stereotypes are "internalized" through negative identifications":

> No individual can escape this opposition of images, which is all-pervasive in the men and in the women, in the majorities and the minorities, and in all the classes of a given national or cultural unit. Psychoanalysis shows that the unconscious evil identity (the composite of everything which arouses negative identification (i.e., the wish not to resemble it) consists of images of the violated (castrated) body, the ethnic out-group, and the exploited minority. (1963, p. 243)

A psychological implication and dilemma for this type of internalization is the *inevitability* of low self-esteem for a minority identity. Minority identification with the dominant group prepares the way for identity conflicts, thus compromising healthy, "normal" development. This view of the impact of minority status on development is part of decades of debate and research. Until very recently the effect of majority identity on development has received scant attention. The relationship between self-esteem and racial/ethnic identity has been vulnerable to "social reductionism." In fact, the understanding of race as a concept often falls prey to this type of reductionism: race is understood primarily as a "social" phenomenon. Thus, lack of *social* esteem is categorically translated into psychological low *self*-esteem. Fortunately, psychic damage resulting from the internalization and identification with minority status is neither inescapable, inevitable, nor simple. We know that the relationship between self-esteem and racial/ethnic identity is magnificently richer and more complex than initially conceived.

In summary, with ego psychology's emphasis on the psyche's protective maneuvers and activities, psychoanalytic understandings of racism and bigotry placed increasing focus on the concepts of "defense" and "identity." Defense mechanisms utilized by majority groups and members such as "projection" and "displacement" of aggressive impulses towards minorities in order to ward off destabilizing anxieties has been seen as a central interpretation. Furthermore, Erikson's focus on the concept of identity, including minority identity, expanded psychoanalytic attention to the impact of culture in psychological development. This expansion helped create a theoretical bridge between the "intrapsychic" (one-person) psychoanalytic psychologies and the "interpersonal," "intersubjective," or "relational" (two-person) models of the mind.

Let us look at a clinical application of contemporary ego psychology from the work of Young-Bruehl (2006) with African American and Latino homeless youths at a drop-in center in New York City. After knowing something of these young men's lives, she saw the ways in which each one protected himself from traumatic histories using racial identifications but in opposite ways. Young-Bruehl began her clinical observations by noting the following pattern in the case of Transformation (the African American youth's self-chosen name):

> This, I came to learn, is the story of Transformation's life, the emblem of his humiliation: someone else is always getting provided for, while he gets beaten up and cannot get what he needs. (p. 324)

She later on noted that Transformation hads formed strong attachments to white teachers. Young-Bruehl continued her observations:

> He loved the white teachers at school and developed another determining idea: that black people—especially very dark ones like him—could never be as

good as whites. When his mother beat him, he cried out for one of the white women teachers, and he had a fantasy that he might go home with her and be her boy. (p. 325)

Transformation was notoriously "sweet to everybody" and became a caregiver and rescuer. Young-Bruehl understood Transformation's character style as one dominated by "reaction formation," a defensive strategy that turns our impulses into its opposite—in this case, rage to sweetness. By projecting and displacing "goodness" (lack of aggressiveness) to whites and "badness" to his own race, Transformation dealt with severe abuse in his personal history, but at a great cost to his racial self-esteem.

In contrast to Transformation, Ricardo, the Latino adolescent, was a "taker," his anger palpable. Ricardo "does not ever want to be seen as a woman" (p. 330), and is ever on the lookout for betrayal and disrespect from others. Young-Bruehl interpreted this way of protecting himself from an extreme history of humiliation and sexual abuse as always wanting to be "on top." She then proceeded to tell Ricardo a story about a woman called Anna Freud, who also worked with "children and adolescents almost a hundred years ago in a European city with some areas that were just as rough as where he grew up" (p. 338). Young-Bruehl then explained to Ricardo that Anna Freud had worked with a boy just like him and she had described him as "identifying with the aggressor." Ricardo apparently felt "very happy" about her giving him "white people's words" (p. 337).

We see here, in Young-Bruehlh's work, a way of understanding the psychodynamics of race using an ego psychological perspective. In this view, race, like any other human experience is used in a variety of ways to identify, dis-identify, to defend, and to cope in life (see Holmes 1992, 2006 for another contemporary ego psychological clinical application to racial psychodynamics).

Before we continue to the more contemporary views, let us take a moment to elaborate briefly on another psychoanalytic idea that was critical in this "bridging" and expansion, the concept of "projective identification."

The psychoanalytic concept of projective identification has been elaborated in ways that are critical in the linking of social theory and psychoanalysis (see Clarke 2003 for an overview of this idea). Highlighting the original definition by Melanie Klein, Clarke cites Klein as proposing:

Split off parts of the ego are also projected on to the mother or, I would rather call it, *into* the mother. . . . Much of the hatred against parts of the self is now directed towards the mother. This leads to a particular type of identification which establishes the prototype of an aggressive object-relation. I suggest for these processes the term projective identification. (Klein 1946, p. 8; quoted in Clarke, p. 147)

These psychological "processes" are seen as basic to our development (see chapter 6). The term has been used in a variety of ways (as defense, normal mechanism of organization and communication, and as an object - relation) and in a continuum (from malignant/pathological to benign/ empathic). The psychological use of the (m)other as "container" of disa- vowed parts of the self is a fundamental psychoanalytic understanding.

The application of this insight to racial hatred and ethnic dynamics is of critical significance to our current understanding. As Clarke points out:

> The most obvious way to view projective identification in terms of the explana- tion of racism and ethnic hatred is as a violent expulsion of affect which ren- ders the recipient in a state of terror and self-hatred. (2003, p. 156–57)

These ideas have tremendous potential for the understanding of racial dynamics at all levels (e.g., the group, the individual, and the clinical dyad). We will highlight contemporary examples of the application of these ideas in the relational section below. Before proceeding to clinical examples, next, I want to highlight an idea that Hamer (2002) adds, that of racism serving as a "condensation":

> In itself, race is a condensation of many meanings (Schachter and Butts 1968); thus, race can mean more than one thing and more than one thing *at once*. Intrapsychic meanings of race exist in the borderland between the body and the social contexts within which the body is recognized and constructed. Sameness or difference in a few body features (e.g., skin color, hair texture) can serve as the basis for a myriad of constructions, which, like anatomical differences between the sexes or generational differences, assume psychologi- cal significance for different reasons and at various moments of urgency. (p. 1221–22)

The idea or "construct" of race as "condensation" opens up and deepens our conversations about racism; it places our dialogues in what Winnicott calls "potential space," a space where we can "play" with old and new ideas.

In the following sections, we will address the psychoanalytic turn in the United States toward what Mitchell and Greenberg (1983) called the "rela- tional schools." This shift evolved out of major epistemological and theo- retical developments beginning with what we now call object relations and self psychology, or the two-person psychologies.

Turning Toward Relationship

Psychoanalysis has always paid attention to the relationship. The con- cepts of transference and countertransference were at its foundational core (e.g., Freud 1912, 1915). What has changed are our views on how the clinical dyad is formed, how it takes shapes (development and dynamics), and how it can be used. From these debates, fundamental assumptions about human development, motivation, and pathology are questioned (see earlier section on key controversies impacting views on the psychoanalytic understanding of racism). In this case the role of the Freudian concept of the "object" is dramatically transformed if not reversed. As Fairbairn's famous quote highlights: " Libido is not pleasure seeking; it is object seeking." Emphasis on the object (internal and external) takes center stage.

Two main schools inform this tradition, object relations and self psychology. More recently, ideas on intersubjectivity, attachment, and postmodern critiques are pushing the theoretical envelope.

Object Relations

"Racial prejudice is, after all, a problem in object relations."

McDonald (1970)

"The place where cultural experience is located is in the *potential space* between the individual and the environment (originally the object)."

Winnicott (1971)

We have now looked at how psychoanalytic drive and ego psychologies view race/racism and ethnic prejudice. Contemporary thinking has shifted the emphasis from concerns over beastly struggles of "civilized" life to the developmental needs of the individual through her relationships. From this perspective, the individual psyche is seen as unfolding *within* a relational matrix. Many relational theorists now believe that experience in relationships form the basis of our internal lives as well as our perceptions of the external world. The relationship between the inner and outer worlds is a more fluid, open, and reciprocal one than the earlier psychoanalytic models implied. These recent perspectives—including postmodern critiques—are discussed at more length in chapter 9 on intersubjectivity. Interestingly, however, relational schools were foreshadowed by Freud (1921):

In the individual's mental life someone else is invariably involved, as a model, as an object, as a helper, as an opponent; and so from the first individual psychology, in this extended but entirely justifiable sense of the words, it is at the same time social psychology as well. (p. 1)

How can we understand racial dynamics from a relational perspective?

Object relations theories focus on the infant's struggle with the emerging awareness of separateness and thus "difference." Our psychological birth follows a slow and eventful differentiation process with a primary "other."

Through differences, we come to recognize and establish a relatively cohesive sense of identity. This developmental process is patterned by the oscillation between two poles, what we perceive as being "me" and "not-me" experiences.

Skin color difference, like genital difference, shapes a major "axis" in the unfolding of identity. Our awareness and experience of our skin color is embedded in our specific caretaker/family/cultural/historical context(s). This relational context gives form and meaning to our racial identities.

Even before we are born, our parents' fantasies, thoughts, wishes, feelings, and anxieties about the color of the baby come to constitute how we "put together" who we are. (See Bowles 1988 for a recent controversy about the internalization of race, or what Dalal 2002 calls "the racialization process," which will be discussed in more detail later.) We know that a child's "discovery" or emerging awareness of skin color difference is neurologically possible before the first year of life, and it can generate skin color anxiety (McDonald 1970). In psychoanalytic terms, Smith (2006) observes:

> I think of difference, like absence, as a primary stimulus to thought and fantasy—in which case one could argue that categorization of difference begins even earlier than language, with the first registrations of difference or otherness. (p. 8)

Initially, a difference is psychologically experienced and "categorized" as "not-mother," subsequently, as "not-me." A difference comes to symbolize what we recognize as Other. We also know from psychoanalytic experience that a recognition of difference early in life—particularly if it is suffused with emotional intensity and/or cultural significance—will be "charged" with basic affective shadings of "goodness" and "badness." In fact, "stranger anxiety" has been considered "the original emergence of the other as enemy" (Fornari, in Volkan 1988, p. 18).

The following dialogue from a therapy session between a clinical social work student and Joey, an African American seven-year-old boy, demonstrates how color comes to be symbolized and expressed:

J: What's your favorite color?
Th: I like lots of colors.
J: I don't like Black. Black jellybeans are nasty.
Th: Black jellybeans are licorice. So you don't like licorice?
J: White ones taste ok, though.
Th: You like the flavor of the white ones?
J: (pause) My teacher's white.
Th: (pause) And I'm white.
J: Well, kind of.

How do we "listen" to Joey's "color preference"? How do we take into account his age, given that we know children do not acquire or stabilize "ethnic constancy" until latency (Aboud 1987)? Is it "defensive" that he says he doesn't like black jellybeans, but finds white ones "ok" (see Young-Bruehl's 2006 interpretation of the defense "identification with the aggressor")? Is it a "transference state" (Hamer 2006)? How do we understand Joey's relational world (his sense of self and objects, his family, and community at that specific point in history)?

Experiences—internal and external—in relation to skin color become part of an inner image of the self that eventually becomes integrated in the child's developing racial identity. The internal representations of self and other are colored by racial tones and become part of us. The current postmodern lens sees identity as more "plural" (identities) and fluid (less stable and integrated) than earlier "modern" psychoanalytic perspectives. The relative "stability" of identity has been a source of continuous controversy, particularly, along "cultural" lines. For example, the Kleinian (British) and Lacanian (French) traditions have always disputed the emphasis placed by ego psychology (U.S.) on identity "consolidation," ego "mastery," and "self-"cohesiveness." The European tradition sees the self as more embattled and fragile.

Nonetheless, for psychological well-being, the child must internalize a loving feeling toward her own skin. These sensations become part of a general sense of self, a unique, special, loved person (Bowles 1988). Anxieties, defenses, fantasies, thoughts, and feelings related to developmentally specific stages or ways of relating can come to be expressed, struggled with and through, tangled, and/or confused with anxieties of difference (McDonald 1970). Thus, in Joey's case, color differences in food could be heard as concerns about "early" or basic preoccupations about what he "takes in" (oral), who provides it (object relations), and in what context (inside, outside the therapy/his family/community/culture).

We noted earlier how psychoanalytic classical theories suggested that racism and bigotry reflected both anal anxieties (excessive preoccupation with order and dirt) as well as genital fears (dark body as castrated or damaged). In her racially integrated nursery, McDonald (1970) came to the following conclusion:

> Separation anxiety can have many determinants, from many developmental levels, and many different kinds of personal experiences. In our clinical experience we found that no matter what the individual developmental or traumatic focal point for the separation anxiety, the dark-skinned child revived it for *all* the children. (p. 134)

Racism—the association of "white" with what is good, and " black" with what is bad—remains an area of vulnerability for psychological splitting for all of us (possibly throughout our lifetime). In a recent article, Altman (2006) looked at this splitting for "whites," a long overdue analysis and reflection. "Whiteness is thus an omnipotent fantasy," he concludes, a "fantasy of mastery and fullness" (p. 55). Just as dark skin stimulates associations to devalued characteristics, light skin comes to symbolize idealized traits. Equally distorted, psychologically speaking, both "parts" of our "selves" are simplified in an either/or literally black-and-white impoverishment of our experience of being human. We *all* remain at risk for the contortions (protective/defensive distortions, wishes, and fantasies) based on our deeply racialized past, albeit from different standpoints, and with very different consequences.

More recently, relational schools have drawn our attention to the inevitability of "enactments" in the therapeutic encounter. Addressing specifically "racial enactments," Leary (2000) defines them as "those interactive sequences that embody the actualization in the clinical situation of cultural attitudes towards race and racial difference" (p. 640). For example, Leary, an African American therapist working with Gloria, an African American middle-aged woman, insightfully comments on an exchange following Leary's request for a change in their session's schedule. This exchange led to Gloria's commenting on Leary's doing "a white thing" (keeping her name after she got married). This period in the therapeutic process opened up a series of discussions where competitive feelings were acknowledged. Leary interpreted Gloria's comments as "retaliation for my relational snub" (p. 647). That "Gloria drew from the powerful arsenal of race for her counterattack is evidence," Leary continues, "of the narcissistic injury I brought" (p. 647). Like many other relational clinicians, Leary is making a case for *both* the inevitable presence of racial dynamics in the therapeutic relationship *and* the possibilities of working with it (or more accurately *through* it).

In this section, we have integrated insights from relational perspectives in order to understand racial psychodynamics. Our experiences of and in relation to primary caregivers, internalized through early childhood, lay the foundation for our sense of identity. Or, as postmodern theorists would emphasize, our relational experiences lay the foundation for our identities. Early anxieties about "separateness" color our awareness and perception of "difference." Our cultural group plays a major role in helping us organize the "good" and the "bad" in all of us. A "malignant spiral of racial misuse" results when certain groups become "seductive repositories" for our devalued parts (Sherwood 1980). The narcissistic implications for this process have been further deepened by the self psychology school, which we will now turn to.

Self Psychology

A prominent feature of this psychoanalytic perspective is its emphasis on "self experience." Experiences that foster self-cohesion are considered the most critical for psychological health and development. These types of experiences depend on the responsiveness—the "empathic attunement"—of our environment to our developmental needs. These needs are fulfilled and/or thwarted through the formation of "self-self object mergers," where we experience important people in our lives as part of the self. Failures in responsiveness or mis-attunement are seen as leading to developmental arrests or deficits, and thus to pathologies of the self.

A distinguishing feature of this perspective is its reconceptualization and understanding of the psychodynamic concept of "narcissism." In contrast to earlier notions, self psychology places narcissistic needs at the center of self-vitality, wholeness, and well-being. The empathic recognition of the child's developing needs for mirroring, idealization, and twinship are pivotal elements of self-esteem (see chapter 7).

Given these assumptions, what is the impact of race and culture in the development, vulnerability, and cohesiveness of the self? Speaking to us from this perspective, Donner (1988) offers us some ideas:

> Everyone experiences assaults on his or her sense of self-worth and self-cohesion. However, everyone does not experience the same opportunities for self-enhancing self-object experiences. Assaults on the self often occur selectively, according to sociological categories of gender, race, ethnicity, class, age, and sexual preference clinical social workers must ask how the larger society contributes to or interferes with opportunities for growth-producing mirroring and idealization. (pp. 20–21)

Hence, our society's "choices" of what to admire and what to devalue impact selectively on processes affecting self-esteem. In this psychodynamic context, experiences of racism and bigotry are considered as assaults on the self. Miliora (2000) suggests that chronic, cumulative experiences of cultural racism can amount to narcissistic trauma, which in turn can lead to a "breakdown, or disenfranchisement" that depletes the self. This disenfranchisement, she argues, "can contribute in deleterious ways to a sense of oneself as 'ungrandiose'" (p. 43).

In a clinical example, Miliora comments on Evette, a middle-aged African American woman who sought help for severe depression. As Miliora observed, Evette's "capacity for self-assertion seemed almost nonexistent" (p. 49). Persistent and debilitating financial problems plagued Evette's history, even though she was gainfully and steadily employed. Evette had a family history embedded in cultural racism. She was raised in the South, in poverty, and sent at an early age to work as a servant for a white elderly woman. Miliorai comments on Evette's impoverished childhood circumstances, "circumstances that limited the capacity of her parents—themselves victims of racism—to mirror her grandiosity" (p. 51). At the same time, Evette "does possess, however, survivor skills and a determination to live an independent life" (pp. 51–52). Responded to with profound empathy, Evette was seen as needing mirroring for her "disenfranchised grandiosity." In this case, Evette's inability to set financial limits with her family was understood as an unconscious expression of disavowed grandiosity, a narcissistic need thwarted by cultural racism. Sustained empathic attunement and mirroring responsiveness by the therapist are seen as crucial mutative components of the therapeutic process, a process that would allow for arrested narcissistic longings to be transformed into a more mature manifestation. In Evette's case, her ambitious strivings were expressed in a more balanced manner, as seen in her ability to set reasonable financial goals and limits for herself and her family.

In contrast to the most common interpretation of racism, self psychologists argue that the psychodynamics of prejudice are less about defending against aggression (through the uses of displacement and counter-aggression) than about "an expression of a vulnerable, fragmentation-prone self-organization struggling to overcome a traumatic history" (Ryan and Buirski 2001, p. 21). Thus, a prejudiced attitude is a by-product of an extremely vulnerable self, protecting its self against further selfobject mis-attunements.

One of the most important contributions of a self psychological perspective is its attention to our narcissistic needs. The normalizing (non-judgmental, developmental) and empathic reflection of the self's narcissistic longings draws our clinical eye to the ebb and flow of self-esteem, the assaults and injuries of dehumanizing interpersonal and cultural practices. Clinicians interested in the negative impact of racism in the development of a minority identity have focused on the importance of parental mirroring in the buffering of social (racist) assaults (e.g., Bowles 1988). However, as we noted earlier, a simplistic assumption that a minority identity is inevitably damaged or "riskier" than a "normal" (dominant) identity remains problematic. After many decades of research, we know that clear conclusions remain elusive and contradictory (see Spencer and Markstrom-Adams 1990 for a review of this literature). There is no question that cultural discontinuity and ethnic or racial devaluing present significant challenges for minority youth. At the same time, we know that minority children are not destined to be poorly "adjusted," nor do they experience lower levels of self-esteem (Cross 1987, Milner 1983, Powell 1985). The minority child's "knowing" and experiencing more than one world presents not only challenges, it also offers possibilities (e.g., more flexibility, endurance, wisdom) given supportive family and community resources. In addition—and conversely—we need to study the impact of the narcissistic distortions (for example, defensive or malignant grandiosity) generated by the identification with "whiteness."

The empathic responsiveness to a racist expression has generated significant controversy. The controversy over the appropriate therapeutic response to racist manifestations in the clinical encounter (see for example, Ryan and Buirski's 2001 stance and recommendations) often centers on our different views on the nature of aggression. Psychoanalytic schools offer diverse ways of understanding the origins and dynamics of aggression in human relationships. The "conflict" schools, such as drive and ego psychologies, view aggression as intrinsic to human nature; relational theories tend to conceptualize aggression as contingent on the relational matrix. In particular, self psychology's view of aggressive expressions as derivatives or by-products of a self struggling against fragmentation remains at one extreme, that is, in this view, aggressive acts are considered primarily as reactive more than a "natural" dimension of our humanity.

Like other relational theories, self psychology places the individual and her society—the inner and the outer worlds—on a more mutual, interdependent plane than earlier psychoanalytic accounts. Our relationships with others shape and sustain our well-being—and our suffering or "pathology"—throughout our lifetime.

Self psychology's primary emphasis on the self has made it susceptible to the same critique held against most psychological theories in our Eurocentric, North American intellectual tradition. That is, its underscoring of individual experience makes it problematic when we attempt to understand groups that conceptualize the person differently. For example, cultures that emphasize or value the family as a more important unit than the individual (what Roland 1988, 1991 has called the "we-self" view versus the "I-self"), tend to clash with psychodynamic accounts of individual development.

POSTMODERN COMMENTS AND OTHER CONCLUSIONS

To conclude, then, let us review key insights on the psychodynamics of race and racism derived from the main psychoanalytic schools. We will then end with some ongoing controversies based on postmodern critiques of psychoanalytic accounts of human development.

- Drive theory offered us the association in unconscious life of darkness (the black body) with beastly impulses (drive theory) or "'badness."
- Ego psychology offered us the importance of aggression (hostility, hatred) and the excessive use of defensive mechanisms such as projection and displacement to deal with primitive fears and anxieties. Ego psychologists also helped us to understand that social devaluation and idealization(s) are internalized through the process of identification.

- Object relations theories provided the concepts of projective identification and splitting to ward off conflicts exacerbated by the complexities, diversity, and alienation of modernity
- Object relations theorists also underscored the relationship between child-rearing practices—punitive, hierarchical (authoritarian) parenting—and intolerance and bigotry in childhood.
- Object relations theorists further identified the tendency to (mis)use devalued racial groups as "containers" for disavowed and unwanted aspects of the self.
- Self psychology offered ways of understanding racism as narcissistic assaults and as a function of lack of cohesion.
- Further, self psychology helped us understand racist experiences—assaults on the self—as impingements on self cohesion.
- Last, self psychology demonstrated how narcissistic distortions (devaluation as well as idealizations) based on racial categories can interfere with the self's capacity to develop a healthy and mature sense of self.

We have seen a variety of ways in which psychodynamic theories have been used to understand or interpret the relationship between society and the psychological development of the individual. We will conclude with a few comments on ongoing debates.

With the turn and inclusion of postmodern critiques to our psychoanalytic discourses, several dilemmas remain in our dialogues on race and racism. For example, a postmodern perspective cautions us against any theory that claims universality. In claiming universality, theories typically attempt to find the "essential" dimension to our psyches, the basic common denominator that governs our minds. Postmodern authors wisely caution us against this intellectual arrogance: No one individual or group can escape the biases, prejudices, and preferences of its historical and sociocultural context. In other words, we will inescapably and (psychoanalytically speaking) unconsciously prefer theories that maintain our power or privileges. Thus, a postmodern clinician will argue that the best antidote to our human grandiosity is to let multiplicity and diversity of views prevail and contest. In the psychoanalytic domain, this bent has meant an appreciation for the fluidity and illusory quality of identities.

At the same time, the "consolidation" or affirmation of a minority identity has been a significant political—and psychological—struggle and achievement. The political implications of intellectual delegitimizing the concept of identity remain problematic. For example, if "essentially" there are no races, a black identity loses its power; thus, we are left with the dilemma of how to identify the problem of racism and advocate for equitable solutions, while not reproducing a racist lens. In a remarkable article, Cole (2001) takes this a psychological step further. He incisively argues that "the conservation of race by African Americans often masks an effort to conserve the trauma of social history"; moreover, he continues, the concept of race, whether "biologically or socio-historically conceived," has the ability to establish a link with the trauma of slavery, while simultaneously offering itself as protection from a conscious encounter with this trauma (p. 58). How can we understand this "link" to trauma? How does it transmit itself intergenerationally?

Other questions remain: Are we illuminating and thus combating racism when we address it in the therapeutic situation, or are we reaffirming its power as a category? Dalal (2006) argues that "the naming of people as *black* or *white* is not so much a descriptive act as an *othering* process—a racializing process" (p. 156). Hence, he calls for the use of the term "racialization," a term that he defines as "the process of manufacturing and utilizing the notion of race in any capacity," rather than racism because of its "emphasis on activity and an activity that requires our continual cooperation" (p. 157). We cannot not "racialize," given our historical and social conditions. Is there no escape from internalizing and therefore reproducing our racist past? Or, in psychoanalytic terms, how do we disrupt our compulsion to repeat?

In this chapter, then, we have given an overview of some of the ways that psychoanalytic discourses have been used—and are being applied in an illuminating way—to our understanding of race and racism. Many psychodynamic questions remain to be asked. Many fights remain to be fought. Many more questions need to be formulated. We welcome the challenge.

REFERENCES

Aboud, F. E. (1987). The development of ethnic self-identification and attitudes. In *Children's Ethnic Socialization, Pluralism and Development*, ed. J. S. Phinney and M. J. Rotheram, pp. 32–55. Newbury Park, CA: Sage.

Adorno, T. W., Frenkel-Brunswik, E., Levinson, D. J., and Sanford, R. N. (1950). *The Authoritarian Personality*. New York: Harper.

Altman, N. (2006). Whiteness. *The Psychoanalytic Quarterly* 75(1):45–72.

Bettelheim, B., and Janowitz, M. (1964). *Social Change and Prejudice*. New York: Free Press.

Bowles, D. (1988). Development of an ethnic self-concept among blacks. In *Ethnicity and Race: Critical Concepts in Social Work*, pp. 103–113. Silver Spring, MD: National Association of Social Workers.

Brickman, C. (2003). *Aboriginal Populations in the Mind: Race and Primitivity in Psychoanalysis*. New York: Columbia University Press.

Brunner, J. (1991). The (ir)relevance of Freud's Jewish identity to the origins of psychoanalysis. *Psychoanalysis and Contemporary Thought* 14(4):655–84.

Clarke, S. (2003). *Social Theory, Psychoanalysis and Racism.* New York: Palgrave Macmillan.

Cole, S. (2001). Trauma and the conservation of African-American racial identity. *Journal for the Psychoanalysis of Culture and Society* 6(1):58–72.

Cross, W. (1987). A two-factor theory of black identity: Implications for the study of identity development in minority group children. In *Children's Ethnic Socialization, Pluralism and Development,* ed. J. S. Phinney and M. J. Rotheram, pp. 117–133. Newbury Park, CA: Sage.

Dalal, F. (2002). *Race, Colour, and the Process of Racialization: New Perspectives from Group Analysis, Psychoanalysis and Sociology.* Hove, UK: Brunner-Routledge.

———. (2006) Racism: Process of Detachment. *The Psychoanalytic Quarterly* 75(1):131–61.

Donner, S. (1988). Self psychology: Implications for social work. *Social Case-work: Journal of Contemporary Social Work* 69(1):17–22.

Erikson, E. H. (1963). *Childhood and Society.* New York: Norton.

———. (1968). *Identity: Youth and Crisis.* New York: Norton.

Fanon, F. (1967). *Black Skin, White Masks.* New York: Grover.

Freud, S. (1912/1913). Totem and taboo. *Standard Edition* 13:1–162.

———. (1912). The dynamics of transference. *Standard Edition* 12:97–108.

———. (1915). Observations on transference-love. *Standard Edition* 12:157–71.

———. (1921). Group psychology and the analysis of the ego. *Standard Edition* 18:65–143.

———. (1930). Civilization and its discontent. *Standard Edition* 21:59–145.

———. (1939). Moses and monotheism. *Standard Edition* 23:7–137.

Fromm, E. (1955). *The Sane Society.* New York: Rinehart & Co., Inc.

Frosch, S. (1989). *Psychoanalysis and Psychology: Minding the Gap.* New York: New York University Press.

Geertz, C. (1973). *The Interpretation of Cultures.* New York: Basic Books.

———. (1984). From the native's point of view: On the nature of anthropological understanding. In *Culture Theory: Essays of the Mind, Self and Emotion,* ed. R. A. Shweder and R. A. Levine. Cambridge: Cambridge University Press.

Gergen, K. (1994). *Realities and Relationships, Soundings in Social Construction.* Cambridge, MA: Harvard University Press.

Gilman, S. L. (1992). Freud, race and gender. *American Imago* 49(2):155–83.

Hartmann, H. (1958). *Ego Psychology and the Problem of Adaptation.* New York: International Universities Press.

Hoffman, I. Z. (1991). Discussion: towards a social constructivist view of the psychoanalytic situation. *Psychoanalytic Dialogues* 1(1):74–105.

Holmes, D. (1992). Race and transference in psychoanalysis and psychotherapy. *International Journal of Psychoanalysis* 73:1–11.

———. (2006). The wrecking effects of race and social class on self and success. *The Psychoanalytic Quarterly* 75(1):215–235.

Kovel, J. (1970). *White Racism: A Psychohistory.* New York: Pantheon.

———. (2000) Reflections of white racism. *Psychoanalytic Dialogues* 10(4):579–87.

Kurtz, S. N. (1992). *All the Mothers Are One: Hindu India and the Cultural Reshaping of Psychoanalysis.* New York: Columbia University Press.

Lacan, J. (1981). *The Four Fundamental Concepts of Psycho-Analysis.* Trans. A. Sheridan. New York: Norton.

Lane, C., ed. (1998). *The Psychoanalysis of Race.* New York: Columbia University Press.

Leary, K. (2000). Racial enactments in dynamic treatment. *Psychoanalytic Dialogues* 10(4):639–53.

Malinowski, B. (1927). *Sex and Repression in Savage Society.* London: Routledge & Kegan Paul, 1953.

McDonald, M. (1970). *Not by the Color of Their Skin: The Impact of Racial Differences on the Child's Development.* New York: International Universities Press.

Miliora, M. T. (2000). Beyond empathic failures: Cultural racism as narcissistic trauma and disenfranchisement of grandiosity. *Clinical Social Work* 28(1):43–53.

Milner, D. (1983). *Children and Race.* Beverly Hills, CA: Sage.

Mitchell, S. A. (1988). *Relational Concepts in Psychoanalysis: An Integration.* Cambridge, MA: Harvard University Press.

Mitchell, S., and Greenberg, J. (1983). *Object Relations in Psychoanalytic Theory.* Cambridge, MA: Harvard University Press.

Moore, B. E., and Fine, B. D., eds. (1990). *Psychoanalytic Terms and Concepts.* New Haven, CT: Yale University Press.

Paul, R. A. (1991). Freud's anthropology: A reading of the "cultural books." In *The Cambridge Companion to Freud,* ed. J. Neu. Cambridge: Cambridge University Press.

Powell, G. J. (1985). Self-concepts among Afro-American students in racially isolated minority schools: Some regional differences. *Journal of the American Academy of Child Psychiatry* 24:142–49.

Roland, A. (1988). *In Search of India and Japan: Towards a Cross-Cultural Psychology.* Princeton, NJ: Princeton University Press.

———. (1991). The self in cross-civilizational perspective. In *The Relational Self: Theoretical Convergences in Psychoanalysis and Social Psychology,* ed. R. Curtis, pp. 160–80. New York: Guilford.

Ryan, M. K., and Buirski, P. (2001). Prejudice as a function of self-organization. *Psychoanalytic Psychology* 18(1):21–36.

Sherwood, R. (1980). *The Psychodynamics of Race: Vicious and Benign Spirals.* Atlantic Highlands, NJ: Humanities Press.

Smith, H. (2006). Invisible racism. *The Psychoanalytic Quarterly* 75(1):3–19.

Spencer, M. B., and Markstrom-Adams, C. (1990). Identity processes among racial and ethnic children in America. *Child Development* 61:290–310.

The Analytic Press (2000) Symposium on race. *Psychoanalytic Dialogues* 10(4).

Volkan, V. D. (1988). *The Need to Have Enemies and Allies: From Clinical Practice to International Relationships.* Northvale, NJ: Jason Aronson.

Watkins, M. (1994). *On the Real Side: Laughing, Lying, and Signing—The Underground Tradition of African-American Humor That Transformed American Culture, from Slavery to Richard Pryor.* New York: Simon & Schuster.

Winnicott, D. W. (1971). *Playing and Reality.* New York: Tavistock.

Young-Bruehl, E. (1996). *The Anatomy of Prejudice.* Cambridge, MA: Harvard University. Press.

———. (2006). Coming of age in New York City: Two homeless boys. *The Psychoanalytic Quarterly* 75(1):323–43.

12

From Theory to Practice

Joan Berzoff, Laura Melano Flanagan, and Patricia Hertz

The preceding chapters have explored psychological concepts from a range of psychodynamic theories, and attempted to integrate biological and social perspectives with these theories. We looked at how forces from the inside and outside combine to influence development and shape the lives of individuals. The content of these chapters can stand on its own, as it is often taught in separate courses on developmental theory or social theory in programs of social work, counseling, nursing, and psychology. However, in our experience as teachers and practitioners, this content is too readily divorced from the practice in which people then engage. Students learn about Freud, Erikson, Winnicott, Mahler, and Kohut during one semester, for example, and then move on to a course in clinical practice or psychopathology or social theory with little integration of the theories they just studied. The theory then becomes a body of knowledge to memorize, but not to use and integrate in the room with clients.

At their best, these theories provide us with hypotheses—socially constructed conceptualizations that help us begin to make meaning of the turmoil and resilience in the lives of our patients and ourselves. They are metaphors that organize our information and enable us to decipher patterns out of our patients' experiences that both enhance and hinder growth. They give us hope that we can offer an idea, a perspective, an interpretation that can engage the curiosity of those with whom we work. As Pine (1998) notes, our theories are our tools, imperfect though they may be.

As we hold these theories loosely in our minds, however, how do we allow them to inform our practice in a meaningful, and possibly transformative, way? How do we hold in our minds a multiplicity of theoretical models without letting them clutter our thoughts or our hearts, or without creating an agenda that may be irrelevant to the person with whom we are sitting? How do we organize what we hear into meaning that does not foreclose other possibilities and other interpretations? To address these questions, we must first acknowledge the paradox inherent in this process. We must "know" and "not know" simultaneously; we must strive to be both "full" of knowledge and theory while being "empty" enough to be surprised, to learn, to appreciate the uniqueness of every person with whom we work. In this era of managed cost and care, we are forced to know too soon, to offer diagnoses and treatment plans, medications and discharge plans with too little information and far too much certainty. If we could instruct every intern and staff member with one axiom, we would ask them to keep their work *complicated*. We would encourage them to believe that the capacity to tolerate uncertainty is a prerequisite for our profession, as is the capacity to welcome the mystery and surprise in our work.

As Freud struggled with the paradox of how to achieve being full and empty at the same time, he developed the concept of "evenly suspended attention"—perhaps the most useful clinical tool of them all because it is the foundation upon which all the other clinical techniques (interpretation, confrontation, clarification, examining the transference, and so forth) rest. Freud (1924) described this complex internal state in the following way:

> It consists simply in not directing one's notice to anything in particular and in maintaining the same "evenly suspended attention" (as I have called it) in the face of all that one hears. . . . Or, to put it purely in terms of technique: "He should simply listen, and not bother about whether he is keeping anything in mind." (p. 111)

This sounds relatively simple, but it is not at all easy to achieve in clinical work and needs to be practiced over a lifetime. Ralph Greenson (1967) believed that evenly suspended attention (sometimes called "evenly hovering attention") is a necessary component in the development of empathy, which places "strenuous and contradictory demands on the clinician." Alfred Bion (1970) took the concept even further, stating that somehow the clinician needs to be without memory, desire, or understanding—a mysterious, hauntingly evocative phrase. For how can a clinician really be "without memory, desire, or understanding?" Are we not supposed to remember our patient's history and diagnosis as well as all the theories we have studied so that we can choose the best possible interventions? Are we not supposed to desire to help our clients heal old wounds and develop new strengths? Are we not supposed to understand our clients' life experiences, joys, and pain? The answer of course is "yes," but also "no," because often the best, most meaningful clinical work is done when the therapist is in the emptiest, most receptive, most impressionistic state.

Nina Coltart (1986), a member of the British Independent Tradition of object relations, was interested in the same phenomenon, and taught that the clinician must always find a balance between reliance on theory and "a willingness to be continually open to the emergence of the unexpected." She wrote:

> It is of the essence of our impossible profession that in a very singular way we do not know what we are doing. Do not be distracted by random associations to this idea. I am not undermining our deep, exacting training; nor discounting the ways in which—unlike many people who master a subject and then just *do* it, or teach it—we have to keep *at* ourselves, our literature and our clinical crosstalk with colleagues. All these daily operations are the efficient, skillful, and thinkable tools with which we constantly approach the heart of our work, which is a mystery. (p. 186)

This harkens back to the Mary Gordon quote in the first chapter about the importance of never knowing *for sure* how a particular experience will affect a person's development. It has been amusing and sometimes touching to notice over the years that students often first hear the phrase "evenly suspended attention" as *"eagerly* suspended attention." This may not quite be what Freud and Bion had in mind, but it does add a nice note of enthusiasm to the process.

The theories that we have presented in the first half of this book, then, should ideally remain available and accessible in our minds in order to teach us *why* a person may come to us with certain struggles and strengths at a given time and in a particular fashion. They can then help deepen our understanding of our clients' emotional turmoil, and help create options for healing and growth. They can offer us empathic windows through which we can see our clients' pain and strengths. They must not, however, become prescriptions for how the work *should* proceed. If we know too much too soon, we stop listening to the unique essence of our clients' lives; we run the risk of deciding where the therapeutic journey will take us, rather than having it evolve out of the interactions unfolding in the therapeutic relationship.

In the first half of the book, we noted that only by appreciating external and internal dynamics can we more fully understand the pain with which many of our clients present. Recall the two clients we described in chapter 1—Martin and Michael. Both had been seen by clinicians in an advanced post-master's program who had effectively intervened on their behalf in the external environment, but who were bewildered by what their clients experienced internally. Michael was a Latino man, raised in a chaotic, physically abusive environment in which conflicting messages abounded. Michael described himself as three Michaels: a good Michael, a bad Michael, and a middle Michael, and his therapist was mystified by the meaning of this. His history revealed severe and persistent physical abuse at the hands of his stepfather and an early abandonment by his mother, who had been abused by the same man.

The therapist who worked with Michael began by helping him adjust to life outside the hospital, focusing on how discrimination, poverty, and the stigma of mental illness affected his ability to function. With the theories we have studied in this book, we can augment the therapist's understanding of Michael's suffering. From object relations theory, for example, we learned that people are not born with integrated senses of themselves and that psychological integration develops over time; babies and young children often feel that they have good parts and bad parts, and that with time and care children can realize that they are a complex combination of both good and bad. We learned that there can be profound effects on a child's sense of self and ability to trust when the child has been neglected, abandoned, or abused.

Using this theoretical knowledge, we can start to make sense of the way Michael "carries" his suffering. His symptoms reflect the way he has integrated external and internal struggles, and found "solutions" to them. We can begin to develop hypotheses about how splitting the "good" and "bad" parts of himself helped him cope with the abuse and neglect of his environment, and with his internal rage and disappointment. We can see how this experience of himself remained fragmented in the face of oppressive and destructive forces from without and from within. The theoretical constructs in this book can then be bridged with the discussion of psychopathology that is to follow.

The story of Martin affords us a similar opportunity. Recall that Martin, a twenty-eight-year-old black Haitian man, came to treatment worried about what terrible thing would befall him next. He had become so preoccupied that he was unable to function in school, work, or his marriage. Martin had grown up in a Catholic Caribbean culture, raised by a father who was a policeman and who set extremely high standards for himself and his son. Prior to contacting the clinic, Martin had been capriciously arrested by white officers and had been the victim of racial assaults by fellow prisoners who had poured buckets of urine on him throughout his night in jail. Upon his release, he could not stop berating himself or feeling that he deserved to be punished.

Each theory we studied can illuminate some aspects of Martin's symptoms and his internal struggle. A drive theorist might focus on Martin's own aggressive impulses and wonder how they were discharged or checked both during and after his arrest. Had the anger he felt toward the white officers and prisoners been turned against himself? Or were Martin's feelings of unworthiness related to his sense that he had failed his church's and father's high expectations of him? An ego psychologist might focus on his overwhelming annihilation anxiety and on the failure of his defenses to ward this off. An object relations therapist might attend to his self and object representations, which under the strain of trauma led him to experience himself as worthless and others as dangerous. An attachment theorist might have assessed Martin's early attachment style, trying to understand how the racial assaults were experienced in light of it. A self psychologist might focus on how this frightening experience caused a tremendous injury to Martin's sense of self. How might his previous trust in his own emotional strength, or his belief in the wisdom of police officers like his father, been shattered by this racist assault? How might this have affected his goals and ambitions? Each theory advances a set of hypotheses about what may have led to the symptoms with which Martin presents. In the second part of this book, we will offer a way to understand both Michael's and Martin's emotional struggles by focusing on several psychopathological syndromes.

Before we move to a discussion of these diagnostic categories, however, we want to reflect for a moment on the concept to which we are devoting the remaining chapters—the concept of "psychopathology." Webster's (1963) defines *psychopathology* as "the science of dealing with diseases and abnormalities of the mind." The word *disease* implies illness or sickness, an entity to be treated—most likely by those who are "disease free." A division and boundary is then created between those who are allegedly "well" and those who are "sick." The notion that the definitions of health and illness themselves are largely social constructions gets lost, as does an appreciation that we all fall along a continuum of mental illness and health that is not static in nature.

If we can move to an understanding of pathology that is more closely linked to its Greek origin, with *pathos* meaning suffering, we can then use the term *psychopathology* to connote not just disease, but the suffering of the mind or soul. Other cultures, such as that of Native Americans, capture this condition with terms that suggest someone is "out of harmony." These descriptions of psychopathology force us to recognize that we are not necessarily so different or separate from those who are labeled with mental illness. We all have experienced elements of suffering and disharmony, with which we are able to cope with varying degrees of success at different points in our lives. Biological, psychological, and social forces combine to determine where we fall in a given moment along the continuum from mental illness to mental health. As Harry Stack Sullivan (1940) noted, "In most general terms, we are all much more simply human than otherwise; be we happy and successful, contented and detached, miserable and mentally disordered or whatever" (p. 39).

How difficult it is actually to live and practice by this seemingly obvious and easy reminder of our common humanity was illustrated quite vividly one summer when a case was being presented to a group of social work students. The class had already met for several weeks and had heard all the cautions about "pathology" and the tendency of clinicians to distance themselves from patients by seeing them as "different" or "sick." The topic was Personality Disorders; the case was of a woman presenting many features of what diagnostically would be called a "low-level borderline." Severe splitting and projective identification were described as major defenses. Instances of disorganizing rage and self-destructive behavior were explained. Then a student asked what work the patient did. When the answer was "she's a social worker," the class gasped in shock and disbelief. Many students asked agitatedly, "How can a social worker be a borderline?" and "How can a borderline be a social worker?" At first, the teacher was very disappointed. Had the lectures failed so thoroughly that no one understood the principles and values that had been stressed? As the class talked further about their reaction, however, everyone understood more powerfully than ever before how deeply ingrained is the desire to distance ourselves from illness and psychic distress. It became clear that "we are all much more simply human than otherwise" is not such a simple tenet to fully espouse and practice by.

What had not happened enough in this class was what often does happen in courses on psychopathology, namely that many students feel in themselves every illness and syndrome that is being discussed. Students should barely be able to leave the room after the lecture on depression, whereas they should fidget and worry all through the description of anxiety disorders, and even experience a loss of contact with reality in the classes on schizophrenia. The old saw about psychopathology courses is that you "get" everything you learn about. *This is how it should be.* This is what we want. In fact, if the students do not "feel" in themselves some of what is being described then they are keeping themselves too distant, too separate, too apart from the material, needing to hold on to the illusion that pathology is something outside of and different from themselves.

There is indeed no magical line dividing the "sick" patient and the "healthy clinician." Health and illness, be they physical or mental, exist along a slippery slope, a fluid continuum that must keep us all humble.

When one of our dear, trusted colleagues was hospitalized on the same psychiatric unit on which she had trained, we experienced with great humility that there is no "we" (the healthy therapist) and "them" (the sick patient), no illness that we could protect ourselves from with our "greater" knowledge and wisdom. Although in hindsight there had been clear signs of this colleague's bipolar illness, we had secretly believed (something of which we are not proud) that her capacity for psychological insight and mental health could make her immune to this illness. How wrong we were; how humble we have since become.

In the following chapters, we review five major psychopathological syndromes—the psychoses, personality disorders, depression, anxiety, and trauma—using the theories we studied in the first part of the book. With a biopsychosocial perspective, we explore the complex interplay between nature and nurture in the creation of these disorders, and discuss the ways in which the disorders themselves reflect the social contexts in which they emerge. We will refer to the *DSM-IV-TR* (2000), the diagnostic manual of psychiatric disorders recognized by the American Psychiatric Association, but have chosen not to present these disorders exclusively according to its standardized nosology. The *DSM-IV-TR* is deliberately atheoretical. It offers a set of criteria that define disorders in terms of symptom lists; it offers an empirical way of ensuring that diagnosis be made on the basis of observable and describable behavior rather than on the basis of psychological ideology. It does not posit any particular reason for a given psychiatric problem, nor does it prescribe any one method for treating it. While this manual allows clinicians of all disciplines and theoretical orientations to make diagnoses based on common criteria, the richness of the internal, subjective psychological experience of "suffering" and "disharmony" is forfeited by this classification system.

A *DSM* diagnosis is something like a snapshot. It is based on the symptom picture. Certain symptoms or combinations of symptoms add up to a certain diagnosis. Just as a snapshot can reveal that someone has black hair or blue eyes, or is very thin or is smiling, so too *DSM-IV-TR* can tell the clinician that if someone manifests signs of excessive anxiety and worry more days than not for at least six months, has difficulty in controlling the worry, exhibits shakiness, experiences difficulty sleeping, muscle aches, and fatigability, they could be diagnosed with Generalized Anxiety Disorder (300.02, p. 476). A failure to conform to social norms, deceitfulness, reckless disregard for safety, consistent irresponsibility, and lack of remorse would result in a diagnosis of Antisocial Personality Disorder (301.7, p. 706). A snapshot can be very detailed and can tell a great deal, yet by its very nature it is also limited, finite, and two-dimensional—all it gives is a flat picture. *DSM-IV-TR* is similar in that it looks at what can be seen, documented, and measured, but does not attempt to explain how or why the symptoms or conditions came to be.

It is important to know what the *DSM-IV-TR* does have to offer. When used thoughtfully and not simply as a reductionistic tool, it can help organize complex information in a way that deepens understanding of a complex symptom picture. It facilitates communication across disciplines, and at times offers a snapshot of a problem in a way that can be very reassuring to a patient. A client who had been overwhelmed with fear when she developed episodes in which her heart raced, her palms became sweaty, and her breathing labored was enormously relieved to find a name in the *DSM* for this ailment. She was not going crazy or having a heart attack, as she had feared. She had developed a panic disorder.

In the second half of this book we want to take the reader inside the snapshot to meet the person. Quoting from the mission statement of the Smith College School for Social Work, where we teach: "Clinical social work appreciates and responds to the complexities of the human condition: its strengths, possibilities, resiliency, vulnerabilities, limitations, and tragedies." This underscores the importance, in the process of diagnosis, of looking not only at the illness but also at all the biopsychosocial aspects of the life of the person suffering from the illness. Even the *DSM* exhorts clinicians to be careful about language and never call a patient a "schizophrenic" or a "bipolar," but rather to say "an individual with schizophrenia," or "a person with bipolar disorder." And even this sensitive use of language is not enough for many patients. In her comprehensive and useful book, *Of Two Minds: The Growing Disorder in American Psychiatry*, Luhrmann (2000) offers the following poignant quote from a patient: "When I talk to people, I have to say, 'I am a person with schizophrenia,' and I don't like that. I'm not 'with' anything. I have severe functional limitations when it comes to certain aspects of living. I'm not 'with' anything, I'm me" (p. 292).

Over the years, the authors of the *DSM* have made a concerted effort to broaden their classification system by making it multiaxial, meaning that they have tried to include more than simply the symptom picture of each diagnosis. Axes I and II cover the Clinical Disorders and Personality Disorders. Axis III asks clinicians to look at General Medical Conditions, such as diseases of the circulatory, respiratory, digestive, and musculoskeletal systems, infections, metastatic disease, and so forth. In Axis IV (Psychosocial and Environmental Problems), cultural, political, and economic factors are alluded to for the first time (!) in the history of the manual. Although by no means perfect, this was a huge step forward. The destructive force of social ills such as poverty and oppression are not described powerfully enough, but we are hopeful that with the passage of time Axis IV will become stronger in subsequent editions. Axis V is the Global Assessment of Functioning, which allows the clinician to look at the highest and lowest level of both past and current functioning, emphasizing that no set of symptoms is fixed in time. Even though it is much more cumbersome and time consuming, it is essential to include all five axes in a thorough diagnosis.

Our goal in the following chapters is to demonstrate how a psychodynamic theoretical orientation can help us understand not just the symptoms of several disorders, but also the person with the symptoms, combined with that person's biology and the outside forces that have shaped her life. Using a biopsychosocial lens, we hope to illustrate how an application of the theories we have studied in the first section of this book deepens our view of the complexities of people's pain. From a biological perspective, we will explore how genetic and neurobiological factors can predispose and/or lead to the development of particular disorders. From a psychodynamic perspective, we will look at how drive theory, ego psychology, life cycle theory, attachment theory, object relations, trauma theory, self psychology, and relational theory help explain the etiology and course of people's inner turmoil and outward dysfunction. From a social perspective, we will look at how gender, culture, class, and the forces of oppression can create the context for and fuel the development of emotional difficulties.

The mental disorders we have chosen to describe do not include the full range of psychopathological syndromes that affect people's lives. They represent an arbitrary and perhaps idiosyncratic selection of several major diagnostic categories, including the psychoses (with a special emphasis on schizophrenia), the personality disorders, the mood disorders (with a special emphasis on depression), the anxiety disorders, and trauma. We chose to explore these five broad categories because they reflect a range of emotional problems with which many people struggle, and because they illustrate how a biopsychosocial lens can help us fully assess people in the context of their inner and outer worlds. They also lend themselves to exploration from a psychodynamic perspective.

In the following chapters, then, we will study psychopathology from the inside out and the outside in. In each diagnostic category, we will look at how what originates from the outside is experienced intrapsychically, and how what is experienced intrapsychically influences a person's perceptions of, and experiences with, the external world. Only then can we begin to appreciate the multiple levels of meaning in our work with our clients.

REFERENCES

American Psychiatric Association. (2000). *Diagnostic and Statistic Manual of Mental Disorders*, 4th edition, Text Revision. Washington, DC: American Psychiatric Association.

Bion, A. (1970). *Attention and Interpretation*. Northvale, NJ: Jason Aronson.

Coltart, N. E. (1986). Slouching towards Bethlehem . . . or thinking the unthinkable in psychoanalysis. In *The British School of Psychoanalysis*, ed. G. Kohon, pp. 185–99. New Haven, CT: Yale University Press.

Freud, S. (1924). Physicians practicing psychoanalysis. *Standard Edition* 12. London: Hogarth Press.

Greenson, R. (1967). *The Technique and Practice of Psychoanalysis*. New York: International Universities Press.

Luhrmann, T. M. (2000). *Of Two Minds: The Growing Disorder in American Psychiatry*. New York: Alfred A. Knopf.

Pine, F. (1998). The four psychologies of psychoanalysis and their place in clinical work. *Journal of the American Psychoanalytic Association* 36:571–96.

Sullivan, H. S. (1940). Conceptions of modern psychiatry. *Psychiatry* 3:35–45.

Webster's Third International Dictionary. (1963). Springfield, MA: G. & C. Merriam Company.

13

The Psychoses, with a Special Emphasis on Schizophrenia

Patricia Hertz

The word "schizophrenia" makes doctors forget everything they've learned about working with people, and makes them search frantically for something magic. I've been in this business for a long time, and I've never yet found any magic. And I've done a lot of looking, believe me.

(Semrad, in Rako and Mazer 1980)

Although written several decades ago, these words are as hauntingly true today as when Elvin Semrad first wrote them. Schizophrenia, and the range of psychotic disorders that affect millions around the world, remain etiologically perplexing and challenging to treat. They can be burdensome to the patients whose minds have betrayed their owners' trust and to those who care for them. The seemingly "crazy" thoughts or behaviors of mentally ill people can alienate us as we attempt to dismiss what we understand least yet often fear most. For beginning clinicians who use logic and linear assessment tools to understand their clients, working with psychotic patients can be a frightening and overwhelming experience. For experienced clinicians, Semrad's words remind us of our need to remain humble in the face of this perplexing illness, wary of "quick fixes," and trusting of the power of the relationships we form with our clients.

In this chapter, we will use a biopsychosocial perspective to help us understand schizophrenia, and explore the factors that impact the illness and the internal worlds of people with the disease. Before turning our attention to schizophrenia, however, let us first turn to the general concept of psychosis, which can emerge in disorders other than schizophrenia. In fact, it is essential that we not assume that the presence of psychotic symptoms means that an individual is suffering from schizophrenia.

The term *psychosis* refers to a mental disorder in which there is a partial or complete withdrawal from reality. Psychosis, or a "break" from reality, can assume many forms. The two most notable symptoms of a psychosis are (1) delusions, which are fixed, false ideas believed by the person that cannot be corrected by reason; and (2) hallucinations, which are sensory experiences leading a person to see, hear, feel, or smell things that cannot be established in reality. Even in the absence of delusions or hallucinations, a psychotic person's capacity to evaluate reality is almost always severely impaired. Let us consider a sampling of people who present with psychotic symptoms. Each of the case vignettes below illustrates a person *experiencing* a psychotic episode yet suffering from a different mental illness.

> Sam presented in his first meeting with his therapist as a well-related, casually attired, and thoughtful young man. He discussed problems he was having in his relationship with his girlfriend in a reliable, reality-based manner. When he returned for a second appointment, he entered the room with a bloody and swollen face, stating that he had been in a fight with the devil the previous evening. The devil, he said, had taken his head in his hands, yelled at him, and repeatedly banged his face against the bedroom floor. When questioned about the events preceding this episode, Sam reported that he had shot a quarter gram of cocaine shortly before the fight.

Sam experienced both auditory and visual hallucinations precipitated by his use of cocaine. He suffered from a *cocaine-induced psychotic disorder*. Illegal drugs, as well as prescription medications, can precipitate psychotic episodes in which visual hallucinations frequently emerge as a prominent characteristic. Psychotic symptoms can be present in a range of *organic mental disorders*, that is, those that have a clear biological etiology, such as *dementia, delirium, substance-related disorders*, and *schizophrenia*. When clients present with psychotic symptoms—especially for the first time—it is essential that they be assessed medically to determine if a general medical or substance-induced condition may have triggered the psychotic episode. Had Sam arrived at a clinic without either reporting his substance history or receiving a medical workup, he could have easily been misdiagnosed and hence mistreated. Mental health professionals are often the first people who evaluate these clients, so it behooves us to develop formulations of their struggles that are based on thorough biopsychosocial assessments.

Our next illustration is of a thirty-three-year-old married woman who was hospitalized on an inpatient psychiatric unit due to her psychotic symptoms.

Carol brought her active, vibrant, and well-fed three-month-old infant daughter into the hospital office. She noted tearfully that her daughter was not moving, was starving herself, and was close to death. When the therapist commented on the medical reports documenting her daughter's good health, Carol angrily replied that the medical staff were actors involved in a plot to torture patients and to kill their babies.

Carol was suffering from a *postpartum psychosis*, which is estimated to occur in one out of every one thousand women following the birth of a child. This type of psychosis, usually brief but invariably disturbing in nature, is precipitated most frequently by the tremendous hormonal shifts that occur after childbirth (Seyfried and Marcus 2003). It is characterized by either severe depression or mania and by delusions and hallucinations that usually center on the baby. We do not yet know why some women are vulnerable to this condition and others are not; psychological, social, and biological theories have all been advanced to explain this phenomenon. Regardless of what triggers it, a postpartum psychosis is terrifying to all parties involved in what we generally expect to be an exciting and hopeful moment in a family's life. For Carol, delusions about her daughter initially robbed her of an opportunity to bond with her infant and to rejoice in the miracle of this birth.

The last vignette we will consider illustrates a woman in the throes of a manic psychosis.

Susan, a thirty-two-year-old mother of two, felt increasingly energized and high. Over the course of several weeks, she went on a spending spree, slept two to three hours a night, and had racing thoughts and pressured speech. She began hearing voices that told her to take leadership of the treatment unit on which she worked as a psychiatric nurse.

Although Susan had no prior psychiatric history, she developed a *bipolar mood disorder* in her early thirties. The onset was gradual for Susan and occurred later in life than is usual in schizophrenia. Susan's mental status was characterized by an elevated and expansive mood, a flight of ideas, a distorted and grandiose self-perception, and ultimately hallucinations and delusions. Her psychosis emerged in a discrete episode and disappeared entirely when she began treatment with lithium. The majority of people who have mood disorders do not become psychotic; when psychotic symptoms do arise, they are usually congruent with the person's mood state. Susan's psychotic thoughts, for example, reflected a grandiosity and omnipotence consistent with her mania.

The conditions noted above by no means represent an exhaustive list of psychotic disorders or of conditions in which psychotic symptoms may appear. They reflect, however, a sampling of the many ways that people's minds can stray from reality and their lives get disrupted from within. None of us is immune from these conditions, which emerge along a continuum from severe illness to relatively good health. People with psychosis are not necessarily psychotic all of the time; they may have moments or periods of great lucidity. Similarly, those of us who pride ourselves on being reality-based may, at times of great stress, become tangential and disoriented. "Crazy," after all, can be a relative term.

Schizophrenia

Steven comes in carrying headphones, looking sluggish, overweight, and unkempt. His clothes are ill fitting and he appears fatigued and distracted. He toys with the headset he puts on the table, winding and unwinding the cord. The week has been uneventful, he says—almost apologetically. No real friends to spend time with, no engaging interests to relieve the emptiness.

Let us travel back in time and visit with a young man in his late twenties, accomplished, handsome, full of promise and vitality. Valedictorian of his high school class, graduate of a prestigious Eastern university, he is now a young physician brimming with ideas and hopes and guided by a sense of mission. Life's possibilities stretch before him like limitless vistas. Hard work yields rewards. There is a sense of order and fairness and justice to life. There is no hint that anything could mar such a beautiful picture, that a decade-and-a-half later, he would say, "I feel like Job, stripped of all my accomplishments."

Yet on the verge of a brilliant career, everything changed in inexplicable fashion. Before his first hospitalization, he prayed frantically in various languages, beseeching the heavens to spare a relative diagnosed with a brain tumor. "Books fell off the shelves and opened to the right pages," he said. "It may sound delusional to some but it was not that I *thought* I was the Messiah, I *was* the Messiah." His descent from the pinnacle was gradual but inexorable, as ten more hospitalizations followed over the next twelve years. (Horowitz 2002)

Steven's story, so poignantly captured by Horowitz, is painfully familiar to those whose loved ones and/or clients are living with schizophrenia. Perhaps with more than any of the other illnesses we will be studying, an overwhelming and unrelenting sense of loss invariably accompanies this illness. It is a loss not just of functioning in the present, but a loss of hopes and dreams nurtured in the past and projected into the future by the individual and the family. As quoted by Torrey (1988), "Schizophrenia is to psychiatry what cancer is to medicine: a sentence as well as a diagnosis" (p. 1). Like many cancers, schizophrenia afflicts people from all walks of life and often has a chronic course. We are uncertain about its causes, unable to prevent it, and have limited success in treating it. Schizophrenia is a syndrome that can alter all aspects of a person's life, as it creates deficits in the cognitive, behavioral, affective, and social spheres. For those afflicted, it can be experienced as a painful struggle for emotional survival. Although the nature versus nurture debate about the cause of schizophrenia raged for decades, research has shown that schizophrenia is a heterogeneous group of disorders of multifactorial origin. The interplay of genetic and neurochemical vulnerabilities is at the core of schizophrenic disorders. In the absence of these vulnerabilities, social and psychological factors alone have not been shown to produce schizophrenia.

Schizophrenia was first classified in the late nineteenth century by the neuropsychiatrist Kraepelin (1896), who used the term *dementia praecox* to describe an illness that progressed toward a state of dementia and began in adolescence (hence *praecox*) as compared to old age. In 1911, the Swiss psychiatrist Bleuler renamed the syndrome *schizophrenia,* a term broadly meaning "splitting of the mind." Although frequently and inaccurately confused with the concept of split or multiple personalities, this term referred to the splitting or fragmentation of various mental functions. Bleuler identified several traits common to schizophrenic patients including disturbance of affect, loose associations of ideas/thoughts, and an autistic-like turning away from reality. It was Freud (1894) who first attempted to explain the psychodynamic etiology of this psychotic process. He initially explored how intolerable ideas, inadequately rejected by the ego, return in the form of hallucinatory wish fulfillments (Arieti 1974). Freud (1924b) later understood psychosis as developing from a conflict between the ego and the external world, leading to a total denial and reshaping of reality. As he noted:

> Both neurosis and psychosis are the expression of a rebellion on the part of the id against the external world, of its unwillingness—or if one prefers, its incapacity—to adapt itself to the exigencies of reality. . . . [N]eurosis does not disavow reality, it only ignores it; psychosis disavows it and tries to replace it. . . . *Thus the psychosis is also faced with the task of procuring for itself perceptions of a kind which shall correspond to the new reality; and this is most radically effected by means of hallucination.* (p. 185–86)

Although his understanding of the causes of schizophrenia reflect the lack of knowledge in his era of the anatomy of the brain and the role of neurotransmitters, Freud offered valuable insight into the psychological mechanisms operative in psychotic disorders. His description of the role of repression, projection, and symbolization remains helpful in exploring the primary process thinking so central to the schizophrenic person's cognitive processes.

Contributions made by various theorists over the decades that followed Bleuler's and Freud's attempts to classify and decode schizophrenia have

been alternately refined, elaborated upon, and discarded. This most debilitating of mental illnesses has defied easy answers in regard to cause and
cure, although social, psychological, and physiological paradigms have
given us a more comprehensive understanding of the etiology and course of
schizophrenia. In the spirit of honoring the complexity of what is actually a
"collection" of illnesses classified as schizophrenia, this chapter will review
the epidemiology and clinical picture of schizophrenia, psychodynamic
ways of understanding the internal experience of the person with schizophrenia, and the relevant social, cultural, and environmental issues.

General Description

A staggering number of people in the United States have been diagnosed
with schizophrenia. Approximately 29 million people suffer worldwide
from this disorder with up to 2.5 million living in the United States. It
occurs in all populations with remarkably similar prevalence rates, ranging
from 1 percent to 1.4 percent, depending on the study (Barbato 1998,
Jablensky 2000, Kulhara and Chakrabarti 2001). Most of us have known
people with schizophrenia even though we may have been shielded from
the reality of this diagnosis. How many of us, for example, have been told
of a great-aunt Jane who had a "nervous breakdown" and was sent off to
live "in the country," or of the high school senior Johnny, who started acting strangely and never came back to complete his final semester at school?
Euphemisms such as "nervous breakdown" have served to cloud our perceptions of this disorder and to prevent us from educating ourselves about
it. Schizophrenia carries the "scarlet letter" of mental illness; the social
stigma of this diagnosis often isolates those afflicted and further burdens
their families.

The onset of schizophrenia usually occurs in late adolescence or early
adulthood. Approximately three-fourths of all people with schizophrenia
are afflicted between the ages of seventeen and twenty-five (Torrey 1987).
Often the onset is gradual, with the most striking characteristic being that a
person gradually develops seemingly odd beliefs and mannerisms. At other
times the onset is acute, with a person suddenly becoming psychotic—
having a "break"—with no clear prior indication of any psychological difficulties. Schizophrenia is often triggered by a significant loss, the
negotiation of a new developmental stage, or chronic feelings of frustration.
The death of a parent, leaving for college, or moving can precipitate a break
for the vulnerable individual. As we have noted, any of these environmental
stressors can trigger neurochemical events in the brain, particularly in the
changing adolescent brain, that sets the schizophrenic process in motion.

The course of the illness is similarly variable. Although all people with schizophrenia undergo an active psychotic phase at some point during the course of the illness, some recover with little residual deficit, some restabilize at a lower level of functioning, and others remain chronically psychotic. In a study of 274 patients assessed five times over fifteen years post-hospitalization, approximately 40 percent showed one or more periods of recovery (Harrow et al. 2005). The most common course of the illness consists of a series of acute phases with increasing personality deterioration between episodes. A fifty-five-year-old schizophrenic man, for example, may become psychotic infrequently, but appear to be a "shell" of his former being. His personality, not just his thoughts or affects, may be altered over time.

Once afflicted with schizophrenia, a person's prognosis is uncertain. Those in the "Recovery Movement" (Ahern and Fisher 2001, Anthony 1993) challenge the prevailing views of a pessimistic prognosis, believing that recovery rates can be much greater when a person is supported in a rehabilitation model that emphasizes self-sufficiency and self-determination, potential for growth, and the presence of someone who believes in their recovery. Most researchers agree that several factors predict a more favorable outcome, including a sudden onset of the illness, a predominance of positive symptoms (delusions, hallucinations, disordered thinking), perceptual changes that are experienced by the individual as strange, and the clear presence of a precipitating event. Supportive networks, comprising of family members, friends, and mental health professionals, can also be important elements in influencing the course of the disease. According to the World Health Organization (1998), the medium-term course of schizophrenia can be summarized as follows: approximately 45 percent recover after one or more episodes, approximately 20 percent show unremitting symptoms and increasing disability, and approximately 35 percent show a mixed pattern with varying degrees of remission and exacerbations of different lengths. Torrey's (1988) older research defined the ten-year course of schizophrenia as follows: 25 percent of people recover, usually within the first two years, and have no more than two psychotic episodes; 25 percent improve significantly; 25 percent improve moderately; 15 percent do not improve; and 10 percent die, mostly from suicide. This last figure is of importance because suicidal ideation and suicide attempts are a common and often overlooked occurrence in schizophrenia. Suicide is sometimes attempted during the first psychotic episode when clients feel bewildered and out of control, or during periods of depression when they feel despondent over the discrepancy between their early achievements and their current level of functioning. This figure is also important because the public frequently misperceives people with schizophrenia as homicidal. They are far more frequently victims of crime perpetrated by others, or, as tragically, by their own hands.

CLINICAL PICTURE

Max is a thirty-seven-year-old man who is paranoid and delusional, but bright and articulate. Christine is a twenty-seven-year-old woman whose speech is frequently incoherent and whose affect is incongruent with her mood and thought content. Bob is a forty-five-year-old man who postures in a rigid, catatonic fashion. How can we understand how all of these patients can be diagnosed with schizophrenia? As we think of it today, schizophrenia is a *collection* of illnesses, a syndrome that manifests diverse symptomatology depending on a combination of organic and external factors. It is a "disease of the brain that is expressed clinically as a disease of the mind." (Andreasen 1999)

In the *DSM-IV-TR* (2004) classification system, people are diagnosed with schizophrenia if they manifest characteristic signs and symptoms of the illness for at least six months, with one month of "active phase symptoms" (i.e., two or more of the following: delusions, hallucinations, disorganized speech, grossly disorganized or catatonic behavior, or negative symptoms) (p. 298). If the duration of these symptoms is less than six months, a person is diagnosed with schizophreniform disorder. The authors of *DSM-IV-TR* also differentiate among subtypes of schizophrenia (paranoid, disorganized, catatonic, undifferentiated, and residual), with each subtype reflecting the predominant symptom picture at the time of evaluation.

Let us turn now to the clinical picture of schizophrenia, to the ways in which this illness most characteristically presents itself in people's lives,

Disturbance in Thought and Cognition

One of schizophrenia's most striking symptoms is the disturbance in virtually all aspects of the afflicted person's cognitive functioning, from the most basic sensory processes to more abstract thinking and complex problem solving. Schizophrenia can be understood as a disease of information processing, as it is characterized by slower processing of and response to stimuli, difficulty sorting out information and excluding nonessential data, and impairments in attention, memory, and all the executive functions. It can lead to a "mental nihilism" (Robbins 1993), as volition—the process of choosing, initiating, and actualizing—is so often compromised by the disease. From a clinical standpoint, this disturbance can be manifested in the *content* and *form* of people's thoughts, and in their *perceptions*. Thought content may be characterized by concrete thinking, as evidenced in the inability to move from the literal or concrete to an abstract thought. Thought content may be permeated by *delusions*, fixed false ideas believed by the person that cannot be validated in reality. Before ascertaining that seemingly bizarre beliefs are delusional, however, it is critical that we assess them in their cultural context. A Haitian man who complains that a curse was put on him through voodoo, or a U.S. political activist who states that the FBI is wiretapping his phone, must be heard in the context of the norms and realities of their cultures. What sounds psychotic may be so only to the ears of the uninformed listener.

Delusions are enormously varied in content, and take shape in the context of a person's societal norms. Delusions of a religious or destructive nature have been reported to be common in Europe, but rare in Asia. In industrialized Western countries, delusions involving witchcraft and magic seem to have been replaced by those involving wiretapping, electronics, TV, and radio. They may also be a form of communication, whose meaning we must work toward understanding. A person may believe, for example, that his thoughts are being broadcast to the world by an electronic device that was secretly planted in his ear. Would it be any wonder, then, if he attempted to gouge out part of his ear to remove it?

People may have *ideas of reference*, believing that things are related to, or refer to, them with no basis in fact. They may "find" messages in billboards or a news anchor's report on television, which they believe are secret communications directed exclusively to them. As described by a woman with schizophrenia: "In psychosis, nothing is what it seems. Everything exists to be understood beneath the surface. . . . An advertising banner revealed a secret message only I could read. The layout of a store display conveyed a clue. A leaf fell and its falling spoke" (Weiner 2003).

Delusions can be persecutory ("The CIA is spying on me."), grandiose ("The peace postcard I mailed to you brought about a cease-fire in Nicaragua and again in the war of Iraq and Iran."), somatic ("There is a knife growing in my stomach and it causes me pain."), and/or religious ("I am Christ.") in nature. Whatever the content of the delusion, primary process thinking in which thoughts are not governed by logic usually prevails. The following comments of a thirty-four-year-old woman with schizophrenia illustrate this disturbance in thought content:

> I heard my name on the radio. They said the Christ child had been born. I am God, but would never admit it. I'd rather be a pathological liar. . . . I saw myself in a Michael Jackson cartoon. I saw my picture in the subways. How did they get it? I thought I looked good. It was scary. I sang and they applauded. I turned on the radio again and they offered me a Motown contract. They must have heard my voice in the underground.

The following letter, written by a man with schizophrenia to his therapist, offers us another illustration. Note his grandiose delusions, and how these delusions provide an explanation for the painful loneliness in his life.

> I am in true birth the living God child and son, kidnapped from Berlin, Germany, of Adolf and Eva Hitler. Yes, dear, Eva Braun Hitler and Adolf physically

are my true Ma and Pa. Because I had been trying to save the American flag from being taken down since June 1959 daily at work, I have not been able to get a date with a girl. I am at war—Honest and True. . . . Please mail a copy of this letter dearest to a man I am very proud of, President Richard Milhous Nixon.

In addition to this disturbance in thought content, "perceptual difficulties" abound in the schizophrenic person's cognitive functioning. These are often in the form of hallucinations. Auditory hallucinations are the most common type and can assume a range of forms: a repetitive sound ("I keep hearing a clicking noise."), a familiar voice ("My [dead] mother tells me to sleep."), or multiple voices of unknown origin ("I hear children's voices outside my window at night."). The hallucinations are often unpleasant and, dynamically, may reflect intense anxieties and unresolved, conflictual thoughts. A married woman with schizophrenia, for example, who was accused by her husband of having an extramarital affair, struggled with her ambivalence about conceiving a child. She confided to her therapist that she was having olfactory and auditory hallucinations: "The smells are in my face. They are not around me but right in my face. I haven't done anything that wrong. God doesn't want me to have kids. I hear bells and a clamping sound in my stomach."

Perceptual difficulties can assume forms other than hallucinations. There can be an increased acuity of perceptions, a flooding of the senses with stimuli. Noises may appear louder, colors may look brighter, and odors may be more pronounced. This intensification of perceptual sensitivity can be very distracting. An adolescent client, for example, could not concentrate on his thoughts in the office because of how loud the ticking of the clock sounded to him. At the other end of the spectrum, there can be a dulling or blunting of the senses, so that a person appears oblivious to noises and activities in his/her environment.

Cognitive impairments are also present in the *form* of a person's thoughts, which is referred to as a "thought disorder." A "loosening of associations," in which unrelated ideas are strung together with no awareness of their lack of logic, continuity, and purpose, is a prominent characteristic of a thought disorder. Words are sometimes associated by their similar sound (referred to as "clang associations"), or can be made up (referred to as "neologisms"). In the following exchange between a woman with schizophrenia and her therapist, note the gradual loosening of associations as the client began discussing her most recent psychiatric hospitalization.

It is my opinion that these three men belong in a Mental Institution. In fact I think all three of them act kind of funny and either belong in a jail or a Mental Institution. They constantly make fun of me and my good name. In fact all of them do, and my name is McAuliffe, same as Dick McAuliffe, formerly of the Boston Red Sox, and also General McAuliffe, like General McArthur. McAuliffe, General McAuliffe that is, said nuts when told to surrender to the Japs or Germans, and is not nuts, and neither am I.

When listening to these thoughts, the therapist initially assumed that the client was describing her experience in the hospital. As is common with tangential thinking, however, this client's associations became increasingly illogical and irrational, even as they remained loosely related to her initial point.

Given the range of cognitive impairments in the minds of people with schizophrenia, from the possible occurrence of delusions and hallucinations to the loosening of associations and tangential and concrete thinking, we can better understand why many frequently choose to spend time alone, keep lights and/or the TV on all night, or struggle to follow seemingly simple directions. The world may seem a frightening place when it is impossible to determine what are external rather than internal stimuli, what are real versus imagined dangers, and what is the intended meaning of a vast array of communications.

Disturbances of Affect and Behavior

Whereas the cognitive disturbances described above are disquieting symptoms for the person with schizophrenia, the "affective and behavioral abnormalities" are frequently the more noticeable and alienating of the symptoms. Behavioral changes can be the most obvious of the disturbances brought about by schizophrenia. Inappropriate or bizarre postures, the reduction in spontaneous movements, pacing, and rocking can all appear as symptoms of the disease. Although these behaviors are often attributed to the antipsychotic medications, they may occur in patients who have never taken medication. When they do occur as a result of the medication, it is important to carefully weigh the risks and benefits of continued drug therapy.

"Affective abnormalities," as evidenced in fewer positive and more negative facial expressions and inappropriate emotional communication, are similarly disruptive. A person may scowl when describing a pleasurable exchange, or laugh when discussing a tragic event, seemingly unaware of the discrepancy between the meaning of the words and the expressed emotion. Problems with the intensity and regulation of affect can also be seen in the schizophrenic person's experience of rage. Rage, understood by some theorists (Bion 1965, Robbins 1993) to be at the core of the schizophrenic person's emotional life, can be expressed globally in the language of destruction, often seen in hallucinations. Poorly organized and often non-specific, this rage can fuel a self-destructiveness, an attack on one's thoughts, feelings, and actual self.

Over the course of the illness, there is usually a loss of a subtle gradation of affect. People's emotions may become *blunted* (a severe reduction in the intensity of their affective expression) or *flat* (no signs of affective expression). A mother of a schizophrenic woman, for example, brought her daughter's therapist pictures of and letters written by her daughter before she became ill. She tearfully recounted how the expressionless woman the therapist had come to know was once a passionate, intense girl whose laughter and tears flowed easily. The disease had robbed her vibrant daughter of her previously rich emotional life.

Etiology

As noted earlier in this chapter, there is general agreement that neurobiological vulnerabilities lie at the core of most, if not all, schizophrenic disorders. Scientific researchers have been unable to pinpoint the exact cause of schizophrenia, as no single factor characterizes all patients who suffer from this illness. The widely held "stress diathesis" theory postulates that schizophrenia results from a mix of constitutional vulnerabilities, and environmental and stress factors (Walker and Difiorio 1997). Genetic, neurobiological, and prenatal factors give rise to constitutional vulnerabilities, which predispose people to this disorder. Subsequent neuromaturational processes, especially those that occur during adolescence, along with exposure to stressful events, can trigger the expression of this vulnerability (Walker et al. 2004). This model moves us away from the dichotomous thinking of "nature versus nurture," and allows us to contemplate the complex interplay of innate factors along with environmental "insults."

Many hypotheses have been advanced to pinpoint the exact nature of these constitutional problems (Encyclopedia of the Neurological Sciences 2003). Rather than attribute causality to a defect in one specific brain region, researchers are focusing on the dysfunction of one or more neural circuits in the brain. Particular neurotransmitter systems (dopamine, serotonin, and glutamate) are believed to be a central element in the pathogenesis of the disorder. For many years, dopamine played the most enduring role in theories about the biochemical basis of schizophrenia. The "dopamine hypothesis" speculates that an excessive level of the neurotransmitter dopamine causes schizophrenia (Creese et al. 1976). This hypothesis explains why antipsychotic medications, which have been shown to block postsynaptic dopamine receptor sites in the brain, have been somewhat effective in treating this disease. More recently, there has been a growing interest in the role of the neurotransmitter glutamate, as researchers (Walker et al. 2004) have found evidence of diminished activity at the glutamate receptors among patients with this disorder. Understanding the impact of a deficit of glutamate, then, may become the next area of hope for researchers still burdened by inconclusive evidence about this painfully perplexing disease.

Many other avenues are being explored to determine the etiology of schizophrenia. With the advent of neuroimaging in the 1960s, attention was drawn to the structural abnormalities in the brains of people with schizophrenia. Enlarged brain ventricles and reductions in the size of structures such as the thalamus and hippocampus were found with the use of this technology. Prenatal and postnatal factors in pregnancy—including obstetrical complications, maternal infections, stressful events during pregnancy, and postnatal brain insults such as head injuries—may also be relevant in the etiology of this disorder (Javitt and Coyle 2004).

The role of heredity is also unequivocally significant in the generational transmission of schizophrenia. Any clinician who has worked with the chronically mentally ill in one community for a length of time has invariably seen family members of different generations afflicted with this disease. The risk of developing schizophrenia is elevated in individuals who have a biological relative with the disorder. The closer the level of genetic relatedness, the greater the likelihood the relative will also suffer from schizophrenia. Twin studies have shown a significantly higher concordance for schizophrenia among monozygotic twins than dyzygotic twins; estimates suggest that identical twins have two to three times the rate of concordance for schizophrenia than their fraternal counterparts (Gottesman 1991). Similar results have been found in some adoption studies, which show that children of schizophrenic parents adopted away from the family develop schizophrenia at greater rates than adopted controls (Kety et al. 1972). Distinctions have been made within this group, however, with schizophrenia found to be more common in the biological relatives of people who have *chronic* schizophrenia. We must remember, however, that there is no definitive linear causality along genetic lines; 90 percent of people with schizophrenia do *not* have a schizophrenic parent, and 81 percent have neither a parent nor a sibling who suffers from schizophrenia (Robbins 1993).

What do these genetic studies suggest, then, about this illness? Given that the concordance rate of schizophrenia for monozygotic twins is not 100 percent, it is clear that genetics alone do not determine who will develop schizophrenia. It seems that a *predisposition* is inherited for some types of the disease, which is more likely to emerge when combined with physiological and/or environmental stressors. Once again, these studies force us to remain humble about our still rudimentary understanding of the causes of this illness.

Many medications have been developed over the years to treat this disorder. Conventional antipsychotic medications such as Haldol and Thorazine, otherwise known as "typical" antipsychotics, were introduced in the 1950s and 1960s, and were found to be somewhat effective in reducing the "positive" symptoms of schizophrenia, such as delusions, hallucinations, overacuteness of the senses, and other debilitating characteristics of a thought disorder. They did not, however, cure the illness, and frequently produced a range of serious side effects. Tardive dyskinesia, a syndrome that causes involuntary movements of the tongue and mouth and jerky movements of arms, legs, and body, was estimated to have been drug induced in approximately 13 percent of those treated with these drugs (Torrey 1988).

The "atypical" antipsychotics, including Clozapine, Resperidol, and Zyprexa, were introduced in the 1990s, with the hope that they could alleviate both the positive and negative symptoms of schizophrenia (apathy, loss of interest, emotional withdrawal) and produce fewer side effects. A recent study (Lieberman et al. 2005), however, found that most of the atypical antipsychotics were no more effective in treating schizophrenia than the older, less expensive medications. Furthermore, almost three-quarters of the patients in the study stopped taking their prescribed medication before the end of the eighteen-month study because of the lack of symptom improvement and/or because of the intolerable side effects. This rate of "noncompliance" is truly astounding, and as we will discuss later in the chapter, has significant implications for clinicians and insurers who use these medications as the first and sometimes only treatment intervention for this population.

In addition, medications today are frequently dispensed in the context of very brief psychiatric visits, where there is little time to explore side effects or assess the fears, wishes, and concerns that clients understandably bring to the decision to embark upon a pharmacological course of action. *It is axiomatic that medications are only a component of care; they are not a substitute for care.* Ideally, they should be prescribed and received in the context of a relationship that allows for adequate dialogue and thoughtful attention.

The contributions made by medical research to our understanding of the cause and course of schizophrenia have been enormous. The biological disease model of schizophrenia has helped destigmatize the illness, and has offered patients far more effective treatment than just "talking" psychotherapeutic interventions alone. However, the biological model of the illness can lead to an exclusive reliance on medication as the only meaningful intervention; *psychological* dilemmas are then minimized, clients' complex inner worlds are left unexplored, and the focus of care all too often turns to the management of behaviors and the treatment of symptoms rather than to the person *with* the symptoms.

For many of the clients with schizophrenia, isolation and loneliness are all too constant by-products of their illness. As Robbins (1993) notes:

A consequence of viewing the mental manifestations of schizophrenia as expressions of an organic disease entity separate from the personality of the sufferer, manifestations that are meaningless and incomprehensible even to the schizophrenic himself, is the direction of so-called treatment measures to expunge these with "tranquilizing" drugs and to persuade the patient to conceal his thinking, symptoms, and limitations from others and try to function as if he were normal. . . . *But the preferred "treatment" of today mirrors and enhances the schizophrenic's basic alienation from others, and, regardless of the impression conveyed by his compliance, lends reality and substance to whatever mistrustful paranoid beliefs he may have that the world is a dangerous place and that others are basically inimical to his well-being.* (p. 187, italics added)

PSYCHODYNAMIC UNDERSTANDING OF SCHIZOPHRENIA

Given our recognition that constitutional, genetic, and environmental factors lie at the etiological core of schizophrenia, why, one may ask, do we invite readers to use psychodynamic theories to deepen their understanding of this illness? Regardless of causality, the person with schizophrenia lives with powerful affects, drives, relational longings, and thoughts that are deserving of comprehension and compassion. Too often, mental health professionals attend minimally to the content of a client's psychotic processes, not recognizing that they may be internally logical and rational to the client. A person may wear sunglasses all of the time in order to block out the lasers he believes are blinding him; another may hold daily conversations with Queen Elizabeth in order to feel connected to a special, seemingly powerful individual. How we understand these *compromise solutions* to internal crises and external pressures will inform our capacity to work empathically with psychotic clients.

Psychosis can leave so many feeling isolated, yet yearning—in spite of their fears—to be heard. As noted by a woman with schizophrenia: "I wanted to learn to talk about my psychotic experiences, to communicate about them, and to learn to see their meaning. I learned that this wish is not accepted as a legitimate need for care" (Boevink 2006). Using the psychodynamic theories described in the first part of this book, we will explore the internal world of people with schizophrenia, so that we may be better able to "hear" what clients such as this woman may be communicating.

Drive Theory

Freud (1911, 1914) initially postulated that schizophrenia resulted from a regression in the face of intense frustration and conflict with others, a literal turning of the energy attached to others (and the representations of others) back onto the self. Although this theory does not satisfactorily explain the etiology and many manifestations of schizophrenia, the psychic energies—in the form of the aggressive and libidinal impulses—significantly impact the cognitive and affective states of people with schizophrenia. Valiant attempts are made to avoid experiencing intolerable rage, anxieties, and other emotions, which are often expressed through bodily symptoms. Semrad, a gifted and talented psychiatrist known for working with the most troubled of clients, would gain access to this hidden but important emotional landscape "held" by the body. He would do a "verbal tour" of the client's body, asking him or her to locate the bodily organ in which he or she felt the pain in order to bring it to consciousness.

We must remember that because schizophrenic individuals have difficulty sorting through and processing external stimuli, they are vulnerable to experiencing the world as a dangerous and frightening place. Statements such as, "You better put me in restraints because I'm dangerous," or "I am powerful enough to stop the war" reflect an aggressive upsurge in the face of a feeling of helplessness or of a perceived (internally or externally generated) threat. This upsurge, frequently accompanied by intense anxiety, can lead to a regression to a primitive psychosexual stage of development, manifesting as themes of orality (i.e., "I swallowed his body when we met"). Sexual and aggressive urges are also frequently poorly controlled and regulated. As illustrated in the following letter, these impulses can become fused as loving relationships can switch precipitously to hostile ones. This letter, written by a man hospitalized after becoming increasingly psychotic, was sent to his much loved and feared therapist.

> Listen i am getting strung out about the whole thing [his attachment to his therapist] you just want to fuck yourself to death, then when your through see if i'm any good—then i thought i remembered the stern looks and when i'd come in your face would be shiny like you had vaseline on it i use to hate that you use to look like you worked there i like it better when you just look like somebody's wife but any way those things scared me I don't want to die.

Feeling abandoned by his therapist, this individual felt enraged by his need for her and discarded for being "no good." He projected both his loving and aggressive impulses onto his therapist, whom he then perceived as dangerous and stern. His fears of his therapist's and of his own aggression threatened the very core of his existence. Consistent with the quality of many schizophrenic people's object relations, his intense longing for an attachment to his therapist was challenged by his terror of it. That which he desired most, he also most feared.

Ego Functions

Early writings on schizophrenia postulated that the ego of the person with schizophrenia was weak, and thus unable to withstand the dilemmas posed by reality (Freud 1924a). But what is meant by a "weak" ego? As with all the illnesses we will be studying, the impairment of ego functions depends on the severity of the illness and on the stage of the illness. Before looking at two of the functions of the ego in greater depth—the management of anxiety and the defenses—we can make the following general comments about the ego functions of many people with schizophrenia. First, perception, memory, and the range of autonomous functions of the ego suffer some degree of impairment. Second, judgment is frequently poor, as is reality testing. Third, thought processes are hindered by the intrusion of primary process material. Fourth, the synthetic-integrative functions of the ego, which help organize and integrate the disparate aspects of one's personality into a coherent whole, are compromised.

As described in the first part of this chapter, the thinking of people with schizophrenia is characterized by what Searles (1965) describes as a lack of differentiation between the concrete and the metaphorical. Idioms are interpreted literally, and the richness of nuances and metaphor in language is lost. Searles suggests that this concreteness of thought in people with schizophrenia serves an important function: it helps maintain various anxiety-laden affects "under repression." When, for example, Searles abruptly told a self-righteous patient, "You can't have your cake and eat it too!" he was met with the following concrete response: "I don't want to eat any cake in the hospital! You can eat cake here, if you want to; I don't want to eat any cake here" (p. 564). Not only did the patient respond literally to Searles's reproach, he avoided the affective meaning of the limit-setting remark.

The Experience of Anxiety

Depending on how well it is managed, anxiety can motivate people to act, or it can paralyze them. In developmental terms, we have said that anxiety can be experienced as threatening on different levels: people may fear losing the love of another; they may fear being abandoned by others; or in more primitive terms, they may fear losing themselves. For the person with schizophrenia, anxiety is usually experienced as the latter: as a *fear of annihilation*. The intensity of annihilation anxiety is so overwhelming that individuals may fear that they will cease to exist, or that their identity will be reduced to a part of a person rather than a whole. Themes of disintegration and engulfment often emerge in sessions with psychotic clients as manifestations of this intolerable anxiety and of the experience of rage. Comments such as: "Nuclear war is here and the world is exploding into pieces," and "I saw myself in the center of the earth swallowed up and found by no one" reflect this experience of annihilation anxiety.

Annihilation anxiety is frequently precipitated by loss, by frightening interpersonal contacts, and by the experience of powerful affects. In the following example, note how Mark, a man with schizophrenia, expressed his anxiety in his first session with a new therapist.

> Mark, a Jewish man with schizophrenia, noted that his father owned a deli. He handed the therapist a bag, saying he had brought her a corned beef sandwich. He then hesitated, appeared anxious and said, "I thought I brought you a corned beef sandwich, but maybe it was a piece of my arm." The therapist, using humor to handle her own anxiety, replied, "Hold the mustard."

Imagine the level of panic experienced by Mark during this first encounter. Most, if not all, of us would approach a first session with a therapist with some trepidation and perhaps fear. For this psychotically vulnerable individual, however, meeting someone new provoked fears of disintegration, if not annihilation, of parts of himself. Establishing a safe relationship with his therapist, in which these feelings could be tolerated and understood, was a crucial part of their therapeutic task.

How can we understand this level of anxiety in dynamic terms? Pao (1977) used the term *organism panic* to describe this state of fear. He noted that due to the great and overwhelming distress experienced by schizophrenic people early in their lives, "the predisposition to anxiety may become so enhanced that each time he should experience anxiety he experiences panic instead" (p. 394). Panic interferes with the development of healthy ego functions and relationships with others. When conflicts arise, the schizophrenic person uses the more primitive "tools" (denial, projection, and primary process thinking) to alleviate this sense of panic. Psychotic symptoms can be the end result. Semrad (1960) also captured how psychosis may be the best possible solution for overwhelming anxiety and intense affect that cannot otherwise be borne (Adler 1978). He believed that in the face of losses, life stressors, and unbearable affects, the "schizophrenia-vulnerable person" retreats from reality in order to avoid the painful experience and the affects associated with it.

> When onset is acute, the patient is faced with three alternatives for dealing with his unbearable pain: homicide, suicide, or psychosis. He chooses psychosis and withdraws from a reality he can no longer endure. Illness emerges as the only option available for the survival of a particular individual, given his genetic background, his early developmental history, and his current environment of pain and frustration. (Day and Semrad 1980)

Although we no longer ascribe to this psychodynamic formulation regarding causality, particularly as related to the issue of *choice*, the level of anxiety and distress described by Day and Semrad captures the "subjective holocaust" (Semrad 1960) experienced by people with schizophrenia. Generated by biological and intrapsychic determinants, annihilation anxiety is a significant factor in schizophrenic people's interactions with others and in their inability to engage successfully with the demands of daily life.

The Defenses

As we have noted, we all use a range of defenses to cope with challenges of processing internal and external stimuli. It is the rigid and pervasive use of what we called primitive defenses (chapter 6) that most disrupt a person's ability to function in the world. For people with schizophrenia, the heavy reliance on *denial, projection, introjection,* and *externalization* helps a person avoid the experience of unbearable loss and frightening contact with others. These defenses are attempts at a solution, and on some level "work"—but at an enormous price. The painful feelings and thoughts are disavowed, but reality becomes distorted. We can see how this process unconsciously unfolded for Karl, a client whom we will discuss at greater length later in this chapter.

> Karl struggled with his sadness and rage as he was repeatedly shunned by his peers. In the face of his isolation, he "constructed" a reality in which he believed that three girls whom he barely knew were in love with him, and other boys were "after him" because of his popularity. His pain was transformed through denial and projection. His delusions enabled him: (1) to avoid real relationships; (2) to feel valued and special; and (3) to attribute his own aggressive fantasies to "the boys" rather than experience them in himself.

In another illustration, we can see how introjection served a function, with a cost, for another client.

> A forty-three-year-old woman, angry and sad about the loss of a relationship that had ended ten years earlier, reported that she had swallowed her ex-boyfriend's head. She heard his voice regularly, an occurrence that was alternatively pleasurable and annoying. Over time in treatment, she recognized that this represented a symbolic taking in and retaining of the "lost object" as part of her internal psychological structure.

While the use of these defenses bring a heavy penalty, they also can help people construct a world in which their external reality is more tolerable and their internal reality is easier to bear.

Object Relations and the Sense of Self

As implied in our clinical description of schizophrenia, many people with this illness have difficulty negotiating relationships with others. Their aversion to contact with others often reflects their difficulty maintaining self-object boundaries and differentiating components of their minds from characteristics of other people and other things. The adult relationships of people with schizophrenia may become characterized by simultaneous longings for, and terror of, fusion; attachments to others are experienced as mergers, and separations feel like death or disintegration of the self or the caregiver. The following comments of a man with schizophrenia and his mother capture this dynamic, as the son implores his mother not to leave, and his mother perpetuates the loss of boundaries between the two of them.

> *Son:* You can't go visit John. If you leave, I'll die. Or if you stay, maybe your spirit will swallow me up.
> *Mother:* You don't feel that way. You can't be angry now. I'm not.

These types of interactions can obviously occur between people functioning at various levels of development; when they occur with a person vulnerable to psychosis, however, they create the unbearable paradox that both separation and intimacy may lead to destruction. It is not surprising that poor differentiation between self and other undermines the development of a clear self image—a self-identity as a whole, intact being *separate* from others and distinct from one's surroundings. This loss of ego boundaries and fragmentation of a sense of self can also lead to extreme confusion about one's identity. This confusion is not an existential-like search to understand "Who am I?" It is instead a shattering of the experience of wholeness. From a self psychological perspective, it is a *disintegration of the cohesive self*, an absence of internal coherence in one's identity. Goals and ambitions, self-esteem, and twinship needs must then be negotiated within the context of this fragmented self-experience, and are inevitably compromised in the process.

ENVIRONMENTAL AND SOCIAL FACTORS

Social Class, Ethnicity, and Culture

Just as personality is shaped and molded by culture, ethnicity, gender, and socioeconomic status, illness itself is given form and meaning by these variables. Social factors such as poverty, discrimination, and inequality can deplete emotional and psychic resources, creating undue stress on people who are already constitutionally vulnerable to schizophrenia. Conversely, favorable social environments may compensate for or mediate against these vulnerabilities. This does not mean that social or psychological factors cause schizophrenia, only that they can influence its development and course.

Studies have repeatedly shown the highest incidence of schizophrenia to occur in the lowest socioeconomic strata of urban communities (Barbato 1998, Eaton 1985, Torrey 1988). In fact, it is estimated that 60 percent of people with schizophrenia live in poverty, one in twenty end up homeless, and fewer than one-third hold jobs. Different theories have been used to account for the relationship between social class and schizophrenia, including the migration of people with illness to cities where more services may be available, the disease itself causing a decline in people's earning potential, poor maternal and obstetrical care in lower socioeconomic neighborhoods, and industrial urban centers providing less support and creating greater levels of hostility than rural agricultural areas. Conversely, traditional cultures with strong family ties and a sense of collective responsibility for all members of the community may account for the more benign course of the illness in patients from these societies (Weisman 2005).

The disproportionately higher rate of schizophrenia falls not only along economic and geographic lines, but ethnic ones as well. The incidence of schizophrenia reported among Blacks and Hispanics is higher than the rate of diagnosis for whites (Strakowski et al. 1993, Torrey 1988). Questions about bias in the diagnosis of minority groups have been raised to account for this difference. Trierweiler et al. (2000) found that clinicians attributed more negative symptoms of schizophrenia to African American patients than their non–African American counterparts. Not surprisingly, the latter were more frequently determined to suffer from mood-related problems. In addition to bias in diagnosis, the higher rates of diagnosis of schizophrenia in minority groups may be attributed to the discrimination and prejudice many in this population face on a daily basis, which create stressors that may exacerbate psychic vulnerabilities (Kohn 1973).

Whether poverty and discrimination are recognized as variables in the etiology and course of schizophrenia or not, both have an impact on the resources available for treating the disease. Options for the uninsured are far more limited than for those with insurance and/or other economic resources. Hospitalizations and follow-up care are frequently determined by financial resources. Although money provides no protection against *developing* schizophrenia, the lack of it creates great stress in people's lives and limits treatment options. We must therefore consider how the *course* of the illness may be adversely impacted by social class and this uneven distribution of wealth and resources.

Gender

Numerous gender-related differences have been found in studies of schizophrenia (Angermeyer et al. 1990, DeLisi et al. 1989, McClashan and Bardenstein 1990, Piccinelli and Homen 1997). A later onset of the illness

in women has been consistently asserted, yet this assertion is mainly supported by studies that equate age of onset with age of first contact with the
treatment system. Other studies reviewing gender differences in schizophrenia found that women tend to develop the illness later in life than men,
to display more affective symptomatology, to respond better to neuroleptic
medications and treatment, and to experience a higher level of functioning
prior to its onset and upon recovery. More men than women are given this
diagnosis, whereas more women are diagnosed with schizoaffective disorders. These gender-related differences raise many questions: Has the diagnosis of schizophrenia been based primarily on studies of men? What
effects might women's greater affiliative behaviors and expression of emotion have on the diagnosis and course of illness? What differential interventions may be needed based on gender differences?

Availability of Resources

No full understanding of schizophrenic people's lives can occur without
an appreciation of the resources, or lack thereof, available to the chronically
mentally ill. Access to housing, mental health and legal services, and supportive networks is a critical variable in determining the quality of life of
people with schizophrenia. In the wake of deinstitutionalization, many
seriously mentally ill clients were discharged into the community, where
community-based services were supposed to provide alternatives to hospitalization. Housing, day treatment, and community mental health services
were established to offer a comprehensive network for these clients. The
positive outcomes of deinstitutionalization can be seen in the establishment of social clubs, transitional employment programs, and consumer
groups such as the Alliance for the Mentally Ill. However, despite the generous and compassionate vision behind deinstitutionalization in the 1970s,
adequate funds were not made available to realize many of its original
goals. The long-term results of this failure are apparent in all parts of society: our city streets and shelters are crowded with homeless, chronically
mentally ill individuals; our jails and prisons are overflowing with people
who are psychotic; our community mental health centers are inundated
with more persistently mentally ill clients than their beleaguered staffs can
handle; the waiting lists for residential programs for the chronically mentally ill are months, if not years, long. In addition, funding for community
mental health centers and state hospitals continues to dwindle at alarming
rates to balance local budgets. While state hospitals close, private for-profit
hospitals compete to serve this population in order to keep their beds full.
The sickest people in our society are frequently "lost in the cracks," as they
are discharged from institutions to poor and inadequate aftercare.

What solutions are there to this crisis? No simple answers exist. On one level, a commitment to the most disturbed members of our society is needed to provide funding for inpatient, outpatient, and outreach community psychiatric services, and for housing alternatives. On another level, a shift in our priorities must occur so that we *all* see the care of society's neediest as our joint responsibility.

Treatment Issues and Case Example

An attitudinal shift has occurred over the last several decades in how we think of treatment for schizophrenia. We have moved away from the belief in "magic bullets," from the exclusive focus on decreasing symptoms as if they are separate from the people in whom they are embedded. We are embracing models of practice that help people make meaning of living with chronic mental illness, that support the creation of relationships that allow for grieving while building on strengths, and that add spiritual dimensions to feed the soul. Psychosocial rehabilitation models (Leclerc et al. 2000; Stromwall and Hurdle 2003) have grown in number and breadth, including services such as supervised shelters, training in social and occupational skills, groups to improve cognitive functioning and teach coping strategies, and case management services that honor people's wishes to live within their communities. The Recovery Movement (Ahern and Fisher 2001, Anthony 1993) has challenged us to focus less on the pathology of the person with schizophrenia and more on the potential for growth, to recognize that recovery does not mean cure but the development of new purpose as one grows beyond the "catastrophe of mental illness." The Alliance for the Mentally Ill has supported the family, once seen as cause of the problem, as an essential resource that needs to be nourished in the face of the depletion that occurs when caring for an ill loved one.

Psychoeducational approaches (Sundquist 1999) have been invaluable in helping clients and their families understand mental illness and plan for the future when aging parents may not be present to care for their mentally ill children. They have also assisted families in identifying some of the "triggers" that contribute to clients relapsing and needing additional hospitalizations. Studies have demonstrated that decreasing the level of "expressed emotion" in family interactions—the number of critical, hostile, or emotionally overinvolved behaviors, comments, and attitudes—has helped people remain out of the hospital for longer periods of time (Weissman 2005). These psychoeducational interventions benefit the client and the family, as they underscore that the symptoms of schizophrenia are the result of an illness and not willful acts aimed at disrupting family life.

As valuable biological and social interventions take center stage in the treatment of schizophrenia, there is less and less written about the psychological world of people living with this disorder. Psychotherapy is often overlooked as a treatment intervention, because it does not cure the illness. It can, however, offer a relationship in which a person's daily struggle is recognized and shared, where tears are shed for the dreams not realized, and new hopes are constructed for the life yet to be led. Describing his brother's battle with mental illness, Neugeboren (2006) asks what had made the difference for the many patients he interviewed who had recovered after years of institutionalization. He answered:

> Some pointed to new medications, some to old; some said they had found God; some attributed their transformation to a particular program, but no matter what else they named, they all—every last one—said that a key element was a relationship with a human being. Most of the time, this human being was a professional—a social worker, a nurse, a doctor. Sometimes it was a clergyman or family member. In every instance, though, it was the presence in their lives of an individual who said, in effect, "I believe in your ability to recover, and I am going to stay with you until you do" that brought them back. . . . [T]he more we emphasize medication as key to recovery, the more we overlook what is at least as important: people working with people, on a sustained long-term basis. . . .
>
> Let's find resources to give people afflicted with mental illness what all of us need: fellow human beings upon whom we depend to help us through our dark times and, once through, to emerge into gloriously imperfect lives. (p. 17)

Let us end this chapter by moving from theories about schizophrenia to the human costs of the disease. The story of the life and struggles of a young man with schizophrenia follows. It is a somewhat typical story in that it chronicles the gradual deterioration of functioning that we see so often in people who are not among the fortunate ones who recover more fully from this illness. It is also a unique story, as is every schizophrenic person's, in that it reflects this particular man's expression of the emotional turmoil in his life.

> Karl is a twenty-four-year-old man who was referred to a community counseling center by a school guidance counselor. School personnel had grown increasingly concerned about his declining grades and obsessive preoccupation with his love for a fourteen-year-old girl. Karl was found stalking this young girl, whom he barely knew, writing her long love letters, and buying her excessively expensive gifts.
>
> When Karl was five months old, his father died of cancer. His mother, who remained depressed for many months, remarried several years later and bore three more children. Karl identified strongly with his biological father's heritage, keeping his last name and maintaining ties to his father's family. A cousin, aunt, and grandfather on this side of the family have all been diagnosed with schizophrenia.

In latency, Karl began spending an increasing amount of time in his room playing with dolls, watching TV, and building houses with cards. The family began to hear Karl's voice from behind the closed door, as he talked to himself about the plot of soap operas and the best strategies for winning college basketball games. By the beginning of his senior year in high school, this academically average student was failing all his courses and isolating himself from his peers.

As the therapist became acquainted with Karl over the first few months of his psychotherapy, she was struck by his persistent inability to greet her, to make eye contact in the hour, and to display any affect regardless of the content of his speech. Showing little insight, he described the auditory hallucinations he had been having since his "rejection" by the fourteen-year-old "girl of his dreams." The hallucinations were most frequently made up of voices of children at play, laughing with one another, and were usually most pronounced at night. Karl slept with the radio or television turned on all night. More significant, perhaps, than these hallucinations was Karl's pervasive distortion of reality. He believed that he became Jason of the *Friday the 13th* movies, a character who was taunted and then drowned by his peers at a summer camp, and who returned to seek violent revenge on his fellow teenagers. When angry or upset, Karl donned a goalie mask (to resemble Jason), grabbed an ax from a storage closet, and acted out his own violent homicidal fantasies in his room. On occasion, he walked the streets in costume, and approached passersby to ask them where he could buy a chain saw.

Karl developed numerous delusions in his life about random girls to whom he would become attached. If he briefly met a girl on a checkout line in a store, he would believe that she was madly in love with him. Love notes, engagement rings, and money would then be sent to her for months as his fantasy grew, although no further face-to-face contact would be initiated by him. He furthermore believed that his connections to the FBI and Mafia would assist him in learning about and doing away with his potential rivals.

During the many hours spent locked in his room, Karl created something he called "my world." With dolls and cards at his disposal, he spent his time reenacting scenes from soap operas or sporting events, adding, changing, and deleting events as he pleased. He assumed a range of parts in each plot, which usually entailed a woman, her suitors, and a jilted lover.

Before we turn to the treatment Karl received, let us consider his emotional difficulties in the context of what we have studied in this chapter. Given the heavy genetic loading for schizophrenia in his family, we can suspect that Karl was constitutionally vulnerable to developing this illness. The onset of his difficulties was gradual, although the emergence of his most serious symptoms occurred following the rejection of his fantasized "girlfriend" in adolescence. Dynamically, both his aggressive and libidinal drives were poorly differentiated as his objects of love were quickly transformed into sources of rage. Given his sense of helplessness (in relation to his own mind and to the world), he was frequently flooded with murderous aggression directed alternately toward himself and toward others. During the first year of his treatment, he was chronically suicidal; he brought the therapist new wills he had written (in a black and white composition note-book) on a biweekly basis, in which he delineated to whom his records, tapes, and TV should be left. He had homicidal fantasies toward his stepfa-ther and toward boys perceived as rivals.

Karl's object relations were impoverished, as actual contact with others felt threatening and overwhelming. His delusions and "his world" served to defend him against the despair and loneliness he felt. People were expe-rienced as extensions of himself, and not as complex, separate individuals. They were most safely present in his fantasy life, over which he had greater control. Karl relied on primitive defenses (denial, projection, splitting, and externalization), and interpreted events in his life in a concrete, distorted fashion.

Working with Karl was a variously frightening, rewarding, boring, and interesting experience. He was given antipsychotic medication at the begin-ning of the treatment, which helped to diminish his auditory hallucina-tions. For the first several years of his therapy, he and his therapist constantly assessed how much of a risk he was to himself and to others. His family's help was elicited in this task, and they were referred to a support group for families of clients with major mental illness. As Karl came in week after week with the same details of imagined and real injustices committed against him, he and his therapist began to explore the disappointments, losses, and limitations in his life. He required two brief hospitalizations, the first following a suicide attempt, and the second when he became more psychotic (he believed he was Jason) and planned to harm another person. As he gradually felt safer in the treatment relationship and more aware of his sadness, he stopped writing wills and threatening to hurt other people. He repeatedly shared the intricacies of his daily rituals, allowing the thera-pist to sense the depth of his despair and loneliness. For years in their work together, the therapist felt as if she were a nonentity, interchangeable with any individual and having no defining characteristics of her own in his eyes. When disruptions occurred in the treatment due to holidays and vacations, however, Karl responded with rage and increasing psychic disorientation.

Over the years, Karl began to use the therapist as an auxiliary ego, some-one who could help him differentiate between fantasy and reality, between his feelings and his actions, and between the impulses arising within him from those expressed by others. He relied on the therapist to help him con-trol his impulses, modulate and differentiate his affect, and at times simply explain confusing aspects of life. They shared the pain of his losses and of the limitations brought on by his devastating illness.

A student once asked the therapist if she thought therapy "cured" Karl. If we define "cure" as Karl no longer suffering from schizophrenia, she would have to reply "no." Karl continued to have delusions about various girls in his life, and to have limited social and vocational engagements. As we have noted, however, the concept of recovery needs to be defined more broadly than "cure." We need to measure Karl's gains in the context of his own life and his capabilities. We need to assess if therapy assisted him in returning to *his* optimal level of functioning. In this framework, significant changes occurred in his treatment. When angered by a perceived rejection, he no longer became Jason, complete with hockey mask and ax; he stated instead, "I'm getting those Jason feelings," and then discussed what he was feeling and assumed others were feeling about him. Although wedded to the rituals with his dolls and cards, he was able to be in the presence of others without feeling humiliated due to his behaving or talking in an obviously bizarre fashion. As he noted in one session, "I can keep my crazy stuff in my room and in this office, so not everyone has to know about my emotional problems." This enabled him to periodically sustain part-time work and to attend social gatherings with his family. As he grew more accepting of himself, the therapist, too, was experienced by him as a more separate person with her own personality traits. Karl greeted her and made eye contact when he entered her office, said "Bless you" when she sneezed, and even asked about her vacation following her absence.

Will society (and insurance companies) deem the work Karl and this therapist completed significant enough to warrant the time and money devoted to his case? We do not know. We are certain, however, that medication alone would not have decreased his sense of alienation, helped him grapple with the very real losses in his life, nor improved his sense of himself in the ways a consistent, caring treatment relationship did. Karl will have to carry the burden of his illness through the rest of his life. At least he was able to share the weight of that burden for a period of time in a relationship that could also bear his pain.

REFERENCES

Adler, G. (1978). The psychotherapy of schizophrenia: Semrad's contributions to current psychoanalytic concepts. *Schizophrenia Bulletin* 5(1):11–137.

Ahern, L., and Fisher, D. (2001). Recovery at your own pace. *Journal of Psychosocial Nursing and Mental Health Services* 39(4):22–33.

American Psychiatric Association. (1994). *Diagnostic and Statistical Manual of Mental Disorders*, 4th ed. Washington, DC: American Psychiatric Association.

Andreasen, N. C. (1999). Understanding the causes of schizophrenia. *New England Journal of Medicine*, 340:645–47.

Angermeyer, M., Kuhn, L., and Goldstein, J. (1990). Gender and the course of schizophrenia: differences in treatment outcomes. *Schizophrenia Bulletin* 16:293–307.

Anthony, W. A. (1993). Recovery from mental illness: The guiding vision of the mental health service system in the 1990's. *Psychosocial Rehabilitation Journal* 16(4):11–23.

Arieti, S. (1974). *Interpretations of Schizophrenia*, 2nd ed. New York: Basic Books.

Barbato, A. (1998). Schizophrenia and public health. *Division of Mental Health and Preventions of Substance Abuse*. Geneva: World Health Organization.

Bion, W. (1965). *Transformations*. New York: Basic Books.

Bleuler, E. (1911). *Dementia Praecox or the Group of Schizophrenias*. New York: International Universities Press, 1950.

Boevink, W. (2006). From being a disorder to dealing with life: An experiential exploration of the association between trauma and psychosis. *Schizophrenia Bulletin* 32(1):17–19.

Creese, I., Burt, D., and Snyder, S. (1976). Dopamine receptors and average clinical doses. *Science* 194:545–46.

Day, M., and Semrad, E. V. (1980). Schizophrenic reactions. In *The Harvard Guide to Modern Psychiatry*, pp. 199–241, ed. A. M. Nicholl Jr. Cambridge, MA: Belknap Press of Harvard University Press.

DeLisi, L., Dauphinius, I., and Hauser, P. (1989). Gender differences in the brain: Are they relevant to the pathogenesis of schizophrenia? *Comprehensive Psychiatry* 30:197–208.

Eaton, W. (1985). Epidemiology of schizophrenia. *Epidemiologic Reviews* 7:105–26.

Encyclopedia of the Neurological Sciences, pp. 209–12. (2003). Elsevier Science Ltd.

Freud, S. (1894). The neuro-psychoses of defence. *Standard Edition* 3:45–61.

———. (1911). Psycho-analytic notes on a case of paranoia (dementia paranoides). *Standard Edition* 12:3–88.

———. (1914). On narcissism: an introduction. *Standard Edition* 14:67–102.

———. (1924a). Neurosis and psychosis. *Standard Edition* 19:149–53.

———. (1924b). The loss of reality in neurosis and psychosis. *Standard Edition* 19:181–87.

Gottesman, I. I. (1991). *Schizophrenia Genesis: The Origins of Madness*. New York: W.H. Freeman and Co.

Harrow, M., Grossman, L., Jobe, T., and Herbener, E. (2005). Do patients with schizophrenia ever show periods of recovery? A fifteen-year multi-follow-up study. *Schizophrenia Bulletin* 31(3):723–34.

Horowitz, R. (2002). Psychotherapy and schizophrenia: The mirror of countertransference. *Clinical Social Work Journal* 30(3):235–44.

Jablensky, A. (2000). Epidemiology of schizophrenia: The global burden of disease and disability. *European Archives of Psychiatry and Clinical Neuroscience* 250:274–85.

Javitt, D. C., and Coyle, J. T. (2004). Decoding schizophrenia. *Scientific American*, January, 48–55.

Kety, S., Rosenthal, D., Wender, P., and Schulsinger, F. (1972). Mental illness in the biological and adoptive families of adopted schizophrenics. *American Journal of Psychiatry* 128:302–6.

Kohn, M. L. (1973). Social class and schizophrenia: a critical review and a reformulation. *Schizophrenia Bulletin* 3:617–31.

Kraepelin, E. (1896). *Dementia Praecox and Paraphrenia*, trans. R. M. Barclay. New York: R.E. Krieger, 1919.

Kulhara, P., and Chakrabarti, S. (2001). Culture and schizophrenia and other psychotic disorders. *Psychiatric Clinics of North America* 24(3):449–64.

Leclerc, C., Lesage, A., Ricard, N., and Lecomte, T. (2000). Assessment of a new rehabilitative coping skills module for persons with schizophrenia. *American Journal of Orthopsychiatry* 70(3):380–88.

Lieberman, J. A., Stroup, S., McEvoy, J. P., Swartz, M. S., Rosenheck, R. A., Perkins, D. O. Keefe, R. S., Davis, S., Davis, C. M., Lebowitz, B. D., Severe, J. K., and Hsiao, J. (2005). Effectiveness of antipsychotic drugs in patients with chronic schizophrenia. *The New England Journal of Medicine* 353(12):1209–23.

McClashan, T., and Bardenstein, K. (1990). Gender differences in affective, schizoaffective, and schizophrenic disorders. *Schizophrenia Bulletin* 16:319–30.

Neugeboren, J. (2006). Meds alone couldn't bring Robert back. *Newsweek*, February 6, 17.

Pao, P. (1977). On the formation of schizophrenic symptoms. *International Journal of Psycho-Analysis* 58:389–401.

Piccinelli, M., and Homen, F. (1997). Gender differences in the epidemiology of affective disorders and schizophrenia. *Division of Mental Health and Prevention of Substance Abuse*. Geneva: World Health Organization.

Rako, S., and Mazer, H. (1980). *Semrad: The Heart of a Therapist*. New York: Jason Aronson.

Robbins, M. (1993). *Experiences of Schizophrenia: An Integration of the Personal, Scientific and Therapeutic*. New York: Guilford.

Searles, H. (1965). *Collected Papers on Schizophrenia and Related Subjects*. London: Hogarth.

Semrad, E. V. (1960). *Teaching Psychotherapy of Psychotic Patients*. New York: Grune & Stratton.

Seyfried, L. S., and Marcus, S. M. (2003). Postpartum mood disorders. *International Review of Psychiatry* 15(3):231–42.

Strakowski, S. M., Shelton, R. C., and Kolbrener, M. L. (1993). The effects of race and comorbidity on clinical diagnosis in patients with psychosis. *Journal of Clinical Psychiatry* 54(3):96–102.

Stromwall, L., and Hurdle, D. (2003). Psychiatric rehabilitation: An empowerment based approach to mental health services. *Health & Social Work* 28(3):206–13.

Sundquist, A. (1999). Family psychoeducation can change lives. *Schizophrenia Bulletin* 25(3):619–22.

Torrey, E. F. (1987). Prevalence studies of schizophrenia. *British Journal of Psychiatry* 150:598–608.

———. (1988). *Surviving Schizophrenia: A Family Manual*. New York: Harper & Row.

Trierweiler, S., Neighbors, H., Munday, C., Thompson, E., Binion, V., and Gomez, J. (2000). Clinician attributions associated with the diagnosis of schizophrenia in African American and Non-African American patients. *Journal of Consulting and Clinical Psychology* 68(1):171–75.

Walker, E. F., and Diforio, D. (1997). Schizophrenia: A neural diathesis-stress model. *Psychological Review* 104(44):667–85.

Walker, E. F., Kestler, L., Bollini, A., and Hochman, K. (2004). Schizophrenia: Etiology and course. *Annual Review of Psychology* 55:401–30.

Weiner, S. (2003). Living with delusions and effects of schizophrenia. *Schizophrenia Bulletin*, 29(4):877–79.

Weisman, A. (2005). Integrating culturally based approaches with existing interventions for Hispanic/Latino families coping with schizophrenia. *Psychotherapy: Theory, Research, Practice, Training* 42(2):178–97.

14

Personality Disorders, with a Special Emphasis on Borderline and Narcissistic Syndromes

Patricia Hertz

The study of the personality disorders is a challenging and rewarding task, full of its share of controversies. The concept of personality disorder has entered the public's consciousness, with portrayals of antisocial characters in shows such as *The Sopranos*, as well as magazines with ominous headlines such as "Borderline Personality: Are You a Victim?" (*Self* 1990). As we examine the classification of these disorders, we will discuss the concept of character, the epidemiology and characteristics of several of the disorders, and the value of a psychodynamic lens in understanding their development. We will also touch upon some of the controversies that have emerged in relation to the diagnosis and treatment of personality disorders. Before turning to these specifics, however, let us begin by considering two brief anecdotes—one from a clinical encounter and one from a movie—to see what they might teach us about the concept of personality styles.

> Catie called the therapist for a first appointment after getting her name from an acquaintance. With a sense of urgency in her voice, Catie told the therapist that all of her previous providers were lousy, that everyone in her life had let her down, and that she felt desperately alone in the world and terribly depressed. Although the therapist was merely a name on a piece of paper she had received from a friend, Catie spoke to her with a kind of intimacy and insistence that left the therapist feeling that only two paths lay ahead of her. She was going to be the one to "fix" Catie's life for her, or she would be yet

another person who would disappoint and abandon Catie as had everyone else.

The next illustration comes from the movie *Goodfellas*, which depicts the life of the Mafia in Brooklyn. The narrator and protagonist, Henry Hill, explains why he chose to live a life of violence, taking what he deemed was his with no regard for the rights of others. Henry brazenly ridicules those who work honestly for their paychecks as "suckers" who have "no balls," and contrasts them to the men in his circle who simply take what they want when they want it. The life of crime to which he was drawn as a teenager—a life of stealing, lying, and killing with no remorse or regret—becomes routine for him. Over time, all of Henry's relationships and aspirations reflect a pattern of deceit, aggression, and disregard for others.

What might these examples illustrate about personality styles and disorders? People are generally *consistent* in how they deal with the world and with other people, and in how they react to life's stressors and demands. Behaviors, attitudes, interests, and aptitudes reflect particular personality styles and character traits, and form what is unique about each individual. When these characteristic patterns are shaped by problematic constitutional, psychological, and/or social forces, they can become maladaptive and ultimately disruptive to one's overall level of functioning. The result can be the development of the psychopathological syndrome called *personality disorders* (also known as *character disorders*, terms we will use interchangeably in this chapter).

For Catie, relationships had come to be equated with disappointment and betrayal. An alternating thread of enmeshment and abandonment wove through her connections to others, leaving her with the conviction that she would always be left hurt and alone. She therefore approached others with anger and desperation, hoping for a different experience, yet preparing for the worst. For Henry, the narrator in the movie, violence at home and in the streets had come together to shape the norms of his culture. To "be someone," to "make it," meant learning how to "score" at someone else's expense and not to care about the pain inflicted on others. His worldview evolved so that he saw only two choices in all of his relationships: "be screwed" or "screw someone else." For both Catie and Henry, the maladaptive patterns established over years led to the formation of their respective personality disorders.

In our study of these disorders, we have chosen to focus on only two of the syndromes delineated in *DSM-IV-TR* (2000): borderline and narcissistic personality disorders. We have done this for several reasons. Although there is an overlap in the symptomatology of many of the personality disorders, understanding the etiology and evolution of these two disorders helps us appreciate key processes in *all* of the personality disorders. Common vulnerabilities underlie many of them, including fears of aloneness and struggles with regulation of self-esteem and modulation of affects. The symptoms of the particular disorders vary, in part, according to which of these vulnerabilities is more pervasive and which defenses are mobilized to manage them. Some individuals, for example, may cope with their sense of inadequacy and aloneness by becoming excessively dependent on people and may develop dependent personality disorders. Others may defend against their anxieties and fears of inferiority by "acting out" in sociopathic ways and may develop antisocial personality disorders.

In addition to the diagnostic value in exploring borderline and narcissistic personality disorders, the treatments for them frequently consume disproportionate amounts of time and energy. Intense, complicated, and alternately loving and hateful feelings are often engendered in both the transference and the countertransference. Therapists are frequently drawn into an enactment of the central conflicts and struggles in their clients' lives, surprised by the intensity of the feelings directed toward them as well as experienced by them. They are often compelled unconsciously to be participants in their clients' narratives, holding the hope that new, more constructive relational experiences may unfold. The work with these clients can thus be an excruciating challenge, but remarkably productive and rewarding.

THE MEANING OF THE TERM "PERSONALITY DISORDER"

The concept of personality or character disorder originated in the psychoanalytic study of character. Before focusing on the development of a *disordered personality*, let us first define what we mean by the word *character*. The *American Heritage Dictionary* (2000) defines character as "the combination of qualities or features that distinguishes one person, group, or thing from another." Psychoanalytic theorists capture the more dynamic aspects of character formation in their definition. Fenichel (1945) described character as "the habitual mode of bringing into harmony the tasks presented by internal demands and by the external world" (p. 467). Reich (1945) defined it as "an armoring of the ego" against the dangers of the outside world and repressed instinctual demands, and emphasizes that it represents "not only the outward form . . . but also the sum total of all that the ego shapes in the way of typical modes of reaction" (p. 171). *Character*, then, reflects a pattern of adaptation, *unique* to each individual; once formed, it is *relatively* constant and enduring. We use the word "relatively" because people's patterns of relating can appear remarkably different when the context for their behaviors is significantly altered. Although controversy remains about what actually forms character, we believe that constitutional factors, psychological influences, and societal conditions all contribute to character formation—both in its normative and pathological evolution. Newborn infants are clearly not blank slates at birth; they have the seeds of a personality that blossom differentially based on the influences of the external environment (family, culture, economic opportunities, forces of oppression) and the organization of their internal worlds. *The forces of nature and nurture shape development;* when problems exist in either or both of these realms, character structure will be affected.

Our characters are made up of numerous traits, some of which can be useful and adaptive in one context, and yet dysfunctional in another. Being obsessional, for example, may be an enormous help during tax season, but a hindrance during crises that require a spontaneous decision. At what point do traits become so problematic that a character becomes *disordered?* According to *DSM-IV-TR*, a personality disorder exists when character traits are so inflexible and maladaptive that they cause either significant impairment in social or occupational functioning, or subjective distress. We are not referring here to a sudden change in a person's behavior, but to features typical of a person's long-term functioning. Character disorders reflect an *enduring,* dysfunctional way of experiencing nearly all aspects of life. As noted in *DSM*:

> The essential feature of a Personality Disorder is an enduring pattern of inner experience and behavior that deviates markedly from the expectations of the individual's culture and is manifested in at least two of the following areas: cognition, affectivity, interpersonal functioning, or impulse control. This enduring pattern is inflexible and pervasive across a broad range of personal and social situations and leads to clinically significant distress or impairment in social occupational, or other important areas of functioning. (p. 686)

EPIDEMIOLOGICAL FACTORS AND CLASSIFICATION OF PERSONALITY DISORDERS

Although an estimated 15 percent of the general population has personality disorders, there is little agreement about the causes of specific disorders. Studies of genetic factors (Livesley et al. 1993, Thaper and McGuffin 1993) have shown a higher concordance for personality disorders among monozygotic twins than among dizygotic twins, although they have not identified exactly what is inherited. Other studies (Chess and Thomas 1978) have suggested that certain temperamental traits identified in children under three years of age may predict the development of a personality disorder later in life. Psychodynamically oriented theorists (Akhtar 1992, Kernberg 1970, 1975, Masterson 1981) have focused on early childhood experience and the "fit" between child and parent in explaining the etiology of these disorders. As in our discussions of all of the psychopathological syndromes, we must allow for the interplay of nature and nurture in understanding psychological development. We must hold multiple perspectives simultaneously as our field continues to grapple with how the interactions of biological predispositions, ecological contexts, and psychological influences combine to produce personality disorders. Despite the lack of consensus about the causes of these disorders, all agree that in their most severe form, they exact a significant emotional cost to afflicted individuals and to their significant others.

Given the complexity of these psychopathological syndromes, how do we classify people with personality disorders? On a psychological continuum from health to major mental illness, they fall between the neuroses and the psychoses. Unlike people with neuroses, their problems are *not* confined to discrete aspects of their lives while other aspects remain free of psychological conflict (Waldinger 1986). Whereas people with neuroses are more fully individuated and "boundaried," and able to take responsibility for their contributions to their difficulties, those with personality disorders are preoccupied psychologically with separation and individuation issues, and are prone to feeling attacked when the "problem is located within them" (McWilliams 1994). People at the neurotic level of development may struggle with internally driven conflicts between what they wish for and what they fear in the context of triadic relationships. Character-disordered individuals tend to be engaged in dyadic relationships often revolving around fears of enmeshment, engulfment, and abandonment, as they grapple with more permeable boundaries between themselves and others.

As we learned in our chapter on schizophrenia, people with psychoses have impaired reality testing as manifested in hallucinations, delusions, and an inability to distinguish what originates within and outside the self. Individuals with character disorders, however, demonstrate an appreciation of reality; if they do have psychotic episodes, these lapses occur infrequently, are of short duration, and are generally ego-dystonic. People functioning at the psychotic level may feel their identities annihilated in the face of their fears, as if they literally do not exist. For people functioning at the character-disordered level of development, there has been some degree of identity integration, albeit one full of inconsistencies and lack of nuanced complexity. Their personalities are relatively stable over time—even if their symptoms are not. This is, in fact, why the diagnosis of personality disorder is not generally made until late adolescence or early adulthood. Although traits may be evident in childhood, it is the relative stability of the character—albeit dysfunctional—that is the hallmark of the disorder.

The authors of *DSM-IV-TR*, interestingly, take a slightly different approach to this set of diagnoses than to most of the others in the manual.

Reflective of its general classification system, *DSM-IV-TR* offers descriptions of the symptoms characteristic of each personality disorder, and establishes diagnostic criteria by focusing on observable behavior. It also, however, refers more directly to psychodynamic concepts such as ego functions, object relations, and sense of self in describing this syndrome. *DSM-IV-TR* groups the personality disorders into three clusters, each of which reflects common general symptoms. These clusters are: (1) people who appear odd or eccentric, and fear social relationships; the associated character disorders are paranoid, schizoid, and schizotypal; (2) people who appear dramatic, emotional, or erratic, and who tend to act out their conflicts directly on their environment; the associated disorders are antisocial, borderline, histrionic, and narcissistic; (3) people who primarily appear anxious and fearful; the associated disorders are avoidant, dependent, and obsessive-compulsive. A residual category exists for people with mixed or unspecified conditions.

Whereas *DSM-IV-TR* primarily offers a snapshot of various behaviors, a psychodynamic perspective adds a greater understanding of *why* a person may act in a particular maladaptive way. It explores a range of factors, such as superego development, quality of object relations, and defensive structure, to determine how particular styles of being, relating, and growing are developed and retained. It invites us to understand how two distinct and interacting dimensions—the development of personality organization and defensive style within that level—shape the ways we experience our inner and outer worlds (McWilliams 1994). This perspective has led theorists such as Kernberg (1970) to classify personality disorders into "higher, intermediate, and lower" levels of organization of character pathology. In lower levels of personality development, as in antisocial character disorders, there is an impaired capacity to experience guilt, a predominance of aggression, and a reliance on primitive defenses such as projection and splitting. In higher levels of organization, such as in histrionic character disorders, there is a well-integrated, albeit severe, superego, an ability to experience a range of affective responses, and a reliance on defenses such as repression and reaction formation. This form of classification describes the presumed *internal states* of individuals, rather than their symptom pictures, to determine diagnosis.

CRITIQUE OF THE DIAGNOSTIC
CLASSIFICATION OF PERSONALITY DISORDERS

Regardless of the perspective used to classify personality disorders, many problems and much controversy surround the use of these diagnoses. Although they are conceptualized as objective diagnostic entities, they are inevitably defined by the prevailing social, cultural, and political norms. Views on what constitutes health and illness are rooted in implicit assumptions about "normal" roles for men and women, about "correct" displays of emotion, and about "reasonable" needs for dependency on others. Who defines these "objective" standards for "adaptive" levels of functioning? Can we fairly label behavior out of its social context as it emerges, for example, in response to chronic abuse or racism?

Written over twenty years ago, but still relevant today, Kaplan (1983) captured the gender bias codified in *DSM-III* in her critique of the criteria for dependent personality disorder. She created the following fictitious personality disorder "Independent Personality Disorder" to satirize *DSM-III*'s assumption that women's dependency needs, and the way they express them, are unhealthy.

Diagnostic Criteria for Independent Personality Disorder
   The following are characteristic of the individual's current and long-term functioning, are not limited to episodes of illness, and cause either significant impairment in social functioning or subjective distress.
A. Puts work (career) above relationships with loved ones (e.g., travels a lot on business, works late at night and on weekends).
B. Is reluctant to take into account the other's needs when making decisions, especially concerning the individual's career or use of leisure time (e.g., expects spouse and children to relocate to another city because of individual's career plans).
C. Passively allows others to assume responsibility for major areas of social life because of inability to express necessary emotion (e.g., lets spouse assume most child-care responsibilities). (p. 790)

Sound familiar? In another society and time, might these "normative" traits associated with "successful" men be labeled as disordered? Might dependency—a reliance on advice, collaboration, reassurance, closeness—be associated with health? As exemplified in this satirical illustration, pathology is determined, in part, by the assumptions and biases of those who define the diagnoses. The traits of the "Independent Personality Disorder" reflect the way many men have been socialized to function in Western society, and have been rewarded for so doing. The characteristics of men, many have argued, have been used as the criteria to ascertain "healthy" psychological functioning, whereas those of women have too readily been deemed pathological.

Other feminist authors have challenged the diagnostic entity of personality disorders because the category does not adequately attend to the profound effects of trauma and oppression on psychological functioning. As Brown (1992) suggests, there are a wide range of behaviors that can result from being powerless, oppressed, and discriminated against in a repetitive, ongoing manner that do not reflect a *disordered* personality. These behaviors may be adaptive responses to experiences of interpersonal trauma, for example, that have become entrenched over time due to repeated exposure to traumatic experiences. "Certain forms of behavior which in isolation may appear dysfunctional or pathological are actually appropriate and precise responses to other aspects of the interpersonal environment" (p. 217). A category such as "battered women's syndrome" (Walker 1984) would account for characteristic behaviors of battered women (e.g., guardedness, passivity) without pathologizing the women in question. Brown suggests that a new diagnostic framework is needed, one that describes how repetitive victimization and/or exposure to sexism, racism, and other forms of cultural oppression affect psychological functioning and personality development.

In addition to the feminist critique of this classification system, other concerns arise in the use of the term of personality disorder. First, a stigma is often associated with this diagnosis, as it is sometimes offered with an implicit judgment and warning—i.e., this client will be "trouble." The complexities and adaptations in people's unique stories are disregarded, as assumptions are made about the reasons for their entitlement and lability. Second, the categories are established in a notably arbitrary fashion, as many people exhibit traits of several of the disorders. Third, as suggested in the previous paragraph, character structure is difficult to assess when significant trauma has occurred. Trauma can temporarily and/or permanently alter character structure, defensive functioning, and the quality of one's relationships with others; clients may therefore present with some symptoms of a particular personality disorder when they are suffering primarily from posttraumatic stress disorder (see chapter 17 for a further discussion of this). Inappropriate treatment may then ensue if therapists focus exclusively on the internal world of character structure and not on the traumatic context in which problematic—and perhaps *situationally adaptive*—behaviors emerged.

The last cautionary comment to make about the use of this diagnostic category involves the issue of cultural context. Given each culture's unique norms in regard to socially acceptable expressions of conflict and pain, symptoms diagnosed out of context may erroneously appear to reflect a disordered character. For example, Mendez-Villarrubia and LaBruzza (1994) note that people in some Hispanic cultures may develop episodes in which they shout, cry, tremble, lose consciousness, and become nervous and angry. These symptoms may reflect an *ataque de nervios* (attack of nerves), a culturally acceptable way to respond to stress. Through this culturally condoned expression of pain, people mobilize the support of the family and community, and are temporarily relieved of their social roles. In a different culture, these very same symptoms may reflect characterological and/or organic difficulties, and warrant notably different treatment interventions.

PERSONALITY DISORDERS AS A DIAGNOSTIC ENTITY

Each of the personality disorders we will be studying encompasses a unique constellation of symptoms and etiological factors. What generalizations, however, might we offer about the character disorders as a diagnostic entity? Broadly speaking, the following characteristics are associated with these disorders:

1. The ego functions (reality testing, capacity to tolerate anxiety and delay frustration, judgment, etc.) of character-disordered individuals are impaired to different degrees and are likely to be relatively inadequate and immature. Responses to stress are usually inflexible and maladaptive, but may change over the course of the life cycle.
2. Individuals with a character disorder usually feel that their problems lie not within themselves but in the environment. How is this manifested? A worker, for example, may be having problems at his job. Rather than consider his own contribution to the problem, he may blame his boss, his coworkers, or his family. We say that the problems for these individuals are *ego syntonic*, that is, they do not create turmoil and conflict within their psychological lives.
3. The ability to sustain loving, consistent, and mutually satisfying relationships with others is impaired to varying degrees. Someone who is schizoid, for example, may choose to be alone, have little contact with people, and seem indifferent to the reactions of others. Someone who is narcissistic may constantly need others to bolster his self-esteem and affirm his value and competence at the expense of others.
4. Individuals with a character disorder are usually not troubled by their behavior and, in fact, perceive themselves quite differently from the way others do. The manifestations of their difficulties, however, are invariably distressing to those in their environment. A man with antisocial personality disorder, for example, was referred for treatment by the court following one of his countless car thefts. He boasted of his accomplishments, claiming there was not a car alarm in existence that he could not dismantle in six seconds or less. Lacking a strong superego, he felt untroubled by his behavior, which, needless to say, greatly troubled his victims. As with many character-disordered individuals, the impetus to change did not originate with him, but with the

friends, family, colleagues, and legal institutions that put pressure on him to alter his behavior.

5. Because the character-disordered individual's issues are so frequently acted out or enacted in the interpersonal realm, the countertransference reactions of the therapist in the treatment relationship are invaluable tools in diagnosing, assessing, and treating these clients.

These generalizations provide us with a backdrop as we turn our attention to the study of the specific personality disorders. As we review each of these disorders, we must remember that we *all* have some of the traits delineated. It is the *prominence*, *rigidity*, and *clustering* of these traits that can lead to a diagnosis of personality disorder.

BORDERLINE PERSONALITY DISORDER

Let us begin our study of the borderline personality disorder with an anecdote that illustrates several of its characteristics.

> The therapist's phone rang at 12:45 A.M. Sandra, a young woman who had been in treatment for three months, was on the other end of the line. Through intermittent sobs she told the therapist that a man to whom she was attracted ignored her at a concert earlier that evening and that she was sitting on the bathroom floor with a bottle of aspirin in her hands. "I can't hold on to anything good anymore," she said. "If I take all the aspirin, the pain will disappear real fast. . . . When I get close to guys, they leave me. Then the little hurt sets off the big hurts, and I feel like total shit. Like what's happening in me will destroy any relationship. When I look at myself, I see a crippled mess. Like I'm running a race with my feet tied. I don't have normal hurts. I feel I have all the outside things. Inside I'm crummy."

Sandra's pain was overwhelmingly acute in the face of her disappointment. She felt abandoned and rageful, became enormously self-loathing, and impulsively grabbed a bottle of aspirin to "blot out" the hurt. She also felt that she could not hold on to any positive sense of herself in the face of the rejection. On the other end of the phone line, the therapist experienced a range of feelings: helplessness, anxiety, concern, and anger at the intrusion. This "crisis," in which both parties carried their feelings with great intensity, is not atypical of the "dance" that unfolds in the treatment relationship between clients with borderline personality disorder and their therapists.

Why has the concept of *borderline* received so much professional and popular scrutiny? The reasons for this attention are varied. Although the prevalence of this disorder is estimated at between 1 percent to 2 percent in the general population, people with borderline personality disorder constitute up to 11 percent of psychiatric outpatients and 19 percent of inpatients (Skodol et al. 2002). Most mental health professionals have thus been involved in offering treatment to individuals with borderline personality disorder, an experience that can alternately be challenging and rewarding, draining and frustrating. Much discussion and supervision time is devoted to the work with these clients, who frequently engage mental health systems to help provide containment for their destructive impulses. Suicidal and self-injurious behaviors are particularly prevalent with this population, with rates ranging from 69 percent to 75 percent (Clarkin et al. 2001). Complicated and intense transference and countertransference reactions are engendered in the treatments of these clients; clinicians may be alternately idealized and then devalued, and seemingly secure attachments may be precipitously disrupted. When therapists are loved and then suddenly despised, they rarely forget the experience of being the recipients of these powerful, at times dissociated, affects.

ETIOLOGICAL AND DIAGNOSTIC DILEMMAS

The concept of *borderline* evolved in an effort to categorize a group of clients who seemed to exist "on the border" between neurosis and psychosis. Unlike people with schizophrenia, these clients seemed to recompensate despite transient psychotic episodes; unlike neurotic clients, they developed problematic transference reactions and manifested primitive defense mechanisms in analysis. The first author who formally used the term *borderline* was Stern (1938), who outlined ten characteristics of a group of patients who were too ill to be treated with the classical psychoanalytic method (Richman and Sokolove 1992). Other theorists followed with different labels to describe this ill-defined population, including the "as-if'" personality (Deutsch 1942), pseudoneurotic schizophrenic (Hoch and Polatin 1949), and psychotic character (Frosch 1964).

Despite the general acceptance of the label *borderline* in current literature, theorists continue to debate the etiology of the disorder and to question who should carry this diagnosis. As we have noted in our discussion of other psychopathological syndromes, it is the interplay of internal and external factors—weighted differently in each individual—that accounts for the degree of severity of the disorder. Biological influences in the form of heredity, events during fetal development, and the impact of trauma on the regulation of emotions, along with the impact of a pervasively invalidating environment (Linehan 1993), transact over time to create the symptoms associated with this disorder. Graybar and Boutilier (2002) explain this "stress-diathesis" model as follows:

It is a model that we believe can account for extreme, moderate, or minimal contributions to personality from either heredity (genes) or environment (nurturance or trauma), and more typically, from the multilayered, bidirectional interaction of both. . . . The nontraumatic model emphasizes the interaction between the individual's constitutional vulnerability, which might include deficits in information processing, affect regulation, mood, and interpersonal relatedness and the vicissitudes of his or her environment, such as being exposed to "good" or "bad," "adequate" or "inadequate," "wonderful" or "horrific" parenting, and according to Millon (2000), social support, social change, and other sociocultural conditions. We believe it is important to note that extremely negative contributions from either end of the nature-nurture continuum have the potential to override or offset very good genes or very good parenting. (p. 154)

Note in the paragraph above the term "nontraumatic," which brings us to another controversial issue in the diagnosis of this disorder. The role of trauma in the etiology of borderline personality disorder has been debated for many years. Patients—particularly women—were diagnosed with borderline personality disorder with no consideration given to the possibility that they were actually suffering from posttraumatic stress disorder. The symptoms many of these women manifested, such as hypervigilence and affective lability, were often "adaptive" responses to traumatic events in their interpersonal world. When their trauma histories were acknowledged and worked through, the borderline symptoms abated for many of these women and an intact character structure was apparent—one that would not be classified as borderline. Molly Layton (1995) explains the importance of acknowledging trauma as follows:

What is added to our treatment of so-called borderline functioning when we locate its roots in a history of trauma? It is a profound shift in focus from character to context, like uneasily observing a person on the crowded street who seems to be gesturing and talking to himself, and then, thankfully, spotting the person across the street with whom he is in conversation. Viewing borderline traits as the fallout of real suffering ineluctably shifts therapy from a mission impossible to a mutually constructed more empathically demanding task of naming and sizing the effects of trauma. (p. 39)

We must recognize, however, that the effects of trauma on some individuals indeed create a character structure that becomes organized at the borderline level of functioning. Studies (Zanarini et al. 2003) have shown that people with borderline personality disorder report rates of abuse, including physical, sexual, verbal abuse, as well as neglect, ranging from 60 to 80 percent. This would explain in part why women, who are victims of sexual abuse more often than men, are diagnosed with borderline personality disorder anywhere from two to six times more frequently than men (Stone 2000).

On the other hand, as Graybar and Boutilier (2002) suggest in their use of the terms "nontraumatic pathways," it is an oversimplification to state that the borderline personality disorder is a trauma spectrum disorder. How could we account, they ask, for the minority of patients who develop this disorder with no history of trauma? There are several nontraumatic pathways that they describe for the development of borderline personality disorder: inheritable personality characteristics, temperamental factors, affective disturbances, and neurological impairments. As any or all of these are "hardwired" into a child, they may create an emotionally reactive, difficult-to-soothe child whose attachments are inevitably strained. In some instances, then, borderline traits develop not as a result of trauma but of the complex interplay of emotionality, attachment, affect regulation, and interpersonal relatedness.

For some, the assaults from the external world, coupled with internal vulnerabilities, create entrenched, dysfunctional patterns that lead to formation of character disorders; for others, psychological and constitutional strengths protect their character in spite of these assaults; and yet, for others, adequate environments are not enough to shield them from the hardwired deficits that lead to the development of this disorder. As clinicians, we must embrace these complexities as they inform our work. These diagnostic dilemmas are an essential part of the challenge in the treatment of borderline clients and add to the richness of our clinical pursuits. Our treatment interventions should be guided by detailed assessments, which work best when they remain hypotheses that are altered and revised as new information is acquired.

With these diagnostic challenges in mind, let us now turn our attention to the clinical presentation and symptom picture of people with borderline personality disorder.

CLINICAL PICTURE

The manifestation of borderline symptomatology can be dramatic and jolting. Because individuals with borderline personality disorder often engage people through intense attachments, those involved in their lives are invariably affected by their symptoms. Virtually all parts of their lives are impacted by their illness. Impulsivity, identity disturbance, and affective instability characterize their functioning. Linehan (1993), in fact, describes borderline functioning as a form of dysregulation in the emotional, interpersonal, behavioral, and cognitive realms. In the following sections, we will explore the prominent features of this disorder using a psychodynamic paradigm. We will look at the traits of the borderline personality disorder in the context of a person's object relations, ego functions, and sense of self. Throughout this discussion, remember that the maladaptive traits we identify are frequently attempts at a "solution" to overwhelming internally and externally generated stressors. They "live on"—maladaptively, perhaps, in the present—as survival strategies to help needs get met and wounds healed.

Object Relations

Individuals with borderline personality disorder usually have relationships characterized by *instability and great intensity*, as their need for attachment to others fluctuates with their need for distance. Reflective of that struggle, they search—at times desperately—for unconditional love and acceptance in relationships to fill the emptiness inside and provide ongoing external support for their fluctuating and frequently poor self-esteem. People in their lives can be idealized one moment then devalued the next, with no affective sense that the person they hate today is the person they loved yesterday. Relationships often end abruptly, while new attachments are made precipitously. Hypervigilant, they look for cues that might reveal that the person they care about does not love them after all and is about to desert them. When their fears seem to be confirmed, they may erupt into a rage, make accusations, sob, seek revenge, mutilate themselves, have an affair, or do any number of other destructive things (Mason and Kreger, 1998). This dynamic may be repeated countless times in their relationships, depleting those who care for them and perpetuating their own inner hell.

The attachment theorists (chapter 8), who describe various attachment styles ranging from the secure to the insecure, might consider these relational patterns as reflective of the insecure attachment style called "ambivalent." Although patterns of attachment do not correlate specifically with diagnostic categories, the ambivalent attachment style, described as inconsistent and preoccupied, is predominant among people with borderline personality disorder. Individuals with ambivalent attachments have not developed a consistent strategy for attachment, often because there was no consistent attachment pattern on the part of their caregivers. In more severe cases of borderline personality disorder, the attachment style may be characterized as "disorganized," reflecting more chaotic and unstable styles of relating than the ambivalent one.

How might the tenets of object relations theory help us understand the challenging relationships so typical in the lives of people with borderline personality disorder? First, although these individuals have a differentiated sense of self and other, the *boundaries between self and other are quite permeable.* Closeness can be experienced as "merger," as they feel engulfed in a longed-for, yet feared, union. This experience of "fusion" is captured in the following comment a client made about her relationship with her boyfriend: "We're so close I feel like we're one person. . . . Sometimes it feels so good—like we're handcuffed together. Other times it feels like he's in my face so I can't breathe." With poor boundaries, an *optimal distance* is difficult to establish. Closeness may be stifling, yet separation may feel abandoning. In fact, as we will discuss shortly, the fear of abandonment shapes most of their interactions with others. This fear is greater than a passing moment of anxiety; it is a terror that can lead to frantic measures (i.e., hurting themselves to manage their pain or to force others to reengage with them). As Mason and Kreger (1998) note, this results in the central irony of borderline personality disorder: people who suffer from it desperately want closeness and intimacy, yet the things they do to "get" it often drive people away from them (p. 30).

How can we make sense of the abandonment fears so central to these problematic dynamics? Many people suffering from this disorder *have not achieved object constancy*, that is, the ability to internalize a whole object as an emotionally soothing inner presence that sustains the person during the other's absence. Without a solid capacity to evoke the memory of others in their absence, individuals cannot retrieve soothing, comforting images when alone. This leads them to feel terror at being alone, a characteristic that Adler and Buie (Adler and Buie 1979, Buie and Adler 1982) consider the central, organizing feature of this pathology. This terror is not simply a fear of being lonely; ordinarily, when people are lonely, they can picture or feel the presence of loved ones whom they are missing. When people with borderline personality disorder feel alone, they experience a total void, an emptiness that renders the world a frightening place. They become fearful of abandonment and deal with this fear in seemingly contradictory ways. At times, they urgently cling to others to ward off their aloneness; at other times, they distance themselves from others to avoid the threat of attachment/abandonment completely.

This struggle is frequently manifested in therapy, when the patient cannot "hold on to" the therapist during absences. Listen to the articulation of this struggle in the following example.

Margie was raised by two alcoholic parents who frequently left her and her siblings home alone while they went bar hopping to all hours of the night. During the first six months of treatment, Margie often called between sessions, stating, "I just need to hear your voice to make sure you're still there." Following the therapist's vacation, she missed several appointments; when coaxed to come back into the office, she reported the following: "I was literally paralyzed when you were gone. I broke out in hives; I felt hollow inside. I couldn't picture your face, hear your words to reassure me. You might as well have been dead. I thought maybe if I did something desperate you'd come back sooner; then I just decided to stay away from you so I wouldn't have to worry about your leaving me again."

Margie could not comfort herself with the therapist's image during the break in treatment. She responded to her ensuing despair and rage by alternately becoming self-destructive (e.g., she made superficial lacerations on her arm), and then by rejecting those with whom she yearned, yet feared, to have an attachment. Although frequently seen in exclusively pathological terms, her attempt to engage her therapist can also be understood to represent a "powerful, healthy energy . . . embodying her lifelong attempt to locate a protective spirit" (Layton 1995, p. 40). As Margie became more able to hold on to the image of the therapist during ensuing breaks in the treatment and to develop a sense of trust that the therapist would indeed return when planned, these behaviors abated.

Another reason for the relational problems of people with borderline personality disorder is their *difficulty integrating positive and negative self and object representations* (Kernberg 1975). Simply stated, people with borderline personality disorder tend to experience themselves and/or others as "all good" or "all bad." When needs are gratified, the other is all good; when needs are frustrated/disappointed, the other is all bad. This splitting of object representations can be seen in the following comments made by a client about her mother: "When I hate my mother, I just hate her. I can't remember her ever being wonderful or nice. When she's nice, she's the best mom in the world, but I know I'll hate her again and never want to see her." Anticipating the therapist's attempt to help her integrate these split representations, the client added: "And when I only feel hate for her you'll remind me that I once thought she was nice." We can see in this client's beginning self-awareness the difficulty she has tolerating ambivalence in her feelings for others. She experiences her mother as either wonderful or loathsome, with no shadings of gray in between these two feeling states. How painful it must be for her that she cannot sustain an inner experience of her mother as someone who can be wonderful and awful, loving and frustrating, gratifying and depriving—the complex realities experienced in most relationships.

The therapeutic relationship provides fertile ground for the emergence of splitting and precipitous endings and reattachments, making the work with individuals with borderline personality disorder feel a bit like a roller coaster ride. The therapist may be idealized at one point, but as a colleague said to us, "it can be a quick trip from the penthouse to the basement." Leah gave her therapist this kind of ride.

Leah, a twenty-five-year-old woman who ultimately completed a five-year therapy, fired her therapist eight times during the first two years of their work. During a stable period of the treatment, she told her therapist, "You gave me words for my thoughts and feelings. I felt mute before. You just seemed to know me and understand me." Two weeks later, when she and her therapist disagreed about the contents of a letter sent to the Welfare Department, Leah shouted over the phone, "I'm never coming back to see you. You don't know a thing about me. You're as incompetent as the rest of them. I can't believe your college gave you a social work degree," and then hung up.

For people in the helping professions, this type of help-rejecting stance can be enormously frustrating and painful—as we noted, like a roller coaster ride over which one has no control. It is critical to understand, however, that these fluctuations are an inevitable part of the work, and may be an adaptive way for clients to survive the fear of abandonment and engulfment, and to manage the intensity of their rage.

The lack of integration of positive and negative representations occurs not only in relation to others; it occurs as powerfully in relation to the self. People with borderline personality disorder tend to be easily flooded by shame and to experience themselves as all good or all bad, with no shadings or nuances in between. In one moment they may be angrily self-righteous, believing that they are entitled to special treatment and that all of their problems result from their victimization in a cruel world. In the face of a failure or disappointment, however, they can lose all sense of self-worth, can become enormously self-loathing, and can invite punishment for their "badness." Prior experiences of competence and adequacy disappear completely, as they perceive themselves as worthless, damaged human beings.

> Carmen described feeling on one day that she was the most attractive, competent woman in her workplace. Following a rejection from a man the following day, she said, "I looked in the mirror and all I saw was this disgusting face; it had bulging eyes and crooked teeth. That, I realized, was me. I wanted to tear me apart limb by limb." Only one reality existed for Carmen then: the reality of that moment. Any experience of herself as an attractive, competent individual dissipated and could not be retrieved; it was replaced by her experience of herself as inherently defective.

Given the central role of impaired object relations in the pathology of individuals with borderline pathology, it may be helpful (and hopeful) to trace a client's object relations through the evolution of a therapy. Cassie, a thirty-year-old woman who successfully completed a treatment of several years duration, described her relationships with others, particularly her mother, in notably different ways during successive stages of treatment. The development of her object relations shifted from merged selfobject representations to a more differentiated sense of herself and others, as can be seen in the following vignettes.

> In the first year of her therapy, Cassie reflected on her relationship with her mother as follows: "My mother is totally dependent on me. She copies my haircuts, takes my advice. I can't get angry at her because she'd fall apart. I can't leave my mother; could you leave a kid who's trying to learn a new dance step while her shoe laces are tied together?" . . . [Turning to the therapist, who had recently returned from a vacation] "I couldn't picture your face when you were away. It was like you were dead—you were so removed from my life."

At this point in the treatment, Cassie's object relations were characterized by poor boundaries between herself and others, and by her lack of object constancy.

> Two and a half years into the therapy, Cassie stated: "It used to be when my mother was upset, I'd spend all night with her. I'm first realizing what the word *separation* means. I don't have to feel all of my mother's feelings. I will always choose to give to my mother, but I can't give her all of what she wants. It's scary—this could be the end of my relationship with her—she could flip out. During her hospitalization, I felt like we were the kids in *Sophie's Choice*, and I had to decide who'd live. . . . I sometimes dream that one day I'll wake up and my mother will be an adult."

At this juncture, Cassie was struggling to develop a separate sense of self. Although she feared that separation would lead to dire consequences, she fought against her fears and depression to establish her own identity.

> During the last year of treatment, Cassie married, was promoted at work, and planned to move out of state. She reflected on her relationships as follows: "My mother taught me how to love as one [hands clasped] but not as my*self*. Now I love as much but from one step back, ya know? Like before it was like I looked at a painting and saw colors up close. I'd find a color I'd like, focus on it, and it was beautiful. But I couldn't see the *whole* painting. If I'd move my face I'd maybe see one other color—like black. Yes, black—it was scary and awful. Now I can see the complex whole."

During her last year of treatment, Cassie had clearly moved toward integrating positive and negative images of herself and of others, and toward a fuller, complex affective life. In a letter she wrote to her therapist following her move, she described the pleasure she felt from a visit from a friend with whom she had once threatened to "cut off" contact because the friend had not been good in keeping in touch with her in the past. Cassie tolerated her ambivalent feelings brought on by her love of this friend along with the disappointment, only to find a true treasure at the end.

I guess I've never given my friend the opportunity to show how loyal and loving she can be with me. I am so glad I took the time and went through the pain of adjusting my expectations of our relationship. With you standing by my side, I worked hard at and won a treasure I could never have imagined—a relationship that "stayed."

Cassie had achieved object constancy, and with it, a sense of hope and trust in how relationships could enrich her life.

Ego Functions

Although there is a range of functioning along the borderline continuum, the ego functions of people with this disorder are impaired to varying degrees. *Cognitive processes* are frequently distorted by the maladaptive beliefs developed in childhood. Exhibiting a poor understanding of their thoughts and emotions, individuals with borderline personality disorder tend to think in dichotomous terms (i.e., experiences of everyday life are assessed as all good or all bad). Cognitive disorientation and transient psychosis may occur under stress, and the capacity for solid evocative memory may not be achieved. People with this disorder may have *difficulty modulating their feelings and impulses,* and can show *poor judgment and a disturbed sense of reality.* Additionally, the *rigid use of more primitive defenses* characterizes the borderline person's defensive operations. Let us look at some of these ego functions in greater detail, so we can better capture the complexity of this experience.

Impulse Control

As evident in the anecdotes thus far described, people with borderline personality disorder tend to act in impulsive and unpredictable ways. They frequently engage in self-destructive behaviors, such as self-mutilation, sexual promiscuity, gambling, violence, and substance abuse, the latter of which has a co-morbidity with borderline personality disorder of more the 50 percent (Stone 2000). These behaviors are usually *ego syntonic* during the act, but *ego dystonic* afterward. Nancy, who frequently engaged in sexually promiscuous behavior, described her impulsivity this way: "I was so mad that I said 'fuck it'—I drank, picked up a guy at the bar, took him back to my place, and had sex. It was fun at the time—I needed it. Now I'm worried I have AIDS."

As described above, impulsive behaviors often occur in response to the threat of abandonment. Suicidal and self-destructive gestures may erupt with no apparent forethought, and with little consideration given to potential consequences. Suicidal acts lead to death in approximately 10 percent of borderline patients, with the majority of self-harm behaviors carrying a risk of low lethality (Sansone 2004). Self-mutilation is a common form of expression for this impulsive behavior and carries with it different meanings that need to be assessed and understood on a case-by-case basis. At times, for example, people may cut themselves with the hope that they will die; at other moments the act may be an attempt to engage others in their lives and to force them to take notice; at still other times people may cut themselves to feel alive, to literally see that they are filled with warm, living blood—to counteract the emptiness and deadness they feel when alone. The blood and physical pain help them know that they exist, help create a sense that "I am bleeding and feel pain so I must be alive." An example of this type of self-mutilation, along with features common to borderline pathology such as rage, self-loathing, and the use of projection, can be seen in the following illustration:

> Cindy entered her therapist's office looking angry and sullen, and wearing a bandage on her arm where she had cut herself following the previous therapy session. She began the hour: "You made me feel like a fucking loser on Monday. I'm pissed. Don't look at me like I have three heads. Turn away! You think I'm some kinda failure. Well fuck you too. I'm such a loser. I feel unsafe, but I won't let you put me back in the hospital. [Looking at her arm] I didn't even feel the pain. Like one minute I was unloading the dishwasher and the next there was blood trickling down my arm. It kinda made me feel like a person again."

Cindy became overwhelmed with feelings of inferiority and rage. Cutting herself made her feel alive again. If there was blood, then she still existed.

When people with borderline personality disorder make these kinds of gestures, they are frequently described as being "manipulative." That characterization, however, does little to help us understand the motivation behind the act. The suicidal and destructive behaviors labeled manipulative are a significant form of communication, an attempt to provoke a response from another or to manage intolerable pain. If the term is used pejoratively to dismiss the serious nature of the person's action, it may ultimately encourage an escalation in the acting-out behavior as the client feels further abandoned. As therapists, we may have a range of responses to this self-destructive behavior, including feelings of anger, helplessness, frustration, and anxiety. We must learn how to recognize these important countertransference reactions and to use them as diagnostic tools in the treatment of our clients.

Defenses

Although we all use a range of defenses to manage our anxieties and powerful affects, those with borderline personality disorder rely more consistently on the more primitive defenses of splitting, projection, projective identification, denial, primitive idealization, and devaluation (see chapter 4 for definitions). Several theoreticians (Goldstein 1990, Kernberg 1975), in fact, consider borderline personality disorder as a condition centered around splitting—as both a defense and as a fixation at an earlier level of development. In addition to splitting, we want to draw attention to two other defenses central to borderline pathology: projection and projective identification. In an attempt to "rid" themselves of toxic feelings, of an internal sense of their own badness, people with borderline pathology project negative thoughts and feelings onto others. With little capacity for ambivalence or nuanced experiences of feeling states, they unconsciously choose to vilify the other ("you're stupid, disgusting, hateful") rather than experience themselves as worthless. In the moment, the projections may "work"; they feel entitled to their sense of superiority, while the other is held responsible for all that is bad or wrong. The victory is short-lived, however, as the relationship may be destroyed and the negative feelings about the self return. Furthermore, as these projections continue in relationships, another complicated dynamic emerges. The target of these projections may resonate unconsciously with what is being projected. They "identify" with the projection, as the feelings and thoughts of which they have been accused are "owned" by them. Frequently this leads to the recipient of the projection acting on the very things that were attributed to them and which they initially denied. John, for example, had promised he would never leave Samantha in spite of her repeated accusations that he did not love her and would dump her for another woman. Eventually, as John began to feel depleted and angry—feelings unconsciously passed back and forth by both Samantha and him—John decided to end the relationship.

In the course of therapy, projective identification serves to promote powerful responses on the part of the therapist. When, for example, a therapist is repeatedly accused of being incompetent and not caring, a chord within the therapist—who may struggle with questions about her own competence and adequacy—invariably responds. Worn down and hating herself and the patient, she may act out in ways that confirm the patient's worst, yet predicted, fears. In the following statement, a therapist spoke candidly about the challenge to her own narcissism when working with a chronically suicidal, borderline patient.

The patient made me feel that if I knew more, the treatment would be going better and she'd be saved. I'd started to think maybe she was right—I should switch her to another therapist, someone more experienced and wiser than me. I'd feel awful about myself, and then start to get mad at the patient for making me feel that way. Part of me wanted her to finally kill herself so I could get out of this treatment. I began hating her for making me feel this way, and of course hating myself for being such an uncaring, incompetent therapist.

Regulation of Affect

Another impairment in ego functioning that is a hallmark of the borderline disorder is the poor regulation of affect. Difficulties with affect regulation have led some researchers (Smith et al. 2004) to consider borderline personality disorder as part of the bipolar spectrum due to their similar etiological features. Although we all experience depression, anger, and dissatisfaction in our lives, the *persistence, lability, and intensity of these affects* is what differentiates the borderline person's affects from everyday affects. Anger and innate aggression, in fact, are considered by many to be the dominant affect that individuals with borderline personality disorder experience (Gunderson and Singer 1975, Kernberg 1970, 1975). Two aspects of their manifestation are noteworthy. First, anger is often *not modulated or experienced with any degree of gradation*; a "little anger" suddenly becomes rage, or, as a client explained: "I go from number one on the scale of anger to number one hundred in two seconds flat." Second, the anger is often not differentiated from other affects. Situations that may engender hurt, sadness, or disappointment in many people are experienced solely as anger. A range of patients, for example, were told that their therapist would be leaving the clinic. Most discussed feeling angry, scared, sad, and disappointed during the weeks leading to the termination. One woman with borderline pathology stated consistently, "I'm just pissed. What else is there to feel? It's black or it's white." There was no shading to her feelings, as they were experienced not just intensely in a given moment but *exclusively*. Borderline individuals tend to show little capacity to experience ambivalence, that is, to be able to hold mutually conflicting feelings simultaneously. The all-or-nothing phenomenon we described in people's interpersonal relationships is therefore also evident in relation to affects.

Helping people with this disorder differentiate among various affects, and integrate them, can be an important part of the therapeutic work. Feelings may not be recognized or modulated, as evidenced in the following exchange between Maria and her therapist.

Maria was discussing her rejection from a previously sought-after college program, and noted that she was not feeling disappointed. In response to the therapist's look of surprise, Maria questioned: "You mean I may be feeling a little disappointed? You mean you can sometimes feel moderately disappointed? I don't get it. That sounds like being a little pregnant to me. I'm either overwhelming disappointed, or not at all." She then explained why she "chose" not to feel anything in response to the rejection. "If I feel disappointed, if I feel anything in fact, how will I know I won't enter that black hole of depression? I can't risk it. . . . It's like the Loch Ness monster—there's always danger lurking in the waters." In not being able to differentiate or modulate her affect, Maria often felt a numbness, a pervasive deadness in her emotional life.

Reality Testing and Sense of Reality

Although people with borderline personality disorder have a capacity for reality testing that is relatively intact, they can be *vulnerable to transient psychotic episodes and to distortions of reality.* In the following example, Cecilia, who suffered from no prior or subsequent episodes of psychosis, briefly "lost touch" with reality.

> Cecilia left for vacation with great fears about being on her own and tremendous guilt—reinforced by her parents—for leaving her children for several days. Despite her thirty-three years of age, she packed an entire suitcase full of stuffed animals to "keep me company" and help soothe her when alone. On the third day of her trip, she walked down the street and "saw" her parents at the corner. She ran over to these two strangers, calling them Mom and Dad. Over the next twenty-four hours, she had auditory hallucinations as her parents "continued to talk" to her, criticizing her for neglecting her children. Cecilia had never before been psychotic and recompensated fully upon her return home.

Brief and transient psychotic episodes such as Cecilia's can emerge in people with borderline pathology, but unlike in psychotic disorders, they are ego-dystonic and unsystematized. Except during psychotic regressions, individuals with borderline personality disorder retain the capacity for reality testing; they can distinguish between fantasy and reality, and between self and other. Their sense of reality can, however, become distorted. They may have experiences of depersonalization, dissociation, or derealization, develop distorted views of themselves, or misperceive others' intentions as malevolent. The following comments reflect some of these phenomena: "It's odd—like I can be in this room and suddenly the room changes," or "I touched my arm and couldn't feel anything; it seemed like it wasn't attached to my body." More persistent distortions of reality can be manifested in their suspiciousness of others, onto whom they may project their sense of "badness" or evil. When there is evidence of these kinds of distortions, it is particularly important to assess whether past trauma has led to a dissociative process.

Level of Anxiety

Individuals with borderline pathology often have difficulty binding their anxiety, which can be experienced as chronic and diffuse or episodically intense and overwhelming. Given their lack of object constancy, they can experience tremendous anxiety in response to real or perceived abandonment. This anxiety can be characterized as *fear of the loss of the object.* Unlike people with schizophrenia, they do not usually fear either being annihilated or having the power to annihilate others. Unlike people with neuroses, they do not fear "loss of love of the object" or "loss of regard for the self." Rather, they fear the emptiness, rage, and aloneness precipitated by the loss of a significant other. In treatment, disruptions, such as when therapists leave for vacation or are ill, can often bring on experiences of intense anxiety. This experience was captured by a young man who became distraught and anxious during the weeks prior to his therapist's planned departure. He was unable to concentrate at work or to sleep through the night. He told his therapist, "When you're away, I become unglued because you don't exist for me. You might as well be on the other side of the planet—I can't even picture your face." Phone contacts, appointment cards, or letters can often decrease the anxiety that arises in the face of these frightening separations.

Sense of Self

Having explored the quality of object relations and the ego functions of people with borderline personality disorder, let us use a self psychological lens to examine their sense of self. Central to the borderline pathology is the *lack of an integrated, cohesive identity and sense of self*. Whether due to temperamental vulnerabilities and/or environmental deprivation and neglect, borderline individuals often struggle with the development of healthy self-esteem, ambitions, and goals. Their early lives are frequently devoid of people who provided the relatively consistent soothing, nurturance, and validation necessary to create cohesive selves. This deficit may make them vulnerable to transient infatuations with, for example, cult-like or religious figures who hold the promise of love and guidance.

Since people with borderline personality disorder tend to experience themselves and others in "all good/all bad" terms, the subtle complexities of feeling and thought are often absent. The self is frequently experienced in unintegrated, diffuse pieces, not consolidated into an enduring, cohesive whole. A client described this state as follows: "I feel fragmented, like there are two parts of me that have nothing in common but that they're a part of me. . . . I used to feel like a tiny speck, surrounded by gelatin." Mason and Kreger (1998) quote Waldinger to describe this identity disturbance:

> Identity diffusion refers to borderline patients' profound and often terrifying sense that they do not know who they are. Normally, we experience ourselves consistently through time in different settings and with different people. This continuity of self is not experienced by the person with BPD. . . . A sense of inner emptiness and chaos renders the borderline patient dependent on others for cues about how to behave, what to think, and how to be. (p. 34)

People may manifest their identity disturbances in a variety of ways, including being chronically confused about their future goals and sexual orientation, making frequent geographical moves, and having shifting, unconsolidated views of themselves and others. Without a coherent sense of self, they may not achieve their full potential despite their considerable talents, as seen in the life of Gary.

> Gary, an extremely bright, engaging man, spoke of functioning well below his professional aspirations as he worked part-time for fifteen years as a home health aide, making ten dollars an hour. He spoke alternately of his wish to do more with his life and of his sense of entitlement about what the world owed him. He was involved in two consecutive long-term relationships with men, which were sexual only during the first few weeks of courtship. He noted that the men with whom he lived over the years provided him with the security of not being alone—but no more. At age forty-one, he stated, "I don't really know what I am—straight or gay. I don't have a clue about my sexual preference—I'm scared of closeness with both men and women. I don't even know what I want to be when I grow up, because I don't have a clue as to who the 'I' in me is."

PSYCHODYNAMIC THEORISTS AND THEIR UNDERSTANDING OF BORDERLINE PERSONALITY DISORDER

Having explored the symptoms of borderline pathology, let us now turn our attention to a developmental understanding of this disorder. Several psychodynamic theorists offer an explanation of the etiology of these traits. Depending on their theoretical orientation, each of these theorists traces the heart of the disturbance to different developmental factors. Each explores how tasks are mastered at various developmental stages, and then hypothesizes how the unresolved issues from these stages are manifested later in life. The work of these theorists helps us understand how poorly negotiated tasks from early developmental stages create a foundation from which problematic patterns may develop; the dynamics that emerge in adult relationships, they speculate, reflect the unresolved issues from inter-actions with primary caregivers. It is tempting but very problematic to look at these models in a linear fashion and to decide, for example, that difficulties in the separation-individuation phase automatically lead to an inability to trust. The impact of friends, extended family, teachers, religious mentors, social forces, physical illnesses, and the like *all* influence psychological development. The following conceptual frameworks offered by several prominent theorists focus most on the pre-oedipal relationships of people with borderline personality disorder.

Kernberg (1967, 1970, 1975), operating from a "drive-defense" model, traces the fundamental pathology in the borderline disorder to problems in early object relations. He believes that due to a constitutionally based predisposition toward aggression as well as rage from conflictual early relationships, some children cannot integrate positive and negative self and object representations. Although their ability to differentiate between themselves and others is intact, their capacity for experiencing ambivalence and a cohesive sense of themselves is impaired. Their good, loving images of self and other are protected from their excessive aggression through the development of a primitive defensive structure. Splitting, denial, devaluation, projection, and projective identification are the defenses used to keep the positive images of self and/or other from being destroyed by rage or "badness." They also serve to ward off the anxiety that would otherwise result from borderline individuals' contradictory experiences of themselves and others.

Due to constitutional vulnerabilities and possible neglect or abuse in their childhoods, people with this disorder have harsh, often sadistic superego introjects. Hostile, "bad" objects are both internalized and then projected, and coexist with overidealized images that lead to unattainable goals. What emerges are punitive thoughts and behaviors alternately directed toward themselves as failures, or toward others whom they experience as persecutors. Kernberg's description of these pathological internalized object relations, as well as his description of their defensive structure, offers us a way to understand the development of many of the symptoms we associate with borderline pathology. As he stated in Lata McGinn's interview with him in 1998:

> When, as children, we relate to important people in our lives, we internalize the memory of intense emotional states we experience during our interactions with them, and these intense emotional states get organized in two parallel series of loving and hateful emotions. These emotions are embedded in the relationship between representations of the self and representations of significant others. . . . [A] prototype of . . . a pathological internalization is what happens as a consequence of severe aggressive trauma or sexual trauma, physical abuse or sexual abuse, extreme long-term physical or sexual abuse. What we find in these cases is that, say in the case of physical abuse, individuals unconsciously identify themselves both as victim, i.e., *internalize the self that has been attacked,* and as abuser, i.e., *internalize the memory of the abusing figure.* Internalizing both these memories as a dyadic self representation–object representation unit brings about the unconscious temptations to reenact these roles again and again as if the only relationships that count in the world are those between the abuser and the victim. (p. 193)

Masterson (1976, 1981), who draws on Mahler's (1975) separation-individuation theory, focuses on abandonment depression and the defenses against it as central to borderline pathology. Recall in our discussion of object relations theory (chapter 6) the developmental struggle called ambitendency: the tendency to swing between two intense wishes (the wish to be close and the wish to be separate) and two enduring, intense fears (the fear of engulfment and the fear of abandonment). Masterson hypothesized that the lives of people with borderline personality disorder are organized around these twin wishes and fears. He suggested that during the rapprochement subphase, mothers with borderline personality disorder withdraw their emotional support as their children attempt to separate and individuate; when the children remain dependent and clinging, they are rewarded. Either way the children pay an enormous psychological price. Those who move toward autonomy are faced with abandonment and depression; those who remain dependent and regressed never develop a separate, boundaried sense of self. In adult relationships, these individuals subsequently seek intimate ties with nurturing substitutes. When those relationships are established, however, the unresolved issues pertaining to autonomy and individuation reemerge. A pattern of unstable relationships then develops, in which intense unions are followed by precipitous ruptures.

Unlike Kernberg and Masterson, Buie and Adler (Adler and Buie 1979, Buie and Adler 1982) focused on deficits, not conflicts, as central to borderline pathology. They integrated Piaget's (1954) theory of cognitive development, Mahler's (1975) theory of separation-individuation, and Winnicott's (1965) concept of the holding environment to develop their theory about this disorder. They hypothesized that due to a lack of "good enough" mothering during the separation-individuation phase of development, a core deficit results—*an impaired capacity for solid evocative memory.* Without the capacity to evoke the positive mental representation of a soothing, holding caregiver, a profound sense of aloneness and emptiness prevails. In times of stress—often precipitated by abandonment—panic and then rage emerge because individuals with borderline personality disorder cannot evoke a positive representation of another, nor rely on their own impoverished resources to soothe themselves. They also state that aggression is not primary in the development of borderline pathology; it is secondary to the despair and panic resulting from the lack of nurturing, soothing introjects. With an impoverished inner world, relationships are alternately experienced as life sustaining or nonexistent. Buie, in more recent years, has described this impoverishment in terms of "self-maintenance deficits"; emotional equilibrium, he notes, is built on the capacity to feel held and soothed, to experience self-worth and self-love, and to experience oneself as having a core. From this vantage point, we can see how people with borderline personality disorder live with a painful void of essential self-maintenance tools.

Dialectical Behavioral Therapy

There are many approaches currently being used in the treatment of people with borderline personality disorder, which we can broadly classify as: (1) supportive psychotherapy; (2) psychoanalytically and relationally oriented psychotherapy; and (3) cognitive behavioral and dialectical behavior therapy. Although discussions of treatment approaches are generally outside the scope of this book (consult, for example, Markovitz 2004 for pharmacological interventions), we want to briefly mention the contributions made by the introduction of dialectical behavior therapy (DBT) to the field. Linehan (1993) devised DBT to help patients who engage in parasuicidal (deliberate self-injury, with or without the intent to die) and self-mutilative behaviors learn to give up these destructive tendencies in favor of more adaptive ways of interacting with others. The most fundamental dialectic addressed by this treatment approach is that of acceptance and change (Robins and Chapman 2004). A "move" toward either pole of this dialectic is counteracted by the force of its opposite. The goals of treatment in DBT range from increasing behavioral control over severely self-destructive behaviors, to experiencing emotions in more appropriate ways, to achieving happiness and improved relationships and self-esteem, and finally to increasing a sense of joy and connectedness. These goals are accomplished through a structured program that includes group skills training, individual psychotherapy, telephone consultation between sessions, and consultation for the therapist as needed (Robins and Chapman 2004). Linehan and her colleagues draw on cognitive behavioral techniques along with mindfulness practices and psychotherapy to attend to the needs of this population. Although there is now a tendency in certain circles to proclaim this treatment protocol as the exclusively effective one, we trust that clinicians can hold multiple treatment approaches in mind as they consider the particular needs of their patients, their own theoretical orientation and comfort with particular models of practice, and of course the "fit" between the two.

The dynamic issues in borderline pathology are complex and rich, and often need time for adequate exploration. The treatment relationships that unfold with this population can be frustrating and draining, but also moving and gratifying. We want to end this section with a comment by Cassie, about whom we wrote earlier, that captures the sense of peace she found in doing the work of therapy. In reflecting on the turmoil and distress of her life, she noted: "I now know what it must feel like to be more 'normal': to have hurts that don't destroy me or the people I care about, to see that I don't have to sacrifice my*self* to my parents, to get to know myself and find I can love and be loved over time. . . . So, how'd we do it???? I guess that's been our work in the therapy!"

NARCISSISTIC PERSONALITY DISORDER

Over the last several decades, authors such as Lasch (1979) have described the emergence of a "culture of narcissism" characterized by self-absorption and the glorification of the self. Devoted to self-improvement at any cost, many people have become obsessed with attempts to perfect themselves. They concentrate on amassing personal wealth and power, and turn to cosmetic surgeons and the latest diet and exercise fads to help prolong life and defy the aging process. The media reinforces this narcissistic preoccupation with shows like *Survivor* and *The Bachelor*, glorifying the ethos of greed and winning at others' expense. Some of this preoccupation with self-improvement may have tangible and meaningful benefits. When it reflects cultural norms, however, individual greed may be valued above collective responsibility, and empathy may be lacking for those who are different or less fortunate. Lasch has described this period as a disordered social time, remarkable for its degree of social fragmentation and its absence of rootedness and connection. Perhaps the diagnosis of narcissistic personality disorder, so prevalent since the 1980s, reflects this cultural phenomenon—one in which people protect themselves against the pain of disconnection and isolation through self-absorption.

In this section, we will explore the concept of narcissism from a clinical vantage point, focusing on the characteristics of the narcissistic personality disorder. Before we study its exclusively pathological manifestations, however, we must appreciate how this concept encompasses normative functions as well. All levels of psychological development include aspects of narcissism. Healthy narcissism, an ability to love oneself and/or to regard oneself positively, is critical in the development of self-esteem. Narcissistic issues are displayed in varied ways across the life cycle and across cultures, and should be evaluated in context before being deemed pathological. Imagine, for example, the pride we may feel in a two-and-a-half-year-old girl who spontaneously stands before a crowd of people and begins to sing, dance, and clap her hands in glee. Many of us might smile at this exhibitionistic display, delighted in this girl's pleasure with her own accomplishments. We would not perceive her as being pathologically narcissistic. Might we wonder, however, about the arrogance and self-centeredness of a thirty-year-old woman who performed at any opportunity in front of others, desperately seeking attention and admiration? Displays of narcissism, such as exhibitionism and grandiosity, assume markedly different meanings depending on when they occur in the life cycle, and in which cultural context they are embedded.

The term *narcissism* was drawn from the Greek myth of Narcissus, summarized by Cooper (1986) as follows:

Narcissus was a physically perfect young man, the object of desire among the nymphs, for whom he showed no interest. One nymph, Echo, loved him deeply and one day approached him and was rudely rejected. In her shame and grief, she perished, fading away, leaving behind only her responsive voice. The Gods, in deciding to grant the nymphs' wish for revenge, contrived that Narcissus would also experience the feelings of an unreciprocated love. One day, looking into a clear mountain pool, Narcissus espied his own image and immediately fell in love, thinking that he was looking at a beautiful water spirit. Unable to tear himself away from this mirror image, and unable to evoke a response from the reflection, which disappeared every time he attempted to embrace it, he gradually pined away and died. (p. 112)

Which features present in this myth do we currently associate with the concept of narcissistic personality disorder? Cooper (1986) delineates some of the traits evidenced by Narcissus: arrogance, self-centeredness, grandiosity, lack of sympathy or empathy for others, poorly differentiated self and object boundaries, and lack of enduring object ties. Let us hold this evocative myth in mind as we now turn our attention to the clinical picture of the narcissistic personality disorder.

CLINICAL PICTURE

Toward the beginning of the movie *Sunset Boulevard*, William Holden comments to Gloria Swanson, the aged, well-past-her-prime silent screen actress, that she was once famous. Denying the reality of her fall from stardom and masking the humiliation she feels about her current life circumstances, Swanson responds with indignation, "I am still big. It is the pictures that have become small." Her desperate attempt to remain special and unique, her unrealistic self-concept, and her devaluation of all that has occurred in the film industry following her departure are captured in this poignant and painful moment on screen. Swanson's character embodies many of the characteristics that *DSM-IV-TR* identifies for the diagnosis of narcissistic personality disorder:

A pervasive pattern of grandiosity, need for admiration, and lack of empathy, as indicated by five of the following: (1) has a grandiose sense of self-importance; (2) is preoccupied with fantasies of unlimited success, power, brilliance, beauty, or ideal love; (3) believes that he or she is "special" and unique; (4) requires excessive admiration; (5) has a sense of entitlement; (6) is interpersonally exploitative; (7) lacks empathy; (8) is often envious of others or believes that others are envious of him or her; (9) shows arrogant, haughty behaviors and attitudes. (p. 717)

In this chapter, we will explore these characteristics in greater detail as we look at the disturbances in the sense of self, in object relations and in ego functions of individuals with narcissistic personality disorder. Keep in mind, as with all the psychopathological syndromes we have studied thus far, it is the *pervasiveness and inflexibility* of these traits that lead to psychological dysfunction.

Self-Concept

As evidenced by Swanson's character, people with narcissistic personality disorder have *difficulty maintaining a realistic concept of their own self-worth*. On the one hand, they can have an inflated and grandiose sense of self-importance. Fantasies of magnificent achievements or unrealistic goals may preoccupy them. Self-righteousness, contempt, and superiority may be conveyed in words or behaviors, reflecting beliefs that they are "better than" or "know more than" or "are more important than" others. Geraldine, a college professor, repeatedly spoke about her colleagues at the university at which she taught in the following terms: "I can't stand their stupidity, their constant drive. I won't waste my time in their committee meetings when I have so many better things to do." On the other hand, the self-concept of people with narcissistic personality disorder may also include a profound sense of worthlessness and propensity toward shame. These feelings of inadequacy, "unlovableness," and self-loathing coexist with arrogance and self-importance. In fact, grandiosity can often serve as a compensatory counterpart to a sense of worthlessness and mask a core sense of vulnerability. Geraldine, who seemingly felt superior to her colleagues, asked in a moment of despair: "What would it mean to no longer feel worthless? It would mean not secretly resenting people for being better than me. I'd have to stop pretending to be competent, because there's nothing worse than being reminded of one's worthlessness." Hear the pain, envy, and shame that so clearly underlies her grandiose stance in the world.

In the following illustration, we see how these themes may emerge in the course of a therapy.

Gerry frequently entered his therapist's office with a demeaning comment about someone in his life, or with a question to the therapist about whether she had read a certain article or novel. The therapist often felt stupid in his presence, wondering if Gerry would not be better served by a more intelligent, better-read clinician. On this particular day, Gerry began his session in silence, more aloof and distant than usual. After a period of time, he asked in a demanding tone, "Who was that professional-looking man you smiled at when he left your office?" The therapist momentarily felt guilty—as if she had done something wrong—then recognized that much of her self-doubt in her work with Gerry was evoked through projective identification. She felt as incompetent and inadequate with him as he felt perpetually in the world. After some exploration of his thoughts, he stated, "I assumed that I was your favorite client—in fact, in my head I pictured myself as your only client." He became devaluing momentarily, defending against his hurt, "My last therapist would never have smiled at another client leaving her office," then added with a sense of sadness and resignation, "If I'm not your special client, I feel like a nobody."

Although Gerry usually presented as arrogantly self-assured, he had a fragile sense of self, a self that deflated—like a balloon full of air that is pricked—in the face of a perceived slight, hurt, or disappointment. His vulnerability was usually concealed by a condescending, critical attitude toward others. Morrison (1986) has described this seeming paradox as follows:

> This need for absolute uniqueness, to be the sole object of importance to someone else, symbolizes the essence of narcissistic yearning. . . . What *are the affective implications of this yearning for uniqueness?* We have noted that it may lead to an outpouring of untamed aggression, or of reactive rage against the offending object. Internally, however, I suggest that such an experience leads to a sense of utter despair, profound depression, and reflects the paradoxical extremes of grandiose entitlement, on the one hand and vulnerability to mortification, on the other. (p. 4)

Those struggling with narcissistic issues have a disproportionate need to attain narcissistic supplies and supports to their self-esteem. This preoccupation promotes a self-centeredness and arrogance that obscures a subjective experience of emptiness, inferiority, and shame. The experience of shame is quite different than that of guilt, which reflects the belief that one has committed a wrongdoing. Shame is the experience of being exposed as not good enough, or weak, worthless, "small." With shame, a person may feel that he or she is losing the competition and everyone can *see* it. With guilt, the critical voice is within the self (super-ego); with shame, the "audience" is outside of the self (McWilliams 1994), ready at any moment to expose and humiliate the individual. As McWilliams notes:

> In every vain and grandiose narcissist hides a self-conscious, shame-faced child, and in every depressed and self-critical narcissistic lurks a grandiose vision of what the person should or could be (Meissner 1979, Miller 1975, Morrison 1983). What narcissistic people of all appearances have in common is an inner sense of, and/or terror of, insufficiency, shame, weakness, and inferiority. Their compensatory behaviors might diverge greatly yet still reveal similar preoccupations. (p. 171)

Implied in the traits we have thus far reviewed is the tendency of people with narcissistic personality disorder to be *self-centered* and *self-referential*.

In spite of the seemingly arrogant pride in their many talents, however, they feel like frauds. Beneath the boasts are profound self-doubts and self-reproaches.

> Jake, a twenty-seven-year-old, African American man, struggled with many of these character traits in his life and relationships with others. The youngest of four in his family of origin, he was raised by a distant, cold father and a critical, depressed mother who gave him daily enemas until he was twelve. Jake felt ignored by his parents, who he remembers attended his siblings' performances and school functions, but never his own. "I could've jumped on the table and they wouldn't have noticed. . . . I wanted my mother to love me, to stop saying I was the black sheep and to say instead I was her miracle child. . . . I preferred being hit by her with a paddle [which she did routinely] than ignored."
>
> When Jake was twenty-seven, he sought therapy because of feelings of emptiness, depression, and a pervasive sense of dissatisfaction with his life. He had begun a career as a stand-up comic, and alternated between thinking he was the next Richard Pryor and believing he had no talent. He was obsessed by what others thought of him, and he married an attractive woman because, "she was beautiful, self-assured—and I thought she'd make me more comfortable with myself." Performing before crowds was the only way he could defend against the dreaded boredom he feared in his life. He noted that he needed the audience to feel alive, and likened the pleasure of anticipation before a performance to a tiger standing tall before the crowds at a circus. When the audience departed, he would "crash," feeling empty and deflated.

Despite the bravado practiced on stage, Jake had a fragile sense of self so typical of people suffering from this disorder. Although intensely ambitious, he felt chronically bored, ashamed, and unable to channel his intellect and talent into any ongoing vocational, academic, or personal pursuits.

Object Relations

People with narcissistic personality disorder have relationships with others that are frequently superficial and shallow and lacking in emotional depth. Showing little capacity for empathy, they can be insensitive to others' needs and exploitative in their behavior. Remorse, which may reflect a "defect," is rarely shown, and gratitude, which may reflect a need, is rarely displayed (McWilliams 1994). Although their psychological boundaries are less permeable than people with borderline personality disorder, they tend to take advantage of others, whom they also envy. At times, they seek out associations with individuals whom they perceive as perfect, basking in the glory of their intelligence, success, or fame. At other times, they search for admirers who can gratify their need for affirmation and idealization. This breeds a superficiality and lack of mutuality in their relationships, as well as a sense of entitlement that the mundane details of life should be the purview of others rather than of themselves.

A colorful illustration of this can be seen in the novel The Prime of Miss Jean Brodie (Spark 1961). The title itself captures a narcissistic woman's desperate need to feel perfect, as well as her denial and fear of the reality of her vulnerabilities. Miss Jean Brodie, an aging teacher, insists she is in the prime of her life despite her failing relationships with others (exemplified ultimately in the betrayal by one of her students). She arrogantly holds on to the belief that she holds the "truth" about life and love, and tolerates no imperfections in herself and others. The students in her class become extensions of her own need for affirmation and admiration; if she can make them "perfect," then she can feel competent and "whole." Miss Brodie refers to them as the "Brodie set," and tells them, "I am putting old heads on your young shoulders. . . . [A]ll of my pupils are the crème de la crème. . . . Give me a girl at an impressionable age, and she is mine for life" (pp. 11–12).

The students in Miss Brodie's class are valued only as they function as narcissistic extensions of their teacher. They matter not because of who they are, but because of what function they fulfill in supporting Miss Brodie's self-esteem. When caregivers convey this type of confusing message—you are highly valued, but only for the role that you play (McWilliams 1994), narcissistic vulnerabilities inevitably emerge. The child learns to suppress feelings and behaviors deemed undesirable by the caretaker and to present a "false self" (Winnicott 1960) that is perpetually reinforced by the praise and criticism of those on whom the child depends.

Intimate relationships are deeply affected by excessive narcissism. People with this disorder may fall in love easily but superficially, and frequently come to devalue what they receive from their partners. As McWilliams (1994) notes, "their need for others is deep, but their love for them is shallow" (p. 175). Relationships become organized around the person's needs for attention, with little acknowledgment that their loved ones may have needs and interests markedly different from their own. Tom, a gay, white man involved with his partner for fifteen years, wryly commented on the success of his relationship as follows:

"The relationship works because Bobby knows that everything has to be about me. I'm incredibly selfish; I just take, and Bobby waits on me. But it's okay. Bobby is a passive guy anyway." When asked about his desire to explore this issue in treatment, Tom replied: "The truth is, I don't want to change anything, change who I am. There is a part of me that if I walked by someone on the street who was dying, I'd walk by."

Despite their seeming imperviousness to others' opinions of them, people with narcissistic personality disorder can be exquisitively sensitive to perceived slights. An unempathic statement, a felt criticism, or an unmet demand can trigger a *narcissistic injury*, that is, the experience of feeling deeply wounded, humiliated, and hurt. When "injured" in this fashion, people with this disorder may respond with intense rage. Following a session in which a therapist made an unempathic transference interpretation, for example, a client angrily noted to his therapist: "I was furious at you after last week. I'm not the least bit interested in what you think of me. I have my own agenda here, an important one that has nothing to do with yours. I know far more than what you learn in your psychiatry and social work texts about what human nature is about." The client felt exposed and misunderstood by his therapist; he subsequently became enraged, assuming a grandiose stand while devaluing her. As we will see in the next section, this posture characterizes the defensive style of the narcissistically disordered individual.

Ego Functions

In contrast to people with borderline personality disorder, the ego functions of those with narcissistic personality disorder tend to be relatively intact. Their judgment, reality testing, and cognitive processes can be distorted by emotional issues to some extent, but they tend to function with greater consistency and proficiency than individuals with borderline pathology. They are often extremely articulate and opinionated, traits that may boost their self-esteem while masking a sometimes superficial knowledge base. This accounts in part for the large number of narcissistic people in positions of power; their intelligence, their sense of certainty and confidence in their own abilities, and their comfort giving orders to others are traits frequently rewarded by promotions to powerful roles. Anxiety is generally masked, lest it expose a weakness or vulnerability in their character. It is nonetheless central in their psychological make-up, and it emerges in their terror of losing approval, acceptance, and love from others. Unlike people with borderline personality disorder who live with the anxiety: "I'm worried you will abandon me once you come too close," those with narcissistic personality disorder live with the anxiety: "You will be disgusted when you see the 'real' me. I will live in shame when exposed." Who among us does not grapple with some of these fears, these hopefully transient pangs of anxiety rooted in self-doubt? Yet for those with narcissistic personality disorder, this type of anxiety is key to their experience of themselves and others, and to the compensatory strategies that are triggered to handle it.

Anxiety, as we will learn in chapter 16, is managed through the mobilization of our defenses. The defenses of people with narcissistic personality disorder serve to protect their fragile self-esteem. A defense such as idealization helps create "perfect" others with whom they can merge; devaluation and projection help rid them of their own imperfections, which they then "see" in others to whom they can feel superior; denial and rationalization assist them in avoiding their own weaknesses and vulnerabilities. The use of some of these defenses, and the function they serve, can be seen in the following case:

> Larry, a twenty-seven-year-old, affluent Hispanic man who talked incessantly about his looks in his psychotherapy, reported that he felt obsessed about his appearance. He applied facial cream eight times a day, was drawn to mirrors on all surfaces to "check up" on his looks, and constantly sought to be sexier or more outrageous than other men. At the beginning of each visit to his therapist's office, he would offer a critical comment about what he saw: "The picture on the wall is crooked." "The tag on the rug is showing." "Your skirt doesn't match your top." When a therapeutic alliance had been established in the work, Larry and the therapist explored why he felt a need to be so devaluing. He noted: "I do say something critical every time I come in here. Maybe I'm trying to make this—and you—imperfect because I feel so insecure. If I saw you as okay, or even perfect, I'd have to deal with how shitty I really feel about myself." Larry was ultimately able to understand that his preoccupation with his appearance reflected his attempt to "fix" his more deep-rooted sense of inadequacy. As he developed a more cohesive sense of self and greater compassion, he became more comfortable with the reality of his physique and more tolerant of imperfections in others. He no longer projected his worst fears about himself onto others, and slowly developed an awareness of the impact of his comments on them.

THE ETIOLOGY AND TREATMENT OF
NARCISSISTIC PERSONALITY DISORDER

Much of our understanding of the causes of narcissistic personality disorder is rooted in the work of psychodynamically and psychoanalytically oriented theorists. Significant contributions to this understanding have been made in recent years by the research in the areas of neurobiology, attachment theory, and temperament. We all know children who, from an early age, are viewed as "overly sensitive" or "thin skinned." They may be constitutionally more sensitive than others to people's emotional cues, and exquisitely attuned to slights, criticisms, and expectations held by others. As demonstrated in the clinical observations done by researchers such as Daniel Stern (1985), these children "bring" this vulnerability to their interactions with caregivers, who face a more challenging task parenting in supportive, nonshaming ways. "Avoidant/dismissive" styles of attachment (see chapter 8) may result from the problematic fit between the attachment styles of these children and their caregivers. Traits we then associate with narcissistic personality disorder, including minimizing the value of connections with others, disliking dependence because it exposes vulnerability, and superiority and aloofness, may be traced to these early attachment issues.

Research on affect regulation (Hotchkiss 2005, Schore 1994) adds another dimension to our understanding of the etiology of this disorder by demonstrating how "brain circuitry" impacts the processing of emotion. Problematic early interactions (i.e., neglect, abuse, abandonment) can impact the neurochemistry of the brain, particularly the part of the brain that manages a person's capacity to self-soothe, regulate affect, and neutralize shame states. Whether hardwired at birth or triggered by invalidating environments or both, these neurologically based vulnerabilities can lead to difficulties in the regulation of affect and emotion and ultimately, to narcissistic disturbances.

Psychodynamically oriented theorists have offered varied accounts of the etiology of the narcissistic personality disorder. In his essay "On Narcissism: An Introduction," Freud (1914) attributed narcissistic problems to a withdrawal of libido from the outer world into the ego, that is, a retreat from attachments to others to a state of self-absorption. He noted that this regressive retreat could be caused by stresses secondary to trauma, disease, or the onset of old age, and/or by frustrations in relationships with others. He believed that an infant optimally evolves from a normative stage of autoeroticisim or self-love to a love for others. If, however, there is an obstacle to the fulfillment of the love for and from others, narcissistic disturbances arise. Britton (2004) described this development as follows: "Those unfortunate enough to find love unrequited are thus deprived of self-esteem as well as the other's love, thus suffering pain and loss of self-regard" (p. 480). Although recognizing that all people have residual aspects of narcissism, Freud believed that the amounts of libido directed toward the self accounted for differences in people's capacities for loving others. Individuals, then, who lavished excessive attention and love on themselves would suffer from the greatest disturbances in narcissism.

In the last several decades, the principal controversy surrounding the theoretical understanding of the narcissistic personality disorder has revolved around the models proposed by Heinz Kohut (Kohut 1977a, 1977b, Kohut and Wolf 1978) and Otto Kernberg (1974, 1975, 1995). Some people have suggested that these theorists developed their models based on two different client populations, with Kohut basing his theory on a healthier and higher-functioning population than Kernberg. We believe, nonetheless, that each model offers an instructive accounting of the many possible causes and manifestations of this disorder, and of treatment interventions that derive from them.

Kohut (as noted in chapter 7) understood pathology in terms of deficits in self structure. He attributed narcissistic pathology to the failure of the environment to provide age-appropriate empathic responses to the child's needs. Without relationships in which they are adequately mirrored and in which they have someone to idealize and feel similar to, children lack the validation, admiration, and modeling necessary for the development of a healthy self-esteem. They become vulnerable to feelings of worthlessness and inadequacy, and turn to others for self-definition. The development of the self is thereby "arrested." A three-year-old child who sings "Happy Birthday" off-key with incorrect words may need to see the gleam in his mother's eyes to support his healthy exhibitionistic display and positive self-regard. Consistent critical or neglectful responses to these types of displays may contribute to the development of the fragile self that is so central in a narcissistic personality disorder. Kohut (1977a) also noted that the environment must provide children with an "optimal level of frustration" so that they can learn to cope with disappointments, anger, and frustration. After all, the three-year-old child who sings off-key will have to recognize, when older, that he may not be the next Pavarotti. If children chronically experience too much frustration or are overly gratified, they cannot take in selfobject functions or experience the world as a safe place; they become hungry for love and affirmation, and prone to idealizations of others to replenish their depleted selves. If they chronically experience too little frustration, they remain entrenched in grandiose omnipotence and self-absorption. Either state can lead to the development of the traits we have discussed in the narcissistic personality disorder.

Kohut's views on treatment derived directly from his understanding of the etiology of narcissistic disorders. Kohut believed that narcissistic issues emerge in the transference, which reactivates clients' needs for mirroring, idealization, and twinship. Through the transference, the wishes for affirmation, connection to idealized others, and twinship can be addressed. As described by Brodie and Gravitz (1995):

> Three distinct components of the narcissistic transference promote completion of the self's arrested development. The initial mirror transference provides continuous empathic mirroring of the grandiose self, followed by the idealizing transference in which the therapist assumes the role of the omnipotent, soothing selfobject. Ultimately, through the twinship transference, the patient is able to relate to the therapist as a separate human presence. (p. 60)

By assuming an empathic stance, the therapist helps clients reconstruct and identify selfobject needs, understand their experience of disappointment in themselves and others, and ultimately seek out appropriate selfobjects. In addition, according to Schore (1994), this kind of empathic attunement helps the brain regulate feelings of rage or worthlessness. In

Kohut's model, rage and entitlement on the part of the client are not interpreted as shortcomings of the client, but rather as understandable reactions to the inevitable empathic failures of the therapist. Kohut believed that when these empathic failures are acknowledged and repaired, the deficits leading to narcissistic vulnerabilities can be addressed.

Kernberg (1974, 1975, 1995) offers a strikingly different view of the etiology of narcissistic disorders. Unlike Kohut who saw narcissistic disorders as reflective of arrested development of the self, Kernberg describes the self in the narcissistic personality as a "grandiose pathological self," formed from the fusion of the ideal self and ideal objects. What is bad or weak in the self is projected onto others, who are then devalued and dismissed. The person's internal world is left devoid of representations of significant others who might otherwise support self-esteem. Rather than feel the pain of their sense of worthlessness and of the unmet need for support and love, people with narcissistic personality disorder valiantly protect themselves from experiencing their neediness. They become self-centered, shallow, and aggressive individuals, seeking excessive admiration from others, whom they also envy. Although Kernberg believes narcissistic individuals function at a higher level than those with borderline personality disorder, he sees narcissistic personality as a subtype of borderline personality organization.

To what does Kernberg attribute this disturbance? He notes (1995) that "the most important cause is the chronic frustration of the need to be loved and a consequent, inordinate development of rage. That rage takes the form of envy—namely, envy of the person who is needed, who has what the patient needs but will not give him—love" (p. 11). Kernberg's "narcissists" are thus full of aggression, which may be both constitutionally and/or environmentally induced. Neglected and enraged, they interact arrogantly and aggressively with others, and protect themselves by believing they have all they need without depending on anyone else.

Kernberg's treatment interventions evolve from his theory about the development of this disorder. He suggests that people with narcissistic personality disorder must renounce their yearning for perfection and accept the terror inherent in true intimacy. Unlike Kohut, who allows the transference to unfold so that the therapist is ultimately internalized as an idealized selfobject, Kernberg challenges this idealizing transference. He interprets clients' idealization of the therapist as a defense and challenges them to acknowledge their envy, rage, and, ultimately, their dependency needs. He advocates a tactful but insistent confrontation of people's grandiosity, so that clients will ultimately be able to love and be gratified based on a realistic appraisal of their behavior.

In practice, most clinicians draw from techniques offered by a range of theorists as they grapple with treating narcissistic clients. Regardless of one's theoretical orientation, however, the treatment of these clients can be enormously challenging. Therapists may alternately be devalued or idealized, and feel as if they are riding a roller coaster. During one part of the ride they may experience themselves countertransferentially as the best clinicians to treat this client population; at a moment's notice, perhaps following an unknowingly unempathic comment, they may come to feel as if they are frauds—the most incompetent, worthless clinicians in the whole clinic. Their value depends in part on how exquisitely attuned they are to the clients' emotional needs in the moment. Therapists may also feel as if they do not exist in the room, their presence "tolerated" until they offer an observation that is different than the client's. This may trigger feelings of shame or annoyance in the client, or an outburst of rage. The lack of curiosity and interest in the therapists' separate views can contribute to a range of countertransference reactions, including boredom, self-doubt, irritability, and a fear that the treatment is not progressing. Ultimately patience is needed in the ongoing work with these clients, and faith that the relationship itself will be curative as narcissistic wounds are healed, and the hope for being loved in an authentic relationship is realized.

REFERENCES

Adler, G., and Buie, D. H. (1979). Aloneness and borderline psychopathology: The possible relevance of child development issues. *International Journal of Psycho-Analysis* 60:83–96.

Akhtar, S. (1992). *Broken Structures: Severe Personality Disorders and Their Treatment.* Northvale, NJ: Jason Aronson.

American Heritage Dictionary of the English Language, 4th ed. (2000). Boston: Houghton Mifflin Company.

American Psychiatric Association. (2000). *Diagnostic and Statistical Manual of Mental Disorders*, 4th edition, Text Revision. Washington, DC: American Psychiatric Association.

Britton, R. (2004). Narcissistic disorders in clinical practice. *Journal of Analytical Psychology* 49:477–90.

Brodie, P., and Gravitz, M. A. (1995). Nurtured narcissism: The developmental origins of narcissistic personality disorder and implications for treatment. *Psychotherapy in Private Practice* 14(1):53–64.

Brown, L. (1992). A feminist critique of personality disorders. In *Personality and Psychopathology: Feminist Reaappraisals*, ed. L. Brown and M. Ballou, pp. 206–28. New York: Guilford.

Buie, D. H., and Adler, G. (1982). Definitive treatment of the borderline personality. *International Journal of Psychoanalytic Psychotherapy* 10:40–79.

Chess, S., and Thomas, A. (1978). Temperamental individuality from childhood to adolescence. *Annual Progress in Child Psychiatry and Child Development*, pp. 223–44.

Clarkin, J. F., Foelsch, P. A., Levy, K. N., Hull, J. W., Delaney, J. C., and Kernberg,

O. F. (2001). The development of a psychodynamic treatment for patients with borderline personality disorder: A preliminary study of behavioral change. *Journal of Personality Disorders.* 15(6):487–95.

Cooper, A. M. (1986). Narcissism. In *Essential Papers on Narcissism*, ed. A. P. Morrison, pp. 112–43. New York: New York University Press.

Deutsch, H. (1942). Some forms of emotional disturbance and their relationship to schizophrenia. *Psychoanalytic Quarterly* 11:301–21.

Fenichel, O. (1945). *The Psychoanalytic Theory of Neurosis.* New York: Norton.

Freud, S. (1914). On narcissism: An introduction. *Standard Edition* 14:67–101.

Frosch, J. (1964). The psychotic character: clinical psychiatric considerations. *Psychiatric Quarterly* 38:81–96.

Goldstein, E. G. (1990). *Borderline Disorders: Clinical Models and Techniques.* New York: Guilford Press.

Graybar, S. R., and Boutilier, L. R. (2002). Nontraumatic pathways to borderline personality disorder. *Psychotherapy: Theory/Research/Practice/Training* 39(2):152–62.

Gunderson, J. G., and Singer, M. T. (1975). Defining borderline patients: An overview. *American Journal of Psychiatry* 132:1–10.

Hoch, P. H., and Polatin, P. (1949). Pseudoneurotic forms of schizophrenia. *Psychiatric Quarterly* 23:248–76.

Hotchkiss, S. (2005). Key concepts in the theory and treatment of narcissistic phenomena. *Clinical Social Work Journal* 33(2):127–44.

Kaplan, M. (1983). A woman's view of *DSM-III*. *American Psychologist* 37(7):786–92.

Kernberg, O. (1967). Borderline personality organization. *Journal of the American Psychoanalytic Association* 15:641–85.

———. (1970). A psychoanalytic classification of character pathology. *Journal of the American Psychoanalytic Association* 18:800–22.

———. (1974). Contrasting viewpoints regarding the nature and psychoanalytic treatment of narcissistic personalities: A preliminary communication. *Journal of the American Psychoanalytic Association* 22:255–67.

———. (1975). *Borderline Conditions and Pathological Narcissism.* New York: Jason Aronson.

———. (1995). Narcissistic personality disorders. *Journal of European Psychoanalysis* 1:7–30.

Kohut, H. (1977a). *The Analysis of the Self.* New York: International Universities Press.

———. (1977b). *The Restoration of the Self.* New York: International Universities Press.

Kohut, H., and Wolf, E. (1978). The disorders of the self and their treatment: An outline. *International Journal of Psycho-Analysis* 59:413–25.

Lasch, C. (1979). *The Culture of Narcissism.* New York: Norton.

Layton, M. (1995). Emerging from the shadows. *Family Networker* 19(3):35–41.

Linehan, M. M. (1993). *Cognitive-Behavioral Treatment of Borderline Personality Disorder.* New York: Guilford.

Livesley, W. J., Jang, K. L., Jackson, D. N., and Vernon, P. A. (1993). Genetic and environmental contributions to dimensions of personality disorder. *American Journal of Psychiatry* 150(12):1826–31.

Mahler, M. (1975). *The Psychological Birth of the Human Infant.* New York: Basic Books.

Markovitz, P. J. (2004). Recent trends in the pharmacotherapy of personality disorders. *Journal of Personality Disorders* 18(1):90–101.

Mason, P. T., and Kreger, R. (1998). *Stop Walking on Eggshells: Taking Your Life Back When Someone You Care About Has Borderline Personality Disorder.* Oakland, CA: New Harbinger Publications, Inc.

Masterson, J. F. (1976). *Psychotherapy of the Borderline Adult: A Developmental Approach.* New York: Brunner/Mazel.

———. (1981). *The Narcissistic and Borderline Disorders: An Integrated Developmental Approach.* New York: Brunner/Mazel.

McGinn, L. K. (1998). Interview: Otto F. Kernberg: Developer of object relations psychoanalytic therapy for borderline personality disorder. *American Journal of Psychotherapy* 52(2):191–201.

McWilliams, N. (1994). *Psychoanalytic Diagnosis: Understanding Personality Structure in the Clinical Process.* New York: The Guilford Press.

Mendez-Villarrubia, J. M., and LaBruzza, A. (1994). Issues in the assessment of Puerto Rican and other Hispanic clients, including *ataques de nervios.* In *Women of Color: Integrating Ethnic and Gender Identities in Psychotherapy,* ed. L. Comas-Diaz and B. Greene, pp. 141–76. New York: Guilford.

Morrison, A. P. (1986). *Essential Papers on Narcissism.* New York: New York University Press.

Piaget, J. (1954). *The Construction of Reality in the Child.* New York: Basic Books.

Reich, W. (1945). The characterological resolution of the infantile sexual conflict. In *Character Analysis,* 3rd ed., ed. M. Higgins and C. M. Raphael, trans. V. R. Carfagno. New York: Farrar, Straus, & Giroux.

Richman, N., and Sokolove, R. L. (1992). The experience of aloneness: Object representation and evocative memory in borderline and neurotic adults. *Psychoanalytic Psychology* 9(1):77–91.

Robins, C. J., and Chapman, A. L. (2004). Dialectical behavior therapy: Current status, recent developments, and future directions. *Journal of Personality Disorders* 18(1):73–89.

Sansone, R. A. (2004). Chronic suicidality and borderline personality. *Journal of Personality Disorders* 18(3):215–25.

Schore, A. N. (1994). *Affect Regulation and the Origin of the Self: The Neurobiology of Emotional Development.* Hillsdale, NJ: Lawrence Erlbaum Associates.

Self, Borderline personality: Are you a victim? *Self,* August 1990.

Skodol, A. E., Gunderson, J. G., McGlashan, T. H., Dyck, I. R., Stout, R. L., Bender, D. S., Grilo, C. M., Shea, M. T., Zanarini, M. C., Morey, L. C., Sanislow, C. A., and Oldham, J. M. (2002). Functional impairment in patients with schizotypal, borderline, avoidant, or obsessive-compulsive disorder. *American Journal of Psychiatry* 159:276–83.

Smith, D. J., Muir, W. J., and Blackwood, D. (2004). Is borderline personality disorder part of the bipolar spectrum? *Harvard Review of Psychiatry* 12(3):133–39.

Spark, M. (1961). *The Prime of Miss Jean Brodie.* New York: Dell.

Stern, A. (1938). Psychoanalytic investigation of and therapy in the borderline group of neuroses. *Psychoanalytic Quarterly* 7:467–89.

Stern, D. N. (1985). *The Interpersonal World of the Infant: A View from Psychoanalysis and Developmental Psychology.* New York: Basic Books.

Stone, M. H. (2000). Clinical guidelines for psychotherapy for patients with borderline personality disorder. *The Psychiatric Clinics of North America* 23(1):193–212.

Thaper, A., and McGuffin, P. (1993). Is personality disorder inherited? An overview of the evidence. *Journal of Psychopathology and Behavioral Assessment* 15(4):325–45.

Waldinger, R. J. (1986). *Fundamentals of Psychiatry.* Washington, DC: American Psychiatry Press.

Walker, L. E. A. (1984). *The Battered Women's Syndrome.* New York: Springer.

Winnicott, D. W. (1960). *Ego Distortion in Terms of True and False Self.* London: Hogarth.

———. (1965). *The Maturational Processes and the Facilitating Environment.* New York: International Universities Press.

Zanarini, M. C., Frankenburg, F. R., Hennen, J., and Silk, K. R. (2003). The longitudinal course of borderline psychopathology: 6-year prospective follow-up of the phenomenology of borderline personality disorder. *American Journal of Psychiatry* 160:274–83.

15

Biopsychosocial Aspects of Depression

Joan Berzoff and Michael Hayes

Depression is probably the first diagnostic category that we have encountered about which it is safe to say that every one of us knows what it is. Depression refers not just to a syndrome, with all of its technical definitions, but also an affective state that we have each experienced: a state of sadness, depletion, deflation, emptiness, hopelessness, boredom. And yet, because we often start from the position that everyone knows what depression is, we can too easily minimize its potentially debilitating impact and its complexity.

Affective disorders are disorders of mood. When we speak of moods, we are speaking of a range of everyday feelings from sadness to joy, anger to acceptance, despair to elation. Moods refer to prolonged emotions that color our psychic lives. Affects, on the other hand, refer to the feeling tones or emotional states at a given moment, and to their outward manifestations. A person's mood, for example, may be sad while her affect is blunted. We may fail an examination and experience a mood of utter hopelessness, as if we are stupid and uneducable, but we may show no affect; or we may get an A on that exam and experience ourselves as exceptional, brilliant, and promising, and our affect may be manic. As with several of the other disorders we have studied, affective disorders are complicated precisely because they clearly derive from an interaction between psychological, social, and biological sources. Two major troublesome affects that people experience are anxiety and depression. This chapter focuses on the depressive affective disorders.

In all of its forms, depression is considered the most widespread emotional disorder in the world, afflicting 2 to 3 percent of the world's population, or 100 million people. Of American children and adults, 10 to 15 percent (20 million) are estimated to have moderate to severe depression, with perhaps half of the reported 31,000 suicides a year in this country attributable to those with major depressive disorders (Hoyert et al. 1999).

Mood disorders occur in people of all ages, and from all social classes. No one is immune to them. Some affective disorders are reactive in origin; that is, they are precipitated by an external event such as the actual loss of a person, of work, of ideals, or of an object of significance. Likewise, an individual may react to a normally positive event—childbirth, a promotion, a new job, moving to a new city, a graduation—with depression, because any of these joyous occasions may also present a loss to that person.

Loss, however, is not the precipitating factor in all cases of depression. Affective disorders may be endogenous in origin; that is, there may be no obvious external event precipitating the shift in mood. There are many biological causes for these disorders that are genetic, hormonal, and/or biochemical in origin. Intrapsychic factors and life-cycle issues can play a role in affective disorders. One life-cycle issue that can precipitate depression for some women is having in the home two or more young children below the age of six (Brown 1991, Brown et al. 1989). Another life-cycle predictor is found in older, single, widowed men, living alone, who have a physical illness. Such men are most at risk for depression and for suicide. Among the elderly, depression occurs equally in both men and women.

Gender plays a significant role in affective disorders. Women are two to three times more likely to be diagnosed as suffering from depression than men. Social class also plays a significant part in affective disorders. Poor and working class women are most at risk for depression. In fact, people in the lowest socioeconomic classes have two times the risk of being diagnosed with a major depression than those in the middle- and upper-middle classes. The risks for depression among the poor may actually be even greater than reported, since poor and working-class people are often overly diagnosed as schizophrenic without adequate clinical justification (Weissman and Klerman 1977).

In this chapter, we first discuss the experience of depression. Next, we draw upon psychodynamic theories to help us understand some of the internal psychological dynamics of these disorders from the perspective of the four psychologies. We then consider depression at different developmental levels. From biology, we consider the influence of genetic, biochemical, and endocrinological factors. Social factors that contribute to depression are explored, including gender differences. We then consider suicide: its risk factors and its demographics. Finally, we describe ways in which the mood disorders affect not only the client, but also the therapist. The order of these factors in no way represents a hierarchy of any one cause over another.

THE EXPERIENCE OF DEPRESSION

How do we draw the line between ordinary human suffering with all of its sadness, ennui, and pessimism, and clinical depression? The term "depression" is used in many ways. In its wider usage, it often refers to a "lowering," for example, of an economy or of barometric pressure. In a person, it often refers to lowered self-esteem and decreased functioning in a variety of manifestations. To help us understand the symptoms of depression, it may be instructive to turn to people who have themselves been clinically depressed. In their own voices, they provide us access to what are perhaps universal experiences of depression.

William Styron (1990), for example, who has written many novels and an autobiography, found himself at a loss for words to describe his own severe depression at age sixty. He writes:

> Depression is a disorder of mood, so mysteriously painful and elusive in the way it becomes known to the self . . . as to verge close to being beyond description. . . .
>
> For myself, the pain is most closely connected to drowning or suffocation, but even these images are off the mark. . . . [It is] as if my brain has to endure its familiar siege: panic and dislocation, and a sense that my thought processes [are] being engulfed by a toxic and impassable tide that obliterate[s] any enjoyable response to the larger world. . . . Instead of pleasure, [it is] a sensation close to indescribably different pain. (p. 6)
>
> The pain of severe depression is quite unimaginable to those who have not suffered it and it kills in many instances because its anguish can no longer be borne. (p. 7)

In this passage, Styron describes many depressive symptoms. He feels inward, flat, and monochromatic. He feels panicked, and anguished, and suffers from a sleep disorder that slows him down and leaves him fatigued. He feels helpless, in pain, inarticulate, suffocating, and lacking in any capacity for pleasure. He considers suicide and is aware that not only his feeling but also his thinking are disordered by his mood. His despair envelops his world in what he later describes as a "visible darkness."

Poet and novelist Sylvia Plath (1971) similarly describes the depression she experienced at age eighteen. Having left home for the first time, she began a glamorous job on a women's magazine. While she imagined herself to be the envy of adolescent girls everywhere, it felt to her as if:

I wasn't steering anything, not even myself. . . . I should have been excited . . . but I couldn't get myself to react. I felt very still and very empty the way the eye of a tornado must feel moving dully along in the middle of the surrounding hullabaloo. (p. 3)

Like Styron, she felt flattened, numb, dulled, and emptied as she moved within an externally stimulating world.

As with many depressed people, Plath is irritable and angry at feeling so removed from her feelings and experience. Like Styron, she is enveloped by a darkness that is colorless and flat. Like Styron, she despairs because she cannot "contain" her darkness. It is as if the darkness, once outside of her, fully inhabits her inner world.

Shakespeare's Hamlet also experiences the losses of pleasure and meaning that characterize depression. Hamlet cries out:

I have of late . . . lost all my mirth, foregone all custom of exercises, and indeed it goes so heavily with my disposition that this goodly frame, the earth seems to me a sterile promontory. This most excellent canopy the air, look you, this brave overhanging firmament . . . why, it appears no other thing to me than a foul and pestilent congregation of vapors. . . . Man delights not me—no, nor woman neither. (Shakespeare 1917, p. 50)

In Hamlet we once again encounter the futility, pessimism, and loss of humor that are signs of a depressed mood. Hamlet is angry—both at himself and at his world, which now seem foul and pestilent. His external world seems depopulated and sterile. People are not only absent but are no longer experienced as valuable. Indeed, what is interesting here is that not only are events and people outside of Hamlet devalued, but also that Hamlet includes himself among those most devalued. It is not surprising when he says to Polonius: "You cannot, sir, take from me anything that I will more willingly part withal—except my life, except my life." Hamlet experiences his life as a burden to be willingly surrendered (p. 47).

What all three authors have described, in different voices and to varying degrees, are the very markers of depression. Each reader, no doubt, has felt these feelings at some time or other, and each has struggled to override them and regain some zest for life.

SYMPTOMS OF DEPRESSION

What, then, are the symptoms of depression? Each of these authors notes in themselves what we refer to as vegetative symptoms: changes in sleep, appetite, weight, interest in love, and/or interest in the world. Each has vividly described fatigue or physical pain. Styron and Plath experience a slowing down, or what we call "psychomotor retardation." Often in depression or in mania, we see the opposite: a state of speeding up or of agitation. Hamlet spoke of his poverty of ideas, and accompanying this, of his own lowered sense of worth. Each author described a prolonged sad mood. Each had difficulty with concentration and indecisiveness. At different moments, two of the authors considered suicide because their numbness, pain, darkness, and withdrawal were so unbearable.

In fact, there can be so many symptoms and combinations of symptoms associated with depression that they become bewildering to the clinician, threatening to make the concept too inclusive. To achieve some useful clarity about depression, we usually focus on three altered mood states described by the aforementioned authors. In Styron, we find a loss of interest ("apathy"); in Plath, a loss of energy ("asthenia"); in Shakespeare's Hamlet, a loss of pleasure ("anhedonia"). None of these states alone, however, constitutes clinical depression. To make the diagnosis of depression, at least two of these states must always be present (Kaplan and Sadock 1985).

What is happening psychologically when people experience such symptoms? Our knowledge of drive, ego, object relations, and self psychological theories may help us to understand the internal worlds of those who are depressed.

Freud's Ideas about Depression

Let us begin with Freud, who provided a framework for conceptualizing the dynamics of depression in his very important paper, "Mourning and Melancholia" (1916). Freud proposed that we understand depression by first looking at grief. He described grief as a normal reaction to the loss of a loved one. When someone we love dies, we feel sad, empty, bereft. We turn away from the world to do the work of mourning, and every culture has its customs to honor the process and to make the reality of death or loss official. In mourning, we remember the person who has died and we retain their images and memories (as we described in chapter 6). When a relationship with a loved person is disrupted forever, memories of that person are "cathected" as if they were the person himself or herself. Freud wrote that we "hypercathect" our memories: we remember a favorite song, how that person laughed, the ways it felt to be with him or her, the places that were shared, and we hold on to those memories tenaciously. Ira Gershwin wrote a song about his brother, who died of a brain tumor, which beautifully describes hypercathecting his memories.

Ira Gershwin wrote a song about his brother, who died of a brain tumor, that beautifully describes hypercathecting his memories. He talked about remembering the way his brother dressed, the way he drank his tea. In remembering each aspect of his brother, he wrote, the tie to him grew even stronger.

Here Gershwin was describing not only how, with loss, we are filled with the memories of the person whom we have lost, but also how we hold on to those memories as a way of keeping that person alive in us. With the passage of time, Freud thought, the energies that are bound up in thoughts and memories of the lost person become free in order to help us form new attachments.

But Freud noted that no one abandons a libidinal position willingly, even when a substitute beckons. That is why we do not fall in love immediately after a significant loss. But with the passage of time and with the acceptance of reality (whatever that may be), and through the process of bringing old memories to consciousness and of experiencing anew the pain of the loss, we gradually begin to reinvest in the world. We are now, to quote Loewald (1980), "sadder but wiser," and with that, more open to new relationships.

But Freud also suggested that we never fully give up the person we have lost—that, instead, we hold on to the lost person by identifying with aspects of her/him, and unconsciously taking in aspects of the lost person as parts of ourselves (Freud 1923). For example, some attitude, behavior, or characteristics of that person (or that which we experienced in our relationship with the person) become part of who we now are. In this way, we are actually transformed by our losses. Mourning changes who we are. A mother who loses her daughter, a writer, to cancer, becomes a writer herself. A senator's wife, who loses her husband in a plane crash, runs for the senate. A social worker who loses her sister writes a book and runs a program about death and dying so others might suffer less. All of these are ways of holding on to the lost object through identifying with him or her.

"Melancholia" (Freud's term) or complicated grief shares many of the same characteristics as mourning. One feels dejection, loss of interest, and inhibition of activity; but one also feels something else in addition: a disturbance in self-regard. Often this is expressed in angry, reproachful, self-blaming, even self-hating statements. Melancholia may include feeling worthless and self-critical, and may occur not only in the instance of an actual death of a loved one, but also when one feels slighted, disappointed, or as if one has not lived up to one's own ideals. Why does the person who is melancholic become self-hating? Freud thought that the clinically depressed person's self-reproaches almost always turn out to "fit someone else the patient loves" and has "lost." He hypothesized that the person's self-criticism is really a "complaint" about the object, but that this is unacceptable to the conscious self. Often melancholia derives from a conflicted and ambivalent relationship with a lost object. When anger at another cannot be acknowledged consciously, it is often turned against the self. Freud suggests two things: (1) that the depressed person is unaware of the more negative or hateful feelings toward the lost object; and (2) that the lost object is too essential to the maintenance of the self to be given up through grieving. In depression, the ambivalently held relationship with the deceased leads the griever to experience self-depletion and self-hatred. Whereas in mourning, it is the external world that has become impoverished and empty; in depression it is the internal world that becomes poor and empty. Freud (1916) wrote quite beautifully that in melancholia, as well as in grief, "the shadow of the object falls upon the ego" (p. 249), suggesting that the quality of the relationship (positive and negative) affects the outcome of grief. Freud wrote:

> One feels justified in maintaining that a loss has occurred, but one cannot see clearly what it is that has been lost. The patient cannot consciously perceive what he has lost either. What gives rise to his melancholia is the sense that he knows whom he has lost, but not what has been lost in him. (1916, p. 245)

Take, for example, Jane:

> Jane, a seventy-five-year-old Italian Catholic woman, began treatment because she was profoundly depressed, having lost her husband of forty years, eight years before. She talked with him daily, said prayers with him in the morning and at night, and visited his grave twice a day. This, in itself, would not be pathological except for the way in which she described her apartment as a "tomb." She could not sleep, shop for herself, make any decisions, pay her bills, or take care of herself or her cat. She had lost twenty pounds and had driven her children away with a litany of complaints about them and about herself.
>
> Jane had married at twenty-seven, after having taken care of her aging parents and her six siblings' children. She had forgone college to do so, and yet denied that she ever felt any anger about sacrificing herself to her siblings or her emotionally abusive parents. In fact, through clenched teeth, she let me know that she was *never* angry. Jane saw herself as something of a saint, and viewed her husband as nothing less than the same.
>
> Jane's husband had been a childhood friend, and she had, on some level, always known that he was homosexual. After their conceiving two children, he moved into another room in the house, and took a lover at work. Jane felt that her children blamed her for the couple's disaffection, and although she could not remember, her children described to me her murderous rages where she would hit them with brushes and shoes.
>
> What made her grief even more unbearable was that on her husband's deathbed, he told her that he had never loved her and wished that it was she who was dying in his bed, not he.

Why had Jane become so depressed and even suicidal? Freud might surmise that Jane was unaware of her unconscious anger toward her husband (or parents and siblings), and that the anger she was now recognizing toward him threatened her ability to hold on to his memory. Her ambivalent feelings about him, especially her anger and hurt, had also now been set up inside herself, directed against herself. The other more difficult problem for Jane was that she needed to maintain in fantasy what was never true in reality. For Jane, and for so many others, it can be simply debilitating to internalize an unresolved and highly conflictual relationship. Melancholia can be difficult to treat because the person who experiences it is so invested in denying ambivalence, and that threatens to obliterate any memories at all, which then further impoverishes the person's inner world.

Ego Psychology

Ego psychology offers a different but complementary theory for understanding depression. We learned in chapter 4 how anxiety may serve as a signal to take action to protect oneself from danger. So, too, can depression serve as a signal—to do the work of mourning that we have seen is a necessary part of growth. In this sense, depression is not necessarily pathological. This is why psychodynamic theorists so stoutly resist the idea that all depressive affects—sadness, bereftness, helplessness—are useless afflictions to be removed or avoided in whatever way possible. In fact, the capacity to bear depression—to live with grief, sadness, and hurt—is one of the greatest and most useful ego strengths (Zetzel 1965) and a hallmark of mental health. Interestingly, it is when we cannot bear depression that we often become clinically depressed.

Edward Bibring (1968), an ego psychologist, proposed an alternative explanation for depression that extended and modified Freud's original views. He noticed that in everyday life, the death or loss of a loved object, country, or ideal is not the most frequent trigger for depression. Rather, depression is precipitated more frequently by a state of felt helplessness brought on by not living up to one's own ego ideals. This state results from "a conflict within the ego" between the universal aspirations to be worthy, loved, and strong, and the ego's experience (judgment) that it cannot achieve those aspirations. Bibring, then, reconceptualized depression as a state, not deriving from aggressive drives directed toward a lost object and now directed against the self, but rather as a conflict between one's ideals and one's perceived inability to achieve them. The loss of self-esteem that is central to depression is not only the consequence of depression, but, in fact, is often the cause.

Daniel is a fifty-four-year-old, successful, well-published scholar and professor of Native American studies. Each time he begins a new writing project, however, he reports feeling overwhelmed at the prospect of condensing so much material into something coherent. He finds himself at a loss for words; he berates himself for how inarticulate he is. He feels deeply and with utter conviction that he doesn't know, and never did know, his content area. He reports feeling low, depleted, lacking energy. He feels helpless, and imagines reproaches from colleagues as he harangues himself for his perceived inadequacy. He finds himself eating too much and sleeping too little.

Daniel suffers from the kind of low self-esteem that most of us have experienced. Although his depressive symptoms are mild and transient, his sense of helplessness is central to his depressive experience.

An ego psychologist, then, would formulate Daniel's experience as helplessness that involves some negative judgment or negative assessment of his ability to effect needed change. With helplessness also comes self-reproach, and an expectation of similar reproaches from others. One can easily see how these elements can trigger a repetitive, self-reinforcing downward spiral of felt helplessness, inaction, loss of self-esteem, and self-reproach. If the ego cannot reestablish a reasonable sense of self-esteem, experiences of unhappiness and self-reproach increase and lead to a greater sense of helplessness. How do we escape such spirals in everyday life? Daniel reports that factors such as the pressure of deadlines (external interpersonal connections), the memory of his past competencies, and the use of some of the energy from self-reproach to "get angry" and "cut the task down to size" and thus to rebut internal criticism, help him to mobilize and to get on with his work.

An interesting footnote is provided by Saari (1989, personal communication), who notes that Bibring used himself as a core example of his theory. Bibring developed his theory of depression when faced with his own helplessness over the diagnosis of terminal cancer. He was able to make his (presumably painful) experience the subject of observation, and thereby gain mastery over his depression by contributing intellectually to the field. Bibring wrote that depression, in the form of lowered self-esteem, is relieved by anything that reverses conditions of helplessness.

At this point, we have presented two complementary theories of depression. From Freud, we have suggested that depression results from unconscious anger directed at the lost object, which is then directed against the self. This depletes and impoverishes a person's self, which can lead to a depressed state. From an ego psychological perspective comes the idea that depression involves a discrepancy between one's ideals and aspirations, and one's perception of one's capabilities and worthiness. The result is helplessness and self-reproach. Here, the problem is one of regulating self-esteem. While the first theory of depression suggests that one identifies with the hated object and that the hatred is directed toward the self, the second implies a superego problem, having to do with not living up to one's expectations or ideals.

Object Relations Theory

An object relations view of depression had already been anticipated by Freud's emphasis on the centrality of object loss to depression. In object relations terms, often a melancholic person cannot mourn successfully because she cannot sustain an emotionally useful, enduring object representation in the absence of a lost other. Perhaps the key contribution of object relations theory is its elaboration of the development of internal object representations and of the relationship of that development to depression. Object relations theorists address two important aspects of this relationship: one focuses on the developmental level of representations at the time that loss occurs, and the other considers the effect of losses at different stages of development.

Recall that object relations theorists depict relationships with others as the organizers of internal experience and functioning from the very first moments of life. Relationships form the structure of psychic functioning. We have seen that central to many object relations theories (Jacobson 1964, Kernberg 1966, Klein 1940, Mahler and McDevitt 1980) is the idea that representations of others (literally, the mental representation of the absent person) undergo a developmental progression from the infant's fleeting, poorly differentiated (between self and other) images, to the adult's enduring, well-differentiated, multifaceted representations. Obviously, the actual loss of a needed loved one, whether due to death, physical absence, abuse, or emotional unavailability, might produce very different depressive reactions, depending on the developmental stages of the representation of that loved one in the person experiencing the loss.

Early attachment theorists, such as Spitz and Wolf (1946) and Bowlby (1958), studied the reactions of infants and toddlers to prolonged separations from their mothers to whom they had become attached. Both noted that in the absence of another dependable caregiver with whom to become involved, these infants became distressed, disorganized, profoundly sad, and finally detached, apathetic, and retarded—almost a prototype of the symptoms we have seen in depressed adults. Some infants even died. Spitz and Wolf called such depression "anaclitic." An anaclitic depression occurs at the stage when the representations of the lost loved object can only be sustained by the almost constant actual visual and physical presence of that person. Loss of the actual person at this stage of object representational functioning produces intense feelings of emptiness, painful aloneness, helplessness, and equally intense cravings for immediate contact with and love for the lost person. Spitz and Wolf and later theorists (Blatt 1974) note that such depressive experiences are not unique to infants but are seen in persons of any age whose internal world of object representations has not gained a measure of object constancy. Such depression will be marked by intense feelings of helplessness, abandonment, and emptiness, with less guilt and lower self-esteem than in other forms of depression. Indeed, it often seems to the person suffering depression at this level that there is no "self" without the lost other.

> Marc was a twenty-eight-year-old married man of Polish-American descent with a history of substance abuse (alcohol and marijuana) and of psychiatric hospitalization for "nervous breakdowns," in which he experienced himself as unable to function at all. He referred himself for individual therapy, despite a stated "hate [for] all shrinks." Suddenly, about eleven months after his father's death, Marc begun having symptoms, including sudden uncontrollable weeping ("for no reason, I just feel so empty and alone"), and an intense fear of going to work alone. Marc reported that if his wife or mother accompanied him to his place of business "I can work just fine." Marc had been in business with his father, whom he described as "the most unhappy, bitter, critical guy anyone who met him ever knew—not just me." He described working with his father as "me doing all the work while my father stood around criticizing [me]." Marc was mystified that now, so many months after his father's death; he could not do the work he had always done "unless someone [a loved one] is there so I know it's all right." When he was alone, Marc felt "like I forget everything, I don't know anything—I'm not sure I can even remember my name."

An object relations approach to Marc's depression would focus on his difficulty maintaining an object representation of his father that could sustain him in his father's absence. He cannot even feel the presence of the angry, critical father he has known, but instead feels no presence at all. He feels empty, depleted of all energy and content, almost as though (in his words) "I don't really exist." Marc is experiencing depression with clear anaclitic features. An object relations theorist would note that he seeks relief from this depression by trying to establish a new relationship with a "hated" person, the therapist. This was exactly the description Marc gave of his relationship to his father before the latter's death. It is as though Marc is trying to reconstitute the same kind of relationship he had with his father, without which he feels he cannot survive.

As a child develops beyond infancy, his or her object representations become more enduring and better differentiated from representations of his or her self. We have seen that object relations theorists picture these newly independent and more stable object representations as first being organized (or "split") along the emotional lines of how the person feels toward the object. Thus, representations associated with pleasurable interactions with the object ("good object" representations) may be kept separate from representations of frustrating interactions ("bad object" representations). Later, under the best of circumstances, the child is able to integrate these representations into a more realistic image of the object in which the same person both pleases and frustrates. This consolidation, as we have seen, is called "object constancy" by object relations theorists, or is referred to as the achievement of the "depressive position" by Klein (1940) (see chapter 6). Object relations theorists consider this to be a major developmental advance in that it involves in itself some depression, as Klein's term suggests. Forever after this developmental step, the individual lives in a more complicated, sadder-but-wiser representational world in which the object, and also the self, can be experienced as good and bad, loving and hating, pleasurable and painful. The capacity to bear this developmental step has impact on the individual's lifetime "capacity to bear depression" (Zetzel 1965), and makes possible the uncomplicated but painful mourning Freud described as normal.

Object relations theorists suggest that when a person who has suffered an object loss lacks sufficient integration of good and bad self and object representations, he or she may feel depletion, object hunger, guilt, self-reproach, and lowered self-esteem (Blatt 1974, Jacobson 1964). Jacobson noted that when children experience a lack of parental understanding and empathy, this diminishes a child's self-esteem. This then leads to angry feelings toward the parent(s), accompanied by guilt, which further lowers self-esteem. In order to protect the parent whom the child needs, the child may turn his or her anger toward him or herself. Disappointment and fury at the person who was emotionally depriving are then experienced as disappointment or fury at the self.

Pedro was thirty-four years old when he came to therapy, depressed by his lack of professional success (he was working as a low-level salesman of computers), by his inability to make a commitment to his fiancée with whom he was living, or to show affection to her two children, whom he planned to adopt. He too had recently lost a parent, his father, and he was very confused by his lack of feelings, by his depressed mood, and by his anger with himself.

Pedro's father had been a successful computer technician. Pedro had two brothers, both of whom were married and occupationally successful, and each of whom had completed college. Pedro had dropped out of college after his first year, because, he said, he partied too much. He came home to live with his parents, and this produced much interpersonal conflict in that he felt he was the object of his parents' constant criticism and disappointment.

Growing up, Pedro felt that his parents preferred and rewarded both brothers. Each was very capable in school and had many friends; while Pedro's only notable success was in hockey. He appeared to have significant learning issues that had never been diagnosed, and he could not recall either of his parents having ever attended a hockey game in which he was successful. In fact, when he was able to make it into the semifinals, neither parent was willing to transport him to either practices or competitions, and so he had to forfeit the one domain in which he felt mastery.

But Pedro felt very guilty about being angry with his parents, and now that his father had died, felt especially guilty and incompetent. He would repeatedly say in therapy, "I wish I had done more; I wish I had done more for him." On one level, it appeared he was lamenting that he wished he had done more for his dying father; on another, he was saying that he wished his father had done more for him. After his father's death, he needed to hold on to an idealized view of him as a highly skilled and competent man, while seeing himself as without skill or value.

Object relations theorists have concerned themselves not only with a developmental understanding of depression at the time it becomes a problem, but also with the study of how losses affect representational development. They note that the kinds of losses that occur—when they occur, and how often they occur—play crucial roles in development. Infant and child studies are beginning to document specific relationships between object experiences and later representational development, and depressive symptoms.

Bowlby (1958, 1961, 1963) was among the first to suggest that different kinds of losses predispose people to different kinds of depression. Bowlby noted that when faced with prolonged separations, children go through three phases: protest, despair, and detachment. His studies of children separated from their mothers revealed that when a caregiver is emotionally or physically absent for significant periods of time, a child will first try to bring back the lost object. If the child cannot mobilize the caregiver's attention or bring her back, the child may become more disorganized. The child may protest, and ultimately may despair. Finally, if over time the child has been unable to reengage the caregiver or a substitute, she may detach entirely, leading to a kind of hopelessness and turning away from the object world.

Attachment theorists point out that early relationships with others that are insecure or unstable can lead to the development of internal working models of the self as unlovable and unworthy, where the experience of others is as attacking or rejecting. Such individuals tend to be vulnerable to depression and experience everyday disappointments as evidence of a lack of self-worth, or of a lack of care and support from others (for further elaboration, see chapter 8 on attachment theory).

Tronick and Granino (1988) have captured this phenomenon in detail on videotape with healthy mothers and their children under experimental conditions. Well-functioning mother-infant dyads were filmed in the process of mutually cueing one another. In one scene, a mother expressively engages her child through smiling and laughing. In the next scene, her face becomes blank. In response, the child first tries to reinitiate the "dialogue." The mother's face still remains blank. When that fails, the infant cries and fusses. When there is still no response from the mother, the child's protest becomes louder and the child's behavior becomes more disorganized. Finally, we see the infant look away, no longer interested in attempting to bring her mother back.

For children with severely depressed mothers, or children who have suffered profound early losses, the experience of withdrawal is not simply an isolated event. When this pattern recurs again and again, depression emerges as a reaction to the accretion of millions of these tiny events. For children who are separated from their mothers for prolonged periods of time, or children who have chronically unresponsive or abusive caregivers, a depressive hopelessness and disengagement is frequently the outcome.

Studies of older abused toddlers and preschoolers reveal that extremes of maltreatment interfere with the development of a representational internal world, which can affect states of self and other, pleasurable interactions between self and others, and a stable, positive sense of the other in fact or in her absence (Cicchetti 1989). Follow-up studies suggest, as object relations theory would predict, that such children are at greatly heightened risks of depressive symptoms by adolescence (Cicchetti 1989). Such extreme cases provide powerful evidence of the object relations view that later self-esteem is constructed by earlier relational experiences.

Self Psychology

Self psychologists conceptualize affective disorders as emerging from a pattern of empathic failures by significant caregivers. Recall that every individual needs to have someone strong to mirror, and with whom to merge for the achievement of her vigor, grandiosity, and healthy self-esteem. Parents, teachers, coaches, neighbors, extended kin, and siblings in a child's interpersonal world can provide these selfobject functions. They can affirm the child and respond to the child's needs with empathy, acceptance, and admiration. When this occurs, the child has the building blocks for mature self-esteem and for the pursuit of realistic ambitions and goals. But when mirroring fails, the child may treat herself poorly—establishing unrealistic ideals, treating herself recklessly, attending neither to danger nor to limits, and being unable to mobilize self-care. How early and how radically these selfobject experiences are missing affects how intact and cohesive the self will be and how vulnerable it will be to depressive reactions to loss.

Liza, the oldest of six children in an African American family that was both emotionally impoverished and financially drained, described herself as always exhausted as a child and as underachieving in school. She grew up in a family in which she felt that there was "no one home." She felt neither noticed, nor special, nor talented in any way. She spent much of her childhood on the couch, simply too tired to move. It seemed to her that no one noticed her existence nor had any sense of who she was. As a consequence, neither did she.

Now, as a forty-year-old adult, she lies on the couch much of every day, unable to mobilize, watching TV, and waiting for her husband to come home and make her dinner. She describes feeling like an irritable baby who simply cannot soothe herself. Nothing seems to engage her interest; she looks around her house and is overwhelmed by all the half-finished projects that require her energy. She lacks the sense that she can accomplish anything.

At one point in therapy, Liza brought in baby pictures, and noticed for the first time that all of the pictures were of her in her crib, on her back. She wondered, first, what kind of baby she must have been, for no one to want to pick her up. Later, she wondered what kind of family she must have had that would let her lie so much alone.

A self psychologist might posit that Liza grew up without sufficient self-objects to mirror her and help her develop healthy goals and ambitions. Her lack of mirroring and of affirmation from others, and the absence of present adults with whom to merge, contributed to her sense of herself as depleted, empty, and like a big baby.

Unlike the drive theorist, ego psychologist, or object relations theorist, who might see her depression as her anger now turned against herself, as not living up to her ideals, or as a result of a failure of integrated self and object representations, a self psychologist would understand her depression as an appropriate by-product of unmet selfobject needs. Her inability to soothe or develop a coherent sense of herself might stem from a developmental failure to attain the capacity for activity, given a lack of transmuting internalizations of available and empathic selfobjects.

The differences in the four theoretical perspectives are not simply academic. They lead to different kinds of clinical interventions and choices. A drive theorist, for example, might help a depressed client become conscious of her unconscious anger and of the ways in which that anger is turned inward in the form of self-hate or self-harm. An ego psychologist might attend to the client's superego ideals and to the client's sense of worthlessness, which results from excessive or unrealistic expectations. An object relations theorist might attend to early losses, lack of nurturance, abandonment, and to the lack of integration of good and bad self and object representations. A self psychologist might serve as a new selfobject to the client, offering strength, affirmation, mirroring, and appreciation for the client's needs. There is no one psychodynamic formulation for depression, nor is there one treatment. Instead, there are multiple dynamics and multiple approaches for treating depression from a dynamic perspective. As with all of these disorders, choices are made based upon the uniqueness of each individual client, the genetic history of that client, and the particular ways in which depression manifests itself.

DEPRESSION AT DIFFERENT
DEVELOPMENTAL LEVELS

Depression is the first diagnostic category we have considered that is defined in terms of an affect or mood rather than in terms of functioning. We have, up until now in this book, studied three different developmental levels: psychotic, borderline, and neurotic. In this chapter we see that depression can be experienced at any of these developmental levels. As clinicians, we encounter depression daily in our clients. A developmental approach offers a way to understand how depression is experienced and how the internal world of that client is "constructed." Only by entering into that world can we join with our client empathically and introduce some discordant and, one hopes, helpful experiences that will be tolerable to the client.

Below, we consider three prototypic cases of depression at the psychotic, borderline, and neurotic levels of functioning.

Depression at a Psychotic Level of Functioning

Recall that psychosis is characterized by the loss of reality testing and the concomitant loss of a sense of self and object relationships. These characteristics are also seen in psychotic depression, in which the depressive affects and symptoms we have been studying reach psychotic proportions. It is important to mention here that biochemical and genetic vulnerabilities predispose a person to psychotic depression.

Mrs. Stewart is a thirty-four-year-old married woman of second-generation Scottish-Irish descent. Prior to the onset of her depression, she was considered a cheerful, outgoing, "perfect" wife, mother, and part-time dental hygienist, who was also active in her church. Gradually she became more somber at work. At home, she spent more and more time alone in her room. Sexual relations with her husband stopped. She became extremely apologetic about minor paperwork errors, worrying aloud that she would be fired by her boss (whom she knew to be benevolent). She became obsessed with worries that, by lack of proper hygiene or through a neglectful procedure, she would hurt her patients. She began to accuse herself, giving voice (in mutters) that she should be fired, that her cleanings were the worst in the world. Now she was retreating to her room at home and berating herself for her failing "to feel better." Eventually, she could "no longer go through the motions." Life became meaningless. She did not leave her room and barely spoke—and only in a raspy low voice. Her husband brought her to the hospital because he was afraid that her having "nothing to live for" might indicate that she was suicidal.

In the hospital, she heard a mocking voice telling her that she was not real, and that she should "die" for an "affair" she had had six months previously with a fellow church member. The affair had never been sexually consummated and there had been little actual time spent with this person. In one early session, Mrs. Stewart confused her therapist (a male) with her mother, who commanded her to "go to your room until you get yourself under control" (a clue to her early object experience). At another time, she thought her therapist was her minister to whom she was confessing.

At the psychotic level of functioning, a person's greatest fear is that death or annihilation to the self has occurred. Mrs. Stewart felt, at a level of stark terror and disorganization, as if she were already dead or disintegrated. Nothing made sense to her—she no longer made sense to herself. With a collapse of selfobject differentiation, Mrs. Stewart was no longer able to tell whether the mocking, reproachful voice she heard came from inside (from memories or internal "dialogue") or from outside herself. At such a primitive level of ego functioning, her reality testing was compromised. Thinking was organized along the lines of primary processes; primitive feelings rather than logic or empirical fact predominated. Thus, Mrs. Stewart experienced a psychotic transference to therapist as mother or minister without being able to test the reality of who was actually in the room with her.

Some other aspects of Mrs. Stewart's experience were also typical of a psychotic depression. There were early hints that some of her self-reproaches about being "not real" or psychically dead were criticisms of an "emotionally dead" parent (or one that was experienced that way), who was being treated as part of her (criticized) self. Indeed, Mrs. Stewart had experienced both parents as extremely reserved and disapproving of any affective display, happy or sad, on her part. At times (not necessarily times of otherwise overt psychotic functioning), she would experience her dead mother as inside or as a part of her body. Such experience reflected her fantasizsed "eating" or incorporation of the loved (and hated) one, a primitive operation that is sometimes the best the ego can do to retain a needed object relationship.

Also typical of a psychotic level of depression is a grossly distorted superego. This client believed herself to be dangerous to others—accusing herself at times of killing her mother and at other times of hurting her family—and sentencing herself to a kind of living "death" or nonexistence in which she felt she could do no more harm. These harsh superego injunctions were at the psychotic level.

What was the usefulness for the clinician of understanding Mrs. Stewart in developmental terms? First, it helped the therapist tolerate Mrs. Stewart's overwhelming feelings of panic, emptiness, and rage, and made these feelings understandable in terms of her internal world. That, in turn, allowed the patient to sense dimly that "someone was with me who seemed to know where we were, but was not afraid." Later, as Mrs. Stewart's ego functioning improved, she still suffered intense depressive affects, but was able to use her therapist's recognition of her experiences to differentiate herself from her feelings. In her words, "Now I feel there is an *I*, who 'had' those experiences" (Hayes 1996, personal communication).

Depression at a Borderline Level of Functioning

We previously characterized borderline level functioning as resulting from a difficulty in integrating a sense of self and others, so that these images are "split" into all good or all bad representations. People who function at this level also tend to experience aggression as un-neutralized and as coming from the outside rather than inside. Depression at this level of functioning does not reach the psychotic state of Mrs. Stewart's, but has an "all or nothing" totalistic quality to it.

Ms. Ramirez, a twenty-three-year-old Puerto Rican mother of a six-year-old son, Raphael, was admitted to the hospital in a diabetic coma because of failure to comply with her medical regimen. As she recovered, she complained of many specific physical pains and symptoms, centered in her abdomen, chest, and head, whose location shifted so frequently that she could not be successfully diagnosed. Ms. R. gradually became friendly with a nurse who became alarmed at what she heard in conversation and asked for psychotherapeutic services.

Ms. R. told her therapist that she and Raphael had moved to the mainland from rural Puerto Rico about a year before for "no special reason." Ms. R. held a clerical job, but was socially isolated except for Raphael, who had become "very hostile" over the past year. He had, in fact, been dismissed from several day-care centers for violent behavior. Ms. R. clearly described a cycle at home in which she experienced Raphael's abundant (but perhaps normal) curiosity and activity as maliciously aimed at "getting on my nerves," and she retaliated by getting very angry and then raging at him. She would become frightened of her wish to hurt him physically, and angrily withdraw all contact, sometimes for many hours. It was during these times that Ms. R. would withhold medication from herself and self-destructively eat dangerous foods. Death, she thought, was the only escape. She had in fact "taken pills" on several occasions before her son's birth in attempts to die.

Initially, Ms. R. described a "happy childhood." Only after some months of outpatient work did she "remember" her father's desertion of the family when she was seven (remember that her son was six), and her mother's alcoholism and physical abuse of her. She had, in fact, left her hometown at age twenty-two to follow an unfaithful lover with whom she reunited for a time. Her hospitalization was immediately preceded by news that this man had left her for another woman who had just moved to their city. That woman turned out to be her father's stepdaughter, for whom "he left me when I was seven"!

Ms. Ramirez, while never manifesting overt loss of reality testing, experienced her depressed moods as timeless and cut off from any hope of improvement. Memories of feeling better held little meaning when she was depressed. She would mainly remember those times when she had been depressed, and then sadness, helplessness, and badness would seem to exist forever in an eternal "now."

Ms. Ramirez's anxiety fluctuated between poles of terror of aloneness, which she experienced when abandoned by her lover or cut off from her son. She struggled with a fear of being invaded, which she experienced when she felt her son was abusing her and when she abused him. She tended to experience her son (and her therapist) as "all good" or "all bad," and was more likely to experience herself in a "split" fashion. She was prone to savage attacks upon herself, including physical pounding and even suicide attempts, as primitive superego retribution for her badness. In punching herself, Ms. Ramirez could be both punishing the (poorly differentiated) abusing mother with whom she was identifying and reexperiencing herself as the abused child.

Work with Ms. Ramirez was also aided by a developmental approach to her depression. Her therapist was able to empathize accurately with her utter hopelessness and the extreme urgency of her need for relief when she and all around her felt "bad" and lonely. Only later, after they had experienced together several cycles of good and bad times, would her therapist begin to bridge these states, which Ms. Ramirez experienced as timeless and "forever" when she was in them, reminding her they had "been here before" and that she had survived. Such bridge building with a reliably available, nurturing other began to address her self and object relations issues underlying depression at this developmental level.

Depression at a Neurotic Level of Functioning

We now consider a developmental approach to understanding depression in people whose depression is at the neurotic level (as we will discuss more fully in the next chapter). A person who has achieved more integrated self and object representations, and whose ego functions are more intact may experience depression as a result of conflicts at the superego level of development. Feelings of low self-esteem, of not living up to one's ego ideal, and of disappointment in the difference between one's aspirations and one's reality are usually experienced at the neurotic level.

> Mr. Jones, a school principal, came to treatment feeling bad about himself. He said that he often could not live up to the expectations of the parents of children with whom he works. He tends to feel overburdened and then becomes angry at home when demands are put on him. He feels terrible for being so

parsimonious with his children in terms of having time or energy for them, and he feels that he consistently disappoints his wife. All of these expectations that he feels he meets incompletely make him disappointed in himself as a father, husband, and principal. (Hayes 1995, personal communication)

Mr. Jones may be seen as an example of someone whose depression is primarily at the neurotic level of functioning. His depression is experienced at the superego level, where he feels unable to live up to his own ideals. His reality testing, judgment, and sense of self and others are intact. He is able to control his angry impulses, but feels bad for having them. Mr. Jones's low self-esteem and his chronic mild hopelessness about himself may stem from experiences of always feeling "in the wrong" with his parents, which further contributes to his current feelings at his workplace and in his family.

BIOLOGICAL FACTORS

There are many biological factors that need to be considered in the etiology and treatment of depression. Genetics, hormones, biochemistry, and temperament all may play significant roles in a person's predisposition to the triggering and prolonging of depressive states. Let us consider each of these factors separately.

Genetics

Next to stressful life events, genetics are the second-largest risk factor predicting depression. In particular, bipolar illness (formerly called manic depression) clearly has a genetic basis. In one study, 31 percent of the children whose biological parents had bipolar disorders were also diagnosed as having a bipolar disorder, as opposed to only 2 percent of the children whose biological parents did not have an affective illness. In another study, if one parent had a mood disorder, the lifetime risk to the offspring of having a mood disorder ($N = 614$) was found to be 27 percent. If two parents had mood disorders, the offspring ($N = 28$) faced an enormous risk (75 percent) of developing the disorder (Gershon et al. 1982).

The mode of transmission of depression remains uncertain, but it does not follow classic patterns. Several studies have cited similarities between blood types in families that manifest these disorders. Researchers are also seeking to isolate other genetic transmitted traits, such as light sensitivity, which may characterize families with mood disorders. While many research groups actively continue to try to find and isolate the gene predominately responsible for depression, none has currently achieved this. It is important in taking a family history that we ask not only about the history of mood disorders, but also about the history of alcoholism and gambling in the family. These two addictions often mask bipolar illness, and may be genetically transmitted, or cluster with depression. Clinicians clearly should always take a family history of affective illness.

Hormonal Theories

Hormonal theories also contribute to our understanding of depression. Female hormones may play a role in the finding that depression is two to three times more likely to be diagnosed in women than in men. Women's menstrual cycles and menopause may have sub-clinical effects on their moods, and may result in irritability, sadness, or hopelessness. Likewise, postpartum depression (which often signals an underlying bipolar affective disorder) and ordinary postpartum blues appear to be related to hormonal changes. Likewise, miscarriage can trigger depression. No single hormone, such as progesterone, has been identified as the causative agent for depression. Rather it seems that multiple hormones may work in concert in predisposition to depression. Also, it is clear that we should not limit our thinking to sex hormones exclusively, as many of the hypothalamic and pituitary hormones are also likely to affect emotions. Agents like prednisone and adrenocorticotropic hormone (ACTH), which are often administered for cancer, inflammatory reactions, and so on, are commonly found to cause mood disturbances.

Biochemistry

There have been enormous changes in the treatment of all affective illnesses as a result of our use of medications that impact the biochemistry of the brain. Our increased understanding of the neurotransmitters and receptor sites has led to the use of pharmacological interventions not just for more disruptive affective illnesses, such as bipolar disorders and major depression, but also for milder yet chronic depressions through the use of SSRIs.

Biochemical theories maintain that, in depression, there are chemical transmitters that are depleted along specific tracts of the brain. Antidepressant medications block the metabolism of the neurotransmitters and make them more available. The newest class of antidepressant medications, called serotonin reuptake inhibitors, selectively acts on one neurotransmitter—serotonin—lifting mood and lessening anxiety, presumably by making this chemical more available for brain cells to use and reuse. In the past, drugs such as MAO inhibitors and tricyclic antidepressants were shown to have significant side effects, often causing cardiovascular problems, and were associated with a higher suicide rate (Roose and Cabaniss 2005).

Today, SSRIs are considered the treatment of choice for many people, except for those with bipolar illness, where such medications may sometimes precipitate an underlying manic episode. The clinician must be especially vigilant in the use of SSRIs with suicidal clients, as concerns have been raised that they may provide just enough energy to actually complete the suicide. Similarly, recent questions have been raised about an increase in violent or suicidal behavior when SSRIs are used by children and adolescents. Yet, medication can be life saving, helping a person regain perspective and psychological mindedness that can help enormously. Remembering back to Styron, Plath, and Hamlet, the muddiness, fogginess, hopelessness, cognitive deficits, and darkness can be lifted with medications so that a client can engage in the work of understanding the underlying causes of their depression.

Interestingly, there is also research in the area of traumatic life events, especially about losses in early life, which suggests that such occurrences may actually change brain chemistry (Van der Kolk 1987). "Kindling" is a concept used in epilepsy to describe the observation that once someone has a seizure, the brain becomes altered, sensitized, and more vulnerable to subsequent seizures. This theory provides a biological paradigm to explain why some adults who were severely abused or depressed in childhood may have repeated episodes of depression later in their lives. The same is true for trauma (see chapter 17).

Temperament

Yet another biological basis for affective disorders can be found in temperament (Kagan et al. 1988, Thomas et al. 1968). This theory holds that we are each born with a unique neural chemistry. Children who are sensitive or shy may be more vulnerable to early loss and separation (Kramer 1993). Children who grow up timid and vulnerable to stress or change may be more predisposed to adult depression. The "fit" between a child's and parents' temperaments is also important (Kaplan and Sadock 1985). In fact, one avenue of research into temperament links congenital neurotransmitter balances with behavioral predispositions, thereby providing a hypothetical connection between temperament and brain chemistry known to be involved in depression (Cloninger 1987).

All of these biological explanations offer us complex windows into some of the multiple causes of depression. It is virtually impossible to consider biological factors, intrapsychic factors, or social factors as being entirely distinct or separate causes of depression. Perhaps more than any others, mood disorders require that we take a fully informed biopsychosocial view of psychopathology. However, with the increased emphasis on symptom reduction, and on brief, intermittent managed care, there can be a pull to treat only the symptoms biochemically and/or with cognitive behavioral treatment. We maintain that one needs also to pay careful attention to the psychological roots of the depression and the social conditions that perpetuate it.

SOCIAL FACTORS

We have observed throughout this book that there are many deprivations and tragedies in the social world: unemployment; social isolation; discrimination based on race, gender, age, religion, and class; lack of access to housing, health care, and education; poverty; disability; and dislocation due to war, natural disasters, or homelessness—to name a few. All of these factors may contribute to an individual's feelings of helplessness, hopelessness, unworthiness, and lowered self-esteem. Furthermore, since, as we noted at the beginning of this chapter, the lifetime risk of a major depressive episode is two to three times greater for women than for men, it is interesting to look more closely at depression in women.

One explanation for the gender difference may be found in the complicated expectations for women in Western cultures. Women may be more stressed than men as they manage a variety of conflicting roles. We said in chapter 10 that many women in Western culture have been socialized to forge identities through their relationships. If women are socialized to be in relationships, then the loss of a relationship or relationships for women may lead to depression (Jack 1987). Often men tend to explain their affective disorders in terms of the loss of a job or a failure to be promoted, whereas women are more likely to attribute their depression to difficulties in relationships.

In a study of 400 women by Deborah Belle (1982), the presence of a confiding intimate relationship with a partner, even in the face of stressful conditions such as poverty, inadequate housing, young children in the home, and young children with illnesses, was the most important factor that women identified in not becoming depressed. Blau (1973) found that among elderly women, having a confiding and intimate female friend was more predictive of women's emotional health than any other factor. In a study of fifty midlife women, Shydlowski (1982) also found that, except for good health, female friends were cited more than husbands, work, or children as sources that prevented depression. In another study of midlife women, Berzoff (1985) found that female friends were consistently cited as enhancing adult self-esteem. All of these studies bear out the premise that in intimate and confiding relationships, women are less vulnerable to depression.

But dependency on others, in a patriarchal culture that rewards separateness and autonomy, can lead to conflicting expectations: to be independent and autonomous, or to be intimate and dependent. Many women fear that if they are really independent, they may lose their relationships. Furthermore, if we think that depression may be anger turned against the self, what then happens to women, who are consistently socialized to internalize their anger? Furthermore, as discussed in chapter 10, we might suspect that this dynamic, for women, may contribute to their depression.

When considering the epidemiology of depression in women, we also need to be aware of many of the other social factors that promote dependency and helplessness. Women are physically vulnerable to violence, particularly domestic violence. Such vulnerability undermines self-esteem. In divorce, women who care for dependent children become economically disadvantaged, often resulting in their downward social mobility toward poverty. In a society that pays men more than women, women's worth in the workplace is materially devalued. In a culture in which the norms are that women work full-time and still maintain responsibility for the household maintenance, women often feel depleted and empty. In a social structural arrangement in which child care is actually shared, it is often still seen as a husband helping out his wife.

> Judy is a member of a women's therapy group. She came to the group feeling depressed. She is a professor, mother, and wife currently writing two books. She works full time. Her income is close to that of her spouse's. In the group she complains, however, that when any of her children are ill, it is assumed that she will cancel her work. She arranges the social life of the family, remembers and handles all medical appointments, attends parent-teacher conferences, is responsible for providing transportation to school and extramural events, and maintains responsibility for the household (shopping, cooking, and so on). She participates in all school and athletic events for her children. Her spouse and children, however, tease and deride her "easy" life. When Judy isn't angry, she feels depressed.
>
> For her, a group that has helped her examine not only her own individual dynamics, but also the social structural causes of her depression has allowed her to make systemic changes in her family life that make her feel more effective.

Gender, however, is not the only risk factor in depression. As noted earlier, families in poverty and women in poverty are at serious risk for depression. Consider the effects on low-income people of early loss, exposure to pathogenic parenting, lack of social supports, inadequate financial resources, limited education, unemployment, sole responsibility for care of dependent children, and lack of access to safe and affordable housing. In fact, psychosocial stressors are implicated in the neurobiology of recurrent affective disorders (Post 1984).

As Bibring (1968) noted, depression is likely to occur when there is a gap between aspirations and accomplishments. Consider, then, the experiences of low-income people who must daily reconcile less-than-average "expectable" environments. As we have described in many of these chapters, families living in urban poverty who experience repeated traumatic losses from violence, gangs, and homicide are at risk for depression. It is also important to remember that, for many disadvantaged families, the anomie that underlies depression often goes undiagnosed and untreated, given a diagnostic tendency to emphasize acting out, substance abuse, and suicide.

Yet another social factor in the epidemiology of depression is the inherent bias in diagnosis. African Americans are diagnosed as schizophrenic at twice the rate of white Americans. This means that depression in the African American community often goes undiagnosed and untreated.

In addition, as with every diagnostic category we have studied, we need to consider the different cultural meanings of depression. Cultures have different kinds of attributions for depression. For example, clients from developing countries may complain of somatic equivalents of depression (e.g., constipation, insomnia, sexual dysfunction, weight loss, a wind in the heart, a pain in the belly). In countries with a strong Judeo-Christian perspective, guilt may be the predominant feature. In some Native American cultures it is considered a mark of maturity, not of pathology, to feel profound grief over losses, sorrow for the pain of causing suffering to others, and sorrow for those less fortunate. In those cultures, depression is seen as a positive sign of interdependence, of connection to the community, and of moral virtue.

We have looked at how psychological, biological, and sociocultural factors affect the diagnosis of affective disorders. We have examined clinical cases of depression at three developmental levels. Let us now consider suicide, one of the most devastating outcomes of severe depression.

SUICIDE

Suicide poses an enormous public health risk and is one of the most tragic outcomes of depression. It can happen when someone is psychotic, or suffers a major loss: losing a life partner, a job, during a divorce or separation, or during a postpartum depression. Suicide may ensue when a person is abusing substances, when there has been a suicide in the family, when there is a history of sexual or physical abuse, where there has been a history of impulsivity, a severe illness, or as said earlier, among widowed older men, living alone, with an illness. Some people with major depression are too depressed to kill themselves, and it is only when they begin to feel better that they have the energy to follow through. Suicide is almost always a response to unbearable anguish and almost always contains both a wish to die and a wish to be rescued.

In 1997, suicide was the sixth leading cause of death in the United States. In fact, 10 out of every 100,000 people died by suicide, and approximately 500,000 people received emergency room care for suicide attempts. In 1997, suicide was the third leading cause of death among teenagers. Among teens and adults, boys and men are four times as likely to kill themselves, while women report trying to kill themselves two to three times as often as men (www.allaboutdepression.com/gen_27.html). African American men are at high risk in young adulthood; white men are those most at risk in older age (Boerum 2006, personal communication). Those who are most at risk are people who believe that their loved ones would be better off without them, those who have actual plans (pills, a firearm, rope), and those who have a day and time in mind. For the clinician, assessment is enormously important, and one must look at the risk factors noted above, and at whether or not the person has made a previous suicide attempt.

Suicide may be understood intrapsychically in many ways. Suicide may be a result of unbearable shame, guilt, dependency, hopelessness, and hostility. It may be a result of wanting to hurt or kill another. Maltsberger and Buie (1980) see suicide as a form of murder, but one that reflects a client's disturbed inner world. From an object relations view, the self is populated by hostile introjects based on angry experiences with others. In the absence of comforting inner presences, a person may split off what is good from what is hostile and dangerous, and suffer from serious disturbances of self. When the hostility inside becomes split off from the self, there may be a desire to get rid of the intolerable part or parts of the self. In this view, suicide may be understood as a way to rid oneself of hostile impulses by murder. A self psychological view is also useful in understanding how narcissistic assaults can lead to a total loss of self-cohesion, resulting in destroying the self.

> David was a fifty-year-old white nurse. He had a family history of depression and a sister who had killed herself when she was in her late twenties, after being asked to take a year off from law school when she was unable to complete the work due to depression. She had hanged herself in her apartment, where her parents were likely to find her.
>
> David now had two children, a wife, and a very satisfying career. He was beloved in his community and known for his kindness in his work with children at risk. To his utter dismay, however, his wife left him for a woman, asking for a divorce. David became extremely depressed, was unable to function at work, wept, railed, had difficulty sleeping or eating, isolated himself from his children and friends, and was finally hospitalized for severe depression.
>
> After two weeks, and begun on medication, David was discharged. He started drinking heavily. His friends and neighbors were very worried about

him and kept an around-the-clock vigil to see that he did not harm himself. His mother came from another state to stay with him, but on the first night that she was there, he hanged himself, again having her find his dead body.

David had many risk factors for depression. He felt worthless without a partner who could mirror back to him his value. He had been quite dependent on his wife, and he was devastated by her rejection and wish for a divorce. His internal world lacked soothing introjects, and his hostility was so great that it overwhelmed his inner world. His own suicide served multiple functions: it was a way to punish his wife for abandoning him, and it was a way to destroy the rage in him that could not be soothed. He was also strongly identified with a sister who had committed suicide, and he carried a genetic history of suicide risk. His use of alcohol to deal with his increasing despair was also a risk factor, as he was mixing substances with medication for his depression. Whereas he had been too despondent to harm himself, his antidepressants lifted his depression enough that he could act. Perhaps most tragically, he had been very conscious of the effects of his sister's suicide on him and on his parents, and spoke often of wanting to make sure that his children never experienced the kind of pain that he had after his sister's death.

Let us finally turn to how the client's experience of depression can affect the clinician.

WORKING WITH DEPRESSED CLIENTS

When faced with a client's hopelessness, despair, or self-criticism, it is not uncommon for the beginning clinician to feel hopeless or anxious too. Depressive affects often feel to the client like dead ends. We, the clinicians, presumably less depressed, may begin to wonder how to help the client move on from a seemingly interminable bleak state. Because depressive affects seem to lead nowhere, it becomes difficult for the clinician to hold on to the conviction that, in the telling of a client's story, there can, in fact, be any relief.

Initially, in sitting with depressed clients, clinicians often find that they are experienced as a kind of medicine. The client may begin to feel better, but gradually, the clinician may seem to become less helpful, and begin to feel herself as lacking in a variety of ways. Finally, the clinician often experiences herself as inadequate, heir to many of the same criticisms once directed by the client against herself. This can induce in the clinician some of the same feelings of unworthiness, ineffectiveness, and helplessness that the client feels. Some clients feel so hopeless that, in sitting with them, we clinicians can feel paralyzed. Sometimes, suicidal clients can lead us, the clinicians, to feel tormented. There may be times when, sitting with suicidal clients, we may begin to hate them, or even worse than hate, feel aversion toward them and turn away (Buie and Maltsberger 1983). This aversion can be lethal to the client. But if we can acknowledge our hopelessness and helplessness to ourselves and to our supervisors, then we clinicians may not need to disavow these feelings. When we can be aware of our depression, our hate, or our aversion, we will not be unconsciously asking our clients to bear our aggression as well as their own.

There are other pitfalls for beginning clinicians who work with depressed clients. One very common error is to try to cheer up or talk a depressed client out of being depressed. To do so may repeat other failures in empathy and lead to the experience of a loss of self-cohesion for the client. In psychodynamically oriented work, we need to empathize with a person's depression, while enlisting her help to find its causes in both internal and external realities. Sometimes, a client's depression may make us want to mobilize to action. We want to give advice or do something that will relieve the suffering. This, too, can lead away from what the client needs—someone who can tolerate painful affects, which up until now may have seemed unbearable. If, as we have said, one of the greatest ego strengths is the capacity to bear depression, then we must be able to do this ourselves if we want to help our clients do the same.

CONCLUSION

Beginning clinicians need to hold a biopsychosocial lens when they work with people who are depressed. Therapists do not treat depression, but rather the person experiencing it. The therapeutic goal should be to alleviate the symptoms and to restore, or create, the capacity to do the constructive rebuilding work that allows for a more creative and flexible use of the self. Cognitive behavioral therapies that cut the problem down to size, reduce negative cognitions, and externalize the problem—along with social support therapies—can be helpful to depressed clients. However, in our current practice of managed care, the danger is that we may be moving toward a model of simply medicating mood disorders, or helping our clients reframe their cognitions, without attending to their complex psychosocial causes. In fact, in the worst kinds of managed care, organized only around diminishing symptoms, the pressure to contain costs by limiting care may unintentionally join with the therapist's unexamined countertransference motives to avoid depression altogether.

Eighty percent of people with affective disorders improve with the combination of medication and talking therapies. In the move toward intermittent therapies, however, we need to still recognize the value of a treatment relationship in understanding the client's inner world and restoring functions that may have become disturbed.

In the Chinese language, the word "crisis" is designated with two characters that mean "danger" and "opportunity." Affective disorders pose enormous dangers, not the least of which is the risk of suicide. But these disorders also provide opportunities: to restore lost functions, to heal internal wounds, to gain sufficient mobilization to make social changes, to become able to bear the affects heretofore unbearable, to be able to return to or find community, and to be able to use a helping person to sort out the meaning of the crisis. The felt danger of a crisis is often the loss of meaning or of loved ones. The actual danger is that, without the crisis, we may never discover our own strengths.

REFERENCES

Belle, D. (1982). *Lives in Stress: Women and Depression*. Beverly Hills, CA: Sage.

Berzoff, J. N. (1985). Valued female friendships: Their functions in promoting female adult development. Unpublished dissertation. Boston University.

Bibring, E. (1968). The mechanism of depression. In *The Meaning of Despair*, ed. W. Gaylin, pp. 145–81. New York: Science House.

Blatt, S. (1974). Levels of object representation in anaclitic and introjective depression. *Psychoanalytic Study of the Child* 9:107–58. New York: International Universities Press.

Blau, Z. (1973). *Old Age in a Changing Society*. New York: New Viewpoints.

Bowlby, J. (1958). The nature of a child's tie to his mother. *International Journal of Psychoanalysis* 39:350–73.

———. (1961). Childhood and mourning and its implications for psychiatry. *American Journal of Psychiatry* 118:481–98.

———. (1963) Pathological mourning and childhood mourning. *Journal of the American Psychoanalytic Association* 11:500–41.

Brown, G. W. (1991). Epidemiological studies of depression: Definition and case findings. In *Psychosocial Aspects of Depression*, ed. J. Beicher and A. Kleiman. Hillsdale, NJ: Laurence Erlbaum.

Brown, G. W., Bilfulco, A., and Harris, T. O. (1989). Life events, vulnerability and onset of depression: Some refinements. *British Journal of Psychiatry* 150:30–42.

Buie, D. H., and Maltsberger, J. T. (1983). *The Practice and Formulation of Suicide Risk*. Somerville, MA: Firefly.

Cicchetti, D. (1989). How research on child maltreatment has informed the study of child development. In *Child Maltreatment*, ed. D. Cicchetti and V. Carlson, pp. 327–431. Cambridge: Cambridge University Press.

Cloninger, C. R. (1987). Neurogenetic adaptive mechanisms in alcoholism. *Science* 236:410–16.

Freud, S. (1916). Mourning and melancholia. *Standard Edition* 14:237–59.

———. (1923). The ego and the id. *Standard Edition* 19:3–66.

Gershon, E. S., Hamorit, J., Dibble, E., et al. (1982). A family study of schizo-affective, bipolar, unipolar, and normal control probands. *Archives of General Psychiatry* 39:1157.

Gershwin, I. (1937). "They can't take that away from me." *Shall we dance?*

Hoyert, D. L., Kochanek, K. D., Murphy, S. L. (1999). Deaths: Final data for 1997. *National Vital Statistics Reports* 47(19). http://www.cdc.gov/nchs/data/nvsr/nvsr47/nvs47 19.pdf.

Jack, D. (1987). Self in relation theory. In *Women and Depression: A Lifespan Perspective*, ed. R. Formanck and A. Gurian, pp. 41–46. New York: Springer.

Jacobson, E. (1964). *The Self and the Object World*. New York: International Universities Press.

Kagan, J., Reznick, S., and Snidman, A. (1988). Biological basis for childhood shyness. *Science* 240:167–71.

Kaplan, H. I., and Sadock, B. J., eds. (1985). *Comprehensive Textbook of Psychiatry*, vol. 4. Baltimore: Williams & Wilkins.

Kernberg, O. (1966). Structural deviations of object relations. *International Journal of Psycho-Analysis* 47:236–53.

Klein, M. (1940). Mourning and its relationship to manic-depressive states. In *Contributions to Psychoanalysis 1921–1945*. New York: McGraw-Hill.

Kramer, P. (1993). *Listening to Prozac*. New York: Viking.

Loewald, H. (1980). *Papers on Psychoanalysis*. New Haven, CT: Yale University Press.

Mahler, M., and McDevitt, J. (1980). The separation-individuation process and identity formation. In *The Course of Life*, vol. 1, ed. S. I. Greenspan and H. Pollock, pp. 407–23. DHSPUB No. (ADM) 80-786. Washington, DC: National Institute of Mental Life.

Maltsberger, J., and Buie, D. (1980). The devices of suicide: revenge, riddance and rebirth, *International Review of Psychoanalysis* 6(61):151–61.

Plath, S. (1962). *The Collected Poems*, ed. Ted Hughes. New York: Harper & Row.

———. (1971). *The Bell Jar*. New York: Harper & Row.

Post, R. M. (1984). *Neurobiology of Mood Disorders*. Baltimore: Williams and Wilkins.

Roose, S., and Cabaniss, D. (2005). Psychoanalysis and psychopharmacology (chapter 17) in *Textbook of Psychoanalysis*, eds. E. Person, A. Cooper, and G. Gabbard, pp. 255–66. Washington DC: American Psychiatric Press.

Shakespeare, W. (1917). *The tragedy: The Prince of Denmark*, ed., E Chambers. Boston: D.C. Heath and Co.

Shydlowski, B. (1982). *Friendship Among Women in Midlife*. Unpublished dissertation. Fielding Institute.

Spitz, R., and Wolf, K. (1946). Anaclitic depressions. *Psychoanalytic Study of the Child* 2:313–42. New York: International Universities Press.

Styron, W. (1990). *Darkness Visible: A Memoir of Madness*. New York: Random House.

Thomas, A., Chess, S., and Birch, H. (1968). *Temperament and Behavior Disorders in Children*. New York: New York University Press.

Tronick, E., and Granino, A. (1988). The mutual regulation model: The infant's self and interactive regulation and coping and defensive capacity. In *Stress and Coping*, ed. T. Field, P. McCabe, and N. Schneiderman, pp. 47–68. Hillsdale, NJ: Lawrence Erlbaum.

Van der Kolk, B. (1987). *Psychological Trauma*. Washington, DC: American Psychiatric Press.

Weissman, M. M., and Klerman, G. L. (1977). Sex differences and the epidemiology of depression. *Archives of General Psychiatry* 34:98–111.

Zetzel, E. (1965). On the incapacity to bear depression. In *The Capacity for Emotional Growth*, ed. E. Zetzel, pp. 82–114. New York: International Universities Press.

16

Anxiety and Its Manifestations

Joan Berzoff

In the preceding chapter on affective disorders, we discussed the experience of depression and the possible biopsychosocial causes that contribute to it. This chapter describes the experience of anxiety and reviews psychodynamic, social, and biological etiologies and treatments for anxiety disorders. Whereas depression is felt when loss, hurt, disappointment, and disillusionment have already occurred, anxiety is experienced around what might be about to happen. Hence, anxiety is an anticipatory feeling. It is related to the future, not the past. It is about something dreadful that might happen outside the self, or something terrible that one fears might emerge from inside.

These days, psychodynamic theories and therapies are currently less in favor than are other treatments, especially in the treatment of phobias and obsessive-compulsive disorders. Cognitive behavioral therapies of many forms—behavioral exposure therapies that desensitize patients, cognitive behavioral interventions that help change distorted thinking, meditation, eye movement rapid desensitization, sensory motor integration therapy, group treatment—have come to be seen as treatments of choice (Ballenger and Tylee 2003). Nonetheless, as we have maintained throughout this book, people with anxiety disorders are more than the sum of their symptoms, and since mind, body, and environment are all implicated in anxiety disorders, understanding them in depth requires more than treating symptoms alone.

THE EXPERIENCE OF ANXIETY

We informally polled some of our colleagues to ask them to describe what it was that they feel when anxious. This is what they said. One reported difficulty falling asleep and staying asleep as he contemplated a promotion at work. He would awaken with free-floating anxiety and a sense of impending doom. He began to dread being with his family and being at work. He was short-tempered, preoccupied, and generally restless. The physical illnesses of coworkers, family, and friends loomed larger than life. He could not put into perspective the newspaper articles he read documenting wars, ecological disasters, or medical illnesses. He began to exercise excessively. Another colleague remembered her terror at having accidentally been locked in a bathroom when she was five years old. As she tried to get out, her head began to pound and her heart raced. She could not breathe, and was left feeling helpless and alone. To this day, she avoids public bathrooms, because when she uses them and the door locks, she feels like that little girl, anxious and afraid. Another described how the sound of a noontime siren makes her heart race and her mouth tingle. Because she was born at the end of World War II, when civil defense drills signaled real danger, sirens in the present still physiologically revive her anxiety from her past. Another recalled her annual terror of lecturing to a classroom of a hundred students. At each first class, she became nauseated, clammy, and dizzy, and her ears rang. Often, she experienced examination dreams in which she failed to bring her notes to class, was unprepared, undressed, and felt humiliated.

What all of our colleagues describe is what every reader has also experienced. Anxiety is a universal affect. It can make our hearts beat faster, our tongues tingle, our palms sweat. Anxiety can make us ruminate or obsess. Anxiety can take the form of irrational fears of such things as planes, bathroom doors, open spaces, supermarkets, bridges, or tunnels. Anxiety can be experienced as flashbacks or nightmares of horrific traumatic events. In fact, anxiety is probably the most common symptom with which clients present. Anxiety affects over one-quarter of the population (Ballenger and Tylee 2003). There is a 2:1 ratio of females to males who report anxiety symptoms.

Anxiety can manifest itself in a variety of forms and in varying degrees of severity. At its most useful, it serves as a signal of danger and motivates us to act: to prepare lectures, to meet deadlines, to attend to what was initially threatening. At its most disruptive, anxiety paralyzes us, preventing us from leaving home, from concentrating on work or family, from sleeping, from traveling, from enjoying pleasures, or from functioning at all.

As in our approach to other psychopathologies, we will use a variety of biopsychosocial lenses when evaluating the symptoms of a person suffering from anxiety. Biological vulnerability, genetics, brain organization, chemical imbalances, drug and alcohol use, and physical illnesses may predispose an individual to anxiety. Intrapsychic conflicts and early developmental issues may contribute to anxiety disorders, which in turn create enormous psychological distress as a person's functioning in relationships and work becomes impaired. Social factors—oppression, trauma, neglect, abuse, and violence—may increase a person's experience of helplessness and vulnerability, and result in the development of anxiety symptoms. An understanding of the interface between these biological, social, and psychological factors allows for the greatest appreciation of the complexity of these disorders.

ANXIETY AND CULTURE

Before exploring the kinds of anxiety disorders described in the *DSM-IV-TR*, it is important to recognize how the expression of anxiety might be different according to culture. Jewish, Hispanic, or Italian families, for example, may express their anxieties with emotion that may appear exaggerated to those of different backgrounds.

> Joshua, an eight-year-old Jewish boy from a middle-class family, had been referred to his school psychologist for an evaluation because he repeatedly said, "Oh my God, I'm gonna kill myself!" whenever he missed the ball at games of kickball, or whenever he forgot his homework. While his predominately white Anglo-Saxon Protestant school thought a suicide evaluation might be in order, within his ethnic family norms, "killing oneself" was idiomatic for the expression of any anxiety or frustration and did not reflect any overt pathology.

In Eastern cultures, anxiety is often expressed physically. People from Eastern cultures tend to experience anxiety when they feel shame or fear of losing face, and may express their anxiety through blushing, somatic complaints, or obsessive-compulsive rituals. Many other cultures also present with psychosomatic equivalents of anxiety. Iranians, for example, often express their anxiety as pains in the heart, as weak nerves, as shaking, or as body pain. In Latin America, anxiety is referred to as *susto*. It is often characterized by phobias, tachycardia, irritability, or insomnia (Ho 1987). In Caribbean and Latina cultures, anxiety is often expressed as an *attaque de nerviosa*, where a person experiences crying attacks, heat in the chest rising to the head, uncontrollable shouting, or verbal or even physical aggression (Craske 1999). In Singapore, anxiety can take the form of a panic-like disorder called *Koro*, in which a person fears that his sexual organs will retract into the body, causing death.

Anxiety may also emerge over different kinds of cultural prohibitions. For white Anglo-Saxon Protestants, whose culture may value independence and stoicism, anxiety may erupt when autonomy is threatened. By contrast, in Asian cultures where interdependence is the norm, anxiety may arise when there has been some inability to rely on others or too much separateness from others. In Japan, for example, there is a particular form of social phobia, *Taijin Kyofusho*, in which a person becomes anxious when he or she fears having offended others through socially inappropriate behaviors, such as flatulence, giving off offensive odors, staring inappropriately, showing inappropriate facial expressions, or having a physical deformity. This violates the cultural norms of extreme politeness and attention to the needs of others. In Western cultures, on the other hand, anxiety may emerge when a person fears being ridiculed, shamed, or humiliated for those same behaviors (Craske 1999). In addition, as a result of differences in attributions for anxiety, many individuals from cultures such as Native American, Latin American, Alaskan, African American, or Asian may not present to the mental health field with anxiety symptoms, nor will they seek medication or psychotherapy for symptom relief. Rather than view anxiety as a symptom, different cultural groups may understand anxiety as a spirit or ghost, for example, and seek cures through magic, shamans, monks, or herbs. Many African Americans often seek spiritual cures, and use their ministers, not therapists, for help with their anxiety (Neal-Barnett and Smith 1997). Thus, it is important to remember that cultures express affects in culturally specific idioms, and that individuals seek culturally prescribed treatments for their pain and discomfort.

ANXIETY AT DIFFERENT DEVELOPMENT LEVELS

Just as we discussed in the previous chapter that depression is experienced at different developmental levels, so too is anxiety experienced differently according to a person's level of psychological development. When assessing a client's internal experience of anxiety, it is important to assess the developmental level of that person's anxiety. We described, in chapter 4, how anxiety can be experienced at the level of castration anxiety (the fear of something bad happening to the body because of unacceptable wishes or desires), as separation anxiety (the fear of loss of love and loss of a needed person due to unacceptable wishes or desires), and as annihilation anxiety (fears felt at the level of the destruction of the self). Each of these anxieties corresponds to a person's psychological level of development: neurotic, pre-oedipal, or psychotic. Below, we discuss how anxiety may manifest at these different levels of psychological development. Whereas, in other chapters, we began first with the most disturbed level of development, in this chapter, we begin with the higher level of development, because anxiety is so often experienced by those at the neurotic level.

Anxiety at the Neurotic Level

Ginny, a thirty-year-old unmarried historian, complained of chronic headaches and anxiety, which were precipitated by her father's recent suicidal ideation. As the middle of three children, she came from a Jewish family that had initially viewed itself as "golden." Her father was a highly successful and attractive businessman, and her mother worked for a music publishing house. Both parents presented an ideal and enviable life to the community. However, when Ginny was five, her older brother, aged seven, became ill. Ginny both loved him and felt him to be her rival. In fact, as an adult, she remembered a song she had sung to her brother: "Die, die, my little darling pie." When he became quite ill with meningitis, he left for the hospital, but not before Ginny kissed him good-bye. Overnight he developed pneumonia secondary to meningitis and he died. Ginny remembers feeling somewhat vaguely as a child that she herself was the "kiss of death," a feeling that made her feel anxious much of the time.

Ginny can remember having tried to comfort her mother and father around this terrible loss, and recalled sitting on her father's lap, reading with him and snuggling after her brother's death. To Ginny's delight, when she was six and a half, her mother announced another pregnancy. With her mother's pregnancy, Ginny felt, in fantasy, that she had had something to do with this blessed event. Ginny felt especially thrilled (and a little guilty) to be having a baby in the family, whom she thought of as hers and her father's. When her new sister was born with Down syndrome, however, Ginny again experienced her loving feelings toward her father as dangerous and destructive, given that her new sister was born severely developmentally delayed. Given one brother's death, which she associated with her aggressive feelings, and her sister's damage, which she associated with her loving feelings, she grew up with a vague sense of danger about both her loving and aggressive wishes.

At age thirteen, she wrote a birthday song for her sister. Her mother had the song published, and it was an overnight success. Ginny was coronated by her classmates for her new-found fame as a children's songwriter. But she renounced the success, not seeing it as her own, and was uncomfortable with her achievement and with the public acclaim it brought her. Her academic successes were henceforth experienced as anxiety provoking and she sought invisibility. Though popular, successful, and intelligent, when angry or frustrated as a child she would literally hide in the back of her closet so as not to be a problem to others. As an adult she experienced both generalized anxiety and headaches, often brought on by an event that disappointed or angered her. Her symptoms required that she retreat to a darkened room. These often came on after she was happy and excited, or furious or frustrated.

We would say that Ginny experienced anxiety at the neurotic level. What do we mean by neurotic? In drive-theory terms, Ginny's anxiety emerged from her unconscious sexual and aggressive wishes and fantasies that occurred at the oedipal stage of development. Freud thought that sexual or aggressive memories, fantasies, and feelings were kept out of consciousness through the defense of repression. When these unacceptable aggressive or sexual impulses broke through, however, she became anxious around anything that made her feel too visible or successful. Using structural theory, Ginny's unconscious aggressive feelings toward her brother had been realized by coincidental damage and death. As a result she suffered neurotic guilt and anxiety over conflicts between her superego and her impulses. In addition, her father's serious depression had heightened her sense that she was somehow responsible for her damaged sister and lost brother.

In ego-psychological terms, Ginny suffered from neurotic anxiety (as distinguished from psychotic anxiety) because her reality testing remained intact. She knew she hadn't really killed anyone. Furthermore, she used the high-level defenses of sublimation, intellectualization, and reaction formation to deal with her unacceptable wishes and urges. She adapted to her family's losses by attempts to be good, quiet, and nonassertive, which became ways of relating that shaped her character. Some of her anxiety also derived from her critical superego, having identified with her parents' high standards both for themselves and their surviving children. But she also had good judgment, humor, and an excellent capacity for insight, which were later invaluable in treatment.

In object relations terms, Ginny's anxiety was at the neurotic level because her early relationships had been secure and she had internalized integrated and coherent representations of herself and others. She could engage in deep and intimate friendships in which affection and mutuality were genuine. She had some difficulties in close relationships with men, feeling that they (like she) could not live up to her expectations. But other people were viewed as being whole, and not part-objects.

In self psychological terms, Ginny's anxiety was neurotic because she had a relatively cohesive sense of self. But because her narcissistically injured parents had needed her as a selfobject to compensate for their many real losses, their own depletion had left them unable to be fully empathic to her. As a result, she sometimes felt that her successes were narcissistic achievements for her parents and not for her. But as she experienced herself to be understood in the course of treatment, and as she came to understand and forgive herself, she began to experience greater empathy for herself and for her parents' losses. She could also acknowledge her family members' less than ideal lives.

Also indicative of her neurotic-level anxiety was a strong observing ego that enabled her to develop a transference to her therapist and to examine it. Initially, she felt that she had to live up to her fantasies of her therapist's expectations, as she had felt she had to live up to her parents' expectations. Often the therapist felt "obligated" to live up to hers. Ginny would bring in volumes of nineteenth-century literature and ask if the therapist had read them. She would discuss in great detail the latest avant-garde music, which the therapist had not heard. The therapist often, through projective identification, felt like a disappointment, and not bright, witty, or urbane enough. This made the therapist anxious, paralleling Ginny's anxiety. In the treatment, Ginny dared to become angry and disappointed with the therapist, and later dared to make a career change that required considerable self-assertion and self-differentiation. She chose a career that was different from that of her therapist's, her father's, or her mother's. She ultimately met a man who she felt was good enough for her. Over the course of treatment, her headaches remitted.

Prior to *DSM-IV*, we would have understood Ginny to be neurotic. Whether looking at her anxiety from a drive, object relations, ego, or self psychological perspective, we would have pointed to her intact reality testing and her superego conflicts around her sexuality and aggression. We would have assessed the quality of her anxiety as oedipal anxiety. We would have identified her defenses as high level, and would have seen her as relatively successful in work and love, noting her ability to form and maintain triadic relationships. Hence, we would have referred to her anxiety as "superego anxiety."

Neurosis used to be one of the main diagnostic categories for anxiety disorders until the authors of *DSM-IV* severed the link between psychodynamic theories of etiology and diagnosis. The authors of *DSM-IV*, and now *DSM-IV-TR* (2000) believe that the standardized diagnostic manual for the country should list only the observable symptoms for each diagnosis and not endorse any particular theory of dynamics or causation. It is important to note that a new, complimentary guide to the *DSM* has emerged from the Psychoanalytic Division of the American Psychological Association and the American Psychoanalytic Association, modeled on the *DSM*, but focusing, like this book, on understanding the human complexity at the root of disorders, rather than simply providing descriptions of the disorders. The *Psychoanalytic Diagnostic Manual* (2006) tries to address the kinds of issues of the "soul" discussed in chapter 2.

The disappearance of neurosis as a diagnostic category does not mean that the neurotic processes cease to exist. An understanding of neurotic anxiety, such as that experienced by Ginny, is still extremely relevant for the treatment of some anxiety disorders today.

If Ginny had been psychotic, her anxiety would have looked very different. She would have experienced anxiety at the level of the annihilation of her self. If she were psychotically anxious, she might have been convinced that she had murdered her brother or had given birth to her father's child. This would have produced anxiety so primitive that it would have been experienced as if her very self were dissolving under the weight of her sexual or aggressive impulses. Were she psychotic, she would have been unable to distinguish wish from deed, thought from action. Her thoughts would have been distorted by delusions that she was powerful enough to either wreak havoc upon her family, or else to save them from destruction. She might have had hallucinations that God or the devil had told her to kill family members. If she had been psychotic, her defenses would have distorted reality. She might have denied her sibling's death, or projected her own badness onto the world outside, making it a dangerous place. Were her anxiety of psychotic proportions, her relationships would have been at the level of selfobject merging with few, if any, boundaries between herself and others. Had her anxiety been psychotic, her capacity for enduring friendships, intimate relationships, or a therapeutic alliance would not have been possible. In short, because her anxiety was at the level of superego concerns, she did not experience "annihilation anxiety," as do people who function on a psychotic level.

Ginny also did not suffer from the kind of anxiety that we associate with people who have severe character pathology. She did not express profound "separation anxiety"—the terror of being alone or of feeling that she would be swallowed up or engulfed if separated from those she needed. She did not exclusively use defenses such as splitting, primitive idealization, or projective identification as ways of keeping contradictory feelings separate, each of which would have seriously distorted her perceptions of other people. As we noted earlier, *she* was the one who suffered; she did not cause suffering in those around her. Had Ginny been suffering from anxiety at the level of severe separation anxiety, she might also have had transient breaks with reality.

The hallmark of anxiety at the neurotic level, then, is that it does not impair reality. The function of anxiety at the neurotic level is to signal intrapsychic danger and to mobilize the defenses. The hallmark of anxiety at the character-disordered level is separation anxiety (fear of loss of the other), and its function is to try to restore psychic equilibrium by holding on to needed others. At the psychotic level, anxiety is experienced as annihilation anxiety, a fear of the loss of the self and the terror of disintegration.

ASSESSING SYMPTOMS AT DIFFERENT DEVELOPMENTAL LEVELS

To understand and assess the source, the nature, and the developmental level of a person's anxiety, it is necessary to go beyond the symptoms to the story. For example, obsessive-compulsive behaviors are often anxiety symptoms, signs that unmanageable anxiety is present. But obsessive-compulsive symptoms (excessive hand washing, checking, counting, obsessions, or rituals) do not reveal what the anxiety is about, nor at what developmental level it is experienced. This point was brought home very forcibly to one of the authors at a time when two of her patients were experiencing severe anxiety that manifested in a very similar manner. Yet the cause, the story, of the anxiety could not have been more different.

Both Darla and Patty described themselves as "neat freaks." Everything in their apartments had to be clean and meticulously arranged. Darla spoke of the sense of "relief and safety" that she felt when she would look in her closet at all her clothes "hanging in perfect order and symmetry." Her shirts were all lined up in one section, skirts in another, and so on; each hanger was facing the same way. If anything was out of order, she would get very anxious, experiencing a nameless dread. Patty spoke of very similar activities and feelings. Any kind of messiness made her very uncomfortable. She needed to feel that "everything was always under control," that "nothing could go wild." Darla could no longer go out to eat with friends who might drop crumbs on the table, and Patty was starting to get frightened of driving. As each examined the sources of her fears the following emerged:

Darla grew up in a chaotic family. Her father was quite sadistic. In the nature/nurture paradigm, nurture was uneven at best, and Darla's nature was very sensitive, finely tuned, and shy. At the beginning of treatment she presented a line drawing of herself with parts not connected at all, a kind of stick figure in pieces. The figure was a poignant manifestation of her internal disorganization, fragility, and vulnerability. As the therapist looked at it, she wondered if Darla's love of and need for order arose out of her internal feeling of falling apart and going to pieces, of never feeling whole, solid, and connected. Darla wept as she felt how desperately she needed her closet to look perfect to reassure her momentarily that maybe she could hold herself together a little longer. Developmentally, her level of anxiety had to do with the fear of total disintegration or annihilation. Relating to the consistent presence of the therapist and telling the myriad terrifying experiences of her childhood enabled Darla to heal in such a way that, eventually, this primitive early anxiety did not recur with any great frequency. She became free to live a much more spontaneous, full, and joyful life.

When Patty talked about *her* life she described a very organized structured family that was quite close, loving, and strictly religious. Patty attended only Catholic schools and had been very influenced by the nuns and priests who taught her. By far the most traumatic event in her life occurred when she was the victim of a rape at nineteen years of age. The rapist had held her locked in his apartment at knife point and had forced her to submit to hours of sexual activity. When she tried to resist, he cut her on the throat and ejaculated for the third time as he licked her blood. Arrogantly, he released her, stating that no one would believe he would do such things and he would never be convicted. Patty did report the crime to the police and after years of legal battles, the rapist was hospitalized in a psychiatric facility for six months. Patty, in the meantime, attended a rape victims' group and worked through many of her reactions, but felt that she nevertheless was growing more anxious and compulsive with the passage of time. She was beginning to have short periods of dissociation when she entered treatment. It took many months to get to the trauma because she had total amnesia about it, but what finally emerged was that Patty had, at one point, experienced an orgasm as she was being penetrated by her rapist at knife point. She had not been able to remember it because both her guilt and shame made having an orgasm under such circumstances unacceptable to her superego. Her anxiety was about having to face what she considered a terrible, sinful aspect of herself. Her symptoms of needing excessive orderliness and control were unconscious attempts at denying the possibility of being as out of control as she felt during her orgasm. Eventually, Patty made peace with the fact that her body had responded to unwanted sexual stimulation. Her great anxiety then diminished because she had faced what terrified her about herself. In Patty's case the danger (following the rape) did not come from hostile forces outside herself but from feared impulses within. Whereas Darla manifested annihilation anxiety, Patty experienced superego anxiety. The latter anxiety, like Ginny's, was at the neurotic level.

Let us now consider the anxiety disorders (generalized anxiety, panic attacks, phobias, obsessive-compulsive disorders) separately, recognizing that often there are multiple causes of anxiety disorders, which may be intrapsychic, biological, and social. PTSD is also among the anxiety disorders, but we have dedicated a chapter to this important diagnostic category.

Generalized Anxiety Disorders

Imagine the anxiety you feel before taking an examination. You have difficulty sleeping the night before. You feel agitated, distracted, your heart begins to race faster and faster. Now imagine being in that state for days, for weeks, even for years. With generalized anxiety disorders (GAD), people are worried and fearful that something will happen to harm them or their loved ones. They may experience anxiety dreams and sleep disorders. Their form of anxiety is usually chronic, and they may see themselves as "high strung." Because of how pervasive and diffuse generalized anxiety disorders are, and because of the intrapsychic conflicts that often underlie them, they are more responsive to psychodynamic treatment and the least responsive to behavioral interventions. They are very responsive to medication, especially SSRIs. More often, although by no means exclusively, generalized anxiety disorders are experienced by women. GAD involves free-floating anxiety, and most often occurs in conjunction with another psychiatric disorder.

> Annette, a fifty-year-old, working-class mother of two teenagers, worked as a telephone marketer, at home, because she felt too anxious to go out of the house or to work next to other people. She came to treatment, sent by her husband, because she could not stop worrying about what would become of

her fifteen-year-old daughter, who, she had learned, had had sex for the first time. Annette found herself obsessing about her daughter, unable to sleep, unable to derive any comfort about her own parenting. Every time her children went out, it felt like she would never see them again; she began to listen in on all of their phone calls and found ways to read their e-mails. While she had always been "high strung," now she could not get through the day without catastrophizing that her husband might have an accident at work, her daughter would become pregnant, or her son (who was an excellent student) might lose interest in school. It appeared that, as her children were becoming more independent, her anxiety was becoming intolerable.

In a brief therapy, Annette was able to explore many feelings about that which she could not control. Her single-mother had been paralyzed with polio during Annette's whole childhood, which had been terrifying to her, and had also limited her freedom. She had come to believe that she could control the outcome of her mother's living or dying by staying close by her mother's side. She did exactly what she was told to do, took care of her mother's physical needs, and developed an early and enduring belief that the same kind of vigilance was required to keep her own family safe. In early adulthood, her first marriage was to a man who totally controlled her (in unconscious ways not so dissimilar to her mother). He would not let her leave the house without permission; he was physically abusive and so jealous of her friends that she stopped seeing them. Now, in her second marriage, her daughter had become sexual, reviving fears about her own life careening wildly out of control, which caused constant and chronic anxiety.

With medication and with six sessions, Annette was able to understand some of the causes of her anxiety and to get symptom relief. Upon terminating, she gave her therapist a gift of relaxation soaps and candles, clearly something she would have wished had been given to her.

People who suffer with generalized anxiety often seek out a medical practitioner because their symptoms—such as sweating, palpitations, shortness of breath, gastrointestinal symptoms—appear to be physical. Often clients with this disorder are reluctant to take medication, except when the medications are prescribed for the treatment of their physical symptoms.

Panic Attacks

We recall that, early on, Freud described a kind of anxiety that was biological. In fact, today, panic attacks are understood largely as a biological phenomenon, even if they are triggered by a psychological response to perceived internal or external danger. A professor described his panic attacks this way:

Scary. It feels like you're not even here on earth. I don't feel human when I get one of these attacks. My heart starts racing, my palms get sweaty, and all I want to do is run! When I experience a panic attack, I feel like I can't breathe, my heart beats very fast, and then I feet like I'm going to die! Everything just gets very hazy, almost but not that. It's like I'm dizzy and I'm going to faint!

People with panic attacks often feel that they are going crazy. They experience intense psychological symptoms: choking, hyperventilating, or heart palpitations so severe that they may fear they are dying. Very often, clients with panic attacks do not recognize that their attacks have a psychological origin, and so they first seek medical help. When their medical findings (often cardiac in nature) are normal, they are often sent home with no treatment at all.

Panic attacks can be devastating because they can so dramatically constrict life functioning. Mark, a potter, spoke eloquently about how his panic attacks made his life a prison. Describing his first panic attack, he said:

I was standing in front of my potter's wheel, when a feeling of absolute terror overtook me. It felt like an explosion, like a reflex, almost like a sneeze. I had no idea what was happening or why. All I can recall is that I next found myself curled in a ball, on the floor, with my heart racing. Tears poured down my cheeks. I was perspiring, and I couldn't breathe. In fact, my fingers had swollen; so had my eyes. My body had become numb. I felt completely out of control.

As Mark's panic attacks worsened, his freedom in the world decreased. Going to exhibits, out for dinner with his wife, or using public transportation became impossible. The boundaries of his world had become increasingly circumscribed. In trying to describe his feelings, he said:

Some people compare panic to what you feel when you find yourself unprepared and have to go on stage; others say it's like having to fight in a war. I think it's more like this: Imagine that you are driving along peacefully when, suddenly, out the blue, a car lurches at you. Try to imagine the terror, confusion, instantaneous racing of your heart, the split-second when the world is utterly out of your control. Remember the out-of-body experience, the way that your nerve endings are almost electrified, and then take that moment and expand it into hours, even days. That's a small scintilla of what a panic attack feels like for me.

As we have said throughout this chapter, people with anxiety disorders such as Mark's may be functioning at a neurotic, personality-disordered, or even psychotic level. While Mark's level of functioning was at the neurotic level, often people with severe character pathology experience panic disorders as a result of separation anxiety. Clients with poorly developed object constancy often experience severe panic attacks when they cannot evoke the image of a needed other. For example, Darla, who also suffered from obsessive-compulsive symptoms, was able to ward off her panic attacks when she called her therapist's answering machine and heard her therapist's voice every night. Her temporary "connection" served as a transitional object that soothed her and diminished her anxiety symptoms. Mark wrote this about his recovery from his panic disorder:

> My recovery will continue slowly. I may have painful and discouraging setbacks. . . . I am not cured. I am still living with, and will for a long time, an illness I am learning to manage, the way diabetics learn to manage their diet and insulin. I have a long way to go, but I have come a long way. I have hope again. The more I speak of my panic attacks, the more I realize that I am not simply a potter with severe or debilitating anxiety. I am a father, a husband, an artist. . . . I am a person with a disorder, not the disorder itself. This is the important piece of a story.

Although vulnerability to panic disorders may lie in our biochemical and genetic make-up, these disorders may develop when dynamic issues trigger their onset. Panic disorders often are rooted in childhood physical or sexual abuse, vicious cycles of parental neglect or rejection, and fears of losing ties to the parent altogether. Often people with panic disorders perceive their parents as overly controlling, frightening, critical, and demanding. Quite often they have difficulties in tolerating anger (Sadock and Kaplan 2004).

Phobias

Phobias are also anxiety disorders. Like panic attacks, they do not have one simple cause or one simple treatment. There are biological, psychological, and social reasons for phobias, and there are different approaches to their treatment. In general, people who suffer from phobias feel dread, panic, or terror when faced with the situations that they fear or cannot control. Their anxiety is anticipatory and very intense. As a result, they go to great lengths to avoid what is feared, even if it interferes with daily functioning.

There have been interesting psychodynamic formulations of phobias. Freud formulated phobias as symptoms that are compromises. Like so many of the anxiety disorders, they partly disable the individual, but they also make anxiety more manageable. They disguise unacceptable instinctual wishes by displacing them onto something else that can be feared and then avoided (Gabbard 1990).

One of Freud's most classic cases (1907) was of a phobic four-and-a-half-year-old boy named Little Hans. This little boy developed terrible phobias of horses and of open spaces. Like many boys his age, Hans both loved his father and feared him. Hans's mother had recently given birth to his little sister, and Hans was quite jealous of her. Hans clung more than ever to his mother. Freud postulated that being an oedipal child, Hans experienced conflicts over his love for his mother and his unconscious and competitive feelings toward his father. Hans also feared that his father would retaliate for the intense feelings Hans had for his mother. Since Hans wanted to be loved by both parents, Freud hypothesized that he "projected" his own aggression onto his father and then displaced the aggression onto horses. By developing a phobia about horses, and not his father, he could keep his father close. But a fear of horses also restricted his movement, as in Victorian Vienna, horses were a common means of transportation.

Hans's phobia had a secondary gain as well; it kept him close to his mother. As long as his unconscious conflict around wanting his mother and fearing, but wanting, his father's love continued unresolved, he became more phobic, projecting and displacing his feelings about horses onto boxcars, railways, and open streets. Now, his freedom was very restricted. It was not until some of his unconscious conflicts were interpreted and made conscious that Hans began to experience some symptom relief and could go out into the world without fear.

A drive theorist, then, would conceptualize phobias as representing unacceptable sexual or aggressive impulses that are defensively displaced onto something outside of the self. But the defense of displacement is not always adaptive because it circumscribes and ultimately limits a person's functioning.

Object relations theorists, on the other hand, formulate phobias differently. In this view, a phobia may encapsulate a wish for, or fear of, merging with significant others. People who are phobic may wish to move toward independence, as did Hans, but may also fear losing others and thus need to hold on to them. From an object relations point of view, Hans's phobia expressed an unconscious dilemma over separation, autonomy, and closeness. Whether from a drive theory or an object relations perspective, the person who has a phobia is truly restricted because the objects, locations, or situations that she fears must be actively avoided. Unlike in Little Hans's day, however, medications and behavioral interventions, such as exposure desensitization treatments, are now considered the most effective interventions to treat the symptoms of phobias. Whereas in Freud's day, clinicians thought of all phobias as the same, today we distinguish between three kinds of phobias: agoraphobia, specific phobias, and social phobias.

Agoraphobia

Ruth entered her sixth anxiety group session with much trepidation. Today she was scheduled to embark on her much feared "mission" with one of the group's co-therapists. She was to drive her car across the bridge that connected her town to the clinic. Ruth sat in the driver's seat, her therapist at her side, and took off toward the city. She chatted comfortably with her therapist for the first ten minutes of the trip until they were about a quarter of a mile from the bridge. Then, silence descended upon the car. Her therapist looked at Ruth and noted several things: Ruth's chest was rising and descending rapidly as her breath became shorter and shorter. Her hands gripped the steering wheel so tightly that her knuckles turned white. Beads of perspiration appeared on her forehead. As they stopped at a traffic light, Ruth began to shake. She turned to the therapist and said, "We can't drive over the bridge. We're gonna die."

People with agoraphobia may be afraid of standing in line, being on a bridge, traveling in a bus, train, or car, or being in open places, such as supermarkets, malls, shopping centers, and streets. All of these fears are of being in situations where escape is difficult, or in which help might not be available.

It is interesting to note that 75 percent of people with agoraphobia are married women. The onset of their phobias usually occurs between the ages of twenty and thirty. Agoraphobia may be more common in women because these symptoms express the stresses in marriage and child rearing for women who either stay at home or try to combine work with parenting. We know that women who are at home full time with small children under the age of five sometimes have limited social support and may feel especially vulnerable. Agoraphobic symptoms may exaggerate their experiences of powerlessness in the larger world, and, at the same time, keep women close to their homes where they feel most oppressed.

Often people with agoraphobia suffer from severe separation anxiety and must be accompanied by a husband, child, or other relative in order to be able to leave their homes. From an object relations perspective, agoraphobia may have the secondary gain of keeping others close and so provide a symptom and its solution. For example, a mother who developed agoraphobic symptoms after her children left home had them return daily to run the errands that she could no longer do. Her symptom represented her early needs to be taken care of, which had been satisfied while she was the caretaker of her children. The symptom provided a solution to her needs for others to remain with her. By becoming dependent, she kept them close. Because the symptoms of agoraphobia often strain interpersonal relationships, it can be important to involve the couple or family in the treatment itself.

Specific Phobias

Specific phobias are persistent, excessive, and unreasonable fears that come from anticipating or experiencing the situations that are feared (e.g., flying, heights, animals, injections, the sight of blood, etc.). Usually people with specific phobias recognize that their fears are unreasonable, but knowing this does not keep them from anxiously anticipating or avoiding what they fear. People with specific phobias feel great distress as their phobias interfere with social relationships, activities, and many other aspects of life functioning.

> Ellen is a twenty-five-year-old secretary who is terrified about becoming trapped in an elevator. Unfortunately, she works in a high-rise building on the thirty-second floor. When she arrives at work each morning, she often thinks she should try riding the elevator. But her ears begin to ring, she becomes dizzy, she cannot breathe, and finally, she takes the stairs. She is exhausted and out of breath by the time she reaches her office. Because each time she leaves the building she faces climbing or descending sixty-four flights, she does not join colleagues for lunch. She has been passed up for promotions because she seems disinclined to go the extra mile for her company: to attend meetings with her boss in other parts of the city, to travel when necessary, or even to attend parties and social functions for work.

For Ellen, in treatment, it appeared that intrapsychic conflicts around her own achievement at work had been displaced onto elevators. She felt that she could not "rise" in her work, and her anxiety about that had been displaced onto the very conveyance that would carry her there.

Social Phobias

People with social phobias fear being humiliated or embarrassed by a social situation. Often they avoid social or performance situations, and when they cannot, experience great distress.

> Like Ellen, Marcia, a fifty-six-year-old single librarian, lives alone and has not had a satisfying intimate relationship. She has also been passed over for jobs that require expressing herself. She experiences her lack of a promotion in her work as yet another proof of her inadequacy. Ellen comes from a large and overburdened Italian Catholic family where being heard and being noticed required acting out boldly and loudly. Two brothers were alcoholic; one was often arrested for petty thievery and her two other sisters were able to get parental attention through a litany of physical complaints. Ellen's response was to be very quiet and hope that she would be noticed for her more saintly qualities. But rather than be noticed, she was largely ignored, and when her father left the family when she was thirteen, she withdrew even more into the church and into herself. Throughout her adult life she has experienced great discomfort speaking at meetings, and even more discomfort imagining discussing anything with her brothers and sisters, all of whom have gone on to have careers and families of their own. Now, she not only avoids her family of origin, but also colleagues at work who have sought her out or men she has met from time to time. She is terribly anxious around other people, feeling that she has nothing to say and that being with others will reveal her inade-

quacy. She is acutely self-conscious and analyzes any interaction she has. She thinks that every shopkeeper, waiter, and service person with whom she comes in contact, scrutinizes her behavior as she does and has come to the same negative conclusions about her that she has about herself.

She always excuses herself from meetings; she either doesn't show up or says she is physically ill because she is so sure she will feel humiliated by what she does not seem to know. She also does not attend parties, workshops, or lunches with colleagues because it feels too painful to think that everyone else views her as she views herself.

Sometimes we do not see people with phobias in our clinical practices at all because they self-medicate, using antianxiety drugs such as Valium to deal with their fears. The appropriate medications, however, are antidepressants such as SSRIs rather than antianxiety agents. Antidepressants tend to motivate change, while the antianxiety agents have a depressant effect and may become addictive.

For people with phobias, behavioral techniques are often seen as the treatment of choice. Clients who are exposed to that which they fear, slowly and incrementally and in conjunction with relaxation techniques, often feel symptom relief. Behavior modification groups may help clients support one another, while teaching them techniques such as assertiveness or systematic desensitization. In these groups people can learn to confront what they most fear in small doses. Groups offer particular support because they provide places to share experiences, information, common symptoms, and methods that have worked. Despite the fact that phobias respond to behavioral, cognitive, behavioral, and biological techniques, individual therapeutic relationships also have value. A client who is phobic feels a great deal of shame. A therapeutic relationship allows the expressions of the shame and the acknowledgment of the fears. It helps put words to the frightening and intolerable feelings, and helps make meaning out of what feels incomprehensible to most people. It can act as a bridge in helping to make behavioral changes. A therapeutic relationship can also help someone understand and resolve some of the psychological sources of their avoidance.

Obsessive-Compulsive Disorders

We mentioned earlier that both Darla and Patty suffered from obsessive-compulsive disorders. Like all of the anxiety disorders, obsessive-compulsive disorders occur at different developmental levels. Because of this they are sometimes confusing. Sometimes they can look like depression or even schizophrenia. They are also confusing because they need to be distinguished from obsessive-compulsive character styles and obsessive-compulsive personality disorders.

Obsessions are intrusive, recurrent, and persistent stereotypic thoughts, images, and ideas. They cause marked anxiety and distress. The thoughts are not simply excessive worries about real-life situations, because the people who have them recognize that their obsessions are products of their own minds. Common obsessions include having committed harmful acts, being contaminated, and harboring unacceptable thoughts or impulses toward others.

Compulsions are repetitive ritualized behaviors that feel obligatory and that attempt to manage intolerable levels of anxiety. Compulsions are by their nature repetitive acts that a person feels driven to perform. Compulsions include such acts as hand washing, counting, checking, touching, praying, or other acts that are ritualized. People with obsessions are often plagued with blasphemous thoughts or are by murderous impulses. They may experience impulses to hurt another person or say something unacceptable. (For a further discussion of some of the intrapsychic factors in these disorders, see the case of Mr. Johannson in chapters 2 and 3.)

> Tanya suffered from an obsessive-compulsive disorder. As is common, her disorder had begun in adolescence. A nineteen-year-old born-again Christian who attended a religious college, she came for treatment because she was washing her hands forty to fifty times a day. They were chapped, raw, and bleeding. When she tried to stop, she would be flooded by intolerable levels of anxiety. She was terrified of germs and would tap three times to avoid them. She was isolated at college and was indeed shunned for her odd behaviors. Tanya was disheveled and had difficulty making eye contact.
>
> At age two, she had suffered a blood disorder and had since been excessively worried about her fragility and her mortality. When she began menstruating at thirteen, her obsessive-compulsive disorder flourished and she began washing her hands.
>
> She often looked very disturbed, almost schizophrenic. Tanya was, in fact, quite functionally impaired. But her symptoms could be distinguished from schizophrenia in that people with schizophrenia often overvalue their thoughts and lack insight, and their symptoms are not alien to them. For Tanya, as for many people with obsessive-compulsive disorders, the symptoms were dystonic. She felt enormous shame and desperation over her obsessions and compulsions and wanted them to stop.
>
> Although Tanya's disorder had intrapsychic causes, she needed to be medicated first to help her manage her anxiety. While psychotherapy was not of particular benefit in helping to extinguish her compulsive behaviors, it did provide a safe context in which she could examine her isolation from others, her rigid use of her religion's rituals to bind her anxiety, and her fears of being away from home, which had revived intense separation anxiety.

For many people with obsessive-compulsive disorders, it is often difficult to make a direct correlation between psychological events and biological responses. A drive theorist working with Tanya might have emphasized her difficulties with her own aggression and concerns about her sexuality as stemming from unresolved anal issues when she first became ill. From this perspective, Tanya's compulsions might serve to control her sexual impulses, which were revived in adolescence. Tanya's harsh superego injunctions, now expressed as rigid rituals, might have had their roots in earlier unresolved pre-oedipal issues. An object relations theorist, on the other hand, might focus on Tanya's attempts to gain control over her fears of separation. Perhaps having faced her own mortality as a child and having been separated from primary caregivers when ill, she was left more vulnerable to severe separation anxiety. Perhaps her blood disease left her filled with self-representations full of dangerous, bad, destructive forces. The obsessions and compulsions might be a solution and a compromise to help her manage her own internal world and make it less dangerous.

Recent work on obsessive-compulsive disorders (Jenike 1990) indicates that, as with many of the anxiety disorders, there is also a strong biological component. Serotonergic antidepressants such as chlorimipramine, fluoxetine, and fluvoxamine have antiobsessional effects. But as with patients with phobias, there is a high rate of noncompliance with drug prescriptions among patients who do not want to ingest substances that they fear may control them.

Cognitive behavioral and behavioral therapies are also useful for people with obsessive-compulsive disorders. Here, as with panic disorders and phobias, clients can be exposed to anxiety-provoking situations, and be behaviorally trained not to engage in typically compulsive responses. As said previously, however, many people with obsessive-compulsive disorders may be resistant to taking drugs or even complying with behavioral injunctions.

Few among us have not at some time experienced a fleeting obsessive thought or compulsive act. Did we remember to lock the door or have to turn off the oven, or suppress an impulse to shout an obscenity at someone who made us angry? But people who chronically suffer from these disorders feel at the mercy of their impulses, which they cannot ignore or suppress. While there is no gender differential in this disorder, it has been found to occur more frequently among upper socioeconomic classes and among the more highly educated.

Post-Traumatic Stress Disorders

Post-traumatic stress disorders are considered the last of the anxiety disorders, but we refer the reader to the chapter on trauma (chapter 17), because we consider these disorders to be so prevalent and complex that they require a separate discussion.

We have now discussed the anxiety disorders: generalized anxiety, panic attacks, phobias, and obsessive compulsive disorders. All of the anxiety dis-orders have complex biological roots and therefore biological treatments that must be understood as well.

Biological Factors

As will be shown in the chapter on trauma (chapter 17), brain develop-ment begins before birth, and continues sequentially. The slow develop-ment of the brain is shaped by social and psychological factors: constitution, good enough parenting, nutrition, safety, consistency. On the other hand, the brain is also shaped by the effects of trauma, neglect, war, severe deprivation, parental psychopathology, genetic and biological diffi-culties, and lack of nutrition and of health care—all of which can have neg-ative effects on brain development. The nature of the environment plays an essential role in shaping a child's developing neural networks and affects memory, emotion, affect regulation, attachment, and a child's sense of self (Schore 2000).

The brain comprises the frontal cortex, the amygdala, and the hippocam-pus. These parts of the brain are made up of millions of neurons that form neural networks. These networks create patterns that help us to complete increasingly complex tasks, feel emotions, and relate to others. How any brain interacts is a function of genetic makeup and of the individual in rela-tionship to the environment. We know that stimulating environments, for example, can expand brain development so children may learn new things; children who are understimulated, on the other hand, may have greater problems with learning, mastery, and the regulation of emotions (Cozol-ino 2002).

Stress is a major force in shifting the biochemistry of the brain. Extreme stress can inhibit learning and growth while moderate stress can stimulate the production of hormones. When there is overwhelming stress such as in severe trauma, the neural networks are disrupted and neural integration does not occur. This affects learning, behavior, emotion, sensation, and cognition. Under extreme stress, the integration of information processing may shut down, as we see in the case of dissociation. The role of therapy and medications, then, are to restore neural network integration and coor-dination, so that emotion, cognition, sensation, and learning can occur without being overwhelmed by stressors from within or outside of the self.

In each of the anxiety disorders, biological factors are implicated in their etiologies and treatments. In the case of generalized anxiety disorders, heightened cortical activity accounts for intense arousal and hypervigilance (Hollander and Simeon 2003). This then causes alterations in the amyg-dala, the part of the brain that controls emotions. Medications such as ben-zodiazepines or Buspar may be very helpful. There is also a genetic link and a higher frequency of people with generalized anxiety disorders among relatives with other anxiety disorders. However, the genetic links are modest (19–30 percent), suggesting that environmental factors play a larger role in the development of generalized anxiety disorders (Wilson et al. 1995) than do biological.

In the case of panic disorders, there are a number of biological explanations. Noradrenergic neurons may misfire into the hippocampus and amygdala, affecting the limbic system and cerebral cortex. These misfires interfere with normal fight-flight responses, which increase cortisol and serotonin. Because serotonin and cortisol are raised, SSRIs and benzodiazepines are effective in lowering cortisol (Ballenger and Tylee 2003) when treating panic disorders. There is also a genetic basis for panic disorders. About 50 percent of people with panic disorders have relatives with panic disorders (Wilson et al. 1995).

Among the biological causes for phobias are blunted growth hormones that lead to noradrenergic dysfunctions (Hollander and Simeon 2003). It is thought that phobias, like PTSD, may involve structural changes in the brain, which begin as environmentally induced, but may lead to changes in the limbic system that then permanently maintains an anxiety response. In addition, for people with phobias, there are strong genetic components. Furthermore, an inborn temperament such as shyness may also play a role in the development of some phobias (Wilson et al. 1995).

Obsessive-compulsive disorders are linked to a number of biological causes: birth trauma, diabetes, dopamine dysregulation, even autoimmune diseases such as strep (Tyree 1999). There is a strong genetic component as well (Tsuang and Tohen 2002). People with obsessive-compulsive disorders may also have other kinds of neurological disorders such as tics or even Tourette's syndrome (Wilson et al. 1995). In addition, these disorders represent potential abnormalities of the serotonin system and the prefrontal cortex, which mediate circular and repetitive thoughts.

Many other kinds of biological factors also precipitate anxiety symptoms. People who are hyperthyroid, for example, may experience a racing heart, have startle responses, difficulty managing emotional feelings, insomnia, or increased anger. Their anxiety symptoms are caused by changes in their hormone levels. Someone with an adrenal tumor may present with a full-blown anxiety attack, often not distinguishable from a panic attack. Those anxiety symptoms are primarily caused by the tumor and are not simply a psychological reaction to the tumor. Clinicians who work with anxious clients always need to ask about the client's medical conditions and medications, and should always keep in mind that physical illnesses may produce anxiety symptoms that require medical treatment.

Substance-induced anxiety disorders can also look indistinguishable from other psychogenic anxiety disorders. When someone is intoxicated or in withdrawal from amphetamines, alcohol, caffeine, cocaine, hallucinogens, sedatives, marijuana, or inhalants, her symptoms of hyperventilation, fear, confusion, derealization, depersonalization, numbness, and/or dissociation may look like anxiety symptoms. It is important therefore to know whether the anxiety disorder has been *induced* by substance or whether it preceded taking it. We cannot stress enough the importance of attending to organic factors, including substance abuse, illness, and medications, in understanding the sources of anxiety.

CONCLUSIONS

We have said in this chapter that under the best of circumstances, anxiety serves to warn us of danger and to help us to mobilize effective defenses. Under less optimal circumstances, anxiety can overwhelm us, or our egos, resulting in a variety of inhibiting symptoms. Anxiety disorders are always compromises, the best adaptation a person can reach to what is experienced as a danger situation. Every anxiety is always experienced at different levels: castration anxiety, anxiety about the loss of love, separation anxiety, and annihilation anxiety. Sometimes anxiety is the result of instincts that break through. Sometimes anxiety may emerge as a function of superego conflicts. Some anxiety may be related to an unresolved developmental issue: for example an obsessive-compulsive disorder may reflect a fixation at or regression to anal conflicts, where we see heightened ambivalence, obsessional doubts, and defenses such as doing/undoing, intellectualization, and reaction formation (Salzman 1980). In phobias, there may be anxiety associated with disavowed sexual or aggressive urges that are displaced onto someone or something else, which can then be avoided (Gabbard 1990). In the case of some phobias such as agoraphobia, the level of anxiety may be related to early losses, neglect, or traumatic separations that then led to severe separation anxiety. Or a phobia or panic attack may arise from client's internal world that is filled with harsh and critical introjects that are then projected onto other persons or things.

In the case of Annette, whose generalized anxiety disorder had disrupted her functioning, understanding the relationship between her overly controlled childhood and marriage to an abusive and controlling man, and her current terror of losing control over her daughter, helped her to regulate her feelings, in coordination with medication that also did the same. In the case of Patty, who had developed obsessive-compulsive symptoms following a rape where she had experienced an orgasm and felt great shame over her sexual impulses, the empathic attunement of her therapist provided a context that helped her to manage and give a name to her complex feelings, all of which resulted in greater neural plasticity. In the case of Little Hans, where fears about his love for his mother, and anger toward and fear of his father resulted in phobias about horses, his oedipal fears could be interpreted, so that he was able to give up the defense of displacement and reenter the streets of Vienna.

Every anxiety disorder, whether the root be superego anxiety, separation anxiety, annihilation anxiety, rejection, physical or sexual abuse, or other forms of deprivation and loss, affects the body. But the process of becoming conscious of the sources of the anxiety, creating new narratives, and developing the use of language to describe what has only been felt in the body, can be very helpful, not only putting into words what was felt as a physical symptom, but in helping clients acquire greater neural integration (Cozolino 2002). In most of the anxiety disorders, medication plays an important part in regulating heightened cortisol and serontonin responses.

Anxiety disorders are complex. They derive from many psychological, social, and biological causes and take many forms. They may express themselves as panic attacks, obsessive-compulsive disorders, phobias, PTSD, generalized anxiety disorders. They may result from medical conditions or substance abuse. They may occur in people at different psychological developmental levels. At their core, they usually express experiences, internal or external, of extreme helplessness and vulnerability. They are intense and their manifestations may seriously compromise a person's freedom, creativity, joyfulness, and ability to work and love. There are important distinctions among the disorders as well as cross-cultural differences in their expressions and their treatments.

While there is no question that some anxiety disorders have a biological basis, there has been a tendency in managed-care situations to treat anxiety disorders exclusively by medicating the patient. Little attention is then paid to the environmental stressors or psychological conflicts that may underlie the disorders. Perhaps our zealousness to see anxiety disorders as exclusively biological and/or behavioral is related to just how overwhelmed we, the clinicians, can feel in the face of many of the anxiety disorders. In treating clients with PTSD, for example, it is simply hard to bear the experiences of brutality or human cruelty that we hear about. Anxious people can be hard to sit with. People who see danger in situations we ourselves don't find dangerous may make us feel impatient and eager to find a "quick fix" to their problems. These clients can evoke a range of negative and helpless feelings in us, the helpers. Anxiety disorders also confront us with our own confusion and our own sense of being overwhelmed.

As we move toward managed-care models of treating symptoms, and not people with symptoms, it may seem easier to just treat the biochemical conditions by giving medication than it is to pay attention to the social condition and/or the intrapsychic conflicts that may underlie the symptoms. As with each of the disorders we have addressed in this book, then, it is essential to pay attention to the ways in which social conditions shape brain functioning, how anxiety may look different at different developmental levels, how whatever the treatment—biological, cognitive behavioral, or psychodynamic—we must appreciate the ways in which creating an attuned, accepting therapeutic relationship is essential for change.

REFERENCES

American Psychiatric Association. (2000). *Diagnostic and Statistical Manual of Mental Disorders*, 4th edition, Text Revision. Washington, DC: American Psychiatric Association.

Ballenger, J., and Tylee, A. (2003). *Anxiety*. London: Mosby Press.

Cozolino, L. J. (2002). The *Neuroscience of Psychotherapy: Building and Rebuilding the Human Brain*. New York: W.W. Norton and Co.

Craske, M. (1999). *Anxiety Disorders: Psychological Approaches to Theory and Treatment*. Los Angeles: Westview Press.

Freud, S. (1907). The analysis of a phobia in a four-year-old boy. *Standard Edition* 10:5–187.

Gabbard, G. (1990). *Psychodynamic Psychiatry in Clinical Practice*. Washington, DC: American Psychoanalytic Press.

Ho, R. (1987). *Family Therapy with Ethnic Minorities*. Newbury Park, CA: Sage.

Hollander, E., and Simeon, D. (2003). *Concise Guide to Anxiety Disorders*. Washington DC: APA Press.

Jenike, M. (1990). Approaches to the patient with treatment refractory obsessive compulsive disorder. *Journal of Clinical Psychiatry* 51(2):15–21.

Neal-Barnett, A. M., and Smith, J., Sr. (1997). African Americans. In *Cultural Issues in the Treatment of Anxiety*, ed. S. Friedman. New York: Guilford Press.

PDM Task Force (2006). *Psychodynamic Diagnostic Manual*. Silver Spring, MD: Alliance of Psychoanalytic Organizations.

Sadock, B. J., and Kaplan, V. A. (2004). *Concise Textbook of Clinical Psychiatry*, 2nd edition. New York: Lippincott, Williams, and Welkins.

Salzman, L. (1980). *Treatment of the Obsessive Personality*. New York: Jason Aronson.

Schore, A. N. (2000). Attachment and the regulation of the right brain. *Attachment and Human Development* 2(1):23–47.

Tsuang, M. T., and Tohan, M., eds. (2002). *Textbook in Psychiatric Epidemiology*. New York: Wiley-Liss.

Tyree, P. (1999). *Anxiety: A Multidisciplinary Review*. London: Imperial College Press.

Wilson, G. T., Nation, P. E., O'Leary, K. D., and Clark, L. A. (1995). *Abnormal Psychology: Integrating Perspectives*. New York: Lippincott and Welkins.

17

Trauma Theories

Kathryn Basham

Throughout history, traumatic events brought about by natural disasters and by interpersonal violence have plagued human beings. Relational violence between individuals and within families and communities persists, while unresolved political, economic, and religious conflicts fuel terrorism and warfare across the globe. Given global environmental shifts in the last few decades, a record number of devastating natural disasters have occurred. In fact, violent hurricanes, catastrophic earthquakes, flooding, and destructive tsunamis have wreaked havoc throughout the continents. Overall, the cost in human life and suffering has been massive. Although many individuals cope with these dire circumstances without suffering long-term negative effects, others respond with a range of mental and physical health problems in response.

Denial of both the enormity and reality of traumatic events further distorts our understanding of trauma. As one adult Holocaust survivor said: "Remembering and acknowledging the horrors of a mass genocide are totally unbearable and unthinkable. . . . and so one stops thinking about the realities of the events and they cease to exist in our minds." In fact, we frequently hear explanations and rationalizations about traumatic events that minimize or negate the reality of relational violence. Often victims are blamed for their own victimization. A form of cultural denial supported by racism and bigotry further contributes to our distancing from traumatic events. An example of this cultural denial of trauma occurred during the aftermath of Hurricane Katrina, which struck the Gulf Coast of the United States in September 2005. Immediately following the disaster, many individuals were stunned by the glacially slow pace of the government's response to provide aid, primarily to economically challenged African American citizens and their families. As denial and inaction persisted, the issue of racism surfaced as a likely basis for the massive neglect of traumatized citizens, already marginalized in our society. Although there is a strong pull to deny these horrific events, we must continually be mindful of the profound impact imposed on these traumatized individuals, especially those additionally burdened by poverty, ill health, and a stigmatized social identity.

This chapter will address the biopsychosocial contexts for our understanding of trauma, the wide range of responses to traumatic events, and the central role of resilience in aiding individuals as they cope with these events. We will explore some of the psychological challenges that arise as a result of traumatic experiences. We will examine the cultural relativity of diagnosis, the neurobiology of the "traumatic stress" response, and the connections with leading-edge research in infant development, attachment, and trauma. We will review how the psychodynamic theories we have studied help us understand trauma-related interpersonal dynamics, both outside and within the treatment relationship. The effects of practice with traumatized individuals will also be discussed, including how the clinician may experience secondary trauma, vicarious traumatization, and transference/countertransference phenomena in the therapeutic work. Finally, implications for practice will be addressed.

HISTORICAL CONTEXT

Our understanding of trauma has changed dramatically over the years, often depending on the social forces that support or discourage an acknowledgment of the impact on individuals, families, and communities. Freud (1905b) grounded his theorizing, early on, in the strong belief that symptoms of hysteria were caused by internal intrapsychic conflicts between traumatic events that were out of consciousness and feelings that remained conscious, but that were not integrated with the trauma. In contrast, Breuer (1893), a contemporary of Freud, maintained that hysterics entered a "hybrid" state, experiencing two states of consciousness following a traumatic event. Breuer understood that his patients dissociated in response to trauma, while Freud thought that patients experienced intrapsychic conflict. An important shift in psychodynamic theory occurred when Freud (1905a) developed his theory of oedipal conflict and abandoned his earlier seduction theory of neurosis (see chapter 2). Freud asserted that the narratives heard from patients regarding sexual abuse were likely based on fantasy and wishes, rather than actual child maltreatment. As a result, the recognition of the pernicious effects of real childhood sexual abuse was then replaced with the notion that children "fantasize" experiences of sexual abuse. To this day, similar denial of childhood sexual abuse exists strongly embodied in part in the "false memory movement" that questions the validity of many allegations of sexual abuse (Loftus 1993, Loftus, Polonsky, and Fullilove 1994).

Societal responses have also been subdued, if not absent, in response to combat survivors. From as early as ancient times, accounts have revealed how war-related stress symptoms impair daily life. For example, descriptions of the physical and psychological plights of warriors are vividly depicted in Homer's *Iliad* (Shay 1994). Historical medical literature clearly documents post-combat distress starting with the Civil War when soldiers described disrupted sleep, heart palpitations, and breathlessness, an enigmatic syndrome that was consequently called "irritable heart" (or the Da Costa syndrome). In the early 1920s, World War I veterans suffered "shell shock" characterized by mutism, amnesia, and blindness. Originally thought to be caused by concussions inflicted by the force of deafening sounds from exploding shells, this syndrome was later associated with psychological origins.

Following World War II, veterans reported re-experiencing their traumatic combat-related events through intense symptoms of hyperarousal, through an acute syndrome referred to as "battle fatigue," or through "combat exhaustion." A persistent and chronic form of battle fatigue was further documented long after World War II had ended (Friedman and Marsalla 1996). However, interest in the biological underpinning for traumatic stress seemed to wane during this post-war time period. After clinicians listened to the narratives of Holocaust survivors and then treated thousands of male and female veterans of the Vietnam War, the mental health community recognized the clear existence of post-traumatic stress disorder (PTSD) as a psychological syndrome. Finally, in 1980, the American Psychiatric Association officially included this disorder in the *DSM-III*. The public recognition of an actual trauma-related diagnosis helped many veterans to affirm the "realness" of their suffering following deployment. Similar legitimacy was also attached to the presenting concerns of Holocaust survivors and their families, and to survivors of childhood sexual abuse, physical abuse, emotional abuse, domestic violence, and other natural and man-made traumatic events.

In summary, several sociopolitical forces led to critical shifts in heightening public awareness of trauma during the 1960s and early 1970s. In particular, the emergence of the "feminist revolution" in the United States ensured advocacy and protection for survivors of domestic violence, rape, and childhood abuses. These influential events confirmed the harsh realities of wartime trauma, both on a national and international scale, as well as within the internal domestic war zones of families and communities, plagued by relational violence.

DEFINITIONS/NOSOLOGY OF TRAUMA

So many traumatic events have disturbed and overwhelmed children, adolescents, and adults throughout the world. Whether a natural disaster (like an earthquake or hurricane) or relational trauma, such as childhood sexual abuse, these events are generally viewed as horrific. However, the ways that people respond to these events vary considerably depending upon other moderating factors, including resilience. Constitutional "hardiness," sociocultural factors, family and community support, and preparation/education regarding trauma-related effects may all mediate trauma (Bartone 1999). All of these factors provide a buffer against the emergence of PTSD symptomatology or other negative aftereffects.

Defining Trauma

What do we mean by trauma? In everyday usage, the word *trauma* is often used incorrectly as a synonym for stress. Stress is typically triggered by a stressor that may range along a continuum of intensity from mild to moderate to severe. Trauma refers to an event or an experience that involves the imposition of severe (or traumatic) stressors.

In the *DSM-IV-TR* (2000), trauma is defined in the context of PTSD. In order to qualify for this diagnosis, a person must have been exposed to "a traumatic event in which both of the following are present: (1) the person experienced, witnessed, or was confronted with an event or events that involved actual or threatened death or serious injury, or a threat to the physical integrity of self or others; and (2) the person's response involved intense fear, helplessness or horror" (pp. 427–28).

This definition focuses narrowly on an actual or threatened death or physical injury and a threat to physical integrity. Many of our clients, though, have suffered severe neglect, terrifying separations, abandonment, and/or emotional abuse that do not involve an actual direct threat to physical integrity. In such situations, a person may face experiences that pose a basic threat to the integrity of the psychological self. Attachment theorists suggest that such maltreatment qualifies as traumatic, also leading to experiences of terror, powerlessness, unpredictability, and uncontrollability (Allen 2001). Although these presenting issues might not meet all of the criteria for a diagnosis of PTSD, we need to be mindful of the potentially destructive traumatic effects of such harmful behavior.

> For example, when four-year-old Arlene is showered alternately with random affection and adulation, followed precipitously by a screaming harangue about her "stupidity," she feels confused and overwhelmed by the harsh contradictory messages. In fact, this unpredictable, uncontrollable treatment trauma-

tizes her. On a symbolic level, Arlene feels terrified for her safety and sinks into an abyss of fear and insecurity.

Figley (1988, 1995) offers a definition of trauma that is particularly useful to clinicians. He refers to trauma as an emotional state of discomfort and stress resulting from memories of an extraordinary, catastrophic experience that shatters the survivor's sense of invulnerability to harm, rendering him acutely vulnerable to stressors. With a slightly different slant, Herman (1992) concludes that trauma overwhelms an ordinary system of care that gives people a sense of control, connection, and meaning in the world.

Clearly, we need to make a distinction between events that are traumatic (i.e., represent a threat to physical integrity along with intense fear, helplessness, and horror) and the trauma response. This "traumic stress response" involves a set of neurobiological reactions (an "allostatic overload") along with an affective experience of terror and powerlessness (McEwen 1999) which is described later in the chapter. Not all people react to a horrific event in the same way. Some respond to traumatic stressors with a temporary traumic stress response. Others respond to traumatic stressors with long-term negative effects. For example, ten persons who live on the same block of a neighborhood subjected to the terror of a catastrophic earthquake will have ten different responses to this traumatic event.

In order to understand the range responses to trauma, Lenore Terr (1999) proposes a typology that explicates the nature of certain traumatic events, including natural disasters along with man-made tragedies. She calls these Type I and Type II traumas. Type I trauma refers to a single discrete horrific event of catastrophic proportion. These events include: (1) natural disasters, such as hurricanes, earthquakes, flooding, and fires; (2) violent acts, including rape, assault, robbery, shooting, school shootings, suicide bombings, and carjacking; (3) witnessing injury or death, killing, handling body parts, and dangerous patrol duty during combat; (4) accidents and diagnoses of life-threatening illnesses; and (5) losses of family, friends, property, community, cultural traditions, and/or primary language associated with refugee or immigrant status.

We can see how Natya exhibited many psychological symptoms in the face of several Type I traumatic events:

After fleeing a camp for displaced persons in Bosnia, Natya, age thirty-one, started to meet with a clinical social worker at a health care setting in an urban Northeastern American city. She complained of nightmares, acute anxiety, "shakiness," hypervigilance, and bouts of weeping, countered by feelings of "deadness" and inertia. While escaping from her war-torn village, Natya and her sisters were raped and her father was brutally murdered. Following these horrors, a neighbor helped Natya to travel twenty miles by foot to reach her temporary refuge—the resettlement camp. Without an opportunity to actually grieve these many losses, Natya secured adequate food, shelter, medical care, and eventual passage to the United States. Upon arrival in the United States, her previously high functioning (albeit detached and dissociated) was replaced by severe hyperarousal symptoms and an acute re-experiencing of her traumatic events.

The traumatic rape and witnessing of the deaths of her father and neighbors were compounded by many devastating losses of her family, primary language, sense of home and community, and the integrity of physical/psychological self. Since sharing personal feelings with a stranger was an anathema in her family of origin, Natya only slowly described her feelings about this transition. Although tentative, Natya gradually started to trust her therapist, who had the added advantage of speaking her native language. The provision of safety, stabilization, and self-care at this point in time was necessary. A full range of supports were extended to Natya, including assistance with housing, health care, vocational counseling, language training, and mental health counseling. For relief from very intense trauma-related physical symptoms, Natya engaged in biofeedback, cognitive behavioral techniques, and Eye Movement Desensitization Reprocessing (EMDR). Slowly, she began to recover within the context of a nurturing, culturally responsive therapy. According to a Winnicottian object relations therapy perspective, a reparative "holding environment" provided a sanctuary for this young woman as she learned to re-connect with people and empower herself to adapt as best as possible to her new life. (Winnicott 1958, 1965)

In contrast to the singularity of Type I trauma, Type II trauma refers to the chronic repetitive abuses experienced by children as they grow up. More specifically, children who have been repeatedly subjected to physical, emotional, and/or sexual abuse endure what is considered Type II trauma. Similarly, adult victims of domestic violence suffer the entrapment of Type II traumatic abuses. Thus, the persistence and chronicity of recurrent maltreatment differentiates Type I trauma from other types of traumatic events. A clinical example illuminates this chronic, repetitive (Type II) traumatic experience.

Jeannie, age forty-one, originally reared in a poor, rural town, presented in therapy with fears of overdosing on barbiturates once again. Concerns with "constant edginess," "despair," "isolation," frequent nightmares, and alienation from her two children plagued her continually. Although she had been hospitalized and stabilized, Jeannie worried about the constant verbal arguments that she experienced with her husband, Johnnie, a Vietnam veteran. As a child, severe physical abuse under the guise of corporal punishment was meted out by her parents to her and her five siblings. Between the ages of seven and twelve, she was sexually abused on a continuous basis by her stepfather. By the time she entered high school, Jeannie was ingesting opiates, barbiturates, and alcohol regularly, had cut her upper arms to "remind herself that she was real," and had abandoned her self-care by binging and purging. And so, by the age of thirty-six, when she met Johnnie in the emergency room of a hospital, she had survived childhood physical and sexual abuses, rape by a stranger, and a gunshot wound to her head inflicted during a soured drug deal. Clearly, the cumulative effects of these Type II traumatic events devastated Jeannie's sense of well-being as well as her functioning in the world.

Theorists have also described Type III trauma, related to the effects of violent torture. For example, hostages from wartime report how they survived continuous threats to their survival through a wide range of ways of coping (Kira 2002). Faced with continuous terrifying threats to his life, a POW who was imprisoned in a cage by the Viet Cong for three years described how he disciplined his mind through word puzzles and fantasy to cope with the enormity of his situation. Such coping allowed him a semblance of agency and the experience of control over his mind, if not his body or life choices.

In recent years, another form of traumatic experience has been proposed, which is described as "cultural trauma" or "racial trauma." Allen (1998) and Pouissant and Alexander (2000) assert that the day-to-day verbal (and, at times, physical) racist assaults inflicted on people of color perpetuate the legacies of slavery and colonization. They strongly assert that such racist attacks, or "microaggressions," should also qualify as chronic repetitive trauma in the same vein as Terr's (1999) Type II trauma. We can also think about the kind of trauma that ensues in the face of daily aggressive verbal and physical assaults hurled against persons who are marginalized by their ethnicity, religion, sexual orientation, or disability.

This form of cultural trauma can be seen in Pahir's story:

A twenty-four-year-old partially blind East Indian-American graduate student, Pahir, described his early childhood years as dominated by continuous teasing and bullying by other children. He recalled an incident, at age seven, when his classmates taunted him at recess. While he was floundering to master baseball, several classmates screamed to him that a bee had landed on his head. They yelled: "Why can't you see it? It will kill you! Aren't there any bees where you came from? Why don't you go back home where you belong?" Pahir was terrified and tried to brush off the invisible bee, while his classmates surrounded him, laughing uproariously. They reveled in his humiliation.

While Pahir lived through this one frightening and shaming incident without emotional scarring, similar situations were repeated continuously throughout grade school and high school as he navigated his way through hostile territory. Regular harassment about Pahir's blindness, his East Indian ethnicity, Muslim religious beliefs, and dark-brown skin color fueled ongoing racist and bigoted remarks from his fellow students. Such mean-spirited treatment functioned in the same coercive ways as Type II cumulative trauma.

On a larger scale, genocide and wartime conflicts are forms of collective trauma (i.e., a form of societally sanctioned violence and destruction). For example, massive psychic traumatization has affected the survivors of contemporary genocide in Bosnia, Rwanda, and Uganda, in the Holocaust, the internment of Japanese Americans during World War II, and the disenfranchisement and colonization of First Nations peoples in the Americas.

Another distinction drawn frequently is between impersonal trauma (i.e., natural disasters) vs. relational or interpersonal trauma (i.e., childhood abuses, domestic violence, criminal assaults, rape, sexual harassment, combat, and other forms of political violence). Some theorists suggest that relational trauma involves the added devastation of a violation inflicted by another person (Allen 2001). For example, a serious car crash may be devastating to those involved, yet an auto accident caused by a drunk driver adds an interpersonal component of intention that stirs feelings of betrayal. Similar experiences of distrust and betrayal are also central in the psychological life of children who have been neglected and abused. We will look at the impact of this form of trauma when we explore the interpersonal consequences of early childhood trauma (Allen 2001, Schore 2003a, 2003b).

RESPONSES TO TRAUMATIC EVENTS

Many individuals who have coped with traumatic events approach their lives with optimism and sound functioning. However, other trauma survivors experience difficulties in developing attachments and managing work responsibilities, while still others develop full-blown neuropsychological symptoms and psychiatric disorders. We will now address the role of resilience in coping with adverse traumatic stressors, as well as explore the role of risk factors and the protective factors that guard against mental and physical health problems. We will then explore a range of responses to traumatic stressors including post-traumatic stress disorder (PTSD), acute stress disorder, and complex post-traumatic stress disorder.

Resilience and Coping

As noted earlier, many individuals respond to catastrophic events without developing long-range negative after-effects. We can learn a great deal about adaptation and survival from these resilient individuals. The question arises as to what is the basis for resilience? What are the protective factors that guard against developing psychopathology? What are the factors during traumatic exposure that support coping? Rutter (1993) talks about constitutional factors that predispose some persons toward resilience, including strong physical health, sound mental health, and innate intelligence. Let us consider Maria and Pablo, who demonstrates noteworthy resilience:

A forty-five-year-old married Latina mother of three children, Maria Sanchez, entered family therapy with her forty-six-year-old husband, Pablo Sanchez. The parents wanted to address the rebellious behavior of their two older adolescent children. In the course of the biopsychosocial assessment, Maria reported that, at age nine, she was abducted by political insurgents in war-torn El Salvador. She and her mother were held captive for several years during which she survived severe physical torture and rape. After her father was murdered in a detention camp, Maria and her mother fled to Mexico. Pablo, who described his family as "bourgeois-elite," escaped to Mexico after pursuit by insurrectionists. Maria also revealed a harrowing retreat to her new "home" country where she subsequently rejoiced in her memories of a happy and fulfilling adolescence. She and Pablo met after graduating from high school and decided to marry. One year later, they gave birth to their first child after moving to the United States.

Neither partner discussed their childhood experiences of torture or their other prior traumatic life experiences. Interestingly, neither Pablo nor Maria exhibited any symptomatology of PTSD or other mental health issues resulting from their previous life events. Both Pablo and Maria had learned to suppress emotions related to their childhood horrors and sublimate their energies into creating a new family. Fortified by a cultural prohibition against expressing strong emotions, Maria and Pablo, instead, reflected on how their trauma legacies affected their daily lives on a cognitive, rather than an emotional, level. They started to recognize how their disowned, projected, trauma-related anger was acted out by both of their adolescent children. As they reflected on their earlier traumatic experiences, they were able to reclaim and own their projected affect. Fortified by support from their family and religious faith, this couple demonstrated a determination to foster healthier and happier lives for their children and extended family.

Current research literature addressing combat stress focuses on "hardiness," defined as a positive, optimistic outlook, a belief in the purposefulness of one's actions, an "esprit de corps," and a hopeful outlook toward the future (Bartone 1999). This worldview combined with a sound constitution may serve soldiers very well in combat. Other factors that aid active-duty soldiers include emotional support from family members and friends, a hospitable and respectful welcome from their communities of origin following a return from combat, and substantial education about trauma-related effects.

Not surprisingly, certain sociocultural factors can also serve as moderating or mediating factors in developing stress disorders. For example, class and race served as mediating factors that increased PTSD for Vietnam veterans (Kulka et al. 1990). During the war, many draftees of color were assigned the most horrific duties and subjected to discrimination from officers as well as from fellow soldiers (Green et al. 1990). Further, they often experienced ethical dilemmas in killing Vietnamese citizens, especially when they believed that the war was unjust. Respectful and consistent leadership can provide salutary effects for soldiers in combat; without this clearheaded vision and adequate training, many soldiers experience enhanced vulnerability and powerlessness, dangerous ingredients for the development of PTSD. If we think that trauma shatters a sense of meaning, purpose, and security, then traumatic experiences will increase when wars are waged for ambiguous reasons.

Mental Health Responses

Post-Traumatic Stress Disorder

Although a relatively recent addition to the *DSM*, post-traumatic stress disorder is a syndrome frequently encountered in clinical settings. Post-traumatic stress disorder, or PTSD, is a psychiatric disorder that occurs following life-threatening events such as natural disasters, serious accidents, violent assaults, abuse, terrorist attacks, and wartime combat. Although individuals with PTSD experience nightmares, flashbacks, sleep problems, agitation, detachment, and numbness, these symptoms are not uncommon during an early adjustment to a traumatic event. In general, seven major factors determine the likelihood that an individual will develop post-traumatic stress disorder following traumatization. They are: (1) a higher degree and intensity of exposure to violence; (2) a higher degree of physical violation; (3) longer duration and greater frequency of abuse; (4) more heightened sense of unpredictability and uncontrollability; (5) a closer, familial relationship with the offender; (6) younger age; and (7) an unsupportive social environment that inflicts stigma, shame, and guilt. Although the research literature points to the intensity of exposure as the most influential factor in mediating the emergence of PTSD, there is a wide range of risk and protective factors that also influence how well an individual and family adapt to the traumatic event (Basham and Miehls 2004; Kessler, Sonnega, Bromet, Hughes, Nelson, and Breslau 1999). When these symptoms occur for a short duration (up to one month), they are classified as an "acute stress disorder." In contrast, PTSD can only be fully assessed as chronic after one month following the traumatic incident, although many individuals present with a delayed onset of symptoms as well. Although the PTSD diagnosis arose in response to the needs of war veterans, the syndrome occurs in a much broader population of men and women, children, and adolescents who have been reared in Western and non-Western cultures and diverse socioeconomic strata.

Research data support a strong link between PTSD and depression and substance abuse and addictions (Southwick et al. 1994). Traumatized individuals may also develop other anxiety disorders, such as panic disorder, phobias, and generalized anxiety disorder. Given this complexity, we must be rigorous in our assessments of these disorders to ensure that a correct diagnosis is completed. Only then is it possible to craft a useful, multi-layered treatment plan that addresses all issues involved. We cannot underscore sufficiently how important it is to explore the possibilities of these other conditions, especially depression and addictions (see chapter 16 on anxiety disorders). The following clinical vignette provides an example of how an Iraqi veteran struggles with PTSD:

Abdul Pakteri, a forty-one-year-old, second-generation Iraqi American, has been working for fifteen years as an accountant in a Midwestern bank while rearing his three children with his wife, Ella, an African American occupational therapist. During this time period, Abdul also participated in an army reserve unit, finding the milieu both supportive and non-discriminatory. During his first tour in Iraq, Abdul believed that the search for weapons of mass destruction and the overthrow of Saddam Hussein proved to be just and fair reasons for war. In the first month, he witnessed the killing of two of his "buddies" during a random explosive attack of an I.E.D. (improvised explosive device). Even so, he survived his six-month tour of duty without suffering any physical injuries or mental health problems.

Eight months later, when he was deployed once again to Iraq, he found himself working with a reconnaissance unit that was investigating homes to "ferret out" terrorist insurgents. One day, his unit mistakenly opened fire on a home occupied by four adult women and six children ranging in ages from about three months to ten years. Four of the children were killed during the raid, while the other children and women were wounded. To this day, even with treatment that included debriefing, cognitive-behavioral therapy, and EMDR (Eye Movement Desensitization Reprocessing) methods (Shapiro and Maxfield 2003), Abdul is still haunted by visual and olfactory images of these terrified Iraqi women and children. From that point onward, his faith in the justness of the war was shattered and he experienced a stronger commonality and kindred feeling with the Iraqi citizens, who spoke his maternal language. Rather than seeing these persons as the enemy, he empathized with their terror. Without intensive pre-combat training, without a strong esprit de corps among his fellow soldiers, and lacking immediate treatment in the field, Abdul struggled to complete his tour of duty. Three months after his return home, he experienced haunting nightmares, regular flashbacks, erratic moods, irritability, and a persistent startle response—all symptoms pointing to full-blown PTSD.

As a reservist, Abdul was less prepared and less well trained than his fellow soldiers from other branches of the Armed Forces. He experienced no on-site treatment interventions for mental health concerns and few social supports during his tour in Iraq. Finally, his traumatic exposure to the killing and maiming of children and women shattered his belief system. These combined factors eroded Abdul's resilience and led to the emergence of PTSD.

At this point in time, the full impact on the mental and physical health of returning soldiers and their families serving in Iraq and Afghanistan remains to be seen, but the current rates of PTSD are reported to be quite high. In fact, one in three soldiers and Marines who served in Iraq sought mental health services as reported in a recent study published by the U.S. Army in March 2006 (Hoge et al. 2006).

Cultural Relativity of Diagnosis

PTSD, as a diagnosis, has been critiqued for its relevance cross-culturally. Several researchers have concluded that the neurobiology of trauma-related responses is universal. What happens to the body in trauma is that an individual experiences an increase in blood pressure, an increase in perspiration, and a racing heart, all the while alternately feeling numb or excited. Different cultures attach different meanings to both the traumatic events and to their physical and psychological responses. In Western cultures, there is often a fight-flight response, while in some Latino families, a response to traumatic stress involves a "pause-collect" reaction. On the one hand, an individual responds to the neurophysiological stress state by seeking out loved ones to protect, rather than fleeing or fighting. The experience of collecting oneself may relate to the numbing or stillness effect that looks like flight in another individual. The end goal here might be to care for and protect vulnerable children and elders, rather than switching into a "fight-flight" mode. In other words, behaviors and reactions associated with PTSD are culturally determined (Friedman and Marsalla 1996, de Jong et al. 2005).

Yoki offers a glimpse into the cultural issues in trauma. Attention to spirituality provided important clues related to this client's presenting concerns.

Yoki, a twenty-eight-year-old Cambodian immigrant who suffered sexual and physical abuse from ages ten to thirteen, reported experiences of seeing ghosts, difficulty sleeping, and nightmares of being killed following her rape by a stranger. In therapy with a culturally responsive clinician, she was able to discuss her fears, yet felt comforted by the "ghosts of her ancestors," who were protecting her. She also benefited from acupuncture to help her with her migraine headaches and generalized anxiety.

From a Western mental health perspective, we need to be careful to avoid pathologizing the nature of the ghosts, since they function as culturally adaptive supports rather than maladaptive hallucinations. In this situation, we observe some PTSD symptomatology along with the understanding that Yoki's "ghosts" are culturally syntonic.

Although chronic PTSD often interferes with all aspects of a person's life, some treatment interventions have been helpful. They include: (1) relationship-based psychodynamic individual therapy, (2) psychopharmacology with SSRI medication and new innovations with an experimental beta-blocker, (3) cognitive-behavioral therapy, (4) eye movement desensitization re-processing (EMDR), (4) group therapy, and (5) couple and family therapy. Traumatized individuals and communities who have been subjected to armed conflict, torture, and warfare in non-Western nations have often found healing approaches that draw upon indigenous storytelling, dance, spiritual rituals, and community building to alleviate trauma-related suffering. Each of these modalities has been helpful, differentially, in remediating symptoms, strengthening connections, and enhancing overall work and social functioning.

Complex Post-Traumatic Syndrome (Complex PTSD)

When an infant or young child is traumatized by neglect or abuse, she may develop problems with establishing basic trust, a cohesive identity, and a capacity for secure attachment. Since ordinary developmental tasks are often disrupted following a traumatic experience, clinicians must rigorously explore how these overwhelming events may have influenced various developmental achievements. Although an Eriksonian life-cycle model is limited by the linearity of the developmental progressions and the absence of an adequate sociocultural context, it can still be useful (Erikson 1980). There is wisdom in exploring the effects of an infant's developing trust or mistrust when traumatized; a toddler's capacity to assert confident autonomy, rather than experiencing self-hating shame; a young child's capacity to express curiosity and initiative, rather than suffer strong guilt based on perceived wrongdoings; or a latency-age child's excitement with mastery and industry rather than retreat into a paralyzing withdrawal. Many resilient children manage to grow up mastering these various developmental challenges while also weathering significant traumatic events. However, many children are not as fortunate.

Without sufficient relationships that repair trauma and/or treatment that intervenes, these children often grow up to develop complex post-traumatic syndrome (otherwise know as DESNOS—disorder of extreme stress not otherwise specified) (Goodwin 1990, Herman 1992). This diagnosis tells the clinician that identity formation may be compromised and that dissociation will likely be used to cope. The symptom clusters associated with complex post-traumatic syndrome (i.e., re-experiencing, numbness, and hyperarousal) combine with three other important factors. They include: (1) a full range of somatic, psychological, and emotional symptoms; (2) re-enacting of traumatic relationships in the present; and (3) distorting identity and diminished self-esteem.

> For example, Jeannie, who was introduced earlier, suffered migraines, colitis, severe asthma, generalized anxiety, panic disorder, self-harming, and suicidal behavior. All of these conditions were trauma-related. Throughout her adult life, Jeannie also found herself in consecutive destructive relationships. After escaping from a physically abusive relationship with an addicted partner, she gravitated, only two years later, to an emotionally abusive relationship with Johnnie. Although adult trauma survivors often seek the familiar attachment of the early victimizer in their adult relationships, they are often unaware that they are preserving some idealization of the original offender by replicating the trauma scenario. We must be vigilant, however, to avoid blaming victims during these traumatic re-enactments, and must hold any emotionally or physically violent offender responsible for his actions.

THE IMPACT OF RELATIONAL TRAUMA

We want to trust our caregivers but their acts may cause betrayal and distrust. Subsequently, in adulthood, people who have been traumatized engage in power and control conflicts, while frequently remaining attached to their victimizers. They may use distance and dissociate interpersonally. They may have problems with boundaries and have trouble communicating. For clinicians, this work may also be traumatizing. Often we see the clinician experience a rupture of boundaries, difficulties healing, and dissociation and distancing as ways of coping with traumatic narratives. We will describe these relational patterns in more depth.

"Victim-Victimizer-Bystander" Dynamic

Trauma survivors have typically experienced victimization at the hands of someone who has hurt them. Usually a bystander has been present who has either failed to help or has remained detached or uninvolved. Occasionally, someone has intervened to rescue the victim and/or interrupt the abuse. These ways of relating predispose a trauma survivor to relate to other people within this trauma scenario. Not only does this pattern appear in day-to-day life in interactions with other people, but trauma survivors internalize this "victim-victimizer-bystander" relationship template, which guides their vision of the world (Herman 1992, Staub 1989).

From an object relations perspective, our traumatized clients often experience internal conflict surrounding this relationship template, they project the outward feelings that are associated with this scenario (through a process of projective identification). In relationships, a person may shift between the roles of victimizer, victim, or bystander. Other people at times are experienced as victimizers (even when there is no apparent objective reality), and in response to a hurtful remark, a trauma survivor may experience augmented anger and victimization. In a relationship, each person may shift back and forth with alternating one-up or one-down power positions. Polarizations in affect, thought, and behavior emerge as they argue about who is right or wrong, or good or bad.

> A clinical example of this "victim-victimizer-bystander" paradigm occurred early on in family therapy with Rod and Yolanda, a dual-trauma African American couple. They engaged in bitter, destructive verbal battles characterized by alternating roles as the victim, victimizer, and bystander. They disrespected and mistreated each other in destructive ways, yet denied the damaging effects of their victimizing behaviors. Each of them could readily express their feelings of victimization, while neither partner experienced anyone in their lives as an especially helpful bystander. During the course of their family therapy, both partners moved toward addressing multiple oppressions related to their childhood abuses and racialized maltreatment. They gradually recognized the compounding effects of abuses of power within their intimate relationship that were also mirrored by societal bigotries and by abusive relating in their respective families of origin.

Power and Control Conflicts

Trauma survivors often engage in battles for power and control in relationships. Once again the alternating "victim-victimizer-bystander" pattern sets the stage for such struggles. Attempts to dominate or subjugate the will of the other person characterize unrelenting conflicts about who will gain power in any number of arenas. For example, at the height of the intense fighting between Rod and Yolanda, they battled regularly about who was the better caregiver, parent, or financial manager.

Attachment to the Victimizer

Let us start with a question that baffles many of us: Why do so many trauma survivors maintain an attachment with their abusers? When a child has been actively hurt and mistreated by a parent, she frequently sustains a strong attachment to the abusive parent. Especially in the case of chronic repetitive (Type II) abuses, traumatized children or adults often assume responsibility for the abuse and blame themselves. In order to hold on to an internalized image (or in object relations terms, an introject) of the offending caretaker, they often blame and hate themselves for the abuse so that they can maintain an idealized tie to their offender. The British object relations theorist, Fairbairn (1952a, b) refers to this internalized object as the "internal saboteur" that undermines healthy growth. In addition to the ambivalent tie that many trauma survivors maintain with their offenders, they may also reenact the trauma scenario by gravitating to an intimate adult partner who is abusive. In speaking about re-enactments, we must be very cautious to recognize this pattern of "traumatic bonding," yet clearly hold an offender exclusively responsible for any violent or abusive behavior. Although a continuing attachment to the victimizer perniciously motivates many destructive re-enactments, we must also vigilantly avoid blaming the victim.

Ellen, a twenty-eight-year-old health care professional, gravitated to a sixty-five-year-old male partner, Ed, who provided for her financial and emotional security. However, after three years of marriage, Ellen felt tyrannized and entrapped when Ed questioned all of her outside friendships, preferring to be the sole focus of her existence. She found herself distancing from all social contacts, feeling despondent, and fantasizing about escape. In therapy, she was shocked to recognize that she had metaphorically "married" her very fragile mother, who had battled both a major mental illness and a life-threatening cancer during her lifetime. Ellen had nursed her mother until her death several years before, ignoring the abusive physical outbursts leveled by her mother during her unmedicated manic states. Ellen sought the security of a familiar, albeit possessive and tyrannizing attachment, which also provided some sustaining nurturance.

Distancing and Dissociation

When a child has been mistreated, she may retreat from the person and situation, setting the stage for a pattern of distancing and withdrawal. After the child grows up, she may well experience persistent distrust and heightened wariness toward other people. Withdrawal from a threatening person serves to protect a traumatized child, adolescent, or adult from further hurtful interactions.

For example, Jane, a second-generation Finnish-American who survived childhood sexual abuse, immerses herself in homebuilding, finding very little time for conversation with her lesbian partner, Maria. As a survivor of childhood sexual abuse, Maria, who was reared in Argentina, maintains distance by providing overly zealous caretaking for relatives and friends, taking her away from home and her partner. Although each partner expressed extreme withdrawal from the other, culturally based explanations were offered. Although their different ethnic backgrounds were significant in shaping attitudes about a "we" vs. an "I" self, and valuing extended family, a sociocultural explanation alone could not fully clarify these augmented trauma-related distancing responses.

Dissociation, as an adaptive defense mechanism, has been observed frequently in clients who have suffered traumatic experiences either in childhood or during their adult years. In the field of traumatology, considerable attention has been paid to understanding the function of dissociation as well as the most helpful clinical interventions that minimize reliance on this adaptation (Briere 1996; Cohen et al. 1995, Courtois 1999, Kluft 1995). Dissociation involves the key features of detachment and compartmentalization, operating on a continuum from mild to severe processes. Clients who have suffered especially brutal childhood abuses often demonstrate the most extreme dissociative responses, resulting in dissociative identity disorder (DID). Evidence of dissociation is often apparent in memory lapses and an experience of internal fragmentation. For example, gaps in memory may last for several seconds to several hours. Providing an example of a common occurrence of dissociation helps people understand the process of dissociation. Most people can identify with a situation that has been terrifying, like a car accident, where a victim automatically detaches her emotion from the event. If you have witnessed an accident or the injury of another person, various questions surface. For example: Have you been aware of a full range of feelings? Have you ever experienced numbness? Have you retained or forgotten the details of this event? Rather than viewing memory lapses related to dissociation as deficiencies, we should regard them as adaptive coping. When dissociation occurs regularly, aspects (or parts) of one's self-structure may be undermined. As a result, the client may experience tremendous internal chaos or mental clutter when memory and feelings are split off.

Boundary Ruptures

Boundary ruptures are common among trauma survivors. A traumatized individual may intrude upon the privacy of another person or may experience another person as intrusive or violating. She may also express the other extreme in attempting to maintain clear and flexible boundaries by disengaging.

A middle-aged, dual-trauma, Eastern European Jewish couple, Rebecca and Harry, struggle with such difficulties in establishing flexible boundaries with each other. As both partners wrestled with depression and intergenerational legacies of the Holocaust, they harnessed their impressive resilience to negotiate a workable balance between connectedness and solitude. When this couple moved into their new home, they discovered no individual space for either of them. Ultimately, Rebecca asserted her desire for a private, isolated sanctuary. A tiny, converted closet became the safe place where she could retreat to read, reflect, and collect herself without feeling the invasiveness of her husband. Harry learned to respect her privacy and recognized a need for his own solitude as well.

Another example of a boundary rupture involved Rhonda, a female probation officer who had survived beatings and sexual abuse during her childhood. In a recent incident, she described her road rage. Rhonda had chased down a car that had driven too close to her while screaming loudly and clenching her fists wildly before careening to an abrupt halt. Having experienced this intrusion as a re-traumatizing boundary violation, she reacted with rage, terrifying her husband, who sat by speechlessly as an unsuspecting passenger.

Sexual Issues

Sexuality may be fraught with fearfulness around sensual and sexual touch. Trauma survivors often defend against emerging anxiety with the defenses of dissociation, repression, isolation of affect, and suppression, often leading to inhibition of sexual desire. At times, touching that is reminiscent of the earlier childhood trauma triggers an experience of re-traumatization, especially if a survivor has been sexually abused.

> Maria, a second-generation Italian-American trauma survivor, shrieked in distress whenever her male partner playfully surprised her. After learning that this teasing reminded her of earlier childhood violations when her father unexpectedly appeared in her bedroom, her partner subsequently understood her fears and no longer personalized her rebuff as rejection. As each partner developed more empathy toward the other, they were both able to gradually change their attitudes and behavior.

Often trauma survivors need to discover ways of relating sexually that do not trigger traumatic memories. At other times, traumatized individuals need to desensitize themselves to feelings of shame and guilt associated with their sexual feelings. For example, a heterosexual dual-trauma couple established verbal "rules" that provided each partner with predictability about which areas of their bodies were safe for sensual touching. Since each partner had experienced non-consensual, violating sexual acts as children, they both needed confirmation "with words" that neither partner felt coerced or intimidated before any sexual activity could ensue. Another common trauma-related pattern is hypersexuality, which one female trauma survivor described as a "compulsive driving pressure" that provides immediate physiological and psychological relief.

Communication Problems

When a person has been betrayed, threatened, or abandoned, she may experience difficulties with expressing ideas and feelings during adulthood as well. If a traumatized child was warned to suppress all feelings surrounding her abuse, or for that matter any other issue, she would learn to withhold her thoughts. A common motto expressed in abusive families is "no hear, no see, and no talk" (Basham and Miehls 2004, p. 146). Not only are there strong psychological directives to remain silent, the neurophysiological traumatic stress response also suppresses the Broca region of the brain, which regulates the expression of speech. This may lead to a profound shutdown in verbal expression. In contrast, trauma survivors may also yell, berate, and denigrate each other in a relational pattern that mirrors the "victim-victimizer-bystander" scenario.

Cultural influences may shape the ways that trauma survivors communicate their thoughts and feelings. For example, a second-generation Japanese American client, Nokai, expressed deep sadness and regret that she could no longer see or talk with her parents, who were now deceased. Captives during World War II in an internment camp in New Mexico, they had never discussed their experiences of torture and isolation suffered during their incarceration, since the cultural expectation was to bear the suffering without using words. As an adult, Nokai suffered inexplicable symptoms of clinical depression, which eventually improved with a combination of non-Western and Western therapeutic approaches. As she learned how she carried the unexpressed projected grief and traumatic loss disowned by her parents and extended family members, she discovered a renewal of spirit. Although her Japanese cultural traditions promoted the restraint of expression, Nokai's bi culturality encourgaged more direct modes of communicating her emotions.

Dearth of Rituals

Finally, a paucity of rituals surfaces as another important relational pattern. When children are abused physically, sexually, or emotionally, they live amid violence and disorganization. A very strong correlation between substance abuse and addictions with childhood trauma sets the stage for incendiary toxic family environments where celebratory or healing rituals are virtually destroyed or absent. Needless to say, when holidays arrive, family chaos often interferes with any ritual that might help a family celebrate meaningful connections with each other. For example, Elana, a middle-aged Polish Catholic trauma survivor, recalls that most Thanksgiving dinners were punctuated by some terrifying eruption of rage. In particular, she recalled that her abusive, alcoholic father threw the festive turkey across the dining room on more than one occasion. Only after recounting these terrifying memories of family gatherings could Elana's husband recognize why she rejected any formal celebrating of the holidays and religious traditions. As couples and families redefine healing rituals for themselves, they are also able to find new ways of honoring their important family connections.

PSYCHODYNAMIC THEORIES AND TRAUMA THEORY MODELS: A SYNTHESIS

Psychological and cognitive development may be undermined or derailed in response to traumatic events during childhood, adolescence, or adulthood. As each psychodynamic theory model focuses on different aspects of the legacies of trauma, each perspective must be synthesized with contemporary trauma theories to yield a more complex assessment. For example, drive theory addresses how trauma interferes with an adequate regulation of aggressive and sexual drives, or impulses, paying attention to the role of repression and unconscious conflicts in response to traumatic events. Ego psychology focuses on how effectively an individual copes and adapts to environmental and developmental challenges with subsequent emergence of a range of defenses in response to trauma-induced anxiety. Such defenses include dissociation and projective identification. From an object relations theoretical perspective, when a child has been abused, she faces a formidable dilemma. On the one hand, she may have to renounce her abusive parent in order to view her self as "good." On the other hand, she might maintain her connection with her parent, yet view herself as deserving of the abuse (perpetuating the notion of the internalized "bad" object). Finally, from a self-psychological perspective, interpersonal trauma may rupture empathic attunement between a child and her most important idealizing and/or mirroring selfobjects, those who provide life-preserving caregiving functions. Traumatic events may cause fragmentation and disintegration anxiety while interfering with the emergence of a cohesive "I" or "we" self. Clearly, traumatic events that occur during the first four to five years of life may have enduring effects that undermine the development of a cohesive sense of self, object constancy, and mature range of defenses. When a young child has received "good enough" caregiving (in a Winnicottian framework), she may then rely on these earlier developmental strengths and capacities to weather devastating events that occur in adolescence or adulthood.

NEUROBIOLOGY OF TRAUMA

Groundbreaking developments in the field of neurobiology, neuropsychology, and traumatology have challenged the mental health community to expand our knowledge base. Relying on positron emission topography (PET) and magnetic resonance imaging (MRI) data, direct associations have been established between relational and nonrelational trauma and effects on the human brain and body (Siegel 1999, van der Kolk et al. 2005). Since the aftereffects of trauma clearly influence an individual's neurobiological and neuropsychological status, I will draw attention briefly to the impact of trauma on an infant's developing health and mental health.

Affect Regulation, Trauma, and Infant Development

For infants, relational stressors are far more "detrimental" to child development than are non-relational assaults, such as an accidental fall (Schore 2000). The neurophysiological status of an infant is based on a combination of factors, including genetic, constitutional, environmental, and psychosocial supports and stressors. Many studies have demonstrated the link between dysfunctional maternal behavior and fetal development, suggesting that mothers who abuse alcohol, tobacco, and other drugs during their pregnancy may interfere with their infant's cognitive and physical development (Espy, Kaufman, and Glisky 1999; Fergusson, Woodward, and Horwood 1998; Streissguth et al. 1994). Ironically, when mothers behave in this way, their activities are not generally considered traumategenic, even though they may cause long-term damage to their babies.

Abuse and neglect from an early caregiver, however, do qualify as relational forms of trauma. Schore (2000), a prolific infant researcher, believes that caregiver-induced trauma basically contributes to more frequent and more intense psychopathology in children. In his groundbreaking research, Perry (1997) reported two separate psychobiological responses to trauma experienced by an abused infant. When a child is threatened, she experiences an alarm or startle reaction resulting in increased heart rate, blood pressure, respiration, and muscle tone. Hypervigilance emerges, followed by crying, and ultimately screaming. Beebe (2000) vividly describes how this overarousal escalates when there is a lack of empathic attunement from the caregiver, whether this is the parent or any designated primary caregiver. In her videotape, after the infant expresses extreme distress, including averting her head totally, arching away, and screaming, the mother continues, unrelentingly, to react with a poorly attuned response. She ultimately fails to soothe the infant. This lays down a way of relating where the infant withdraws into her internal world and dissociates. A state of numbness, withdrawal, compliance, and restricted affect occur. This parallels the familiar "traumatic stress response," which vacillates between hyperarousal and numbness.

We now understand that early trauma alters the development of the infant's right brain, the hemisphere that is responsible for processing social and emotional information, bodily states, and attachment (Schore 2001). The right hemisphere, more so than the left, is involved with the limbic system and the sympathetic and para-sympathetic components of the autonomic nervous system. Therefore, it plays a central role in emotional processing, on cognitive as well as physiological levels. In addition, the right hemisphere secretes stress hormones and activates vital functions that support survival. Executive control functions are regulated in this area as well. Since the right prefrontal cortex of the brain is critical in processing emotions, any intense and unregulated stress usually induces heightened negative affect, chaotic biochemical reactions, and a developmentally immature defective right brain. Needless to say, these are serious long-term effects that bear scrutiny (Schore 2001, 2003a, 2003b).

When a person lacks efficient right-brain functioning, she inevitably experiences problems with self-soothing during times of stress. Often, heightened aggression is associated with these decreased right-brain functions as well as the development of a disorganized/disoriented ("Type D") attachment style (Lyons-Ruth, Alpern, and Repacholi 1993; Lyons-Ruth, Repacholi, and McLeod 1991). As children protect themselves from the ravages of cumulative relational trauma, they then retreat both psychologically (through dissociation) and neurobiologically (by overly restricting their yearnings for attachment). Social interactions are then replaced with withdrawal and dissociation as predominant defenses.

Without any intervening reparative caregiving, these stress-induced responses start to organize the neural system, resulting in enduring after-effects. As a result, permanent shifts in the affective centers of the limbic system may result, which ultimately influence affect regulation and the attachment pattern for the child, adolescent, and the adult trauma survivor. The infant posttraumatic stress reactions of hyperarousal and dissociation may well set the template for symptomatology in later life, including adult posttraumatic stress disorder (PTSD) or complex PTSD. When infants express stress responses to threatening stimuli, their immature brain processes resemble appropriate "flight-flight" responses (Nijenhuis et al. 1998). However, adults who were traumatized as children retain these immature responses to stress. As a result, when confronted with severe stress in adult life or triggered by an event reminiscent of the earlier traumatic experience, the adult brain will then regress to an infantile state. Because of the consequent alterations in brain neurophysiology related to childhood trauma, these adults experience a state of re-traumatization. A clinical example illuminates this process:

> Patricia, a thirty-seven-year-old social worker, recalls an incident during the past week when she returned home from work to find her partner, Alice, toiling away cleaning the house. Although Patricia felt initially appreciative of her

partner's efforts, she suddenly felt overwhelmed by nausea, terror, and agitation. She smelled a strong solution of Clorox, which was being used as a cleaning agent.

In therapy, what emerged was Patricia's connection of these olfactory sensations to a triggering of traumatic memories stored in her body. Her right-brain activity was subdued at the time, while her stress response activated automatically in reaction to the olfactory stimuli of the bleach smell. What eventually emerged was a narrative of physical abuse during infancy where her day-care provider hit and scratched her frequently. She often tended to the wounds by first applying a strong antiseptic solution. As a result, Patricia's body "remembered" the physical injury through the associated channel of smelling the cleaning agent. Within seconds, her early traumatic body memory was triggered with the associated "traumatic stress" response.

Somatic Responses to Traumatic Stress

Researchers have demonstrated the ways in which overwhelming traumatic experiences are stored in somatic memory and expressed with significant changes in the body (Siegel 1999, van der Kolk 2003). There are complex neurobiological processes involved in the response to traumatic stress as compared with ordinary life stressors. Further, a traumatic stress response in reaction to a traumatic event influences the encoding of body memories.

Typically, a person in an ordinary low-stress situation registers information through various visual, auditory, olfactory, or tactile senses. This information is then passed on to the neocortex, or the "thinking brain." Information is typically organized and assigned appropriate meaning after being ferried to the limbic system, which attaches emotion that is congruent to the situation. Then, this information is stored in the hippocampus, the brain's "filing cabinet," in logical, declarative memory. In this low-stress scenario, emotions accommodate and facilitate the orderly functioning of laying down logical memories in the hippocampus.

> For example, a forty-five-year-old Cambodian refugee, Phum Sreng, who fled the Pol Pot regime as a young adolescent, moved with her family, initially to Thailand, and then later to the United States at the age of thirty. Soon after arriving in the Pacific Northwest, Phum Sreng attended E.S.L. (English as a Second Language) classes. Phum reported learning new words, grammar, and sentence structure fairly rapidly in spite of apprehension about her accent. Since she did not worry a lot, Phum was able to hear and see new English words, integrating the content quite rapidly as her new language was being stored in a structured, logical manner in the hippocampus.
>
> This contrasted with her almost complete paralysis when she first entered school in Thailand. At that time, she recalls her total incapacity to take in new learning. Flashbacks of her earlier traumatic experiences of witnessing multiple

executions of trusted relatives interfered with any deliberate purposeful processing of new information. During that time, she experienced regular nightmares, mood changes, intense fears, and physical symptoms of headaches, stomach upset, and hyperventilation. With this full-blown PTSD symptomatology, she was unable to take in new information until her acute distress eased.

We know that adults respond to auditory, tactile, and olfactory stimuli. When the thalamus (a section of the brain) registers these messages as dangerous, the person responds with a "fight-flight" reaction. First, the sympathetic regulatory system, anthropomorphized as "the agitator," excites the amygdala, the brain's "alarm system," which mobilizes to defend and protect the person from harm. When the amygdala hijacks the ordinary process of information processing, it broadcasts distress and disaster, thus triggering a cascade of physiological responses. Instead of laying down a logical, clearly defined memory of an event, the hippocampus is flooded with intense emotionally laden stimuli that are then laid down as body memories. They are also referred to as "iconic" or "symbolic" memories.

Concurrently, the parasympathetic regulatory system (or the "paralyzer") activates as well. When this system is aroused, opiates are released in the brain, contributing to a state of numbness. Other physiological changes include an increase in cortisol levels along with a decrease in blood pressure. In this state, a person may experience restricted affect, withdrawal, and "freezing," or emotional paralysis. For example, many survivors of wartime combat describe a calm state of detachment devoid of feeling when they are actively involved in a violent exchange. During these times of extreme stress, both the "agitator" (the sympathetic system) and the "paralyzer" (the parasympathetic system) are activated simultaneously, creating a chaotic toxic neurochemistry. Therefore, when a person's cardiac system is stimulated and inhibited at the same time, the body freezes.

Metaphorically, this is like riding the gas and applying the brakes of a car at the same time. This familiar state translates into the blank, dazed look of a traumatized child or the frozen watchfulness of a traumatized adult. When an individual repeats this draining stress response over and over, all systems become challenged and compromised, ultimately leading to ill health.

CLINICIAN RESPONSES TO WORKING WITH TRAUMATIZED INDIVIDUALS

Clinical practice with traumatized clients typically stirs strong emotional responses in the clinician. Not only must we, as clinicians, be mindful of countertransferece responses, we must also be aware of the impact of becoming traumatized through the processes of vicarious traumatization traumatization or secondary traumatization (Chu 1998, Figley 1995, Pearlman and Saakvitne 1995). As we think about the complexity of the intersubjective space between the clinician and client, many questions emerge. For example, how do client and clinician affect each other in the ongoing work? How does hearing another's violations influence the clinician's sense of safety? How are these various influences recognized and addressed? In cross-cultural practice with trauma survivors, how are cultural assumptions and biases addressed? How do personal and professional values shape the clinician's response? What methods are useful in addressing countertransference? Vicarious traumatization? Secondary trauma?

Vicarious Traumatization and Secondary Trauma

Clinical practice with trauma survivors evokes strong feelings and alterations in one's own belief system. Pearlman and Saakvitne (1995) state that, especially in work with survivors of sexual abuse, we, as clinicians, are vulnerable to vicarious traumatization. This process is defined as "the transformation in the inner experience of the therapist that comes about as a result of empathic engagement with the clients' trauma material" (p. 3). Trauma shatters assumptions not only in the client but also in the worldview of the clinician. This is an insidious process, which starts off at an unconscious level but gradually erodes a sense of hopefulness, coherence of self, and meaning. Unlike countertransference, which is understood as specific to the therapist-client dyad and omnipresent in all therapies, vicarious traumatization exists in a more generalized way in response to intensive continuous therapeutic work with trauma survivors.

Many who work with traumatized individuals, couples, or families—or with communities in disaster work—experience compassion fatigue (Figley 1995), or what is also referred to as secondary traumatic stress (Stamm 1999). These responses may involve full-blown PTSD symptomatology, including the hyperarousal-numbness pendulum, affect dysregulation, startle reactions, and re-experiencing including flashbacks and nightmares. Yet, these helpers do not always experience the complete transformation or dismantling of the clinician's inner world that occurs when someone is traumatized.

There are numerous approaches that can assist a clinician in dealing with vicarious traumatization. First, it is important to understand that the experience is normative and expected in practice with trauma survivors. Second, clinical supervision and supportive clinical teams provide clinicians with an opportunity to connect with each other and talk about their experiences. Not only does this help to counteract a sense of despair or powerlessness, but the actual talking helps to change neo-cortical brain activity. For these interventions to be successful, institutions and organizations need to support their viability (Catherall 1995). Furthermore, one might take care of oneself through: (1) sustaining self-care practices, including exercise, nutrition, and stress-relieving practices; (2) developing of a sense of spirituality that counteracts a loss of hope; and (3) ongoing self-awareness (Pearlman and Saakvitne 1995, Yassen 1995).

Transference/Countertransference Phenomena with Trauma Survivors

In most therapeutic relationships with trauma survivors, there are a number of predictable countertransference traps based to a large extent on the "victim-victimizer-bystander" relationship template. These countertransference traps may occur through the processes of projective identification. For example, the clinician might slip into a passive and indifferent bystander stance that mirrors the client's numbness and detachment. Another trap leads to helpless victimization, or not knowing how to proceed. When a clinician finds herself extending the boundaries of sessions, losing clarity around professional role and financial compensation, or shifting into an overly zealous omnipotent helper, she may be succumbing to a rescuer enactment. An eroticized countertransference trap is very common as well, where a clinician may experience a range of sexual feelings activated within the therapeutic relationship, especially in practice with survivors of childhood sexual abuse. Understandably, caution is urged to avoid eroticized re-enactments that recapitulate the earlier childhood trauma. Behaving aggressively toward a client may be another form of countertransference enactment while identifying with a victimizer role. And finally, reaction formation represents a trap where the clinician, while disavowing anger, may act in a false and overly solicitous manner. For example, a clinician may avoid dealing with conflict or negative transference responses by steering away from the conflict, while behaving in a vaguely supportive, jocular manner.

In summary, enactments on the part of the clinician are inevitable. However, it is very important to understand the nature of the countertransference enactments to both strengthen the empathic connection with our clients, to repair therapeutic ruptures when enactments occur, and to minimize the occurrence of enactments, as best as possible.

IMPLICATIONS FOR CLINICAL PRACTICE

Although this chapter has focused primarily on the basic constructs of trauma theories, we will briefly address some relevant implications for clinical practice. Since many trauma survivors have been mistreated physically and/or psychologically, they often neglect their physical and mental health. Living with PTSD symptomatology undermines the ease with which traumatized individuals navigate their lives. As a result, many contemporary trauma therapy practice models are phase-oriented and synthesize knowledge about the neurobiology of trauma along with psychodynamic constructs within social context (Allen 2001, Chu 1998, Courtois 1999, Davies-Frawley 1994). The first phase of therapy involves helping the client to attend to her physical and mental health by strengthening self-care. Symptom relief and safety are sought. When the client is relatively stabilized in these areas, she may start to talk about the effects of her traumatic experiences on her current day-to-day life. This phase-two trauma work focuses on narrating the trauma while reflecting on the meaning of the legacies of trauma. After gaining some perspective on ways that the traumatic experiences have affected a person's psychological, social identity, and relational development, the client and clinician then move along to address phase-three psychotherapy tasks. In fact, many clients who strengthen their self-care capacities ultimately transform their identities from a position of "victim," defining themselves almost exclusively through the traumatic experiences, to a "survivor" of tragic, traumatizing events. Here, clients move from a state of powerlessness and hopelessness to positive agency and ultimately toward heightened creativity and assertiveness. Intersecting social identities including race, ethnicity, gender, and sexual identities cohere as well during this transformative process. As clients move beyond therapy and a self-definition that relates to their legacies of trauma, they often begin to view themselves as "thrivers" who are living their lives with vitality and purpose.

CONCLUSIONS

It is important to remember that many trauma survivors have prevailed in coping with traumatic events without developing subsequent psychopathology. They continue to lead healthy and zestful lives. However, other trauma survivors struggle with the legacies of childhood trauma, with war, or with natural disasters that undermine their capacities for growth in their relationships and life dreams. Trauma can disable a person and lead to shattered assumptions and shattered lives. Yet traumatic experiences can also be addressed in ways that lead to renewed strength, convictions, and hopefulness in the face of adversity. Most compelling are the tales of individuals who have overcome tremendous adversity and emerge from their journeys all the stronger.

Toward the end of her psychotherapy, Claire, a thirty-six-year-old woman who had suffered severe physical abuse during early childhood years, brought me a large, variegated conch shell that she had discovered along a rugged Jamaican beach. To her surprise, it was intact. On most beach walks, Claire carefully selected multicolored and geometrically shaped stones, pebbles, and shells along with twisted driftwood that had been buffeted and dispersed by cross currents. "Just as I design a colorful mosaic with this debris from the sea, I have also re-collected 'the fragments of my mind.'" Claire spoke metaphorically about the healing forces of the ocean that washed away her terrors and self-hatred. "But I want this weathered conch shell to be a continual reminder of our powerful connection," she said. Like the flow of tides and tumultuous waves of strong emotion—I am grateful to be able to live with myself and also feel more connected to the world." In parting, Claire hoped that whenever I picked up this shell and placed it to my ear, I, too, would be "lifted up by the soothing sounds of the sea." To this day, I look with deepening respect at this weathered artifact, settled into my bookshelf as a continuous reminder of our transformative work together.

REFERENCES

Allen, I. A. (1998). PTSD among African Americans. In *Ethnocultural Aspects of Post-traumatic Disorder: Issues, Research and Clinical Implications*, ed. A. J. Marsalla, M. J. Friedman, E. T. Gerrity, and R. M. Scurfield, pp. 209–38. Washington, DC: American Psychological Association.

Allen, J. G. (2001). *Traumatic Relationships and Serious Mental Disorders*. New York: John Wiley & Sons, Ltd.

American Psychiatric Association. (2000). *Diagnostic and Statistical Manual of Mental Disorders,*. (4th edition, Text Revision). Washington, DC: American Psychiatric Association.

Bartone, P. T. (1999). Hardiness against war-related stress in army reserve forces. *Consulting Psychology Journal: Practice and Research* 51(2):72–82.

Basham, K. K., and Miehls, D. (2004). *Transforming the Legacy: Couple Therapy with Survivors of Childhood Trauma*. New York: Columbia University Press.

Beebe, B. (2000). Co-constructing mother-infant distress: The microsynchrony of maternal impingement and infant avoidance in the face-to-face encounter. *Psychoanalytic Inquiry* 20:412–40.

Breuer, J., and Freud, S. (1893). Studies on hysteria. *Standard Edition* 2:3–305.

Briere, J. (1996). *Therapy for Adults Molested as Children: Beyond Survival* (rev. ed.). New York: Springer.

Catherall, D. (1995). Preventing institutional secondary traumatic stress disorder. In *Compassion Fatigue: Coping with Secondary Traumatic Stress Disorder in Those Who Treat the Traumatized*, ed. C. Figley, pp. 232–47. New York: Brunner/Mazel.

Chu. J. (1998). *Rebuilding Shattered Lives*. New York: John Wiley.

Cohen, L. M., Berzoff, J. N., and Elin, M. R. (1995). *Dissociative Identify Disorder: Theoretical and Treatment Controversies*. Northvale, NJ: Jason Aronson Inc.

Courtois, C. (1999). *Recollections of Sexual Abuse: Treatment Principles and Guidelines*. New York: W.W. Norton.

Davies, J. M., and Frawley, M. G. (1994). *Treating the Adult Survivor of Childhood Sexual Abuse: A Psychoanalytic Perspective*. New York: Basic Books.

de Jong, J. T. V. M, Komproe, I. H., Spinazzola, J., van der Kolk, B. A., and Van Ommeren, M. H. (2005). DESNOS in three post-conflict settings: Assessing cross-cultural construct equivalence. *Journal of Traumatic Stress* 18(1):13–21.

Erikson, E. (1980). Elements of a psychoanalytic theory of psychosocial development. In *Infancy and Early Childhood*. Vol. 1 of *The Course of Life: Psychoanalytic Contributions Toward Understanding Personality Development*. In *Infancy and Early Childhood*, eds. S. I. Greenspan and G. H. Pollack. Washington DC: National Institute of Mental Health.

Espy, K. A., Kaufman, P. M., and Glisky, M. L. (1999). Neuropsychological function in toddlers exposed to cocaine in utero: A preliminary study. *Developmental Neuropsychology* 15:447–60.

Fairbairn, W. R. D. (1952a). *An Objects Relations View of the Personality*. New York: Basic Books.

———. (1952b). *Psychoanalytic Studies of the Personality*. London: Routledge & Kegan Paul.

Fergusson, D. M., Woodward, L., and Horwood, L. J. (1998). Maternal smoking during pregnancy and psychiatric adjustment in late adolescence. *Archives of General Psychiatry* 55:721–27.

Figley, C. (1995). *Compassion Fatigue: Coping with Secondary Stress Disorder in Those Who Treat the Traumatized*. New York: Brunner/Mazel.

———. (1988). A five-phase treatment of PTSD in families. *Journal of Traumatic Stress* 1(1):127–41.

Freud, S. (1905a). Three essays in sexuality. *Standard Edition* 7:135–243.

———. (1905b). The aetiology of hysteria. *Standard Edition*. 3:191–225.

Friedman, M., and Marsalla, A. (1996). Post-traumatic stress disorder: An overview of the concept. In *Ethnocultural Aspects of Posttraumatic Stress Disorder: Issues, Research and Clinical Applications*, eds., A. Marsella, M. Friedman, E. Gerrity, and R. Scurfield. Washington, DC: American Psychological Association.

Goodwin, J. (1990). Applying to adult incest survivors what we have learned from victimized children. In *Incest-Related Syndromes of Adult Psychopathology*, ed. R. Kluft, pp. 55–74. Washington, DC: American Psychological Association.

Green, B. L., Grace, M. C., Lindy, J. D., and Leonard, A. C. (1990). Race differences in response to combat stress. *Journal of Traumatic Stress* 3(3):379–93.

Herman, J. (1992). *Trauma and Recovery*. New York: Basic Books.

Hoge, C. W., Auchterlonie, J. L., and Milliken, JC. LS. (2006). Mental health problems, use of mental health services, and attrition from military service after returning from deployment to Iraq or Afghanistan. *Journal of the American Medical Association*, 295:1023–32.

Kessler, R. C., Sonnega, A., Bromet, E., Hughes, M., Nelson, C.B., and Breslau, N. (1999). In *Risk Factors for Posttraumatic Stress Disorder*, ed. R. Yehuda, pp. 23–59. Washington, D.C.: American Psychiatric Press.

Kira, I. A. (2002). Torture assessment and treatment: The wraparound approach. *Traumatology* 8(1): 23–51.

Kluft, R. P. (1995). The confirmation and disconfirmation of memories of abuse in DID patients: A naturalistic clinical study. *Dissociation* 8(4):253–58.

Kulka, R. A., Schlenger, W. E., Fairbank, J. A., Hough, R. L., Jordan, B. K., Marmar, C. R., and Weiss, D. S. (1990). *Trauma and the Vietnam War Generation: Report of Findings from the National Vietnam Veterans Readjustment Study.* New York: Brunner/Mazel.

Loftus, E. F. (1993). The reality of repressed memories. *American Psychologist* 48(5):518–37.

Loftus, E. F., Polonsky, S., and Fullilove, M. T. (1994). Memories of childhood sexual abuse: Remembering and repressing. *Psychology of Women Quarterly* 18:67–84.

Lyons-Ruth, K. Alpern, L., and Repacholi, B. (1993). Disorganized infant attachment classification and maternal psychosocial problems as predictors of hostile-aggressive behavior in the preschool classroom. *Child Development* 64:572–85.

Lyons-Ruth, K., Repacholi, B., McLeod, S., and Silva, E. (1991). Disorganized attachment behavior in infancy: Short term stability, maternal and infant correlates, and risk-related subtypes. *Development and Psychopathology* 3:377–96.

McEwen, B. S. (1999). Allostasis and allostatic load: Implications for neuropsychopharmacology. *Neuropsychopharmacology* 22(2):10–124.

National Center for Posttraumatic Stress Disorder. (n.d.). "What Is Posttraumatic Stress Disorder (PTSD)? www.ncptsd.va.gov/ncmain/ncdocs/fact_shts/fs_what_is_ptsd.html.

Nijenhuis, E. R. S., Vanderlinden, J., and Spinhoven, P. (1998). Animal defensive reactions as a model for trauma-induced dissociative reactions. *Journal of Traumatic Stress* 11(2):234–260.

Pearlman, L., and Saakvitne, K. (1995). *Trauma and the Therapist: Countertransference and Vicarious Traumatization in Psychotherapy with Incest Survivors.* New York: W.W. Norton.

Perry, PB. (1997). Incubated in terror: Neurodevelopmental factors in the "cycle of violence." In *Children, Youth and Violence: The Search for Solutions,* ed. J. Osofsky. New York: Guilford Press.

Pouissant, A., and Alexander, A. (2000). *Laying My Burden Down: Unraveling Suicide and the Mental Health Issues Aamong African Americans.* Boston: Beacon Press.

Rutter, M. (1993). Resilience: Some conceptual considerations. *Journal of Adolescent Health* 14:626–31.

Schore, A. N. (2000). Attachment and the regulation of the right brain. *Attachment and Human Development* 2(1):23–47.

———. (2001).The effects of early relational trauma on right brain development, affect regulation, and infant mental health. *Infant Mental Health Journal* 22:201–69.

———. (2003a). *Affect Dysregulation and Disorders of the Self.* New York: W.W. Norton.

———. (2003b). *Affect Regulation and the Repair of the Self.* New York: W.W. Norton.

Shapiro, F., and Maxfield, L. (2003). EMDR and information processing in psychotherapy treatment: Personal development and global implications. In *Healing*

Trauma: Attachment, Mind, Body and Brain, eds. M. F. Solomon and D. J. Siegel, pp. 196–220. New York: W.W. Norton.

Shay, J. (1994). *Achilles in Vietnam: Combat Trauma and the Undoing of Character.* New York: Scribner.

Siegel, D. J. (1999). *The Developing Mind: Toward a Neurobiology of Interpersonal Experience.* New York: Guilford Press.

Southwick, S. M., Bremner, D., Krystal, J. H., and Charney, D. S. (1994). Psychobiologic research in post-traumatic stress disorder. *Psychiatric Clinics of North America* 17(2):251–64.

Stamm, B. H., ed. (1999). *Secondary Traumatic Stress: Self-Care Issues for Clinicians, Researchers and Educators.* Lutherville, MD: Sidran Press.

Staub, E. (1989). *The Roots of Evil: The Origins of Genocide and Other Group Violence.* New York: Cambridge University Press.

Streissguth, A. P., Sampson, P. D., Olson, H. C., Bookstein, F. L., Barr, H. M., Scott, M., Feldman, J., and Mirsky, A. F. (1994). Maternal drinking during pregnancy: Attention and short-term memory in 14-year-old offspring—a longitudinal prospective study. *Alcoholism, Clinical and Experimental Research* 18(1):202–18.

Terr, L. (1999). Childhood trauma: An outline and overview. *American Journal of Orthopsychiatry* 148:10–20.

Van der Kolk, B. A. (2003). Posttraumatic stress disorder and the nature of trauma. In *Healing Trauma: Attachment, Mind, Body and Brain* (pp. 168–95), eds. M. F. Solomon and D. J. Siegel. New York: W.W. Norton.

Van der Kolk, B. A., Roth, S., Pelcovitz, D., Sunday, S., and Spinazzola, J. (2005). Disorders of extreme stress: The empirical foundation of a complex adaptation to trauma. *Journal of Traumatic Stress* 18:389–99.

Winnicott, D. W. (1958). *Collected Papers: Through Paediatrics to Psychoanalysis.* London: Tavistock.

———. (1965). *The Maturational Processes and the Facilitating Environment.* London: Hogarth.

Yassen, J. (1995). Preventing secondary stress disorder. In *Compassion Fatigue: Coping with Secondary Traumatic Stress Disorder in Those Who Treat the Traumatized*, ed. C. Figley, pp. 178–208. New York: Brunner/Mazel.

18

Conclusion

Some Final Thoughts

Joan Berzoff, Laura Melano Flanagan, and Patricia Hertz

What, then, have we learned in this book? We began our journey with Freud, the "father of psychoanalysis," whose explorations into the unconscious life of individuals helped us enter into an uncharted, inchoate underworld of internal forces governing psychic life. We learned about how passions, when unknown, may lead to human suffering, while we studied the absolute value of self-knowledge for effecting psychological change. We came to see how important the therapeutic relationship can be to both therapist and client, and examined the symbolic and real aspects of that relationship to the people within it. We came to appreciate the complex ways in which drives shape child development, resulting in lifelong symptoms, character structure, and strengths. We learned how Freud and his contemporaries conceptualized most of mental life as a battleground in which unconscious conflicts between the drives, the self, and society were played out within and between the structures of the mind. We came to see how intrapsychic conflicts result in compromises, called symptoms, and how our understanding of unconscious conflicts can set us free.

We studied the increasingly central role of the ego in mediating between the drives and society and its important functions in providing an individual coherence and equilibrium. We studied the ego's capacities and strengths in adapting to and mastering the environment and we learned about the kinds of defenses it employs to ward off danger. We learned about the ego's other autonomous functions: thinking, feeling, and motility. In addition we saw how the ego seeks coherence and continuity over the entire life cycle, as each individual negotiates psychological and social tasks at every stage of life-cycle development. We learned that ego development is mediated by psychological *and* social forces (race, class, gender, culture, age, ability) so that the individual always interacts within the sociocultural context in which she develops.

We studied some of the many ways in which an individual develops an *internal* sense of self, occurring first through earliest relationships with others. Conceptualized by object relations theorists, we examined the central place of early maternal relationships on a child's sense of self and began to see how external relationships come to be uniquely metabolized as internal representations of the self and of others. We looked at the tragic consequences that can accrue when the external world cannot provide the necessary nurturance for achieving internal psychological wholeness. We looked at the absolute importance of attachment to the developing child, and we studied the kinds of attachment difficulties and styles that may develop based on caregiver/child relationships, which may enhance or derail development.

From self psychology, we came to see how a person's self-esteem and self-cohesion are based on the attunement and empathy provided by others in the environment, as we continued to move away from models that located psychological problems as deriving only from problems in the earliest years of life. Self psychology offered a more hopeful view of the curative power of ongoing relationships (including the therapeutic relationship) for promoting healthy self-esteem.

From a relational perspective, the therapeutic inquiry began to shift its emphasis from the individual to the ways in which the *relationship* between the therapist and client became the unit of study and of change. Here we looked at the intersubjective field between client and therapist, the ways in which each of their subjectivities influences the other, and how self-disclosure and therapeutic authority are reconceptualized. We considered the influence of postmodernism on the therapeutic relationship, with its emphasis on the influence of race, class, gender, and sexual orientation as inevitably interwoven into the dialogue. We also considered how relational theories decenter therapeutic authority and emphasize mutuality.

We studied the consequences of racism on the individual and the particular contributions offered from drive theory, ego psychology, object relations, and self psychology in understanding the dynamics of racism and its pernicious effects on the individual. We again gained another way of conceptualizing how what is *external* and *outside* of the individual comes to be experienced internally. We learned the ways in which individuals develop their ethnic and racial identities and the value of this knowledge for any cross-cultural therapeutic encounters.

As we looked at the relationship between gender and psychodynamic theories, we again encountered the ways in which psychodynamic theories have both oppressed and liberated our understanding of female development. We came to see the complex relationship between women's internal lives and their places in the social structures in which they live. We saw how a cross-fertilization of social and psychological theories helps us more fully understand intrapsychic and social oppression.

In the second half of this book, we learned about the biopsychosocial aspects of psychosis, borderline and narcissistic conditions, depression, anxiety, and trauma. We studied how each diagnosis is rooted in its social times and expresses particular dilemmas of the culture and the society. We learned the ways in which people with these disorders are more than their symptoms, and we stressed, throughout, our own conviction about the power and value of a therapeutic relationship to effect meaningful change. In each of the diagnostic categories, we exhorted the reader to attend to neurobiology, genetic endowments, biochemistry, hormones, internal psychological processes, and social oppression.

Throughout this book, we have held to a stance that "We are all much more simply human than otherwise" (Sullivan 1940, p. 39), expressing our conviction that every fear, symptom, sense of unreality, passion, urgency, longing, need, defense, and desire that our clients express may be similarly experienced by us, the clinicians. Therefore, as we have attended to the internal experiences of the clients we serve, we have encouraged the reader to attend to the experiences of the helpers, ourselves, who work with people in psychological pain. We have held that we are not different, not other, and that in many ways, if we do not suffer our own moments of psychosis, or borderline and narcissistic longings, depression, anxiety, and early trauma, then we are keeping ourselves too separate from the people with whom we work.

What do we hope that the readers have taken away from this book? Some awe for the complexity of psychological life, and some appreciation for the unique ways every individual has of mediating between psychological, cultural, gendered, racial, and biological variables within and outside of the self. We hope that the readers will be able to enter into and understand the inner worlds of the clients with whom they work, approaching each person with a sense of wonder with which all human phenomena must be clinically approached. We hope that all readers will keep alive their own sense of "not knowing," continually learning anew from each individual client with whom they work. We hope to convey that with every client with whom we work, we are changed in the process.

George Bernard Shaw said, "For every complex problem there is a simple solution—and it is wrong!" As we move toward very brief, often cognitive or biological mental health managed-care models that tend to treat the symptoms but not the person in the environment with the symptoms, we hope that each reader will grapple with the complexities of a biopsychosocial perspective, rejecting simplistic solutions that attempt to reduce people to their manifest problems. In short, it is our hope that the practitioners/readers/clinicians will, whenever possible, continue to keep the work as complicated as they can!

REFERENCES

Sullivan, H. S. (1940). Conceptions of modern psychiatry. *Psychiatry* 3:35–45.

Index

About the Editors and Contributors

Kathryn Basham, MSW, PhD, received her BA in psychology from the George Washington University in Washington, D.C., her MSW from the University of California at Berkeley, and her PhD from the Smith College School for Social Work in Northampton, Massachusetts. She is currently a professor and chair of the Human Behavior in the Social Environment Sequence at the Smith College School for Social Work. She is a coauthor of the book *Transforming the Legacy: Couple Therapy with Survivors of Childhood Trauma* and is a member of a committee formed by the Institute of Medicine to explore the effects of deployment-related stress on soldiers, veterans, and their families. She writes and presents regularly, in both national and international venues, on the topics of clinical practice with traumatized couples and families, and the interface of psychodynamic theories and cross-cultural practice. She is also in private practice in Northampton, Massachusetts.

Joan Berzoff, MSW, EdD, received her BA from Washington University in St. Louis, her MSW from Smith College School for Social Work, and her EdD from Boston University. She is currently a full professor and the codirector of the doctoral program at the Smith College School for Social Work, where she also directs the End-of-Life Care Certificate Program. She is a coeditor of the books *Dissociative Identity Disorders: Controversies in the Diagnosis and Treatment* (1995) and *Living with Dying: A Handbook for End-of-Life Care Practitioners* (2004), as well as the author of many publications related to women's friendships; intersubjectivity; feminist theory; death, dying, and bereavement; and educational curriculum. She presents both nationally and internationally and is the recipient of a Project on Death in America Social Work Leader Award and the Outstanding Scholar Award from the

463

National Academies of Practice. She is in private practice in Northampton, Massachusetts.

Laura Melano Flanagan, MSW, graduated from Manhattanville College and received her MSW from the Hunter College School of Social Work. She received a certificate from the Advanced Institute for Analytic Psychotherapy in New York City. She has taught as an adjunct instructor at the Hunter College and New York University Schools of Social Work in the post-master's certificate program, and she is currently an adjunct instructor at the Smith College School for Social Work. Ms. Flanagan is in private practice in New York City.

Martha Hadley, PhD, is a psychoanalyst and researcher who received her doctoral degree in psychology from the Graduate Center of the City University of New York and her postdoctoral training in psychotherapy and psychoanalysis at New York University Post Graduate Institution. She currently teaches as adjunct faculty at Smith College School for Social Work, maintains a private practice in New York City, and does research focused on children and adolescence with the Michael Cohen Group in New York. She has written on the topics of relational aggression among girls, and unconscious communication in psychotherapy and supervisory contexts. She serves as executive editor of *Studies in Gender and Sexuality*.

Michael Hayes, PhD, graduated from Georgetown University, and received his MSW and his PhD from the Smith College School for Social Work. He is a professor in the Department of Social Work at Providence College, Providence, Rhode Island, has taught and served as a research advisor for over twenty years at the Smith College School for Social Work. He is also in private practice.

Patricia Hertz, MSW, graduated from Cornell University and received her MSW from the Smith College School for Social Work. She has taught at the Boston Institute for Psychotherapy and the Simmons College School of Social Work, and is currently an adjunct professor at the Smith College School for Social Work. She maintains a private practice in Boston, Massachusetts, and consults to a variety of agencies and organizations, including Beth Israel Deaconess Medical Center, the Big Apple Circus, and the Dana Farber Cancer Institute.

Maria de Lourdes Mattei, PhD, graduated from the University of Puerto Rico. She received her doctorate from the University of Massachusetts. Dr. Mattei is associate professor of clinical psychology at Hampshire College, Amherst, Massachusetts, and is in private practice in Northampton, Massachusetts. In addition, she is on the adjunct faculty of the Smith College School for Social Work, and the Massachusetts Psychology Internship Program at Brightside/School Street Counseling Institute in Springfield, Massachusetts. She consults to community mental health centers in the area on the topic of psychotherapy and culture.

Gerald Schamess, MSS, graduated from Columbia University and received his MSS from the Columbia University School of Social Work. He is professor emeritus at the Smith College School for Social Work and the editor of the *Smith College Studies in Social Work*. He currently maintains a private practice in Northampton, Massachusetts, where he provides long-term treatment and clinical supervision.

Cynthia J. Shilkret, PhD, received her BA from Barnard College and her PhD in clinical psychology from the State University of New York at Buffalo. She was an intern and also a postdoctoral fellow at Mount Zion Hospital and Medical Center, San Francisco, where her postdoctoral fellowship was in the area of psychotherapy research. She is a founding member of the San Francisco Psychotherapy Research Group. She has been an adjunct member of the faculty of the Smith College School for Social Work since 1980. She is in private practice in South Hadley, Massachusetts, and writes on various clinical topics.

Robert Shilkret, PhD, received his BA from The Johns Hopkins University and his PhD in clinical psychology from Clark University. He interned at Judge Baker Guidance Center in Boston and was a postdoctoral fellow in clinical psychology at Mount Zion Hospital and Medical Center in San Francisco. He is the Norma Cutts DaFoe Professor of Psychology at Mount Holyoke College, where he has also been department chair, dean of studies, and acting dean of faculty on three occasions. He has been a visiting faculty member of the Smith College School for Social Work since 1975. He is a member of the San Francisco Psychotherapy Research Group. He writes in the areas of college students' development and relations with their families and in developmental theory.